The legislative system

the Legislative System

EXPLORATIONS IN LEGISLATIVE BEHAVIOR

John C. Wahlke, Vanderbilt University

Heinz Eulau, Stanford University

William Buchanan, University of Southern California

LeRoy C. Ferguson, Michigan State University

John Wiley and Sons, Inc., New York · London

To Joan, Cleo, Vivian

Preface

THE RESEARCH ENTERPRISE which we report in this book has a unique intellectual history. It began even before any one of the four authors was personally acquainted with all the others; it ended as a reasonably unified effort by a four-man team. Its inception as a cooperative research venture did not come about through simple coincidence of research interests of the four members of the team. Rather, it was the product of a confluence of theoretical and research interests from many sources. The particulars of intellectual biography are set forth in our report, but we must acknowledge here the heavy and diverse debts incurred by us in the process of completing this research.

The project was inspired by the Committee on Political Behavior of the Social Science Research Council which, in December, 1954, had circulated an appeal for "the devotion of additional effort to the comparative study of state politics" as "an especially advantageous way to advance the margins of our knowledge about politics" and to make "significant methodological and substantive advances in political science." The four of us, each at that time in the early stages of work on some project dealing with politics in some particular state, were among the scholars brought together by the Committee in New York City, July 1–2, 1955, to discuss ways and means of promoting such study. From such beginnings the project evolved into its final form with the constant support and encouragement of the Committee on Political Behavior, which generously provided us with individual grants, funds to permit us to come together to coordinate our work, and administrative, clerical, and individual expenses. Just as important as the original stimulus and the continuing monetary aid was the help and advice given by the Committee collectively and its members individually, particularly in the crucial formative stage of the project.

Our acknowledgment here cannot adequately express our gratitude to the Committee on Political Behavior and to its members—Chairman David B. Truman, Angus Campbell, Conrad M. Arensberg, Robert A. Dahl, Oliver Garceau, Alexander Heard, V. O. Key, Jr., Avery Leiserson, Dayton D. McKean, and M. Brewster Smith.

To David Truman and Avery Leiserson we owe special thanks for their unfailing willingness to hear about our research problems and to counsel with us. Similar thanks are due President E. Pendleton Herring, Dr. Bryce Wood, and other staff members of the Social Science Research Council, who not only helped us with their professional advice but also solved many of our practical day-to-day problems. To the extent our study constitutes progress toward the objectives of the Council and the Committee, theirs is a great share of the credit. For our errors or failures, only our own shortcomings are to be blamed.

One of our most rewarding—and humbling—experiences has been the wholehearted encouragement, support, and assistance given us by a wide circle of institutions and persons. Our own universities,* of course, granted the indispensable leaves of absence for field work, provided essential research and secretarial facilities, and supplemented the grants from S.S.R.C. by further grants from their own research agencies. We are particularly indebted to the Governmental Research Bureau and the All-University Research Fund of Michigan State University, the Institute for Research in the Social Sciences of Vanderbilt University, and the Legislative Internship Program of the University of California (Berkeley). Nor can we forget that Paul Bixler, Librarian of Antioch College, and A. F. Kuhlman, then Librarian of the Joint University Libraries, Nashville, provided excellent facilities for short conferences during the early stages of the project.

The sources from which we received help were by no means limited to agencies of our own academic institutions. The Citizenship Clearing House of Southern Ohio, then under the guidance of Professor Howard White of Miami University, helped meet the costs of interviewing in Ohio. The Western Data Processing Center (University of California, L.A.), the Survey Research Center and the Computer Center (University of California, Berkeley) provided machine facilities and assistance in the analysis of some of the data. Some of the analysis carried out in Nashville was partially supported by the Na-

---

* At the time the project began Mr. Buchanan was at Mississippi State University and Mr. Eulau at Antioch College. Mr. Buchanan and Mr. Wahlke both served subsequently as Visiting Professors at the University of California (Berkeley).

tional Science Foundation (grant number NSF-G1008 to Vanderbilt University).

Moreover, academic institutions to which we had no ties except respect and friendship played an indispensable part in our work by providing space and facilities for extensive conferences of four peripatetic researchers who could not easily have met together otherwise. We are particularly indebted to Professor Charles S. Hyneman who enabled us to meet at Northwestern University in the summer of 1956, to Professor John A. Vieg who enabled us to meet at Pomona College in the summer of 1957, and to Dr. Ralph Tyler, Director of the Center for Advanced Study in the Behavioral Sciences, for permitting us not only to meet there in the summer of 1958 but to use the Center's superb facilities in our work.   For help at that time we owe our collective thanks also to Preston Cutler, Assistant Director, Mrs. Jane Kielsmeier, Assistant to the Director, and John Gilbert, Mathematician-Statistician, of the Center.   Mr. Eulau is even more indebted individually to the Center and its staff for the opportunity to devote himself intensively to analysis of our data while residing at the Center for a year as a Fellow.

In the course of our meetings at all these institutions and on many other occasions we profited from the sympathetic attention and the thoughtful comments of other professional colleagues too numerous to mention.   While we should like to thank them all individually, we must limit our acknowledgments here to thanking Jean Driscoll (then at Northwestern University), Joseph P. Harris and Jay Doubleday of the University of California (Berkeley), Totton J. Anderson of the University of Southern California, and Everett K. Wilson, sociologist, and Victor Ayoub, anthropologist, of Antioch College. Needless to say, all of them are totally innocent of any sins and mistakes we may have committed.

Similarly, though we cannot here thank individually all those, mostly our students, who helped us at various stages, particularly in the interviewing of legislators, we should like to mention our gratitude to Peter Toma, Lee Layport, and Charles Mayo for their assistance in California; to Murray Frost and Emory T. Trosper for their help in several places; to Stanley Newmann, Peter Orleans, and Suzanne Berger for their assistance in Ohio; and to Mrs. Jo Ann Bennett and Charles Kelso for their aid in Tennessee.   We are indebted to Mrs. Helena Austin of the Center for Advanced Study, Miss Sandra Levinson of Stanford University, and Mrs. Cleo Wescoat Sandlin of Vanderbilt University for invaluable secretarial assistance, and to Mrs. Anna B. Luton for typing the bulk of the final manuscript.

Finally, we wish to express our gratitude to the 474 members of the California, New Jersey, Ohio, and Tennessee legislatures and their associates who cooperated as fully and freely as did our professional colleagues. We are particularly grateful to Representative Herman K. Ankeney of Greene County and Senator Lowell Fess of the Fifth and Sixth Districts for their help in introducing the Ohio senior researcher to their colleagues, and to Speaker Roger Cloud and President pro Tempore C. Stanley Mechem for acquainting the members of their respective chambers in Ohio with the purposes of the research. For similar assistance in Tennessee we are indebted to Speaker of the Senate Jared L. Maddux, Speaker of the House James Bomar, and the late Damon R. Headden, then Administration Floor Leader in the House. For especial assistance in California we are indebted to Senators James A. Cobey and Robert I. Montgomery, and Assembly-men Luther H. Lincoln, Gordon H. Winton, Jr., Edward E. Elliott, Charles J. Conrad, Jesse M. Unruh, and Bruce Sumner. We were greatly aided also by the late Dr. William S. Carpenter, Director of the New Jersey Division of Legislative Information and Research, and his assistant, Ralph Eisenberg, by Dr. Franklin M. Bridge, of the Ohio Legislative Service Commission, by the late John H. Green and Mrs. Green of the Tennessee Legislative Service, and by Thomas A. Johnson, Executive Director of the Tennessee Legislative Council Committee. We hope they will all feel that helping us understand their work has been at least a small contribution to the public good which they serve.

For permission to use material previously published in several journals, we wish to thank the *American Political Science Review,* the *Journal of Politics,* the *Midwest Journal of Political Science,* the *Western Political Quarterly,* the *American Behavioral Scientist,* and the *International Yearbook of Political Behavior Research.*

It may seem strange that, in a book aspiring to represent a unified effort, we named the authors of individual chapters. We have done so largely for the convenience of readers who may wish to query any one of us about special aspects of the research. However, as we continuously checked each other's analyses and drafts, we are prepared to take collective responsibility for the research as a whole and for what any one of us has written.

Aix-en-Provence, France
April, 1962

JOHN C. WAHLKE
HEINZ EULAU
WILLIAM BUCHANAN
LeRoy C. FERGUSON

Contents

PART ONE INTRODUCTION   1

1. Theory: A Framework for Analysis *by John C. Wahlke*   3
2. Method: Research Design *by John C. Wahlke and Heinz Eulau*   29
3. Context: Settings of the Study *by William Buchanan*   40

PART TWO THE LEGISLATIVE CAREER   69

Introductory Remarks *by Heinz Eulau*   69

4. Recollections *by Heinz Eulau*   77
5. Orientations *by Heinz Eulau*   95
6. Expectations *by Heinz Eulau*   121

PART THREE THE LEGISLATIVE ARENA   135

Introductory Remarks *by John C. Wahlke*   135

7. Rules of the Game *by John C. Wahlke and LeRoy C. Ferguson*   141
8. Leadership Roles *by William Buchanan and Leroy C. Ferguson*   170
9. Subject Matter Experts *by William Buchanan*   193
10. The Bonds of Friendship *by William Buchanan*   216

PART FOUR LEGISLATIVE ROLES   237

Introductory Remarks *by Heinz Eulau*   237

11. The Legislator as Decision Maker: Purposive Roles *by Heinz Eulau*   245

12. The Legislator as Representative: Representational Roles
by Heinz Eulau — 267
13. The Legislator and His District: Areal Roles by Heinz
Eulau — 287
14. The Legislator and the Interests: Pressure-Group Roles
by John C. Wahlke — 311
15. The Legislator and His Party: Majority and Minority
by Heinz Eulau — 343

PART FIVE THE LEGISLATIVE SYSTEM — 377

Introductory Remarks by Heinz Eulau — 377

16. The Network of Legislative Role Orientations by Heinz
Eulau — 384
17. Legislative Role Structure and Political Conflict by
Heinz Eulau — 414

PART SIX LEGISLATIVE RESEARCH — 433

18. Strategy and Tactics of Legislative Research by Heinz
Eulau and John C. Wahlke — 435

APPENDICES

1. Construction of Role Types — 465
   1.1 PURPOSIVE ROLES — 466
   1.2 REPRESENTATIONAL ROLES — 467
   1.3 AREAL ROLES — 468
   1.4 PRESSURE-GROUP ROLES — 468
2. Construction of Other Scales and Measures — 471
   2.1 MEASURES OF PARTY COMPETITION IN DISTRICTS — 471
   2.2 LEGISLATIVE EFFICACY SCALE — 474
   2.3 LIBERALISM-CONSERVATISM (IDEOLOGY) — 475
3. Legislative Officers—How They Are Chosen and What
They Do — 476
4. Behavior Expected of Formal Leaders — 483
5. The Legislators: Their Backgrounds and Characteristics — 486
6. Interview Schedule and Instructions to Interviewers — 492
7. Bibliographical Note — 505

INDEX — 509

PART ONE

Introduction

CHAPTER 1

Theory: a framework for analysis

THE RESEARCH TO BE REPORTED did not begin with a theory to test nor did it end with one. It was designed to study a number of different questions within a common conceptual scheme, to see if that scheme deserves to be utilized in developing legislative theory "properly." Consequently, the chapters of this book, while they lead to some fairly general conclusions and, we hope, form a more or less coherent whole, do not "cover" the subject of legislatures. Rather, they present closely related studies of some important topics concerning legislative institutions and processes. Moreover, the studies are exploratory, not definitive. Some of them explore new ground, examining questions little touched by previous research; others examine familiar topics in ways and terms not so familiar. To the extent that they help illuminate the topics they treat, they serve also to demonstrate the theoretic utility of the conceptual framework within which they were made. In any case, we have sought throughout not merely to report particular findings but to speculate broadly about their implications for theory and future research. This chapter explains the conceptual scheme which served as a "roadmap" to guide our research.

THEORETICAL OBJECTIVES

The basic concern of this book is with the functioning of legislative institutions in modern democratic political systems. Its findings are relevant to questions which should be familiar to political scientists and other students of those institutions: What are the functions of the legislature in the various political systems possessing such institu-

This chapter drafted by Wahlke.

tions? What are the crucial features which determine how well or poorly those functions are performed?

Historical and analytical knowledge. The data to be reported concern four particular state legislatures (California, New Jersey, Ohio, and Tennessee) during one particular legislative session (1957). But the key generalizations have much wider import. The aim of research was not to construct descriptive accounts of the institutions and processes of legislation in the four states studied, or of the political forces and factors which operate from day to day through their legislatures. Nor was it to discover precisely what happened in these four states in a particular session or to acquire understanding of the unique historical events of those particular situations. The objective, rather, was to gain knowledge about generic problems of legislative institutions and processes in American state government, and of similar institutions and processes (by whatever name they might be called) in other political systems. In other words, the four particular state legislatures are viewed here primarily as four cases of a possible fifty. For certain purposes, if appropriate care is exercised in specifying the assumptions being made, they may be viewed as cases from a still larger population including certain non-American legislatures as well as those of the states of the American union. It is analytic knowledge, not historical (much less journalistic) comprehension which is sought.

Legislative institutions, legislators' behavior and legislative functions. The book focusses upon the perceptions and behavior of the men and women who were members of the four legislatures in 1957. The attempt to study institutions by looking primarily at behavior will seem paradoxical to anyone accustomed to think of "institutional" and "behavioral" approaches to the study of government as fundamentally antithetical to each other. But a major methodological theme of this book is that the two are, in fact, interdependent: the empirical data of "institutional study" consist only of some record of human behavior. At the same time, to contribute to political analysis, accounts of human behavior must be guided by recognition of the institutional context of most behavior which is relevant to government and by concern for the questions which have traditionally occupied students of political institutions.[1]

[1] The relations of the "behavioral approach" to the 'institutional" are discussed in David B. Truman, "The Impact on Political Science of the Revolution in the Behavioral Sciences," pp. 202–231 in Stephen K. Bailey, et al., *Research Frontiers in Politics and Government* (Washington: The Brookings Institution, 1955), and

Such concepts as "legislature" and "legislative institution," as these terms have already been used here, provide an initial illustration of this interdependence. The legislature is a construct which assumes the existence of institutionalized human groups identifiable with appropriate proper names, such as The Legislature of New Jersey, or The General Court of Massachusetts. Legislatures, for purposes of empirical research, are constituted by certain uniformities and regularities in the behavior of men acting in such visible or "concrete" institutionalized groups.

At an elementary empirical level, the basic behavioral uniformities are so obvious and commonplace that they sometimes produce conceptual confusion. For example, regular performance of routine actions like making motions to pass bills, participating in formalized debate, or taking of votes where each member counts equally is usually considered a defining characteristic of any institutionalized group called a legislature. Selection of membership by some method of popular election is likewise often taken as a defining characteristic of such a body. But the generic name, "legislature," given to them, derives from more than just descriptive generalization of these particular uniformities of behavior. It derives also from assumptions about the functions performed by bodies called by that name, and about the part they play as subsystems in larger political systems.

It is often taken for granted that the legislative subsystem is preeminently concerned with that central political function which has variously been called "willfully or purposefully controlling men's actions and behavior,"[2] "deciding who gets what, when, and how,"[3] or "authoritatively allocating values for society."[4] The commonplace notion that "legislation" is the chief task of a legislature and that it involves decisions by the legislature about what shall and shall not be law tends to equate "legislation" with such a general decision-making function. But not all so-called legislatures "legislate" in a clear decisional sense. The Supreme Soviet of the U.S.S.R., to take the most obvious example, certainly does not do so. Whether or not any

---

Muzafer Sherif and Bertram L. Koslin, "The 'Institutional' vs. 'Behavioral' Controversy in Social Science with Special Reference to Political Science," (Theoretical and Research Reports, Norman: University of Oklahoma, Institute of Group Relations, 1960).

[2] George E. G. Catlin, *A Study of the Principles of Politics* (London: Allen and Unwin, 1930).

[3] Harold D. Lasswell, *Politics: Who Gets What, When, How* (New York: McGraw-Hill, 1936).

[4] David Easton, *The Political System* (New York: Alfred A. Knopf, 1953).

particular legislature does perform genuine decisional functions in the larger political system is essentially a question for empirical investigation.

A better way to look at the problem, however, is to ask *how* a particular legislature contributes to the decisional function in the society of which it is a part. Some serve only to "ratify" decisions made elsewhere; others perform an essential function of "promulgation," without which decisions made elsewhere do not become effective. Many perform important "information-gathering-and-organizing" as well as "deliberative" functions. Any of these may be performed as specialized routines in a process where the legislature genuinely makes major decisions; they may also be performed by "legislatures" in systems where the genuine decisions are made by extralegislative agencies. Again, whether and how any given legislature performs such decision-related functions or subroutines of the decisional function is a question for empirical investigation.

Most legislatures play a major part in the performance of still other important political functions which cannot be comprehended under the rubric of decision making. Above all they ordinarily have a great deal to do with "legitimizing," or making authoritative, important classes of decision, wherever those decisions might be made in the particular system. This involves in almost all cases a process and function of "representation" of important political groups and interests in the community. It usually involves also a high degree of ritualistic "symbol-manipulation" which provides cues to political publics for responding to legislative actions. Legislatures may facilitate catharsis of political grievances by providing a forum for the verbal expression of anxieties, resentments, and aggressive desires, thus contributing to stability in the political system. "Administrative oversight," "adjudication," and other functions might be added to the list without exhausting the repertoire of functions performed by various legislatures.

Some political scientists advocate studying political systems by identification of the institutions and processes which perform these and other functions in each system and by comparison of the functional equivalents in the various systems.[5] We have chosen instead to examine one particular institution in four different systems. Although, as emphasized above, the functions performed by that institution in each case must ultimately be determined by empirical inquiry, we have proceeded on the assumption that our four legislatures (and those of other American states, the U.S. Congress, and

[5] See especially Gabriel A. Almond and James S. Coleman (edit.), *The Politics of the Developing Areas* (Princeton: Princeton University Press, 1960), Chapter 1.

many parliamentary bodies in other systems) do in fact perform decisional, legitimizing, representative, and other functions. We have assumed that examination of the behavior of legislators will yield insight about performance of these functions by legislators in the four states and by legislative institutions more generally. But, just as institutional and behavioral political study are interdependent, so, too, are structural and functional approaches. One can investigate the same problems by asking what functions are performed by a given institution, and how, as by asking what agencies or institutions perform a given function, and how? In other words, the theoretical conceptions guiding this research are behavioral, institutional (structural), and functional—not any one or the other.

THE CONCEPT OF ROLE AND THE MODEL OF THE LEGISLATIVE ACTOR

The interdependence of these three approaches has not always been taken into account in studies of legislatures, largely from the lack of any clear-cut and generally accepted conceptual scheme for describing and analyzing behavior in that institutional context. Recent theoretical and research developments in various social science fields suggest that the concept of role can serve well as the key in organizing such a conceptual scheme. "Role" has been used with relatively minor variations of meaning by analysts in sociology, anthropology and social psychology, which indicates its probable utility for tying together the concerns of "institutional," "functional," and "behavioral" studies in political science.[6]

[6] The seminal work for all theories of role is that of George Herbert Mead, especially his *Mind, Self and Society* (Chicago: University of Chicago Press, 1934). For the meaning and use of role concepts in cultural anthropology consult Ralph Linton, *The Cultural Background of Personality* (New York: Appleton-Century-Crofts, 1945), especially pp. 76–77; S. F. Nadel, *The Theory of Social Structure* (Glencoe, Illinois: The Free Press, 1957). Sociologists' use of the concept is illustrated by Talcott Parsons, *The Social System* (Glencoe: The Free Press, 1951), especially pp. 25–26, 39–40, 236–242; Talcott Parsons and Edward A. Shils, *Toward a General Theory of Action* (Cambridge, Massachusetts: Harvard University Press, 1951), especially pp. 19–20, 208–218; and Robert K. Merton, *Social Theory and Social Structure* (Glencoe, Illinois: The Free Press, 1957), Chapters 8 and 9. For use of the concept in social psychology see Theodore M. Newcomb, *Social Psychology* (New York: The Dryden Press, 1950), Chapter 9; and Stansfeld Sargent, "Concepts of Role and Ego in Contemporary Psychology," in John H. Rohrer and Muzafer Sherif (Editors), *Social Psychology at the Crossroads* (New York: Harper and Brothers, 1951). The case for using the concept more precisely and formally in political science is argued by Jean Viet in "La

Better than any alternative concept in social science, the notion of role yields a model of the legislator as an acting human individual which is consistent with the basic understandings of individual and group psychology. At the same time, it yields a model of the legislature as an institutionalized human group which logically incorporates the model of the individual legislator and which relates the behavior of legislators to problems of legislative structure and function which are the traditional concern of students in the field.[7]

Role, for any individual legislator, refers to a coherent set of "norms" of behavior which are thought by those involved in the interactions being viewed, to apply to all persons who occupy the position of legislator.[8] It is important to emphasize the normative aspect of

---

Notion de Rôle en politique," *Revue Française de Science Politique* **10**:309–334 (1960).

Good summaries, as well as bibliographical information, are available in Frederick L. Bates, "Position, Role and Status: A Reformulation of Concepts," *Social Forces* **34**:159–163 (1956), and "A Conceptual Analysis of Group Structure," *Social Forces* **36**:103–110 (1957); Neal Gross, Ward S. Mason, and Alexander W. McEachern, *Explorations in Role Analysis* (New York: John Wiley and Sons, 1958), pp. 11–69; Lionel J. Neiman and James W. Hughes, "The Problem of a Concept of Role: A Re-Survey of the Literature," *Social Forces* **30**: 141–149 (1951); Theodore Sarbin, "Role Theory," I, 223–258, in Gardner Lindzey (Editor), *Handbook of Social Psychology* (Cambridge, Massachusetts: Addison-Wesley, 1954); and Ralph H. Turner, "Role-Taking, Role-Standpoint, and Reference-Group Behavior," *American Journal of Sociology* **23**:316–328 (1958), reprinted in (and hereafter cited from) Lewis A. Coser and Bernard Rosenberg (Editors), *Sociological Theory* (New York: The Macmillan Company, 1957), pp. 272–290.

[7] Several writers have hinted strongly at such a use of the concept of role in a study of legislative bodies. See Earl Latham's discussion of "officiality" in *The Group Basis of Politics* (Ithaca, N. Y.: Cornell University Press, 1952), pp. 33–40, and David B. Truman's discussion of the status (office) of legislator and its associated role in *The Governmental Process* (New York: Alfred A. Knopf, 1951), pp. 346–360. Norman Meller has also observed that "a legislator's decisions are . . . influenced by the dictates of his role and the roles of others." ["Legislative Behavior Research," *Western Political Quarterly*, 13 (1960), 144.]

[8] The term "position" is preferable for our use to "status" which is often used in this way, especially by writers following the usage of Linton. As Ralph H. Turner has pointed out, roles are associated with "a particular status in society (e.g., doctor or father)," with "informally defined position[s] in interpersonal relations (e.g., leader or compromiser)," and with "particular values in society (e.g., honest man or patriot)." (*Op. cit.*, pp. 272–273.)

The term "norms" incorporates the meaning of "*expectations* of behavior" used in many definitions of "role." Certain behavior is expected of occupants of positions because it is assumed they will comply with the norms of the position. In other words, a role is "normative" in both principal senses of that term: statis-

the concept in order that the role of legislator not be confused with the office, or position, of legislator. It is the normative aspect, also, which gives psychological validity to the concept: the concept postulates that individual legislators are aware of the norms constituting the role and consciously adapt their behavior to them in some fashion. In order to avoid any possible confusion, it is convenient to use the specific term "role behavior"[9] to refer to those overt actions which result from legislators' acting in conformity with norms included in the role. Although the term role itself refers to conceptions (in the form of norms) in the minds of the legislative actors, where it is necessary to emphasize the perceptual aspect of role phenomena it is also useful to adopt the somewhat redundant term, "role concept." A basic postulate of our research, then, taken from general role theory, is that the office of legislator is a clearly recognizable position in the four states studied, that legislators and many other persons in those societies associate certain norms of behavior with those positions, i.e., expect certain types of behavior from occupants of the position of legislator simply because they occupy that position, and that a significant portion of the behavior of legislators is role behavior consistent with legislators' role concepts. To study the role of legislators, then, is to study particular sets of norms which underlie relevant legislative behavior.

The chief utility of the role-theory model of the legislative actor is that, unlike other models, it pinpoints those aspects of legislators' behavior which make the legislature an institution. In the light of most other models, the actions of any given individual legislator appear highly individualistic, to be explained by factors operating uniquely and distinctively for each individual member. For example, according to what may be called the "rational-man model," the legislator is somehow or other apprised of an end and engages in deliberate actions which he consciously conceives to be, and chooses as, means to that end. Thus many democratic reformers, as well as Edmund Burke, visualized the ideal legislator in the well-functioning legislature as an individual with a clear conception of the public good who seeks

---

tical, insofar as the role can be described as particular behaviors which are statistically normal (and expected, accordingly); and ethical, insofar as the role embodies behaviors which others think they have a right to expect.

[9] The term "role behavior" corresponds to the terms "role enactment," "role performance," or "role playing," also in common use. Such behavior, involving compliance with norms, is to be distinguished from what Turner calls "'playing-at' a role," or overt enactment of a role as form of pretense. (Turner, *op. cit.*, p. 273.)

intellectually and rationally to devise means of promoting it. Even the undesirable type of legislator so despised by Burke and others, who recognizes some selfish or "bad" interest of his own, of his friends, or of some group, and seeks to promote that interest by rationally devised means, is a rational man patterned on the same model. So too is the legislator who rationally perceives the actions demanded of him by various "forces" outside the legislature—political parties, pressure groups, constituents, etc.—and who rationally weighs the strength of those pressures against his own rational preferences for the various courses of action urged on him, then strikes a balance and acts accordingly. The behavior of individual legislators would be even more individualistic according to what might be called the "psycho-analytic model," which explains significant portions of an individual's behavior by subconscious motivations.[10]

But the behavior of legislators is clearly "institutional behavior," not merely aggregated or symbiotic behavior of individuals. Institutions, it has been said, are regularities or uniformities of behavior. The concept of a role associated with a position of membership in any institutionalized group refers to precisely those behavioral uniformities or regularities which constitute the institution. No legislature or other institution could be "seen" by the analyst if the human actors did not exhibit behavior in conformity, to at least some minimal extent, with the norms of behavior constituting their roles. If one is interested in the structure and functions of an institution, it would seem proper to ascertain and analyze those forms of behavior which are central and constitutive to the institution as such before attempting to describe or explain uniquely individual actions or individual deviations from some unspecified model of behavior.

An important characteristic of role is that it always relates to an actor's confrontations with other actors in a role relationship. It is a concept which assumes the existence of interpersonal relations. The set of norms which make up a person's role can be divided into subsets of norms according to the position, status, or character of the other person (the alter) with whom the role player in question (ego) is called upon to deal. Any role, therefore, can analytically be divided into role sectors, each sector comprising those norms appropriate to

[10] See, for example, Harold D. Lasswell, *Psychopathology and Politics* (Chicago: University of Chicago Press, 1930). The only application of this general conception to legislators is by John B. McConaughy, "Certain Personality Factors of State Legislators in South Carolina," *American Political Science Review* 44:897–903 (1950).

some particular "counter-role," i.e., to encounters with persons occupying some particular counterposition or status.[11]

Because legislators are public officials and because representation is generally understood to be a principal function of the legislature, attention has most often been concentrated upon legislators' relationships with persons, groups, and a general public outside the legislature. Nevertheless, the overwhelming bulk of a legislator's transactions and interactions are with his fellow legislators in the course of his daily life in and around the legislative chamber. An important sector of his role, therefore, is what might be called the "core-roles sector," which includes all the norms guiding the legislator's behavior with reference to other legislators perceived simply in their character (or role) as one of all coequal legislators, or with reference to the legislature perceived as a type of social situation or a sort of "generalized other."[12]

For purposes of political analysis this core-roles sector may be subdivided still further according to the functional significance attributed to certain norms in it by the analyst or by the legislators themselves. Because the legislatures in question are working groups made up of individuals playing roles which (in the core-roles sector) are common to all members, there must be some minimal level of agreement about how the legislative game is to be played, some "working consensus" or, as it has been called, "a kind of inter-actional *modus vivendi*."[13] In the modern legislature such a working consensus is based in large part on norms of two sorts: written prescriptions or precepts in constitutions, statutes, rules of procedure, etc., that tell legislators how they are expected to act in certain situations—all of which may be conveniently described as enacted role requirements; and those unwritten but informally understood norms sometimes called rules-of-the-game. Since interest in such norms arises from a concern with their function, they may be called "consensual norms" and referred to collectively as the "consensual role." In Chapter 7 we shall examine some of the characteristics of the working consensus, with emphasis on the rules of the game.

Other categories of norm included in the core-roles sector may also

[11] The concept of role-sector is used by Gross, Mason and McEachern, (*op. cit.*, pp. 50–56, 62) to describe that part of a role relating to only one counterposition, whereas we use it to refer to the part of role relating to counterpositions of a particular class.

[12] For discussion of "generalized others" see Mead, *op. cit.*, pp. 86, 232, and elsewhere.

[13] Erving Goffman, *The Presentation of Self in Everyday Life* (New York: Doubleday and Company, 1959), p. 9.

be analytically distinguished. Each legislator has some purposive or functional conception of the ultimate aim of his activities which will be embodied in certain types of norms for his relations with his fellows in the day-to-day legislative operation. Those which have to do with behavior appropriate to the substantive goals or purposes of legislation and the legislative operation, as he conceives them, will be referred to as the "purposive role," discussed in Chapter 11.[14] Closely related to this is another set of norms which it is yet possible and, as we shall see, important to distinguish analytically. These concern the method or process of individual decision making deemed appropriate to pursuit of the substantive goals. The term "representational role" will be used to refer to this area of the core-roles sector, which will be explored in Chapter 12.

Elements of the core-roles sector go far toward fixing the character of the legislative institution, since they govern a large part of the legislators' behavior in encounters with other legislators "inside" the legislature. But no legislature is an isolated, autonomous body operating without reference to events, persons, and groups beyond the legislative walls. The concept of role takes into account one important linkage between the legislature as an institution and all relevant persons, groups, and events outside it. Citizens and legislators alike expect legislators to deal routinely with a variety of other political actors. The most important of these, indeed, are recognized by legislators and laymen alike as so many counterpositions, with associated counter-roles, from the legislators' viewpoint. The role of legislator includes norms for his behavior in encounters with the occupants of these various counterpositions. The list of counterpositions varies greatly from one political system to another, but in American state legislatures at least four are likely to be of major importance: political party organizations and agents, constituents and constituency organizations, organized interest groups, and executive or administrative officers and agents. Because the role of legislator (in American society, at least) normally includes the expectation that legislators will, in some sense, be alert to their possible views and wishes, that sector of the legislator's role made up of norms of behavior for dealing with such persons can conveniently be labeled the "clientele-roles sector," and the various subsets of norms in it can be

---

[14] We are not presenting a model inclusive of all aspects of behavior, perception, or attitude for the individual as a total personality. Although norms in the area called purposive-role are no doubt related to general value-beliefs, social philosophy, life-goals, etc., the concept in question is but one aspect of such larger problems.

called respectively the "party role," the "areal role" (since constituencies in the cases to be considered are defined geographically), the "pressure group role," and the "administration role." Chapters 13 to 15 will examine three of these clientele roles.[15]

Like any sizeable and complex group existing to perform certain tasks, a legislature requires organization to do its work. This means that the role of legislator includes a "specialized-subroles sector," comprising norms of behavior for occupants of various positions and statuses within the legislative group. Whereas the various roles in the core-roles and clientele-roles sectors are played by every legislator, the subrole relationships involve norms for the behavior of occupants of certain specialized positions or statuses toward all other legislators. The various positions of formal office or leadership within the legislature, for example—Speaker, Committee Chairman, Party Leader, etc. —are the basis of various "formal-leadership roles." There are other important subroles not formally prescribed or defined by occupancy of a formal organizational office but associated with certain statuses that may be achieved by some legislators. The "subject-matter-expert role" is an example of this type. These two varieties of subrole will be discussed in Chapters 8 and 9.

The last sector to be described here is not generically part of the role of legislator as such. It has to do with the fact that every individual occupies many positions and statuses in his society. Both legislators and scholars have noted that "the personal factor,"—relations between individual members or between members and various "outsiders" in statuses other than those already described—have something to do with decisions made by legislators and may, in the aggregate, influence the legislature's actions. Kinship, friendship, fraternal or recreational associations, give rise to extralegislative, extraparty role relationships. If there are also qualities of "leadership" which inhere in certain persons who become "influential" because of them, this phenomenon would be included among such incidental factors. (It would, of course, be distinguished from formal leadership statuses, which we treat elsewhere.)

Because these roles grow out of largely non-political and non-legislative social circumstances, and because they will vary idiosyncratically not only from one legislature to another but also temporally

---

[15] The administration role was omitted from the study primarily because none of the four authors' individual projects was focussed on the administration. Several relevant questions were included in the interview schedule (see Appendix 6), but the scope of the present work is already such as to discourage exploitation of the data from these few questions here.

within each legislature as its membership changes, they may be appropriately labeled, from the analysts' standpoint, as belonging in the "incidental-roles sector." While we had no systematic postulates about the structure of the network of these incidental roles, we study in Chapter 10, as one example, the "friendship role."

The conception of the role of legislator can be summarized in graphic form. While the role sectors and their various components set forth in Figure 1.1 are not a complete inventory of all norms making up the role of legislator, the conception is intended to be comprehensive enough to apply to most aspects of legislative behavior which have interested students in the past, and detailed enough to guide research based on the concept of role.

Role consensus, role conflict, and role orientation. It does not follow from role theory that all behavior in the legislature is appro-

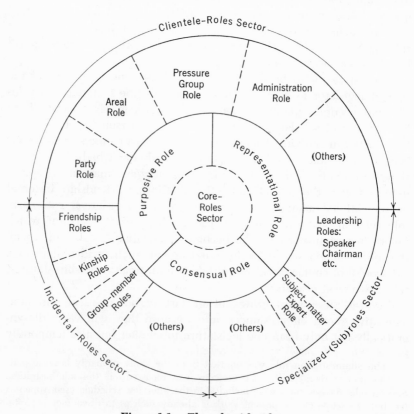

Figure 1.1. *The role of legislator.*

priate role behavior, and that legislative role concepts, therefore, strictly determine the course of events. To deal with the relationship of legislators' role behavior to other variables in the legislative process, one must first describe the role of legislator by abstracting it from legislators' behavior and perceptions. This raises the question, to what extent can legislators' role concepts and behavior be expected to vary from one member to another within a given legislature? Unless there is some minimal level of agreement about what constitutes the legislative role and its various component sectors the role could not be said to exist. Without some minimum of consensus the legislature would cease to be an institutionalized group. Yet complete agreement is hardly to be expected among any group of human legislators.

Two different sorts of consensus are involved in the problem. First, each member of a role relationship—e.g., legislator and lobbyist—must agree to some extent about what behavior is appropriate for himself and the other in their encounters. In this case the problem is one of "*inter*position consensus."[16] Where a system includes a number of actors some or all of whom play common roles, i.e., roles which all are expected to play in relation to various counter-roles, the problem is not one of agreement between ego and alter but of agreement between a number of egos about what they should all do in relation to a common alter. In this second case, the problem involves "*intra*position consensus." To describe any role system completely one must determine to what extent there is consensus, both *inter*position and *intra*position, among all role players in the system.

The behavior of each role player depends in important respects upon the extent of compatibility or conflict among the various norms or expectations making up his own role or roles, as he conceives them. Whenever he faces contradictory expectations, he may be said to experience "role conflict." In some cases, the conflict arises because he sees different "alters" in a particular role relationship expecting different behaviors of him, i.e., confronting him with conflicting definitions of his role. Such would be the case, for example, if two different sets of lobbyists expected two different sorts of role behavior of him. This kind of conflict has been called "intra-role conflict." In the example given, there are conflicting definitions of the legislators' pressure group role. In other types of situation, the actor may be faced with the apparent necessity of choosing which role to play. For example,

[16] The discussion and conceptualization here follows essentially that set forth in much greater detail by Gross, Mason and McEachern, *op. cit.*, pp. 116–143, 244–257.

in a given situation, his party role might require a legislator to act one way, while his administration role might require him to act quite differently. In this case he is faced with "inter-role conflict."

The exact relationship between role consensus and role conflict in any particular situation must be determined empirically. It is quite possible, theoretically, for a legislator to be faced with acute inter-role conflict even though there is perfect consensus (both interposition and intraposition) among all role players concerned. It is also possible that no legislator feels role conflict even though there is little role consensus. On the other hand, the *intra*-role conflict experienced by any legislator will certainly vary according to the degree of consensus obtaining about his role. Role analysis of legislatures, therefore, must ultimately undertake careful investigation of role consensus and role conflict in different situations.

Our research did not permit exhaustive investigation of the full range of these problems. Because the research was primarily exploratory, and because we were interested primarily in questions of institutional structure and function, we have concentrated upon the problem of *intra*position consensus. Our data permit some remarks about the problem of interposition consensus only with respect to formal-leadership roles. They permit no analysis of problems of role conflict.

Specifically, we have sought to discover the major patterns of role concept held by legislators in each of the role sectors described above. We have found that there are, in each legislature studied, different "role orientations" or different conceptions of the purpose, style, and limits of each sector of the role of legislator. Thus, all legislators seem to recognize norms making up what we have called their representational role. But some conceive of that role in a way we have found it convenient to describe as that of the "trustee," others as that of the "delegate," and still others, as "politico." Different purposive-role concepts of legislators can be described as those of the "broker," the "tribune," the "inventor," or the "ritualist." Similarly, with respect to pressure-group roles, some legislators have the orientation of "facilitator," some, of "resister," and others we call "neutral." The character of these different role orientations is discussed in detail in the relevant chapters of Part Four. The point here is simply that the term role orientation refers to a pattern of norms making up a particular role which may be contrasted with other patterns for the same role. In other words, it refers to systematic differences in legislators' conceptions of a particular component of the role of legislator. Although it emphasizes differences in role concepts, it still allows for the existence of widespread agreement (intraposition consensus) about the role in question.[17]

Finally, we must recognize the likelihood that, where there are several different orientations current in a legislature, the individual legislator may well be aware of more than one of them. In particular, we should not think of any given role orientation as a fixed attitudinal attribute of each person, which invariably leads him to act and react the same way in every situation. It is more likely that most legislators pattern their behavior in the light of one role orientation in one situation, but according to another under other circumstances. We can therefore conceive of the "role set" of each legislator as all those orientations in any given component of his role which he is capable of entertaining.[18] If his armory of role concepts includes all identifiable role orientations in a given typology, he possesses the full role set and, presumably, will exhibit extremely versatile role behavior. If his range of role concepts is more limited, it will be of interest to determine in what respects it is so. While our research did not permit us to explore "role segmentalization"—the richness of role concepts or the versatility of role behavior—systematically or intensively, the theoretic importance of the problem must not be overlooked.

THEORETICAL IMPLICATIONS OF THE MODEL

The major objective of this research has been to delineate the principal legislative role orientations. It may be helpful, even though not strictly necessary for the immediate purposes of this particular research, to consider how the conception of legislators as role players fits into a conception of the larger political system.

The legislature as a system of roles. It follows fairly directly from the model of the legislator just presented that the legislature can be thought of as a network of relationships among legislators and others,

[17] The language of role theory is unfortunately ambiguous on this point. What are described above as different orientations are sometimes referred to by others as *roles*—e.g., "the role of tribune," or "the role of trustee." "Role orientation" is intended to connote a general type of attitude in a particular role, or an inclination to play a particular role in a certain way or style. This usage focusses attention upon patterns of consensus (or dissensus) about what the role is.

[18] Whereas we use the term "role set" to refer to available orientations (or styles) for playing one particular role, (i.e., one component in one sector of the role of legislator), it is used by Merton (*op. cit.*) to refer to the available roles upon which a person may draw in acting in a given situation.

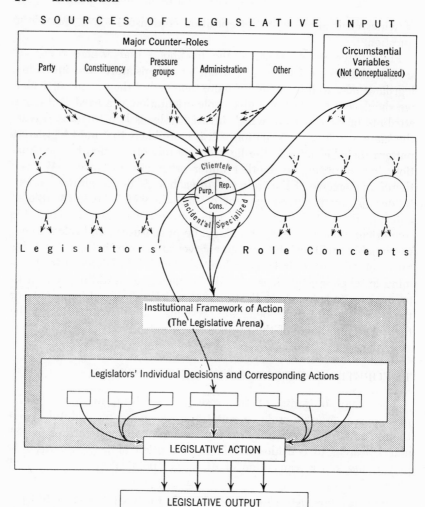

Figure 1.2. *The legislative system and the legislative process.*

all taking roles in certain ways. Figure 1.2 offers a graphic summary of the resulting conception.

From the perspective of the larger political system, the analyst's attention is first drawn to the "legislative actions" which are the most obvious manifestations of the legislature at work. Legislative actions are, of course, aggregates of particular actions by individual legislators, each of which may be conceived to result from an individual decision to act, so long as the term "decision" is not interpreted too strictly to refer only to highly self-conscious mental determinations based upon carefully articulated processes of reasoning.

The essential point, however, is that these individual actions occur within a determinate institutional framework of action, a particular legislative arena. As we have seen, this framework is largely constituted by legislators' concepts of the consensual role and the various specialized subroles recognized in the system, although certain incidental roles may also form a part of the structure of role relationships which remains relatively constant over the shorter run. The legislative arena, therefore, comprises role relationships primarily among legislators themselves and persons more or less formally identified with them (e.g., clerks, sergeants-at-arms, etc.).

The legislative "system," however, comprises not only these but also a considerably wider set of relationships. It includes, notably, all those in the various clientele counter-positions, as well as those who otherwise become salient as sources of information, cues, and other stimuli to legislators' perceptions. Again, we are interested primarily in those more or less stable features of these wider relationships discernible as role concepts and role behavior. To call the legislature a system is to assert that the distribution of roles and role orientations within it is not random. It also implies that the combination of role orientations making up the role concept of any particular legislator is likewise not random. Succeeding chapters will explore the patterns of role orientation and role combination in the four states studied and suggest their consequences for the functioning of those legislatures. Questions relating to these problems are the exclusive concern of Part Five of this book.

The legislative process. Assuming successful description of the four particular legislatures as functioning systems of roles, it is still necessary to relate that description to other major theoretical questions and problems of political study. One theoretical problem in legislative study is how to take into account the particularities and accidents of the historical, day-to-day progression of events. In our conception, these are all comprehended as circumstances affecting "legislative input."[19]

From the standpoint of the legislative actor, party, administration, pressure groups, and constituents are all sources of legislative input

[19] "Legislative input" and "legislative output" (to be discussed shortly) are comparable to, though at a somewhat lower level than, the concepts of "political input and output" proposed by David Easton, "An Approach to the Analysis of Political Systems," *World Politics* 9:383–400 (1957).

into the system—major sources, but certainly not the only ones. (See Figure 1.2). The activities of these extralegislative actors, in their multitudinous encounters with legislators, provide behavioral stimuli to which legislators respond with appropriate role behavior. What encounters occur and what particular stimuli these various persons and agencies present to legislators are obviously variables which are largely independent of the role concepts of legislators. Role theory helps us predict certain general types of response by legislators, given certain types of stimuli from key extralegislative role players, and given certain types of role concept entertained by legislators. It can not tell us much about the probable specific character of the critical stimuli. Other fundamental concepts and more comprehensive theoretical formulations are required to deal with such questions.

Similarly, the legislators' definitions of the situation[20] in which they feel called upon to play their roles at each given moment will be responsive not only to their role concepts but to variables largely independent both of those role concepts and of the particular stimulus behavior of others. What party has a majority in the legislature? Which controls the governor's office? Is the legislature operating in a time of peace and quiet or a time of crisis? In a society that is generally prospering or experiencing economic distress? Economically and socially expanding and changing, stagnating, or shrinking? What historic events (deaths of political figures, birth or activity of political movements, etc.) have occurred or are occurring? The identification and classification of such "circumstantial variables," though it is a theoretical task of obvious importance, is well beyond the needs or capacity of this particular research.

It is our belief that the concept of role, applied to the analysis of the behavior of such individuals as governors, political party officials, lobbyists, and voters, and to the behavior of news reporters, editors, and others who play a vital part in communicating the information which is vital to legislators' definitions of their day-to-day situations, can contribute much toward conceptual clarification in this area. Nevertheless, we may treat all inputs as independent variables of the legislative process. Although we have tried to describe and analyze

---

[20] Actors' "definitions of the situation" is a central concept in role theory. An excellent discussion of it, though not explicitly in terms of role theory as such, is given in Goffman, *op. cit.*, pp. 1–16. Lippmann's conception of public opinion (the "pictures in people's heads" as distinct from supposedly "objective facts" of the world situation) anticipated all important elements of this viewpoint and applied them specifically to political problems. See Walter Lippmann, *Public Opinion* (New York: The Macmillan Company, 1922).

the dimensions and attributes of legislators' role concepts as critical factors in the legislative system, we do not attempt to investigate empirically the relationship between roles and circumstantial variables.

Variables determining legislators' role concepts. Of more immediate relevance to the limited purposes of this research are questions about why a particular pattern of role orientations might be given in various cases. Again, the answers to such questions were not a major research objective. But our data do permit us to offer suggestions throughout the following chapters. The theoretical conceptions which underlie those suggestions, graphically portrayed in Figure 1.3, can be briefly summarized here.

Because the role of legislator is associated with occupancy of the position, it seems likely that a great deal of the role concept must be built up only upon entry into and continued occupancy of that position. We have already seen that the legislator's role includes what have been called "enacted role requirements." This amounts to saying that constitutions, statutes, rules of procedure, and similar "formal enactments" help determine the character of the role by dictating at least the skeletons of roles for all legislators, as well as the skeletons of various official specialized subroles.

Closely related to formal enactments as determinants of legislative role are certain features of organization and structure so permanent and fixed in the legislative landscape as to constitute major landmarks for every actor in the legislative situation. These "situational landmarks" include the number of chambers; the size of each; the length and type of the legislative session; staffing, servicing, and facilities for legislative work.[21] We have attempted, in Chapter 3, to summarize the principal situational landmarks in the four legislatures under study.

General role theory suggests another important source of role concepts in its assertion that roles, being functionally specific to systems of action, are always in some degree "entailed" or "engendered" by the system itself. Formal enactments and situational landmarks serve as important agencies in this engendering process, but they are by no means identical with it. Day-to-day involvement in the legislative

---

[21] "Situational landmarks," which, though they vary from one legislature to the next, remain constant for any given legislative body, must not be confused with the "circumstantial variables" discussed above, p. 20. The latter vary temporally *within* any given political system, as well as from one system to another. From the standpoint of general political theory, both are important varieties of "situational variables"; from the standpoint of legislative analysis, they are concepts relevant to different questions and different types of inquiry.

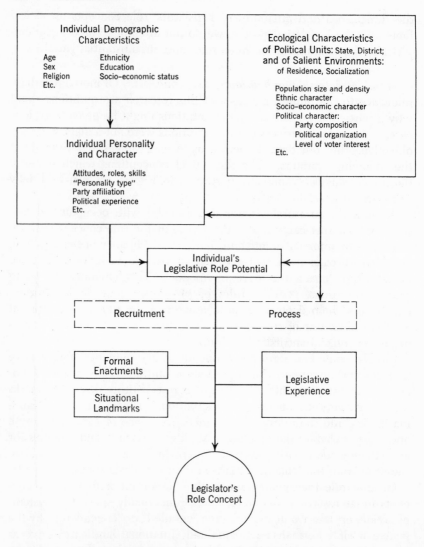

Figure 1.3. *Schematic summary of inter-relationships of major variables in the generation of legislators' role concepts.*

system plays an equally important part, so that legislators are in some degree driven by necessity to construct appropriate concepts and orientations for themselves, especially so long as maintenance of the system itself is a value at all controlling their attitudes and behavior. Thus legislative experience, by which we mean not just the quantity of time but rather the quality and character of experiences, is an important variable shaping the legislative role.

Legislators do not begin to acquire and form their legislative role concepts and orientations only at the official dawn of their legislative careers. Before that moment they have probably heard and thought about legislative work more than has the average citizen and, in many cases, even before it occurred to them that they might some day hold such office. Then, too, like other persons, they hold other attitudes and play other roles which have some effect on their self-conceptions on becoming legislators. We can, therefore, conceive that each legislator-to-be possesses some sort of "role potential," according to the attitudes, roles, and other personal characteristics shaped by such "demographic variables" as age, sex, ethnicity, religion, education, and socio-economic status, and by such "ecological variables" of his salient environments, particularly his state and his legislative district, as size and density of population, political character (party competition or dominance, political organization, etc.), ethnic character, and socio-economic character (see Figure 1.3).

All these demographic and ecological variables affect the individual personality and character of the legislator-to-be in various ways and quite generally, contributing to the development of attitudes, skills, and roles which are antecedent to and independent of his later legislative position and role. They do not, of course, totally fix and shape his personality and character. So it is necessary to view individual personality and character as a third major variable underlying the legislator's role potential. It is also necessary to recognize that ecological variables play a direct part in the legislative process insofar as they are consciously taken into account by legislators as circumstantial variables. Needless to say, we are not attempting here to give a full theoretical account of all these variables, but only to locate them approximately.

Whatever the would-be legislator's role potential, he becomes a legislator only after passing through a "recruitment process" which allows voters to make the final decision whether or not he will occupy that position. He must play the role of candidate, and it is obvious that not only his skill in this role but also the ecological characteristics of his district will have much to do with the probability of his being called upon finally to transform his role potential into guiding role concepts. While politicians' and voters' concepts of candidates and legislators and the congruence between them are fertile fields for investigation, they are beyond the bounds of this study.

We have attempted to explore some of the relationships between some of the demographic and ecological variables described above and the role concepts of legislators, and, in particular, to examine (in Chapters 4 to 6) legislators' political socialization and recruitment. But comprehensive and systematic explanation of the general problem of "origins" of role concepts was not a major objective of the research, and no attempt has been made even to list all the relevant variables in Figure 1.3 or the related discussion.

Legislative output and the end variables of political inquiry. Investigation of the questions and problems suggested in the discussion up to this point should lead to an understanding of how the legislature works and why it works that way. To understand the functions of legislatures in a larger sense, as component subsystems in larger political systems, and as institutional entities in the social system, requires consideration of the consequences of the legislature's doing what it does as it does. We cannot hope to present here a general theory of politics. But we should set forth the major theoretical concepts and assumptions about these larger topics which underlie and which have affected, probably in some ways we have not clearly recognized ourselves, the design and conduct of our research.

From the standpoint of the persons making up society—who receive or lose values, are controlled, obey laws, are informed, entertained, or antagonized, and so on—and from the standpoint of other actors in related political sub-systems, the activities of legislators (legislative actions) will appear at any given moment in time to result in a "legislative output" embodying various expectations and dictates about the behavior and attitudes of citizens and others. Acceptance of these intimated dictates and expectations by citizens and others as legitimate (rightfully deserving attention, controlling behavior, etc.) gives legislative output its authoritative character, and enables the legislature over a period of time to continue performing its functions.

Earlier in this chapter we stated our basic assumption that the legislatures we are studying have functions comprehensible above all as "lawmaking." Most important legislative actions are best conceived of as decisions by the legislative body, in the sense that predicting the outcome of any particular choice situation in the legislative arena would require mastery of a great many variables. The various services, simple communicative acts, and other actions not directly describable as "authoritative decisions" but nevertheless viewed by some clientele or public as an important part of the legislative output, whether or not they serve to make the decisional part of the output more acceptable (authoritative), are peripheral to the primary function of legislation. In any case, to conceive of a "legislative output" in these terms focusses attention upon the consequences of different legislative outputs defined in terms of the expectations, evaluations, and resulting behavior of other individuals, groups and publics.

A major theoretical problem for legislative research, if it is to be relevant to more general problems in political theory, is therefore to achieve adequate conceptualization of legislative output, i.e., to specify the dimensions or variables of legislative output which are related to different consequences of that output. We have not attempted to deal with this problem in this book.

For general political theory, the corresponding problem is to specify the dimensions or variables of response by individuals or groups to different legislative outputs, and the dimensions or variables of functionality of those outputs in the social system. The concept of representation, with all its ambiguities, is the concept most often used in attempting to cope with this problem.[22] This concept will be examined in some detail in Chapter 12, but we should note here its connotations with respect to the perceptions of legislative output by those who are, as it were, the recipients of output. Usually, of course, "representation" is used as a term describing a particular process or method (direct election by citizens) for choosing legislators. But such usage implies that the process serves the function of making legislative output congruent with expectations of the various persons and groups composing society. The term "responsibility" is also often used to refer to the goal of congruence between legislative output and citizens' preferences. In other words, representativeness or responsibility is a commonly recognized dimension of legislative output. Such concepts could be indexed for systematic research only by the expectations and perceptions of persons outside the legislature who pass judgment on legislative output.

Even if such dimensions of legislative output as representativeness or responsibility were precisely and rigorously formulated, there would remain the necessity of clear conceptualization of the functional consequences of variations in output so analyzed. Most analyses of legislative output appear to deal with the distribution of values consequent to particular outputs or patterns of output.[23] But systematic political

[22] For a convenient and comprehensive summary of definitions of representation see John A. Fairlie, "The Nature of Political Representation," *American Political Science Review* 34:236–248, 456–466 (1940).

[23] See, for example, Holbert N. Carroll, *The House of Representatives and Foreign Affairs* (Pittsburgh: University of Pittsburgh Press, 1958); Robert A. Dahl, *Congress and Foreign Policy* (New York: Harcourt Brace, 1950); Marian

theory has yet to devise concepts and categories for analyzing this variable. The familiar categorization of legislative decisions as "pro-labor," "pro-farmer," "anti-business," and so on, which compares output with preferences or expectations of discrete segments of the public, represents an attempt at such conceptualization. So, too, do such familiar value-oriented concepts as "liberal" and "conservative."

Other analyses of legislative output appear to relate to problems considered by so-called equilibrium theories and general systems analysis, problems involving functional consequences of wider import and of more abstract character than those just described. For example, the general legitimacy of the legislature as a decision-making system ultimately depends upon the character of its output. So does the assuasion or exacerbation of individual and group tensions or conflicts in society which potentially threaten to rupture the bonds of political community and destroy the basis of government itself. The degree of stability, or lack of it, and the potentiality of degeneration, solidification, or transformation of the total political system are also affected by the character and quality of legislative output.

We have not attempted to list exhaustively or precisely what may be called the functional consequences of legislative output for the general political system. In each case, the task of conceptualization is formidable and hardly begun. Because the kinds of variables described are not clearly formulated, the inter-relationships among them are even less clear. General political theory, for example, must essay to describe not only what is meant by "legitimacy" of the legislature but also how that relates to stability of the political system or the probability of political change.

Theoretical progress in these respects is as necessary for advancing the study of legislative institutions in particular as for developing general political understanding. For legislative output reacts back upon the continuing legislative process and the legislative system through various "feed-back" mechanisms. Functional consequences for the legislative system itself can be analyzed in two different categories. In one, the legislative output affects the legislative institution directly; in the other it affects it more indirectly, through the eventual

---

E. Ridgeway, *The Missouri Basin's Pick-Sloan Plan: A Case Study in Congressional Policy Determination* (Vol. 35, Illinois Studies in the Social Sciences. Urbana: University of Illinois, 1955); Fred W. Riggs, *Pressures on Congress: A Study of the Repeal of Chinese Exclusion* (New York: Kings Press, 1950); and H. Bradford Westerfield, *Foreign Policy and Party Politics* (New Haven: Yale University Press, 1955).

effects upon the legislature of the kinds of general political consequences discussed in preceding paragraphs.

Under the first heading falls, for example, the possibility that a given decision or decisions may so alienate one group of legislators as to affect drastically the course of all future deliberations and debate. That is, the state of conflict, tension, and group cohesion within the legislature itself is directly affected by its own output and its process of arriving at that output. In the same way, legislators' sense of concern, apathy or efficacy may be affected by prolonged stalemate or continuing dissatisfaction with the legislative product on the part of individual legislators.

The second type of consequences of legislative output for the legislature itself includes all those cases where the attitude or behavior of clienteles, having been affected by legislative output, react back directly upon the legislators in a temporal sequence. Electoral effects are an instance of this process, as indicated by the widespread

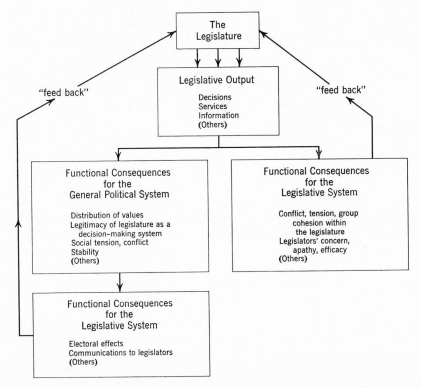

Figure 14. *Legislative output and the end variables of political inquiry.*

belief that what the legislature does and how it does it will significantly determine whether some legislators are defeated or re-elected. Communications to legislators from constituents and others are likewise commonly assumed to follow varying patterns depending upon how those persons react to legislative output. Dissatisfied clients may take their business elsewhere—for example, pressure groups may begin to deal with administrators instead of legislators. In the long run, the legislature as a decision-making system may atrophy as a result of such developments, and the function of the legislative institution in the system become something quite different from what we have called lawmaking.

Bearing in mind that the foregoing discussion does not pretend to offer a genuine theoretical formulation, we can summarize the relationships among the classes and types of variables discussed in graphic fashion, as shown in Figure 1.4. The result can hardly be called a model of the political system, for the relationships described are essentially logical relationships, useful for guiding classification and data collection, perhaps, but not for stating theoretical propositions about *how* any given factor will vary concurrently with any other. The major point to be made is not that the particular "variables" described here should immediately become the basic concepts of political research. It is simply that a principal and pressing task of general political science is to conceptualize, in terms suitable for empirical research, what can be called the "end variables" of political inquiry.

CHAPTER 2

Method: research design

T HE PURPOSE OF THIS CHAPTER is to describe what data are being reported, how they were collected and analyzed, and to point out the connections between decisions of research strategy and the theoretical framework which guided the research. Our research incorporated several innovations in conception, design, and conduct which may be of special interest to professional readers who are concerned with methodological problems ranging beyond the particular subject of this research. But these more general problems of method are reserved for consideration in Chapter 18, where they are treated in some detail.

Our fundamental working hypothesis, as explained in Chapter 1, was that a significant proportion of legislators' behavior is role behavior, that this behavior is substantially congruent with their role concepts, and that insight into the working of legislative bodies can therefore be gained by ascertaining their role concepts. The principal objective, therefore, was to discover the main role orientations of legislators. More specifically, we sought to explore the dimensions and range of this variable and to relate it both to the functioning of the legislatures dependent on it and to a few key variables which might influence legislators' role concepts.

RESEARCH SITES AND SAMPLE

Because of the interest of the Social Science Research Council's Political Behavior Committee in comparative research, it was early determined that the research would focus on several American states. A large element of fortuitous circumstance entered into the selection of the sites in which the research was eventually carried out, however. The controlling reason for operating within American states, rather than including at least some non-American legislatures, was un-

This chapter drafted by Wahlke and Eulau.

doubtedly that the project grew out of four different projects focussing on various problems in different states which the authors individually had already under way before the project came into being.

The choice of the particular four states was likewise the result of largely accidental factors. Three of them were the home states of three authors at the time of research; New Jersey was deliberately selected somewhat later because its legislature is smaller than the other three, it is located in a different region, and its socio-economic character differs from the others.[1]

Despite the accidental character of the choice, selection of California, New Jersey, Ohio, and Tennessee suited the purposes of the research quite well. The four states differ considerably with respect to such matters as the size of legislative chambers, the continuity and intensity of the legislative operation, salaries, staff and facilities for the members, and character of the party system in the legislature, as well as with respect to such demographic and ecological characteristics as education level of the population, proportion of urban to rural populations, degree of industrialization, and geographical region of the country. In other words, they exhibited sufficient variation on all those variables which we might wish to relate to variations in legislators' role concepts.

Although these four legislatures in no sense constitute a representative sample of any universe of legislatures, comparison of what legislators do in these four institutional environments affords a much sounder basis for generalization than would inspection of one legislature only. Because one can specify certain respects in which the four institutional environments are similar and others in which they are different, it is to some extent possible to test hypotheses (or suggest new ones) concerning differences between systems as such. But, equally important, study of four legislatures yields data for comparing eight legislative chambers, sixteen legislative party groups, and other units which can be viewed as so many experimental and control groups, depending upon the particular problem one wishes to investigate. Insofar as one seeks generalizations applicable to all legislators as such, it should not be forgotten that studying four states yields a potential population of hundreds, where study in one yields comparatively few cases on which to base analysis.

---

[1] But the selection of New Jersey was made possible by the willingness of one author's institution to supplement the research funds for that purpose. Originally the project included the states of Michigan, Mississippi, Ohio, and Tennessee. The final selection of states was determined, however, before construction of the interview schedule.

One particular decision relative to sampling deserves mention here. That is the decision to attempt to interview all members of all four legislatures, i.e., to seek a 100 per cent sample. This decision was made to avoid sampling worries at least so far as concerns the problem of making statistical inferences from a sample to the particular population studied.[2] Although we did not succeed in interviewing our entire populations, we came so close to the 100 per cent mark that some potentially thorny sampling problems were obviated (see below, Table 2.4).

INTERVIEW DATA

The decision to attack the problem of legislators' role concepts with data obtained from interviews with them is justified above all by the theoretical assumptions discussed in the preceeding chapter. The choice made was essentially a choice between collecting data about legislators' perceptions and collecting data about their overt behavior. The enormous difficulties of observing overt behavior in real life, as distinct from experimental, situations have often been pointed out[3]— selecting what classes of action to observe, from the innumerable actions which are observable; actually classifying the actions which are observed; securing access to observe actions ordinarily performed in private or in secret; and others equally troublesome. But our reasons for choosing the interview method had little to do with seeking to avoid these difficulties. It was not our primary purpose to ask respondents for information about their overt actions, though such a course might be justified for some research. Our interviews were designed rather to secure data primarily about legislators' perceptions, so that we could inferentially construct portions of their cognitive and evaluative maps.[4]

Generally speaking, the direct question put to a respondent provides evidence about his perceptions which is no more circumstantial than data collected by other methods. More specifically, however, the concept of "role" refers to perceptual aspects of phenomena as well as to overt physical actions. It describes something in the minds of legisla-

[2] See below, Chapter 18, pp. 455–462, for more detailed discussion of this and other statistical problems.

[3] See, for example, George Homans, *The Human Group* (New York: Harcourt, Brace, 1950), pp. 24–47.

[4] The rationale for focussing upon political actors' "cognitive maps" is succinctly presented in Angus Campbell, et al., *The American Voter* (New York: John Wiley and Sons, Inc., 1960), pp. 42 ff.

tors, and not just the gross physical mechanics of their behavior. Of course, since role theory asserts overt actions (role behavior) conform to perceptions (role concepts), it would be possible to attack the problem in other ways—for example, by observation of legislators' role behavior or through investigation of the expectations about legislative role behavior entertained by others. But there is no sound theoretical reason for preferring one of these methods over another.[5]

The more pressing question here is the empirical one: how reliable, truthful, and complete are the responses of legislators to questions probing their role concepts? Validation of the role concepts discovered in our research lay beyond the scope of this particular project, which seeks primarily to delineate the role (i.e., role concepts) of legislators. The usual limitations of time and resources, as well as the methodological difficulties of doing otherwise, have forced us to concentrate upon the perceptual data and to forego systematic comparison of overt behavior with corresponding role concepts. Wherever behavioral data (i.e., data about behavior not elicited in response to interview questions about role concepts) could be compared directly with role perceptions—as was the case with respect to expert roles and friendship roles, and in connection with the questions on education issues—it became apparent that there was substantial agreement, but invariably some deviation. Less systematic observation of the activities of individual members playing known roles appeared to substantiate this less-than-perfect relationship. Whether such discrepancy as occurred was due to interviewing inadequacies, to members' rationalization of their own roles, or deliberate intent to mislead, we cannot say. Our intention was to delineate the roles as accurately as we could, realizing that perfect accuracy was unlikely.

Questions about the accuracy of interview data in reflecting legislators' role concepts must not be confused with questions about the congruence between role concepts and role behavior. The assumptions of role theory tell us that there should be substantial conformity but that there is not likely to be a perfect one-to-one correspondence. The discrepancy between role concept and role behavior in particular cases is, indeed, an extremely important datum in any role analysis. But

[5] Nadel suggests three different ways for empirically investigating roles— establishing how frequently and regularly assumed attributes or behaviors of the role appear together in fact; examining the explicit statements and assertions of people as to the conduct deemed appropriate to given roles; and examining the maintenance, or sanctions, machinery of the society. In Nadel's words, "the first and third method involve the piecing together of the role, while the second may furnish us with the total picture." (S. F. Nadel, *op. cit.*, p. 25.) It is a variety of Nadel's "second method" which has been followed in our research.

our research concepts and instruments are not sufficiently refined to enable us to say, in the event of difference between the way legislators are seen to behave and their role concepts as inferred from interview data, whether that difference is attributable to divergence of role concept from role behavior or to inaccurate representation of the role concept. The important point for the limited purposes of this research is the finding of sufficient congruence to make us confident we achieved reasonably accurate delineation of legislators' role concepts.

The interview schedule.[6]   Theoretical justification of the interview method did not, of course, solve the practical problem of formulating questions to elicit the kinds of data required. The schedule of questions used was a formidable one, requiring an average of one and a half to two hours for completion. It opened with a series of questions about the respondent's personal background which moved from simple factual questions (about education, occupation, etc.) to increasingly complex ones concerning the respondent's political career and interests. Then came a series of questions probing perceptions of the working of the legislature and the tasks of legislators and legislative officers, followed by a series concerning the working of political parties and pressure groups. A succeeding set of questions dealt with an issue of substantive policy, that of "school needs," and legislators' perceptions of the bearing of parties, pressure groups, and other factors on that issue. Before the interview was closed with several personal questions (about religion, income, etc.), respondents were asked some twenty-five agree-disagree type questions designed for the construction of various measures and scales.

The key questions seeking data about legislators' role concepts were open-ended questions which gave the respondent the widest possible opportunity to structure his response and to introduce whatever categories of information or comment seemed to him to be relevant to the question. Because there has been no previous formulation of legislators' roles which might indicate critical questions legislators should be "forced" to answer, we did not feel justified in imposing on them by closed questions any preconceptions we might have. Instead we sought to devise questions pinpointing as clearly as possible the area or topic we wished legislators to talk about, to insure, by appropriate probing questions, that they talked as fully as possible, and thereby to amass enough essentially qualitative data to suggest to us the critical categories of legislators' thoughts and perceptions.

[6] The full interview schedule and instructions to interviewers are presented in Appendix 6, pp. 492–504.

Interview procedures and experience. One author was responsible for completion of the interviews and other aspects of the field stage of the research in each state—Buchanan in California, Eulau in Ohio, Ferguson in New Jersey, and Wahlke in Tennessee. The method of arranging for and conducting interviews varied from state to state, according to the particular modes of legislative operation and the size of the job in each. Somewhat over half the interviews were conducted by the authors themselves, most of the remainder by graduate or undergraduate students, and a few by professional colleagues or friends interested in the project.

In general, interviews were begun only after the authors had been present in the legislative chambers for several weeks and had become known to a number of the members. Begun in late January or early February, interviewing continued to early June, 1957.

The place of interview was largely dependent upon the structure, customs, and facilities of the several legislatures. In New Jersey, where the legislature meets only one day a week, it was necessary to conduct the interviews in the homes, offices, or places of business of the respondents. This was facilitated by the relatively short distances involved in getting around the state. Only 16 of the 79 New Jersey respondents were interviewed in the legislative chambers. In Ohio, on the other hand, with its large legislature and great geographical distances, but where the legislature met from early January until the middle of June, a determined effort had to be made to conduct and complete as many interviews as possible within the legislative session and in the legislative chambers. In Tennessee, by contrast to Ohio, the short duration of the legislative session—January 7 through March 22—required that approximately half of the interviews be conducted after adjournment in respondents' homes or places of business. In Ohio and Tennessee where, except for the leadership, legislators have no office facilities whatsoever, interviews in the capitol had to be held at respondents' desks on the floor at the beginning or close of the legislative day or during recesses, in lounges, committee rooms, and other nooks. In California 27 legislators were interviewed in their homes or offices during the February recess following the introduction of bills, and the remainder in Sacramento where legislators have spacious private offices which provide almost ideal interviewing conditions. The problem was finding them in those offices long enough to complete the interviews, and toward the end of the session several members had to be interviewed at the rear of the chamber. As Table 2.1, summarizing the locations of the interviews in the four states indicates, in all states some interviews took place in hotel rooms and restaurants, and some in such unlikely places as the embalming room of a funeral parlor, at a hospital bed, a fish dock, an automobile, or a bale of hay in a produce barn. While field interviewing in New Jersey was easy because of the state's limited geographical extent, the post-session interviews in Tennessee involved a heavy investment of time and money, since they required four roadtrips from Nashville, each lasting from one to two weeks, and each requiring thousands of miles of travel by automobile.

Table 2.1: Location of interviews in the four states

	N.J.	Calif.	Ohio	Tenn.
Capitol building (floor or office)	16	83	153	40
Hotel rooms, restaurants	5	2	3	31
Homes	15	10	1	8
Place of business	42	16	4	35
Miscellaneous (including combination of above)	1	2	1	6
Total	79	113	162	120

Table 2.2: Abridgment of interviews

	N.J.	Calif.	Ohio	Tenn.
Issue series omitted	8	23	8	6
Scale items omitted	0	1	0	2
Issue series and scale omitted	0	2	0	0
Otherwise abridged	1	5	0	0
Interview complete	70	82	154	112
Total	79	113	162	120

In view of the complexity of the interview schedule it is hardly surprising that there was considerable variation in the duration of interviews. They ranged generally from one to five hours in length (the average, as previously noted, being approximately two hours), although one Tennessee interview—surprisingly full despite its brevity, thanks to this respondent's terse and rapid-fire manner—was completed in one-half hour. In many cases, the interview could not be completed in the initial visit and one, or occasionally two call backs were necessary. In some instances, it was not possible to complete an interview, in spite of efforts to arrange call backs at the time it was interrupted. The number of incomplete interviews and the character of the abridgments is shown in Table 2.2.

In spite of the demanding nature of the interview, the heavy competition for the time of busy legislators, and the physical and logistical difficulties of interviewing 504 persons in four states, remarkably complete coverage was obtained. From 91 per cent (in Tennessee) to 100 per cent (in New Jersey) of all members were interviewed. Of the 30 persons not interviewed, only 8 refused outright to be interviewed, although another 14 were suspected in some degree to have evaded being questioned. The data concerning total number of interviews and failures of interview in each of the four states are shown in Table 2.3.

Table 2.3: Interviews and failures to interview

	N.J.	Calif.	Ohio	Tenn.
Refused outright	0	3	3	2
Evaded interview	0	3	7	4
Died or hospitalized	0	1	1	0
Contact failure	0	0	0	6
Total not interviewed	0	7	11	12
Total interviewed	79	113	162	120
Per cent interviewed	100	94	94	91
Total membership	79*	120	173	132

* Constitutionally, the New Jersey legislature has 80 members. One seat was vacant in 1957.

More important than the sheer number of interviews completed, however, was their quality. All four authors and all interviewers were impressed with the relative accessibility, the cooperative attitude, and the frank and open responses in all four states. At the end of each interview, interviewers were required to rate the frankness and sincerity of respondents' replies. Although ratings of this kind are highly subjective and likely to vary a good deal from interviewer to interviewer, they tend to become standardized and to acquire greater validity where interviewers accumulate experience in a particular situation and acquaintance with a particular population, and where they not merely interview but also observe respondents daily at their work on the floor, in committee, and elsewhere, and hear what their colleagues say about them. In such circumstances, interviewers rapidly formulate standards and criteria which make their ratings credible. As Table 2.4 shows, comparatively few respondents in the four states were judged evasive or not very frank by those who interviewed them.

In addition to the interview data we have, of course, made use of certain types of documentary data, which require little explanation. Each of the authors accumulated another sort of datum, however, which has no doubt entered into the analysis, although it was not systematically collected or applied. From the beginning, we were keenly aware of the unfamiliarity of the territory to be explored with a research method that had not previously been used for this purpose. In order to accumulate all the experience and the unsystematic data possible, each author observed at first hand, through practically the

Table 2.4: Interviewers' ratings of respondents' frankness

	N.J.	Calif.	Ohio	Tenn.
Very frank	13	32	51	58
Frank	59	48	86	52
Not very frank	7	22	19	9
Very evasive	0	7	5	0
Not recorded	0	4	1	1
Total	79	113	162	120

entire sessions of 1957, the operations of one legislature. In addition, each visited, observed for at least a short period, and conducted some interviews in one or more of the other three legislatures.

METHODS OF ANALYSIS

The size of the population studied (504, of whom 474 were interviewed) dictated the use of machine methods of analysis. The various data were coded, punched into Hollerith cards, and processed through I.B.M. 075 or 082 counter-sorters, 101 statistical and 402 tabulating machines, or 650 or 704 electronic computers, depending upon the complexity of the problem to be handled. The code for punching the data was constructed jointly by the four authors after completion of the interviews. Each was then individually responsible for preliminary analysis of assigned portions of the data.

A major problem in analysis was the coding and processing of data from the numerous and important open-ended questions, which allow the respondent to phrase his answers in his own words. The resulting heterogeneity of verbal responses required many classificatory judgments both in the construction of codes and in the coding of often complex and diverse forms of verbal behavior. Moreover, because this was an essentially exploratory study, it was difficult to anticipate the variety and extent of responses to open-ended questions. Consequently, many of the major categories and concepts used in subsequent chapters were devised at the stage of coding and analyzing the data, not devised a priori and used as categories for collecting them. That is, they were constructed inductively out of the manifest content of legislators' responses, not deductively out of our theoretical conceptions of role or of the character of the legislative system. Our theoretical task was in large part to relate such inductive, a posteriori concepts to the theoretical framework.

The chapters which follow range over a great variety of problems and arrive at many different kinds and levels of generalization. It is inevitable, therefore, that the data are presented differently, depending upon the hypothesis in question or the problem under consideration. Where we generalize about all legislators, we have aggregated the data from all interviews; where we generalize about interstate differences, we have grouped the data by states; where we discuss differences between parties which persist throughout states, we have grouped the data by party; where interstate differences are thought to reflect underlying differences between party members, we have grouped the data by parties within states; and so on. In some cases we have based analysis not upon the number of respondents in a given legislature, chamber, party, or other category, but upon the number of responses made by them. Such variations in the bases of analysis, depending as they do upon the questions to which the data are addressed at any given point, should occasion the reader no difficulties. The justification for using each one is, we hope, made clear when it is used.

For various reasons, however, there are slight variations in the number of cases representing each of these different bases from one use to the next. In some cases this results from failure of a few respondents to answer a particular question. In others, it results from the open-ended character of a question, whereby some respondents might give answers codable in a given category but others fail to give them (even though they did answer the same question in ways codable under other headings). To alert the reader to this variability in N's we have, in all cases, indicated the basis for computing each table of data.

A number of difficult and complex statistical problems were encountered in the analysis. These are discussed below (Chapter 18, pp. 455–462), but several points should be noted here. Because the studies which follow were conceived of as exploratory, we have not hesitated to make inferences from small differences, fully recognizing that we have not definitively established generalizations of this kind. Similarly, we have relied more upon internal replication than upon magnitude of differences as evidence supporting our findings.

Finally, as the reader will discover, we have not confined ourselves to reporting just quantitative results of the interviews. We have quoted generously from the interview protocols, not only to illustrate the meaning of one or another abstract concept or category of analysis but to lend depth to that analysis by giving the reader some realistic feeling for the way legislators talk and think about their problems. We have not generally drawn any conclusions from the impressions conveyed by legislators' words, except as those impressions have been subjected to systematic comparison with the words of all others.

The actual writing of the book, like the design, conduct, and analysis of the research, was a joint venture of the four authors. One member of the research "team" was responsible for drafting each particular chapter on the basis of an outline jointly planned. In some cases, owing to the individual interests of another, the writing of a chapter became a joint enterprise by two members. A footnote at the beginning of each chapter indicates who was responsible for its original drafting. But the words in print are the product of criticisms, comments, and suggestions made both individually and collectively *en conference* by all four authors. This research was an experiment not only in comparative but also in collaborative methods. To methodological problems associated with this aspect of the research we have also given considerable attention in Chapter 18.

CHAPTER 3

Context: settings of the study

THIS CHAPTER SEEKS TO PROVIDE enough background to make the four legislatures as institutions comprehensible. The descriptions which follow are offered on the assumption that certain "organizational facts" and "situational landmarks" are perceived in substantially the same way by all the legislators in a state, and that journalists and academic observers share this common perception. We are dealing here only with features where it seems reasonable to assume the consensus in perception is so high that the phenomena may be adequately described without recourse to our interview data.[1] The account is not a complete description, but emphasizes those similarities and differences which are relevant to the rest of the study.

The four systems are described as they existed in 1957, when Ohio, New Jersey, and California were all in the hands of Republicans. Party balance, elections laws and procedures, and problems faced by legislators have changed since then, but such changes are immaterial to our analysis (except on rare occasions when they highlight the situation existing in 1957).

Size and party composition in the legislatures. The number of members of each chamber, their distribution by party, and the party controlling the executive branch are given in Table 3.1. There are large and basic differences in the dimensions of the chambers. It is evident that a freshman Republican in the Ohio lower house, to take one extreme, is surrounded by a necessarily complex organization. His term may be half over before he can identify his 138 fellow

This chapter drafted by Buchanan.

[1] Concerning documentary and other sources of information on particular states and their legislatures see Appendix 7.

40

members, or for that matter his 96 fellow Republicans. At the other extreme, a freshman New Jersey senator finds himself a member of what is called "the 21 Club"—a circle that could easily meet in his own living room. Other chambers fall somewhere in between. None of the houses we studied is large compared with some New England legislatures or with Congress. Only two of the eight chambers are as large as the United States Senate. Some of the consequences of size will become apparent in Chapter 10, dealing with interpersonal relationships between members.

Deadlocks between a governor of one party and a legislature controlled by the other, or between two legislative chambers controlled by different parties, occur with some frequency in American states

Table 3.1: Size of chamber and party balance in the four legislatures

| | Calif. | | | N.J. | | | Ohio | | | Tenn. | | |
	House	Sen.	Gov.	House	Sen.	Gov.	House	Sen.	Gov.	House	Sen.	Gov.
Democratic	38	20*		20	7	x	42	12		78	27	x
Republican	42	20	x	38	14		97	22	x	21	6	
Total	80	40		58	21		139	34		99	33	

* The California Senate was organized by Democrats.

due to the combination of bicameralism, separation of powers, and a two-party system.[2] However, in 1957 the potentiality for such a deadlock was present only in New Jersey, where Democratic Governor Robert B. Meyner confronted a heavily Republican legislature. Republicans were safely in control in Ohio; Democrats in Tennessee. The situation in California may only be understood in terms of the peculiar politics of that state, which will be discussed below, but it amounted to Republican control of both branches. The particular balance that existed in 1957, however, may be understood only in the context of the historical balance between the parties in each of the states studied.

PARTY SYSTEMS IN THE STATES

Most of the efforts to categorize state party systems have involved an assessment of the extent to which they deviate from the two-party competitive system prevailing at the national level. Whether a given state is classified as "competitive" or "one-party" or somewhere between depends on whether the criterion is presidential, congressional,

[2] See V. O. Key, Jr., *American State Politics, An Introduction* (New York: Alfred A. Knopf, 1956), Chapter 3.

gubernatorial, or legislative elections, or some combination of these, and also on the period chosen for study. Except for Tennessee, these four states are as difficult as any to classify.

When presidential, senatorial, and gubernatorial races are combined for the period 1914–1954, California, New Jersey, and Ohio are "two-party" states, Tennessee a "modified one-party" system.[3] There is a difference between these top-of-the-ticket offices and legislative elections. On the criterion of party majorities in the lower houses from 1924 to 1956, Key puts Tennessee in the predominantly (above 90 per cent) Democratic group, New Jersey is "strongly Republican," and California and Ohio become bracketed in the intermediate group which leans toward Republican control.[4]

The American Political Science Association Committee on State Legislatures a few years ago categorized the states by their current party balance, and also asked observers in each state to appraise the party system. Ohio was classed as a two-party state, but one with only moderate party cohesion. New Jersey was classed as one with a weak minority party (Democratic) but with strong party cohesion in legislative competition. California was classed as a two-party state on the basis of Democratic membership, but as a state with extremely weak party cohesion. Tennessee of course was a one-party state, though not among the extreme ones.[5]

By whatever standard, Tennessee is on the borderline between a one-party state and one with a weak minority party. Perhaps a dozen states are more extreme. California is further up the line, and its placement depends upon whether one gives weight to the long Republican dominance or the brief Democratic ascendencies in the 1930's and since 1954. Similarly, New Jersey is inconsistent, being either Republican-dominated, competitive, or Democratic-dominated, depending on what offices are examined in what period. It is less competitive on the legislative than on the gubernatorial level, where until 1958 no Democratic governor since Woodrow Wilson had commanded a majority of even one legislative chamber. By any standard, Ohio is among the most competitive two-party states in the Union, and has been so in national elections since the Civil War. Republicans

[3] Austin Ranney and Willmoore Kendall, *Democracy and the American Party System* (New York: Harcourt, Brace and Company, 1956), pp. 161–164.

[4] Key, *Politics, Parties and Pressure groups*, 4th ed. (New York: Thomas Y. Crowell and Company, 1958), pp. 314–315.

[5] Belle Zeller, Edit., *American State Legislatures* (New York: Thomas Y. Crowell and Company, 1954), Chapter 12.

have nevertheless maintained an advantage, though not an insuperable one, in legislative elections.

Let us examine the party balance in each state in more qualitative, less statistical terms:

Tennessee. In contrast to some Southern states, Tennessee has for many years had a Republican delegation in Nashville. It comes largely from East Tennessee. It has not altered appreciably in size or origin in half a century, since its reason for being is more closely related to the politics of 1861 than of 1957.[6] In legislative voting, as in state elections, the Republicans numerically are too weak even to hope to gain control, yet they are strong enough to determine occasionally which of two competing Democratic factions will govern.

California. Until 1910 California politics were not strikingly different from those of other states. Election-law reforms introduced at that time by Hiram Johnson Progressives—non-partisan local elections, over-regulation of state parties, easy direct legislation, and above all cross-filing—tended to vitiate the party system in California. In the late 1940's as many as three-fourths of the legislators gained office by the non-partisan route of cross-filing, a tactic at which Republicans seemed more skillful than Democrats. It is not surprising that some of them in this atmosphere of independence from parties were able to keep alive Johnson's antipathy toward political parties.[7] Beginning in 1954, when amended election laws required candidates to indicate their party affiliation on the primary ballot, voters could again without difficulty distinguish Democrats from Republicans. They started sending more Democrats to the legislature forthwith. Cross-filing was still in effect when this study was made, but only one-fourth of the members gained their seats in this way in 1956. A good many more, however, had entered politics when non-partisanship was not only a valued tradition but a highly successful electioneering technique.

New Jersey. The strength of both parties in New Jersey lies in the county organizations, and there is wide variation among the counties in the nature of party membership, discipline, and policy orientation. South Jersey Republicans, whose center of power is the smooth-work-

----

[6] V. O. Key, Jr., *Southern Politics in State and Nation*, (New York: Alfred A. Knopf, 1949), Chapter 4.

[7] James C. Findley, "Cross-Filing and the Progressive Movement in California Politics," *Western Political Quarterly* 12:699–711 (1959); Joseph P. Harris, *California Politics*, 3d ed. (Stanford University Press, 1961), Chapter 1.

ing Atlantic City machine, tend to be quite conservative. In the northern counties such as Bergen and Passaic there are more "modern" Republicans, and even some affiliated with the C.I.O.

Twenty years ago the Democratic party organization was hardly more than an appendage of Frank Hague's Hudson County machine. Democratic strength first increased in the Camden and Trenton areas, and those former Republican strongholds, as well as Middlesex County, are now considered safely Democratic. At the time of this study, Republicans still controlled the Passaic and Essex county delegations in the Assembly, and hence had a safe legislative majority. Governor Meyner was on the verge of forging a state-wide Democratic organization, despite only luke-warm support from the Hudson County machine.

Though neither party had managed to coordinate the activities of the legislators with those of the state party organization, in the larger counties there was close supervision by local party organizations of their respective delegations. The large county organizations controlled the nomination of assembly candidates, and "rotated" these nominations to reward the party faithful and at the same time to keep close control of the delegation. Large delegations had their own leaders, conferred frequently, and customarily voted as a unit.

The New Jersey Senate, consisting of one man per county, seems safely Republican for some time to come. The lower house (Assembly) passed over to Democratic control for the first time in a generation in 1958, following our study.

Ohio. Democrats have controlled the legislative and executive branches on two occasions in the recent past: once in the mid-'thirties and again in the late 'forties. Democratic governors had been in office more frequently than that—actually about half the time since the early 1920's—but they have considered themselves lucky if they had a slim majority in one chamber to support their programs.[8] Republican governors usually had supporting majorities in both houses, and this was the situation in 1957.

The state Republican organization extends down to the county level, where it controls access to the legislature, and this was an essential element in the strength of the chamber leadership. Democrats, by contrast, were not united. Their city organizations were fighting for control of the state party, and there was also a difference of opinion on strategy between those legislators who were willing to negotiate with the Republican leadership and those who believed that militant

[8] Key, *American State Politics, op. cit.,* Fig. 10, p. 72.

opposition would pay off in the long run. Democratic governors (most recently, Frank J. Lausche) have not been unwilling to come to terms with the dominant Republicans in the legislative branch. This willingness to cooperate across party lines has heightened the contrast between "strong" party cohesion in New Jersey and the "moderate" cohesion in Ohio that was noted in the A.P.S.A. report.

The Democrats were divided into three factions in 1957: the pro-Lausche conservatives, often from rural, down-state counties; the Cleveland-based anti-Lausche group which numerically dominated the delegations; and a loosely knit "New Deal" faction who looked to Michael V. DiSalle of Toledo for leadership. In 1958 Democrats won control of both houses, organized behind DiSalle as a successful gubernatorial candidate.

Party balance, contemporary and historical. Because of these many different kinds of "partisanship" it is not easy to array the states in order of partisanship. However, in electoral terms there are few exceptions to the order: Ohio, New Jersey, California, and Tennessee in order of descending competitiveness. On the other hand, when one focusses on the enthusiasm with which members go about being partisan, the array: New Jersey, Ohio, Tennessee, and California may better express the historical pattern, although there is a judgment here, particularly with respect to the last two states, that cannot be expressed in strictly quantitative terms.

When the chambers are arrayed in order of the party balances existing in 1957 (which is done simply by putting Table 3.1 into percentage terms) still a different pattern emerges:

California	Senate	50%	each
California	House	53	Republican
Ohio	Senate	65	Republican
New Jersey	House	66	Republican
New Jersey	Senate	67	Republican
Ohio	House	70	Republican
Tennessee	House	79	Democratic
Tennessee	Senate	82	Democratic

California in 1957 was quite clearly the most closely balanced legislature. With the advantage of a hindsight that the legislators interviewed then did not have, we may attribute this to the fact that California was in a rapid state of transition to Democratic control. Ohio, too, though the legislature in 1957 appeared to be safely in Republican hands, was in transition.

It must be recalled that our concern in this chapter is not with structural factors for their own sake, but instead as boundary elements that presumably shape the legislators' views of their situation. The question may be asked: To which do legislators give more weight, the situation as they have learned to know it during their tenure of office, or the situation that clearly faces them at the moment? We cannot answer this in advance (beyond suspecting it will differ for individuals), but we may avoid concentrating exclusively upon contemporary party balance at the expense of an out-of-date historical balance, for it may be that legislators, like others, are victims of cultural lag.

APPORTIONMENT AND DISTRICTING

Apportionment of state legislatures is notorious for the weight given to rural constituencies, and these four are not exceptions. Tennessee and Ohio were among the twenty-two "where distortions from democratic theory can be considered substantial," according to Gordon Baker; and New Jersey and California were among the eight states where urban under-representation was "especially severe."[9] The standard set by an American Political Science Association committee for apportionment of Congress was 15 per cent above or below "normal" (the number obtained by dividing the population by the number of seats).[10]   Table 3.2 shows how wide is the departure from this standard in every chamber except the Ohio Senate.   It is always the metropolitan areas that are under-represented, except in the New Jersey House, where the middle-sized, rapidly growing suburban counties have fewer members in proportion to population than either the most or the least urban areas.

The apportionment system determines what segment of the population, geographically defined, has the larger share of the votes in a chamber, but the controlling segment may be divided, or may not perceive any common interest, so that it does not exercise the power mathematically at its disposal.   Dominant non-metropolitan blocs must vote together (or effectively threaten to do so) if they are to get their way, and they may not do this.[11]   Just as relevant as apportion-

[9] Gordon E. Baker, *Rural versus Urban Political Power* (New York: Doubleday and Company, 1955), pp. 15–17.

[10] "The Reapportionment of Congress," *American Political Science Review* 45: 153–154 (1951). See also, *Law and Contemporary Problems*, Vol. 17, No. 2 (Spring, 1952), issue on legislative reapportionment.

[11] David R. Derge, "Metropolitan and Outstate Alignments in Illinois and Missouri Legislative Delegations," *American Political Science Review* 52:1051–1065 (1958).

ment—perhaps more so—are other aspects of the formula determined by state population, the size of the legislature and law regarding multi-member districting.[12] These parameters, in several possible combinations, determine (1) over how many constituents a legislator must spread himself, (2) with how many other legislators he must share each constituent, and (3) with how many legislators he must interact.

For contrasting examples, take two of the largest counties: Los Angeles, represented by 31 members in the 80–man California lower house, and Cuyahoga (Cleveland), represented by 18 members in the 139–man Ohio House. Each Los Angeles member is elected from a

Table 3.2: Apportionment and malapportionment: district population as a percentage of average district population

Population in Proportion to Average District Population*	Calif. House	Calif. Sen.	N.J. House	N.J. Sen.	Ohio House	Ohio Sen.	Tenn. House	Tenn. Sen.
Over 220% of average	—	3	—	3	—	—	12	5
115% to 219% of average	23	5	10	4	70	5	33	7
85% to 114% (within 15% of normal)	33	3	40	2	13	23	11	3
55% to 85% of average	21	3	5	3	13	6	28	8
Under 55% of average	3	26	3	9	43	—	15	10
Total seats	80	40	58	21	139	34	99	33

* Population of multimember district is divided by the number of members representing it.

single-member district. Central city representatives are Democrats, suburban ones Republicans. Each member is responsible to constituents numbering from 110,000 to 160,000; he is their sole representative in the Assembly. Each comes from a contiguous, if not compact, area more or less homogeneous with respect to socio-economic characteristics. By contrast, Cuyahoga's delegation is elected at large. Each member represents all 1,400,000 persons in the county. Most of the members are Democrats, since Democratic strength in the central city districts gives that slate an advantage. Each member represents a scattered, heterogeneous mass public, sharing the responsibility for it with 17 other members. These differences alone are enough to account for the fact that the Cleveland Democratic contingent is often able to dominate the Democratic party delegation and can easily

[12] Maurice Klain, "A New Look at the Constituencies: The Need for a Recount and a Reappraisal," American Political Science Review 49:1105–1119 (1955).

elect its man minority leader, while the Los Angeles delegation is split into two parties, three factions, and several mavericks, and often can agree only on the most basic geographical issues. What other differences in style of representation may result remain to be seen.

All Californians, about three-fourths of Tennesseans, one-half of the Ohioans, and one-third of the New Jerseyans represent single-member districts. In the two largest counties in New Jersey (Hudson and Essex) the combination of local machine strength and multi-member districting has produced a peculiar system of rotation. The party organizations controlling access to the slates balance them nicely by racial, ethnic, religious, and occupational background. They commonly permit a member only two terms in the legislature before they move him on to a local or national candidacy or return him to the obscurity from whence he came. As a result, representatives from these counties are likely to have more experience in local government than in legislative procedure, and they do not accumulate seniority. There are a few exceptions where a member is particularly useful to the party in the Assembly, or has enough local strength to avoid being "rotated."

District lines in Tennessee coincide with county lines (as in New Jersey and the Ohio House) but 17 of 33 seats in the Tennessee Senate and 23 of 99 seats in the House represent multi-county districts. The latter are called "floterial districts" and ordinarily consist of two counties, though they may have as many as five. A system of rotation is practiced in at least 17 of these 40 constituencies, whereby Democratic county organizations agree to pass the nomination of candidates from one to the other in some regular order. By terms of the rotation agreements, all but one of the county organizations in the district refrain from nominating a candidate in any given election. Courts have upheld these rotation agreements in contested elections. Although some legislators manage under this system to "rotate" from House to Senate as their county rotates the two seats, the general effect of the system is to reduce the level of experience in the legislature by interrupting the tenure of a number of members and reducing the chances of their eventual re-election.

TENURE, TURNOVER, AND EXPERIENCE OF LEGISLATORS

One of the most striking differences between chambers is in the length of service of the members. Nearly half the Tennessee House turns over each session. More than half the New Jersey Assembly is rotated out after two terms. By contrast the Ohio and California legislatures consist of older persons, with considerably more legislative experience. (The distributions are given in Appendix 5.) Factors which appear to be relevant to turnover are the rate of compensation, responsibility sufficient to make the job attractive, electoral laws and practice which favor incumbents or discourage rotation, as well as the constitutional length of terms of office.

The amount of time spent on legislative business is quite variable as well. The New Jersey member commutes to Trenton every Monday for perhaps six months of every year. Ohio and Tennessee legislatures meet for several months continuously in the spring of odd-numbered years. California legislators alternate between one-month and four-month annual sessions, but many of them spend two additional months on interim committee meetings scattered through the period. In Table 3.3 the approximate number of days per year spent

Table 3.3: Index of average legislative service in each chamber

	Calif. House	Calif. Sen.	N.J. House	N.J. Sen.	Ohio House	Ohio Sen.	Tenn. House	Tenn. Sen.
Number of days in session per year*	59	59	22	22	49	49	28	28
Median tenure†	5.2	8.4	3.5	5.0	4.8	8.0	2.2	4.6
Index of experience (days × tenure, rounded)	310	500	80	110	240	390	60	130

* Based on Book of the States, Vol. 12, 1958–1959, pp. 50–51.
† From Appendix 5, Table A-12.

in session, exclusive of interim committees, is given, based on the 1957 session. California and Ohio spend approximately twice as much time in session as Tennessee and New Jersey.[13]

In view of the wide variation, tenure alone becomes a poor index of the amount of legislative experience acquired by the average member of a chamber, or the actual time the legislators have associated with each other in solving policy problems. A better index, though still quite rough, is obtained by multiplying median years of tenure by the

[13] Length of sessions is, of course, quite variable, and some states pay on the basis of time in session, others at an annual rate. The number of days spent in session during the 1956–1957 biennium was figured from Council of State Governments, Book of the States, Vol. 12, 1958–1959 (Chicago, 1958), and divided by two to get the annual figure to compare with salaries. A check of earlier volumes indicated the 1956–1957 biennium was not unrepresentative.

days in session annually. This is approximately the number of days of legislative experience acquired by the average member of each chamber. This further differentiates between the states. One would expect one sort of "group life" in the California and Ohio legislatures, where members are old hands at the business and are familiar with the subject matter of legislation, as well as with one anothers' philosophies, capabilities, and idiosyncracies. One would look for quite another atmosphere in the Tennessee legislature or the New Jersey Assembly, which have a large proportion of novices in transit.

Compensation, working conditions, staff and facilities. To compare pay schedules it is necessary to make rough allowances for the difference in time demands just discussed. Table 3.4 does this. Despite the factors not taken into account when legislative pay is reduced to a simple dollars-per-day basis, the differences are so large that one must conclude that Tennessee legislators are "underprivileged" by almost any standard. New Jerseyans, in addition to a better rate, have an ideal system for fitting their legislative work into their business schedules with a minimum loss or interruption of regular income. The one-day-a-week schedule in effect for most of the time they are in session would of course be impossible in a less compact state. Californians have longer distances to travel than the others, and heavier demands on their time. A few of them move their families to Sacramento for the biennial long session and enter their children in school there. In addition, some of them spend more than a month per year on interim assignments (for which they are more than adequately compensated in mileage and per diem). Most of them consider being a legislator a half-time job, some spend full time at it, year in, year out.[14] In demands and compensation the California legislator's job is larger than the others', but he may still suffer because in time and pay it is too much for a part-time job but not enough for a full-time one.

The California legislature has by far the most impressive working facilities. Each member occupies a modern two-room office suite, with a full-time secretary guarding the outer room, answering mail, keeping track of his bills, and making appointments for constituents and lobbyists to see him. A Legislative Counsel with a staff of 26 lawyers and 22 clerks is available 13 hours a day during the week and eight hours a day on weekends to draft bills or estimate their constitutionality. There is also a Legislative Analyst, with 44 assistants, responsible to the Joint Budget Committee for combing the $2 billion

[14] The Mangore Corporation, *The California Legislator* (Los Angeles, 1958), pp. 32–33.

executive budget and recommending revisions in line with legislative policy. The University of California Bureau of Public Administration makes long-range studies of specific problems; interim committees with specialized staff work on medium-range ones. The Legislative Bill Room performs prodigious feats of overnight printing to give each

Table 3.4: Annual salary, other compensation, and approximate number of days in session, averaged for 1956–1957 biennium

	Calif.	N.J.	Ohio	Tenn.
Base pay (annual)	$6,000	$5,000	$5,000	$375
Per diem (annual)	$1,200	——	——	$190
Schedule of sessions (approx.)	5 day wk., Jan., March, Apr., May odd yrs.; Mar., even yrs.	1 day wk. Jan. thru June; few days in fall	3–5 day wk. Jan. thru May, odd yrs. only	4–5 day wk., Jan. thru Mar., odd yrs. only
Legislative days served per year* (approx.)	59	22	49	28
Total pay per day in session (approx.)	$120	$230	$101	$20
Other compensation and allowances	To $1,300 for interim mileage, per diem; to $4,000 for secretary, etc.	Mileage, RR pass, small secretarial allowance	Mileage; $2,500 more for presiding officers	Mileage; extra pay for special sessions

* From Table 3.3.

member (and lobbyists subscribing) copies of (1) every bill with its latest amendments, (2) a "History" which shows the current progress of all bills, (3) yesterday's "Journal," with roll calls, and (4) today's agenda (the "Daily File") for both houses and all committees. Except during the heat of parliamentary contest and amendment, no member has an excuse for not knowing what he is voting on; action on extensive amendments is held up until members have copies before them.

In New Jersey each member receives a small allowance for secretarial help which ordinarily goes to his wife or to his office secretary for keeping track of legislative affairs from his home or business office. There are no offices for members and few committee rooms in Trenton, but there are caucus rooms—the Senate's is air conditioned. This lack of facilities in the Capitol must be seen in the light of the Mondays-only schedule, which makes it possible for members to do the bulk of their homework while they are in their districts. A Law Revision and Legislative Services Commission has research and bill drafting offices, there is a Counsel to the Legislature and a Reference Bureau in the State Library. Records of the session are commercially published.

In Ohio the legislator's desk serves as his office for the session. Here he keeps his files, reads bills, answers mail, and interviews lobbyists and constituents. He shares a secretary with a number of other members. A Legislative Reference Bureau, staffed by part-time law students at Ohio State, aids in drafting bills, maintains a file of back measures, and also serves as a reference library. A bipartisan Legislative Service Commission consisting of 14 legislators and a professional staff of 12 persons investigates longer-range problems, using the customary power of a legislative investigating committee when necessary. Some subjects are referred to it for study by the legislature, others originate with the staff or director. Although the choice of subjects bears the stamp of majority-party policy direction, the reports themselves are comprehensive, detailed, and "objective." The staff, while outside civil service, is professional and free of patronage appointees.

The Tennessee legislature operates with a minimum of paperwork. Members work at their desks or in their hotel rooms. They have available, for absolutely essential secretarial chores, a small pool of stenographers on leave from administrative agencies for the session. The Legislative Reference Service has a staff for bill drafting, but some of the members who feel the omnipresent influence of the Governor here prefer to take their bills to the office of the independently chosen Attorney General. The Legislature provides each member with a subscription to the private "Legislative Service," which daily duplicates copies of general bills and, occasionally, important amendments (but not local bills or resolutions). Floor proceedings are tape recorded, but not transcribed until after the session is over.

THE LEADERSHIP STRUCTURE

Allowing for minor differences in nomenclature, the structure of formal leadership in chamber and party is quite similar in all four legislatures. There is always a presiding officer, almost always minority and majority party leaders, generally some kind of steering committee to attend to housekeeping and/or control the calendar, always a committee system with about a dozen or more standing committees whose titles indicate that the subjects of legislation are organized in about the same way from house to house.

Examination of the regulations governing the selection of these formal leaders indicates a slightly greater variety of enacted role requirements between chambers. A closer look at the prevailing customs and practices, many of them unrecorded, that are actually followed in the process of selecting these officers reveals that the variety is even greater than the printed rules would indicate. Finally, when we note what these officials actually do, we discover that the same essential functions may be performed by quite different officers or committees in each of the chambers. Thus the original similarity of title may turn out to be superficial. The necessary jobs—appointing committees, referring bills to them, floor management on major legislation, controlling the calendar—have to be performed. Who performs them and whether he wields the requisite power in his own behalf or in behalf of some other agency within or outside the chamber are matters that cannot be determined merely by observing the formal structure. Though detailed compilations of titles of legislative officers may be made, the 1953 survey indicated that the variety of practice is so bewildering that they are meaningless without evaluation.[15]

Some of these allocations of power are the product of long-standing agreements within the majority party as to how things shall be run. Where the majority party has been in control of the legislature for a generation, as it had been in California or New Jersey, we cannot say with certainty whether we are describing a legislative institution or a party institution. "Majority" means "Republican." "Democratic" means "minority." Of course, all sorts of legislative arrangements might change considerably if the minority were to succeed to power. But when the Democrats in 1958 took over chambers they had not held for decades, they did not, on the whole, immediately make basic changes in chamber organization and structure. This suggests that the structures we describe here are rather persistent over a period of time, regardless of which party is in power.

Appendix 3 summarizes the formal titles, the route of entry to each office and the powers, duties and functions that are attached to it. Beneath some of the surface inconsistency there is a genuine logic

---

[15] Zeller, op. cit., pp. 192–199.

that will become more apparent when we examine each chamber as a coherent, on-going institution, working within the boundaries that the society and the political and constitutional system set for it.

California. In the Assembly the Speaker is an extremely powerful person. He appoints nearly every significant officer. He selects the personnel of committees and their chairmen as well, and then he decides what bills each committee will consider. Though he is invariably chosen from the majority party, the Speaker attains office by organizing about himself a bipartisan faction—or in some instances by gaining the support of an existing faction. Because he has made implicit or explicit promises to certain majority and minority members in return for their commitments to vote for him for Speaker, he does not have an entirely free hand in appointments. He is, however, substantially independent of the Governor, of his own party, and—in recent years at least—of the lobby.

The formal role of the Majority Floor Leader was in process of evolution in 1957, the office itself having achieved official recognition only two years before. The post happened in 1957 to be held by the Republican who voted with the Democrats more often than any other member of his party. But the Majority Leader himself, the other members, and even the formal Handbook rule specifying his duties (which he, incidentally, had written), all envisioned that he would represent the Speaker, not the majority party. The Democratic Minority Floor Leader, on the other hand, carried out his job in a highly partisan fashion, needling the Republican Governor at every opportunity and opposing bills introduced by Republican members—notwithstanding the fact that he, too, was a member of the Republican Speaker's faction.

The California Senate is run by a five-man Rules Committee, chaired by the President pro Tempore, who is by all odds the dominant figure in the chamber. The Rules Committee appoints all other standing committees, refers bills to them, and handles housekeeping affairs and senatorial perquisites. Though two members of Rules come traditionally from the minority party, regardless of its strength, the committee is actually selected by the Senate as a whole. In 1957, with the chamber divided 20–20, all the Democrats and two Republicans voted for the Democratic candidate for President pro Tempore. This gave the Rules Committee a Democratic chairman and a 3–2 Democratic majority. The President pro Tempore, however, was a senator who had acted in that capacity in an earlier Republican administration when the incumbent was ill. The other Rules members who had been elected when the chamber was Republican continued to hold their seats in 1957. No party leaders existed in the California Senate, and no caucuses met. So one should not think of the Senate as being organized by the Democratic party in the usual sense, though we are forced to treat it that way.

Neither house has a person or agency primarily concerned with the calendar or agenda, though the Rules committees are technically responsible. Bills are considered in the order they arrive, at the presiding officer's desk, in committee, and on the floor. Every bill is given a hearing in committee if the author requests it, and all but a few bills reported out of committee come up for a floor vote before the session is over. Important measures are set in advance as "special orders" but this is done by vote of the membership. This "automatic calendar" is an outgrowth of the highly individualistic process where each member "carries" dozens of bills. Any officer or committee with power to advance or retard these bills would be swamped with petitions and would find the pressure unbearable.[16]

New Jersey. On paper, the New Jersey structure is similar to that of the California Assembly. The same officers and substantially the same committees appear (except for Rules committees) and they ostensibly have the same powers. In practice, the Speaker has relatively little personal influence beyond the formal leadership function. Members of the majority party are rotated into and out of the post each session as though it were a game of musical chairs. The person appointed chairman of the Appropriations committee one year can count on being elected Majority Leader next year and Speaker the year after, assuming his party continues to organize the House. Then he joins the company of ex-Speakers among the membership, some of whom may be more influential than the incumbent Speaker. Though there is a full-fledged committee structure on paper, these committees rarely meet. Bills are referred to them, but never reported out except on demand of the majority caucus. The exception is the Committee on Appropriations, whose members come to the Capitol an extra day or two during budget session to hammer out the state's fiscal policy.

The majority party caucus makes all crucial legislative decisions, both procedural and substantive, as a body. It decides who the

---

[16] Slight variations between Assembly and Senate in procedure are overlooked here in the interest of brevity. In the Senate bills are referred by the Rules Committee rather than the presiding officer alone, Senate committee chairmen and committees are more powerful because they are more cavalier about the formalities, and so on.

officers will be, which bills will be advanced on the calendar and which will die, and how these bills will be combined or amended.   A "conference committee" of elders guides these decisions in an informal way.   The officers and the majority members on standing committees merely implement the decisions of the caucus.

The system is substantially the same in the Senate, in that the majority caucus makes all important decisions, and the presiding officer is changed every year.   One important reason for the retention of the rotation scheme in both houses is the absence of a Lieutenant-Governor and the fact that first the President of the Senate and then the Speaker succeeds to the governorship.   In the same order they become Acting Governor whenever the Governor is out of the state.   By custom both officers manage to become Acting Governor at least once during the year that they are in office, and the rotation system insures that this prestigious experience is widely shared.   The Democrats since 1958 have also rotated the speakership.

Ohio.   The Ohio structure is the easiest to understand since it most closely follows the federal prototype in theory and practice.   It is both a committee and a party system.   In the House the Speaker serves as party leader, and the Speaker pro Tempore as his assistant.   In the Senate, where the elected leader is relieved of the responsibility of presiding (due to the presence of the Lieutenant Governor) he is able to function as party leader without an assistant.

The presiding officer in each chamber dominates the Rules and Reference committees and the chairmen of standing committees and committee "sections" (i.e., subcommittees).   This interlocking clique is in fact the leadership of the Republican party in the legislature. The Republican caucus, with 97 members in the House, is entirely too large to function as a collegial body, as does its New Jersey counterpart.   Committees in Ohio meet, hear testimony, amend bills and recommend them to the chamber; but the chairmen decide what bills are to be taken up in committee, and the presiding officers, through their handpicked Rules committees, keep tight control of the agenda, in contrast to the free-for-all in California.   The Ohio Senate works on about the same system as the House, but having fewer members and more senior ones it requires less formal machinery.   Minority members in both chambers have a share, through criticism and participation in committee proceedings, in the shaping of legislation—a share that is denied the New Jersey minority members.

Tennessee.   Here the selection of leadership personnel is almost invariably dominated by the Governor.   Both parties hold presession caucuses to nominate candidates for Speaker in each chamber, and the Democratic nominees are elected at the organization session by a strict party-line vote. (In this respect one-party Tennessee operates more like a two-party system than the more competitive California legislature.) The Democratic nominees, however, are usually more than acceptable to the Governor; quite often they are in fact nominated at his express desire. Thus despite a seeming tendency for Speakers (particularly in the House) to be elected for several terms, and despite the biennial presession gossip about the availability of "independent" candidates for the post, there is rarely even token opposition in Democratic caucus to the gubernatorially approved candidates, and the Speakers in both houses continue to be key men in the Governor's legislative-leadership nucleus. As such their roles involve the exercise of personal influence with members individually and in leadership strategy sessions. Yet recent Speakers have tended to be scrupulously neutral in the performance of their official role as presiding officers.

Whereas Ohio and New Jersey have majority party leaders, Tennessee has "administration floor leaders." Either one leader or two co-leaders may be designated by the Speaker for each chamber. They are so appointed on the informal recommendation of the Governor, without the formality of nomination by a party caucus and (usually) without much informal consultation beyond the narrow circle of those key legislators most trusted by the Governor. The floor leader's primary job is as legislative strategist and planner. He participates in top-level conferences (with the Governor or his aides, the Speaker and a few key legislators) to schedule consideration of bills. He is recognized as the chief actor on the floor, usually making all key motions for passage, amendment, tabling, reconsideration, adjournment, etc. He either presents and defends all administration bills himself (being listed as cosponsor) or selects spokesmen to do so. He performs corresponding functions when it is necessary to oppose bills hostile to the administration.

The administration floor leader, therefore, performs traffic-control functions which are commonly considered useful by all members, even those hostile to the administration, as well as providing a cue to the political significance of many bills—the same sort of cue a party label provides in many other legislatures. These functions gain indirect recognition by what might be called "legislative sterilization" of the administration floor leaders. So that they may serve clearly as traffic control agents of the whole house and as cue givers for the administration, floor leaders are expected to refrain from using their office to push legislation of merely personal interest to themselves, and to make absolutely clear (by leaving the chair, and often by express declaration) when they speak as private members. The practice of choosing coleaders facilitates the task, by making it possible for one coleader to divest himself of his administrative hat when the administration takes a position which he cannot support for personal reasons.

In both the Senate and House in Tennessee there are Republican floor leaders, chosen by vote of their party caucus early in the session. But this post is more honorific than functional or influential. The Republican floor leader who is recognized by his fellow partisans and by the opposition as a spokesman for his group usually attains such recognition because of his personal skill and zeal, and not because of his office. Few do attain it. The usual practice for Republican rank and file is to look to the administration forces for leadership and to accept from them whatever crumbs are to be caught.

In addition to the Speakers and administration floor leaders, the leadership group includes the chairmen of important committees. All chairmen are appointed by the Speakers, but are usually selected in fact by the administration's leadership group, and usually upon either the suggestion or the approval of the Governor. The scant importance of both committees and parties in the Tennessee system is indicated by the fact that Republicans regularly receive posts as chairmen and vice chairmen of several committees.

Although important decisions are made by the administration leadership group, the lesser decisions necessary to carry them out involve a slightly wider circle, formally constituted as the Calendar Committee, which is made up of the Speaker and all committee chairmen. Since it formally sets the agenda for the following day at the close of each day's business, its members are the focal points of legislative intelligence. For the end-of-session rush, usually several weeks before adjournment sine die, the Calendar Committee is enlarged slightly and renamed the Steering Committee. The latter relieves all standing committees of whatever bills they have not discharged—often a substantial number—and until adjournment proceeds to act as both a calendar or scheduling committee and a subject-matter committee. Thus standing committees, which are hardly active early in the session, vanish entirely at the critical stage of it.

At the risk of being obvious, we should point out some very general functional similarities in the eight chambers. There seems to be a necessity for some organizing principle, some rallying point for leadership and initiative, whether it be party, faction, clique, caucus, or governor. This dominant force in the membership needs in large chambers two official figures: one to preside in ostensibly impartial fashion, the other to manage a program, or at least expedite the work of the house, from his position on the floor.   Around these two arise a group of powerful members who share in the major decisions, either officially or informally, and in the job of implementing them.   What this means in terms of the roles played by legislative officers will be further explored in Chapter 8.

LEGISLATIVE PROCEDURES

The four legislatures all follow a standard pattern in the formal process of passing laws: introduction of bills, referral to committee, recommendation, floor debate and vote, repetition of these steps in the other house, negotiation by conference committee if necessary, and signature by the governor.   There is from house to house a great deal of difference in the importance of each step and the elaborateness with which it is conducted.   There are also differences in the legislative workloads, reflecting in part demands made upon the legislative branch, and in part the way past legislatures have defined the role of that branch.

California.   The process here is geared to handle four to five times as many bills as the other states receive, and to enact six to ten times as many general bills.   It does this without the screening and programming services contributed by parties in some other systems.   In the absence of a partisan organization, the individual legislator who authors a bill is the central element, and under these circumstances the individual has a great deal of work cut out for him if he carries a normal load.   In other states members refer to the "party program" or the "Governor's program."   California legislators refer to "*my* legislative program."   This is a reasonable phrase where the average legislator gets a score of bills enacted into law.   He receives these measures in embryo form from constituents, lobbyists, and departments. He is only moderately concerned, or for that matter informed, about some of them; others are introduced only for strategic purposes, and are allowed to die along the way.   But there are always numerous measures in which he is personally involved, and unless he takes positive and strenuous action at several points in the process, none of his bills will advance.   If he does not shepherd several significant measures through the legislature and get the Governor's signature on them, he will regard himself—and will be regarded by his colleagues— as "ineffective."

It is normally such an "interested" individual legislator who takes an outline of a bill to the Legislative Counsel to be drafted, who gathers signatures from coauthors, and who puts the bill "across the desk." Once the bill is referred to a standing committee by the Speaker, who only occasionally uses his power of referral for political purposes, it is the individual member who asks the committee chairman to set it for a hearing, who appears with supporting lobbyists, administrators, and/ or citizens, and who presents it to the committee. This he does in rather stylized manner, telling what group or agency "gave" it to him, what changes in the law it is designed to make, and so on. It is normally the individual sponsor who is approached by lobbyists, opposing legislators, or other interested parties seeking to have the measure amended, for an "author's amendment" offered before the bill is considered is always adopted by the committee.

Committees meet at least weekly, and bills to be heard are announced in advance. The committee process has the earmarks of a public decision-making operation, attended by 10 to 500 persons, depending on the interest in the bills set for a hearing. Executive sessions are never held, and committees do not "write" bills except by the give and take of the amendment process. After hearings, bills may be reported out "do pass," with or without amendments, or they may be retained in committee until such time as committee approval appears likely. A majority is required for a quorum or to pass a bill. Such influence as chairmen exert during the process is dependent on personal rather than party commitments.

Once out of committee, a bill takes its place on file and reaches a floor vote in due time. Again it is the individual interested member who "works the floor" to mobilize support and offset opposition. Once the bill is passed (by a constitutional majority, as recorded on electric roll call machines), the member must repeat his performance in the other chamber, except that he must find a member of that chamber, preferably the one who shares his constituency, to present it on the floor there.

From beginning to end, therefore, it is individual members, rather than parties or other agencies, who play the key roles.[17] The process has been described in terms of the Assembly; it differs in some minor particulars in the Senate. But the salient aspects of the process in

[17] Tabulation of roll call votes (based on a preliminary analysis by Richard Wright and further processing using facilities at the Survey Research Center and the Computer Center at the University of California) showed that overall party cohesion in California in 1957 was substantially less than in any of the states studied by Malcolm E. Jewell in "Party Voting in American State Legislatures," *American Political Science Review* **49**:773–791 (1955). Similar comparisons for the other three states could not be made at this time.

California can be summarized as follows: (1) the vast number of bills, (2) the essential part played by the author, (3) the open committee hearing and the overt part taken by lobbyists in decision making, (4) the "automatic calendar" which gives every bill some consideration if the author asks it, (5) the importance of the floor vote, (6) the wide range within which the outcome of any given issue is unpredictable, depending as it does upon the actions of certain members who remain until the last essentially free agents, and (7) the irrelevance of political parties.

New Jersey. There can be no greater contrast than between the process in California and in New Jersey. Here the majority caucus (38 persons in 1957) is small enough to engage in a frank, confidential, and somewhat informal discussion of the merits of any piece of legislation profferred by one of its number. The author of the bill or the party leaders seek to persuade the members to support it. After a discussion there is a counting of heads. A floor vote of 31 members (a constitutional majority of the house) is needed to get a bill through the Assembly. If this many members of the caucus approve it, the bill is to all intents and purposes on its way to the Senate—all the subsequent steps are pure technicality. It has become a "policy bill." If the bill should get the support of a majority of the caucus but less than a majority of the chamber, as is more frequently the case, it may still go "on the board" (i.e., the calendar) as a "non-policy bill." In this case its supporters hope to pick up enough votes from minority members to get it passed. Even with these bills it is expected that a member who objects will speak up in caucus, and that all who do not oppose it in caucus will support it on the floor.

Technically a bill approved by the caucus still has to be recommended by committee. The committee need not meet formally to do this, for it is assumed that since the caucus has approved the bill the majority members, who control the committee, also do. So the chairman needs only to circulate the copy to these members for their signatures, and the bill has committee approval.

On many local and technical bills, the parties are not in disagreement. These go through unanimously or with large majorities. Even here, however, the minority member is at a disadvantage. He must go through the majority leadership or get support in caucus from a majority member to get his bill on the board, for nothing moves without the approval of the majority caucus. Occasionally they will prevent action on a minority member's local bill if they think they can beat him at the polls next year by demonstrating his "ineffectiveness."

Members of large delegations, when introducing bills, will often approach their delegation leaders first, to get their support before going to the caucus with their bills. When a bill has passed his own house, the author will go to his opposite number and ask him to bring it up in the caucus of the other house, and then on the floor. If both are of the majority there are few problems. If the author is of the majority, but his county is represented by a minority member in the other house, he may go through someone from an adjacent county or through the party leadership. But a minority member, even after he is lucky enough to get a bill through his own house still faces the perplexing problem of other-house sponsorship. The chances of a minority member's bill surviving both screenings are rather slim, unless it is merely a local or technical bill.

Minority members are not entirely without bargaining power. In 1957 the Republican majority's strength was two votes short of the two-thirds necessary to put an emergency bill into immediate effect or to override the veto of a Democratic governor. On non-policy bills, moreover, individual Republicans have to come to terms with individual Democrats. Therefore the system has some play in it.

With a virtually moribund committee system, minority members have trouble keeping informed on the content of measures, and with the calendar tightly controlled by the majority they may be caught without time to prepare debate. Knowing they have little chance to affect legislative policy, even through vocal opposition, they speak to the gallery and to the public beyond, pinning their hopes on next year's election. (Although the Democrats protested the caucus system when in the minority, they found in 1958 they could hardly do without it when they became the majority. It hardly occurs to anyone that the game might be played by other rules.)

There are few differences between Assembly and Senate, and these are usually due to the small size and personal intimacy of the 21-man Senate.

The essential features of the New Jersey legislative system, then, are (1) the small size of the legislature, (2) the strength of partisanship, (3) the dominant part played by the majority caucus as a group, (4) the irrelevance of committees, (5) the impersonalism achieved by rotation of members in the Assembly and officers in both chambers, and (6) the inability of the minority to make a responsible contribution to policy development.

Ohio. The legislative process in Ohio resembles in some respects the California system, and in others the New Jersey system; but more than either its strongest resemblance is to the federal system. It is definitely a party-oriented legislature, but it has a larger stratum of personal leadership since the majority caucus (97 persons in 1957) is too large to make policy itself in informal meeting, as in New Jersey, yet one or two officers cannot handle the administrative burden alone. This leadership layer consists of the Rules committees, and in the House the Reference committee, plus the chairmen of standing committees, who are powerful because these committees have an important function in Ohio.

As bills are introduced they are assigned (by the Reference committee in the House and the President pro Tempore in the Senate) to standing committees. The hearings are public and are well attended by members and lobbyists. Both sides are heard, though the proceedings are less elaborate and less formal than in California. Where there is a partisan element the results are more predictable, for the committees reflect the party distribution in the chamber. Bills referred to committee are the property of the chairman, who may hear them when he chooses or not at all. Members spend a good portion of their time in committee sessions and minority criticisms may be reflected in the revised bills that come out of them. Even after being reported out, House bills go back to the Reference committee for screening as to "form and legal effect" before being sent to the floor.[18] This gives the Speaker a final chance to hold or sidetrack them if he chooses, through action by the Chairman of the Reference Committee.

Until the last weeks floor sessions are short. They serve more the function of a cash register than a deliberative body, though lively debate sometimes develops in the Senate. Republican members are expected to follow the caucus decision in their vote, but their leaders are quite willing to "give leave" to individuals who explain their objections to voting for particular bills.

Minority members in Ohio, though they appear to be more active than in New Jersey and to have a better chance to get their bills through, pay a price for their right to participate. In order to accomplish their individual objectives, many Democrats go along with the Republican organization and abstain from pointed criticism. In turn, the presiding officers, sometimes working through minority leaders, can generally find the votes necessary to reach the two-thirds majority required for emergency bills.

The real leaders of the majority party are the Speaker in the House and the President pro Tempore in the Senate. They are the hub of

[18] See Roscoe Baker, "The Reference Committee of the Ohio House of Representatives," *American Political Science Review* 34:306–310 (1940).

activity; they maintain liaison with the Governor and the state party chairman, they control the calendar through the Rules committee, and they keep tab on, and influence, committee action through the chairmen. Though presiding rather impartially, the Speaker of the House is able from the rostrum to work with his chief lieutenant (the Speaker pro Tempore) on the floor, and together they expedite action on bills of importance to the party. The House differs from the Senate in practice principally in promoting able young Republicans to positions of responsibility after only a few years of experience. The Senate relies heavily on members with long tenure in its choice of officers and chairmen.

The essential elements of the Ohio process are (1) the complete fusion of chamber and majority party leadership, administered by the presiding officers, (2) the smooth functioning of this leadership to the point where it is secure enough to treat the opposition permissively on occasion, (3) the importance of committees as the heart of the legislative process, (4) the general resemblance to congressional procedures, and (5) the formalization of structure and process required by the size of the lower house.

Tennessee. Turning to Tennessee we find a process that bears little resemblance to that in the other states. It differs most obviously in the prevalence of local bills or "private" legislation. Although a 1953 constitutional amendment requiring two-thirds approval of a county board or city council to put local bills into effect has tended to curtail both the practice and its importance, the legislature still spends much time in ratifying local decisions. Approximately half the measures passed in 1957 were of this sort. The end of each legislative day, and all of the Monday and Friday floor sessions until very late in the session are usually devoted to local bills. By almost invariable custom, each member or delegation is given unanimous approval for measures applying only to the local district. This approval is given tacitly in most cases, since the local bill procedure ordinarily consists of the Speaker's, the Clerk's and the interested member's droning through the formalities of reading the bill and the Speaker's then announcing some fictitious and arbitrary but legally sufficient majority of "votes" for passage. Custom also requires unanimity of a delegation where a district has more than one representative if a measure is to receive this kind of approval. If a delegation is split and if some of its members insist on carrying the issue to the floor, members outside the delegation concerned usually report themselves "present but not voting," thereby depriving the bill of its constitutional majority.

The procedure for general bills is considerably simpler than is the case in the other three states. Though a full roster of committees exists, only two—Judiciary; and Finance, Ways and Means—are in the habit of meeting regularly and frequently, debating, and taking decisions as a body. Many of them meet rarely, and then on short notice. The result is ordinarily to approve what bills are presented by the chairmen; if he does not want them approved he simply neglects to mention them. Whenever serious controversy arises, as when some major revision of program is a principal item on the Governor's agenda for a session, the committee which has jurisdiction will be brought into action for that session only, and may hold hearings and discuss the bill. Committees may recommend amendments, but these are reported separately and are incorporated in a bill only by formal vote in floor sessions of the chamber.

A larger proportion of the decisions are made on the floor in Tennessee than in any of the four states. Members spend a good share of their time in formal session, where the action for the most part is straightforward, with little parliamentary intrigue. On administration bills the floor leader or a manager selected by him takes the initiative, as noted above. The antiadministration side of the debate will be carried by individuals who object to that particular measure. Once in a while some member becomes identified as an administration opponent in some substantive area (as the chairman of Judiciary did in 1957 with respect to education bills) and the others will watch him for cues as to their action. Very occasionally an opposition leader will reappear on a number of issues, or the Governor's opponents will call a strategy meeting, but such opposition is never very sustained or formalized. In many of these ad hoc alliances, Republicans are hardly distinguishable from Democrats.

The essential elements of the Tennessee process, then, are (1) high turnover and brief sessions, (2) initiative almost entirely in the hands of the Governor, represented by his floor leaders, (3) the importance of floor action as the central point of decision, (4) the amount of time and attention devoted to local bills in a variation of the "unanimous consent" procedure, and (5) the negligible part played by political parties.

These procedural differences between legislatures have an influence on many other facets of the process. There is a functional relationship between the formal and the informal rules. The role behavior expected of officers is quite dependent on what the constitution, statutes and rules demand of them as the elementary and minimal part of their job (see Chapter 8). The committee system and the system of informal specialization that has grown up beside it are interlocked (see Chapter 9). The legislator's view of his own relationship to the constellation of other actors in the process may be influenced by the routine actions a particular system demands, whether it be listening to committee witnesses or flipping a switch on his desk (see Part Four). His role as a partisan obviously is affected by whether parties have everything or nothing to do with the procedure for passing bills (see Chapter 15).

THE SOCIAL AND ECONOMIC SETTING

These legislative systems do not exist in a vacuum. The characteristics of the state's population, the background, occupations, and income of its citizens, its natural resources and geographical position, the money available for public services—these are some of the limitations on the actions of legislative bodies. As each legislature and political system has particular features not found in others, so do each state's economy and society. We can list only the major, available indicators of differences, of course, and these in very summary form.

Table 3.5 describes the population of the four states, with the items that make particular states stand out indicated by italics: New Jersey's

Table 3.5: Population characteristics (figures rounded)

	Calif.	N.J.	Ohio	Tenn.
Estimated population (1956)* (millions)	*13.4*	5.4	9.1	3.5
Population per square mile (1950)†	68	*643*	194	79
Percentage urban (new definition)†	81%	87%	70%	*44%*
Increase, 1940 to 1950†	*53%*	16%	15%	13%
Born in state of residence†	*42%*	68%	76%	80%

* *Book of the States*, 1958–1959, p. 197.

† *Statistical Abstract of the United States* (1953), pp. 11, 29, 18, 43.

density of population, Tennessee's rurality, California's size and rapid in-migration.

The financial limitations within which these legislatures worked are indicated by the figures in Table 3.6 on the income and fiscal situation for 1956—the fiscal year preceding this session. Tennessee was obviously handicapped by more straitened circumstances than the other three states, but in terms of current budget it was making relatively as great an effort as any. California, with per capita resources about equal to those of New Jersey and Ohio, was demanding more of its citizens than they were. New Jersey had the highest debt and the lowest tax level. The refusal of earlier legislatures to enact either a sales or an income tax, and the unwillingness of either party to accept the onus of initiating them, left the state in financial difficulties. Local government agencies have always had a heavy share in providing and paying for services, including education, and New Jersey was the only one of the four states where local taxes were

Table 3.6: Personal income and state expenditures, per capita, 1956*

	Calif.	N.J.	Ohio	Tenn.	United States
Average personal income	$2,419	$2,443	$2,154	$1,317	$1,937
State taxes	122	52	74	76	87
Taxes as % of income	5.0%	2.1%	3.4%	5.8%	4.5%
State debt	$73	$166	$66	$32	$79
Debt as % of income	3.0%	6.8%	3.1%	2.4%	4.1%

* Cited in or derived from *Book of the States*, 1957–1958, pp. 171, 196, 197.

Table 3.7: Major components of the labor force, 1950*

Employed in	Calif.	N.J.	Ohio	Tenn.	United States
Manufacturing	20%	38%	37%	21%	26%
Wholesale, retail trade	22	18	18	22	19
Agriculture, forestry, fishing	8	3	7	17	12
All other	50	41	38	40	43
	100%	100%	100%	100%	100%

* Derived from *Statistical Abstract of the United States*, 1953, pp. 211–212.

higher than state taxes.[19]   The principal object of state expenditure in California and Tennessee was education; in Ohio and New Jersey it was highways.[20]

Table 3.7 gives the major occupations in the labor force. Tennessee obviously is the most agricultural state. Ohio and New Jersey would be classed as industrial states, while California has the most diverse economy of the four.

Particularities of economy and society not revealed in the above tables also play a large share in determining the kinds of problem

[19] *Book of the States*, 1957–1958, p. 197.
[20] *Ibid.*, p. 170.

with which each legislature must deal and the kinds of clients and constituents most visible to it. Thus, part of New Jersey's economy is an adjunct to the Manhattan financial complex; many of its citizens are commuters; and it is the home of large national corporations. Ohio's society and economy gives the impression of being balanced and stable, the product of evolutionary growth. Both urban-industrial and rural-agricultural extremes are present, but in a peculiarly balanced geographical distribution. Tennessee's geography has tended to make its government a holding company for disparate economic interests spread over a wide sliver of territory with great differences in both culture and economy between East, Middle, and West Tennessee. California's economy and society is not only balanced but diverse. Its multiplicity of industries (shipping, mining, oil production, motion pictures, logging, etc.) is matched by a heterogeneity of races and nationalities (Latins, Orientals, Jews, Negroes, southern whites, etc.).

From this brief account of the context—institutional, political, economic and social—within which legislators in the four states must work, we now turn to consider the persons who, in 1957, did that work, and the ways in which they came to assume legislative office.

PART TWO

The legislative career

LEGISLATORS DO NOT RESPOND to expectations—from whatever source—
as incumbents of a particular kind of public office alone but in terms
of qualities and characteristics which define them as human beings.
How they respond and why they respond as they do are questions influenced by the whole sequence of their prior experiences, attitudes, and
predispositions; by their current perspectives and goals; and by their
anticipations of the future. This sequence is nothing less than the
political career. Subjectively, as Everett C. Hughes has put it, "a
career is the moving perspective in which a person sees his life as a
whole and interprets the meaning of his various attributes, actions,
and the things which happen to him."[1] The legislator's personality
and career perspectives, already substantially embodied in what we
described in Chapter 1 as his role potential, shapes, in part at least,
his actions in the performance of legislative roles.

Ideally, we should connect a legislator's taking of particular roles
and combinations in which they occur with his whole personality.[2]

This introduction drafted by Eulau.

[1] Everett C. Hughes, "Institutional Office and the Person," in Men and Their
Work (Glencoe: The Free Press, 1958), p. 63.

[2] Political scientists, with a few exceptions, have not followed up Harold D.
Lasswell's pioneering effort in Psychopathology and Politics, first published in
1930, despite the theoretical importance of Lasswell's formulations. In a recent
essay, "Afterthoughts: Thirty Years Later," attached to a new edition of his
classic, Lasswell has re-emphasized his belief in the desirability of "seeking to
connect the playing of a political role with the whole personality system as it is
found at any cross-section of adult life; and further, [of] attempting to connect
the personality of the adult with the developmental sequence through which the
person has passed." See Harold D. Lasswell, Psychopathology and Politics, A
New Edition (New York: The Viking Press, 1960), pp. 275–276.

But data secured by way of the few survey-type questions which asked about legislators' earliest interest in politics, their decision to become politicians, and their future career plans are inadequate for motivational analysis. Therefore, even though some respondents used motivational language in explaining "why" politics came to interest them, or "why" they became political activists, we are not prepared to take such "explanations" at face value. We shall be concerned in the following three chapters not with "why" state legislators chose a career in politics and in the legislature, but rather with "how" they perceive its development. Recollections, orientations, and expectations of this perceptual kind need not, and probably cannot, be given motivational meaning. Yet, they are significant, for they have a functional reality of their own in being "definitions of the situation" in which legislators may take relevant roles.

There is another largely technical difficulty in the way of linking legislators' career perspectives with particular roles. The open-ended character of the questions made for so wide a range and so great a variety of responses that data are quantitatively insufficient for such analysis.[3] We must speak here, therefore, of the legislator as such— his "generalized role," so to say—in spite of the fact that such simple identification of a "position" or "office" with a single role is an artifact of analysis and not a description of reality. What defines the incumbent of a legislative office as a legislator is the complex set of multiple relationships in which he is involved and which give rise to role expectations and orientations. Nonetheless, there probably are aspects of the political or legislative career shared widely enough to make for more or less typical career sequences and orientations.

Our starting point, in Chapter 4, will be legislators' "political socialization": the process by which, in their own views, they selectively acquired the values, attitudes, interests or knowledge that fit them for legislative roles and make them take these roles in characteristic ways. As long ago as 1925, Charles E. Merriam, assessing the promises of behavioral research in politics, proposed that "the examination of the rise and development of the political ideation and the political behavior of the child has in store for us much of value in the scientific understanding of the adult idea and conduct."[4] Yet, thirty-five years later, we know very little about political socialization. We do know that, under certain conditions, family tradition can be an important

---

[3] For further discussion of the advantages and drawbacks of open-ended questions, and of the statistical problems involved, see Chapter 18, pp. 459–460.

[4] Charles E. Merriam, *New Aspects of Politics* (Chicago: University of Chicago Press, 1925), p. 85.

factor in a person's orientation towards politics, influencing the degree, kind, and direction of his political involvement.[5]   We also know that religious, ethnic, and class perceptions and attitudes are formed rather early and, through time, become integrated into a system of values which tends to shape a person's social outlook and changes only slowly when it comes into conflict with opposed social values.[6]   But the studies along these lines shed little light on the part which political socialization plays in the developmental pattern of a political career.   The developmental context is important because, as we shall see in Chapter 4, political socialization may occur at almost any phase of a legislator's career and is part of a continuous process of growth.[7]

If little is known about the political careers of people generally, not much more is known about the careers of those for whom politics is a matter of central concern—politicians.   Biographies, of course, tell us a great deal about particular, usually distinguished, public figures, but they represent unique cases which cannot be generalized.[8]   A political career, like careers in other pursuits, is a more or less typical sequence of events, a developmental pattern in the life histories of politicians moving into positions made available by the framework of institutions.   It is for this reason that political careers can tell us a great deal about governmental institutions as formalized and regularized patterns of action which both shape and are shaped by political roles.   Moreover, a political career is not simply determined by the politician's skill in occupying available offices.   On the one hand, it may be facilitated or impeded by the politician's initial position in the social structure from which entry into politics is gained.   On the other hand, it may be furthered or limited by the ways in which the political system itself is structured.   From the patterns of political careers in a given system, therefore, we can indirectly learn something

[5] See, for instance, Eleanor E. Maccoby, Richard E. Matthews, and Alton S. Morton, "Youth and Political Change," *Public Opinion Quarterly*, 18:23–39 (1954); Robert E. Lane, *Political Life* (Glencoe: The Free Press, 1959), pp. 204–208.

[6] Herbert Hyman, *Political Socialization* (Glencoe: The Free Press, 1959), summarizes and appraises relevant research findings.

[7] Talcott Parsons (*The Social System, op. cit.,* pp. 207–208) uses the term socialization in a broader sense than that of the   process of child development— "to designate the learning of *any* orientations of functional significance to the operation of a system of complementary role-expectations.   In this sense, socialization, like learning, goes on throughout life.   The case of the development of the child is only the most dramatic because he has so far to go."

[8] See Morris Janowitz, "The Systematic Analysis of Political Biography," *World Politics,* 6:405–412 (1954).

about the recruitment process for various institutionalized groups, and the patterns of role potential among their members.

How the social structure and the politician's social attributes promote or obstruct the recruitment and mobility of political elites has long been a concern of research.[9]   Numerous studies seek to discover the class origin, occupational status, educational level, religious or ethnic affiliation, and other socially relevant attributes of public office holders.[10]   Although many of these studies may be only exercises in fact gathering, they suggest and sometimes answer important questions about the social bases of politics.[11]   This type of research has shown that the social sources of recruitment may be significant avenues of political mobility, enabling the rise to power of those favorably situated in the social structure of a particular society, and impeding or preventing a political career for those less propitiously located.   Moreover, some of these studies have related changes in the composition of elites to changing patterns of politics in diverse systems and to changes of whole systems themselves.[12]

In view of the continued research interest in political recruitment and its effect on political ascent, it is surprising that research has neglected the effect of political structures on the development of

[9] Donald R. Matthews, in *The Social Background of Political Decision-Makers* (Garden City, N.Y.: Doubleday and Company, 1954), examines some of the theoretical assumptions and empirical implications of speculative and research writings concerned with the relationship between political institutions and the social structure of society.

[10] The bibliography in Harold D. Lasswell, Daniel Lerner and C. Easton Rothwell, *The Comparative Study of Elites* (Stanford: Stanford University Press, 1952), pp. 43–72, is brought up to date in Dwaine Marvick, Editor, *Political Decision-Makers* (Glencoe: The Free Press, 1961).

[11] Richard C. Snyder, in his introduction to Matthews, *op. cit.*, p. iv, has summarized these questions: "Does the decision-maker's socio-economic status and previous life experience make any difference in the way he looks at policy problems? in the social groups he will listen to and agree with?   Are certain strata of the population over-represented or under-represented because decision-makers do or do not share their basic characteristics?   What kinds of people enter politics?   What kinds are predominantly successful?   Are everyone's chances of a political career roughly equal?   Are decision-makers recruited from all citizens who have the requisite ability, or are some excluded?   Is the balance of power and influence among various groups reflected in the social composition of the decision-makers?   Do the most high-ranking social groups dominate the decision-maker roles?   Does the social status of the government official have anything to do with who has access to him?"

[12] See, for instance, the Hoover Institute Studies of political elites, especially Robert C. North, *Kuomintang and Chinese Communist Elites* (Stanford: Stanford University Press, 1952).

political careers.[13]   The many excellent case histories, usually in the form of biographies or autobiographies, give much insight into particular political career lines, but they are essentially non-typical and do not permit generalization.[14]   There exist, to our knowledge, no systematic studies which either trace the effect of differential political structures on the career patterns of politicians, and especially elective officeholders, or which are concerned with the career perspectives of politicians at a particular point in their life histories.[15]   As a result, impressionistic accounts of political career patterns may find their way into the textbooks, such as that political mobility follows a regular series of steps from the local to the state to the national level.[16]

The notion of a career line in politics, of a more or less typical sequence of successive office holding within a determinate institutional setting, does not imply that political careers follow a regular series of steps from lower to higher positions.   It is theoretically difficult and empirically impossible to specify such a series, particularly in a political system like the American with its horizontal, federal structure cutting across vertical hierarchies.   Harold D. Lasswell has given a colorful précis of the model: "In American politics the escalator to the top is not a regimented, orderly lift, but a tangle of ladders, ropes, and runways that attract people from other activities at various stages of the process, and lead others to a dead end or a blind drop."[17] Contemporary career perspectives may be symptomatic of aspirations, but no motivational hypotheses about politicians' desires for "higher" office need be advanced, especially in democratic societies where a large sector of the community participates in determining who shall fill governmental positions,[18] and where the recruitment process "tends

---

[13] This lack was recently noted by Avery Leiserson who generously refers to the familiar elite studies as "approximations." *Parties and Politics* (New York: Alfred A. Knopf, 1958), p. 200, fn. 3.

[14] The few systematic case histories which exist are discussed by Lucian W. Pye, "Personal Identity and Political Ideology," in Dwaine Marvick, *op. cit.,* pp. 290–313.

[15] But see a recent study by Robert M. Rosenzweig, "The Politician and the Career in Politics," *Midwest Journal of Political Science,* 1:163–172 (1957). However, the data in this study come from interviews with only sixteen candidates for public office in western Massachusetts and are hardly systematic.

[16] See, for instance, the model presented by Hugh A. Bone, *American Politics and the Party System* (New York: McGraw-Hill, 1949), p. 740.   Most recent texts simply and, in view of the lack of research evidence, rightly ignore the matter of political careers.

[17] Lasswell, "Afterthoughts," in *op. cit.,* p. 303.

[18] See Harold D. Lasswell, "The Selective Effect of Personality on Political Participation," in Richard Christie and Marie Jahoda, Eds., *Studies in the Scope*

to transform power-centered persons into multi-valued individuals, or to reject them entirely."[19]

Nevertheless, careers may be subjectively conceived as real and, because they are so conceived, may have real consequences for the taking of political roles and political behavior.[20] As a subjective experience a career is a developmental sequence of images which links past with present and future. A complete portrayal of political careers as subjective events must include recollections of the past, orientations toward the present, and expectations concerning the future.[21]

A distinction may be made, then, between the *social* recruitment patterns of political elites and their career patterns and perspectives. Whatever the recruitment patterns may be, political careers as such are probably less dependent on recruitment and more dependent on structural conditions of the political system. Recruitment and career patterns may, of course, overlap, as in patrician societies where the identity of social and political structures makes for stable expectations with regard to who shall take what political roles, and where preparation for public service is part and parcel of the training of those who, by birth and social status, are destined to become political leaders.[22] On the other hand, recruitment and career patterns may diverge widely, as in bureaucratic systems. The promotional process in a bureaucracy is relatively rigid. Social origin and training are less likely to determine the career pattern and more likely to determine the level of entry into the hierarchy and the level at which a career will probably terminate.[23]

No such fairly simple models can be constructed concerning the career patterns of elective politicians in a democratic and pluralistic

---

and Method of "The Authoritarian Personality" (Glencoe: The Free Press, 1954), p. 221.

[19] Lasswell, "Afterthoughts," *loc. cit.*

[20] For the social-psychological notions involved in this formulation we are indebted, of course, to W. I. Thomas. See Edmund H. Volkart, Ed., *Social Behavior and Personality—Contributions of W. I. Thomas to Theory and Social Research* (New York: Social Science Research Council, 1951), especially pp. 1–32.

[21] For the notion of development in systematic analysis, see Heinz Eulau, "H. D. Lasswell's Developmental Analysis," *Western Political Quarterly* 11:229–242 (1958).

[22] See the classical study of Sir Lewis Namier, *The Structure of Politics at the Accession of George III* (London: Macmillan and Company, 2nd ed., 1957), pp. 2–4: "Predestination: The Inevitable Parliament Men."

[23] See Arthur W. MacMahon and John D. Millett, *Federal Administrators* (New York: Columbia University Press, 1939).

system as found in the United States. Given the fact that in the United States politicians are recruited from a great variety of levels in the scheme of social stratification, it may be hypothesized, however, that the structure of the political system, and notably of the party system, will significantly influence political career patterns and perspectives.

It would be a mistake, of course, to think of a single, invariable political system in the United States. "The American political system," is inordinately complex and composed of many subsystems which differ a good deal in the degree of popular participation in the choice of officeholders and in political competition. In the United States, therefore, politicians are likely to give varying emphases to different aspects of their careers, according to the differential structure of politics in different jurisdictions. For instance, there may be differences as one moves from highly competitive to non-competitive party systems in regard to the level of office where entrance into political life is gained, the sponsorship of political careers, the skills deemed appropriate for politics, the goals sought in the pursuit of political activity, and the opportunities considered relevant for political mobility. Research along these lines, it has been suggested, "may be another way of describing and analyzing the political process itself."[24] (We shall deal with state legislators' perceptions of these matters in Chapter 5.)

Although bright or dim career expectations are partly rooted in the relatively idiosyncratic components of personality, politicians are particularly skilled in reality testing. They are likely to be especially sensitive to those political conditions which may either facilitate or obstruct their careers. Among these conditions, the structure of the party system in which the political future is planned is probably a perceptually most salient factor, though by no means alone determinative. Just how career orientations and expectations are likely to be formulated in differently structured party systems is difficult to predict, for there exist neither a theory of political career patterns nor a body of empirical data about political careers which could serve as sources of viable hypotheses. How the multi-level structure of the American political system introduces much perceptual ambiguity into legislators' career expectations is the focus of Chapter 6.

The three chapters of Part Two, then, present some data on the political career perspectives of a particular type of politician—the American state legislator. Hence the data cannot be generalized to

[24] From a research proposal by Joseph A. Schlesinger, entitled "A Description and Analysis of Movement Between Political Offices in the States."

the political careers of other formal types, such as state executives, local judges, or Congressmen. Moreover, it is important to keep in mind that the great majority of the men and women included in this study were not professional politicians. They did not, to borrow Max Weber's famous expression, live *off* politics or *for* politics as a vocation. There were some who did meet these criteria of the professional politician, but only twenty of the 474 respondents whom we interviewed (about 4 per cent of the total) gave "politician" or "legislator" as their occupation. For most of them political work was a part-time career superimposed on their ordinary callings. But neither were many what Weber called "occasional politicians" for whom politics is only an avocation—"who, as a rule, are politically active only in case of need and for whom politics is neither materially nor ideally, 'their life' in the first place."[25] Rather, American state legislators would seem in most cases to be mixed-type politicians who are neither devoted professionals nor inspired amateurs. But if they do not live off politics or for politics, they are, nevertheless, very much *in* politics as something more than an occasional incident in an otherwise non-political career.

[25] Max Weber, "Politics as a Vocation," in H. H. Gerth and C. Wright Mills, Eds., *From Max Weber: Essays in Sociology* (New York: Oxford University Press, 1946), p. 83.

CHAPTER 4

Recollections

Any system of interpersonal relations depends for proper functioning on the ability of actors to form and follow reasonably common and stable expectations concerning each other's behavior. Without some minimum consensus as to what roles must be taken and how they should be taken no political system can be viable.[1] Indeed, no political system leaves it to chance whether or not appropriate roles are taken and role takers share certain values, attitudes, or orientations. In the modern state, in particular, "training for citizenship," or "civic education," is a crucial function which must be performed if a political system is to be maintained and perpetuated.[2] The notion of "civic education" has strongly rational and consciously manipulative connotations, but it focuses attention on the fact that certain ways of behavior are expected from members of a political system.

"Political socialization" is a more useful concept from a scientific point of view because it refers not only to the formal and rationally designed processes but also to the informal psychological, social, and cultural mechanisms by which newcomers are related to and integrated into the political system. Furthermore, it sensitizes the observer to the broad range of values, attitudes, and orientations relevant to political role taking, to such matters as the internalization of standards for political judgments, the development of feelings

This chapter drafted by Eulau.

[1] David Easton has pointed out that consensus in a political system may be minimal on the "level of government," but is likely to be greater on the "level of regime" and is probably maximal on the "level of political community." See David Easton and Robert D. Hess, "Youth and the Political System," in Seymour M. Lipset and Leo Lowenthal, Edits., *Culture and Social Character* (New York: The Free Press of Glencoe, 1961), pp. 226–251. Our own research on political socialization refers, of course, to the governmental level and only peripherally to the other two.

[2] See Charles E. Merriam, *The Making of Citizens* (Chicago: University of Chicago Press, 1931), and other studies in the series it summarizes.

77

toward and attitudes about political processes, the formulation of values which serve to legitimize political institutions, or the creation of identifications, demands, and expectations necessary for political survival. A society's ways of behaving politically involve political perspectives generally as well as particular roles, and they are taught and learned in contexts much wider than the formal political setting. The family, the voluntary association, the occupational group, the mass media of communication, and so on, may serve as agents of political socialization.

The concept of "socialization" has been primarily used by psychologists to describe and explain the processes by which the infant and child are transformed into adult and mature persons.[3] From the point of view of political socialization, it has also been generally recognized that the political development of the young is a critical factor in the success of the political system to perpetuate itself across generations.[4] There has been some interest in just how the child acquires his approach to figures of authority and political symbols,[5] and there has been research on his reactions to "authoritarian" and "democratic" group situations.[6] It may be true that, as the bulk of research findings suggests, an American youngster has acquired at the age of sixteen the basic set of social and political attitudes which characterize him through life.[7] But there is reason to believe that the process of political socialization may also take place in various stages of maturity in so far as it involves political roles requiring much greater attitudinal and behavioral differentiation than the child or adolescent can envisage. It would be most valuable to know, therefore, just when and how a legislator "discovers" the specialized functional roles which he is most prepared to take. It may be, of course, that the learning of particular functional roles is not characteristic of a particular stage of development, but that it is a discontinuous process. A boy may "learn" to be a "broker" in his group of friends

[3] For a survey of the literature, see Irvin L. Child, "Socialization," in Gardner Lindzey, op. cit., II, Chapter 18, 655–692.

[4] For an interesting theory of cross-generational socialization as a result of "spiral" development, see R. E. Money-Kyrle, Psychoanalysis and Politics (New York: W. W. Norton and Company, 1951), pp. 106–122: "The Group in its Relation to the Individual."

[5] See Sebastian De Grazia, The Political Community (Chicago: The University of Chicago Press, 1948), pp. 80–98.

[6] See Ronald Lippit, An Experimental Study of Authoritarian and Democratic Group Atmospheres (Studies in Topological and Vector Psychology, I, University of Iowa Studies in Child Welfare, No. 16, 1940).

[7] See Herbert H. Hyman, Political Socialization, op. cit., pp. 51–68.

or "boss" of the school yard. He may have to give up these roles in subsequent stages of his career, but they may be reactivated in later opportune situations. With these kinds of question our limited data do not allow us to deal.

In this chapter, we shall present legislators' responses to the question: "How did you become interested in politics? What is your earliest recollection of being interested in it?" We did not entertain any particular hypotheses about differences in political socialization from one state to the next, but we assumed that political socialization is closely connected with the process of socialization in a culture generally, and that some continuity exists between socialization and other cultural patterns.[8] Whatever cultural variations existed among the four states could be easily articulated by virtue of the open-ended nature of our question, and we were given, indeed, a wide and heterogeneous range of responses.

MAJOR SOURCES OF POLITICAL INTEREST

A summary of the major "sources" of political interest as spontaneously reported by our respondents reveals some obvious state-to-state patterns. The differences are small, but the fact that patterns do occur suggests that the variations may not be arbitrary. Table 4.1

Table 4.1: Major sources of political interest[*]

Source of Interest	Calif. $N = 113$	N.J. $N = 79$	Ohio $N = 162$	Tenn. $N = 120$
Primary groups	34%	47%	43%	42%
Political or civic participation	70	60	49	43
Particular events or conditions	42	25	21	18
Personal predispositions	52	53	52	33
Socio-economic beliefs	16	10	6	3

* Percentages total more than 100 since some respondents gave more than one answer.

presents the responses as they were coded in the major categories, each of which is explained in further detail below. As the table shows, in all categories except "primary groups" and "predispositions" greater proportions of California legislators responded in relevant

[8] This has also been recognized by the students of comparative politics. See Lucian W. Pye, "Political Modernization and Research on the Process of Political Socialization," *Social Science Research Council Items*, 13 (Sept., 1959), 25–28.

terms than New Jersey legislators, and the latter in greater proportions than Ohio legislators who, in turn, exceeded the Tennessee respondents.

The most obvious difference to be noted is between California and the other states in regard to the influence of primary groups as agents of political socialization. One possible explanation of the relatively low percentage in the California column is that primary groups are less effective as socializing sources because primary group influence, especially that of the family, is predicated on a reasonably stable population structure. But California is distinguished from the other three states by the fact that it is still an "immigrant" state, and it may be that the continued population movement into the state has not permitted the formation of stable primary groups which can act as effective agents of political socialization.

What California may lack by way of primary group influence, it seems to make up in the categories of participation and events or conditions as stimulants of political interest. With regard to participation, it may be that social and political activity is seized upon by an immigrant population to make itself feel at home in a new environment. In newly created communities, fewer legislators are "born into" politics, more become politically interested and active in the process of community life. Similarly, political beliefs seem to play a slightly more important role in a state where stable political party patterns have been less crystallized than in states characterized by very definite party-system structures.

The pattern of variation from state to state invites more detailed inquiry. We shall, in the following, deal only with those respondents who gave answers appropriate to a particular category.

Time of legislators' political socialization. In a recent review of relevant studies, Lipset and his associates reported that "it is difficult, if not impossible, to make any reliable estimates, on the basis of empirical evidence, of the age at which politics becomes meaningful to children or youth." After examining the skimpy research evidence, they inclined to focus on the period of adolescence—"the period in the life cycle where the individual first encounters strong influences outside of his family and must proceed to define his adult role.[9] Assuming this conclusion to be correct, our data, summarized in Table 4.2, suggest that politicians may be affected by exposure to the political environment at an earlier stage of personal development than the

[9] Seymour M. Lipset, Paul F. Lazarsfeld, Allen H. Barton, and Juan Linz, "The Psychology of Voting: An Analysis of Political Behavior," in Gardner Linzey, *op. cit.*, II, 1145.

average citizen, at least as recalled by themselves. About a third or slightly more of the legislators in all four states referred to their childhood or the grammar school period as the time when they first became interested in or aware of politics. But only 13 to 16 per cent mentioned the period roughly coinciding with adolescence or high school. Altogether, one half of the respondents, more or less, had recollections locating their first political interest in the precollege age period. The childhood-grammar school period is perceptually more salient than the time of adolescence or any single later period.

Nevertheless, as Table 4.2 shows, sizeable proportions of legislators in all four states reported first paying attention to politics in and

Table 4.2: Time of earliest political interest recalled by legislators

Time Recalled	Calif. $N = 110$	N.J. $N = 57$	Ohio $N = 156$	Tenn. $N = 98$
Childhood or grammar school period	40%	32%	36%	40%
Adolescence or high school period	16	14	15	13
College or equivalent period	8	14	13	8
After college or equivalent period	18	19	11	23
At entry into politics	18	21	25	16
Total	100%	100%	100%	100%

after college or equivalent periods, or at the very time of entry into active politics. A typical comment from a legislator in this last category was:

Well, this might come as a surprise to you, but I was never interested in politics. I first became interested in politics after I was elected.

Although the variations from state to state are small in each time period, college experiences seem to have a more formative influence in New Jersey and Ohio where, in addition, more legislators than in California and Tennessee date their first interest at the time of actual entry into politics. These, it may be recalled, are the two states where the two political parties are most developed and most likely to serve as agents of political socialization. In general, the data suggest that political socialization may occur at almost any phase of a person's development. Differences in the time of political socialization would seem to be a function of different influences which come into play in different periods of an individual's life history.

Primary group influence in political socialization. An interest in politics is probably related to the opportunity to hear about it or directly experience it. Thus, having parents, relatives, or close friends in politics is likely to facilitate an individual's own awareness of and familiarity with public affairs. The strong influence exerted by primary groups on voting behavior is well documented.[10] In non-political social activity, too, family members tend to be either all participants or all non-participants.[11] It is likely that legislators too tend to come from families which are much more involved in politics than the average American family. As Table 4.3 indicates, from

Table 4.3: Relatives of state legislators in politics

Number of Relatives in Politics	Calif. $N = 113$	N.J. $N = 78$	Ohio $N = 162$	Tenn. $N = 120$
One or more	43%	41%	59%	59%
None	57	59	41	41
Total	100%	100%	100%	100%

41 per cent, in the case of New Jersey, to 59 per cent, in the case of Ohio and Tennessee legislators, reported that one or more of their family had been or are active in politics, although in a few cases they went back several generations to find them.

As Table 4.1 has shown, between 34 per cent, in the case of California respondents, and 47 per cent, in the case of New Jersey, mentioned members of their immediate circle as agents of their political socialization. Of those who attributed their earliest political interest to persons with whom they were in direct and sustained relationship, we find that many more mentioned family members than friends and associates as having been instrumental in this respect. Moreover, as Table 4.4 reveals, New Jersey and Ohio legislators

[10] See Paul F. Lazarsfeld, Bernard Berelson, and Hazel Gaudet, *The People's Choice* (New York: Columbia University Press, 1948), pp. 140–145; Angus Campbell, Gerald Gurin, and Warren E. Miller, *The Voter Decides* (Evanston: Row, Peterson and Company, 1954), pp. 199–206; Bernard R. Berelson, Paul F. Lazarsfeld, and William N. McPhee, *Voting* (Chicago: University of Chicago Press, 1954), pp. 88–109.

[11] W. A. Anderson, "The Family and Individual Social Participation," *American Sociological Review*, 8:420–424 (1943).

were substantially more likely—68 per cent and 73 per cent, respectively—to recall that their family had been active in politics and attribute their own political awakening to this fact.   In California and Tennessee, on the other hand, more legislators reported that family members or relatives had been interested but not active in politics. Whether these differences between the two-party states and traditionally nonpartisan California or one-party Tennessee are meaningful reflections of the greater pervasiveness of politics in the former, with possible consequences for the nuclear family as an agency of political socialization, can only be a matter of conjecture.

Table 4.4: The influence of primary groups on legislators' socialization°

| Primary Group | Proportion of Those Mentioning Primary Group Influence | | | |
	Calif. $N = 38$	N.J. $N = 37$	Ohio $N = 70$	Tenn. $N = 50$
Family members or relatives *active* in politics	53%	68%	73%	46%
Family members or relatives *interested* in politics	34	5	19	38
Friends or associates active or interested in politics	21	27	9	20

* Percentages total more than 100 since some respondents gave more than one answer.

Political interest is seen as a matter of family tradition or inheritance: "I was born into a political family . . . I grew up in politics"; or, "I guess it's pretty much a combination of environment and heredity . . . We are all sort of involved in politics," were typical comments.   Other respondents were more explicit:

My first recollection of politics was when I was four years old and my father was a member of the House. . . . I played here in this room when I was a little boy.   Then, too, I experienced a brief congressional campaign when my father was a candidate for Congress.   He was defeated, but the whole thing left a deep impression on me.   I met lots of people in politics through my father.

A legislator might recall that his family had always been active in public affairs as far back as a great grandfather who had been a state Attorney-General and member of the state Senate—"in other words, a big man in politics.   He was held up as a person worthy of being emulated."   Another might recall that: "People around home took their politics serious. I had a grandmother who took me to political rallies where they had entertainments and refreshments. I guess I took in more of those than of politics. But my family was always interested."

The vividness of these and other accounts testifies to the important role played by family members in shaping the politician's orientations. Ties with a political party, consciousness of public issues, knowledge of both the serious and pleasurable aspects of political behavior, or sense of public responsibility, appear as by-products of political socialization in the most intimate form of primary group life.

What strikes one in reading some of the comments is the casualness of the socialization process when the agents are friends or associates. As one respondent put it, "some of the boys I was going around with were interested in politics, so I just went along." Another reported:

I would say that I was catapulted into politics without any approach. My law partner had been city councilman and had held other political jobs. So I had naturally worked in his behalf in these campaigns. This I did for a number of years. So from there I was asked to run for the legislature. I didn't seek the job, I was asked.

In the first case, political interest stemmed from the general social need to be accepted by one's peers; in the second case, it derived from activity on behalf of a politically involved professional associate. In both cases, apparent political apathy is transformed into political awareness and even participation by membership in a socially compelling primary group.

Political interest as a result of participation. Political socialization, our data suggest, does not necessarily precede some form of political activity. A person can participate in political activities of one kind or another without any previously clearly crystallized political affect. For instance, he may find himself involved in "school politics" because his political potentialities are sensed by his peers; he may become active in political campaigns because of other social but originally non-political ties with other campaign workers; or he may even participate in low-level political party work, as an errand boy or leaflet distributor, without really understanding the meaning of the activity. As Table 4.5 indicates, these types of participation are reported as stimulants of earliest political interest in proportions which may vary a good deal from state to state, but without any recognizable pattern. California respondents, in particular, as we noted earlier in Table 4.1, mentioned these types of participation as sources of their political interest and involvement.

A person may be exposed to politics by experiences which as such are non-political in character, but which are close enough to politics to serve the function of political socialization. For instance, school learning, or even self-education, may arouse political interest; so may participation in non-political civic or community work, as well as activity in occupational, professional, or minority groups. Finally, a person may become politically conscious by performing professional

Table 4.5: Political interest as result of political and non-political participation*

Type of Participation	Proportion of Those Mentioning Participation			
	Calif. $N = 78$	N.J. $N = 47$	Ohio $N = 79$	Tenn. $N = 52$
Activity in school politics	17%	6%	9%	1%
Study of politics in school, by self	28	15	29	19
General political work (campaigns, meetings)	28	13	22	29
Party work	17	53	22	15
Civic, community work	15	13	11	19
Activity in occupational, professional groups	12	6	13	1
Activity in ethnic, religious groups	1	4	0	0
Legislative lobbying	4	2	0	4
Politically-related job (teaching civics, journalism, law, public job)	12	6	6	15

* Percentages total more than 100 since some respondents gave more than one answer.

tasks which are relatively close to politics, like lobbying, newspaper work, law practice, teaching of civics, or public employment. As Table 4.5 shows, all of these forms of participation were recalled by state legislators as sources of their earliest political involvement.

Two aspects of the distributions in Table 4.5 deserve special mention. First, the study of civics, politics, or related subjects in school does not seem to have served as a potent lubricant of political socialization for these legislators. Though in California and Ohio somewhat less than a third of those classified as having become interested in politics through "participation" pointed to education as having been relevant, much smaller proportions did so in New Jersey and Tennessee. Typical responses were: "I guess it started with my getting interested in the study of civics in grade school and high school. I suppose this study of civics was my first inspiration"; or, "I became interested in city government in high school and made a habit of attending city council meetings on Monday night." Another legislator paid tribute to a particular college teacher:

> The man who did the most and stimulated me the most was Dr. X., the head of the government department at the university. He was a Roosevelt New Dealer and I was a good Republican. We had some wonderful fights. I still drop in to see him whenever I'm down that way.

What is called "school politics" as a source of an interest in politics generally is described in this response:

> I have been interested ever since I was in high school. There was no particular reason. I guess it's the same reason as people being interested in tennis or anything else. I was class president of the sophomore, junior and senior classes in high school; I was class president at the university, and president of the student council, and I was president of the student body at the business school I attended.

This legislator's orientation to politics was probably formed long before he came to hold, so consistently, the positions of leadership in school to which he attributed his interest in politics. But the fact that he mentioned them in some detail suggests that "school politics" may have a reinforcing effect on the budding politician.

Secondly, it seems that party work or political work more generally may serve to initiate an interest in politics. This, as Table 4.5 shows, seems to be particularly the case in New Jersey where over half of these respondents referred to party work, followed by a fifth of the Ohio respondents. This is likely to be due to the more solid institutionalization of party politics in these two states, and in New Jersey to the highly politicized atmosphere characteristic of that state's metropolitan areas. In other words, party politics seems to operate as its own socializing agent. Getting involved in political work, either occasionally in connection with a campaign, or by doing regular party work, may precipitate a more permanent dedication to public life: "I campaigned for people I thought would do a good job before I was old enough to vote, and I contributed small amounts to political campaigns for years." Running errands, distributing handbills, or door-to-door canvassing were recalled as early political stimuli, usually by those whose family had been active or interested in politics. But for others, being recruited by a party to run for party or public office seems to have been the source of a political orientation. As one respondent said, "I got politically interested in 1938 when I became involved in county and state politics. I then became the chairman of the county committee."

Among non-political forms of participation mentioned by legislators as decisive in their political socialization, activity in civic affairs and community work was prominent:

This is actually an extension of my activities in the school and community. I was interested in service clubs, civic progress and community problem-solving. It was getting so I was going to meetings ten nights a week. It's only a short step from this to public office.

Through the Junior Chamber of Commerce, no doubt about it. I had worked closely with city officials and in city affairs. The contacts with officials I made while in Jaycee work aroused my interest.

Activity in occupational and professional groups, or contact with politics through actually non-political but politically connected jobs, were recalled as initial points of interest. A newspaperman would say that, of course, he became interested because of his profession. Another "became interested in political intrigue as a young cub reporter, and was hired to write publicity for a state senator." A former union leader recalled that he became politically interested when politicians catered to him to win the support of his membership. A lawyer mentioned his work for a property owners association before government agencies, or a civics teacher claimed that his political interest was stimulated when he took his classes to visit the state capitol. A former school superintendent explained:

After I retired from the school business, I missed the public life and the chance to meet people and appear before the public that I had had as a superintendent. I did not think of politics before this, except that as a superintendent you're always in the political business. There's a lot of politics—you have to keep everyone happy. Politics is always entering. For instance, you have to control the board.

Finally, contact with politicians through work in public service jobs was reported by some respondents as having been instrumental in their political awakening. A woman member mentioned her work as a typist for a Congressman in Washington; a male member mentioned a job as an elevator operator in Congress which he was given because his folks knew a Congressman. A number of legislators had served as pages in the state legislature while in college. Public employment, in administrative departments of the state government or in such elective offices as that of county trustee, was a further source of earliest political interest in legislators' reports.

These recollections convey an idea of the great variety of agents and activities which seem to function as influential stimuli of political socialization. Outstanding is the great heterogeneity of the sources at the earliest focus of political attention. Most of this particular group of respondents became interested in politics—at least in their own definition of what it means to be "politically interested"—rather late in their personal development. Political socialization, it seems, is not restricted to the earlier years of the life cycle, but a process which takes place at later phases as well. One must, of course, treat these recollections with caution. But it is noteworthy that many respondents interpreted "political interest" not just as an orientational stance, but as actual "involvement," and it is this point in the personal career which stands out in perception of the past as the critical time in the political socialization process. The foundations of political interest may have been laid earlier, but "real interest," so to speak, is dated at the time when some kind of participation takes place.

The place of events and circumstances in political socialization. Great public events, either of a periodic character, like election campaigns, or of a more singular though far-reaching nature, like wars or economic crises, may have a politically mobilizing impact on persons not previously concerned with public affairs. Similarly, relatively unimportant local or state problems may become public issues which involve people who, before the occurrence of such issues, had paid no attention to politics. As Table 4.1 indicated, 42 per cent of California, 25 per cent of New Jersey, 21 per cent of Ohio, and 18 per cent of Tennessee legislators recalled particular political events or conditions. A look at Table 4.6 shows that among these respondents rather large proportions in California, Ohio, and Tennessee—77 per cent, 60 per cent and 57 per cent, respectively—mentioned presidential or other political campaigns, while in New Jersey, with its highly charged local politics, local circumstances and issues were prominent in recollections of earliest political interest.[12] The tone of these recollections suggests that political socialization occasioned by public events or issues may be accompanied by a special intensity of feeling not generally experienced in other connections.

The presidential campaign, in particular, seems to have an important, if latent, socializing function in the American political system. It

[12] This finding for New Jersey is undoubtedly related to the fact that, as we shall see in Chapter 5, much greater proportions of New Jersey respondents held local government jobs before becoming legislators than was the case elsewhere. See Table 5.1, below p. 95.

serves not only to activate voters, but the excitement, the turbulence, the color, the intrusion of the campaign into the routine existence of a relatively little politicized society like America's seem to make a profound impression, so that many years later a particular election or administration may be recalled with a great deal of relish as a source of political interest—as if the election had been held only yesterday:

In the Hughes campaign of 1916 my grandfather said to me: "My boy, I'll meet my maker, but there's only one thing I regret—that I voted in the re-election campaign for Cleveland's second term." People streamed through the house to find out from the old man how to vote.

Table 4.6: Political interest as result of particular events or conditions*

| Type of Event or Condition | Proportions of Those Mentioning Events or Conditions | | | |
	Calif. $N = 47$	N.J. $N = 20$	Ohio $N = 35$	Tenn. $N = 21$
Presidential campaigns or administrations	32%	15%	49%	43%
Other political campaigns	45	20	11	14
	77%	35%	60%	57%
War	4	10	11	14
Depression	11	0	9	0
Local conditions or issues	11	60	11	24
State conditions or issues	11	0	6	0

* Percentages total more than 100 since some respondents gave more than one answer.

During the Bryan-McKinley campaign I hanged a picture of McKinley on my bedroom wall. My father took it off and I hanged it up again. He took it off and took me to the woodshed. I've been a Republican ever since.

Remarks made about gubernatorial, senatorial, or other election campaigns were less colorful than recollections of presidential contests. But war was recalled in very intensely personal terms by the few who ascribed their first political interest to this experience. "Many of us, when we came back, had a new awakening, a new interest in civic affairs," or, "In prison camp I decided that we should do everything that we could on a local level instead of joining big organizations to influence grand policy." Another recalled:

I had served two years in the Marines, and we were getting ready for Okinawa. In Guadalcanal, the staging area, we were sitting around and talked about the war and what it meant and what should come after. We had a general interest in it, we concluded collectively, I mean. We decided that we would do our utmost after we came back. The war shook us out of our rut.

A few California and Ohio legislators mentioned the depression as the origin of their political awareness. One respondent said, for instance, that in the thirties, while he was employed in county agricultural work, "the plight of the farmers brought my interest." Another said that "during the depression everybody was politically conscious, and that interest stayed with me." For some of those who claimed to have become politically interested in the depression, politics seems to have meant a job. As one of them put it, "Well, during the depression, we weren't selling any automobiles. The situation was favorable for me to get on the ticket for county auditor." In this case, a first interest in politics seems to have coincided with the respondent's active entry into politics.

Finally, state or local conditions were reported by a few legislators as having been instrumental in their political socialization: "Well, I was driving the school bus, and there was muddy roads. I got the county commissioners to do something about it"; or, "We had a crooked Justice of the Peace and a group in town wanted me to run for council"; or, "Our representative bought up land and sold it to the state government for deer, fox, and such. Mad foxes were biting families. There were rattlesnakes all over. My friends and business-men wanted to get the land back"; or, "In 19__ the Seed Producers Association threw father and me out, because we in the corn seed business thought we were entitled to University products the same as anyone. We thought we ought to change the laws."

Personal predispositions and political socialization. Although our research sought to find out "how" state legislators became interested in politics, not "why" they became interested, it is noteworthy that, as Table 4.1 shows, over half of all respondents in California, New Jersey, and Ohio, and a third in Tennessee, seized our question as an opportunity to reflect on certain personal predispositions which, they apparently felt, preceded or accompanied their political socialization. Even if we are not prepared to interpret these responses as anything more than current rationalizations, they are probably quite genuine perceptions and, as such, constitute significant elements in legislators' self-definitions as politicians.

Of those who expressed themselves in predispositional terms, a good many simply said that they had always or long been interested in politics, and left it at that. But much larger proportions did so in Ohio and Tennessee than in New Jersey and California.

Perhaps the most interesting finding revealed by Table 4.7 is that only very few of these politicians spontaneously mentioned desire for political power, influence, or authority as predispositions toward a political orientation. Although it is impossible to say, of course, whether such power motives were really present or absent among those who admitted to them and those who did not, there is no reason to suppose that in a democratic society, where a large part of the community participates in the selection of public officials, politicians

Table 4.7: Personal predispositions and political socialization*

| Type of Predisposition | Proportions of Those Mentioning Personal Predispositions | | | |
	Calif. $N = 59$	N.J. $N = 42$	Ohio $N = 84$	Tenn. $N = 39$
"Long interest"	25%	45%	63%	72%
Ambition for political power	5	12	5	10
Admiration for politicians	36	5	10	5
Indignation	17	14	10	5
General sense of obligation	29	10	16	3
Sense of obligation to special groups	5	12	1	3
Desire for sociability	3	10	2	5
Physical handicaps	2	0	1	3

* Percentages total more than 100 since some respondents gave more than one answer.

are recruited from power-oriented persons. Even though politicians differ from average citizens in the degree of their political involvement, values other than power are likely to bring would-be leaders to public attention.[13] The fact that only very few of these state legislators referred to power or equivalent terms as a predispositional correlate of their political socialization is, therefore, not surprising. The following illustrate this type of response: "I've always had some sort of responsibility in groups I have been in and wished I could have avoided it." Only a few were as explicit as the legislator who said it was hard for him to determine just what first interested him in politics, but who continued:

[13] See Harold D. Lasswell, "The Selective Effect of Personality in Political Participation," *op. cit.*, p. 221, for a discussion of political personality in democratic settings.

I would say that I'm the sort of person interested in doing things. I feel I should contribute from the policy point of view. I'm not a good joiner. I feel the same sort of thing carries over into government and politics. I have always some desire not to be in the crowd. I'm never content to go to meetings and just listen and go home. I like to get my oar in.

Admiration for other politicians, as ego ideals, was suggested by some respondents as having had some influence on their developing political interest. It is plausible that favorable impressions of this kind formed at an early age should have some impact on political awareness, as the following examples illustrate:

I do remember that one summer I was staying with my uncle. I guess I was about 13. I attended an old-fashioned town meeting. My uncle was quite active at the meeting, and it made quite an impression on me.

When I was a young man I admired a Congressman by the name of . . . , although I did not myself go into politics for many years.

I admired Bilbo's speeches as a child. Huey Long was fascinating to me. I lived a long time in Louisiana.

But other respondents reported having become interested in politics for just the opposite reason—because they were indignant and dissatisfied with incumbent officeholders or political situations:

This is a somewhat long story. I was an officer of a sports club, and in this capacity I had to call upon a city councilman to speak to him about getting the use of a hall. He promised me to look into it and have my request heard before the commission, but he never did. He just ignored me.

The reason I was interested was that I felt that I could do the community a service. I wasn't quite satisfied with the way things were going. I could have been wrong, but that's my opinion.

Sense of obligation appears, not surprisingly, as a relatively frequent category of predispositional responses. This kind of answer is, of course, part and parcel of a politician's armor of rationalizations and can hardly be taken at face value. Yet, there seems to be a real difference between the politician who said:

The fact that the Constitution is so flexible gave me the feeling that I would like to serve the public as guaranteed by the principles as set forth by the Constitution; . . .

and the politician who put it this way:

Well, it came about twelve or fourteen years ago when I decided I had spent all my life tending to our business and had done nothing for the community.   I looked around to see how I could help out and decided to run for the legislature.   I thought my business experience would be useful in the legislature.

There is an element of genuine commitment in this second response that is in sharp contrast to the obvious rhetoric of the first.   In other words, a distinction must be made between the politician who really feels a sense of public service, and the politician for whom "public service" is a convenient device of avoidance or deception.

A few legislators suggested that their first interest in politics was stimulated by the "social" possibilities which politics offered, as for instance, the former school superintendent (already cited), who upon retirement missed the chance to meet people which his occupation had given him and who, for this reason, became interested in politics. Finally, three respondents attributed their initial interest to the existence of a physical handicap and implied that politics offered them a compensatory opportunity.   As one of them pointed out, "As a kid I had a bad leg, couldn't participate in sports and developed an interest in politics.   I thought a legal background qualified a fellow for anything in public life."

It requires re-emphasis that our data do not tell us "why" these legislators were "moved" to become interested in politics to the point of taking a political role, while others in the general population, with similar ostensible experiences, were not so moved.   The perceptual data on legislators' prepolitical activities, or the events surrounding their earliest political interest, or even what they described as pre-dispositional factors, cannot be interpreted in a motivational sense.   If there is a personality syndrome of which one may speak as "political man," the data do not and cannot reveal its existence among these state legislators.

Ideology and political socialization.   Not unexpectedly in a society like America's, where politics is pragmatic rather than ideological, political beliefs seem to play a very minor part in the process of political socialization.   As we noted in Table 4.1, only very small proportions of respondents in all four states linked our question of how they had become interested in politics with a discussion of political beliefs.   It is possible to compare this distribution with a similar one of the American electorate as a whole.   As reported in a recent study, only $3\frac{1}{2}$ per cent of American voters in 1956 expressed themselves on issues in ideological terms.[14]   It would seem, therefore, that state

[14] Angus Campbell, Philip E. Converse, Warren E. Miller, and Donald E. Stokes, *The American Voter, op. cit.*, p. 249, Table 10-1.

legislators are only slightly more ideology conscious than the electorate as a whole.

This result is all the more significant because the open-ended character of our question represented a good opportunity for ideological discourse if the respondent wished it. One can only guess, of course, that in a European country where ideology is a more important component of political culture, a legislator would probably have taken this opportunity to justify his interest in politics by expressing political opinions or beliefs of an ideological sort. It is interesting to note, nevertheless, that in spite of the very small numbers involved, Californians seemed somewhat more prone to mention political beliefs than legislators elsewhere. But those who did mention beliefs gave them only most cursory expression. The California exception suggests, perhaps, that the less disciplined the parties are, the more important are political beliefs likely to be.

CONCLUSION

What do our data tell us about the political socialization of American state legislators? In general, it seems that a great many sources are operative in initiating political interest, at least as recalled by respondents themselves. Perhaps the most significant finding is tentative support for the hypothesis that political socialization—the process by which people are introduced into political roles and acquire appropriate attitudes, values, and beliefs—may occur at almost any phase of the life cycle, even among men and women whose eventual concern with public affairs is more intense and permanent than that of the average citizen. But it seems to take place more often than in the case of the average citizen at a relatively early age, for many of them in childhood. Whether the differences from state to state, either with regard to the source or the time of socialization, are significant as evidence of differing political subcultures requires more detailed and systematic investigation than we were able to make in this survey in which the problem of political socialization was restricted to a single question and of only peripheral interest. But one's over-all impression is one of great diversity, suggesting that many roads may lead to an interest in politics for those whose careers lead them into legislative office.

CHAPTER 5

Orientations

A COMPLETE STUDY OF POLITICAL CAREER LINES would, of course, trace the order of succession in which governmental or party offices are held by politicians as they move from one institutional context into the next, from one formal position to another. Our data tell us only what positions had been occupied by the respondents before they entered the state legislature. This limits us to examining what kind of previous governmental or political experience, if any, is particularly conducive to a career in the state legislature.

Prelegislative career. Table 5.1 presents the data concerning prelegislative governmental experience. From one-third of the legislators (in the case of New Jersey) to one-half (in the case of

Table 5.1: Prelegislative career: level of government

| | Proportion Having Different Types of Experience | | | |
Career	N.J. $N = 79$	Ohio $N = 162$	Calif. $N = 113$	Tenn. $N = 120$
No previous experience	34%	43%	51%	51%
Local alone, or local and/or state, national experience	62	50	41	39
State and/or national experience	4	7	8	10
Total	100%	100%	100%	100%

California and Tennessee) had not held any governmental office before entering the legislature. It seems that an apprenticeship in some other governmental office is by no means a necessary condition

This chapter drafted by Eulau.

95

for a state legislative career. However, whether or not the state legislature can be a direct port of entry into politics without a previous apprenticeship in some other office seems to differ somewhat from state to state. In the table, the four states are arranged in order of degree of party competition on the electoral level; (the same order will be used in the tables throughout this chapter).[1] It appears that the more competitive the state's party system, the more likely it is for legislators to have had some prior governmental experience.

It also appears that the more competitive the system, the greater is the likelihood that the apprenticeship has included service on the local level of government. On the other hand, the less competitive the system, the more likely it seems that there was prelegislative service on the state and/or national levels alone. Although the number of respondents in this category is small, the pattern is consistent. In other words, if an "escalator model" of political ascent is applicable it seems likely the escalator must be boarded at lower governmental levels in competitive systems than in less competitive systems.[2] These findings are not surprising. In competitive political systems, party organization is more likely to be effective and the party is more likely to participate actively in the nominating process, and state legislative office is likely to be looked on as a reward for service to the party on the local level.

What kind of governmental experience most appropriate for holding legislative office will state legislators have had before entering the legislature? Our data indicate that about one-fifth of the respondents in all four states had held executive and/or judicial jobs alone before their entry into the legislature. But greater proportions had held jobs which were legislative or quasi-legislative in character, such as service on city councils, county boards, school boards, and so on. Of course, this may be due to the fact that simply more legislative-type offices than executive or judicial positions are available. But, again, the data suggest that differences from state to state may be related to the degree of competition in the state's party system. Of the experienced New Jersey respondents, 48 per cent had legislative-type experience; of Ohio respondents, 36 per cent; of California respondents, 32 per cent; and of the Tennesseans, 30 per cent. Although, with the exception of New Jersey, the differences among the states

[1] The operational criteria used in determining competition are reported in Appendix 2.1, pp. 471–474.

[2] For the conception of the "political escalator" which may be boarded or left at various levels, see Lester G. Seligman, "Recruitment in Politics," *PROD*, 1 (1958), 14–17.

are small, the pattern is consistent. Apparently, demonstration of some legislative ability is more highly valued where competition between the parties is keen.

It is not surprising that holding a party office or being active in party work as a condition for a legislative career seems to follow a similar pattern. Comparing the percentages of governmental experience with the data in Table 5.2, even fewer respondents in all four states had held party office or done party work than had held

Table 5.2: Prelegislative career: party activity

| | Proportion Having Party Activity Experience | | | |
| | N.J. | Ohio | Calif. | Tenn. |
Career	$N = 79$	$N = 162$	$N = 113$	$N = 120$
No party office or work	41%	62%	52%	66%
Local party alone; or local and/or state; local and/or national party	41	30	29	19
State and/or national party	18	8	19	15
Total	100%	100%	100%	100%

Table 5.3: Party activists—California and Ohio°

| California | | Ohio | |
| Democrats | Republicans | Democrats | Republicans |
$N = 54$	$N = 59$	$N = 51$	$N = 111$
59%	37%	35%	40%

* Numbers on which per cent is based are the number of party activists mentioning agencies sponsoring their legislative career.

governmental office; but considerably fewer legislators in competitive New Jersey than legislators in the less competitive states, and especially in one-party Tennessee, had no party record at all.

There is reason to believe that the break in the pattern for California and Ohio is due to the California Democratic Party's organizational revival spurred in recent years by the local Democratic club movement in which many Democratic legislators are involved.[3] When party activists in the two states are examined in terms of their party affiliation, as in Table 5.3, it is seen that the California Dem-

[3] See Francis Carney, The Rise of the Democratic Clubs in California (New York: Henry Holt and Company, 1958), p. 16.

ocrats in fact reported having been much more active in party work than the California Republicans, while Ohio Democrats and Republicans differed only little in the proportions of those who had been party activists before becoming state legislators.

One tentative inference from the data might be that in competitive party systems political careers are likely to be more professionalized than in less competitive systems. There seems to be greater emphasis in competitive systems on entry into politics at the local level of government or party organization, and on having had some governmental and especially legislative experience before running for the state legislature. State legislative service is more likely to be a step on the political escalator which must be boarded early and, if the party is well organized, as the "deviant" case of the California Democrats suggests, under the auspices of the party.

Career sponsorship. If the structural character of the party system is a critical factor in the unfolding of political careers, one should expect that politicians in more competitive systems would be more likely to see the party as a necessary vehicle for a career than politicians in less competitive systems, and that they would consider sponsorship by party essential for electoral success. Indeed, in response to a question of how they became state legislators, a number of respondents in all four states mentioned their party. But, as the totals in Table 5.4 show, only in competitive New Jersey did great

Table 5.4: Proportion of legislators perceiving their careers as party sponsored

New Jersey		Ohio		California		Tennessee	
Dem.	Rep.	Dem.	Rep.	Dem.	Rep.	Dem.	Rep.
$N = 27$	$N = 44$	$N = 49$	$N = 108$	$N = 48$	$N = 55$	$N = 68$	$N = 18$
74%	66%	12%	24%	42%	22%	15%	28%

proportions of the respondents spontaneously refer to their party as sponsoring their legislative career. That only a small percentage would mention the party in almost non-competitive Tennessee was to be expected, but that so few respondents mentioned it in Ohio and California is rather surprising.

But the data in Table 5.4 also suggest that whether or not party sponsorship of the legislative career is considered salient may be a function of a party's discipline and morale. In New Jersey, where the parties are well organized, great majorities in both mentioned their party as sponsor. But in Ohio, where the Democrats were organizationally weak, the Republicans referred to their party twice as frequently as the Democrats. The result is reversed in California where, in line with the greater party activism of the Democratic legislators already noted, Democrats not only mentioned their party to a considerable extent, but did so almost twice as frequently as the Republicans. In Tennessee, finally, more of the greatly outnumbered Republicans acknowledged their party as the sponsor of their career than did the majority Democrats. Party support seems to be seen as essential by members of a minority party in a system where the minority ever struggles for survival in the face of the overwhelming majority.

A number of respondents who did not suggest their careers were party sponsored recognized that their party was nevertheless influential in making available to them the opportunity to be promoted as a candidate.

After I was president of the Young Republicans, I became secretary-treasurer of the executive committee for ten years, with the idea in mind of becoming a legislator. You might say that I came up through the ranks.

I was endorsed by the county central committee and I abided by their decision. . . . I hadn't sought it but, as a member of the central committee myself, I had indicated an interest in politics and they made the opportunity available to me.

The data (not shown here) reveal that such perceptions, exactly as in the case of perceptions of parties as career sponsors, were more frequent in competitive than in non-competitive systems, with California Democrats again accounting for the relative frequency with which the response was encountered in that non-competitive state.

There are different ways in which the party seems to enter the nominating process. When an incumbent decides not to run again, he may be the party's agent in approaching a possible successor:

The Representative who preceded me had enough. We were well acquainted. We decided that he would withdraw and I would run. I was unopposed in the primary.

At times the party may be hard put to find suitable candidates, and it may go so far as to nominate a candidate without his prior consent:

In 19——, the Republican Committee, after many years of not even filing a candidate for the office, wrote my name in without my knowing it. I was elected. At first I was mad because they had done it without asking me. But I'm the first Republican to hold that office and the only Republican in office in the entire county at the present time.

On the other hand, a legislative career may be said to have been "self-started." Fifty-five per cent of the Ohio legislators, 33 per cent of the California respondents, 31 per cent in New Jersey, and 23 per cent of the Tennesseans made this claim. But a closer look at the interview protocols may reveal the party in the background, these self-serving declarations notwithstanding. Whether actually true or not, these self-images may be quite genuine and behaviorally relevant aspects of the legislator's career perspective. Two from among many remarks must suffice to illustrate what are evidently considered prestige-giving self-conceptions:

I was county treasurer. Well, I left the office in 19——, and it wasn't very long that I found that my expenses were the same whether I had a job or not. I sat in the office one day and a fellow politician came in. He asked me whom we Democrats were going to run for the Assembly. My predecessor had been a six-termer and was running for the Senate. I said to this fellow: "Do you know whom we are going to run? You look right at him."

Twenty years ago I developed the desire of becoming a legislator after practicing law awhile. . . . Nobody told me to run. One of my associates is Democratic county chairman; he didn't know until I told him. . . . It was a long-planned thing. I was very active in club work, local politics, had extensive acquaintances. I was in a position to run and win.

If the party is the major agency facilitating a legislative career mainly in competitive systems or when it is especially well organized, one may ask whether there are functional equivalents in the less competitive systems which take over the role of sponsoring legislative candidates. Our interviews revealed that either interest groups or "friends" or "associates" may perform the sponsoring function. Even though this task is one interest groups are thought not to cherish, Table 5.5 shows that 16 per cent of the Tennessee respondents and 9

Table 5.5: Interest groups and friends as sponsors of a legislative career

State	Interest Groups	Friends/Associates
New Jersey ($N = 71$)	1%	8%
Ohio ($N = 157$)	2	19
California ($N = 103$)	9	24
Tennessee ($N = 86$)	16	54

per cent of the Californians referred to interest groups as sponsors, while they were hardly mentioned at all in the more competitive states of New Jersey and Ohio. Apparently, the less competitive the political party system, the more likely it is that interest groups will serve as functional equivalents of party in promoting political careers.

Friends or associates were mentioned somewhat more often as sponsors of a political or legislative career. Again, as in the case of interest groups, the interstate pattern noted in connection with party sponsorship is reversed. As Table 5.5 indicates, friends or associates were more likely to be mentioned as sponsors in the less competitive than in the more competitive systems, and especially in one-party Tennessee. This finding is in accord with those of others that "friends and neighbors" are important political factors in the South generally.[4]

It may be that there is hidden behind the naming of friends, especially in California and Tennessee, the struggle of factions whose identity is concealed by the reference to "friends." The following remarks in one of the interviews are suggestive in this respect:

> I attribute that to about four close friends—a member of the legislature, a member of the county central committee, the county superintendent of schools and the secretary of the election board. They said to me, "Hell, why don't you throw in your hat?" So I got my petition and away I went. I got entangled with the political leader in the county. He had a candidate he could dictate to. He knew he couldn't get to first base with me. He got his candidate to oppose me in the primary, but I won. The same thing happened with the second term.

Career skills. An important consideration in the choice of a career is the possession of talents or skills which are conducive to successful performance of the tasks which an occupation calls for. In governmental administration, civil servants take examinations that are geared to particular levels of *expertise.* But in politics the skills whose mastery is presumably a condition of professional success are much less specific. In many respects, politicians are generalizers rather than specialists. Their careers involve so wide a range of activities that to speak of skills seems almost paradoxical. Nevertheless, politicians themselves are likely to insist that certain qualifications, talents, or skills—broadly conceived as also including certain personal characteristics—are necessary and desirable requisites for a career in politics.

That this is the case appears quite clearly from our data. Though the question we asked in no way directed the respondent to appraise his skills or qualifications as a candidate or politician, quite a few

---

[4] See V. O. Key, Jr., *Southern Politics in State and Nation* (New York: Alfred A. Knopf, 1949), pp. 37–41, or 131–135.

legislators made it an occasion to discuss the matter. At least 75 per cent or more did so in New Jersey, Ohio, and California, but in one-party Tennessee only 40 per cent of the respondents made spontaneous comments about career skills or qualifications. Whatever skills they may actually possess, it would seem that in one-party systems politicians place relatively little value on specific qualifications as requisites of professional success.

A great variety of skills, experiences, or attributes were offered in this spontaneous self-assessment, but three main categories emerged from the interview material: personal, occupational, and political qualifications.

A few legislators (never more than 13 per cent in any state) emphasized such attributes as a "sense of sociability" or "general ability" for political or legislative work. The differences from state to state were small and insignificant. But these personal qualifications were somewhat more frequently mentioned in the less competitive than in the more competitive systems. Those referring to their sociability would simply say that they went into politics because they liked people: "I like people and being here you get all kinds", or, "The ability I have of being able to mix with people. I have always enjoyed mixing with people and getting along with them." Another respondent would say, "Well, I'm gregarious at heart." Those who mentioned their general ability would identify it as being "smart," "well equipped," or having "broad experience." The following two illustrations are typical:

That I picked the legislature? I had attended sessions in other states accidentally. I was impressed. And I did have experience. I felt that a smart man like I (sic) would stand out like a sore thumb. But I wasn't a member long before I found out they weren't so dumb.

Damned if I know! I liked the idea of writing the laws that I'd have to live under. I also feel that there is need, not to be boastful, for better-equipped people here in the House. I thought I could do a better job than some of the fellows I'd seen around here.

Somewhat larger proportions in all four states, but nowhere more than 15 per cent, mentioned non-political occupational skills or experiences in assessing their careers. Though the differences were again very small, there was a slight tendency for legislators in the more competitive systems to stress legal skills or previous experiences with the legislature in some non-legislative capacity.

Politics as a career intersects with many other vocational roles in business, unions, real estate, insurance, and so on. Law, in particular, has long been noted as the one vocation most prominently connected with politics. If, as we have reason to believe, the political career is more professionalized in competitive political systems, we should expect to find there more lawyer-legislators than in less competitive systems. In fact, 52 per cent of all legislators in New Jersey were lawyers; 36 per cent of all Ohioans were also members of the bar, followed by 30 per cent, respectively, of all the legislators in California and Tennessee. Of course, some lawyers will pick a political career for really non-political objectives, as an avenue of advancement in their profession, but others may look on their legal training as a qualification for legislative service:

I don't consider myself a politician. I just availed myself of the opportunity because I was interested in legislative law in my capacity as a lawyer. It was an opportunity to expand my knowledge of the law. Also good during the lean years of practice.

The fact that the legislature is the most important political office in the state, next to the executive. It is a position which would not interfere with my profession because it is only in session six months. And the lawmaking branch is the most compatible with the profession of law.

Previous service with the legislature in appointive positions may be considered a suitable experience for a legislative career. A former secretary to a Congressman claimed to have learned about the nature and demands of legislative work in the Congress. A former Congressional assistant valued the opportunity he had "to watch the House and Senate in action." Another respondent had been counsel to a Congressional committee, and the experience had stimulated him to seek elective office.

Similarly, local elective office, such as county commissioner, county treasurer, or probate judge, may acquaint politicians with the legislature, and this experience will be perceived as relevant in choosing a legislative career:

For eight years I served on the County Treasurers' Legislative Committee. During the course of that time I came down to the legislature often. While on the committee, I worked on bills such as the County Officials Pay Bill. I decided that I had some good experience and that I should run for the legislature.

When I served on the probate bench, I was often required to appear before legislative committees to testify as to the legality of certain bills. That experience caused me to become interested in the legislature, and I decided that I would rather make up the bills than have to come afterwards to decide if it was legal.

Political skills or qualifications proper were mentioned by much larger proportions of legislators in the four states. Here the differences from state to state, as Table 5.6 shows, were more marked, but a consistent pattern is difficult to discern. Yet, as the italicized figures on the diagonal indicate, the pattern may be obscured here by the somewhat different emphases given in the four states to what we lumped together as "political skills and qualifications"—a matter of cultural variation in expressions.

For instance, New Jersey legislators were more inclined than those elsewhere to stress political "know-how"—including such things as experience in local government, wide previous political contacts, demonstrated vote-getting ability, experience in campaigning, and so on—all evidence of the greater professionalization of politics in that

Table 5.6: Political career skills and qualifications*

Political Skills and Qualifications	N.J. $N = 61$	Ohio $N = 122$	Calif. $N = 94$	Tenn. $N = 48$
Political "know-how"	*59%*	3%	25%	2%
Involvement in politics	13	*34*	19	25
Civic commitment	13	15	*34*	15
Political ambition	23	24	27	13
Political "availability"	13	7	12	*21*

* Percentages total more than 100 since some respondents gave more than one answer.

state. In the states where local and state politics is apparently less professionalized than in New Jersey, yet less amateurish than in one-party Tennessee, respondents were more likely to express themselves in appropriate attitudinal terms. Ohio legislators, in particular, emphasized their involvement in and fascination with politics as an important attribute of the successful political careerist. Politics appears as a game, a challenge, or sheer fun. By implication, persons who don't like the game are not qualified to be politicians:

> Oh, I just think it's lots of fun. Election time isn't too much fun, matter of fact it's a pain in the neck. But the legislature is fascinating business.

> It was more or less a challenge. No Democrat ever was elected to county or state office from our area except on rare occasions. I used the direct approach in running. I represent what was once, if not still now, the strongest Republican county in the state. I went right direct to the people while running. I met with small groups and went to see individuals in every nook and cranny of the county.

There is especially much gusto in the statements of those whose career was begun in defiance of the party organization:

Mainly wanting to get my feet wet, to see what it's like. I did it just through campaigning. I had one endorsement, a newspaper. I never solicited organization support. I just did it on my own. It was a lot of fun that way. They wouldn't let me speak at some meetings, but the harder they kicked, the harder I tried. I'm not a party politician, yet.

Being civic minded and devoted to the public interest as a requisite qualification was more often mentioned in California than elsewhere. This may be, of course, a standard response, designed to camouflage either lack of self-awareness, or to portray oneself in a favorable light. But politicians may take their stereotypes of themselves seriously, seek to live up to them, and have a genuine commitment to the public welfare:

I felt it a civic duty to run. The people weren't being well represented. The first time I wasn't elected. But that encouraged me to run again. I ran for the good of the people of the county.

Politics is a means rather than an end. It is a means to an active interest in government. It is a vehicle for doing something. . . . How did I decide to go into it? Well, I liked the legislative job and you know you have to figure out how to get it, to wit, run.

Somewhat more respondents in New Jersey, Ohio, and California than in Tennessee pointed to their ambitions as requisite qualifications, and a few suggested "power" as a desirable aspiration. Yet, interestingly, power is a concept only very rarely used by politicians themselves who prefer terms like "urge" or "ambition" to denote what is evidently considered a legitimate career qualification. As a first termer put it, "I just wanted to be a legislator. I just had the urge. I thought of it all the time, and I just wanted to become one." Frequently politicians seem to find it difficult to articulate this orientation. As another respondent said, "I don't know quite how to answer that; there was just the fact that I always felt that I might like politics." Finally, legislative office may be viewed as a good jumping-off place for a career, a testing ground for the ambitious to acquire further political skills:

I came back from . . . and I wanted to run for some office, either prosecutor or legislator. I talked it over with my father, and we decided that the state legislature was better because it would lead some place more than being the prosecutor of a small county. A prosecutor of a city might go some place, but a small county man isn't likely to go far; he usually ends up pleading property claims; and whereas I don't mind property claims, that isn't my ambition.

A few legislators, but, as Table 5.6 shows, more in one-party Tennessee than elsewhere, ascribed their career to the fact that they had been "available." That this rather passive qualification is most frequently mentioned in the least professionalized political system is not unusual. In a one-party system political recruitment lags, and candidates are likely to be selected to attract supporters of competing factions, just as in competitive systems this consideration may determine the choice of party candidates in primaries. The fact that "availability" was more frequently mentioned in Tennessee only underlines the fact that in competitive systems, counter to some political folklore, more is required of a candidate than a "right" name or religion.

In spite of its wide use, both in political circles and the academic literature, the concept of "availability" is poorly defined. Its most frequent connotation seems to be that a candidate must have certain qualities or characteristics, and that he must lack certain attributes, in such combination that his candidacy is more acceptable to diverse interests than the candidacy of another man who possesses those characteristics or lacks others in a less fortunate combination. Part of one's availability is to be widely known and to have cultivated wide contacts, but this is not enough. *Not* having been a controversial figure may facilitate it. As a respondent put it, "I had no political scars, so I guess somebody thought they could use me." *Not* being identified with a particular interest may increase availability. This was expressed by a non-labor legislator who comes from a strongly unionized metropolitan area:

When a vacancy in the Senate occurred, the incumbent who's a CIO leader asked me to run, and I was endorsed by the CIO. I guess they asked me to run because they did not want another labor man.

On the other hand, availability may mean that the candidate has a single quality which, it is assumed, will attract a particular clientele. For instance, being a woman may be seen as a condition of being picked for the ticket: "There is usually one woman on our county ticket." That a "right" name may be a qualification for being a candidate is familiar enough, and voting studies have shown how widespread the practice is. State legislators seem to share this criterion of availability:

You need a good name in politics, a simple name that appeals to people. Mine is a good name, which helped me. Other good names are those like Marshall or Brown. Funny names are a handicap. Several people have changed their names when they went into politics. Funny names wouldn't appeal down-state. We often get funny names from the city, you can notice them in the Senate, names like Bacigalupi or Radzinsky.

Finally, a few among the respondents who appraised their skills or qualifications—2 per cent in Ohio, 13 per cent in Tennessee, and 17 per cent in California—characterized themselves as essentially "non-political," at least at the time of their candidacy: "I ran and won without knowledge of the election process or a machine of any kind to back me"; or, "I was asked to run for the legislature. I talked it over with my wife. I was never really interested in it until then." Perhaps the most candid remark along this line was: "I don't consider myself 'in,' very deep, very permanent, or very long."

Career opportunities.   Relevant skills and experiences are likely to be of little use in politics unless those who have them can seize appropriate opportunities to apply them.   "Opportunity" means here the particular sets of circumstances which must be harnessed as they arise, whether accidentally or not, rather than that condition of political mobility which stems from advantageous location in the social structure.

Our data suggest a welter of ways in which would-be politicians can define political opportunities.   In general, recollecting the circumstances of their entry into politics, our respondents tended to mention two types: (1) a relatively small proportion—roughly one-fifth—described the broad social or political context of their entry; and (2) much larger proportions of those giving relevant answers—roughly two-thirds—referred to more directly personal conditions.

Because the number of respondents in the first category is so small, and because no meaningful interstate pattern was apparent, we prefer to aggregate the data for descriptive purposes.   For instance, only 3 per cent of the 95 legislators in all states who dealt with the broad context of their career choice mentioned the Depression or economically difficult times, and 6 per cent mentioned war.   It would seem that for the great majority of politicians active at the state level, few of whom are likely to advance much further in their political career, the "great issues" are relatively devoid of salience.   Moreover, those who came to politics in time of depression fall into two quite distinct groups: some entered politics to help others, and some did so to help themselves.   As one of the former group put it:

> In Harding's and Coolidge's times it seemed as though democratic government was to fall apart because of lack of good leaders.   They were taking gold out of this country and that is the life blood of this country.   Roosevelt called a bank holiday and knew where he was going.   The miners and underprivileged people felt that they needed representation.   They talked me into it.   I've been elected five times, mostly by these people.

For the second group, politics was an alternative to unemployment and promised a chance to make a living. The context was to be exploited for personal interest rather than to be changed by political means:

The only job it was possible for one to get during the depression years was some sort of political one. I was just starting to work, had to make some money to get back to school. It seemed like the politics business was all that was open.

Respondents who mentioned war and war's aftermath as conditioning their career choice also seem to fall into two groups. An "idealistic" view appears in this comment:

Getting out of the service for the second time and feeling that as long as the world is in turmoil young lives are affected. Feeling that young people should get into politics and do something about it, possibly correct previous mistakes of our elders.

On the other hand, the more directly personal consequences of war as they relate to the career choice may be expressed as follows:

The Second World War had put me out of business. We couldn't get any merchandise. When I came out of the Navy, I was wholly free, nothing to do, absolutely nothing. At that time the man who represented our district in the Senate was retiring. I remember being in a restaurant with a friend. He said, "There goes the Senator, he isn't running anymore. Why don't you run for the Senate?" I thought it over and decided to run.

Much greater proportions—32 per cent and 43 per cent, respectively— mentioned "dissatisfaction" with general or specific situations or politicians as the context of their career choice. Squabbles over village zoning or waterworks, fights over local sales taxes or public school expenditures, struggles with local political machines or special interests dominating local government, are the kinds of context in which political careers may be initiated. The failure of a politician to respond to local demands may serve as the stimulus:

I'd say that what triggered it was that we wanted two judges here. The man in the legislature would not introduce it. I threatened to run against him. So he introduced the bill and I was told that I could have one of the legislative jobs.

Or there may be a feeling that the incumbent has been in office too long. How dissatisfaction with an incumbent may start a political career is described by a respondent in some detail:

After serving as a page in the legislature I attended the Republican caucus in the Spring of 19—. There was some discussion or comments made that perhaps a Republican should run against the incumbent. The incumbent was a solid Republican, but some people had some gripes against him. I went to a member of the precinct committee, who was also vice-chairman of the party, and said I was interested in running. A few months later there was a party picnic and from several comments made I felt that I would have some support.

How local situations can serve to mobilize a political career was explained by another legislator:

I was disturbed and disgusted by the very corrupt conditions in my home town. The city government had surrendered to and was in collusion with the illegal rackets. That was in the twenties. Prostitution and gambling and so on were protected. I knew some members of the city council and approached them, but they shrugged their shoulders. I told them that if I were on the council. . . . Well, this was the germ of an idea, and I ran and was elected.

More often the local context was factional fights in the party and dissatisfaction with the party organization:

I was cats-paw for my party leaders. I didn't know it was my party. I ran for the city council, but the incumbent made amends, the leaders double-crossed me and I lost by twelve votes. I started campaigning on my own for the next term.

Finally, the fact that certain well-known national leaders were running could serve as a stimulus—the hope evidently being, though not expressed, that the leader's coat tails might be helpful:

Bob Taft was running and labor was opposing him. Personally, I thought he should get in. When some labor people asked me if I would run with him, I accepted, hoping to do anything I could to get him elected.

Well, actually on my own initiative. FDR was running for his fourth term. Nobody thought he had a chance. The regular Democrat didn't run. I ran to show my belief in FDR and I was willing to fight even if the ship was sinking.

On the other hand, a national figure like Roosevelt could serve as a negative symbol stimulating a career:

FDR—I hated his guts, and I still do. He did more god-damned harm to the country. I was in business then. Some guy named Isidore Lubin sent forms all the time wanting to know what I was doing. I was peed off.

A majority of the legislators in all states except Tennessee indicated some sensitivity to the more personal chance or opportunity aspects of their political or legislative career. As we already noted, there seems to exist a direct relationship between perceptions of the opportunity made possible by party promotion and the structure of political party systems, depending on the degree of competition between the parties. On the other hand, there seems to exist an inverse relationship between an emphasis on opportunity to combine political office with one's private occupation and the structure of the party system as patterned by competition. As Table 5.7 shows, regardless of whether they are Democrats or Republicans, legislators in the less competitive states were more likely to say that the possibility of combining their political career with their private employment or occupation gave them an opportunity to go into politics. The differences between the states also reflect other factors such as the greater time demands made on legislators in the competitive systems or better legislative pay which lead to greater or lesser professionalization of

Table 5.7: Proportions of legislators who mentioned opportunities for combining a legislative career with their occupation

N.J.		Ohio		Calif.		Tenn.	
Dem	Rep.	Dem.	Rep.	Dem.	Rep.	Dem.	Rep.
$N = 18$	$N = 39$	$N = 28$	$N = 73$	$N = 47$	$N = 47$	$N = 34$	$N = 7$
0%	5%	7%	12%	11%	17%	24%	43%

the political career in the various states. Occupations most likely to be paired with a legislative career were real estate and insurance which permit the legislator to have control over his own hours, and, of course, law. Retirement was also mentioned as an opportunity to enter politics.

In the same way, opportunity in general, or specific fortuitous opportunities, were more frequently cited by legislators in the less than in the more competitive states, except in the case of Tennessee. This deviation may be explained, in part at least, by the fact that Tennessee legislators, as did Californians, reported that their opportunity to enter politics stemmed from there being no other candidates available (see Table 5.8, below). But the data (not shown) seem to support the notion that career "opportunities" in politics are more a matter of chance in the less competitive systems than in the more competitive structures.

Again, the interview protocols may throw some light on the dynamics of political or legislative career choices as they are seen in terms of "opportunity." Although there is much lore and some evidence to the effect that politicians cherish the combat and challenge involved in campaigning, it may be that just the opposite is preferred. Few legislators, it seems, like to run against incumbents:

A vacancy came up and I had been building up towards it when the opening came. Then I made the move. All politics contains a certain amount of *opportunity*. If opportunities don't come, like in anything else, you don't go any place. One has to be at the right spot at the right time. I happened to be.

Local party strength may also determine the level at which a political career is sought. While it may not be possible to succeed locally, the opportunity may exist at a higher level:

Well, it's the first step for a politician in politics. For me, it's probably the last step. As a Democrat, it was the only thing I could do. At the county level, although there are Democrats elected, all the incumbents were running again and I would not have had a good chance. There was more chance on the state level.

Even the choice of party under whose label to run may be dictated by exigency:

I went to the county chairman of both parties and offered my services. The Democratic Party took more interest in me and therefore I became a Democrat.

The fact that only three candidates entered a primary for two available seats, a legislator felt, "made a good climate for me to run in." On the other hand, a large field of candidates may favor the candidate with the best-known name. As a legislator from a one-party area whose father had been a well-known state and national figure pointed out:

A fellow with the name of . . . had five terms; he died after the May primary in 19—. So the committee had to meet to nominate a candidate. Some people didn't know my father was dead. So I put my hat in the ring. There were 12 or 13 wanting the nomination. They started the process of elimination 'til three were left. One fellow then swung to me and I was selected by the committee.

Finally, the opportunity for political office may present itself under very particular conditions. As a respondent admitting to having "the political bug" pointed out, "we had a fellow here who went bad and took money. I ran on my own hook."

Another set of responses involved more immediately personal circumstances which legislators perceived as salient in molding their career. As Table 5.8 shows, the proportions of respondents in the relevant categories are small and no consistent pattern can be discerned. Yet, it is noteworthy that more respondents in the less competitive states of California and Tennessee attributed the opportunity to enter on a political career to the fact that nobody else was available for taking office. This result is in line, of course, with other findings concerning differences in the political vitality of differently structured systems.

The chance to enter political life is enhanced if the candidate has made a reputation for himself in some other pursuit. As the following comments suggest, some would-be legislators had cultivated wide contacts for many years:

I've occupied a position for some years in which I've been well known; I've been active in veterans' affairs, retail merchandising and financial interests, as well as in the educational system, having taught for several years in the district school. The local party chairman figured I was a likely candidate and asked me to run. I hadn't been at all politically active until then.

Table 5.8: Miscellaneous opportunities for political career

Type of Opportunity	Proportion of Legislators Mentioning Each Type of Opportunity			
	N.J. $N = 57$	Ohio $N = 101$	Calif. $N = 94$	Tenn. $N = 41$
Nobody else available	2%	2%	16%	15%
Reputation from other pursuit	11	8	12	10
Family conditions favorable	—	5	4	2
Earlier defeat encouraging	7	14	13	2

My experience in organized labor, fighting for union hours and working conditions. I joined the ITU when I was 23. We had to serve six years of apprenticeship. It was a democratic union. Then I was active in social work, on the boards of the TB and health organizations in . . . , and one of the organizers of the United Fund and on the original March of Dimes committee in 1937.

One ex-football player mentioned exploiting his reputation as an athlete, pointing out he campaigned with the slogan: "I held the line for [college]—I'll hold the line for you!" In some cases accidentally gained notoriety may precipitate a political career which had not been previously planned:

I was drafted into politics. In 19— the member of the House here was drafted into the Army after he had been nominated. He, of course, had to withdraw and the Republican executive committee asked me to run in his stead, which I did and was elected. Now, here's what happened. It was about that time that a law was passed requiring a license for selling real estate. About that time Congress gave money to build an airport. I was employed to buy the property for the site of the airport. The publicity I got from this is the reason I think that the Republican committee picked me. I'd never been active in party politics before. It was a lot of publicity.

A few respondents mentioned family conditions as favoring their entering on a political career. One legislator reported that though he had always been interested in politics, he did not seek office because his father was in it, and he waited until his father had died. Another commented:

What clinched my taking a political position was that my children were grown up, and my wife is a school teacher, so when they came to ask me I felt that I could do it. Since my financial responsibilities to my family weren't great, I was able to take them up on their request.

Even having been defeated in a first try may encourage rather than discourage a political career. As one respondent put it, "the first

Table 5.9: Major types of goals in career choice

| Types of Goals | Proportions of Legislators Mentioning Each Type of Goal | | | |
	N.J. $N = 79$	Ohio $N = 162$	Calif. $N = 113$	Tenn. $N = 120$
Altruistic-contributive	27%	37%	47%	29%
Selfish-exploitative	12	16	23	23

time I wasn't elected. That encouraged me to run again." Even several defeats may be seen as an opportunity rather than as a handicap:

About the time I was deciding to run, I was quite active in the union. I had held some pretty important positions. So they knew me pretty well. Didn't do me much good, though, because although they were on my side, no one else seemed to be. I was defeated for the first times I ran, for three successive times. I got a larger percentage of the votes each time, though. Finally, all of organized labor and the newspapers gave me some support which I guess must have finally helped because on my fourth try I finally got in. Been here ever since.

Career goals. As politics involves the allocation of values, a political career may be chosen because the possession of public office is likely to facilitate the achievement of goals. The responses of legislators who voluntarily referred to goals in explaining how it came about that they entered politics or the legislature fall into two major categories: (1) goals which one may call altruistic or contributive, and (2) goals which are essentially selfish and exploitative. Table 5.9 reveals an interesting, but not fully satisfying pattern—for, once more, the Tennessee respondents defy the pattern, at least in the first category. But, in general, it appears that the more competitive the political system, the less is the proportion of legislators who perceive their career as a means of goal achievement. On reflection, this is to be expected. In competitive systems party discipline is greater, and the goals to be attained by politics are likely to be party-determined objectives; the legislator not only has less leeway in what, as an individual, he can or cannot do, but as a consequence he also need not concern himself too much with the problem of goals. Indeed, he is quite realistic if he does not overestimate what he can personally accomplish by becoming a politician or legislator. On the other

Table 5.10: Service and ideals as political goals

Service or Ideals	Proportions of Legislators Mentioning Type of Service or Ideal			
	N.J. $N = 21$	Ohio $N = 61$	Calif. $N = 53$	Tenn. $N = 35$
Service: general	24%	51%	28%	37%
Service: special	5	5	15	37
Ideals	24	18	30	6

hand, the less competitive the party system is, the more freedom there is likely to be for the individual politician to select among alternate objectives.

The politician, as Max Weber has suggested, in addition to enjoying the possession of power, is conscious that "his life has meaning in the service of a cause."[5] It is, of course, a commonplace that politicians, when asked what brought them to and keeps them in politics, will express noble sentiments about their devotion to "public service." But "service" is a so widely held stereotypic response of politicians that it is difficult to discriminate between those who really mean it—who are characterized by that "inner balance and self-feeling" which Weber noted as a condition of living for politics—and those for whom it is only a convenient cliché to rationalize their political career.

Table 5.10 presents one category of response that could be considered as expressive of an altruistic-contributive orientation. Some respondents indicated "service" as a goal in the most general terms;

[5] Max Weber, "Politics as a Vocation," in H. H. Gerth and C. Wright Mills, op. cit., p. 84.

others mentioned particular problems they hoped to solve by public service; and still others stated more remote ideals as goals of their career. Though no consistent pattern is apparent, some aspects of the distributions in Table 5.10 may be noted. Tennessee legislators mentioned particular problems as a source of their desire to serve more frequently than did respondents elsewhere. Possibly, in a one-party system, the legislator has more of a chance to concern himself with and do something about special objectives, particularly if, as in Tennessee, he can do this through passage of local legislation. California legislators, on the other hand, mentioned ideals somewhat more often than legislators in the other states. This finding is in line with the earlier finding, reported in Chapter 4, that California respondents, in recalling what first attracted them to politics, emphasized ideological beliefs. It may be that political beliefs and ideals play a somewhat more important role in systems where stable party patterns, either competitive or one-party type, have not crystallized.

Those who mentioned service in general terms would simply say: "I like the idea of service to the people"; or, "Well, I don't know what to say, I wanted to be of public service"; and so on. Those interested in serving for the purpose of solving special problems mentioned things like hospital construction, mental health, county roads, revision of welfare laws, child welfare, taxation, school financing, and a miscellany of other matters. A variety of "ideal causes"—liberalism, conservatism, fighting socialism or corruption, doing something about a world in turmoil, and so on—were professed as career objectives.

A second category of altruistic–contributive responses referred to the struggle of group interests in the legislature, but only very small proportions of legislators mentioned "group interests" as career goals (data not shown). Business, labor, farmers, and ethnic or religious groups were cited as foci of career objectives. The following quotations from the interviews may convey some of the flavor of this approach in some of the categories:

A good many people urged me to run, with the argument that the *business* point of view represented in the legislature might be in the public interest. Many problems of legislation are identical with those of business—such as judicious spending of public funds, efficient administration, a clear philosophy of government.

They need people down here, laymen, that will represent the average viewpoint. The legislature needs people that aren't lawyers, that are for the common man. With my training and background in *labor*, I felt I could represent the average viewpoint, I mean the viewpoint of the people that work for a living. I thought I could do something that could better the position of the working man. I had no fancy slogans when I ran; this one thing was all I wanted.

I naturally have a desire to make advances beneficial to my *race*. Money isn't everything, and I'm not here for that. I wanted to make a contribution to this cause. Some must bend their shoulders to bring others up. Whatever I can do to help will be my satisfaction as my reason for being in politics.

I was also interested in maintaining the place of a person of the Jewish *faith*, there are so few of them in public life. . . . The man who held this position before me became a judge. He was of the Jewish faith, the only one in the legislature. When he resigned there was a vacancy. The head of the Republican Party was looking around, and he suggested that I run. If I hadn't, we would have lost the Jewish seat, and we never would have been able to get it back.

It is interesting to note that no Democrat in any of the four states mentioned business interests, while Republicans in New Jersey, Ohio, and California did. More of the Democrats than of the Republicans mentioned the interests of labor as a career focus, and the few Republicans who did came from New Jersey and Ohio, the two more competitive states. Of course, the numbers are so small that these results must be treated with very great caution—though they do correspond to what is generally known about the connection between business and Republicanism and between labor and Democracy.

Finally, service to party or district were mentioned by a number of legislators as career goals. Illustrative of this orientation are comments such as: "I wanted to protect the interests of local government"; or, "I wanted to present local views in the legislature, and I don't necessarily mean rural views, to keep local government strong and stable"; or, "I was in some of the local offices and active in the Young Republicans. We decided that no elected position should be lost through default. So I ran for the state legislature." It might be noted, although the data are not shown, that no New Jersey respondent mentioned service to his district as a career goal. This result is somewhat anomalous since in competitive systems representatives, as we shall see in Chapter 13, are particularly sensitive to their constituencies. However, it may be that in this connection the interests of district and party are perceived as identical. Second, whether or not service to party is seen as a career goal may depend on the morale of the party. In California, as noted in other connections, the Democratic Party seems to loom much larger in the career orientations of Democrats than the Republican Party does among Republicans. Moreover, where little value is placed on service to party, as is the case with California Republicans and Ohio Democrats, the district appears more prominently as a focus of career goals. Finally, where a party is greatly outnumbered, as in Tennessee in the case of the Republicans, the members of the minority seem to be inclined to place relatively high value on service to their district as a career goal, possibly because their survival as partisan politicians depends on maintaining the district's loyalty. The data suggest that career goals of legislators may be related to their partisan roles in differently structured systems, but this can only be considered a very tentative inference.

Even fewer respondents in all four states mentioned what we termed selfish-exploitative goals. Table 5.11 presents the kinds of

Table 5.11: Selfish-exploitative career goals*

| Types of Goals | Proportions of Legislators Mentioning Each Type of Goal | | | |
	N.J. $N = 10$	Ohio $N = 27$	Calif. $N = 26$	Tenn. $N = 18$
To make money	20%	19%	4%	—%
To occupy time: enjoyment	10	15	31	44
To make useful contacts, get publicity	—	22	4	22
To get away from previous occupation	—	—	19	6
To find out about legislature	—	7	15	22
To gain experience	—	33	8	22
To gain by combining legislative work with occupation (secure laws for own interest)	20	11	15	56
To maintain/improve own political standing/influence	50	4	35	6
To meet people, make acquaintances	—	—	4	11

* Percentages total more than 100 since some respondents gave more than one answer.

answers given by these relatively few respondents. Although the number of respondents is too small for them to be considered in any way a representative sample and no pattern of response is evident, the data may suggest questions for future research.

It would seem that New Jersey legislators, characteristically, felt they could improve their political influence, or at least maintain it, by choosing a political or legislative career; Ohio legislators thought they could gain experience from being in politics or in the legislature; and Tennesseans were particularly prone to see in politics a way to advance their personal interests, or they saw, more than respondents elsewhere, politics as a pastime. But these particular distributions should not obscure the great variety of other selfish-exploitative goals which may be linked to the choice of a career.

The few respondents who mentioned making money out of their political career—"living off politics"—were quite frank:

Well, the legislature meant income. If you start in the . . . business from scratch, and I was strictly on commission, the legislative salary helped.

It's getting to be kind of a matter of necessity. I like the income, and this is my only source. I'm dead set against the idea of looking forward to retirement and getting a check from the government. I expect to remain active for quite awhile for I'm completely opposed to the government supporting people.

Other legislators simply stated that they are in politics or in the legislature because they had nothing else to do. As one of them put it, "When I came out of the Navy, I was wholly free, nothing to do, absolutely nothing"; or another: "To be a candidate? I was too old and not able to get a position." These respondents certainly do not seem to have much commitment to politics as a career.

It is widely assumed that for some people politics is an avenue of social or occupational mobility. Those respondents who thought a political career would allow them to make useful contacts or get publicity, particularly young attorneys, were quite candid:

It was not so much for the political aspect of it. I went into politics really for selfish reasons. I'd been practicing law for less than a year and this is a very good way to become better known in the community. Consequently, that was my initial reason for going into politics.

Well, real frankly, I graduated from law school and couldn't take the bar examination 'til Spring. I had no practice to go to. Running for political office seemed expedient. Once again, selfishly speaking, an attorney is prohibited from advertising. I thought it was better to go around meeting people through politics.

Few appropriate remarks are available from those who said they chose a political career because it promised to get them away from their occupation, but a number of respondents echoed the doctor who felt that "politics is a hobby to get relief from the rut of medical practice." Another small group indicated that they became legislators because they were simply curious about the legislature: "Mainly wanting to get my feet wet, to see what it's like." Those who wanted to gain experience from legislative work were more explicit: "You can learn more of the ground work of politics here than anywhere else except the governorship."

Quite a few said that they chose a legislative career because it would be directly advantageous to their business. One respondent wanted to protect his fishing business; another admitted to a personal interest in a sales-tax refund to service-station operators; a third was particularly interested in legislation affecting the automotive industry. The close connection between law practice and politics again was articulated in this connection:

While in law partnership, it was decided that I would be the first one in the firm to run for office. I also felt that it would help the firm in general and me in particular to be in the legislative process. . . . So I was then chosen by the senior partners in the firm as having the best chance.

Finally, a few legislators stated that they chose a legislative career because the legislature seemed a promising step to political influence. Some of the remarks in this connection have been cited earlier, but one further comment may illustrate this orientation:

I thought this is a good place to start; it would be beneficial to me personally more than any other political job.

CONCLUSION

The data concerning state legislators' career patterns and orientations reviewed in this chapter were ordered on the basis of a hunch: that while in democratic-pluralistic societies political recruitment patterns are related to social stratification, political career patterns and orientations are likely to be shaped by the structure of the political system—the structural index employed being the degree of party competition found in a given system. This very general idea was not translated into particular research hypotheses, for at the time the study was designed neither appropriate theory nor empirical data were available to formulate such hypotheses. Although the data are in many respects inadequate from a sampling point of view, the overall patterns show enough internal consistency to support at least the plausibility of the guiding assumption. It seems desirable, therefore, to pull together, if only as ex post facto hypotheses for future research, those findings which suggest viable propositions.

The more competitive the structure of the political party system, the more likely it is that:

1. State legislators have had some prior governmental experience, on the local level and in a legislative or quasi-legislative capacity.

2. State legislators have held party office or done party work at the local level of politics.

3. State legislators will perceive the political party as a sponsor of their legislative careers.

4. State legislators will recognize the political party as an agency for promoting their candidacies.

5. State legislators will *not* perceive interest groups and/or friends or associates as agents sponsoring their careers.

6. State legislators will place value on the possession of particular skills thought relevant to a political career.

7. State legislators will have legal training and skills.

8. State legislators will *not* see an opportunity to combine their private and political careers.

9. State legislators will *not* stress "opportunity" in general as a factor facilitating their careers.

10. State legislators will *not* look upon their political careers as a means for achieving personal goals—whether altruistic or selfish ones.

In addition, the data suggest that not only the structure of the party system, but also varying degrees of a particular party's organizational strength and morale may be an important factor affecting career patterns and orientations. The better organized the party, the more salient it is likely to be in legislators' careers and outlooks. This feature in the structure of the political system is probably related to the degree of competition between the parties, but, as the case of the California Democrats in one direction, and of the Ohio Democrats in another direction, indicates, it may also operate independently of it.

CHAPTER 6

Expectations

For most state legislators the political career is only a part-time occupation. Politics being a sideline, the decision to run for legislative office is not a "big decision" comparable to choosing a non-political occupation or profession.[1] Under certain favorable circumstances it may turn out to have been an important career step, as when it leads to a full-time political or governmental position. But for most, the state legislature is likely to be a terminal point of their political career.

Commitment to state legislature. While these observations are commonplace, they have never been based on solid empirical data. Studies of tenure and turnover of state legislative personnel have been suggestive, but they do not reveal the character of the commitment that is involved in political career choices.[2] In order to determine just how committed our respondents were to the legislative office they were occupying, we asked them whether they expected to run again for the state legislature.

Table 6.1 presents the findings. As in the case of career orientations discussed in the previous chapter, but with the single exception, once again, of the California Democrats, the data show a consistent interstate pattern. It appears that the more competitive the party system of a state, the greater is the proportion of legislators who expect to run again for their legislative seat. The fact that a relatively large percentage of California Democrats indicated continued commitment to their present office probably reflects their party's organizational strength and morale, compared with the Republicans. In general, however, the data suggest that politicians in more competitive

This chapter drafted by Eulau.

[1] For the notion of occupational choice as a "big decision," see Morris Rosenberg, *Occupations and Values* (Glencoe: The Free Press, 1957), pp. 1–9.

[2] These studies were pioneered by Charles S. Hyneman. See his "Tenure and Turnover of Legislative Personnel," *Annals of the American Academy of Political and Social Science*, 195:21–31 (1938).

situations seem to be more inclined to see their legislative career as a continuing enterprise than do legislators in less competitive situations. Where the structure of the political system approaches a one-party character, as in Tennessee, the proportion of legislators with a continued commitment is significantly smaller than anywhere else.

If we look at the differences between the two parties in each of the states, another interesting result is apparent. In highly competitive New Jersey, though outnumbered by a ratio of almost two to one, the Democrats do not seem discouraged by their minority status from seeking the same office again. In fact, a slightly larger percentage

Table 6.1: Expectation to run again for the legislature

Expectation to Run Again	Democrats				Republicans			
	N.J. $N = 27$	Ohio $N = 51$	Calif. $N = 54$	Tenn. $N = 97$	N.J. $N = 52$	Ohio $N = 111$	Calif. $N = 59$	Tenn. $N = 23$
Yes	78 %	57 %	78 %	36 %	75 %	62 %	56 %	26 %
Don't know, perhaps	15	27	15	42	12	30	36	39
No	7	16	7	22	13	8	8	35
Total	100 %	100 %	100 %	100 %	100 %	100 %	100 %	100 %

of the New Jersey Democrats than of the Republicans expect to run again. Similarly, Ohio Democrats do not appear to be very much discouraged by their minority status in the legislature. On the other hand, in Tennessee, where the status of the minority party in the legislature is permanent, only a fourth of the Republicans, as against somewhat more than a third of the Democrats, expect to run again, and over a third definitely disavowed any such intention. The data suggest that a party's minority status may tend to make against continued candidacy only in a system where its hope for organizational control of the legislature is severely limited or non-existent. On the other hand, as will appear later on, minority status on one level of government, such as the state level, may encourage politicians to seek office on another level, such as the local or national, wherever their party may anticipate or actually enjoy more favorable prospects.

Some comments spontaneously made by respondents who were not sure that they wanted to run again illustrate the effect of minority status on their legislative career commitment. "I don't know," said one legislator; "I consider that prospect with mixed emotions. It's very tough to be elected in my county as a Republican. The breakdown is about 65:35, and I'm a member of the 35 per cent group.

That makes it very difficult." Another said: "I'm from a tough district. Right now most of the court houses are Democratic. One county in my district is Republican, but it is too small; you must carry the metropolitan county to win."

One may speculate on the consequences of the difference between competitive and non-competitive systems on career commitment. It is certainly likely to affect legislative deliberation and action. In a state where only about a third of all incumbents expect to return— and not taking into consideration the further possibility that some of these may be defeated in the primaries or election—it means that every session of the legislature will include an inordinately large number of new members with no or little legislative experience. It is likely that the legislature will be dominated by a few old hands with almost oligarchical control over legislative action. On the other hand, a legislature such as that of New Jersey, where three-fourths of the members expect to run again, though some or even many may fall by the wayside as a result of election turnover, can more readily be expected to be a smoothly functioning institution.

Reasons for commitment to state legislature. In spite of the fact that legislative career commitment seems to be related to the character of the party systems and the varying roles played by the parties in different systems, only relatively few respondents in all four states saw their continued incumbency in a political frame of reference when asked why they expected to seek their legislative seat again. Of the 252 legislators who gave "reasons" for their intention to run again, only 15 per cent mentioned some sort of political contingency, 13 per cent referred to status considerations connected with holding office, and a bare two per cent acknowledged a responsibility to their party. The great majority expressed themselves in highly personal terms: 58 per cent spoke of their "involvement" in the legislative job, and 33 per cent gave the standard response of "public service." Strictly private reasons, economic considerations of a personal character, service to special groups and what can only be called "apathy" were each mentioned by less than ten per cent.

Moreover, the variations between the states in most of these response categories were very marginal (probably due to the very small number of cases in the categories), and they revealed neither meaningful patterns nor plausible differences. Only interstate comparison of respondents who attributed their intention to run again to their involvement in the job seems to indicate that this "reason" may be more salient in more competitive party systems. Seventy-six per cent of the New Jersey, 63 per cent of the Ohio and 58 per cent of the

California respondents reported "personal involvement," but only 35 per cent of the Tennessee legislators did likewise. It may be that a competitive system calls for greater personal commitment to politics than a less competitive system.

"Involvement" in the legislative office or in politics generally may, of course, mean a great many different things to different legislators. Many would simply say that they enjoy the work or experience in the legislature, that they like the people they come in contact with, or that they feel they are doing a good job. Some say that they would like to be on the job full time, and one respondent was willing to serve even without compensation:

I'd say that this is the service I prefer, I dearly love it. If I had independent means, I'd run without compensation. It's entirely possible that I'll run again.

This sense of personal involvement was often expressed in more picturesque language:

What else is there that's so nice to do? It gets into your blood and you like it.

I didn't intend to run the last time, but then the bell rings and the old fire horse wants to go.

When the whistle blows I get carried away and decide to run.

Other respondents emphasized the feeling of achievement which their office gives them, or their increasing experience:

It takes more than one term to make yourself felt. The first term seems to be a training period in spite of your familiarity with the routine. I felt that in my position as a . . . I would have time to do it, but am convinced that I would be better off financially if I had stayed at home. But selfishly I enjoy the work. Now salary helps to soften the financial loss. Before it was so low.

Interestingly, a few legislators frankly admitted to just the opposite of "involvement"—that they were committed to a legislative career because they had nothing else to do. These "apathetics" might say:

I'm too old to have aspirations for anything else, too old to step up. Maybe I'm too old to be here now. My aspirations end right here.

You might say that I'm sort of unemployed now and am here for lack of a better job. If I was offered a good appointment, that could change my mind. Naturally, then I'd give up the legislature. Any legislator would.

"Public service" as the rationale of the politician's continued career commitment is, of course, the bread-and-butter symbol by which he justifies his devotion to politics. Nevertheless, a sense of social responsibility may be a genuine concomitant of the legislator's commitment:

> You'd be surprised at the things you can do as a representative. So many people come to you and ask for your help, and then you help your district to get home industry and highways. I find it very satisfying helping all these people.

Of course, the service motive need not be unrelated to a fascination with the political game. As a financially independent respondent pointed out, "I like to be in on it—each bill is a crossword puzzle and has something wrong with it." Another said in this connection:

> I enjoy being a legislator. I am interested in government and politics. Maybe because I'm a freshman; what may be old stuff to the others is not old to me. I like solving problems with people both at home and here. I feel that I have a job that I like, and I want to keep it. I'm certainly not here for the money; but I'm not complaining about the money.

The financial reward of "public service" may not be irrelevant: "I need the money. No, take that out. I have continued interest. I do have an interest in industrial relations and education. I'm interested in all that junk that goes on." In spite of this respondent's disclaimer, the money rather than the "junk" seems to be more salient. But others would mention particular projects which, they said, made them want to seek office again, such as: a twelve-month school schedule, strip-mining legislation, a mental health program, natural resources conservation, and so on.

For another group of legislators their career commitment was closely linked with an appreciation of the influence, prestige, or status which they attributed to the legislative role. In particular, seniority was recognized as something worth preserving by seeking re-election:

> It would be illogical to stop running now, as in government work it's seniority that counts. Your responsibility increases as the duration of your service is extended. There is no substitute for experience in the legislature, and that's recognized by seniority.

The lure of politics as a source of influence is seen as committing the politician to his career in the following interview comment:

> I swear off every year. When you see the possible things that can be done, you always hope that next time you can get rid of your frustrations, that something can be accomplished. When . . . became governor, we could do things. I have a very strong feeling that in politics you have to take it on your own terms, otherwise you become a hack. There must be standards of accomplishment and goals, not just handshaking. I like being in the main stream of things.

Finally, returning for another term is considered a "must" for those politicians who view the legislative job as a way station to some more influential or prestigious political position:

> Well, not necessarily in a legislative capacity . . . either in a judicial capacity or a legislative capacity. This may be a spring board for some other office.

A number of respondents made continued service in the legislature dependent on such personal matters as the condition of their business, their health, or family considerations. If the legislative career can be harmonized with the incumbent's business affairs, the commitment may be all the stronger:

> I'm interested in it; I enjoy it. I commute from north of here, so there's an opportunity to carry on my practice in the morning at home. It doesn't interfere and probably helps my private business, if anything.

In fact, legislative tenure may be seen as a way of directly safeguarding one's private interest, as in the case of the respondent who frankly stated, "I have to protect my fishing business." Finally, the salary itself may be considered attractive enough to remain committed:

> I'll run one more term or as long as the people want me. You know a man of seventy can't find $5,000-a-year jobs so easy. It's a good pastime, it's educational and interesting.

One should expect that sensitivity to the ongoing or emerging political situation would be an important consideration in legislators' career expectations. Yet, only 15 per cent of those who gave reasons for seeking re-election articulated such "political contingencies." Some took a rather passive view, making their own intention dependent on their being drafted by party committees or being guaranteed support by the voters. Others indicated a healthy respect for grassroots approval. As one respondent said, "It depends on the people. I now have the intention to run, but I can change my mind, and will, the minute I have an indication the people don't want me"; or another: "Well, that's a question. . . . It depends a great deal on the political picture. If I feel people are satisfied . . ."; or a third:

> I don't know where I stand. My county gets changes of ideas every year. My constituency is becoming more liberal in their thinking. A public officeholder who was doing a good job, they would insist on running for more than two terms.

Some others would make their intention to seek office again dependent on the decision of their party to support them:

I promised myself that I would stay in the legislature for ten years if I could keep getting elected. This was the only way in which I felt I could do a truly effective job. It is up to the Party. They may want a younger man to run for the office.

Reasons for withdrawal. Just as no particular state-to-state pattern characterized the responses of those intending to seek their legislative office again, so no regular pattern is evident in the reasons given for withdrawal from office. Moreover, of the 220 legislators giving reasons for not running for the same legislative seat again, at most one-fifth would agree on a particular condition: 20 per cent gave economic reasons, 18 per cent personal reasons, 13 per cent found the job too demanding, and 12 per cent thought they had served long enough. Some 13 per cent intended not to run again because they were planning to seek another office, and 12 per cent mentioned political considerations. A few confessed to a feeling of inadequacy in the legislative job, and a few others simply said they were bored with it.

Most noteworthy of these results is, again, how very few legislators appraised their career in political terms. Most sensitive to political considerations were, of course, those who were seeking another political office, and who sometimes felt that another term in their present office might show a lack of political ambition:

That is difficult to answer. In five terms I have been Speaker twice. To my knowledge this honor has been granted to only one other person in the history of this House. The Speakership has tremendous responsibility and is very time-consuming. I don't know whether I'll be back. I would like to sit in Congress, but I wouldn't run against the incumbent representative from my district. He is a personal friend. Politics depends on circumstances.

I have been urged to run for Congress and I must decide whether to stay here or go. I wouldn't have any trouble in getting the Democratic nomination. The Congressional and the State Senate districts are almost identical and I can get lots of votes. Last time I didn't campaign much, just went to two picnics. I wanted to see if I could get votes without campaigning. But there's one ethic of politics you must always live up to. That is to be a true friend. The present Congressman is a very close friend of mine, and if he wants to run, I won't. But he is on the fence, he might be interested in running for governor. If so, I'll probably run for Congressman.

One important contingency in not seeking re-election, then, is the availability of another position. If a friend occupies a coveted office, the politician is unlikely to seek it, even if he would like to get it. Re-election is also out of the question if the legislative seat is subject to rotation in office: "I'm running now, but I doubt that I'll do it again.

They usually limit you to two terms.   In such a large county it has to
be spread around."

As already mentioned, one-fifth of those not intending to seek their
seat again said that their legislative work adversely affected their
private business affairs.   The following comments are typical:

I think it's time I devoted myself to my law practice.   Being in the
legislature has hurt my practice and cost me money.   Also, I don't think
anyone should make a career of serving in the legislature.   You do your
part and then make room for the next guy.

Anyway you look at it, the job means a sacrifice to you, your home, and
your business.   Most people don't realize that there are continual demands
on your time outside the legislative sessions as well.   I don't intend to make
a career of politics.

It depends on business.   If it gets bad I won't be able to run.   That's
the way it is for a businessman.   It's different for a lawyer.   I can't depend on the pay up here.   It doesn't even pay the food bill.   I have four
children.   And the expenses are high, hotel bills and everything.

Apart from losing financially, these legislators find the demands of the
legislative job greater than they had anticipated when they first ran for
office.   The irritations of politics are expressed in this comment:

It's a big problem.   It's a problem of time.   Legislative duties are bad
enough, but handshaking, dinners and speeches are the worst part.   My
phone rang 68 times yesterday.   Politicians get a bad break from most
newspapers and political scientists.   A guy in his right mind wouldn't continue.   I'm not going to worry if I get knocked out like these guys who
make a complete career of it.

A few legislators felt that they had served long enough and expected not to run again for this reason,   But, next to economic reasons,
personal, usually family, considerations were given as obstacles to a
continuing political career in the legislature:

I recently got married and I'd like to be home.   I don't know if I'll ever
be a candidate again, but I know I'll always be interested in politics, maybe
on the local level.

I don't think I should stay too long.   The law is my career.   And there
are family considerations—being away from them.   A political career is too
uncertain and hazardous.

Others tended to express unease, discomfort, disappointment, and
similar feelings about the legislative career:

You have to take a beating.   We have great problems in the party which
affects my disposition.   This is a very difficult area in which to be humble.
That's the worst feature of the whole business.

It's a nervous life.   Some can just sit it out—maybe they are wise.   If
somebody awful good ran against me, I'm afraid he wouldn't have much
trouble.

One gets in the middle of a lot. The more service a man has, the more enemies he makes.

Less than a handful of respondents were simply bored with the legislative process. "You can spend too much time here and get stale," said one of them. "There are three types of legislators up here: first, the young fellows who are here to use this position as a stepping stone. Second, the old, semi-retired men who like to be active; and third, those incapable of doing anything else." Another respondent put it this way: "I'm going to retire, I think. I might come back, but I doubt it. After so many years it all becomes routine."

Finally, two legislators gave "ethical" reasons for their decision to terminate their political career. As one of them stated, "If you want to stay on you have to play footsie with the lobbies and say 'yes' to everybody."

Career aspirations. At any one point in his career, the politician's perspective consists not only of past recollections, current orientations and immediate expectations, but also of those more distant aspirations which probably mold a good deal of political behavior. In order to gain a more systematic picture of all respondents' career aspirations, we asked them whether they would like to seek any other political or governmental position at the local, state, or national levels.

On theoretical grounds, we have no reason to expect that aspirations will follow a pattern geared to the degree of competition on the state legislative electoral level. For aspirations must necessarily refer to offices in other political subsystems where the party system may be differently structured. Indeed, as Table 6.2 demonstrates, no inter-

Table 6.2: Aspiration for other office

Aspiration for Other Office	Democrats				Republicans			
	N.J. $N = 27$	Ohio $N = 51$	Calif. $N = 54$	Tenn. $N = 97$	N.J. $N = 52$	Ohio $N = 111$	Calif. $N = 59$	Tenn. $N = 23$
Yes	37 %	45 %	39 %	27 %	42 %	31 %	36 %	35 %
Don't know, perhaps	22	31	24	21	35	25	18	30
No	41	24	37	52	23	44	46	35
Total	100 %	100 %	100 %	100 %	100 %	100 %	100 %	100 %

state pattern predicated on the ordering of the four states from most to least competitive in terms of the state legislative electoral level is discernible. Yet, the results are not necessarily arbitrary, but quite explicable. For instance, while Ohio Democrats or Tennessee Republicans by virtue of their minority status may be discouraged from returning to their seat in the state legislature, they may be encouraged to seek another office at a level where they can expect to feel less frustrated—as where their parties control Congressional districts, counties, and muncipalities, or where they can count on administrative appointments—Tennessee Republicans from a Republican federal administration, Ohio Democrats from state or local Democratic executives. Just why New Jersey Democrats with no aspirations differ so markedly from their Republican colleagues we cannot say. But California Democrats seem to be somewhat more aspiring than California Republicans, again possibly evidence of their party's organizational revival in the years just preceding the 1957 session.

More insight can be gained from a glance at the kinds of office or level of government that were sought. Table 6.3 shows that Ohio

Table 6.3: Kinds of office and levels of aspiration*

Kinds of Office & Levels of Aspiration	Democrats				Republicans			
	N.J. $N = 15$	Ohio $N = 34$	Calif. $N = 29$	Tenn. $N = 41$	N.J. $N = 32$	Ohio $N = 49$	Calif. $N = 24$	Tenn. $N = 14$
Local								
Executive	—%	12%	3%	17%	6%	2%	4%	14%
Legislative	7	9	3	2	13	—	13	—
Judicial	7	6	—	12	3	27	—	21
State								
Executive	13	9	24	10	19	8	25	7
Legislative (other House)	33	18	17	29	34	12	21	21
Judicial	7	—	17	5	6	4	8	—
Federal								
Executive	7	—	3	—	3	2	—	—
Legislative	40	62	45	32	28	59	42	36
Judicial	—	3	—	—	—	—	—	—
Mention level but not office or office, not level	7	15	7	20	13	—	13	29

* Percentages total more than 100 since some respondents mentioned more than one office.

Democrats with career aspirations looked toward federal legislative office (Congress) almost as much as did Ohio Republicans, and that Tennessee Republicans did so only slightly more than Tennessee Democrats. Ohio Democrats and Tennessee Republicans (but also Tennessee Democrats) had their eyes on local executive office, and Tennessee Republicans apparently felt that local judicial office was not beyond their reach. Both California Democrats and Republicans more than legislators elsewhere saw state executive office as a possibility—a fact which may reflect the more competitive structure of the gubernatorial and other state-executive-office subsystems in California.

Finally, New Jersey respondents, regardless of party, seem to place high value on service in the state Senate. The reasons for this were given in the interviews:

Being State Senator is as good as you can do in New Jersey in elective office—better than Congress. I would like to be in Congress if the district were safer. But you have to be away in Washington and it would not be easy to keep in office.

A lot of people have asked me about Congress, but I don't know. Congress is not a good job. The terms are too short. When you come back you are out of work. You can have more influence as a State Senator.

Of the 474 respondents, 155 volunteered some explanation of why they might seek another office. Almost half of these, 46 per cent, expressed some desire for personal advancement or simply admitted to being ambitious. But almost as many, 42 per cent, pointed out that political mobility depends a great deal on the availability of positions, the kind of competition that could be expected, or particular circumstances such as the retirement or death of incumbents—in short, on "opportunities." Ten per cent indicated some sensitivity to political difficulties that might prevent political ascent, and 8 per cent referred to their ability or experience as grounds of their aspirations. Only two legislators out of the 155 mentioned special goals they hoped to achieve. And there were, of course, a miscellany of other comments (10 per cent).

If one compares these explanations with those made in connection with continued service in respondents' present legislative seats, one is struck by the greater sensitivity of these politically ambitious legislators to the complexities of political life. Many of the remarks suggest awareness of the fact that in a democratic society political aspirations are severely circumscribed by the exigencies of political circumstance. The politically aspiring must be able to seize the "breaks" and adjust to the discontinuities of the political process. There must be the "right opportunity" or "right situation"; there must not be too much opposition; money and backing are requisites of success; the incumbent's plans must be taken into account; even God may enter the picture. The following excerpts from the interview protocols elaborate these points:

I'd say that about 90 per cent of political decisions depend on circumstances. Some have the opportunity. You don't altogether make an opportunity, you avail yourself of it.

There's one thing in politics—you have to take advantage of opportunities. The timing is important. But unless you have the money or backing you have difficulty to make your own opportunity.

Oh, I keep an open mind. If the opportunity comes, I wouldn't be averse to it. You should be ready to meet the breaks. I don't beat the drums, but I believe that if one is qualified, the opportunity comes.

I'd like to be—I'm interested in the judicial branch—federal judge. You can't sit down and make out a schedule; people and time enter into it. You can't plan your whole life; God enters into it.

A number of respondents would further emphasize some of the political difficulties which they anticipated: the strength of the opposition party, factionalism in one's own party, troubles in finding financial support, or the qualities of the immediate opponent were cited as road blocks in the path of a smooth political career:

I'd like to run for Congress. But I'll stay here until the time is ripe. The difficulty is that I'm a Republican from a Democratic Congressional district. It will be difficult to win. I have to wait for the right time and the right opposition. Maybe next year. If I were a Democrat, I could win now, I think.

Well, Congress is a vague possibility. At present I'm not too much interested in the Congressonal picture as things look in my district. As you get into larger positions, you got to have support. If you can't get it, it's foolish to try on your own. You have got to know how the cards are played. A fellow named . . . in my district has run every time and never has won a primary. When it comes to the votes, he just can't make it. Most men who run for Congress have quite a bit of finance or moneyed interests that support them. Since our Congressional district has changed, considerable division has developed in the Republican ranks. There are old factions, and until some of the old–timers die out, regardless of peace overtures, underlying feelings have not yet healed.

On the other hand, some respondents would ignore political opportunities or difficulties, and they would simply state their ambitions or justify their aspirations by referring to their abilities and experience:

I'm conceited enough to think that I could fill another job better than some of the people now in them. There's nothing at the moment that I'm considering, but it has been suggested to me that I run for the State Senatorship from my district. The job pays exactly the same, but you have the additional advantage of being called a Senator.

I have the hope, I would like to be, mayor of my home town. I have served on the national and state level, and now I would like the challenge of local affairs. I have no desire for federal office now.

Reasons for not seeking other office. Ninety-three respondents gave some explanations of why they intended to terminate their political career with their present legislative job. Of these, 37 per cent simply said they preferred their current office to anything else. Another 23 per cent denied having any political aspirations. Others gave business or occupational and personal reasons. Some 11 per cent referred to political difficulties. A few—only three, in fact—gave strictly political reasons for not wanting to seek another office: they said that they preferred their present seat because it could best serve their political interests:

> Operating a newspaper and being in the state legislature is as close to the people as you can get. I wouldn't take two seats in Washington for my position here.
> In fact, the State Senatorship is better than Congress—if you are interested in legislation and not in doing errand-boy work. You get a greater sense of accomplishment. Congressmen, at least many of them, live a dog's life in running errands.
> It's not worthwhile to go to Congress for two years unless you are from a safe area. I would be more interested in Congress if it was for a four-year term.

Respondents without political ambitions generally settled the matter of why they did not seek another office in a few words: "I don't want anything but this"; or, "I have no political ambition whatever"; or "politics is a hobby, not a career." Some feared another office would interfere with their private career in business:

> To hold any other political office would mean either giving up or making a radical change in my law practice which I am unwilling and cannot afford to do.
> I have been with my firm 17 years. I'd lose the job because it wouldn't allow for a full-time political job.

Others mentioned age, ill health, or family problems as reasons for their lack of political aspirations beyond their current legislative position.

CONCLUSION

We have reviewed, in this and the previous two chapters, the careers of legislators in four American states as they are seen by these legislators themselves. Our analysis was guided by the assumption that the politician's career course and career perspective are circumscribed by his sense of realism—his cognitive sensitivity to political circumstances as they really are. We have suggested that the structure of the party system on the state legislative-electoral level can serve as at least an explanatory variable in accounting for state-to-state variations in legislative careers, orientations, and expectations.

To the propositions suggested in Chapter 5 we may now add at least two others relevant to career expectations and aspirations:

The more competitive the structure of the political party system, the more likely it is that:

1. State legislators will be committed to their legislative career by planning to run for their present seat again
2. State legislators will attribute their continued commitment to their "personal involvement" in the legislative job

The qualitative material drawn from the interview protocols has shown that though a good many respondents were quite aware of those political conditions and contingencies which might facilitate or obstruct their careers, many more were thinking of problems which were wholly non-political. Only relatively few indicated political aspirations beyond the state legislature. In fact, of course, even fewer are likely to move on to other governmental positions. One gets the impression that though they are *in* politics, the bulk of these state politicians do not expect to live *off* politics or *for* politics. Their legislative career appears to be only a temporary episode in their total life space, to be cherished while it occurs, but an episode, even if protracted, nevertheless.

The men and women who serve in the state legislatures seem to be so different from each other as to defy easy pigeonholing as "political types." Yet, they all must take roles in a common institutional context. The choice of these roles is probably not unrelated to the kind of person a legislator has become in the course of his political career. Unfortunately, to link the legislator as a person with a definite career perspective with the legislator as a role taker in the legislative system would require much more systematic analysis than we were able to undertake. The problem of the legislator's political career was peripheral to our main research interest—the analysis of state legislatures as role systems.

PART THREE

The legislative arena

Every legislature is a gathering of individual human beings. Its members have been politically socialized in various ways and in varying degrees. They have travelled diverse routes from the status of private citizen to that of legislator. Their political aspirations differ both in direction and in altitude. They conceive and evaluate their legislative status differently, each according to his own political experiences, perspectives, and conceptions. It is therefore important to consider, as we did in Part Two, the different career patterns and the corresponding types of political actor who commonly enter the legislature in each system.

But even more fundamental to understanding the legislature is the fact that, in taking office, with all their differences in background and outlook, legislators gather together in a common arena to take actions appropriate to that arena, not for doing whatever might randomly come into their individual minds to do. The legislative arena is not just a locus for so many persons to behave as they idiosyncratically choose or wish. It provides boundaries to legislative behavior by providing each member with certain premises which must underlie his discretionary actions. The collection of individuals becomes a legislature instead of a crowd only to the extent that the members accept premises of decision common to all. In assuming office, the individual legislator accepts a set of severe limitations on his discretion to act for whatever purpose he pleases or on whatever impulse might seize him.

The most important premise of decision "forced" on the citizen-becoming-a-legislator is the accepted social rationale for the existence

This introduction drafted by Wahlke.

of the legislature he serves. Members, like citizens at large, know that the legislative group exists in order to do certain things and not others. The purpose or function of activity in the legislative arena is specified for the legislator just as the object of the game is specified for the football player in the stadium. One acting wholly without reference to recognized legislative purposes and functions would be quite as *mal á propos* as a lion tamer in the Rose Bowl on January 1st. Actions in pursuit of strictly private goals, or of any goals, can be rationalized only insofar as they are relevant to the recognized object of the legislative game.

In the four legislatures we are studying, the major "object of the game" is recognized to be "legislation," the making of certain types of authoritative decision. Other purposes, functions, and objectives of legislative activity subsidiary, complementary, or independent of this there may be. But in these states the individual governing his actions wholly by these incidental objectives and not at all by the principal task of lawmaking is not considered to be acting as a legislator at all. In any legislature, some few members' actions may be relevant only rarely to the principal group function. But if large numbers of them so behaved that body would be a totally different institutional group and we should have to discover what different kind of "game" it was then playing. We shall take up questions about legislators' conceptions of the "object" of their activity in the legislative arena in Chapters 11 and 12, dealing with their purposive and representational roles. But these questions can best be dealt with after some examination of the institutional framework within which legislators play these particular roles.

Action in the legislative arena can no more be wholly comprehended by merely recognizing that its object is primarily to "make laws" than can football be comprehended by knowing its object is to score more points than the opposing side. The necessary implements and the acceptable procedures or "moves" for that task are specified for legislators just as they are for the football player. Writing agreed-on words on certain paper in certain forms (as Acts, Resolutions, etc.) and delivering them to certain non-legislative officials constitutes a legislative "score" just as pushing a football across a goal line constitutes scoring in athletics. There is an accepted length (or range of length) of legislative sessions, as there are innings and quarters in athletic contests. The numerous legislative rules calling for introduction of bills in certain ways, readings of them after introduction, certain types of action by committees, specified forms and amounts of discussion on the floor, registration of so many votes at one or another of these stages, and other specific "moves," as well as the customary positioning of players in particular seating arrangements, seniority orders, etc., can similarly be compared to the equally numerous rules of football requiring that the game begin with a "kick-off," that possession of the ball be retained for four "downs," and so on.

The structure of the game of football or baseball includes regularized ways of organizing the teams of players. Legislative activity, involving many more "players," is likewise structured by rules differentiating the moves of players in different positions. Baseball teams must have nine men on the field and no more than a specified number on the bench; legislatures must have a quorum out of a total membership similarly specified. Legislatures do not have team captains, referees, umpires and field judges, but they do have floor leaders, committee chairmen, speakers and presiding officers pro tempore, all trying in important respects to do more or less what any individual in their status would do.

The positions and the moves of the players or "pieces" are regularized in many non-formal ways, both in football and in legislatures, more than they are in, say, chess. The written rules of football, for example, require a backfield of not more than four men, but they do not specify it to be made up of fullbacks, halfbacks, and quarterbacks, or wingbacks, slotbacks, and other backs, or that any of these act as running backs, blocking backs, or some other specialized type of performer. In the same way, written prescriptions of the positions and moves of legislators may require that there be a presiding officer but leave to informally evolving custom the development of positions and moves of floor leaders, or the approved modes of activity for speakers, committee chairmen, and others.

Finally, knowing what the game is all about, in legislatures as in football, requires knowing when and how to do many things that are not comprehensible in terms of simple ends-means, cause-effect, or function-performance relationship to the ultimate object of the game itself. Playing the *Star-Spangled Banner* before a baseball game or lighting torches at the opening of Olympic Games have little to do with who wins what in the ensuing contest, just as taking of oaths of office or opening legislative sessions with invocations are relevant hardly at all to the legislative function itself. And just as professional football players seek free passes for their friends, or Olympic hurdlers address Y.M.C.A. banquets, as part of their normal athletics-related activity, so legislators honorifically introduce constituents on the legislative floor, speak to business groups, labor unions, and church guilds, and indulge in countless other activities not because these are immediately relevant to the legislative function (or even to staying on the team, in many cases), but because they are otherwise deemed appropriate aspects of their behavior as legislative performers.

In short, activity in the legislative arena proceeds on the assumption that all legislators are aware of and are in basic agreement about the objectives of their actions there, about the types and modes of action appropriate or inappropriate in various circumstances to those objectives, about their individual assignments within this structure of activity, and about the appropriate occasions for certain types of ceremonial and other not essentially "legislative" behavior. A legislator is expected to "know what it's all about" before he acts as a legislator, much as every player on the football field is expected to know what it's all about before he enters the stadium. There is probably more variation in the basic character of the "game" played in our four legislative arenas than in the game of football played in all American stadia. But not so much variation that different American legislatures are playing essentially different "games." More important, the "game" being played in any given legislative arena does not vary greatly from one season to the next, and few prospective legislators need ever familiarize themselves with more than one arena.

We have not sought to examine in detail the legislative "game" as played in any of the four arenas we have studied. As already explained in Chapter 3, where these have been summarily described, we have heuristically assumed that legislators in their respective arenas perceive the "games" more or less as we have described them there, and that these perceptions form an important part of their role concepts. Nor did we investigate the origins and evolution of the various practices constituting the legislative "game" in any of the four states. Instead we have assumed, again heuristically, that the legislator is already familiar with the bold outlines and major features of the "game" to be played in the legislative arena when he first enters, though his familiarity may increase greatly with experience there. We have assumed, too, that the formal provisions of constitution, statutes, and duly enacted rules of procedure roughly describe those outlines as the legislator sees them. We have further assumed that there are likely to be important features of the legislative "game" not described in formal, documentary sources which are nonetheless recognized as permanent and legitimate by the actors in the arena. We have assumed, finally, that the effective, or "real" structure of the legislative "game" is that which is embedded in the perceptions of legislators, whether its major features be traceable to constitution, statute, bylaw, or unwritten custom. But questions about the extent to which "formal" and "informal" aspects of structure are congruent, contradictory, or mutually supporting, about the relative stability or legitimacy of one or the other type feature, or about the relative merits of different versions of the "game" played in different legislative arenas, are questions not of immediate concern to our research. Our concern is rather with exploring some of the consequences of particular structural aspects of the "game" itself. Assuming that everyone in the legislative arena is playing the same game and playing it pretty much by the rules—an assumption we believe quite as justifiable for American legislatures as for American football teams— what difference does it make if the basic outlines of the game are varied in some particular respect? How is quality of performance related to the basic requirements the game imposes on the players? What particular styles of play are developed and adopted by the players themselves as effective means of reaching the objectives set for them?

In every sport, athletes and spectators alike take considerable interest in the constitutional rules and structure of the game because these influence what kinds of players are likely to win. "Rabbit balls" disadvantage teams with good pitchers and poor hitters; "two-platoon" football is said to give the advantage to teams having a wealth of average talent over teams with a few star performers but little depth. Political scientists, however, have in general been somewhat less curious and far less energetic in amassing data relevant to the differential consequences of different types of rules for playing the game than have sports enthusiasts.

Many years ago, Jeremy Bentham set down what he thought were the functional consequences of a great many legislative rules of procedure, including rules about enforced attendance by members, impartiality of presiding officers, publicity to be given to debates, cloture of debate, seating arrangements of members, forms and stages of bill drafting, organization of committees, duration of legislative assemblies, and numerous other points.[1] But few writers since Bentham have attempted to pursue the subject so comprehensively. Modern literature dealing with legislative structure is generally either purely descriptive, highly polemical,[2] or content to deduce a few broad functional consequences from a priori principles much in the manner

[1] Jeremy Bentham, "An Essay on Political Tactics," John Bowring (ed.), *Works*, II, 299–373 (Edinburgh: William Tait, 1843). See also H. R. G. Greaves, "Bentham on Legislative Procedure," *Economica* 33:308–327 (1931).

[2] The literature on "unicameralism" or that on "legislative reorganization" is illustrative of such polemical focus.

of Bentham and with very Benthamite results.[3]   Only recently have there begun to appear empirical studies of the relationship of salient legislative structural features to the output of the legislative process.[4]

We have therefore singled out four areas of legislative structure for attention in this section.   Chapter 7 examines those generally recognized informal norms of legislative behavior often called "rules of the game" which we postulated in Chapter 1 as an important element in legislators' consensual role concepts.   In Chapter 8 we look at several of the formally recognized specialized subroles which constitute an equally important part of the legislature's institutional structure.   Chapter 9 deals with another variety of specialized subrole, that of the subject-matter specialist, which is not provided for in formal documentary fashion, but which nevertheless appears to emerge as a significant feature of legislative structure in all legislatures of the sort we are studying.   Finally, in Chapter 10, we consider the character and consequences of a more changeable element of legislative structure—that provided by the bonds of friendship between one member and a few of his fellows, bonds expressed in role relationships which seem quite incidental to the legislative function but which nonetheless operate in the legislative process in patterned and regular ways.

While the structural elements treated in these four chapters hardly comprise the total legislative structure, they are certainly among its most important elements.   Moreover, by examining the ways in which key features in one category are related to key features in another we can gain insight into generic problems of legislative structure not attainable by description of formal elements or of informal elements alone.   In other words, our purpose in this section is not merely to provide an amplified description of the more permanent structural features of the legislative institution in the four states.   We wish also to investigate how those features are interconnected in a given legislature, and how different structural patterns relate to the day-to-day processing of legislative business.

[3] The familiar proposition that legislative rules necessarily ("obviously") give the advantage to those opposing action over those proposing positive action is one example of the purely deductive conclusion. Despite the persuasive logic on which it rests, the hypothesis remains untested, supported only by very indirect empirical evidence.

[4] See, for example, Howard E. Shuman, "Senate Rules and the Civil Rights Bill," *American Political Science Review* 51:955–975 (1957).

CHAPTER 7

Rules of the game

FORMAL ENACTMENTS provide skeletal definitions of the legislator's role by formally requiring certain classes and forms of behavior for all legislators. It is therefore often possible to "translate" highly formal "institutional" studies into "behavioral" studies by simply singling out those formal rules seen to regulate legislators' behavior directly and consistently.[1] But there are also in every human group less formal but no less important rules which are particular to each group. These are considered legitimately binding upon every member of the group. They speak to him in much less general, more specific and detailed terms than do the formal requirements of his role.

Small-group analysis, which has generally been concerned with informal groups rather than complex institutionalized groups, discusses such rules under the heading of "group norms." In the words of George C. Homans:

> A norm is an idea in the minds of the members of a group, an idea that can be put in the form of a statement specifying what the members or other men should do, ought to do, are expected to do, under given circumstances. . . . A statement of the kind described is a norm only if any departure of real behavior from the norm is followed by some punishment.[2]

The relationship of norms to the concept of role is also succinctly stated by Homans:

> Some norms . . . define what a single member in a particular position is supposed to do . . . [A norm] that states the expected relationship of a person in a certain position to others he comes into contact with is often called the *role* of this person.[3]

This chapter drafted by Wahlke and Ferguson.
[1] See Sherif and Koslin, *op. cit.*, for discussion of "translation" between "institutional" and "behavioral" studies.
[2] George C. Homans, *op. cit.*, p. 123.
[3] *Ibid.*, p. 124.

The rules for behavior indicated by the term "group norm" are relevant not to behavior associated with a unique position in a group, but to behavior expected by virtue of group membership generally. They are an important element in what we have described (Chapter 1, p. 11) as the legislators' consensual role concepts.

Political scientists have long been sensitive to the importance of the phenomena so described. A. F. Bentley, for example, early emphasized the "habit background" of group activity in a legislature in closely related terms.[4] More recently David Truman has said:

> A legislative body has its own group life. . . . It has its own operating structure, which may approximate or differ sharply from the formal organization of the chamber. When a man first joins such a body, he enters a new group. Like others, it has its standards and conventions, its largely unwritten system of obligations and privileges. To these the neophyte must conform, at least in some measure, if he hopes to make effective use of his position. The claims and imperatives of his other group attachments must be accommodated and adjusted to those of the new one.[5]

Truman has likewise stated more clearly than any other analyst the relevance of group norms to study of the legislature as an institution:

> These norms, values, expectations, "rules of the game"—call them what you will—largely define the institution of government along with other institutions of the society. . . . For the legislator, they set the approximate limits within which his discretionary behavior may take place.[6]

There has, however, been little research investigating systematically the character and consequences of "rules of the game." Some writers have identified impressionistically some of the specific rules detectable in this or that legislature. Roland A. Young, for example, has pointed out that the new member of Congress "will be expected to work through given units within Congress, to assume certain habits of thought, and to exercise his influence in a prescribed fashion. He will also find a fairly well stylized type of behavior to which he, as a legislator, will be expected to conform." Young has listed some of the more specific rules embodied in such general expectations.[7]

[4] Arthur F. Bentley, The Process of Government (Bloomington, Indiana: The Principia Press, 1949), p. 218.

[5] David B. Truman, The Governmental Process, op. cit., pp. 343–344.

[6] Ibid., pp. 348–349. The "rules of the game" discussed by Constantin Melnik and Nathan Leites are "those tendencies, beliefs and feelings that determine parliamentary life." They represent generalizations by analysts about legislators' behavior more than legitimate standards of legislators for their own behavior. See The House without Windows: France Selects a President (Evanston, Illinois: Row, Peterson and Company, 1958), p. 1.

[7] Roland A. Young, The American Congress (New York: Harper and Brothers, Inc., 1958), p. 48. The list of specific rules appears on pp. 48–52.

Truman has also described a number of informal rules thought to apply to legislators generally.[8] More recently, Donald R. Matthews has investigated directly and empirically the conceptions of "folkways" or "rules of the game" entertained by United States Senators.[9]

In order to explore this aspect of legislative behavior, we asked respondents in the four states the following questions:

We've been told that every legislature has its *unofficial* rules of the game —certain things members must do and things they must not do if they want the respect and cooperation of fellow-members. What are some of these things—these "rules of the game"—that a member must observe to hold the respect and cooperation of his fellow members?

Some members don't seem to have the respect and cooperation of their fellow members because they don't follow the "rules of the game." What are some of the things that may cause a member to lose the respect and cooperation of his fellow members? How do the other members make things difficult for these people when they don't follow the rules of the game?

AGREEMENT AND DISAGREEMENT: THE WORKING CONSENSUS

In view of the paucity of previous empirical data it is worth emphasizing that our findings do give strong evidence that legislative rules of the game constitute a body of specific rules of behavior generally accepted and understood by all members. Of all respondents, only two perceived no rules of the game; over half readily named at least four rules (the median number of rules named being 3.14). Even those who had apparently never thought of the existence of such a set of rules—like the Tennessean who said, "Dadgum if I know! I never had anything specifically directed to my attention as to what I should or should not do"—had no difficulty in mentioning rules they thought existed. Most responded with immediate assent to the suggestion that such rules existed and were important guides to legislators' behavior—"Yes, there are those rules. Customary is a better term than unofficial"—and proceeded to name the rules as they saw them.

[8] Truman's list can be found in *The Governmental Process, op. cit.*, pp. 348, 359, 373, 376, 458.

[9] Donald R. Matthews, "The Folkways of the United States Senate: Conformity to Group Norms and Legislative Effectiveness," *American Political Science Review* 53:1064–1089 (1959). Matthews lists six categories of rules of the game recognized by the Senators: Apprenticeship, Legislative Work, Specialization, Courtesy, Reciprocity, and Institutional Patriotism.

Rules recognized in the four states. Those interviewed demonstrated a degree of agreement upon the provisions of the rules of the game which is quite remarkable in view of the open-ended character of the questions asked. Counting each mention of a rule by a respondent as an item, some 1,942 items were mentioned by 461 respondents. Of these, 95 items (just under 5 per cent) were items named by only one individual and not clearly similar to any other item mentioned; the remaining 1,847 items could readily be coded into one or another of 42 categories.

Most frequently mentioned in three states (and third most frequent in Tennessee) was a rule requiring from all members *performance of obligations* which they may specifically take on, for whatever reasons, in the course of their legislative activities:

It's sort of like honor among thieves—the main thing is to stick to your promises—make your word your bond.

Don't violate your word. You may be a thief and a crook, but on the floor your word must be unquestionable. We are so dependent on a man's word for what happens to legislation—it's an essential part of the operation.

Keep a pledge even though it goes against the best interest of party or district.

If you pledge a vote, follow through even if it costs you your seat.

Almost as salient, judging from the frequency with which it was mentioned by respondents, is the rule requiring legislators to *respect other members' legislative rights.* In describing this rule, respondents made clear their recognition of a number of specific legislative rights belonging to all members, as the following comments show:

When a bill concerns only affairs of a particular county you support it if the Senator from that county wants it even though you think it's an outrage.

Don't meddle in others' business—if a bill doesn't affect you, vote for it.

The author of a bill is permitted to make amendments to it before it becomes committee property—so they can discuss it initially in the form he wants it.

Another frequently mentioned rule requires all members to exhibit *impersonality* in all their legislative actions:

Never use any personal matter you might know about a member—for example his employment connections which affect his stand on a bill. Maybe it's something that should be brought out, but it's something you just can't do.

You have to have respect for other people's opinions and refrain from personal abuse. I mean you have to exhibit a spirit of cooperation regardless of party or urban-rural residence. You might even vote with the other group when you think they are right. Also, give constructive criticism

—don't tear a bill down just because it was introduced by a certain party or individual. Don't make fun of ridiculous measures either, or ridicule witnesses when they come before committee. You have to hear everybody and not abuse or hurt anybody's feelings.

It is difficult in a short space to show the qualitative richness of responses to questions about rules of the game, but we have paraphrased in Table 7.1 the most frequent responses for each of the forty-two rules mentioned, as well as indicated the frequency with which each rule was mentioned in each of the four states.[10]

Rules of the game and institutional structure. The data in Table 7.1 suggest that rules of the game are best comprehended as a device to secure what has been called a "working consensus," a "kind of interactional *modus vivendi.*"[11] Such a consensus is based not upon "heartfelt" agreement of each individual in the group with the expressed feelings of all other members; it is rather a "surface of agreement," a "veneer of consensus," acceded to by individual group members, all of whom accept the desirability of avoiding certain types of open conflicts among group members in order to permit collective actions by the group for purposes upon which the members are basically in agreement. Rules of the game, by this definition, represent "not an absolute imposed by a superior power . . . but a convention . . . accepted by a body of equals as the first condition of their cooperation."[12]   As one respondent put it, "The basic reason for the rules of the game is to avoid feuds and personal bitterness, which would be very easy to lapse into." In the words of another, "A legislature works pretty much as a team. You can't be a lone wolf; you have to have good judgment and common sense."

In very few instances is there contradiction or conflict between any two or more of the rules listed in Table 7.1. In these few instances the conflicting rules represent two poles of behavior between which legislators must steer or choose on any given occasion, and such occasions may well face them with very difficult choices. For example, rules 17 and 22 tell the legislator he must to some extent act as an agent of some party organ, but rule 41 sets certain vaguely

[10] The italicized phrases in the table represent categorizations of a rule by the authors, based upon the manifest content of responses and not set up a priori by them; phrases not italicized are direct paraphrases of the legislators' own words. The number preceding each rule represents its ranking with respect to frequency of mention in the four states combined, and is offered here as merely a rough clue to its relative salience.

[11] Erving Goffman, *op. cit.*, p. 9. The discussion of "working consensus" here follows very closely that presented by Goffman (pp. 1–10).

[12] Homans, *op. cit.*, p. 315.

Table 7.1: "Rules of the game" perceived by legislators in four states*

Rules of the Game	Calif. N = 104	N.J. N = 78	Ohio N = 160	Tenn. N = 119
	Percentage of Respondents Naming Rule			
1. *Performance of obligations:* Keep your word; abide by commitments.	64 %	47 %	28 %	24 %
2. *Respect for other members' legislative rights:* Support another member's local bill if it doesn't affect you or your district; don't railroad bills through; don't appear before another committee (than your own) to oppose another member's bill, don't steal another member's bill; respect the rights of a bill's author; accept author's amendments to a bill.	32	26	24	47
3. *Impersonality:* Don't deal in personalities; don't make personal attacks on other members; oppose the bill, not the man; don't criticize the moral behavior of others; address other members through the Chair; don't refer to another member by name; observe the "Golden Rule."	30	27	32	31
4. *Self-restraint in debate:* Don't talk too much; don't speak about subjects on which you're uninformed.	17	9	18	59
5. *Courtesy:* Observe common courtesies; be friendly and courteous even if you disagree, even if you are of opposite party to opponent.	19	19	24	26
6. *Openness of aims:* Be frank and honest in explaining bills; don't conceal real purpose of bills or amendments.	24	8	22	12
7. *Modesty:* Don't be a prima donna, an individualist, an extremist, or a publicity-hound; don't talk for the press or galleries.	9	19	23	21
8. *Integrity:* Be honest, a man of integrity, sincerity.	13	19	18	11
9. *Independence of judgment* (Being independent of outside control): be objective; don't be subservient to a political organization, a boss, a machine, an interest group, lobbyists, or clients.	16	19	11	14
10. *Personal virtue:* Exhibit high moral conduct, no drunkenness or immorality.	13	0	24	8
11. *Decisiveness:* Take a stand; don't be wishy-washy; don't vacillate.	10	8	11	15
12. *Unselfish service:* Don't be a careerist, an opportunist, or overambitious; don't use your legislative position for your personal advantage.	5	19	14	4
13. *Advance notice of changed stand:* Notify in advance if you are going to change your stand or can't keep a commitment.	26	9	6	1
14. *Openness in opposition:* Don't conceal your opposition; notify in advance if you're going to oppose or introduce amendments.	17	4	13	2
15. *Sociability:* Be sociable; develop and maintain friendships with other members.	6	6	9	11
16. *Conciliation:* Be willing to compromise; don't be a perfectionist; accept half a loaf.	7	12	10	5
17. *Agency for party or administration:* Support the governor, administration, party leaders (of own party); don't vote to over-ride a veto by governor of your own party.	1	6	20	0
18. *Restraint in opposition:* Don't fight unnecessarily; don't be opposed to everything.	4	1	11	13
19. *Application:* Be punctual and regular in attendance at sessions, caucuses, committee meetings; don't leave after your own bill has been considered.	5	3	13	5

20. *Respect for other members' political rights:* Respect the incumbent status of other members; don't campaign against a member in his district; don't do anything that would embarrass him in his district; build him up before his constituents.	23	5	3	1
21. *Objectivity:* Be fair, show good judgment, maturity, responsibility.	4	5	13	4
22. *Agency for legislative party:* Follow caucus or conference decisions; go along with majority of your party.	1	23	7	0
23. *Gracefulness in defeat:* Keep your temper; accept defeat gracefully, learn to take a licking; don't take opposition personally.	10	4	4	9
24. *Ability and intelligence:* Show ability, intelligence; not ignorance, stupidity.	2	8	9	5
25. *Non-venality:* Don't sell vote; don't take money; don't introduce cinch bills, shake-down bills.	6	4	3	13
26. *Restraint in bill-introduction:* Don't introduce too many bills or amendments.	2	1	5	2
27. *Maintenance of confidences:* Don't divulge confidential information; don't violate confidence of caucus, committee, executive session.	1	19	5	3
28. *Avoidance of trickery:* Don't engage in parliamentary chicanery, tricky maneuvering.	8	4	6	4
29. *Apprenticeship:* Respect older members; (new members) don't try to accomplish too much too soon.	5	10	8	1
30. *Caution in commitments:* Don't commit yourself too soon; be cautious about making promises; study bills before you decide how to vote.	4	0	3	8
31. *Commitment to job:* Take the job seriously.	4	6	1	7
32. *Institutional patriotism:* Defend legislature and members against outsiders; don't do anything to reflect on the legislature as a body.	12	1	3	0
33. *Respect for opposition groups:* Don't be too partisan; be considerate of minority members.	6	8	3	0
34. *Negotiation:* Recognize the necessity and/or acceptability of log-rolling, horse-trading, swapping-out.	0	0	3	7
35. *Limits to negotiation:* Vote according to the merits of the bill; don't horse-trade, log-roll, or swap-out.	0	3	1	6
36. *Seniority:* Respect the seniority-system.	3	1	3	1
37. *Acceptance of committee system:* Respect committee jurisdiction; don't vote to discharge a committee, withdraw a bill; don't vote to amend budget on floor.	7	3	1	0
38. *Self-restraint in goals:* Don't be overeager; don't try to accomplish too much at one time.	2	4	2	1
39. *Senatorial courtesy:* Observe senatorial courtesy (in a narrow sense—control of appointments, etc.)	0	9	0	1
40. *Compliance with group:* Go along with majority when ⅔ vote is necessary; don't refuse unanimous consent.	2	5	0	0
41. *Limits to partisanship:* Don't delay by being too partisan, too political.	3	0	2	0
42. *Abstinence from dilatory actions:* Don't call attention to absence of a quorum; don't demand call of house at inconvenient times.	2	0	1	0
Miscellaneous others	3	28	11	30

* Percentages total more than 100 since most respondents named more than one rule.

147

defined limits to such actions in agency.   Similarly, rule 34 tells him
it is essential he be willing to negotiate, to compromise, to give and
take, in the legislative process, but rule 35 tells him that some unspecified higher standard imposes limits upon the extent of acceptable log-rolling activity.   On the whole, however, the set of rules of
the game comprises a body of mutually compatible rules which does

**Table 7.2: Average differences between various groups of legislators in
proportions of group naming each of 42 rules of the game**

Groups Compared	Average of Difference in Proportion Naming Each of 42 Rules
All legislators of state*	
California versus New Jersey	6.69%
California versus Ohio	6.29
California versus Tennessee	7.45
New Jersey versus Ohio	5.79
New Jersey versus Tennessee	7.48
Ohio versus Tennessee	6.05
Average of all interstate differences	6.62%
Senators versus representatives†	
California	4.52%
New Jersey	7.00
Ohio	4.95
Tennessee	4.00
Average of all interhouse differences	5.12%
Democrats versus Republicans†	
California	3.38%
New Jersey	5.93
Ohio	4.29
Tennessee	3.64
Average of all interparty differences	4.31%

* Original data in Table 7.1.
† Original data not shown.

not normally confront legislators with the dilemma of choosing among
contradictory rules.   It is significant in this respect that not a single
respondent suggested the existence of conflicting sets of rules, each
with its own set of proponents; nor did any respondent suggest any
of the rules he named conflicted with other rules he named or rules
which might be mentioned by his fellow members.   All accepted
without any question whatsoever the belief (tacitly assumed in the

wording of the question, it is true) that rules of the game are the same rules for every one in the chamber. The differences in proportions of legislators mentioning the various rules, therefore, must be interpreted not as indicating different degrees of legitimacy or acceptability of those rules but as possibly reflecting different degrees of emphasis on them.

Table 7.2 shows some additional grounds for this interpretation: differences in proportionate emphasis upon the various rules are greatest from state to state and least between members of the two parties within the states, with differences between the two chambers of a legislature ranking in between.

The precise nature of the differences between states, chambers and party members is perhaps more instructive than the simple degree of difference, however. Table 7.3 lists the differences in relative

Table 7.3: Differences in emphasis on various rules of the game
by legislators in four states

Rule	Difference between Proportion Naming Rule in Given State and Proportion Naming It in			
	Calif.	N.J.	Ohio	Tenn.
California				
1. Performance of obligations		+17%	+36%	+40%
7. Modesty		−10	−14	−12
13. Advance notice of changed stand		+17	+20	+25
20. Respect for other members' political rights		+18	+20	+22
37. Acceptance of committee system		+12	+14	+15
New Jersey				
1. Dependability	−17%		+19%	+23%
22. Agency for legislative party	+22		+16	+23
27. Maintenance of confidences	+18		+14	+16
Ohio				
10. Personal virtue	+11%	+24%		+16%
17. Agency for party or administration	+19	+14		+20
Tennessee				
2. Respect for other members' legislative rights	+15%	+21%	+23%	
4. Self-restraint in debate	+42	+50	+41	

emphasis upon various rules between legislators of the four states for all those rules of the game where the legislators of one state varied by at least 10 per cent from those of the other three in the frequency with which they mentioned a given rule. The table shows that California legislators, comparatively speaking, put a premium upon abiding by commitments made, upon notifying other members in advance when finding it necessary to change their position on an issue, upon refraining from embarrassing fellow members politically with their constituents, and upon accepting the decisions and operations of the committee system. But they seem to insist less than legislators in the other three states upon modestly refraining from publicity-oriented speaking to the galleries or for the benefit of the press or similar "prima donna" behavior. This pattern appears to reflect the uncontrolled, individualistic character of the legislative process in that state (see Chapter 3, p. 60, above). New Jersey legislators, while somewhat less insistent upon individuals' abiding by their commitments and living up to their word than Californians, still emphasize this rule comparatively more than either Ohio or Tennessee legislators, and emphasize more than their fellows in all three other states the related rule concerning keeping inviolate any confidences they might share.

It is instructive to note that behavior supportive of party or administration is emphasized more in both New Jersey and Ohio, but where New Jersey legislators look to the legislative party in this respect, Ohio legislators look to the administration or the party outside. The proportionately greater emphasis given by Ohio legislators to such personal virtues as moral conduct (in the sense of abstinence from drunken or immoral behavior) suggests an interesting difference in outlook from that of legislators in the other three states. The data also reveal the great responsibility assigned the individual member in the Tennessee legislative process. Not only do Tennessee legislators emphasize the desirability of respecting the legislative rights of individual members, but, in emphasizing the necessity of individual self-restraint from "hogging the floor" reveal also a sensitivity to some of the consequences of such individualistic operations. In short, the "rules of the game" applicable in each legislature embody some of the institutional differences often noted in impressionistic commentaries comparing the legislative processes in the different states. We have here an excellent illustration of the way in which informal expectations concerning appropriate and inappropriate behavior (roles) of legislators flesh out and animate the formal skeleton of the legislative body.

Although there are smaller and fewer differences between members
of different political parties than between members of different
chambers of the same legislature or between members of different
legislatures, it is worth noting wherein party groups do differ significantly in their emphasis on various rules of the game. Table 7.4
presents such comparisons, which reveal that differences between
parties are greatest in New Jersey (both in number and magnitude),

Table 7.4: Differences in emphasis on various rules of the game
between parties in four state legislatures

Rule	Difference between Proportion of Democrats and Proportion of Republicans Naming Rule*	
California		
13. Advance notice of changed stand	−10%	(More emphasis by Republicans)
New Jersey		
3. Impersonality	+32	(More emphasis by Democrats)
5. Courtesy	+11	(More emphasis by Democrats)
33. Respect for opposition groups	+11	(More emphasis by Democrats)
8. Integrity	+10	(More emphasis by Democrats)
2. Respect for other members' legislative rights	−10	(More emphasis by Republicans)
16. Conciliation	−12	(More emphasis by Republicans)
24. Ability and intelligence	−12	(More emphasis by Republicans)
13. Advance notice of changed position	−14	(More emphasis by Republicans)
1. Performance of obligations	−16	(More emphasis by Republicans)
27. Maintenance of confidences	−23	(More emphasis by Republicans)
Ohio		
3. Impersonality	+16	(More emphasis by Democrats)
5. Courtesy	+13	(More emphasis by Democrats)
15. Sociability	+12	(More emphasis by Democrats)
6. Openness of aims	−15	(More emphasis by Republicans)
12. Unselfish service	−17	(More emphasis by Republicans)
Tennessee		
7. Modesty	−11	(More emphasis by Republicans)
1. Performance of obligations	−14	(More emphasis by Republicans)
10. Personal virtue	−17	(More emphasis by Republicans)

* Only those rules where interparty difference exceeds 10% are shown.

least in California, with Tennessee resembling California and Ohio approaching New Jersey in this respect. As will be seen below (Chapter 15), the pattern resembles those obtained in connection with other correlates of party-relevant behavior. This suggests that the mobilization of a legislature into two permanent opposing bodies, whatever its utility for encouraging party responsibility, may pose some problems so far as concerns maintaining a working consensus of the larger group comprising the two parties. It would seem that the more clear and effective the division of the legislature into two opposing party groups, the more likely it is that members of the two groups will entertain different conceptions of what is required of every member as a legislator. It will be seen later (Chapter 8, p. 183) that the consensus on officers' behavior is similarly attenuated in New Jersey. Our data do not permit us, however, to speculate further concerning these differences except to suggest that, if division into increasingly clear-cut party groups tends to increase certain tensions between those groups, the consensus on rules of the game appears to contain such tension within tolerable grounds.

ENFORCEMENT AND SANCTIONS

Almost all respondents recognized the problem of securing universal observance of the informal rules. Some of them spontaneously mentioned this problem when asked what rules of the game applied in their own chambers; 89 per cent of them cited specific sanctions for enforcing the unwritten rules when asked,

How do the other members make things difficult for these people when they don't follow the rules of the game?

Only 7 per cent were unable to recognize any sanction at all.

The 11 per cent who did not mention any specific sanctions for enforcing the unwritten rules still indicated their belief that such a body of rules exists. One variety of these replies (volunteered by 4 per cent) suggested that violations of the norms was not a frequent problem, hence the question of sanctions was unimportant: "All [members] are respected—there's a club atmosphere." Another variety of reply suggested that the rules are not enforced as effectively as might be desirable:

They don't make it difficult for a fellow member of the club.

They actually don't [make things difficult for deviant members]—that's the sad part.

There's no way we punish them. They've gone on to Congress.

A few respondents took refuge in reluctance to divulge the mysteries of the sanction system: "It can be made quite difficult. I don't want to get specific."

But the overwhelming majority had no difficulty identifying for the interviewers what they considered potent sanctions to enforce compliance with the rules of the game. As one member said:

> There are all sorts of tricks of the trade. You give 'em false leads, run 'em around in circles, not vote for their bills, give them no place on sub-committees, don't get their bills out of . . . Committee. It happens much too frequently.

By far the most frequently mentioned sanction was *obstruction of a member's bills:*

> [They] don't support their cat-and-dog bills.
> [They] block their legislation, either openly or behind the scenes. Unfortunately this sometimes involves legislation that is very good.

Another frequently mentioned sanction was *ostracism* of the offending member in one form or another:

> They make you uncomfortable and you feel that you don't belong to the club. It's intangible but you feel it.
> They won't let him in on any of the pre-game practice meetings on bills. They may talk to him individually, but leave him out of group discussions.
> He's shunned socially—you can feel the tenseness and resentment when he stands up.

Table 7.5 summarizes the different types of sanction mentioned by respondents in the four states.[13]

Again, the interstate differences in pattern of response are instructive. While the powerful sanction of blocking a misbehaving member's own legislation is the leading one in all four states, it is mentioned with significantly greater frequency in Tennessee, where, as we have seen, a greater premium is placed on the legislative initiative and discretion of the individual member than in the other three legislatures. But the fact that even in New Jersey, where individual discretion and initiative have been superseded by the disciplining directives of party, some 42 per cent see obstruction of individual members' legislative projects as a potent sanction shows clearly that political conflicts in all four states are much more the product and

---

[13] As in the case of rules of the game in Table 7.1, the italicized phrases are the authors' categorizations, based on manifest content of the responses rather than devised a priori. The phrases not italicized are paraphrases of the legislators' own words most commonly used in the responses.

Table 7.5: Sanctions for enforcing rules of the game perceived by legislators in four states*

| Sanction | Proportion of Legislators Naming Each Sanction in | | | |
	Calif. N = 92	N.J. N = 74	Ohio N = 161	Tenn. N = 116
Obstruction of his bills: abstain or vote against him; bottle up his bills in committee; amend his bills; pass them only if of major importance to general welfare.	55%	42%	57%	72%
Ostracism: give him the "silent treatment"; subtly reject him personally.	24	14	31	29
Mistrust: cross-examine him on floor, in committee; don't put any trust in him.	34	14	25	12
Loss of political perquisites, inducements and rewards: Take away patronage, good committee assignments; report to constituents, local party organization.	15	9	19	4
Denial of special legislative privileges: denial of unanimous consent; otherwise delaying bills.	9	8	4	2
Reprimand: in caucus, in private.	—	12	†	1
Overt demonstrations of displeasure: ridicule, hissing, laughter, etc.	3	1	2	3
Miscellaneous other sanctions	5	12	†	3
No sanctions perceived	7	14	11	10

*Percentages total more than 100 since most respondents named more than one sanction.
† Less than 1%.

expression of demands voiced by individual legislators and much less the expression of regularized and institutionalized divisions between party than is the case in national legislative bodies in America or most other Western countries.

The lesser reliance on the sanction of denying political perquisites in Tennessee and New Jersey, as compared with California and Ohio, illustrates related institutional differences. In Tennessee, relatively little patronage is channeled through the representative, and, committees being of comparatively scant significance in the legislative process, committee assignments are matters of comparatively less interest to Tennessee legislators than others. In New Jersey, however, distribution or denial of such rewards and punishments is within the power of political party agencies, so that the membership of a chamber is far less able to grant or withhold them than is the full body in the other states.

We conclude, then, that the informal enforcement-mechanism embodied in members' perceptions of appropriate sanctions is another element of legislative institutional structure, built up side-by-side with the rules of the game themselves. Together these sanctions and the informal rules they support occupy a central place in legislators' consensual role concepts and thereby serve to maintain the legislature as an institution.

RULES OF THE GAME AND THE FUNCTIONING OF LEGISLATURES

In most cases the over-all tone of replies to our questions was clear enough to justify a judgment by the analysts concerning the attitudes of legislators toward rules-of-the-game as a general set of behavioral directives. The great majority in all states (from 75 per cent in California to 89 per cent in Tennessee) appeared to accept the functional utility of such rules by matter-of-factly describing what the rules are without any suggestion of suspicion or doubt about their utility. Most of the remaining members gave clearer indication still of their positive evaluation of the functional utility of the rules of the game—some by stating clearly that observance of the rules contributes to legislative efficiency or by giving reasons why certain rules are necessary, others by indicating in various ways a moralistic or traditionalistic attitude toward them. Only a very small fraction in any state (from 7 per cent in California to 1 per cent in Tennessee) exhibited some degree of ambivalence toward the rules of the game as functionally useful imperatives, and still fewer (in no case more than 3 per cent) demonstrated a belief that those rules were genuinely dysfunctional. The reasons given for this latter view are by no means clear, but it would seem that some of the dissatisfaction stems from a belief that the rules are not widely nor dependably observed, and some from a feeling by some individuals that the rules constitute barriers to their individual desires with respect to legislation. Typical of the remarks by legislators passing unfavorable judgment on the functionality of rules of the game are the following:

There are a million rules of the game.   Sometimes they stifle good legislation.   I care about results, not rules of the game.   Some rules lead to bad
results; mostly they are used negatively.

These commitments are not incontrovertible or dependable.   It is an
unstable thing at best.   There's a lot of lip service to it, but actually it's
only good until the roll call, which is where you need it.   As for courtesy,
these guys are insulting each other all over the place—I think independence
on the floor is healthy.   Quite frequently fellows who are apparently
amoral are extremely effective.   Then you have people of the highest moral
character who couldn't pass a county amendment.   You see people who
operate continuously in an alcoholic vapor who are of considerable legislative strength, skill and experience.

Sometimes it's better to be inept and not follow the rules of the game.
When I first came here I was advised to sit tight and catch on.   When I
caught on, I felt that I didn't like what I caught.

Research in group dynamics and previous legislative research offer
little data and few generalizations about the precise ways in which
rules of the game function to maintain a working consensus within the
group.   It is commonly said that the two primary functions of such
rules are (1) to help the group maintain its existence and, (2) to help
the group achieve its goals.[14]   A distinction is also frequently drawn
between groups which are valued intrinsically by their members and
groups valued   instrumentally.   In groups having high intrinsic
value—families, clans and tribes, class-conscious social-class groups,
for example—members are likely to subordinate many values to preservation of the group as such without reference to specific group
"purposes" or "goals."   In associational groups, supposedly having
primarily instrumental value—labor unions, business corporations, or
other voluntary associations, for example—the value of maintaining
the group as a group might logically be thought subordinate to the
achievement of specific group goals or purposes.   But if the existence
of the group is prerequisite to the main goal, its instrumental value
must, in some cases, be so high as to be almost indistinguishable from
intrinsic value.   Moreover, the tendency of any group once formed to
perpetuate itself and to acquire an intrinsic value for its members even
after its functional or purposive basis has disappeared or been transformed has been often observed.

In general, therefore, one would expect group norms or "rules of
the game" in any human group, including a legislative one, to have
much to do with promoting and maintaining solidarity and cohesion
among its members, with defending the group against all outsiders

[14] Dorwin Cartwright and Alvin Zander, *Group Dynamics: Research and
Theory* (Evanston: Row, Peterson and Co., Inc., 1953), p. 139.

and consciously seeking to avoid or to minimize activities by any member which might threaten solidarity. But one would also expect legislative rules of the game, since the legislature is far more an instrumental than an intrinsic group, to be couched in terms directly relevant to specific legislative functions and purposes.

Moreover, membership in the legislature is controlled neither by individuals who aspire to membership and therefore "join up" to cooperate toward shared aims nor by the members who actually constitute it at a given moment and choose to admit or coopt like-minded prospective members, but by thousands of individuals (party politicians, voters, etc.) who are in no sense members of the group at all. It might be supposed, therefore, that the psychological process of identification with the group plays a different, and probably lesser, part in the case of a legislature than it does in any of the other varieties of group heretofore studied.

In general, our data suggest legislators do accept the instrumental character of the legislative group almost without thinking. Thus, the rules call for legislators to buckle down to performance of a job which is assigned to them, rather than defined on their own initiative (see rule 19, Table 7.1); they admonish legislators to govern their various actions by conscientious effort to perform their assigned job instead of by self-seeking motives of personal ambition (rule 12) or pride (rule 7). The legislature as a group is regarded as having a distinctive purpose, as further indicated by the fact that only thirteen respondents volunteered the belief that legislative rules of the game are the same as those in any other group.

Moreover, legislators' conceptions of the purpose of their group seem clearly to embody the concept of authoritative decision making by representative bodies in the Western tradition. The job is seen to involve legislators' individually passing judgment and making choices with respect to adoption or defeat of legislative proposals. The rules of the game recognize the existence of a standard which can loosely be called the "public interest" by which legislators are expected to guide their individual choices and decisions. But they recognize it in primarily negative fashion, by admonishing legislators not to base their decisions on various other standards—not on orders from party, executives, administrators, lobbyists, or clients (rule 9); not on personal interests or ambition (rules 7 and 12, again); not on venal rewards (rule 25). Insofar as the rules of the game offer positive guides for decisions in the public interest they do it not in terms of any objective definition of the character or content of the public interest but in terms of faith in whatever products the independent judgment of conscientious legislators turns out (rules 8, 9, 21, and 24)—terms reminiscent of the well-known Burkean conception of the "compleat" representative, which will be further discussed in Chapter 12. The following is typical of many comments expressing this thought:

> There's a lot of legislation where we might disagree but we don't hold grudges. We don't hate one another. If I think it's bad, I must vote against it; or if I think it's good, I must vote for it. If I step on some one's toes, there is nothing personal about it.

That legislative decisions will necessarily involve differences of opinion about what constitutes the public interest on any specific issue is recognized in the rules of the game which call upon legislators to tolerate the opposition of others, to seek compromises with them where conflict occurs, and to avoid rigid insistence on the utter correctness of their own personal conceptions (rules 14, 16, 18, 23, and 34).

Many rules of the game, however, do not seem to have direct and immediate relevance to the function of orienting legislators' behavior toward the standard of the public interest; and many of those which do relate to so orienting them appear to have other functional significance as well. We have therefore coded all the rules mentioned into six different functional categories, with the results shown in Table 7.6.[15]

Some rules, it can be seen, contribute to the legislative function only indirectly by *promoting the group cohesion and solidarity* without which the group could not exist or function at all (category A, Table 7.6). Individual members must avoid "being cliquish," said several respondents. "The Senate is a mutual protection society," said another. "Members must protect each other's local power in their county, maintain close personal relations regardless of party." Above all, said still another, every member must "show and maintain respect for the legislature itself." Usually respondents offered quite explicit and detailed rules, however, rather than generalized statements about the importance of group solidarity. Some of these direct group members to treat others as equal individuals in various explicit respects; others direct members to place membership in and loyalty to the legislature above particular group loyalties or personal

---

[15] These are analytic categories, constructed by the analysts out of legislators' responses which do not manifestly mention those categories. But the classification was based upon the full context of legislators' responses, so that clues as to the functional significance of one or another rule were provided by the respondents themselves.

interests which might at times disrupt the legislature.   The following
rather extended comment well illustrates this category of rules:

Well, I'd say there is an effort made to protect the individual legislator
regardless of party—not taking a position to his detriment by putting him
unduly on the spot.   The converse also happens: an effort is made to help
the individual in the eyes of the people back home—if visitors are there,
you let him have the play in committee and to a certain extent on the floor.
If it's a bill of local appeal, the leadership gives the benefit to the fellow.
In the Senate, there is much more definitely a feeling of a club.   They go
along with what you want.   In the House we are more inclined to vote on
the merits; in the Senate they take it more as a personal offense when
somebody votes against you.

It would seem, however, that group cohesion is of more instrumental
than intrinsic value.   The individual rules which serve to promote it
are usually stated specifically in terms of activities which are legislative in character—proposing bills, voting on bills, moving amendments,
and so on.   It is primarily in those activities which relate directly to
performance of the group's purpose or function that members are
urged to foster solidarity.

A second set of rules (category B) appears to operate for different
purposes, which might be described as *promoting predictability of
behavior within the system.*   "Tell them the truth, whatever comes
up—no pussyfooting!" said one respondent.   In the words of another,

A member should make up his mind first what he wants to do, then take
a stand and keep it.   I feel sorry for these wishy-washy guys; they got the
book thrown at them; nobody thought much of them.

Still another reply suggests why such rules are considered especially
important:

Never knowingly sell them a bill of goods.   You have to trust the other
member when he comes up with a bill.   You don't have time or energy to
study every bill.

The effect of rules in this category would appear to be to force members to play the game with all cards on the table, or, to change the
metaphor, to advise all members what position on what team is being
played by each legislator at any given point in the game.   This seems
to be the thought behind the following comment:

Your word—it's your bond.   This is the only way to command respect
around here.   You're always dealing on top of the table.   You don't have
to agree on a proposition, but you must let people know where you stand
and you must respect the opposition.

Table 7.6: Legislators' perceptions of rules of the game according to function

Rules, in Categories by Primary Function*	Calif. N = 104	N.J. N = 78	Ohio N = 160	Tenn. N = 119
A. *Rules primarily to promote group cohesion and solidarity*				
2. Respect for other members' legislative rights	32%	26%	24%	47%
3. Impersonality	30	27	32	31
7. Modesty	9	19	23	21
9. Independence of judgment	16	19	11	14
12. Unselfish service	5	19	14	4
20. Respect for other members' political rights	23	5	3	1
27. Maintenance of confidences	1	19	5	3
32. Institutional patriotism	12	1	3	0
33. Respect for opposition groups	6	8	3	0
B. *Rules which primarily promote predictability of legislative behavior*				
1. Performance of obligations	64	47	28	24
6. Openness of aims	24	8	22	12
11. Decisiveness	10	8	11	15
13. Advance notice of changed stand	26	9	6	1
14. Openness in opposition	17	4	13	2
28. Avoidance of trickery	8	4	6	4
C. *Rules which primarily channel and restrain conflict*				
16. Conciliation	7	12	10	5
17. Agency for party or administration	1	6	20	0
22. Agency for legislative party	1	23	7	0
29. Apprenticeship	5	10	8	1
36. Seniority	3	1	3	1

Rule				
37. Acceptance of committee system	7	3	1	0
39. Senatorial courtesy	0	9	0	1
D. Rules which primarily expedite legislative business				
4. Self-restraint in debate	17	9	18	59
18. Restraint in opposition	4	1	11	13
19. Application	5	3	13	5
26. Restraint in bill-introduction	2	1	5	2
31. Commitment to job	4	6	1	7
35. Limits to negotiation	0	0	3	7
40. Compliance with group decisions	2	5	0	0
41. Limits to partisanship	3	0	2	0
42. Abstinence from dilatory actions	2	0	1	0
E. Rules which serve primarily to give tactical advantages to individual member				
5. Courtesy	19	19	24	26
15. Sociability	6	6	9	11
23. Gracefulness in defeat	10	4	4	9
30. Caution in commitments	4	0	3	8
34. Negotiation	0	0	3	7
38. Self-restraint in goals	2	4	2	1
F. Desirable personal qualities cited as rules				
8. Integrity	13	19	18	11
10. Personal virtue	13	0	24	8
21. Objectivity	4	5	13	4
24. Ability and intelligence	2	8	9	5
25. Non-venality	6	4	3	13

* The number preceding each rule indicates, as in Table 7.1, the ranking of that rule in frequency of mention in all four states combined.

A third set of rules (category C) seeks to *put limits upon the conflict* which is the legislative game, to *channel* it in certain directions and certain forms. Especially striking here is the insistence on conciliatory attitudes and efforts—an insistence which, even while postulating harmony as a goal, implicitly recognizes that the existence of conflict is not merely probable but even necessary, and comes close to stating the business of the legislature as the manufacture of compromise in conflict situations:

> You can have a *lot* of disagreements in the course of activities.   In fact, you should have disagreement in the legislative process.   And often a healthy respect is developed for a man as a result of the arguments he has. He gains more respect *through* them.
>
> Despite protests of individuality, any legislator has to bend some convictions in hope of attaining ends that he considers more important.   Many things that I would decide otherwise are not serious enough to make me yield.   Any legislator who says he is unyielding is either a poor legislator or a liar.
>
> A legislature is designed to pass laws and no one person can have his way on everything.   Most legislation is composed of compromise measures.   If you voted "no" on every bill you didn't understand not much would be passed.   Legislation depends on judgments as to whether a bill is good or bad.   Lots of legislation is passed on the faith of what others say.

A number of respondents indicated that the choice between compromise for the sake of resolving conflict and steadfast pursuit of one's own objective is not always easy:

> [One important thing is] your ability to give and take—to respect their viewpoint, to make a decent compromise without compromising yourself.
>
> We must cooperate but that does not include compromising on what you think is right and wrong.   I mean, if you feel that something is right or wrong, then you shouldn't compromise on that issue.

The rules serving to limit and channel legislative conflict are by no means confined to general exhortations to hold conciliatory attitudes, however.   They include many specific directives stating what types of agency or partisanship are appropriate to legislative conflict and others (like the rule of seniority) which seek to make certain types of decision automatic.

A fourth type of rule (category D) seems designed to accomplish *expeditious performance of the legislative business.* Quite a few respondents placed a high premium on a business-like devotion to the legislative job and, like the members quoted in the following comments, judged harshly failure to render such devotion:

This job can be done in two ways: (1) by just being present, not really wanting to do a job, but feeling that the legislature is a pleasant change from their ordinary life; (2) by really being conscientious. It gets known who fits into the first category, and they lose respect.

Members constantly on the floor offering arguments or amendments of an extremely minor nature, which are strictly irrelevant to the pending legislation, [lose respect]. The person who always assumes an arbitrary attitude and generates argument for the simple reason of arguing. Those individuals who assume responsibility as a matter of course and do not do their fullest to be good legislators. And then, of course, there's always the apathetic individuals who don't care. You know, no one likes them in any situation.

The patience of most legislators is very short particularly with respect to members who monopolize the floor or who engage in sheer obstructionism. The picturesque language in which such impatience was frequently expressed indicates how sensitive members are to behavior blocking the smooth flow of legislative business: "The crowd don't like this spoutin' off on every bill"; "Don't be on the floor too much or keep whammin' amendments in there"; "Be regular in attendance, instead of lyin' around in hotels."

Two categories of rules mentioned have a somewhat different functional orientation than the first four types discussed. One of these (category E) consists of "rules" which, although their observance would, in many cases, serve one or another of the previously mentioned functions, were mentioned by respondents in such a way as to make clear their belief that observing them would *contribute mainly to the individual advantage of the legislator living by them*, whatever their consequences for efficiency of the legislative system. The other (category F) consists of rules which are not really rules at all, but *personal qualities* which ought to be possessed or exhibited by legislators. All the qualities named, it can easily be seen, are those normally valued highly in the surrounding society and have little or no special significance for legislators that they would not have for members of any other group. Preoccupation by any legislator with such personal qualities would seem to indicate either an inarticulateness about group norms or a lack of perception regarding them, or both.

Comparison of the four legislatures in terms of their relative emphasis on the various categories of rules of the game again yields some interesting insights into differences of institutional structure and processes. The relevant data are set forth in Table 7.7. As already noted, rules promoting group cohesion are among the most salient for legislators in all four states, an indication, perhaps, of the peculiar character of "membership" in a legislative group, which makes it necessary to "manufacture" group sense there whereas group cohesiveness is in some degree more "natural" in most other types of group. The freewheeling character of the Tennessee legislative process, in comparison with all three other states, again shows up, this time in the negligible recognition given to rules which channel conflict, in the substantially greater emphasis upon rules which promote the successful accomplishment of individual aims, and in the slightly smaller emphasis upon rules which introduce predictability into the system. And the necessary consequences of individualization in the legislative process again show up, this time in the proportionately

Table 7.7: Proportions of legislators in four states naming rules of the game in six different functional categories

Functional Category	Calif. $N = 104$	N.J. $N = 78$	Ohio $N = 160$	Tenn. $N = 119$
Promoting group cohesion	75%	87%	68%	85%
Promoting predictability of legislative behavior	78	56	55	45
Restraining, channeling conflict	19	56	37	10
Expediting legislative business	33	27	39	71
Tactical advantages for individual member	33	32	40	56
Personal qualities	32	35	51	38

greater emphasis in Tennessee upon rules which serve to expedite legislative business.

By the same token, the relatively disciplined nature of conflict in New Jersey (and to a lesser extent in Ohio) is reflected in the proportionately greater emphasis in those states upon rules which restrain and channel conflict. And in New Jersey, where legislative business is managed and scheduled more than in other states by party agencies, we find less recognition of rules which directly bind all members to behavior expediting legislative business. The pattern in California is unique in one interesting respect: although the low proportion of legislators mentioning rules limiting and channeling conflict suggests a highly individualized legislative process, like that in Tennessee, more Californians than legislators in any of the other three states mentioned rules promoting predictability of behavior, which would have the contradictory effect of limiting individual initiative and imagination. Apparently the "automatic calendar" and dispersed management of legislative business do not quite suffice as substitutes for party machinery. Informal rules to increase predictability help to fill the gap.

In summary, then, by analyzing the functional significance of the rules of the game recognized by legislators, we begin to see how performance of the legislative function is promoted or inhibited by obligatory patterns of behavior embedded in legislators' consensual role concepts. Formal documents and public expectations may proclaim the general goals and purposes of legislative activity, but legislators, being members of a human group, in working toward those ends, respond to a more immediate and pervasive set of directives embodied in the rules of the game. On the other hand, rules of the game appear to be not random customs and habits but informal norms which develop in systematic ways to complement more formal directives in promoting accomplishment of the legislature's recognized primary functions.

RULES OF THE GAME AND THE INDIVIDUAL LEGISLATOR

We have so far considered differences in institutional structure and processes from state to state as shown by differences in legislators' perceptions of rules of the game. There are also important differences from one individual legislator to the next within each state. These too will have an important bearing upon the working of the legislature.

To explore such differences we have roughly classified legislators according to both the number of rules they mentioned and the diversity of rules mentioned. The assumptions here are, first, that (other things being equal) the legislator most identified with the legislative group will be the one most able to articulate the group's unwritten rules of the game and, second, that naming a proportionately greater number and diversity of rules in response to our open-ended question is a sufficient index of a member's greater articulateness on this score. The most articulate legislators for purposes of this analysis are those who named both more rules than the median number mentioned and a greater diversity of them (i.e., rules in more of the functional categories discussed above) than the median; least articulate are those who ranked below the median on both counts; we have classified as moderately articulate legislators who ranked above the median on one dimension but below on the other.

To one obvious question our data provide generally inconclusive answers. This concerns the bases of legislators' differential sensitivity to legislative rules of the game. It might be suspected that differences in education account for such differences to at least some extent. But there are only negligible differences in articulateness toward the rules of the game among legislators of different educational backgrounds (data not shown). There are noticeable but not especially large differences between legislators coming from urban (city or small town) backgrounds and those from more rural backgrounds (data not shown). The data presented in Table 7.10 seem to indicate

Table 7.10: Legislators' articulateness with respect to rules of the game related to their primary occupation

Articulateness	Professional and Technical $N = 215$	Managers and Proprietors $N = 161$	Farmers, Farm Managers $N = 46$	Clerical and Sales $N = 22$	Craftsmen, Foremen, Operatives, Skilled Labor, Others $N = 13$
Most articulate	43%	39%	30%	23%	8%
Moderately articulate	19	26	24	18	31
Least articulate	38	33	46	59	61
	100%	100%	100%	100%	100%

that the character of the occupational groups in which legislators have worked is of more significance than either educational status or urban-rural background in determining legislators' levels of articulateness. Such a hypothesis seems consistent with the generally accepted proposition that for every occupation there are "customs and folkways which arise out of the nature of the occupation, or out of the traditions of the occupational group," as well as "standards of conduct which are enforced because of the real or supposed effects which their violation would have on the performance of the job."[16]

It might seem reasonable to suppose that differences in sensitivity to the legislative rules of the game bear some relation to differences in experiences in the legislature itself. The four legislatures we are examining are essentially occupational "colleague groups," wherein the relations are, "by definition, relations between members of the same (i.e., political or legislative) occupation." Members of such "colleague groups" are thought to be bound together by a more

[16] Theodore Caplow, *The Sociology of Work* (Minneapolis: University of Minnesota Press, 1954), p. 124.

distinctive group sense or *esprit de corps* than are members of a "work group," whose distinctive characteristic is that the members "[come] together to do a job cooperatively."[17]   It might therefore be hypothesized that members having the longest experience in the group would be the most articulate of rules of the game. The data (not shown) fail to support this hypothesis, however.

Speculating in a different direction, whatever might account for legislators' varying ability to articulate rules of the game, what are the consequences of those differences in the way legislators go about their business? To begin with, it is perhaps surprising that high articulate-

Table 7.9: Legislators' articulateness in rules of the game and respect nominations

Named as being respected for following rules of the game*	Most Articulate $N = 175$	Moderately Articulate $N = 101$	Least Articulate $N = 178$
By more than 10%	23%	22%	13%
By 1–10%	54	54	44
By none	23	24	43
	100%	100%	100%

* In response to the question, "Would you name four or five of your fellow-members, regardless of party or position, who are most widely respected for following these 'rules of the game'—I mean people that a new member should look up to when he's just learning the ropes?"

ness with respect to rules of the game does not appear to be associated with high sense of legislative efficacy (data not shown).[18] The most plausible explanation is that some knowledge of rules of the game is so basic to individual operation in the legislative arena that every member readily acquires sufficient familiarity to feel in command of them. The clearest result of differences in articulateness with respect to rules of the game is the differential evaluation of members by one another. Not only are legislators able to recognize that some of their colleagues better understand the rules of the game than do others, but they are ready to grant those with the greater under-standing a greater measure of respect because of it, as Table 7.9 shows.

[17] Edward Gross, *Work and Society* (New York: Thomas Y. Crowell Company, 1958), pp. 222 ff.
[18] The scale used to measure sense of legislative efficacy is described in Appendix 2.2, pp. 474–475.

In both respects the data suggest that a minimum perceptiveness is needed, but that, beyond this point, no advantage accrues to the exceptionally insightful member.

CONCLUSION

The unwritten rules of the game in legislative bodies provide an almost virgin field for empirical research. That such rules exist in every legislature seems clear beyond doubt. Although there appear to be important equivalences and similarities from one body to the next, only empirical inquiry can determine precisely what the rules are for any given legislature. We have set forth what appear to be the most salient of them in the four states studied.

Such inquiry is essential for understanding of the institutional character and function of legislatures in general or of any particular legislature. Unwritten rules of the game contribute in important ways, as we have seen, to maintaining the institutional structure by supplementing the formal provisions which initially define the institution. They are not merely quaint and curious folkways, of interest primarily to students of the exotic and the mysterious in human behavior. On the contrary, they are directly relevant to and supportive of the purposes and functions of the legislature as these are conceived of by legislators: they maintain the working consensus essential to legislative performance. Toward this end, they appear to take specific form in relation not only to the formal provisions constituting the particular legislature but also to such more elusive structural characteristics as those provided by the party system, or the work habits of the legislature.

Rules of the game are not pious platitudes about good behavior. They are rules enforceable by clearly recognized sanctions which all members have in their power to impose on errant members. Their observance would nonetheless seem to be obtained not primarily through members' fear of such punishment but through their general acceptance of the functional utility of the rules for enabling the group to do what a legislature is expected to do.

Understanding of rules of the game is sufficiently important that the individual legislator's possession of it will affect the part he plays in the legislative process. His colleagues will judge him, in part, by his understanding. Not only does he gain stature in their eyes by virtue of that understanding, but he is more likely to be granted differential status—for example, as a subject-matter expert—because of it.

But the maintenance of group norms which constitute the working consensus appears to be independent of the power or influence acquired through holding formal office. Rules of the game are the property and the creature of the group membership at large, not a reflection of requirements set by either personal or formal leadership. Formal leadership, to which we turn in the next chapter, operates within the working consensus provided, in large part, by legislators playing their consensual roles.

CHAPTER 8

Leadership roles

The INFORMALLY RECOGNIZED NORMS treated in the last chapter and the formally adopted rules of the chambers are the laws that give form and coherence to the legislative process. The mere existence of these laws, of course, is not enough to keep the legislature from drifting toward a chaos of conflict. There must also be leaders for lawmaking task groups. There must be judges—known, authorized, and indifferent—for settling intralegislative squabbles.

The "typical" legislative structure outlined in Chapter 3 above consists of a presiding officer, majority and minority floor leaders (and we saw that the "majority," while usually a party, may be a faction), a series of committees headed by chairmen, and a steering committee. There is a characteristic form to this organization, though it departs from the usual hierarchial, pyramidal organization chart of administrative theory. It looks something like this:

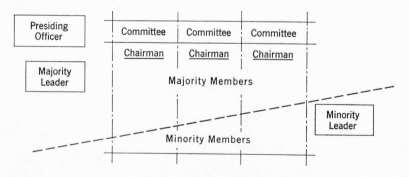

There are two organizational dimensions, as it were, one partisan, the other substantive. Since there is no one outside or above the

This chapter drafted by Buchanan and Ferguson

legislature to make organizational decisions for it, each session selects its staff and fits itself into this pattern in two convulsive shrugs: the first to select the leaders, the second to have the leaders select the committees and chairmen. The two efforts are usually related by a complex of reciprocal understandings. Where committee tenure and a seniority system exist, these tend to reduce the number of decisions to be made. There is also in these chambers a steering committee going by various names which should be considered part of the organizational pattern, though it is not diagrammed above. This chart, it should be stressed, is intended to be nothing more than a point of departure for listing variations.

Our questionnaire asked for descriptions of the behavior the members thought appropriate to officers at three of these levels (the steering committee was omitted). The responses, when taken in conjunction with the "enacted role requirements" and the unofficially sanctioned deviations therefrom, give a rounded picture of the functions of any legislative officer—the "role expectations" of members with respect to these offices. The law and the rules tell an officer *what* he may or should do; for example they tell the presiding officer of a chamber to preside, to appoint committees, to refer bills to them, and so on. They do not tell him *how* to do it: whom to recognize, when to brook delaying tactics and when to curb them, which of two aspirants to appoint to a committee or chairmanship, where to refer a bill if two committees' jurisdictions overlap. These are likely to be the crucial decisions: whether the speaker favors his personal prejudices, his political party, some interest group, or the governor; or whether he withholds any advantage, and lets some existing balance of forces have its sway. This presumably is what political scientists are seeking to describe when they frame generalizations about the power of the speaker, the party system, the rules committee, or standing committee chairmen.

Of the 474 legislators interviewed, 467 responded to two or three of the following questions (those who answered only one were eliminated from the analysis):

Now I'd like to ask you a few questions about the various jobs here in the House (Senate). First of all, what role ought the Speaker of the House (President, President pro tem., of the Senate) to play in order to be most effective in his job?

Now, how about the committee chairmen—what role ought a committee chairman to play in order to be most effective in his job?

And what about the party leaders (floor leaders)—what role ought they to play in order to be most effective in their jobs?

LEGISLATIVE OFFICERS: A FUNCTIONAL APPROACH

To analyze the responses, we might have sought hypotheses about "leadership qualities" or "leadership functions" and set up codes to test them, or we might alternatively have worked from manifest content categories. Early in the analysis, however, it became apparent that the responses were susceptible to coding by the categories just developed empirically to fit the "rules of the game," and that (subject to some minor alterations) the functional categories were nearly interchangeable. The following categories and subcategories were therefore used to classify responses concerning officers' roles:[1]

A. *Behavior making the legislative system stable and predictable*
   1. Maintain order, "be firm," be a "stable leader," "be calm"
   2. Know the rules and procedures, be experienced
   3. Follow the rules, "be fair," preside impartially, be a referee, arbitrator
B. *Behavior focussing the issues and resolving conflict*
   1. Give "due regard" for the rights of members, let them bring out the issues, assign bills fairly
   2. Focus conflict, narrow the alternatives, "organize hearings," "present the issues clearly"
   3. Promote and defend party or factional positions, "get the program through," bring up party and administration bills
   4. Let the majority rule, "let the committee determine the fate of the bill," "don't push personal views"
C. *Behavior leading and administering the system*
   1. Guide and lead the group, "coordinate members' ideas," promote teamwork, be diplomatic with members
   2. Help individuals, "be accessible," assist with personal problems
   3. Expedite business, organize, "be concise," "start on time"
   4. Coordinate, communicate, provide liaison with other officers and political systems
D. *Knowledge of the content of legislation*

[1] Here we were dealing with three different kinds of officers, so each code category had three parallel subdivisions. For example, the demand that the speaker preside fairly over the chamber, the committee chairmen preside fairly over their committees and the party leaders preside fairly over their caucuses are obviously parallel. For a less obvious example: the demand that the speaker give his fellow party members an advantage in committee appointments, that the chairman give preference to his party's bills, that the majority leader work to get through his party's program, and that the minority leader attempt to block it—these were also coded as equivalent in purpose and function, being behavior designed to gain an advantage for their respective parties.

Less than 2 per cent of all responses did not fit into one of these categories. The full cross-tabulation of these twelve categories, for the three officers, in eight chambers, is given in Appendix 4. It is the source of the percentages that are excerpted for closer analysis in this chapter. Table 8.1 presents the gross figures and compares them with the relevant data concerning rules of the game.

Rules of the game and officer roles. One of the most significant conclusions to be drawn from these data is that predictability, stability, restraint of conflict, and preservation of cohesion are functions both of the informal rules which members impose on themselves and of the formal system of leadership. Thus members subject their leaders to restraints and requirements quite similar to those which they impose upon one another. They expect these officers to perform functions which have quite largely to do with maintaining the legislature as a decisional system. This suggests that the legislative leadership system is a group-centered one, a situation of interaction in which leaders serve largely to help the members accomplish their group objectives.

Would one expect any other sort of leadership system in a body which must organize itself, being answerable to no central higher authority—a body composed of members independently chosen and not beholden one to another? Is not member-responsible leadership the only kind of legislative leadership conceivable? The answer is: chief executives, national and state, and political party chairmen, national and state, regularly do imply that there should be another sort of leadership, more susceptible to their influence. The literature of the American party system revolves in some respects around the observation that legislative presiding officers, party leaders, and above all, committee chairmen, react "irresponsibly" to the programmatic leadership supplied by party organs.

Of course we will find a number of specific response items in which many members call upon officers to implement party programs. This is the defined function, in fact, of the party leaders. However, these specific mandates occur within the broader context of the requirement that officers primarily devote themselves to maintaining the legislature itself as an on-going system.

Roles versus rules. Responses indicated clearly that roles of officers were not identical with norms for members, though the functional similarity was great enough to demonstrate their common purpose. Particularly, it was apparent that behavior sustaining cohesion and solidarity among the group, when engaged in by an officer rather than a rank-and-file member, can hardly be distinguished from administrative and executive behavior. Sustaining morale is an executive function. This accounts for the combination of the two categories that were kept separate for studying rules of the game. The category of "personal qualities" which was similar to the same rubric under rules of the game has been deleted from the analysis except for one content item which was relevant: knowledge of the subject matter of legislation (see Table 8.1).[2]

Table 8.1: Norms for the behavior of members compared with officer roles specified (eight chambers combined)

| Norms (Rules of the Game) for Members N = 461 | | Behavior Expected of Legislative Officers | | |
		Presiding Officer N = 467	Committee Chairmen N = 467	Party Leaders N = 433*
Promoting predictability		Promoting a stable and predictable system		
	38%		72%	49%	15%
Restraining, channeling conflict		Focusing issues and resolving conflict		
	29		57	63	63
Expediting legislative business	44	Administering the system, expediting business and promoting harmony		
Promoting group cohesion	77		56	47	52
		Knowledge of content	6	22	10

* There are no party leaders in the California Senate. Percentages in all columns add to more than 100 per cent.

Keeping the legislature running in familiar, predictable grooves is the function of both members and officers, except the party leader. The reason for exempting him from this most pervasive demand is presumably that his loyalty is to the party—a competing and in a sense potentially disruptive force. The responsibility for focussing issues and sharpening, and then resolving conflict is more that of

[2] Another irrelevant category, "formal role behavior," was also omitted. This covered such remarks as "The speaker should preside" or "The chairmen should hold hearings" without indicating how the role should be played. These were essentially non-responses to the request for a role description. The respondents are retained in the base for percentages, however.

officers than of members. But the members rather than the officers are predominantly responsible for maintaining the group's harmony and cohesion.

These expectations with regard to officers, as we shall see, are rather consistent and well structured, and they may be as much a boundary on what officers are allowed to do as are the formal rules. If so, the "power" of particular officers—chairmen, speakers, rules committees—cannot be appraised apart from the system in which they find themselves.[3] The evidence already is that legislative officers are far from free agents, that they are hedged about by commandments from the membership as to what they should and should not do if they are to perform effectively. There is substantial consensus as to how each officer shall act, which is expressed in these appraisals of their roles. The consensus determines, in Bentley's phrase, whether the speaker is "Moses the law giver" or "Moses the registration clerk."[4] Whether a particular speaker, or an average speaker, is more powerful, or less powerful, than the Speaker of the national House of Representatives depends upon how the respective memberships intend for this power to be exerted upon them.

ROLE CONCEPTS AND OFFICERS' FUNCTIONS

Promoting a stable, predictable system. By "representation"—taking the part of the several elements in the society—legislators act out the society's potential goal conflicts in their small arena, substituting "arguments for fisticuffs" as Churchill put it. Whether the analogy is a fight, a game or a debate, there always arises the need for a judge, referee, umpire, arbitrator, or scorekeeper. But the legislature, being theoretically at the apex of the political system next to the "constitution" and the "people," can afford to accept no outside arbiter for its daily battles. It must make do with its own judges, whose representative character sometimes makes them "advocates and parties to the causes they determine."

Many years ago the British Parliament arranged for the Speaker to be elevated above the party struggle and given the authority to referee the game. He is neutralized so far as party politics is concerned, and this neutrality is preserved even to the point of election contests. This arrangement was effected, incidentally, by a reciprocal agreement on the part of both parties and the speaker to alter

[3] Roland Young, *op. cit.*, Chs. 5 and 6, organizes member and officer roles in comparable fashion.

[4] Arthur F. Bentley, *op. cit.*, p. 163.

their common role expectations regarding his behavior. With ample years to do so, Congress and American state legislatures have not chosen to follow the British precedent.[5] (Conceivably, the majority, in the absence of a strong tradition of party discipline, never feels able to make an irrevocable sacrifice of the speaker's vote.) Yet the referee role must be played, and the speaker is the one to play it, as Table 8.2 indicates.

Table 8.2: Proportion of all respondents suggesting various behaviors making the legislative system stable and predictable

Kind of Behavior Suggested	Presiding Officer $N = 467$	Committee Chairmen $N = 467$	Party Leaders $N = 433*$
Maintain order, "be firm," be a "stable leader," "be calm"	21%	24%	1%
Know the rules and procedures, be experienced	18	5	8
Follow the rules, "be fair," preside impartially, be a referee, arbitrator	61	32	6
One or more of the above	72%	49%	15%

* There were no party leaders in the California Senate.

The kinds of behavior necessary if an officer is to contribute toward maintenance of legislative stability and a climate in which members may compete for their individual and subgroup objectives can be put in three categories.

The first of these is *maintaining order*. The speaker must exhibit decisiveness, calmness, firmness, and stability himself, he should "control the tenor of debate." Some characterizations of the speaker's role were:

He's the symbol of authority—his attitude and demeanor are important in regard to the decorum of the House.

He should weigh the things he does before he goes off at a tangent and does things that cause dissension in the chamber.

As Table 8.2 indicates, about the same proportion of members expect this sort of behavior of the committee chairmen, but the language in which the role is described is less temperate. Committee

[5] See Kenneth R. Mackenzie, *The English Parliament* (London: Penguin Books, 1951), Ch. 8, also Young, *op. cit.*, Ch. 3.

chairmen, some say, should be "little dictators," they should "run a tight chair," or "rule with an iron hand."

The second category involves no more than *knowing the rules and procedures*. Presiding officers must "be good parliamentarians," must "know how to use a gavel—and when."

The third category was the most frequently volunteered of any of the prescriptions concerning the behavior of any of the officers. It was mentioned in one Tennessee chamber by almost every member, and in most of the other states by a substantial majority (see Table 8.3). This was the demand that the speaker *follow the rules* in presiding, that he "be fair" in his decisions, that he act as an umpire or referee. Some of the typical comments were:

In presiding he should not do it for a partisan purpose. He should play no favorites in recognition.

Be fair. Don't make hasty rulings. Recess and look it up if necessary.

He should play the role of a judge.

Only half as many legislators expected this impartiality and detachment to be displayed by committee chairmen. In the more intimate, face-to-face committee situation, it may be suggested that personal forcefulness is more appropriate and more successful than resort to the rule book; standards of official conduct are more flexible and less precise. Also, as we shall note shortly, the chairman bears part of the responsibility for getting a program through, and he may have to be less tender of minority sensibilities.

The party leaders are absolved by nearly all from any responsibility for maintaining a stable, "fair" and predictable system. Even the 8 per cent who expect party leaders to "know the rules" are disproportionately members of the minority party. They expect their leader to use this knowledge to prevent the majority from manipulating the rules to its own advantage. The minority leader is enjoined to follow the rules principally when something is to be gained by it for his side.

When the 61 per cent of all legislators who expect their presiding officers to follow the rules and to "be fair" in presiding, is further broken down by chambers, some revealing differences appear. In two chambers—the senates of California and Ohio—the proportion giving this response is substantially below the others, as Table 8.3 shows. While the behavior being referred to is that of the *elected* presiding officer, the president pro tempore, these happen to be the only two chambers where the constitution provides that the lieutenant governors shall preside over the Senate (see Appendix 3, pp. 477–478).

In neither state is the lieutenant governor considered a potent political figure, nor is he thought to be a substantial factor in legislative decisions. Nevertheless, these responses indicate he serves an important function in absolving the president pro tempore from some of his responsibility for judicious, restrained, impartial conduct. The president pro tempore is freed to become a more active, aggressive partisan or programmatic leader, while the lieutenant governor acts as a non-partisan presiding officer in the tradition of the Speaker of the House of Commons.

Table 8.3: Proportion saying presiding officer, and committee chairmen, should "follow the rules," "be fair," etc.

State and Chamber		Presiding Officer	Committee Chairmen	Respondents
California	House	56%	35%	(75)
	Senate	32	50	(34)
New Jersey	House	62	7	(56)
	Senate	57	—	(21)
Ohio	House	59	41	(130)
	Senate	16	35	(32)
Tennessee	House	81	34	(88)
	Senate	94	32	(31)
All respondents		61	32	(467)

The striking contrast to these two senates in Tennessee, where in both houses a very high proportion of members expect that their presiding officer will "know the rules" and "abide by them." In fact, "fairness" was the sole requirement of many Tennesseans. Part of the rationale may be traced to the fact that a larger part of the legislative process in Tennessee occurs in floor sessions, where the speakers of the two houses may exert an influence. It is possible also that the governor's part in selecting the presiding officers, together with the undisciplined character of floor contests in Tennessee, makes the members insist that the speaker play the role, as many expressed it, "of a judge."

With respect to the proportions demanding the same sort of behavior of committee chairmen, we observe the same effect of structure and process on the responses. Where committees are important, in California and Ohio, many demand restraint on the part of their chairmen; where they are less influential, in Tennessee, somewhat fewer; and in New Jersey, where they are quite irrelevant, almost no one.

Focussing the issue and resolving conflict. The four kinds of be-havior imperatives that were combined to make up this category are given in Table 8.4. They are in a sense comparable to four steps in the decision-making process, and as such are worth a detailed analysis.

Bringing out the issue centers about the category of "due regard" on the part of officers for the rights of members of their respective houses, committees, or parties, especially their right to make known

Table 8.4: Proportion of all respondents suggesting various behaviors focussing issues and resolving conflict

Kind of Behavior Suggested	Presiding Officer $N = 467$	Committee Chairmen $N = 467$	Party Leaders $N = 433*$
Let members *bring out issues*, give "due regard" for rights, assign bills fairly	23%	33%	12%
Focus conflict, narrow alternatives, "organ-ize hearing," "present issues clearly"	5	28	6
Promote and defend party or factional posi-tion; "get the program through," bring up party administration bills	18	6	42
Let the majority rule, "let the committee determine the fate of the bill," "don't push personal views"	22	24	14
One or more of the above	57	63	63

* There were no party leaders in the California Senate.

and defend their positions on legislative issues. Presiding officers are enjoined not to "bottle up" bills or to "railroad" them through. They are expected to "give each member a chance to express his opinion" and to "be fair in the referral of bills." They are to "give consideration to the minority." In the more partisan chambers some members felt it necessary to qualify their demands for fairness. The speaker, said one New Jerseyan, should "be as completely non-partisan as he can, recognizing that the majority put him there (in office)."

Committee chairmen should give consideration to minority-spon-sored legislation, should "handle bills fairly" and they should even, one legislator said, "call a meeting whenever a committee member wants it." They should not "pressure members" or "stifle legislation." In summary, the chairman should:

. . . avoid back-room deals that kill some bills and pass others regardless of their merits—know what's going on in the background and get it out in the open.

Even party leaders are expected by some members not to be "too partisan." For examples: "Don't omit the catches when explaining bills." "Don't rely on parliamentary tactics to entangle any legislation." "Encourage full debate—keep the minority happy." The extreme examples from this class of responses were from the California members who in their enthusiasm for the Hiram Johnson tradition of non-partisanship so hedged about the party leader's role that he might have been more harm than assistance to his party if he had followed their advice:

He should see to a cooperative climate between the two parties when the welfare of the state is involved, sublimating party activities where necessary.

Particularly he should bring to the attention of the caucus where they might join with the other party in the harmonious settlement of issues that could get out of hand. He should impress on the caucus that partisanship should not enter into debate except on rare occasions. It rarely does enter in.

Focussing conflict and narrowing the alternatives is a second stage in the process. Although at certain times and places members are to be given a free rein to open up differences of viewpoint, there comes a time when unrestrained debate is inappropriate, for the legislature and its committees cannot argue endlessly. Though comparatively few members suggested that the speaker play this role, one who did so typified the category:

He should ride herd on the chairmen and floor leaders, working early to resolve difficulties so there is not a lot of debate on things that really are not debatable.

It is the committee chairman's responsibility to "present the issues clearly," and "give equal time to proponents and opponents" to this end. But he must also exercise some discretion to "kill bad bills," or to "give special considerations to those bills affecting most people." Two summary statements were:

In a standing committee he should set up hearings at proper times for bills in some relation to their importance. He should conduct fair hearings, limiting the time opponents and proponents of the bill speak. He should prevent improperly drafted legislation from going through . . . he should see that all effects of a bill are thoroughly explored and ask sufficient questions if the others don't.

He can be efficient in being fair to both sides of the proposed measure. He should not spend too much foolish time on one bill just because it's his pet bill. Last year there was a bill that had twelve hearings in a Senate committee. . . . I would try to say to the sponsors: "Now let's only say something if it adds to what's been said already. Don't repeat. If you have anything new, fine. If not, sit down!" You have to give everybody an opportunity to add something, but if you just get people who stand up and say "I like this bill" you'd be there all night.

Promoting and defending the party position and thereby clarifying the major proposals before the legislature, is the third category. As members expressed it, the party or faction in power must "get the administration program through" while the minority leader tries to criticize the majority's program, to "find party issues" and to "develop a constructive opposition." The presiding officer's mandate here is a potential source of role conflict, as we shall see. For the committee chairman it is a minor duty. But for the party leader it is of course his most important function. He must:

Deliver the votes—guide the party program through the legislature.
Determine policy and program—and put it through.
Hold party members together and exercise party discipline.

Resolving differences through majority decisions involves two different, though related, behaviors required of the officers: majoritarian behavior, and impersonal behavior. The speaker is warned not to use his powers to "stack" committees in favor of some faction when this would exclude capable seniors or would thwart decisions acceptable to the majority. He is also warned not to use his position to advance his own bills or make his personal views prevail. One Tennessean put it with biblical simplicity: "He should treat his enemies as his friends." (This category is distinguished from the "be fair" category above in that it is not restricted to behavior on the rostrum.) The speaker's peculiar position was summarized this way:

His own actions must be above criticism so far as legislative work and bills he is interested in are concerned. He shouldn't pull any tricks.
Be tolerant and considerate of all opinions, though he may get tired of hearing them.

One member would go so far as to deprive the speaker of the privilege of introducing bills. Others merely indicated that he should not participate in debate without yielding the chair.
As for the chairman, this kind of behavior includes accepting the committee's decision when it goes against him, and also hearing bills

to which he is personally opposed, as well as vacating the chair when he argues a bill. The strictures here included such demands as:

Don't try to arrange committee meetings so members can't attend.
Let the committee make its decision without interference.
All bills should be considered by the whole committee.
Allow as much time as possible for discussion.
Be an adviser rather than a dictator.

Though the party leader was least subject to this sort of demand, it was mentioned that he should avoid using his office for personal prestige or to advance his own legislation. He should "have his finger on the pulse of the rank and file so he can make decisions based on the will of the majority."

It is obvious that the behaviors called for in these four categories are conflicting at times, for they are in a sense stages in a dialectic process in which differences are first opened up, then sorted out, crystallized, and finally dichotomized and a choice made. At some points officer behavior is permissive and democratic, and at others restrictive and authoritarian. That these behavior requirements are not entirely compatible need not pose problems. The same person may play different roles at different times, and different officers may be assigned to conflicting tasks.

The last line of percentages in Table 8.4 shows that all officers are expected to play some part in this contest that structures the decision to be made, but the variation in cells shows how specialized the performances of the various officers actually are.

The presiding officer is charged with the two most permissive and democratic-oriented behaviors: letting the members bring out the issues (23 per cent) and letting them decide them on the basis of a majority vote (22 per cent). These are the behaviors most compatible with the requirement that he preside in an impartial manner. That 18 per cent expect him to take a partisan position, however, indicates that the speaker is subject to role conflict.[6] This conflict occurs only in the partisan chambers, for only a very few members demand this sort of behavior in either California or Tennessee. In Ohio and New Jersey, the presiding officer must act at times as an impartial referee and at times as a partisan leader. Comparatively few legislators seemed to be aware of the potential for conflict in the way they

[6] The conflict inherent in the office of the U.S. Speaker is discussed in George B. Galloway, *The Legislative Process in Congress* (New York: Thomas Y. Crowell Company, 1955) pp. 345–350.

structured the speaker's role, but two from partisan states indicated that they perceived the problem:

> He has one of the most difficult positions as leader. He always has to find some kind of balance in what is being considered. He must let every member have his views considered and yet retain enough control, influence and respect so that he can rally the support when he needs it. The speaker can't be a dictator or a neutral party; he must be a blend of the two, and this is very difficult to do successfully.

> He should be fair to both sides—except in a real pinch.

The role conflict seems to be inevitable: the speaker or elected senate president must referee because he is the highest ranking official, beyond whom there is no appeal except to the membership itself. Yet he must also be a partisan leader when an organized majority caucus is responsible for his holding office and any appeal over his head would in effect be an appeal to this same majority, voting on the

Table 8.5: Role conflict for the speaker: summary of selected responses indicating partisan and non-partisan behavior demanded

| | Partisan Chambers | | | | Non-partisan Chambers | | | |
| | N.J. | | Ohio | | Calif. | | Tenn. | |
	House	Sen.	House	Sen.	House	Sen.	House	Sen.
The presiding officer as referee:								
Follow rules, be fair	62%	57%	59%	16%	56%	32%	81%	94%
Bring out issues, "due regard"	16	—	23	9	27	29	32	26
Let majority decide	21	19	8	9	51	26	23	23
			Mean: 25% *				*Mean: 42%* *	
The presiding officer as party leader:								
Focus conflict, narrow alternatives	2%	—	7%	31%	4%	—	1%	—
Clarify party position	12	33	36	50	8	—	2	—
			Mean: 21% *				*Mean: 2%* *	

* These means are simply the arithmetic averages of the percentages, and are inserted to summarize and highlight the differences between the four categories.

floor. Table 8.5 highlights the differences between the role of the presiding officer in partisan and non-partisan chambers.

The 12 per cent in the New Jersey Assembly and 33 per cent in the New Jersey Senate who demand that the presiding officer act in a partisan fashion are all members of the Republican majority. This is one of the rare examples of extreme partisan differences in role perceptions. It suggests that party competition in the New Jersey legislature approaches the point where consensus underlying the legislative system is threatened.

Another distinct difference between states occurred with respect to the category of members who asked that officers defer to majority decision. The 22 per cent of the total demanding this sort of inhibition from the speaker (Table 8.4) covered a range from less than 10 per cent in the two Ohio houses to 51 per cent in the California Assembly. Why, aside from the partisan nature of the job which we have just noted, the Ohio legislators do not choose to restrict their speaker is not apparent. Why California assemblymen do so is rather obvious from the nature of the selection process (above, Chapter 3, p. 54). Though a member of the majority party, the California speaker is put into office by a highly personalized majority-minority coalition that has no official status. He has broad grants of power from the rules, but no caucus to restrict the way he uses them. We might put it that members are quick to stipulate that he act impersonally for the very reason that he holds a highly personal office, in terms both of access route and uninhibited power. Legislators disadvantaged as persons may be expected to bear the discrimination less philosophically than those disadvantaged as members of a minority party. In a party system, minority members presumably realize they would do the same if the tables were turned, and hope to have that privilege eventually.

One would expect pronounced differences between majority and minority members with respect to the roles delineated for the party leaders, but this was not apparent. Majority members tended by an insignificant margin to suggest the more aggressive roles for party leaders, but there was a notable exception—the California lower house. Two-thirds of the minority Democrats felt that party leaders should push for the party position, compared with 42 per cent for the entire group of respondents (Table 8.4). Only one-fourth of the Republican majority members felt the same way. This may easily be related to the transitional nature of the party system in California (above Chapter 3, p. 45), and to other aberrant views held by California Democrats (below, Chapter 15, p. 356).

To summarize, all three kinds of officers studied contribute to this central leadership function of enabling the membership to focus issues and resolve conflict, but each by a different pattern of behavior. Committee chairmen are charged with seeing that the issues and the individual positions on them are at least briefly aired, and then with narrowing the range of conflict and making clear what the points of difference are. At this stage party and administration leaders enter to contend for support of their programs, and in so doing they provide the members with cues to make their own determination. Whether the speaker maintains his aloofness as a predominantly impartial official, or shares with the majority leader the responsibility of pressing for a particular course of action, is one of the distinctions between a partisan and a non-partisan system.

Leading and administering the legislature. The functions previously discussed are those characteristic of a legislative body. There are other kinds of leadership behavior which might be demanded of the heads of any organization of comparable size. How the expectations concerning this sort of behavior are distributed appears in Table 8.6.

Table 8.6: Proportion of all respondents suggesting that officers lead and administer the legislature

Kind of Behavior Suggested	Presiding Officer N = 467	Committee Chairmen N = 467	Party Leaders N = 433*
Guide, lead the group "coordinate members' ideas," promote teamwork	43%	13%	16%
Help individuals, "be accessible," assist with personal problems	25	1	5
Expedite business, organize, "start on time," "be concise"	22	29	15
Coordinate, communicate, provide liaison with other officers and systems	14	13	25
One or more of the above	56	47	52

* There were no party leaders in the California Senate.

Guiding the group includes such generalized demands as promoting "teamwork" or "harmony," "coordinating everyone's ideas," "ironing out differences and disagreements among members," "inspiring confidence," acting with diplomacy and tact to keep the group working together, or simply being, as a great many members said, "a good leader." With respect to the speaker:

He, with his organization, committee chairmen and others on whom he depends must establish an overall policy and give direction to the total legislative program. He must maintain control of the house on the floor and in committee, and have the ability to do it in a democratic manner, which is not basically just an arbitrary procedure.

He has to be a diplomat—he's working with eighty individualists . . . eighty potential governors.

I think he should be effective in determining a legislative program which he should then sell by persuasion, not by hitting over the head, and if he can't he should modify it so that the final program will represent the consensus of the majority.

The same sort of behavior was expected of committee chairmen and party leaders with respect to their relations with the members of their smaller groups. Party leaders were urged particularly to rally support for the party by "reasoning" with the members rather than by demanding cooperation.

Helping individuals adds to the manifold duties already assigned the speaker or senate president that of "keeping the members happy," being accessible to them, particularly to freshmen in their adjustment period, to assist with personal problems. For example:

He has to hold himself available to all members—talk over individual problems here and back home—even if they're not of major importance.

He wipes their noses and changes their diapers—he hears more confessions than a parish priest.

These two categories include acts which soothe ruffled feelings and keep the legislature working together. It is this behavior, as we noted earlier, that would be classified as "promoting cohesion or solidarity" if it had been suggested as "rules of the game." As official behavior, it comes under "functions of the executive," particularly since the top officer of the group is expected to perform it.

Expediting the business of the house, committee, or party, both at the beginning of the session and later as log jams occur, is a function shared by all officers. It includes starting sessions on time, keeping to the schedule, and distributing the work load among the membership as well as staging it throughout the session. It is the speaker's duty to:

See that committee chairmen function properly and schedule bills for hearing on time.

Keep the floor clear of lobbyists who clutter up the floor.

Committee chairmen should:

Crack the whip in the interests of time and smooth operation.

Don't get bogged down for a week or two on a bill about whether to shoot cats, and then have to spend ten minutes on an important bill.

Coordination, communication, and liason with the governor, with administrative departments, with the other chamber, with the outside public, and among the chamber officers themselves is the final category in this functional scheme. For party leaders this is an important function. They must keep their members informed on the program and the strategy for getting it through, and keep in touch with their opposite numbers in the other house and the other chamber. They can save time when they are able to decide in advance that they are "agreed to have a battle." Party leaders must also:

Get publicity and credit for the program—build up candidates.
Push forward personalities for the party to stand on at the next election.
Supply party members with information—to know what the pitch is.

Though all three officers contribute to this function, the presiding officer's contribution is heavily in the first two categories—keeping the group working as a team and healing the bruises acquired in legislative combat. Party leaders and chairmen have more technically administrative duties. In the California Senate, where party leaders are lacking, the president pro tempore inherits these administrative functions.

Knowledge of the content of legislation summarizes a series of actions, occasionally by the speaker but most frequently expected of committee chairmen. (See Table 8.1 above.)

He should be well versed on the subject of the committee he is chairman of. For instance the chairman of the Insurance Committee or Finance Committee should be well versed on state finances. If possible, he should know more than the other members. Members who go to him must know they will get correct information. He should not be biased, but fair to both sides. He should not be dictatorial, but informative.

He should prevent improperly drafted legislation from going through. Advise and assist the speaker by informing him as well as the caucus as to the bill's subject matter. . . . Take the floor himself when there's a need to clarify a matter. Above all else he should eliminate or indefinitely postpone a bill that is totally bad so that necessary time isn't expended on it by the legislature as a whole. The legislature must count on what the committees say. If they say it's good, it's good; and bad, it's bad. He should also see all effects of a bill are fully explored, and ask sufficient questions if others don't.

Should have a personal occupation akin to the subject—know what he's talking about. A school teacher should be chairman of Education, a lawyer of Judiciary.

This rationale of the chairman's function as a legislative subject-matter specialist may be a justification of the seniority system of selecting chairmen. It puts into the chair a member with long exposure to the subject matter of the committee (see below, Chapter 9).

It has been noted that New Jersey chairmen had few responsibilities for maintaining the legislative system because their committees as such very seldom met (see Chapter 3, p. 55). In virtually every subsequent category the proportion mentioning committee chairmen is lower in New Jersey than in other houses. However in subject-matter knowledge and in coordination-communication behavior, New Jersey chairmen are as frequently or more frequently mentioned than chairmen in other chambers. This illustrates rather vividly the several levels at which officer behavior may be described in an institution, with different conclusions reached. Here examination of the formal record would lead to the conclusion that committees and their chairmen played the same part in New Jersey that they do in other states. A second look from the balcony or lobby over a period of time would lead to the conclusion that they play practically no part at all in the process. A third look—at the expectation of a fair proportion of members (27 per cent of the Assembly, 43 per cent of the Senate) that chairmen will know the subject matter of bills in their fields and that they will engage in some administrative behavior (36 per cent and 19 per cent respectively)—suggests that chairman do, after all, play a part in the proceedings. How they act the part of specialists is not entirely clear—perhaps they do it in some informal and unobtrusive manner in caucus or in personal conversation.

Self-perception versus others' expectations. The roles of speaker and party leader, as these officers themselves described them, were compared with the norms of the membership to see how congruent were self-perception of role and the role expectations of others. With only a few exceptions, from which no pattern could be deduced, the eight presiding officers and eleven party leaders interviewed conformed quite closely to the prevailing norms. To determine whether officers' responses reflected differences between chambers in the way officers conceived of their duties, we compared the responses of officers to the pattern for their own chamber and to the composite pattern for the other seven chambers. The resemblance to chamber norms was closer than to general norms, but the differences were rather small. Similar tests with chairmen produced only one distinct difference between chairmen and members who were not chairmen: the former were more likely to emphasize the administrative, coordinative part of their job. Thus there is no evidence that norms concerning officer conduct are not shared by officers and members alike. Instead, there is a rather high incidence between the conduct specified by officers for officers, by members for officers, and (as we noted in the last chapter) by members for members.

THE PROBLEM OF GENERALIZATION

To get on with their business of making laws and decisions (and such other affairs as may concern or distract them), legislators need a structure of official positions. Each chamber develops such a system of offices; certain familiar titles are given the holders of these offices; powers are formally allotted to them.

These enactments may substantially contribute to leadership roles, but the behavior expected of officers goes considerably beyond the stereotypic description of the enacted role requirements. The leadership roles played by officers are an essential link between structure and function. These officers appear to perform services useful to the membership as a whole.[7] A tentative scheme for classifying the functions of legislative officers is the following:

Institutional: Maintaining the system; seeing that it works in a familiar, stable and hence predictable pattern, following known rules.

Decisional: Organizing the conflict inherent in the legislative situation so that decisions are made; soliciting alternatives, narrowing them, focussing on differences, structuring party positions, reconciling them or choosing between them.

Administrative: Providing circumstances under which the legislature may work: keeping house, dividing labor and privilege, resolving personal differences, keeping the group working together, expediting business.

Informational: Providing factual background for substantive matters being considered by the legislative groups.

This scheme, though it is on the whole compatible with the observations of Truman and Young with respect to Congress, should be regarded only as a beginning to the task of outlining a framework by which the significance of legislative officers and rules may be examined and evaluated. It may overcome some of the obvious shortcomings of the existing standard for generalizing about officer systems in the legislatures of American states. This standard, a sort of implicit power calculus based upon the allocation of authority that happens to be characteristic of the federal legislature, leads to somewhat discrepant conclusions about the influence of the holders of various legislative offices. The following sentences excerpted from

[7] Our data did not permit us to demonstrate systematically that they did so. This is an inference from the finding that members expected them to perform such functions, and the officers' assent to these expectations.

several state and local, or national, state, and local government textbooks will illustrate the point.[8]

On the power of presiding officers of state legislatures:

. . . he is today relatively more powerful in the legislative process than is the speaker of the national House. . . .

Unlike the national House of Representatives, in which the speaker is the real number-one man of his party, state legislative speakers and senate presidents are not necessarily the actual party leaders. Some of them are puppets rather than political "powers."

On the power of committee chairmen:

State committee chairmen are apt to lack the dominance over their committees enjoyed by congressional chairmen. . . .

Committee chairmen are frequently powerful and at times autocratic figures.

On the power of party officers and organizations:

Although there are party caucuses in the various state legislatures, and although caucus action is significant in a number of instances, the caucus by and large is far less important in the conduct of state legislative business than in congressional proceedings.

Except in Minnesota and Nebraska, legislatures are everywhere elected and organized along party lines. Such leadership as emerges is, therefore, of party origin. As at Washington, the regular, official machinery of each house . . . is paralled by unofficial party machinery, including caucuses . . .

On the power of the rules committee:

The powers of the rules committees vary somewhat in nature and extent, but they are always sufficiently broad to insure a large measure of control over legislation.

. . . and in less than half the states are the rules committees significant.

The difficulty in arriving at generalizations about the "power" of particular title holders in a number of states has several sources. In the first place, it is obvious even without resort to interview that officers with the same titles perform different functions. Even within our four states there were majority leaders who led the majority party, majority leaders who represented the governor, a majority leader who consistently voted with the minority; committee chairmen who called committee meetings and presided over them, and committee chairmen who did neither. At the same time there were identical functions performed by different officers—bills referred to committees by presiding officers, by rules committees, and by committees formed for the express purpose of referring bills; there were parties led by presiding officers, parties led by floor leaders, and parties led by persons unspecified. It is unlikely that the variety of arrangements is

[8] These statements were taken from six texts published since 1953.

characteristic only of these four states. A comparable diversity may be found in the fifty states. Another problem is the transactional quality of roles, wherein members have decided expectations regarding officer conduct which appear to apply particularly to those chambers where officers "on paper" are most powerful. Where the presiding officer represents a factional group or one oriented to the administration, the membership seems particularly eager to circumscribe his freedom of action. On the other hand, where he represents an effectively organized majority party in the legislature, the scope of the speaker's power may be considerable. But in this instance he is wielding consensual, not personalized power. The classic example is the New Jersey legislature, where presiding officers have broad powers under the rules of the chambers, and where in addition they are expected to behave aggressively—to forward the party program, to be firm in presiding, to lead and guide the group. The hollowness of this apparent power is evident when one notes the convention that the office is rotated each session, (Chapter 3, p. 55). So authoritative are caucus decisions that it really is not at all important who sits upon the rostrum.

Comparison of expectations with respect to the three sets of officers suggests that there are similarities in their function despite the variations just noted. Presiding officers, party leaders, and committee chairmen all have responsibilities classified as "administrative" in the scheme above. Committee chairmen have "informational" responsibilities with respect to the subject matter of their committees. All three sets of officers have responsibilities toward the "decisional" system, but their contributions are made in quite different ways. Maintaining "institutional" continuity is largely the job of the presiding officer.

From every evidence—number, specificity, and variability from chamber to chamber of expectations—it appears that the presiding officer is the central figure. His important contribution is preserving a climate of impartiality, stability, and predictability, an atmosphere in which controversial matters may be brought up and settled with some finality without gnawing doubts on the part of the losers that the outcome could have been different. In a non-partisan legislature this role may carry over in the members' expectations to impersonality, majoritarian acceptance of members' views, and permissiveness in letting everyone air these views. Where parties are powerful the chamber president is also expected to play another role that appears to conflict: the role of a party leader who strives to put through the majority party's program. We have no data on the effect of this inter-role conflict upon the officers concerned, but the members seem well enough attuned to it to recognize when the speaker should play each role. In fact, only a few of them perceive the potential conflict. There was some evidence, though highly tentative, that the system may get slightly out of adjustment if an officer is too personal, too partisan, or suspect of too close an attachment to a non-legislative power center (such as the governor in Tennessee).

In their less formal surroundings, chairmen of committees are admonished to play the same role as the presiding officer, but they are less bound by written rules and have to rely more on personal fairness and forcefulness. The chairman plays the leading role in screening legislation, thus expediting the work of the body, but he must be careful in his treatment of the minority. He is expected to use his knowledge of a specialized field of legislation. Even where committees do not appear to be active, the chairmen may still play a genuine leadership role, though in an obscure fashion.

Party leaders were found to have coordinative, liaison functions which provide cues useful to members in making decisions. This is far less aggressive conduct than might be associated with the customary terminology ("binding" decisions, "discipline," "party whips") but it is characteristic of party leadership in Congress as well.[9] Party leaders serve as points of reference, valuable alike to supporters and opponents.

It should again be made explicit that we have no direct data on the performance of functions by officers. We have only the members' descriptions of officers' roles (in which descriptions the officers do tend to concur). This sort of evidence might be expected to overstress the officers' contribution to the common objects of all members and to overlook the officers' "power" to accomplish goals not shared by the membership. Making allowance for this, one is still struck by the similarity of expectations with respect to officers and those with respect to chamber norms of conduct. "Power" is granted to officers so they may accomplish what the majority party and, to a larger extent than an outsider would suppose, what the entire membership wishes to accomplish. "Leadership is not an affair of the individual leader. It is fundamentally an affair of the group. Pomp and circumstance are but details."[10]

---

[9] "Given the mediate function of the Congressional party, the powers of its leaders, especially its principal elective leaders, cannot be expected, except in very small measure, to be formalized, codified, and at all times fully adequate for meeting the vicissitudes of their roles." Truman, *The Congressional Party, op. cit.*, p. 294.

[10] Bentley, *op. cit.*, p. 223.

CHAPTER 9

Subject matter experts

In most of the rest of the government, federal, state, and local, and throughout the society being governed, specialization in the division of labor and of authority is now the rule. One would suppose that members of legislative bodies—the persons principally charged with making decisions authoritatively for the society and government —would be forced by the increasing complexity of the problems they face to devise an appropriate system of specialization.

To what extent Congress has done this is not entirely clear. Most summary studies treat specialization only incidentally.[1] Yet Matthews' recent interviews with United States senators indicate that they recognize and defer to the specialists among them, and that this custom gets their work done more efficiently.[2] Truman and Finer, in more generalized studies of the legislative process, note the occasional relevance of particular substantive information to legislators' performance of their duties.[3] However, neither of them challenges the prevailing conception that bodies of special "subject matter" knowledge lying outside the legislative halls must be revealed and interpreted *to* legislators, rather than known or interpreted *by* them to one another.

The view that specialization is inappropriate in the legislative process is supported by long-standing assumptions about the function

This chapter drafted by Buchanan.

[1] Such references to specialization may be found in George B. Galloway, *op. cit.*, p. 315; Roland Young, *op. cit.*, p. 107; Stephen K. Bailey and Howard D. Samuel, *Congress at Work* (New York: Henry Holt and Company, 1952) pp. 203, 342 ff.; Bertram M. Gross, *The Legislative Struggle* (New York: McGraw-Hill Book Company, 1953) p. 388; Holbert N. Carroll, *op. cit.*, pp. 274–276.

[2] Donald R. Matthews, "The Folkways of the United States Senate . . . ," *op. cit.*, pp. 1064–1089.

[3] David B. Truman, *The Governmental Process, op. cit.*, p. 334; Herman Finer, *The Theory and Practice of Modern Government* (New York: Holt, Rinehart and Winston, 1949) pp. 382, 446.

and desired behavior of lawmakers.   Consideration of technical problems has been associated with the kind of "detailed" regulation deemed more fitting for administrative agencies.   It has commonly been thought proper for legislators to perform, instead of such "administrative" chores, other functions more closely related to broad policy decisions: compromise, adjustment, integration of conflicting goals and values.[4]   Young even suggests that if Congressmen know too much about the fields they regulate as committeemen, Congress would begin to have trouble "making decisions as a corporate group" and determining "the actual location of authority" within the body.[5] Related notions are the assumed omnicompetence of the legislator and its corollary, the theoretical equality of all members of the chamber. These are embodied in the structural features and common practices of legislative bodies—equality of voting power, reliance on administrative or interest-group experts to explain complex matters, reliance on staff experts and committee secretaries to lead in cross-examining these experts.   Indeed, legislatures have often delegated their rule-making power to independent commissions, reluctantly choosing to divest themselves of some of their authority rather than to develop the expertise necessary to maintain it.

The familiar legislative device which has counteracted these principles of generalization and has permitted sustained, specialized consideration of substantive matters is of course the standing committee system.   It is a century old, at least, and predates specialization in some sectors of the economy and society.[6]   But committees are denied the formal authority that might accompany specialized responsibility. They remain, in theory, representative of the whole house; their purpose is ostensibly economy of attention; their decisions are revocable by a bare majority.   It is by tradition and informal agreement that their authority is in fact recognized and their decisions only occasionally over-ridden.   It is also by informal acceptance that committees have come to be organized as mechanisms for developing and authenticating specialists through the practice of recognizing seniority within the committee.   This convention puts at the head of the committee the majority member who, while not always best informed on subject matter, is at least the longest exposed to information about it.

Of course, the constitution of legislative bodies makes practically impossible any explicit attempt to recruit or to develop specialists

---

[4] See Finer, *op. cit.*, Part IV; Carl J. Friedrich, *Constitutional Government and Democracy* (Boston: Ginn and Company, rev. ed., 1946), Ch. 16.

[5] Young, *op. cit.*, p. 107.

[6] Galloway, *op. cit.*, Ch. 12.

among the membership. No mechanism exists to bring a person with specialist qualifications into a district electoral campaign at the moment the legislative body needs his particular brand of knowledge. If by accident such an individual enters the electoral contest, the legislature's need for him in no way helps him to win the election. If by further coincidence he should happen to win, he may yet have to wait for accumulating seniority or a shift in party fortunes, to gain the committee post best providing access to his area of specialty. Finally, after he has been trained, recruited, and given power by some such series of happy accidents, his local constituency may choose to cut him off in his prime on some quite irrelevant ground—or perhaps on the relevant but perverse ground that he spends too much time on larger affairs and not enough on local ones.

Between the structure that inhibits specialization and the philosophy that denies its value, or at the least ignores its relevance, we should expect specialists to arise only where they are badly needed. In the House of Representatives this seems principally to be the foreign policy area. Both Dahl and Carroll describe the crucial role of the "bellwether"— the member who, though he may occupy no formal office, possesses the reputation for understanding some particular international problem or area and is watched by others seeking cues as to the position they should take on issues in this area. The bellwether, Dahl says, is "one whom his colleagues regard as relatively more 'expert' than they, and yet sufficiently akin to them to be trustworthy." He acts as a communication link:

> Just as one function of Congress, taken as a whole, is to mediate between the non-expertness of the citizen and the expertness of the executive-administrative branch, so one function of the Congressional policy specialist is to mediate between the non-experts in Congress and the experts on fact and policy in the executive-administrative. . . .[7]

The expert describes the consequences of proposed actions, Dahl says. He "interprets reality" and formulates the alternative ways a decision might influence the course of events, given this reality. The non-expert decision maker, on the other hand, tends to see alternatives in the light of values—his own or his constituents'. Foreseeing, with the expert's help, the consequences of some policy these values suggest, he is able to clarify his preferences and choose between the relevant alternatives. "Thus the function of the specialist at any point in the line is to define preferences to the more specialized at the 'higher' level of competence, and to define reality to the less specialized at the lower level." The Foreign Relations Committee

---

[7] Robert A. Dahl, *op. cit.*, pp. 60, 150. See also Carroll, *op. cit.*, p. 276.

defines congressional preferences to President and State Department, and in turn helps to define to the members of Congress the world in which their preferred policies must survive. At the next level the non-expert Congressman helps the committee to understand what his constituents want, and then describes to his constituents the reality he has learned from committee members. "Some such policy of 'translating' preferences and reality views at different levels is indispensable to the functioning of most modern organizations. In complicated situations requiring group organization it is usually the only way by which human purposes can be achieved."[8]

In the broader context of any "decisional system" (executive, legislative, or non-governmental) Snyder, Bruck, and Sapin have described the function of such a mechanism as conveying "information regarding the state of the relationship of the system to its setting" so that the decision makers may have a "current picture of the success or failure of their actions and the relative adequacy of the system." The functions include "information storage and organizational memory."[9]

Although states do not need foreign policy specialists, we would expect them, by analogy, to need specialists in fields which are particularly complex, remote, or abstruse.[10] Because a legislature is a representative institution, we might also expect the communication function to link the body to various clienteles or constituencies outside the legislative halls. In this case, the incidence of expertise should reflect the principal problems of the surrounding society which it is a particular legislature's business to solve.

At the same time, the specialization system would not be entirely independent of the structural peculiarities of the chamber. How the jurisdictions of committees are divided, whether staff services exist to perform communication functions through alternative channels, the role of the parties in providing decision cues, constitutional provisions which entrust the legislature with authority in some areas and deny it in others, the size of the chambers, the tenure and turnover of members—all of these might in some circumstances be expected to shape the structure of a particular legislature's system of informal expertise.

[8] Dahl, op. cit., p. 162.

[9] Richard C. Snyder, H. W. Bruck, and Burton Sapin, Decision-making as an Approach to the Study of International Politics (Princeton: Organizational Behavior Section, 1954) pp. 82–91.

[10] Charles E. Merriam and Robert E. Merriam, The American Government (Boston: Ginn and Company, 1954) is one of the few texts which treats this phase of the state legislative process, pp. 224, 232.

THE EXTENT OF SPECIALIZATION

Our original study design did not include direct study of informal expertise. But numerous unanticipated voluntary comments during the pretest period revealed that legislators were preoccupied with specialization, self-conscious of their own fields, and apparently able to agree in part on who were the experts in other fields. The following questions were therefore put to 471 members:

Is there any particular subject or field of legislation in which you consider yourself particularly expert—I mean when it comes to dealing with proposed legislation in that field? What [field] is that?

Why is that [i.e., that you are expert]?

Could you name five or six members of the House [Senate] whom you consider particularly expert in their respective fields? [Interviewer recorded name and field of each.]

Specialization was widely regarded as accepted and acceptable practice: 91 per cent named one or more members they considered specialists in some substantive field, and 83 per cent named fields in which they themselves were, or were becoming, experts.[11]

The objections to specialization by legislators were a very minor theme in the responses of the legislators themselves. Only 3 per cent considered specialization on their own part undesirable, unwise, or impossible, and only 2 per cent denied there were experts in the legislature. Those who denied its existence or objected to its presence did so on a variety of grounds:

There are no real experts. What we need is more people with honor and common sense . . . the last one above all.

Some people are "experts" in a special field but are not necessarily interested in what's good for the people.

Experience in the legislature is equivalent to a college education. You become a specialist at nothing, but develop a knowledge of practically everything.

I'm not really interested in the legislature as a specialized agency. I rely on lobbyists for detailed information.

Interestingly, even a few of these members who denied the relevance of specialization were accepted by a number of their colleagues as specialists in one area or another.

[11] The term "expert"—a rather strong one—was used because that was the word employed by legislators in the pretest. When respondents balked at the term, interviewers recorded the fact, but continued questioning in terms of competence, specialization, interest, or concern. The majority of respondents (61 per cent) did not object to the word.

Table 9.1: Fields of specialization (expertise) in which nominations were made

Law	legal and judicial matters, code revision, enforcement, civil rights, constitution, criminal law	19%
Finance	taxation, ways and means, revenue, budgeting, appropriations	13
Education	public schools	12
Agriculture	farming, livestock and dairies, specific commodities	9
Conservation	water, natural resources	6
Local government	municipal and county government and administration, metropolitan problems	5
Labor	industrial relations	5
Transportation	highways, trucks, traffic, safety, railroads, aviation	4
State government	organization, administration, civil service	4
Banking	commerce, investment, loans, mortgages	4
Welfare	social welfare, juvenile delinquency, pensions, adoptions, problems of women, the aged	3
Health	medicine, mental health	3
Insurance		3
Fish and game	commercial fishing	2
Business	wholesale and retail trade	2
Manufacturing and mining	oil, gravel	2
Military and veteran affairs		1
Other	(less than 1% each): liquor regulation, utilities, elections, real estate, communications, independent authorities, licensing, logging, entertainment, construction	3
Total	(2,105 nominations made by 429 legislators in four states)	100%

Altogether 2,105 "nominations"—each consisting of the name of a person and the field in which he specialized—were made by the 91 per cent who named one or more experts.[12]   Since the legislators were unrestricted as to what fields they might mention, the responses were recorded verbatim and subsequently coded into 27 categories, of which 20 accounted for 97 per cent of the nominations.   The distribution of subject-matter fields, with percentages based on all nominations in the four states, is given in Table 9.1.

[12] A legislator might name one person as expert in two fields, or two persons as expert in the same field.   In either case, two "nominations" were counted.

SUBJECTS OF EXPERTISE

The fields of law and finance, which account for about a third of the nominations, have two common characteristics. First, they are complex and technical. Second, they involve the two important techniques—law writing and budgeting—through which the legislature exercises control over the economy, the society, and the government. The ranking of the other fields appears to be more in order of their importance than of their complexity. This suggests that, in contrast to Congress, expertise in the states is not so much a matter of familiarity with genuinely esoteric affairs as of simple distribution of the work load. Limitations inherent in the part-time nature of state legislative office encourage each member to devote his attention to matters with which he is already to some extent familiar, and rely upon others to guide him in his decisions on unfamiliar ones. This may be why specialization is more obvious in state legislatures than in Congress.

These cumulated results do not reveal the variations between states with respect to the subjects where experts most frequently appear. The fields in which nominations totalled 5 per cent or more of the nominations made in any chamber are given in Table 9.2.

Two of the expected sources of difference between states—socio-economic characteristics of the population and structural-political characteristics of the legislative system—are reflected in this distribution. As an example of the first, the California legislature, which for years has been struggling with a 12-billion dollar proposal for conserving its water resources, shows the greatest need for experts in the conservation-and-water field. Though it is an industrial state, strikes had been comparatively rare in the years preceding this study, and fewer experts in labor-management relations appear there than in the other three states. On the other hand, Tennessee, the most rural state of the four, requires the most agricultural expertise. New Jersey, where national corporations have their headquarters near the Manhattan financial complex, requires the most expertise in banking and commerce. These differences also suggest that the expertise system adapts itself to the changing problems of a state, and that a different distribution may be expected in other states, or even in these a few years hence. Such adaptability is one of the strengths of an informal system. The standing committee system, though technically flexible, since it may be altered by simple resolution, often preserves an inconsequential or virtually idle committee (such as Engrossment and Enrollment) so that someone may be chairman of it.

The second source of differences—legislative structure—is best illustrated by Ohio, where financial expertise appears in abundance despite the fact that the state's budget is reasonable and its debt low compared to its resources. (See Chapter 3, p. 67.) These experts

Table 9.2: Major fields of expertise in eight chambers

Fields Where Nominations Totalled More Than 5% of Nominations in the Chamber*	Calif.		N.J.		Ohio		Tenn.	
	House	Sen.	House	Sen.	House	Sen.	House	Sen.
N =	397	159	286	74	643	169	258	119
Law	9%	9%	9%	24%	25%	27%	29%	27%
Finance	12	6	11	8	21	17		
Education	11	14	16	7	11	16	7	11
Agriculture	7	6	9		10		17	13
Conservation	19	19						
Local government	6		13	9	5			
Labor			8	5		10		8
Transportation		13		5				8
State government	8	7	7					
Banking			7	18			7	
Health						10		
Insurance						6		
Fish and game				9				
Business								8
All others (less than 5% each)	28	26	20	15	28	30	24	25
	100%	100%	100%	100%	100%	100%	100%	100%

* The question called for each respondent to name "five or six" experts. Some named more, some could not think of this many, some did not name experts for various reasons. There was, of course, a wide variation in the size of the chambers. Use of percentages of all nominations in a chamber equalizes for these differences as well as any single measure can, and permits comparison between states where nominations were few and those where they were many. The 5 per cent cut-off point is approximately equivalent to nomination by 20 per cent of the membership, subject to some variation from chamber to chamber.

have apparently been spawned by the subdivision of the Committee on Finance into three "sections" (i.e., subcommittees). Legal expertise also is in great demand in Ohio, where bill-drafting is formally entrusted to Ohio State University law students. As one legal expert explained:

Members started coming to me to read their bills and see if they were all right constitutionally. Pretty soon I got a reputation for having experience in these matters and everyone started coming to me.

By comparison, California's lack of interest in legal specialization may be explained by the existence there of a Legislative Counsel bureau employing a large staff of attorneys to draft bills, index them, and estimate their constitutionality (see Chapter 3, p. 50).[13]

Over-all differences in the amount of attention paid to specialization are summarized in Table 9.3. California is the legislature most

Table 9.3: Awareness of specialization

State and Chamber		Perceive Selves as Specialists in One or More Fields	Name One or More Other Members as Specialists	Number of Respondents
California	House	95%	97%	(78)
California	Senate	94	94	(34)
New Jersey	House	86	98	(58)
New Jersey	Senate	86	86	(21)
Ohio	House	82	97	(129)
Ohio	Senate	77	94	(31)
Tennessee	House	74	81	(89)
Tennessee	Senate	71	81	(31)

aware of specialization; 90 per cent or more of the membership of each chamber consider themselves specialists and also name others as specialists in one subject or another. At the other extreme, only some three-fourths of the Tennesseans regard themselves—and the same proportion regard others—as specialists. In the lower house, where turnover is quite high (see Chapter 3, p. 49), many members were unable to name the "five or six" experts requested. Between California and Tennessee fall New Jersey (with an inexplicable difference between chambers), and Ohio, where members are quick to recognize others' expertise but slow to advance their own pretensions. Hypotheses that the states would differ with respect to the importance attached to expertise according to their relative levels of tenure, the strength of their party systems, the importance of the part played by committees—none of these could be clearly demonstrated,

[13] There are further differences that have not been treated, e.g., Tennessee's relative unconcern about financial expertise, and the appearance in the New Jersey Senate, but not the House, of legal experts. No explanation for these differences occurs to us. It is apparent that socio-economic and legislative-structural differences have not exhausted possible differentiating factors.

though the data did not, on the other hand, indicate that these factors were entirely irrelevant. The most striking finding was the most obvious: that even in the least concerned state—Tennessee—awareness of expertise was characteristic of a three-fourths majority.

Tentatively, we may conclude that specialization varies between chambers slightly in amount but considerably in detail. It conforms to the political and constitutional configurations of particular states, and becomes especially relevant when legislatures face problems amassed by very complex economies. It is a widespread reality, even to the point where one may surmise that specialization and division of labor are prerequisites for the successful functioning of American state legislatures.

THE EXPERTS

Thus far we have considered only the fields of expertise, without regard to what legislators, and how many, shared these nominations. Now we turn to gauging the consensus on who were the experts in each field. For example, take the insurance experts in the Tennessee House and fish and game experts in the New Jersey Senate, two of the smaller categories. In the first instance there were 15 nominations; they were shared among four members with 3 nominations each, one with 2 nominations, and one with 1 nomination. The "top ranking" expert got only 20 per cent of the nominations (and so did the second, third, and fourth ranking experts). There could hardly be less consensus than this. In the second instance, all 7 nominations by New Jersey senators for fish and game expert went to the same member—100 per cent consensus among those who named an expert in this field.

By ranking major experts, computing their percentages as above, and then averaging these percentages for all the fields listed in Table 9.2, we may construct an index of consensus on expertise for each chamber. These are given in Table 9.4.

The 51 first-ranking experts in these major fields averaged 55 per cent of the nominations in their field. In simplified, "on-the-average" terms, we may say that more than half of those legislators seeking a particular kind of expert will pick the same person, and more than four-fifths (84 per cent) will pick one of the top three. Of these 51 top experts, 33 (65 per cent) occupied the chair of one of the committees having jurisdiction in the field. This indicates substantial correspondence between the formal and informal systems of specialization, although the difference is great enough to demonstrate that

Table 9.4: Consensus on leading experts, by chamber

Average Level of Agreement in Choice of:	Calif. House	Calif. Sen.	N.J. House	N.J. Sen.	Ohio House	Ohio Sen.	Tenn. House	Tenn. Sen.	All
First-ranking expert	55%	54%	60%	70%	42%	52%	46%	51%	55%
Second-ranking expert	18	21	19	22	16	24	19	18	19
Third-ranking expert	8	10	11	4	10	11	13	13	10
All other nominations	19	15	10	4	32	13	22	18	16
	100%	100%	100%	100%	100%	100%	100%	100%	100%
Number of nominations	283	119	229	64	464	121	194	89	1563
Major fields, averaged*	7	7	8	8	5	4	6	6	51
Size of chamber	80	40	58	21	139	34	99	33	

* The names of these fields will be found in Table 9.2.

203

"expert" is not merely a synonym for "chairman" in the vocabulary of these legislators.

A comparison of chamber sizes (given on the last line of Table 9.4) with consensus (given on the top line) will make apparent the most striking relationship in the table: the strong inverse correlation between size of chamber and consensus on experts. From the 21-man New Jersey Senate, where consensus on top experts is 70 per cent, down to the 139-man Ohio House, where consensus is only 42 per cent, the houses fall in perfect rank-order with only one minor deviation, the California Senate. The rank ordering is not unexpected. In a large chamber, members cannot know everyone's capabilities, and mere size increases the likelihood that several qualified specialists will be available.

The bases of specialization. Further clues to the part specialization plays in the legislative process may be found in the ways individual legislators acquire the reputation and the sense of being specialists or experts. Table 9.5 shows the reasons given by respondents when they were asked why they were expert in one field or another.

Table 9.5: Reasons legislators give for their own expertise

Responses*	Calif. $N = 217$	N.J. $N = 107$	Ohio $N = 188$	Tenn. $N = 124$	All States $N = 636$
Experience in occupation	25%	30%	42%	55%	37%
Other personal experience	19	14	14	10	15
Political experience	7	15	1	1	5
Problems important to district	16	11	4	5	9
Other personal involvement	15	19	14	18	16
Legislative assignment	18	11	25	11	18
	100%	100%	100%	100%	100%

* Since respondents could name more than one field, and different reasons for expertise in the same field, or in different fields, percentages are based on the total number of responses, 636, given by 395 members.

More than a third of the responses (37 per cent) dealt with occupational experience. For example, one member said:

Certain of us are better equipped along certain lines. I have a B.A., but I've specialized in farming and the dairy business, so I'm rated as one of the agricultural experts. There are not too many members familiar with it

in a practical way.   This is a job of specialization, and we carry most of
the agricultural legislation.   It's easier for us to explain a bill.

In the more industrial states, this response category was smaller,
suggesting that occupation alone is not considered adequate background for dealing with complex problems, even by those who would
like to be experts.

The second category, with 15 per cent of responses, includes those
who advanced membership in a minority group, experience as a
soldier, parent, sportsman or fisherman, experience with a physical
handicap, or educational contact with a problem as a rationale for
specialization.   For example, one transportation expert said:

> I did a term paper on the economics of transportation at college and it
> interested me very much.   I carried this interest over into my work with
> the Chamber of Commerce.

The category of "political experience" was a minor one (5 per cent),
except in New Jersey, where the parties practice informal rotation of
officeholders from local to state positions and back.   (See Chapter 3,
p. 44.)

Typical of the 9 per cent of responses citing the importance of some
field of expertise to a legislator's district were these:

> (Agriculture)   I come from a farming district and I'm sympathetic to the
> problems of the farmer.   I've tried to fit myself to represent agriculture.
> (Fish and game)   All the fish canners live in my district.   . . . I've
> lived in the atmosphere all my life.
> (State government)   If I don't become an expert in civil service legisla-
> tion I'll be out on my ear.   It's dictated by my constituency, with a tre-
> mendous number of governmental employees.

The "personal involvement" category (16 per cent) includes replies
attributing expertise to a feeling that some problem is important to the
individual legislator or to the state, as well as those indicating that
specialization is itself necessary or worthwhile.   Examples of the
range, and the mixed motivations, in this category are:

> (Labor)   I feel some problems . . . I'm interested . . . well, the
> strong groups have competent lobbyists who push their bills.   I know
> injustices, but I don't know the technicalities, in unemployment compensa-
> tion, for instance . . . and I try to influence the experts.
> (Conservation)   Each legislator looks for a specialty for two reasons:
> (1) It's a vehicle to travel on, and (2) To satisfy himself . . . to feel he's
> doing some good.   . . . I examined the fields to see what were the most
> important subjects of statewide interest, which each area would see as

important for years to come.   I was looking for a vehicle to move forward in state politics.

(Transportation)   It's not that the subject (highway safety) appeals to me particularly, but people are interested and you don't hurt somebody by working on it.   It's an ideal field—high publicity content without controversy.

The fact that "legislative assignment" is the second largest category, with 18 per cent of responses, reinforces the suggestion that the needs of the system play an important part in selection of a specialty.   This category includes responses attributing expertise to information or interest acquired as a result of experience as a committee member or a legislative investigator.   This class of responses appears more frequently in Ohio and California, the two states where committees play an important part in the decisional process.

Especially revealing among these responses are those calling attention to the importance of quite fortuitous events in the acquisition of a field of specialization:

I have spent a great deal of time with alcoholic beverage control because my first assignment was to it, when it was an important issue, and I became identified with it.

I was on the Welfare Committee my first session.   We had a big baby-selling stink at the time.

On the whole, the distribution of "reasons" for specialization suggests that personal and occupational background may determine a legislator's preference for a particular specialization area, but the political demands and functional needs of the legislative system play a major part in determining his eventual choice of a field.

Confirmation of this is found in the fact that legislative tenure and formal education are the factors most closely related to attribution of expertise by others, as indicated in Table 9.6.   Apparently one must stay in the legislature long enough to demonstrate that his skills are useful before he achieves wide recognition as an expert.   Although formal education has been acquired before entering the body, it is presumably the demonstrated consequences of this education, rather than the possession of the diploma itself, that the members use as a criterion for selecting experts.

The one irregularity in the table—the lower proportion of experts among law graduates—suggests the importance of legislative demand as a factor in expertise.   Law and education are each chosen by a fourth of the legislators as the field in which they are, or desire to become, expert.   By the very minimal standard—nomination by only one fellow member—only 17 per cent may be called legal, and only 9 per cent educational "experts." Quite obviously there are more candidates than positions in both fields. However, 36 per cent of legislators are lawyers, but only 3 per cent are teachers by profession. Hence many lawyers do not even offer themselves as experts in this field, and, of those who do, not all are chosen. By contrast, there are hardly enough teachers to fill the seats on the Education committees, so one with any legislative competence stands a good chance of being nominated as an expert as soon as he becomes known.

Table 9.6: Tenure and education as factors in the recognition of expertise

Length of Service in Legislature	1–4 yrs. $N = 306$	5–9 yrs. $N = 116$	10 yrs. up $N = 82$
Experts*	16%	38%	54%
All others	84	62	46
	100%	100%	100%

Educational Background	Grade school only $N = 11$	High school only 85	College incomplete 110	College grad., exc. law 86	Law school grad. 163	Other graduate study 26
Experts*	—	14%	30%	36%	26%	50%
All others	100%	86	70	64	74	50
	100%	100%	100%	100%	100%	100%

* Those selected by 5 per cent or more as expert in any field.

A closer look at the best known experts (those nominated by 25 per cent or more of the membership) bears this out. The eight leading legal experts were attorneys, but only three of them were chairmen of Judiciary or comparable committees, suggesting that informal consultation with members on the technicalities of constitutionalism and bill drafting is a function of these legal experts. These lawyer-legislators were more hesitant than others to describe themselves as experts; among their comments were:

No, I'm not an expert, but as a lawyer I know the statutes. I've been chairman of the Judiciary committee for . . . years.

There's very little down there I don't know something about. I'm always getting the dirty job.

This may reflect the role of lawyers as "professional representers," to use Hyneman's phrase.[14] Or it may, instead, indicate the lawyers' awareness of the potential distrust by lay legislators of their legal brethren. One non-lawyer remarked:

> They draw up a law so nobody, including themselves, can understand it. It makes business for them. . . . Laws could be drafted that would be clear and simple if they wanted to.

In contrast, only one of the five education experts picked by a fourth of the membership was an educator by profession, which bears out the finding above. Two education specialists were in fact lawyers, both of them attorneys who had been in contact with school affairs before entering the legislature. Another was an editor, who headed the Education committee of his house. He explained, almost apologetically, that he "backed into that chairmanship, really." The fifth education expert was a member with somewhat limited formal education, who explained that he had become interested in the subject as a parent. A conservative Republican, his interests included the economical administration of schools and the protection of the curriculum from "alien" influences. Of the five education experts, only two were chairmen of the Education committees in their chambers.

Though legal and educational experts were not all chairmen, the four financial experts were. Two of them were lawyers, the others were real estate and insurance men. Altogether, at the top level of specialization, as at the lower level we examined statistically, we find profession a partial but an incomplete explanation of how members become experts.

Further examination of the responses to this question suggests that in playing the role of an informal expert or specialist, the legislator fulfills a dual responsibility which is quite distinct from the behavior expected of an administrator, lobbyist, or citizen who might bring somewhat the same information before the legislative group. These latter may appear to the members as "special pleaders," as "interested" (i.e., biased) sources of information. When the same material is interpreted by a fellow legislator considered an expert in the matter, a person subject to known and understandable pressures from his district and his party, this information becomes more dependable as a guide for legislative action. The responsibility of the specialist toward his fellows is implicit in the following accounts of how certain legislators acquired and perform the role of expert:

[14] Charles S. Hyneman, "Who Makes Our Laws?", *Political Science Quarterly*, 55:556–581 (1940).

(Insurance)   I never discussed [a compensation bill] on the floor because people would think I was doing it because I'm in the insurance business.   I *voted* for putting it in the hands of the private companies . . . and that was all right because the others expected me to . . . but I felt I would lose the respect of other members if I fought for the bill on the floor.

(Licensing)   Licensing has always been requested by the group concerned.   Since that was behind all the legislation, it had been piecemeal—not consistent.   I saw nothing was being done, and I have no ties with any pressure group in the field.   I've made an effort to become an expert in a field in which there was a vacuum.

(Judicial affairs)   They organized a committee to reorganize the court system and they wanted two non-lawyers to carry the legislation who wouldn't ever be appointed to the bench.

Of course, it is impossible to say how far this implied restraint and avoidance of interest representation is carried in fact.   At least there is the feeling that the legislator-expert should play a dual role, responsible in some degree to his colleagues.   The allegiance of the lobbyist-expert, or the administrator, by contrast, lies entirely outside the body, subject to no conflicting claim.

The final observation that should be made about selections of experts is that legislators tended to select members of their own party, though not to the exclusion of those across the aisle.   This again reflects the usefulness of the expert who is a functioning part of the decisional system, who may be appraised as a partisan, as a person, as a fellow legislator—not simply as a conveyor of special information.

In sum, a genuine winnowing process takes place in the informal selection of experts.   Previous experience, occupational, educational, or incidental, is not of itself a guarantee of recognition.   Assignment to a committee by accident or by design; concern with a pressing problem; political ambition; the supply of and demand for information within the legislature as a whole or within one of its parties; demonstration over the years that one is a trustworthy guide to action—all these influence the choice of specialists.   Those who are chosen play a joint role, that of expert and that of legislator, and the latter component is apparently the more important one.

Education experts: a case study.   The interview data permitted one area of expertise, education, to be explored in somewhat greater detail, through a battery of questions about "school needs" in each state in 1957.[15]   We may compare the responses to these questions of:

[15] The story of educational legislation in the four legislatures in 1957 is told in LeRoy C. Ferguson's "How State Legislators View the Problem of School Needs," a report to the United States Office of Education, 1960.

1) "Self-styled" experts—those who said they were experts, or were becoming experts, in education.

2) "Recognized" experts—those who, regardless of how they responded, were named by 5 per cent or more of their fellow members as education experts. This criterion included in each chamber the top-ranking education expert and one to three second-level experts.

3) "Others"—those who did not see themselves, and were not seen by others, as education experts.

Of course the first and second groups overlapped, since most of those who were named by others as education experts were aware of their status.

As Table 9.7 indicates, there are minor differences between both kinds of experts on one hand, and non-experts on the other, in their perception of school needs. Although nearly all legislators pay lip service to the importance of education, concern over school needs is somewhat greater among experts, and experts are somewhat more likely to see the problem in positively toned, sympathetic terms. In other words they tend to have the sort of view that school administrators presumably would like them to have. The greatest perceptual difference, though, is that experts tend to see the problem as a complex one, with administrative, financial, and curricular aspects; while the non-experts are more likely to describe it as an uncomplicated, single-factor affair.

The recognized experts also differ sharply from both the "self-styled" experts and the non-experts in their reported source of information and advice. They are much more likely to go to state-level administrators than are the non-experts and much less likely to go to school officials in their district. They are somewhat more likely to seek advice and information from the Education Association. The "self-styled" experts occupy a middle position between "recognized" experts and non-experts. This suggests that becoming a qualified expert consists of learning where to go for information of a broader scope than is available to the district-bound legislators.

Both kinds of experts are more active than non-experts in authoring or sponsoring education bills, in committee work, in debate on the floor and in informal negotiation with others. The "recognized" experts take on a larger share of the visible activities, introducing bills, and explaining them. "Self-styled" experts work in less prestigious ways, in committee, and by seeking to amend others' bills.

Altogether, we find expertise apparently does not serve a legislator primarily to resist or counter the suggestions of bureaucrats and lob-

Table 9.7: Education experts: their attitudes, information sources, and activities with respect to "school needs" (four states combined)

Responses to Items Concerning "School Needs"*	"Recognized" Experts N = 21	"Self-Styled" Experts N = 81	Non- Experts N = 339
Express "great concern" over needs	90%	89%	75%
Characterize needs . . .			
in positive, sympathetic terms (need federal aid, more state aid, new taxes, higher salaries, new buildings, etc.)	50	51	43
in negative terms (cut out frills, keep expenses down, make more local effort, no further federal/ state aid needed, etc.)	15	13	20
Describe needs as complex matter, combining financial, administrative *and* curricular aspects, rather than as a problem with only *one* aspect, or not a problem	45	42	26
List most trusted source of advice and information as . . .			
Education Association (at state or local level)	43	37	36
state school administrators (Department of Education)	62	45	26
local school officials	14	33	40
Reports action taken (or planned) with respect to school needs as . . .			
authoring or sponsoring bill	48	46	18
offering amendments	14	24	14
working in committee	62	68	27
speaking on floor	67	49	25
convincing others in private	76	73	48
Reports no action taken (or planned)	5	12	33

* Since these are selected responses to several questions, percentages do not total 100 per cent.

byists, but rather to adapt and to use their suggestions, fitting them into an ever more sophisticated pattern of information about the problem. We cannot say whether we would have found the same pattern with respect to highway or conservation experts, or some other kind. Our percentages with respect to education are aggregates, and they are only suggestive. However, they are supported by the finding (Chapter 14, pp. 337–338) that legislators in general are willing to accept the information functions of interest groups, and that those members most willing to accept them tend to be the more experienced and effective legislators (Chapter 14, pp. 341 ff.).

THE CONSEQUENCES OF SPECIALIZATION

The comparative success of experts and non-experts in securing passage of bills they sponsor may serve as a crude measure of the importance of specialization as a factor in the legislative process. If it is important, then one would guess that, other things being equal, the expert in any particular subject-matter field would more often see passed the bills he introduces in that field than would the non-expert. But in other fields, where he is not expert, his success would probably be no greater than that of others. Holding the chairmanship of a committee having jurisdiction over the subject-matter area in which he is specially competent should lead to even greater success on the expert's part, so far as concerns bills he sponsors in that area. Finally, if specialization is genuinely significant, the success of a legislator who is an expert but not chairman of the committee having jurisdiction in his field of expertise should compare favorably with that of the legislator who is chairman but not expert in that field.

Methods of recording and reporting legislative proceedings in California, together with certain features of the committee structure there, make it possible to test these hypotheses with respect to that one legislature. Table 9.8 shows the average number of bills passed in the legislator's fields of specialization and in other fields for legislators who were both chairmen and experts, for experts who were not chairmen, for chairmen who were not experts, and for members who were neither chairmen nor experts.[16] The differences between the average numbers of non-specialized bills passed by the four groups are negligible, suggesting that the groups were fairly well matched in overall legislative influence. Thus any difference in ability to influence the passage of bills in their specialties is much more meaningful.

The averages for bills within their respective areas of specialization are quite different, and these differences prove to be statistically

---

[16] The data concern experts in twelve different fields. The selection of the fields, of experts, and of non-experts, and other details are reported in William Buchanan, et al., "The Legislator as Specialist," *Western Political Quarterly* **13**: 636–651 (1960).

significant when experts are compared to non-experts. As Table 9.8 indicates, experts authored an average of about 18 successful bills in their fields if they were chairman, 13 if they were not. Chairmen who were not experts authored only 7 successful bills in the field of their committee jurisdiction during the course of the session, while the control group of legislators who were neither chairmen nor experts authored only 5 such bills, though they were members of the committee that considered them.

Table 9.8: Comparison of authorship (co-authorship) of successful bills in fields of specialization and outside of these fields

Group	Non-Specialized Bills Mean Passed	S.D.*	Specialized Bills Mean Passed	S.D.*
1. Expert chairmen (16)	37.3	43.2	17.6	12.1
2. Non-expert chairmen (8)	29.4	31.2	7.1	3.5
3. Expert non-chairmen (18)	39.4	77.0	13.0	13.7
4. Non-expert non-chairmen (12)	35.5	52.2	4.8	5.1

Significance of differences between:

Groups 1 and 2	< .50	> .99
Groups 1 and 3	< .50	.68
Groups 1 and 4	< .10	> .999
Groups 2 and 3	< .68	> .90
Groups 2 and 4	< .25	.75
Groups 3 and 4	< .50	> .95

* Standard deviation.

One obvious way that an expert could influence those members who considered him to be especially well informed on bills in an area would be through his action in voting on controversial matters. Surprisingly, a tendency for those who considered certain persons to be experts to follow them in voting could not be demonstrated from the roll call votes.[17] Those who named a person as expert were more likely than other members to vote as he did, but no consistent difference could be found between their votes on matters within his field and matters outside it. One must conclude that the expert's success in getting his bills enacted hinges upon his control in the early stages of bill shaping and committee revision and consideration, rather than

[17] The technique is described in Ch. 10 below, p. 231.

upon his influence at the final stage. By this time the issue has been recognized as controversial, differences between members have been structured and sides have been chosen. These observations apply to the California legislature. Though experts appeared in all the chambers studied, it is quite probable that they exercised their influence at different stages of the lawmaking process or upon different subgroups of the legislative group, depending always upon variations from state to state in the procedures of the lawmaking process.

CONCLUSIONS

Specialization—the process by which an individual legislator brings to the group's deliberation the product of his personal competence in a subject-matter field—appears to be a characteristic of the functioning of state legislatures. This should not be surprising in a specialized society with a specialized government were it not for the tradition that the job of a legislature in a system of separated powers is to determine broad policy, to referee group conflicts, to allocate values, to represent citizens in their geographical clumps—and to leave technical, substantive, narrow, specialized affairs to the administrators.

Especially at the state level it appears that legislatures are perennially confronted with decisions where a technical minutia of no obvious significance to the layman may be the precise point on which policy, broad or narrow, turns. The effect on highways of an increase in the truck weight limit, how much paregoric may safely be dispensed without a prescription, the size of a standard prune crate, the limit on balloon payments to second mortgages, the effect on sanitation of fishing in reservoirs, the closing date of squirrel season, the relation of attorney to physician in private adoptions, the impact of oil severance taxes on petroleum production, salaries of beginning teachers versus experienced ones—something more than a coherent political philosophy is required to take a comfortable position on such matters.

As a framework for distributing the legislative load, the committee system permits specialization, but it creates as well as solves problems: How may committees be kept flexible enough to deal with changing conditions; on what basis are chairmen to be selected; on what criteria are committee decisions to be evaluated by the chamber as a whole? In response to the need of members for better guidance than the committee system provides, an informal system of expertise appears to have developed alongside and overlapping it. Trusted legislators who are believed to have a superior knowledge of certain complex subjects achieve recognition as specialists. They guarantee to their fellows the feasibility of some proposals, challenge others. They process and digest raw facts, they acquire information and advice from lobbyists and bureaucrats, they evaluate these incoming messages and pass them on to their colleagues in the form of "do" or "don't" recommendations—recommendations expressed through the authorship of bills and the endorsement implied in co-authorship, through questions asked in hearings, through stands taken in caucus, through amendments offered, through "debate," through remarks made at lunch or over cocktails or in brief conferences on the floor. The experts appear, to some extent at least, to be responsible to their fellows for exercising restraint in their espousal of their personal interests. Thus they help others distinguish "reality" or "technical knowledge" from "values," "preferences," or "political knowledge" in areas unfamiliar to them. In recompense for their efforts they are given the confidence of their fellows—their bills go through, they shape policy—they have power.

How expert are these experts, really? They have a more detailed understanding of legislative problems than do their colleagues, to be sure. But the comparison should be confined to other legislators, rather than to lobbyists or bureau people. The best answer to this question is in terms of the communication function performed by experts: they are sufficiently informed to be able to translate the arcana of a segment of society into terms that permit legislators, who after all are part-time officials, to estimate the relative merits and probable consequences of proposals. They may also, especially in the case of legal experts, help translate the wishes of their fellows into laws that constrain, rather than confuse, the public affected by them.

The limiting factors on the development of genuine expertise are the inability of the legislature to recruit specialists in the fields where they are needed, to retain the ones it develops in view of the district system of elections and high turnover, and to get the ones it has into the right posts in face of partisanship, factionalism, and seniority. The strength of the informal system of expertise lies in its ability to bring whatever talent is at hand to bear on particular problems, recurrent or non-recurrent, and to adapt to the constitutional and political limitations placed upon the legislature.

That legislative bodies manage to bureaucratize to the extent they do is testimony to the demand upon them. Apparently informal specialization meets a felt need, for it appears to be generated by the problems of the particular society being governed, to correspond to the internal requirements of the legislative system, and to affect the output of laws that govern the society.

CHAPTER 10

The bonds of friendship

I T IS GENERALLY ACCEPTED that personal relationships—friendships, antagonisms, alliances, and feuds—between legislators as individuals and as members of informal cliques play some part in the decisions made by legislative bodies. Journalists, lobbyists, inside dopesters about our capitols, political scientists, and legislators themselves subscribe to this belief. The following comments, selected from interviews, attest to the importance legislators attach to these peer relationships:

Those who don't drink and don't socialize with the others are respected, but there is no camaraderie. They are not as effective.

On (my) basic bills I will go to the members and emphasize not so much what (the bill) does as what it means to me politically and personally. I only do it one or two times a year; but I'm very responsive to others if they're not chronic about it.

You can get together with three or four people and have a drink. . . . That's where you get in your most effective licks.

A lot of people will vote for a bill just because a particular man introduced it.

During the series of questions on the "school needs problem" the legislators were asked to rank several possible influences on their own perceptions of this particular educational issue. "Views of friends in the legislature" was one of the items on the list to be ranked. In the composite judgments of the legislators in the four states it was ranked approximately equal to the "recommendations of legislative committees" and the "views of administrative agencies." Though well below "word from people in the district," it was ranked above both the views of party leaders and the views of interest groups and lobbies. About a fourth of the respondents ranked "views of friends in

This chapter drafted by Buchanan

the legislature" above all these other sources as influential in leading them to see the issue of school needs as they saw it.[1]

That legislative friendships play a part in the lawmaking process has received recognition by academic observers as well as participants. The structure and consequences of the ties of legislative friendship have been treated as follows:

> The need to do social favors involves an incessant vigilance for friends who have social graces and power. Their value may be justly estimated— that is, their value in the political exchange—and they must be held in corresponding regard and offered corresponding respect and political favors.[2]
>
> The relationships of a legislator with his fellow legislators do much to moderate the conflicts inherent in the legislative process and to facilitate the adjustments without which the process could not go on. Skill in handling such relationships, moreover, generates influence that is reflected in leader-follower patterns within the chamber.[3]
>
> Expertness in the art of parliamentary persuasion and manipulation, (although) of the same stuff which underlies all interpersonal contacts . . . is hedged by written and unwritten canons of behavior, decorum and practice; and it is informed by observation of the situation and the personalities involved. . . . Once reasonably well developed, this skill makes its possessor an equal among his legislative colleagues in fact as well as in theory.[4]
>
> Since it is within reasonable physical limits for one man to establish some sort of personal contact with 48 or even 95 others, it is possible and fairly common for one (U.S.) senator, or a handful by concerted efforts, to affect materially the proceedings and decisions of the upper chamber.[5]

Compared to the extensive analysis of the effect of constituency, party, and group affiliation on legislative decisions, there have been comparatively few research efforts in this area. Part of the reason no doubt lies in the inaccessibility of data. The pair and clique connections among legislators may be ascertained only by research directed toward this end. For these are not individual characteristics, but rather reciprocal, transactional relationships. A's friendship with B, or his attachment to a clique consisting of C, D, and E, or his habit of looking to F for leadership or regarding with suspicion whatever G advocates—these are phenomena which demand, at a minimum, the description of two persons plus the nature of the relationship between

[1] The role of friendships with respect to the education issue is treated in LeRoy C. Ferguson, *op. cit.*

[2] Herman Finer, *op. cit.*, p. 383.

[3] Truman, *The Governmental Process, op. cit.*, pp. 344–345.

[4] Garland C. Routt, "Interpersonal Relations and the Legislative Process," *Annals of the American Academy of Political and Social Science* 195:129–136 (1938).

[5] Truman, *The Congressional Party, op. cit.*, p. 96.

them. They are role relationships, involving a "self," an "other," and some sort of expectation of behavior relating the two.

Research directed at this problem includes a unique study of the interaction of members on the floor of a senate, based on observations at periodic time intervals. Certain officers were seen to confer with high frequency, an informally recognized clique leader was in contact with a number of members, the minority leader appeared to be a go-between, and, in general, the number of contacts within parties was higher than between parties. "Such contacts," it was concluded, "are ingredients of the social cement which bound divergent factions of the Senate together into a functioning whole."[6]

Utilizing the familiar "sociometric" technique of asking respondents to name persons who stand in a specified relation to them, Samuel C. Patterson was able to delineate several cliques of three to nine members within each party of the Wisconsin lower house. These appeared to be based on geography, tenure, earlier political alliances, seating in the chamber, or some combination of these elements. The cliques held together on certain votes and organizational decisions. Patterson concluded:

Friendship roles are functional in the legislative group. . . . Perception of friendship by members can be related to leadership in the sense that leaders will tend to be perceived as playing friendship roles by more members and non-leaders. . . . The legislator brings to the decision-making process not only his own sociological and psychological make-up and his multiple-group memberships, but also his informal associations within the legislative group. He is part of the informal social structure of the legislative group, and is affected by the norms of these informal groups in his own decision-making behavior.

Individuals who assume the legislative role have diverse backgrounds and diverse social, political and economic experience, and different reference groups are salient for them. The informal friendship structure of the legislature tends to lessen such differences, to mitigate against the development of potential conflicts, to provide channels of communication and understanding among members who share goals, and to facilitate logrolling.[7]

The existence of clique structures may be pursued by a third technique, using as data the recorded votes of legislators. The relationship between two or more members is expressed as the extent of their common agreement on certain legislative issues. Though complex mathematical techniques have been used to analyze the relation of many men linked by common characteristics and common view-

[6] Routt, op. cit., p. 135.

[7] "Patterns of Interpersonal Relations in a State Legislative Group: The Wisconsin Assembly," Public Opinion Quarterly, 23:101–109 (1959).

points on many issues, we can learn a great deal without resorting to them.[8]

LEGISLATORS' EXPRESSION OF FRIENDSHIP CHOICES

The principal source of data for our analysis consists of responses to the question:

Now, who are some of your closest personal friends in the House (Senate) —I mean the members you see most often outside the chamber, at lunch or dinner or parties or social gatherings.

Since some of the conclusions we reach depend upon the way in which the data were gathered, it is important to call attention to certain features about the research technique:

1. It follows the traditional specifications for sociometric inquiry, except that it calls for a perceived relationship (who are your friends?) rather than a "choice" in the strictest sense (whom would you like for friends?).[9]

2. It asks for "extra-curricular" relationships, and not for the names of members with whom the respondent agrees, votes, or interacts on the

[8] Beyle's pioneer exploration of "attribute-cluster blocs" [Herman C. Beyle, *Identification and Analysis of Attribute-Cluster Blocs* (Chicago: University of Chicago Press, 1931)] is analogous in certain respects to the more restrictive analysis of selected roll calls by Guttman scaling. It leads in its ultimate refinement to some form of factor analysis, as Duncan MacRae, Jr., has pointed out [*Dimensions of Congressional Voting* (Berkeley: University of California Press, 1958), p. 207.] Matrices setting out the relationships between persons in a group have been employed in intricate examination of the party system in Congress (Truman, *The Congressional Party*). In this last, Truman notes the comparability of sociometric choice and roll-call agreement (p. 44) and evaluates the techniques from Stuart Rice's *Quantitative Methods in Politics* (New York: Alfred A. Knopf, 1928) to date. High-speed computers have now made previously laborious techniques quite feasible. Among authors of papers (duplicated) which deal with these are MacRae (University of Chicago), Edward E. Cureton (University of Tennessee), Alan B. Wilson (University of California). The technique used later in this chapter—the calculation of percentage agreement between each pair of legislators—has been used as the first step in a cluster analysis of the U.S. Senate. David J. Fitch, *Predicting Votes of Senators of the 83rd Congress, a Comparison of Similarity Analysis and Factor Analysis* (Ph.D. dissertation, University of Illinois, 1958). See also Duncan MacRae, Jr., and Hugh D. Price, "Scale Position and 'Power' in the Senate," *Behavioral Science* 4: 212–218, (July, 1959).

[9] For appraisal of the method and a summary of results, see Ch. 11, "Sociometric Measurement" by Gardner Lindzey and Edgar F. Borgatta in Lindzey, *Handbook of Social Psychology*, and Ch. 17, "Analysis of Sociometric Data," by C. H. Proctor and C. P. Loomis in Marie Jahoda, *et al.*, *Research Methods in Social Relations*, Part 2 (New York: The Dryden Press, 1951).

floor or in committee. Thus we are able to test for coincidences between these two kinds of behavior.

3. Of the 504 members of the four legislatures, 6 per cent were not interviewed, and another 3 per cent were not asked this question. Of the *remainder*—those who were given an opportunity to respond—13 per cent did not.[10] This included 2 per cent who refused to "name names" of other members, 6 per cent who evaded politely by saying they were friendly with "all the members" and 5 per cent who said they "had no friends" in the legislature. The last group included some, at least, who accurately described their status, for no other member named them. Non-respondents of all types pose a problem in analysis of pair relations that is not present in other tabulation—one is never certain whether they might have reciprocated the "choices" other members extended toward them.

4. In asking such a question, some "cutting point" is established on the continuum that reaches from the respondent's most intimate friend to the persons he barely knows by name. Calling for a certain number (say five) when practicable, makes for ease in statistical analysis, but at the expense of accuracy in describing the perceptions of the respondent who sees three, or seven, members in substantially the same relationship to him. Refusal to set any numerical standard would encourage diversity of interpretation of the question. Our decision was to compromise: the question omitted a number, but interviewers were instructed to probe until five or six names were elicited, but to accept more or fewer if the respondent appeared to be referring to some clear standard of his own.

5. The word "friends" and the amplifying remark about dinners and social affairs give us our only information on the kind of relations elicited. We may extend this a little with our knowledge of the sort of arrangements characteristically made between peers in the same organization in our "shop-talking" society. Further inference that the relationship is of the sort suggested by other analysts—leadership, self-conscious manipulation, sociability as an item on the political exchange, coincidence of viewpoint, etc.—remains to be substantiated. What we do have is evidence of a closeness or linkage, a potential communication channel, between certain members that does not occur between others.

Certain hypotheses derived from the statements of legislators and scholars may be tested against the data at hand. The testing process

[10] This is exactly the rate of non-response encountered by Patterson. It was substantially the same in the four states, suggesting a potential ceiling on results from this method.

cannot be a rigorous or conclusive one with the evidence we have, but we may at least determine whether the structure of relationships is of the sort that would promote or would inhibit the function hypothesized:

1. That the social linkages promote compromise and accommodation between legislators of differing persuasions.
2. That they stem from personal force or attractiveness ("skills, "graces," "arts"), which gives certain legislators a wide circle of influence.
3. That they link persons of like characteristics.
4. That they provide cues for decision making.
5. That they are reciprocal, and facilitate the exchange of influence.
6. That they follow the lines of force represented by the formal structure of the body.

Considered as categorical generalizations, it is evident that some of these (1 and 3, 2 and 5, for example) are not entirely compatible. Since they may exist as tendencies, however, it is quite possible for them to exist side by side. Such a generalized relationship as that of "friend" could serve several functions.

The range of individual influence. The basic element in any pattern we may discern is the scope of the average individual's influence through his social relationships. Though interviewers encouraged respondents to give up to six names, some two-thirds of the legislators who listed some friends indicated that they did not have this many. Only one in ten voluntarily went above the scheduled six. The distribution of choices made is given in the dotted histogram in Figure 10.1. We have a check on this in the distribution of choices received, the solid line in Figure 10.1. The larger proportion of the membership received one to four choices, and even allowing for the additional choices that might have been made by the non-respondents would not increase the norm substantially. The maximum number of choices received by any one person in the eight chambers ranged from 8 to 19. We have a check on this too, in the responses to the two questions calling for the same number of nominations of persons recognized as "experts" in some substantive field, and as respected for "following the rules of the game." Here the choices coincided on a few persons in each chamber, and the maxima ranged from 20 to 85 for experts and 11 to 86 for respected members, compared to the range of 8 to 19 for friends. (The higher numbers were in the larger chambers in every case, of course.) All

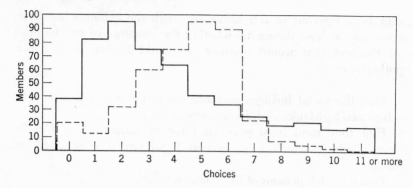

Fig. 10.1. *Distribution of choices made (dotted line) and choices received (solid line). Cumulation for eight chambers.*

these evidences lead to the conclusion that legislative social circles are severely restricted in size, and are subject to an absolute limit rather than one relative to the size of the chamber. The obvious source of such a limit would be the human capacities of time, energy, space, and attention in a busy legislative session—frailties that restrict the average member to perhaps three to five close friends and even the most gregarious to fewer than 20. By contrast, the quality of "leadership," which does not necessarily demand personal contact, but may be exercised by example and embodied in reputation, recognition, and respect even when it is not dressed in the robe of formal office— this quality is virtually unrestricted in scope.

This limitation of a physical nature on the capacity of an individual to make friends is reminiscent of the early administrative concept of "span of control" which sets limits on the number of subordinates an executive can effectively supervise in person.[11] It points up Finer's dictum: "If you wish to waste time on useless people you may do it of course, but it should be recognized as waste."[12] Our numerical limits (which are quite comparable to Patterson's incidentally) are to some degree a function of the way the question was asked; a different technique might set higher and possibly more realistic limits. Making all due allowance for the crudeness of the measure, it seems unlikely that a legislator in any chamber can exert personal influence over a sustained period on more than a dozen members. Rather, it seems

[11] See V. A. Graicunas, "Relationship in Organization," pp. 181–187, in Luther Gulick and L. Urwick, *Papers on the Science of Administration* (New York: Institute of Public Administration, 1937).

[12] Herman Finer, *op. cit.*, p. 383.

likely that whatever influence is exerted is brought to bear within small, interlocking, overlapping, permeable circles.

SOME CORRELATES OF FRIENDSHIP

The contrasting propositions that social relationships will occur among members with similar characteristics and that they promote accommodation between members with different views may be examined by setting up opposing groups and determining the proportion of choice within and across group lines. The tendency to choose persons of like characteristics is called "homophily" and one measure of it is "h," which gauges the extent to which this occurs over and above the amount attributable solely to the relative sizes of the groups.[13]

Tenure, which is in many respects the legislative equivalent of social status, suggests itself as a possible correlate of friendship choice. We might expect to find two tendencies: one for veteran legislators to choose within their own powerful subgroup; the other for freshmen to choose their seniors, using friendship as a channel of upward mobility.[14] Both tendencies are found, as Table 10.1 indicates. Veterans choose overwhelmingly within their own group. Freshmen do so to a considerably lesser extent, indicating that some of their choices are upwardly directed. Where veterans form a tightly knit group, freshmen are thrown back on friendships with their own classmates.

[13] The derivation of h is explained in William L. Nicholls II, "The Measurement of Homogeneity in Pair Relationships," paper read at the New York City chapter, American Statistical Association, April 24, 1956. The measure varies between 0, when exactly the expected number of in-group choices occurs, and 1, when every member of the group chooses another member of it. The formula is based on an expected value: $E = C[(G-1)/(N-1)]$, where G is the number of members in a group, N is the number in the chamber, and C is the number of choices made by members of the group. (Subtracting 1 from each element allows for the fact that no member may choose himself.) Thus E is based on the assumption that choices will be distributed to any group in proportion to the number of persons in it who are available for choice.

The formula for h is: $h = (O-E)/(C-E)$, where O is the observed frequency (the actual number of in-group choices made). If O should be less than E, then $(C-E)$ in the denominator is replaced by E to give minus values for an excess of out-group choices. We do not use this, since all observed frequencies exceed expectation.

[14] Comparable tendencies have been found among college students, Lindzey and Borgatta, *op. cit.,* p. 430.

On the whole it appears that social life in the legislature performs about the same function it does elsewhere, providing companionship and status reassurance. Altogether, only 24 per cent of choices are made across the line that separates freshmen from veteran legislators. In every legislature stratification is more rigid in the large lower house than in the smaller senate. However, in the chamber with decidedly the largest proportion of new members, the Tennessee House (46 per cent), there is comparatively little in-group choice on either side of

Table 10.1: Friendship choices of freshmen versus veteran legislators

State, Chamber	Freshmen as Proportion of Members	Freshman In-Group Choice Tendency, "h"	Veteran In-Group Choice Tendency, "h"
California			
House	16/79*	.32	.81
Senate	5/40	.12	.52
New Jersey			
House	15/58	.34	.63
Senate	4/21	.10	.53
Ohio			
House	32/139	.19	.71
Senate	3/34	.00	.39
Tennessee			
House	46/99	.17	.38
Senate	9/33	.00	.00

* One member of the 80-man Assembly died during interviewing, so the chamber is counted as having only 79 members throughout this report.

the line. Our conclusions about the functional significance of "friendships" in accommodating and integrating new members into the life of the chamber must be limited. Wide variation is apparent: certain chambers have an "open-class" system, while others are rigidly structured, and we do not have enough cases to determine the institutional factors that might account for the differences. In general, since no chambers produced the negative "h" values that would indicate a concerted effort to "adopt" freshmen into existing cliques, we may say that the social life of the legislature does more to reinforce existing differences than to acclimate freshmen to their new surroundings.

Party is a second natural boundary within the legislature, and one with more relevance to the political process than seniority. Table 10.2

gives the "*h*" values for each chamber. Several phenomena are apparent:

1. Both the majority and the minority party tend to choose members of their own group to a large extent, with one exception—the small and stable New Jersey Senate.

2. This tendency is greater among majority than among minority party members, again with one exception—the Ohio Senate.

Table 10.2: Friendship choices of majority vs. minority party members

State, Chamber	Party in Majority	Majority as Proportion of Members	Majority In-Group Choice Tendency, "*h*"	Minority In-Group Choice Tendency, "*h*"
California				
House	Rep.	42/79	.51	.42
Senate	Dem.*	20/40	.41	.37
New Jersey				
House	Rep.	38/58	.74	.65
Senate	Rep.	14/21	.71	.00
Ohio				
House	Rep.	97/139	.73	.63
Senate	Rep.	22/34	.50	.60
Tennessee				
House	Dem.	78/99	.73	.60
Senate	Dem.	27/33	.70	.50

* Though the California Senate was evenly divided, Democrats were counted as the majority party because a Democrat was elected President pro Tempore.

3. In-party friendship is more prevalent in lower than in upper houses.

4. Party exercises a much more regular and consistent effect than tenure, the range of "*h*" values being narrower and the differences between chambers smaller, though the values themselves are consistently high.

These findings, which may be summarized roughly by saying that only 18 per cent of all friendships are formed across party lines, suggest that interpersonal relationships are so structured as to be unlikely to perform one function suggested by several of the writers mentioned above—accommodating different points of view. Instead, they are more likely to *reinforce* team spirit and party competition.

We find here, as with tenure, that the senates have the more permeable party boundaries. The "club-like" atmosphere of the United States Senate and the loyalty of its members to the chamber as an institution have received considerable attention.[15]   The size of the group compared to a House of 400-odd members, has been credited as the important factor.   Similar remarks about the clubbiness of state senators when compared to lower house members occurred in our own interviews.   State senates in the United States average less than half the size of the U.S. Senate, while lower houses in the states average 120 members—not much larger than the U.S. Senate.   The absolute as well as the relative aspect of size should be taken into consideration along with length of service and other factors in any appraisal of the impact of structure on legislative decision making.   Our data support the belief that small size, leading to a more integrated social system within the chamber, may blunt partisanship slightly.[16]

FRIENDSHIPS AMONG LEGISLATIVE LEADERS

The occupants of formal status positions in the legislature might be examined in the same way that party and tenure subgroups were, except that they constitute a rather small group for statistical manipulation.   They have additional significance because of their power: if they constitute a clique this is evidence that an informal channel exists for decision making.   They may easily "consult" and perhaps "concur," to use the Wilsonian phraseology.

In general, legislative leaders are much more likely to be regarded as friends, as Patterson noted.   Formal leaders of house and party receive nearly twice as many choices as do rank-and-file legislators,[17] with committee chairmen falling in between.[18]

[15] Truman: *The Congressional Party, op. cit.,* pp. 96, 314; Donald R. Matthews, "The Folkways of the United States Senate," *op. cit.;* William S. White, *Citadel* (New York: Harper and Brothers, 1957).

[16] In the eight legislatures studied by Malcolm E. Jewell, "Party Voting in American State Legislatures," *op. cit.,* the tendency, though slight and inconsistent, appears to be in the direction of greater party cohesion in the lower houses.

[17] The median for formal leaders is 5.3 choices, for rank and file, 2.6 choices. The former group is composed of presiding officers, party floor leaders and whips, and steering committee chairmen, a segment of the leadership corresponding approximately to Truman's "elective leaders" (*The Congressional Party, op. cit.,* pp. 99–101).

[18] Their median was 3.7 choices. Except that steering committee members were included, they would correspond in function to Truman's "seniority leaders"

Since each leader occupies a specified formal status, and there is a great deal of similarity among the eight chambers in their table of organization (see Appendix 3), we adopt a different technique of analysis. Here we examine the frequency with which a choice (in either direction) occurs between occupants of the same status position in all eight chambers. As representative of chamber leaders we used the elected presiding officer, the majority and the minority floor leaders. To represent chairmen we selected three, the heads of the finance, education, and judiciary committees, which appeared in all chambers, though not always by these names. From the rank and file we chose randomly three members of the majority and three of the minority.[19] By totalling for the eight chambers the number of links between occupants of the same status, and expressing this as a proportion of the number of possible links, we may generalize about the intensity of social interaction between different parts of the typical legislative structure.[20]   The data are given in Table 10.3.

It is apparent that there is a close relationship between the typical presiding officer and his majority leader, and also between these two officers and the chairman of the finance committee. The last, though technically at the second level of legislative organization, generally occupies a critical coordinative position due to his responsibility for the state's budget.

Table 10.4 shows on a similar basis the relationships between the two groups of officials, and within the two groups (the proportions given here being but weighed averages of those in Table 10.3), and

---

in Congress, although in the states they may or may not be chosen on the basis of their seniority.

From the medians alone one might reach the conclusion that persons who were widely chosen as "friend" reached legislative and committee office because of their popularity. That this is probably *not* the case is suggested by the fact that they did not make appreciably more choices than others and that they were no likelier to be chosen to fill vacancies in office that arose after the survey was made. It is safer to conclude that the additional choices they received are due to the prestige and visibility an office gives them.

[19] In two small chambers where almost every majority member held some chairmanship, chairmen of minor committees had to be counted as rank and file.

[20] For example, take the speaker and majority leader. If both responded in a chamber, there are two possible choices, one in each direction. If both responded in all eight chambers, there are 16 possible choices, and the number actually made is taken as a proportion of 16. If one of these officers in any chamber did not respond (whatever his reason) the number of possible choices is reduced to 15, and so on. Where one of the offices did not exist, possible choices are reduced from 16 to 14, since this officer may neither choose nor be chosen.

also the relations between these two official levels and the rank and file, both of the majority and the minority, as represented in our sample.

We find here a high rate of interaction among the chamber officers, and between them and the chairmen, but not among the chairmen

Table 10.3: Proportion of possible choices as "friend" (in either direction) between occupants of the same status position in eight legislative chambers

	Majority Leader	Minority Leader	Chairman Finance	Chairman Education	Chairman Judiciary
Presiding officer	60%	10%	64%	21%	31%
Majority leader	X	22	25	45	30
Minority leader		X	0	0	0
Chairman, Finance			X	27	10
Chairman, Education				X	8

Table 10.4: Proportion of possible choices as "friend" (in either direction) between occupants of three status levels in eight legislative chambers

	Officers	Chairmen	Majority Members	Minority Members
Officers	31%	25%	7%	9%
Chairmen		15	12	5
Majority Members			13*	3*
Minority Members				11*

* These proportions are based on the sample of three members in each house, and are given for purposes of comparison with the rates for officers, rather than as reliable indices of majority-minority interaction.

to the same extent. We find minority members rather isolated except for their contacts with the minority leader, who accounts for most of their friendships in the officer level. (Computed separately, his interaction rate with minority members is 28 per cent, compared to 13 per cent between majority leader and majority members.) These differential rates have been sketched out in Figure 10.2, with the connecting links drawn wider where there is a high proportion of friendship choice. If these social channels bear policy communications, then majority members have the choice of two routes—via the

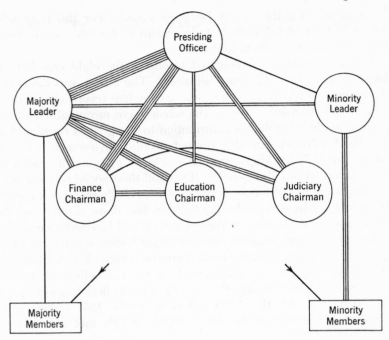

Fig. 10.2. *Level of interaction between legislative officers, chairmen, and members. Based on cumulated friendship choices for eight chambers.*

chairmen or via their party leader—while the minority have only one.[21] In general, the picture confirms the impression we gained from the earlier analysis: that informal, social relationships follow rather closely the formal, official structure of the legislature.

FRIENDSHIPS IN THE DECISION PROCESS

So far we have dealt with the consequences of these social relationships only by inference, concluding from an examination of their pattern and structure that they appear to be well adapted or poorly adapted to perform some function they have been reputed to perform. Now we shall try to appraise the effect of these friendship cliques on the actual lawmaking behavior of legislators and their resultant

[21] In view of the "mediate" character of the legislative party in Congress, Truman attaches considerable importance to the communication functions performed by its leadership structure. See *The Congressional Party, op. cit.*, pp. 130–131.

consequences for the society being governed. For this purpose we use an index which is entirely independent of the interview method—their votes on the bills before them.

This examination was confined to one of the eight chambers, the lower house (Assembly) in California. The choice was dictated by three considerations: (1) there was a complete record of votes available;[22] (2) recorded votes on the whole were meaningful indices of each individual legislator's contribution to the group's decision;[23] and (3) the California Assembly presents a fluid environment where the interpersonal "friendships" studied would be expected to play a part in members' voting decisions.[24]   If we find these social relationships to be influential in California, it does not necessarily mean that they will be influential in every other legislature; but if we do not find them relevant here, it is rather unlikely that they will be effective elsewhere.

To compare our data on "choices" with voting records we need a generalized index of agreement between pairs of legislators on a variety of subjects.   At the same time we may eliminate the non-controversial bills which neither require difficult decisions nor produce disagreements.   Of the 4,250 roll calls in the 1957 session of the California Assembly, 316 were selected which met the following specifications:

1. More than 10 per cent (8 members) were on the losing side.

2. Where successive roll calls were on the same matter, at least 5 per cent (4 members) shifted position.

3. Issues were substantive, not adjournment or housekeeping.

[22] We are indebted to Richard Wright for his initial processing of these roll calls and for his digests of the votes concerned.

[23] The importance of recorded votes varies from one legislature to another. Where the important decisions are made in caucus and followed by straight party-line votes, these record votes would be a poor indication of any member's contribution to the group's decision.   Other practices that diminish the relevance of roll calls as an index of individual positions: automatic unanimous ratification of committee decisions; much time spent in committee of the whole, with heavy reliance on voice votes or standing votes; high rates of absenteeism; "carrying over" roll calls from one bill to the next, thus recording members as for or against who have actually left the chamber.   None of these were common in the California Assembly in 1957.   The record is not, of course, a perfect index of each individual's contribution to the decision.   Nor do we assume that the vote indicates how a member "really" feels about the issue.   For further discussion, see below, pp. 238–239.

[24] Parties were relatively weak, discipline negligible.   Each member "carried" his own bills and lined up support for them by his own efforts.   (See Chapter 3.) In this situation one would expect ad hoc alliances and reciprocal arrangements to be of maximum utility to the individual member.

This procedure avoided judgment on the relative "importance" of the measures, except the judgment of the legislators that is implicit in the time and attention devoted to measures that were contested by amendments, motions for postponement, or reconsideration, and the various parliamentary tactics that make for many votes on contested bills and few on those not considered worth a fight.[25]

For these 316 votes an index of agreement was computed for each pair of legislators, consisting of the number of times they voted the same way (either "aye" or "nay") divided by the number of opportunities for them to agree (i.e., the number of roll calls when neither was absent).[26] The 3,081 pair-indices ranged in value from 27 per cent to 93 per cent, with 59 per cent as the mean.[27]

The influence of friendship. The average of the agreement indices for those pairs of members who mutually chose one another as friends was 77 per cent; for those pairs linked by a uni-directional choice (i.e., A chose B, B chose other members or did not respond) it was 67 per cent; for the pairs who did not choose one another it was 58 per cent. It is apparent that members who are "friends" tend to agree in their votes.

It is apparent from the earlier discussion of structure, however, that social groups conform to party lines, and it is necessary to control for the effect of party. At the same time we shall control for another structural division peculiar to the California Assembly, the division of the membership into "Speaker's Coalition" and "Opposition" factions which occurs in connection with the contest to organize the Assembly. These factions appear to have considerable stability over time. The data, with mutual and uni-directional choice pairs combined for the sake of stability, are given in Table 10.5. It will be noted that the differences are small but they are consistently in the expected direction,

[25] See William H. Riker, "A Method for Determining the Significance of Roll Calls in Voting Bodies," in John C. Wahlke and Heinz Eulau, Edits., *Legislative Behavior* (Glencoe, Ill.: The Free Press, 1959), pp. 377–384.

[26] This is quite comparable to the index Truman used for studying Congress, except that we used all contested roll calls, regardless of level of party cohesion. See Truman, *The Congressional Party, op. cit.,* pp. 320 ff.

[27] Each pair index was based on 316 comparisons and a percentaging operation made possible by a program written by Pete Tenney for the IBM 704 computer at the University of California. For advice we are indebted to J. O. Neuhaus of the Computer Center and Rod Frederickson of the Survey Research Center. The theoretical limits are 0, for no agreement, and 100 per cent, for perfect agreement. That the mean was 59 per cent, not 50 per cent, reflects the characteristic one-sidedness of legislative votes. Had more controversial, or less controversial, bills been included the mean would have been different, so it is also a function of the cut-off point.

Table 10.5: Relation of friendship choice to party voting in the California assembly (party and faction controlled)

	(1) Voting Agreement Between Pairs of "Friends"		(2) Voting Agreement Between All Other Pairs		(3) Difference: Col. 1 less Col. 2	(4) Weighted Mean of Cols. 1 and 2	
	Av.*	N†	Av.‡	N†		Av.	N†
Members of same party *and* faction							
1. Coalition Democrat	66.8	49	63.7	251	3.1		
2. Opposition Democrat	72.5	15	64.5	51	8.0		
3. Coalition Republican	75.8	55	69.1	246	6.7		
4. Opposition Republican	72.1	25	68.7	108	3.4		
5. Total (weighted)	71.8	144	66.7	656	5.1	67.6	800
Members of same party *not* same faction							
6. Democrats	68.8	17	60.5	283	8.3		
7. Republicans	65.0	21	61.6	407	3.4		
8. Total (weighted)	66.7	38	61.2	690	5.5	61.7	728
Members of same faction *not* same party							
9. Coalition	59.1	30	53.6	595	5.5		
10. Opposition	59.6	19	58.6	185	1.0		
11. Total (weighted)	59.3	49	54.8	780	4.5	55.0	829
Members *not* of same party *or* faction							
12. All combinations	56.9	20	51.2	704	5.7	51.4	724
13. Column totals	67.4	251	58.2	2830	9.2	58.9	3081

Recapitulation (weighted averages)	Av.	N
Within party (Col. 4: line 5 + line 8)	64.7	1528
Between parties (Col. 4: line 11 + line 12)	53.3	1553
Difference (influence of party)	11.4	
Within faction (Col. 4: line 5 + line 11)	61.3	1629
Between factions (Col. 4: line 8 + line 12)	56.4	1452
Difference (influence of faction)	4.9	
Among pairs of friends (Col. 1, line 13)	67.4	251
Among other pairs (Col. 2: line 13)	58.2	2380
Difference (influence of friendship)	9.2	

* Average of the percentage agreement between every pair of members choosing one another, either mutually or in one direction only.

† The number of mutual and uni-directional pair choices in the category.

‡ Average of the percentage agreement between all other pairs in the category; i.e., all members of the category who mutually ignored one another in the "friend" choices, taken as pairs.

233

whether the linkages lie within or cut across party and factional divisions.

At the bottom of the table we subtract out to get a rough approximation of the relative influence of party, faction, and friendship, and we find that in percentage terms the social relationship has an effect comparable to the two political relationships. However, the numbers involved must be considered in evaluating their relative impact on the total process. If social relationships may be thought of as falling along a continuum from cordiality at one end to hostility or indifference at the other, our sociometric question (for reasons treated earlier) cuts the continuum near the "cordial" end. While friendship choices cover only a small number of pairs, a common party affiliation is shared by half the pairs. Thus a given level of voting cohesion resulting from common party has a greater impact on the total process than one resulting from friendships. Party cohesion also has a systematic effect, while friendship alliances may cancel each other out.

CONCLUSIONS

Returning to the hypotheses (p. 221 above) we may conclude:

1. There is evidence that where social relationships occur between members of different persuasions (as indexed by party and faction) they do result in some accommodation, and perhaps compromise (as indexed by a common stand on the generality of issues). But the structure of social relations is such that it rarely links unlike legislators, so the effect on total output is almost negligible.

2. Whatever the personal qualities behind legislative friendships may be, they give their possessors only a limited range of consistent influence, due to physical limitations on interaction with more than about 20 persons. But qualities of "leadership" based instead on reputation may embrace a much larger segment of the body.

3. On all the criteria we examined (and presumably others as well) social contacts occur more frequently between members with similar characteristics.

4. The higher agreement among mutual than among unidirectional pairs suggests that exchange of influence does take place.

5. Structural characteristics very strongly influence the location of social linkages. In general, these linkages reinforce the stratification of the chamber horizontally by tenure and officer status, vertically by party and/or faction.

To sum up, we may say that the political roles of a legislator, as a member of a party, an officer of the chamber, or chairman of a committee, are more compelling than his social role as a friend, a good fellow, and a dinner companion. The latter does have an effect in the one chamber where we were able to test it, but on the whole it was not large. So there are occasions when interpersonal social relations may account for otherwise inexplicable behavior on the part of certain members. But we must be careful, when we observe that X and Y appear to be bolting their party because of their cordiality toward Z on the other side of the aisle, that we do not overlook the fact that A, B, C, and D at the same moment may be hewing to the party line because of their friendship ties with each other and with E, their floor leader.

PART FOUR

The roles of legislators in the legislative process

How and why a "bill" becomes a "law" has long fascinated the political imagination. Formally, the legislative process may seem as routine and standardized as production on an assembly line. Every schoolboy learns about the many "steps" in the long road from the introduction of a bill to its final passage. Travel along this road requires a great deal of skill, acumen, and patience. Few ever master it completely. It makes the legislative process as intricate and complex a series of procedures as can be found in democratic politics.

There are, of course, several ways in which one can study what is often rightly called the "legislative maze." Much understanding can come from case studies which follow in detail the progress of a bill from its conception in the minds of single persons or a group to its passage or defeat.[1] It is difficult to convey a sense of the labyrinthine and often idiosyncratic working-outs of the legislative process by methods other than the case study. Yet, by definition, a case is "only" a case. It may well be that, as in the judicial process, legislators are guided by precedents, and in the formal sense of legislative process they certainly are. But alternate strategies and tactics in different

This introduction drafted by Eulau.

[1] The best available case study is still Stephen K. Bailey's *Congress Makes a Law* (New York: Columbia University Press, 1950). Based on documentary materials, formal and informal interviews, and direct observation, this study of "The Story behind the Employment Act of 1946" uses the case method for what it should be used: not as proof for but as a source of hypotheses about the legislative process.

stages of the process, often in response to a multitude of unexpected and ever changing circumstances, make codification of case findings inordinately difficult.

It has been found convenient and economical, therefore, to seek understanding of the legislative process by concentration on its "showdown" phase. When the "ayes" and "nayes" are counted, no legislator can consistently avoid the final choice which he is expected to make. Whether, in fact, the roll call is the most important step in the legislative process—an implicit assumption, certainly, in many roll-call studies—is a matter of argument. By the time a bill comes up for final action, it has been scrutinized, debated, and amended in committee or on the floor, if not compromised in the cloakroom. The final vote may conceal more than it reveals. It is, undoubtedly, *the* authoritative decision. And if one is interested in the impact of authoritative decisions on the life of a community, careful analysis of roll-call votes can convey a great deal of the legislature's place in the political system. Whether a bill finds unanimous support, is reluctantly accepted, or acrimoniously contested, just as the alignment of legislators along partisan, rural-urban, and other lines of cleavage, can tell us much about the functioning of the political system as a whole. Much important work has been done along these lines.[2]

There is a solid body of opinion, shared by independent observers and legislators themselves alike, that the committee phase is the crucial focus of the legislative process. Committees are "miniature legislatures," subject to all the influences characteristically found in the larger body, and they are of enormous importance in determining the course of legislative activity and the fate of legislation. Moreover, because they are "microcosms," committee actions are easier to observe and analyze than the actions of a whole legislature. As Ralph K. Huitt has pointed out, Congressional standing committees are promising research sites for at least four reasons: the greater frequency of interaction among committee members, their exposure to common stimuli, manageable size, and continuous life.[3] But precisely because these conditions do not prevail in the legislature as a whole, the study of committees does not really allow generalization about the legislative process as such, but only about one phase, if a critical one, of the total process.

[2] The many roll-call studies, pioneered by A. Lawrence Lowell and Stuart Rice, are summarized in Norman Meller, *op. cit.*

[3] Ralph K. Huitt, "The Congressional Committee: A Case Study," *American Political Science Review* 48:340–365 (1954).

Roll-call analysis has not only been employed to discover the articulation of the legislative process in the political system, but also as a tool for the study of the behavior of individual legislators. There is much to be said in favor of studying the legislative process in terms of legislative behavior. But whether the roll-call vote is the best unit of analysis is another matter. The assumption is that what "really counts" in legislative behavior is the ultimate and public commitment symbolized by the vote. If a legislator consistently votes with the majority of his party colleagues on a great many issues, it may be legitimately inferred that he is "partisan" in behavior not only in the roll-call stage of the process, but also in earlier phases. But the roll-call vote cannot be taken as proof of this. The fact that a legislator is a loyal party man on roll calls does not preclude his being an important agent of pressure groups in introducing bills, his making determined efforts to change a bill in committee to make it more advantageous to the interests of his district, or his attempting to bring about compromises in line with his own personal principles or convictions. Behaviors such as these, so characteristic of the legislative process, cannot be discovered by way of roll-call analysis. A legislator's conduct in the final voting provides little basis for inferences about his behavior at other stages of the legislative process.[4]

The alternative would seem to be direct observation of behavior in earlier stages of the legislative process, during committee hearings or floor debates. But, again, this research procedure is limited to a particular phase of the process, and the size of most legislative bodies makes direct observation, for all practical purposes, impossible. Moreover, given the often confidential character of legislative politics, it is not feasible to follow a legislator's daily rounds in the many situations where his behavior is private. Direct observational studies have, therefore, been rarely attempted.[5] Furthermore, it is doubtful whether observation of behavior is a particularly fruitful method. Behavior as such is meaningless. A five-year old girl hacking away

---

[4] The effort to make inferences from roll-call votes to individual legislative behavior is most evident in the work of those who subject roll-call votes to scaling techniques. See Duncan MacRae, Jr., *Dimensions of Congressional Voting, op. cit.;* or George M. Belknap, "A Method for Analyzing Legislative Behavior," *Midwest Journal of Political Science* 2:377–402 (1958); and Charles D. Farris, "A Method of Determining Ideological Groupings in the Congress," *Journal of Politics* 20:303–338 (1958).

[5] But see the lonely attempt (and failure) by Garland C. Routt, "Inter-personal Relationships and the Legislative Process," *op. cit.,* for further discussion of the possible uses of observation.

on a typewriter is not a secretary. It is not what she does which is the meaningful datum in the little girl's case, but rather what we ourselves, as observers, expect her to do. We know that the girl is not a secretary but a child, and we expect her to give up typing soon and do something else. We expect her to play. It is this expectation which defines the girl's behavior and makes it meaningful. It is the girl's role of "child" which prevents us from thinking of her as a secretary. So it is with legislators: it is the roles they take in what they do which give their activities social meaning. It is possible to infer a man's role from his conduct. But the important point is that his role has been defined prior to his behavior in the performance of this role.

It is for this reason that identification and description of the roles which a legislator takes in the course of his participation in the legislative process seems to be a promising research strategy. If one is interested in the legislative process as a whole as it emerges from the behavior of legislators, the roles taken by legislators in various phases of the process are particularly fit targets of investigation precisely because they can be assumed to reflect different aspects of the process For different phases involve different expectations from different people and require legislators to take different, though situationally appropriate, roles. For instance, partisan roles may be quite suitable in floor debate where the legislator's party stand becomes a matter of public record, but they may be quite dysfunctional in committee discussions where the roles of expert or specialist are required to solve a technical problem in taxation. The many opportunities existing in the legislative process for informal, private negotiations are likely to require roles particularly suited to the legislature's "brokerage function." Similarly, roles taken in response to the expectations of pressure groups may be more appropriate in the committee stage of legislative activity than in the final stage of voting when the watchful eyes of local constituents may require the legislator to take a role congenial to his district—the public image in terms of which he is likely to be judged on election day.

However, it would be too simple to assume that roles invariably "correspond" to various phases of the legislative process. Some, of course, can only be taken at a certain stage. But others are more pervasive. For instance, the legislator who is predominantly oriented toward his district may take an appropriate role, if it is not attenuated by other roles, in all phases of the process: he will introduce a piece of legislation favorable to his district, defend it in committee and on the floor, mobilize pressures in its support, bargain with fellow legislators in behalf of his bill, refuse to have it changed, and go down to defeat on the final roll call.

Each phase of the legislative process is, of course, not a sharply differentiated time unit. The legislative process is a developmental pattern, but it is not a simple sequence of steps or stages as the formal model would suggest. Criss-crossing each sequence of events are "processes in depth," vertical relations between legislators themselves and between legislators and their clienteles of functional significance for the articulation of the political system. For this reason, we can think of the legislative process not simply as a step-by-step procedure to translate a bill into law, but as a series of processes directed toward the institutionalization, crystallization, and resolution of conflicts. These processes cut across the developmental patterns, but they are difficult to investigate and analyze because they have latent rather than manifest consequences for the political system. Ultimately these processes form a structure of role relationships which constitutes a network. We shall deal with this in Part Five. Of interest here are the roles which legislators take in connection with those processes which involve the institutionalization, clarification, and resolution of conflicts. But as these processes are not necessarily sequential, the same role may be mobilized for different purposes in the course of legislative activity, regardless of whether it involves lawmaking as such, or other functions like communications or services. For instance, what we shall call the role of facilitator serves the dual function of institutionalizing the conflicts of pressure groups as well as resolving them. But the main point to be made is that the incidence of roles, whether geared to the institutionalization, crystallization, or resolution of conflicts, can tell us just what kinds of processes are more characteristic of one legislative system than another.

The roles which legislators take are especially useful units of analysis because they call attention to the interactional nature of the legislative process, the vertical rather than horizontal patterns of conflict institutionalization and resolution. However "role" may be defined theoretically or operationally (the formulations are many and diverse), the concept sensitizes the investigator to the inter-relatedness and interdependence of political actors.[6] It is through the taking of roles that people are linked in their mutual relations, and role-taking, we shall suggest in Part Five, makes possible the coupling of different "outside" groups, organizations, or agencies with the legislature in a single behavioral system.

[6] Our own definitions and usages have been spelled out in Chapter 1, above, pp. 7–17. See also the references cited there.

But the first task of research is to discover those "significant others" in the legislator's environment who, through their expectations, define his role, and towards whom he, in turn, entertains expectations as well. The most immediately "significant others" in a legislator's environment are, of course, other legislators. We have, in Chapters 7 to 10, reviewed and analyzed some of the roles which legislators take by virtue of the interactions with other legislators—roles which stem from their occupying formal positions of leadership in the legislature, roles which stem from the specialized division of legislative labor, and roles which are rooted in the existence of informal friendship relations among them. We have also described and analyzed those "rules of the game" which serve as behavioral norms in defining the legislature as a "task group," and which provide sanctions for legislative role performance in general. Other roles "internal," so to speak, to the legislature will be treated in Chapters 11 and 12. They "correspond" to functions which are at the core of the legislative process—the articulation of popular needs and demands, the coordination and integration of conflicting interests, the formulation of public policies, and the execution of the legislative business as such. They are roles taken less in response to the expectations of identifiable others, but in the performance of those functions for which the legislature has been set up in the first place. These functions have changed through time, of course, and they may be given different emphases through time, depending on the legislature's place in the political system. They are, in some respects, legislators' responses to community-wide, consensual expectations concerning the legislature as an institutionalized group.

The legislative process in democratic political systems symbolizes, in many respects, the increasing importance of popular participation in the councils of government. Legislators are *par excellence* the main links between government and people. As representatives they may approach their legislative tasks in characteristic styles which may or may not be conducive to the performance of their lawmaking and other functions. How the alternatives of mandate and trusteeship give rise to appropriate representational roles, and how these roles are defined by legislators, will be treated in Chapter 12.

Equally important as "significant others" are those individuals and groups more or less directly involved in legislative processes, especially legislators' constituents, party leaders and party activists, pressure groups and lobbyists, and executive officials and agencies. They constitute the legislator's many and diverse "clienteles." They are, we shall point out in Part Five, the major sources of legislative "input" and the major recipients of legislative "output." Though not themselves legislators, they are actors in the legislative system and central participants in the legislative process. These clienteles maintain expectations concerning the legislator's behavior, expectations which he cannot escape without risk to the very position he occupies as a legislator. It is in terms of expectations coming from these clienteles that the legislator orients himself to his tasks in the legislative process. And clientele expectations, just as the legislator's own role orientations vis-à-vis his clienteles, reflect the vertical patterns in the legislative process which so often belie the flat, horizontal, and formal model of what is called "parliamentary procedure." For reasons explained elsewhere (Chapter 1, p. 13), the legislator's role orientations vis-à-vis executive agencies, and especially the governor, were omitted from this research. Chapters 13 through 15 describe and appraise legislative role orientations vis-à-vis the other three major clientele groupings in the legislator's environment.

A distinction can be made, then, between legislative roles focussed on the legislative process from a substantive point of view, the wherefrom or what-for of legislative action, and representational roles focussed on the legislator's style as an actor in the legislative process. How purposive role orientations, clientele role orientations, and representational role orientations are related to each other in the making of a role system will be treated in Part Five. Our task here is to suggest why roles or role orientations are not only useful conceptual tools for investigation of legislative processes, but also why they are critical in legislative behavior.

Behavior, we suggested earlier, including legislative behavior, is meaningful socially only when it occurs in the performance of appropriate roles. This does not mean that knowing a man's role allows us to predict all or even most of his behavior in every concrete situation. In the legislator's case, the roles he can take are many, and the situations in which one or more roles become activated are numerous. But roles or role orientations are at least relatively stable points of reference in terms of which a legislator will conduct himself and give meaning, both for himself and others, to his behavior. Even if, at this stage of research development, we cannot in every case link roles or role orientations to behavior, the fact that legislators do articulate what they think they should do by virtue of their relations among themselves and between themselves and clienteles suggests that roles are effective indicators of behavioral possibilities.

We can assume, therefore, that while legislators' verbalizations in response to interview questions are only behavior "in the the second degree," their "definitions of the legislative situation" and the role orientations derived from these definitions do probably constitute long-range premises underlying legislative behavior in typical instances. One cannot assume otherwise: to assume that verbal behavior prior to action is invariably "false" would doom all human behavior to irrationality. It is much more plausible to assume that men will behave in terms of the roles they are expected to take and which, of course, they redefine for themselves, and to seek explanations for deviations from expected behavior patterns after they have occurred.

CHAPTER 11

The legislator as decision maker: purposive roles

As a structure of power, the legislature is functionally interdependent with other structures of power in the political system—the executive establishment, the political parties, the gamut of interest groups, and the aggregate of constituencies, to name only the most significant. Of course, these relations are subject to numerous constitutional requirements and limitations, but within the parameters of the formal institutional context they are forever subject to changing conditions. If the executive branch of the government is dominant, the legislature may primarily function as an agency ratifying executive decisions or attempting to check executive usurpation of power. If the political parties are effective instruments of policy making, the legislature may chiefly function as a disciplined organization of partisans following and supporting the majority or minority leaderships. If the constituencies effectively assert themselves, the legislature may function mainly as a body carrying out the popular mandate. If pressure groups permeate the political system and project their interests into the public sphere, the legislature may be more of an institution compromising between and integrating conflicting group demands.

In a system as complex as the political, comparative institutional analysis is difficult. For the institutional variables are gross, and their isolation for the purpose of analysis is not easy. Moreover, the power situation in the political system is never as clear-cut as ideal-type constructions of the relationships among institutions suggest. Em-

This chapter drafted by Eulau.

245

pirically, mixed situations are more likely to occur than not. Constituencies may vie with interest groups for the attention of the legislature. The parties may be effective fronts for special interests. The executive may be the voice of grassroots opinion. For these reasons gross institutional analysis may not permit the degree of refinement necessary to identify those legislative functions which are correlates of the power situation, and to relate them to observable legislative behavior.

POLITICAL POWER STRUCTURE AND LEGISLATIVE ROLE ORIENTATIONS

Analysis of legislative role orientations is therefore one way of studying the power position and the functions of the legislature in different political systems. Role orientations are legislators' own expectations of the kind of behavior they ought to exhibit in the performance of their duties. They may be considered as providing the premises in terms of which legislators make decisions.[1]

Since "lawmaking" is accepted as the central function of American state legislatures, participation in the making of decisions is not only expected of the legislator but is authorized and legitimized by his occupancy of the official position. But "participation in lawmaking or decision making" is hardly a satisfactory characterization of the role of legislator. Rather it is role orientations which are the specifications of the legislative role, without which the central concept of "legislator" does not, and probably cannot, have much analytical meaning.

His role orientations are probably not unrelated to the legislator's perception of the power pattern of a political system and the kinds of functions which the legislature is called on to perform. For instance, in a party-disciplined legislature the individual legislator is unlikely to find much room for independence or inventiveness; the purely routine aspects of his job probably loom large in his legislative role orientations. In a legislature particularly exposed to the pulls and pressures of interest groups, role orientations are likely to derive from the need to arbitrate, compromise, and integrate group conflicts. In a legislature subservient to the whims and wishes of the electorate, the spokesman function is likely to be accentuated in legislative role orientations. In a legislature which enjoys relatively great independence from the executive, legislative role orientations may stress the creative, policy-

---

[1] For an interpretation of role as setting "premises" in decision making, see Herbert A. Simon, *Models of Man* (New York: John Wiley and Sons, 1957), p. 201.

making aspects of the job.   Moreover, legislative role orientations need not occur in pristine singularity.   Two and three, or even more, orientations may be held by a legislator.

The complexity of institutionally-derived legislative role orientations becomes even more apparent if we place them in a historical perspective.   They may be, and probably are, patterned by past as well as current configurations in the power structure of the political system.   For as institutions, legislatures are phenomena in time, with memories of their own going beyond the limitations of time.   These memories are transmitted by legislators themselves from generation to generation, consciously or unconsciously shaping the perceptions of the present.   The past may thus continue to serve as a model for contemporary role orientations.

A legislature is the product of a long and slow growth over centuries, with a veritable maze of rules, procedures, privileges, duties, etiquettes, rituals, informal understandings and arrangements.   Every phase of the lawmaking process—from the introduction of bills through their deliberation in committee and debate on the floor to the final vote—has gradually become circumscribed by appropriate strategies and tactics.   The legislator was always expected to master the rules of parliamentary procedure and be familiar with available strategies.   Hence the legislator could traditionally orient himself to the job of lawmaking in terms of the parliamentary rules and routines, rather than in terms of legislative functions as they may be shaped by the power situation in the political system.   Parliamentary ritual rather than parliamentary goals would absorb his attention.   One may call this orientation to the legislative role that of the *Ritualist.*

A second orientation is particularly deeply rooted in American political history.   It was probably generated by the conflict between the British Crown, acting through the agency of the appointed governor, and the colonial legislatures.   In the course of this conflict the legislature came to be viewed as the instrument through which colonial interests could be defended against what were perceived as royal encroachments on colonial rights.   It does not matter, in this connection, that the colonists differed among themselves with regard to the proper object of legislative activity—whether the defense of property rights or the natural rights of man were the goals of colonial claims.   The crucial point is that the legislature and legislators were expected to be advocates or defenders of popular demands.   Wilfred E. Binkley has aptly described the role orientation of the colonial legislator—what we shall call the role orientation of *Tribune:* "The assemblyman, chosen by popular election as a representative of his neighborhood . . . set forth to the provincial capital, commissioned, as he believed, to fight the people's battle against the governor."[2]

A third major orientation seems to have originated at a later stage of colonial-executive relations, the stage when the legislature asserted itself as an institution capable of performing independent, policy-making functions. As Alfred De Grazia has summarized this later development, "The Colonial legislatures already conceived of themselves as possessed of a positive legislative capacity removed from the ancient English idea of Parliament as an agency for wresting concessions from the Crown. They had learned well the lessons of the seventeenth century revolutions as well as those to be obtained from the Bill of Rights. Legislatures, they had come to realize, could govern."[3] Once the colonial legislature was expected to be an instrument of governance, rather than an instrument of obstruction, a role orientation more appropriate to the legislature's new function was likely to emerge. We shall call this the orientation of *Inventor*. The legislator was now expected to be sensitive to public issues, discover potential solutions and explore alternatives, both with regard to means as well as ends. The problems of government were deemed soluble by way of rational deliberation and cogent argument in debate, partly because the issues were relatively simple, not requiring technical, expert knowledge; partly because the range of governmental activity was seen as very limited.

Just as the role orientation of inventor derived from the conception of the legislature as a creative, policy-making institution, a fourth orientation—we shall call it that of *Broker*—developed in response to the rise of interest groups and the increasing number of demands made on legislatures by pressure groups. The legislature became, in the course of the nineteenth century, a major integrating force in the pluralism of American political, social, and economic life. This development had been foreshadowed by the struggle of interests in the Constitutional Convention, in early Congresses and state legislatures, and had suggested to the authors of *The Federalist* the balancing function of legislative bodies. The role orientation of broker was probably implicit in Hamilton's notion of the disinterested representative,[4] and though everyday politics seemed to confirm this conception of the

[2] Wilfred E. Binkley, *President and Congress* (New York: Alfred A. Knopf, 1947), p. 4.

[3] Alfred De Grazia, *Public and Republic, Political Representation in America* (New York: Alfred A. Knopf, 1951), p. 70.

[4] *The Federalist*, No. XXXV.

legislator's role as a working principle, it was not articulated in political theory until fairly recently.

This review of legislative role orientations, whether theoretically derived from the legislature's place in the power structure of the political system or historically reconstructed, has suggested four major types—ritualist, tribune, inventor, and broker. There may be others. For example, journalistic accounts suggest many legislators have an orientation which might be called *opportunist*—the legislator who holds the office without really "taking" the associated role, who accepts the bare minimum of expectations, such as voting on roll calls and attending committee meetings or sessions as a passive participant, but who mainly uses the legislative office, or "plays *at*" the legislative role while concealing that he is really playing other, essentially non-legislative roles.[5]

CONTEMPORARY PERCEPTIONS OF THE PURPOSIVE ROLE

Our primary concern here is with how legislators themselves might formulate or define the legislative role as it relates to the lawmaking function in the contemporary setting. We therefore asked our respondents an open-ended question:

How would you describe the job of being a legislator—what are the most important things you should do here?

It was found, in analyzing the interview protocols, that responses to the succeeding question also contained a good deal of the respondents' relevant perceptions:

Are there any important *differences* between what *you* think this job is and the way *your constituents* see it?   (What are they?)

Responses to these questions yielded the typology of purposive role orientations, as well as others to be discussed later. The way responses were coded and combined to select the members representing role types in the cross tabulations is explained elsewhere (Appendix 1.1, pp. 465–467, below). At this point we must explicate in greater detail the various purposive role orientations which have been theoretically and historically suggested.

Ritualist.   So numerous and complex are the formal rules and procedures of the legislative process that their mastery may appear as

[5] Our data do not permit any analysis of such a role orientation (opportunist). It might, however, be profitably investigated by future research.

the essence of the legislator's role. In the knowledge of parliamentary rules, Finer has pointed out, the legislator "will find all the permissions and prohibitions affecting his right to intervene in discussion. He will discover weapons to defeat his rivals and opportunities to advance his own cause. . . . By adroit use of these rules he may exact concessions by threatening to obstruct his opponents' path with amendments. . . . He will also be able to obtain concessions by the intrinsic merits of his argument, his rhetoric."[6]

Although the rules and procedures of the legislative process are designed to regulate conflict about goals, so overwhelming may be the routine of the process, so consuming its daily impact, that the member's preoccupation with and involvement in legislative maneuvering can become an end in itself rather than remain a means to an end. The legislator then relates himself to the task of lawmaking in terms of the parliamentary routine alone, and he may fail to rationalize his actions by any purpose or goal other than performance of the legislative routine. He is content to list for himself the various tasks which he feels he is expected to perform as a cog in the legislative wheel. In the role orientation of ritualist, therefore, the legislator is particularly sensitive to the flow of legislative business, the intricacies of the legislative maze and the bureaucratic organization of the legislature. The following response is more explicit than most, but its very fullness illustrates the ritualist orientation:

The majority of work is done in committees and then tested by vote on the floor. A legislator should be interested in all legislation. The Speaker has tremendous responsibility as does every committee chairman to determine arbitrarily from a procedural standpoint which bills get precedence and which ones lag. The reference committee and the rules committee in the House determine when a bill moves and to what committee. We're supposed to give out every bill, but that's never enforced as there isn't enough time. Obviously important bills go first and minor ones subsequently. Personal bills of no general interest to those outside of a specific locale get precedence or they are lost in the shuffle. Less than one in twenty bills is partisan. While there are some major conflicts in political philosophy, everyone wants to improve the law, to amend and clarify and repeal the unworkable.

Apparently the minimum expectation of the ritualist is that "the legislature in the last analysis involves voting." Voting is seen as crucial because "you must understand that some of your colleagues and friends may disagree, and this can be cannon fodder for present and future opponents." Through voting, another ritualist suggested, "you can 'backstop the catcher'—stop bills that hurt your county or the

---

[6] Herman Finer, *op. cit.*, p. 383.

state." Indeed, as a ritualist the legislator may really be opposed to lawmaking. As one respondent reported, "an old gentleman once suggested to me that all we should do is pass the budget and go home. He didn't like laws. I agree with him in some respects." The ritualist does not see the budget process as a creative series of acts full of policy implications, but as part of the minimum routine. In this routine the "killing" of bills is seen as more appropriate behavior than enacting needed legislation. At most, lawmaking is seen as a patching-up job if it cannot be helped. The ritualist does not stick his neck out:

Of course, we must review situations, and old situations must be corrected. For old laws have bugs in them. But this way we never get into too much trouble, though we may make mistakes. But then we meet again in two years.

However, the routines of legislative work may be seen as helpful in the performance of some other role, like that of representative:

Primarily, I should acquaint myself with parliamentary procedures and rules and regulations, and finding out where I may avail myself of the necessary information to enable myself to represent my constituency to the highest degree.

But this functional linkage of the ritualist role and another role is rarely articulated. The ritualist emphasizes some particular aspect of parliamentary procedure without concern for consequences beyond those of the lawmaking process as such. One may feel that "the work itself is 90 per cent research—determining the facts." Another may say that it is important to attend sessions faithfully and analyze bills before voting. Watching bills may be a passion:

The most important thing, which isn't done enough, is to watch the type of bills that pass and to watch the language of bills. A legislator will serve the highest purpose if he watches every bill to be passed. For when it comes to the floor, this is the last opportunity there is to scrutinize the bill before it will become the law. Too many members will look at a bill but not see certain features that should not be included. I can't stress how important I think it is for every legislator to read and understand every bill before he votes on it.

The concern here is not with the policy content of a bill, but with its technical perfection.

Committee work looms large in the ritualist's orientation. If the legislator cannot hope to understand all the bills, as the perfectionist would have him, he is at least expected to know the bills that come to the committees of which he is a member. The ritualist is impressed by the committee, for it is here that much important work is done. "Voting on the floor is far less important than anything else," a ritualist pointed out; "I guess I would say that committee work is maybe the most important thing. You ought to know the bills that come before your committee." Committee work is central, another respondent said, because "it's in committee that bills are won. You can't understand a bill from floor discussion. It's work on committees and subcommittees I follow religiously."

Knowing one's way around the legislature and various state departments is another facet of the ritualist's orientation: "If you get requests for information, you can't stumble around. I have seen people with experience of four terms not knowing, old-timers not knowing departments." Finally, the ritualist seems to be particularly sensitive to the need of maintaining good relations with his colleagues:

> People don't realize that one of the most important jobs here in the legislature is that of making friends—especially on the other side of the aisle. You really have to be friendly and cultivate friends in the legislature, because the more friends you have, the easier it is to get your bills passed.

The ritualist, then, tends to stress the mechanisms of the legislative process and the mechanics of the legislator's job. As an orientation it appears, of course, quite frequently with some other orientation. But it may also appear alone. As a role, the ritualist orientation is highly functional to the maintenance of the legislature as a system and its internal cohesion. But a legislature composed only of ritualists would not be a viable system. In combination with other role orientations, the ritualist's definition of the legislator's job brings a good deal of rationality into the legislative process.

Tribune. In approaching his lawmaking tasks, the legislator may primarily perceive himself as the discoverer, reflector, advocate, or defender of popular needs and wants. It is not relevant, in this connection, whether he sees himself as being guided in his decisions by a mandate from the people he feels he represents, or by his own principles and judgment of what the legislative situation requires him to do.[7] Initially the role orientation of the tribune may have been negative—in the sense that the legislator's primary task was to prevent executive encroachment on what he deemed to be the people's rights.

---

[7] What, from the standpoint of the legislator as a *lawmaker*, appears as the orientation of tribune, may become, from another standpoint, his orientation towards the area he thinks he represents. This "areal" orientation may, of course, be independently analyzed in terms of different conceptions as well. This will be done in Chapter 13.

But the contemporary orientation of tribune includes neutral and positive aspects as well. The tribune may express one or more of three conceptions of his role. He may perceive himself as the discoverer or connoisseur of popular needs, as the defender of popular interests, or as the advocate of popular demands. Different as these conceptions undoubtedly are, their generic focus of attention is invariably the popular environment within which the legislator relates himself to his lawmaking task.

At the very minimum, therefore, the tribune considers it an essential part of his legislative role to discover or know the feelings of the people, their needs, hopes, and desires. He sees is as part of his role to stay close to popular problems, to make himself available to people, to sound out and understand public opinions, if not on each issue, at least on major issues. This does not mean that the tribune must commit himself to popular views, though he may do so. If commitment is thought necessary, it may be counter to the legislator's conviction, as appears in this plaintive note:

It's the same old story of any public official. Once he was expected to furnish leadership, now he's expected to find out what the masses want and go along with them. Legislators now must feel out public opinion and commit themselves to it.

The process implicit in this attitudinally neutral interpretation of the tribune role may be quite conscious:

Well, most important is to keep in close touch with your constituents and find out what they want. That's your primary job. I'm right where they can get hold of me. That's why I come back—because I offer myself to the people. Other guys were farmers and you could never find them, or they were retired and spent most of their time in Florida.

But the process of knowing people's problems may be unconscious, resulting, it is alleged, from the basic similarity in the experiences of the legislator and his people:

Basically, you represent the thinking of people who have gone through what you have gone through, and who are what you are. You vote according to that. In other words, if you come from a suburb, you reflect the thinking of people in the suburbs; if you are of depressed people, you reflect that. You represent the sum total of your background.

This neutral conception of the tribune may be elaborated in terms of a negative view of the legislative process. The tribune then sees himself not only as a mirror of popular experiences, but he thinks of himself as the guardian and defender of people's interests, either as they are communicated to him, or as he senses them.   He considers himself a watchdog of the people's welfare, their liberties and rights:

A legislator has an obligation to protect people's rights; every time you pass a law you take some away from them.   The main job is to take away as few as possible.   The legislature is a poor man's court, especially the House.   Here you can protect him against banks, corporations, insurance companies, and so on.

With me the only reason is to improve things for the ordinary man and the underdog.   Big business and rich people have attorneys, accountants and loopholes in the laws, but damn few people are interested in the underdog and minorities.

This negative conception of the legislative process expresses the strongly populist component of the legislator's role which has been traditionally at the core of the tribune orientation.   But the tribune may have a positive conception which also derives from the populist tradition.   He will indicate not only sensitivity to the people's concerns and interests, but also responsiveness to popular demands and commitment to act on behalf of the people.   The tribune appears then, not as a defender, but as a spokesman and advocate.   He "must do the most good for the most people to benefit the people"; he must be "an agent of the people's will"; or he "must represent the welfare of the community as he sees it."   Here the populist conception is reinforced by a strong dose of utilitarian ideology.

The tribune orientation is one having considerable functional significance in a democratic political system.   Although one may take a cynical view of this role, tribunes may be major communication links between the legislature and a more or less clearly differentiated popular environment.   From the point of view of democratic politics, tribunes are the "consciences," so to speak, of the legislature.   In so far as their commitment to the role is genuine, they serve an important function in the legislative process.

Inventor.   Once the technological development of society has reached a scale where expert knowledge rather than lay enlightenment has become a condition of effective government, where the scope of governmental activities has increased so enormously that general understanding is not sufficient as a source of decision making, the formulation of public policy tends to be either a function of the executive, with its corps of expert civil servants, or the product of policy suggestions from well-informed, interested groups outside the formal governmental apparatus.   Under these conditions, the individual legislator tends to become less the creator and more the register of public policy.   Finer pointed out that "in modern legislatures everywhere, the large

majority of members does little more than vote, . . . only a few discuss, and . . . only a very small minority thinks effectively."[8]   Sophisticated state legislators are aware of this.   As one of them put it:

> We're the policy-making body for the state government, and basically we
> should give leadership necessary to meet the problems the state faces.   In
> practice it comes from the executive branch.

In spite of the transformation in the distribution of power between
executive and legislature, contemporary legislators may continue to
perceive themselves as initiators of policy.   The type we shall call
inventor still sees as his primary task the formulation of the general
welfare or of particular policies.   He directs his attention to what he
considers to be the creative aspects of the legislative job.   As one inventor said, the legislator "should try to work for something, rather
than just work against things.   Also, he should try and seek out
problems and use some imagination to solve them."   The inventor is
interested in solving the current problems of his state—public welfare,
education, highway construction, the rehabilitation of the mentally
ill, and so on.   His self-image is that of the thoughtful and far-sighted
legislator, a man of "vision, fortitude, and imagination."   The analogy
may be made with the role of the doctor:

> One has to have certain qualities to be a good legislator.   Like a doctor,
> his job is to cure ills.   This state has many economic and social problems,
> and a legislator with lots of background can grasp these problems and intro-
> duce legislation to better them.   He can cure just like a doctor can.

But amelioration is not enough.   As another inventor put it, the
legislator "should be in front of things."   Fair employment practices,
increased workman's compensation, unemployment insurance and
minimum wages, regulatory and tax problems were mentioned as the
kind of legislation in which inventive effort is called for.   That
creative endeavor along these lines is still considered possible, despite

---

[8] Finer, op. cit., p. 379.   In a study of the origin of bills introduced in the
Ohio Senate in 1929 and 1939, Harvey Walker found that only about one-fourth
of the bills were "member bills," while the remainder were "lobby bills" or
"public bills."   Of the bills enacted into law, only 8 per cent in 1929 and 16 per
cent in 1939 were member bills.   Fifty-two per cent of the bills passed in 1929
were "public bills," as were 45 per cent in 1939.   See Harvey Walker, "Well
Springs of Our Laws," National Municipal Review 28:689–693 (1939).   The type
of legislator Garceau and Silverman have called "policy oriented" bears interesting
resemblances to our "inventors."   Similarly, their "Non-generalizers" resemble in
some ways our "ritualists."   See Oliver Garceau and Corinne Silverman, "A
Pressure Group and the Pressured: A Case Report," American Political Science
Review 48:672–691 (1954).

the severe limitations under which the legislature must work as a result of the concentration of expertness in the administrative service
and executive dominance in policy making, appears in this response:

> My primary interest is in legislation as such. I'm amazed and delighted
> with the freedom I have as an individual to present my own views in terms
> of what I believe is to the public good.

Is the inventor orientation wholly outdated and unrealistic in view
of contemporary requirements for expertise and executive power in
policy making? It may well be, and we shall return to this question
later on. But it may be that, precisely because modern society depends so much on governmental action, because its technical problems
are so perplexing and the pressure of a great variety of special group
interests is so urgent, a legislature's effective performance will depend
on the presence of members whose orientation to their legislative role
is in terms of social inventiveness. These, it seems, are the legislators
who, by virtue of a broad view of the lawmaking task, can give meaning to the whole legislative business.

Broker. The idea that the legislature referees the struggle of
interest groups, constituencies, and executive agencies, and that in this
struggle the legislator plays the role of broker, is probably the dominant theme in studies of the legislative process.[9] But the legislature's
function in the context of group pressures and conflicts involves more
than the simple notion of brokerage might suggest. As Latham has
pointed out:

> . . . in these adjustments of group interests, the legislature does not
> play the inert part of a cash register, ringing up the additions and with-
> drawals of strength, a mindless balance pointing and marking the weight
> and distribution of power among the contending groups. For legislatures
> are groups also and show a sense of identity and consciousness of kind that
> unofficial groups must regard if they are to represent their members
> effectively.[10]

It would seem, therefore, that because of this feeling of identity the
broker role is not only to compromise and arbitrate, but also to coordinate and integrate conflicting interests and demands.[11]

[9] The conception of the legislative process as a struggle among groups in conflict is the dominant theoretical assumption in such works as David B. Truman,
The Governmental Process, op. cit.; Stephen K. Bailey, *Congress Makes a Law,*
op. cit.; or Bertram M. Gross, *op. cit.* But these works are primarily interested
in the group character of political conflict rather than its impact on legislators'
roles or behavior. For further discussion, see Chapter 14.

[10] Earl Latham, *op. cit.,* p. 37.

[11] The broker role focus is internal, directed towards integration and coordination *within* the legislature, rather than towards the outside, towards compromise

The broker may define his role as a legislator in a variety of ways. He may, perhaps naively, interpret it as involving a rather automatic operation which requires him to maintain, within the context of opposing pressures, an "overall picture," best gained by "looking at all sides of a question." The broker may say that "you must not give undue consideration to one group over another"; or, "you must solve the state's problems without being unduly influenced by the feelings of persons who are committed and paid"; or, "you should not make up your mind until you hear both sides, keep an open mind, listen to both sides of any issue, draw your conclusion, and vote accordingly."

The balancing function may be seen largely in terms of personal attributes—"you should be unbiased and tolerant, see both sides, be broadminded"; or:

> Most important is to be honest, not only in your dealings, but also intellectually. That's a prime requisite for a politician or statesman. "Politician" has a bad connotation. It's important to see the other man's point of view. Even if you feel that what you want is the absolute best, give a bit and get the next best thing.

Some legislators interpret the broker role in judicial terms:

> My job is quasi-judicial. I try to solve differences of opinion within the county to bring out in advance a solution in the best interests of the constituency.

> The job is similar to that of a judge. One is faced with a problem. In order to solve this problem, he must have the various facts involved. He must weigh these facts, and make a fair decision.

In this conception of the broker role not only is the fiction perpetuated that all sides must be heard, but the assumption is made that all sides are of equal importance and must be given equal weight. The public interest is expected to emerge from the judicious weighing of all sides, and the decision is assumed to be "just" because it has been judiciously weighed. This elaboration of the broker role reflects a rather undifferentiated view of the structure of the group struggle in politics.

The more sophisticated broker does not see his clienteles as undifferentiated, but is sensitive to the fact that he is exposed to the conflict of group interests whose reconciliation and integration does not simply require impartiality on his part, but an appraisal of opposed claims and demands in terms of their moral worth, the power potential of the groups in combat, and the political consequences for his own position. The following comments illustrate these considerations:

among pressure groups. See Chapter 14 concerning role orientations toward pressure groups.

There are always some groups who see things differently and don't agree with the way you vote. Union people want us to vote one way and get mad if we don't. The doctors and insurance people act as a group and want you to vote certain ways, and they all want favors from you.

It's important to watch out that pressure isn't exerted on you from a very vocal minority group where it's against the general public interest. The majority of mail is almost all by special interest groups, while those who support you you don't hear from. Take this dog bill. You hear from all those damn humane groups, but the doctors, whom the bill would benefit, don't even vote. You've to get used to getting somebody mad at you. The more times you are right, the more enemies you'll make.

It's difficult to use the term "constituents" to give a complete picture. Generally speaking I feel I have to find out what's best for the whole county, but particular groups have particular interests that sometimes interfere with the common good. Most constituents feel I'm *their* representative rather than a common representative, and, as a result, I must weigh the conflicting desires of various groups to determine what will benefit the most people in my district.

Others holding the broker orientation differentiate between competing demands in terms of the geographical units with which they may more or less identify themselves. The dichotomy of local district and the state is a major focus of attention associated with the broker role, and it is seen as a source of continuing conflict:[12]

It is my duty and job to introduce laws of interest to my constituents which, of course, are not detrimental to the state. Then I have to make decisions on prospective laws on the basis of how they affect my constituents and the state as well as the nation.

Every legislator is faced with two facts. First, he should be interested in legislation as it affects his district. Sometimes, and I have had it happen, I have had interests at home which were more or less selfish, and there were conflicts. The legislator must look towards problems facing the state and his district and should be introducing and supporting measures for the welfare of both.

These comments suggest that the broker legislator, in Friedrich's words, "is a specialist in diagnosing group opinion in his constituency, and knows just how far to go in order to strike a balance between the pressure from various special groups and the resistance (passive pressure) from the group as a whole."[13]

PURPOSIVE ROLE ORIENTATIONS IN THE FOUR STATES

Table 11.1 presents the state-by-state distribution of legislative role orientations in the purposive-role set, regardless of whether they occur in combination or isolation. These afford a basis for speculation about

[12] See Chapter 13 for a more detailed discussion of this problem.
[13] Carl J. Friedrich, *op. cit.*, p. 319.

the character of the respective legislatures and their position vis-à-vis other structures of power in the four state political systems. The most obvious aspect of the distribution is that in all four states the orientation of ritualist appears more frequently than any other. This is not surprising. It is an orientation which is "built in," so to speak, the role of legislator. It may be more salient for some legislators than others, but concern with the procedures and routines is unavoidable. The continuing routines and rituals of the legislative business occupy an important part of legislators' attention. Evidently, the legislative process itself does not allow escape. It serves as a

Table 11.1: Distribution of purposive role orientations*

Role Orientation	N.J. N = 79	Ohio N = 162	Calif. N = 113	Tenn. N = 120
Ritualist	70%	67%	58%	72%
Tribune	63	40	55	58
Inventor	49	33	36	30
Broker	33	48	27	15

* Percentages total more than 100 since respondents could hold more than one orientation.

potent parameter for role taking. Not only does the orientation of ritualist provide a minimum definition of the legislative role, but there also seems to exist considerable consensus on its centrality in legislative behavior.

The tribune orientation as a component of the legislative role is not only old, but, as Table 11.1 suggests, it seems to find continued expression in modern state legislatures. In all states except Ohio, the tribune orientation was mentioned more frequently than any other if we set aside that of the ritualist.

Of the various orientations, we suggested earlier, that of inventor is probably the least realistic under modern conditions. In three states —California, Ohio, and Tennessee—only about a third of the legislators were prepared to entertain it. But in New Jersey almost one half of the membership mentioned the inventor orientation as a part of their purposive-role set. This result may well reflect the unique constellation in the power structure of the New Jersey political system in 1957. Unlike in the other three states, party control of the legislative and executive branches was divided—the governorship being held by a Democrat, the two legislative houses being controlled by the Republicans. In a situation where power is divided between the parties in a strong two-party state, the legislature is likely to be relatively more important as a policy-initiating body than when the governor belongs to the same party as the legislative majority and is the acknowledged center of policy making. This need not mean, of course, that the legislature is, in effect, successful as a policy-making body. As we shall see later on, New Jersey inventors did not feel particularly effective in this role. But the distribution would seem to support the hypothesis that role orientations may be partly shaped by the contemporary configuration in the power structure of the political system.

Perhaps the most surprising finding of Table 11.1 is the relative scarcity with which, except in Ohio, the broker orientation appears. An interpretation of these results is difficult. Particularly in California, where the parties have traditionally played a minor and the interest groups a major part in the legislative process, we should have expected more frequent mention of the broker orientation. The fact that it did not appear more frequently in New Jersey is less surprising. In the relatively strict two-party system of that state the individual legislator has apparently less leeway as an individual to perform the compromising-integrating functions associated with the broker role.

In general, then, the data on purposive-role orientations seem to support the assumption that orientations are shaped by both historic conceptions of the functions of the legislature and by contemporary circumstances in the governmental power structure. In all four states, the traditional institutional requirements of the legislative office, centered in the legislative mechanisms, make the ritualist conception an appropriate orientation in the task of lawmaking. In three states, the tribune orientation is held widely enough to suggest that the state legislature continues to be an important link between the electorate and the government. The inventor orientation seems to be relatively unimportant, except in New Jersey where legislature and executive were controlled by different parties and where the legislature may attempt to compete with the governor in the making of state policy. The broker orientation, probably the most realistic but also perhaps the most difficult to take under modern conditions, was less widely accepted than one might have expected, except in Ohio where economic geography would seem to have made it more salient and central in the total legislative role.

PURPOSIVE ROLE SEGMENTALIZATION

Of course, any one legislator may hold more than one purposive-role orientation. The more orientations he holds, the more may his legislative role be said to be segmentalized. Different role orientations, in combination, constitute a role set. The purposive-role set, then, can at its fullest consist of four orientations: ritualist-tribune-inventor-broker. Or it may consist of only three, two, or one orientations. The average number of role orientations in the purposive-role set is about two in all four states—2.26 in New Jersey, 1.90 in Ohio, and 1.80 in both California and Tennessee. The characteristic content of role sets—i.e., the particular combination of orientations—however, is probably more important than the amount of role segmentalization. Presumably, each possible combination of orientations gives the purposive role a typical organization, a structured content which calls for appropriate behavior in the execution of the total role. Two questions may be asked: (1) Do certain combinations of role orientation, or certain forms of segmentalization, occur more frequently than others? and (2) are there significant differences among the four states in the distribution of role sets?

Because the ritualist orientation is so pervasive in all four states, it seemed feasible to omit it from those role sets where it appeared. In other words, it can be assumed that where the ritualist orientation occurs in conjunction with other orientations, it is less salient, and that its importance can be appraised best if it is treated in isolation from the other orientations. Moreover, this procedure has the advantage of reducing the number of role sets from a potential fifteen to a more manageable eight. Table 11.2 presents the combinations of purposive-role orientations with the ritualist orientation omitted from the segmentalized role sets.

Table 11.2: Distribution of purposive-role sets

Role Sets	N.J. $N = 78$	Ohio $N = 160$	Calif. $N = 112$	Tenn. $N = 115$
Tribune-inventor-broker	12%	2%	5%	3%
Tribune-inventor	17	11	13	15
Tribune-broker	9	7	9	5
Inventor-broker	6	12	4	4
Multiple roles: subtotal	44%	32%	31%	27%
Tribune only	27%	20%	29%	37%
Inventor only	15	9	14	10
Broker only	6	27	8	3
Ritualist only	8	12	18	23
Singular roles: subtotal	56%	68%	69%	73%
	100%	100%	100%	100%

As Table 11.2 shows, the triple role set of tribune-inventor-broker is, with the exception of New Jersey, relatively scarce. On the other hand, the dual set of tribune-inventor appears quite frequently in all four states. Moreover, the tribune orientation is more often associated with that of inventor than with that of broker, or the latter with that of inventor, except in Ohio where the inventor-broker set appears more frequently than in the other states.

Among the singular roles, the tribune orientation now outranks the ritualist, followed by the inventor and broker orientations, in that order, except in Ohio where the broker orientation is held more frequently than elsewhere. Moreover, it now appears that California and Tennessee have more pure ritualists than the other two states. This tends to confirm the earlier findings that in these little-disciplined systems the individual legislator must rely more on his own skill to get his bills through the legislative maze than in the more disciplined legislatures of New Jersey and Ohio where the parties usually come to his support and possibly carry the bill for him.

In general, the pattern of role orientations revealed in Table 11.1 is maintained when purposive-role orientations are combined in role sets. In Ohio, the dominance of the broker orientation is reflected not only in the continued strength of the singular broker role, but also in the frequency of the inventor-broker set. In Tennessee, on the other hand, the most traditional roles—ritualist and tribune— are taken somewhat more frequently than anywhere else. Finally, as Table 11.2 shows, segmented or multiple roles are taken most frequently in New Jersey, followed by Ohio and California with almost equal proportions.

What do these data tell us about the character of the legislatures in the four states, and particularly about the position of the legislature in the larger political system? Any answer to this question can, of course, only be very tentative. Yet, comparison of purposive-role orientations suggests a somewhat greater complexity in the total political situation in New Jersey than in the other states. New Jersey legislators apparently feel a need to hold more orientations towards their legislative office than legislators elsewhere. This may perhaps be due to the much smaller size of the New Jersey houses. In larger chambers, greater specialization may be possible and yet meet the requirements of the legislative process. In Tennessee, on the other hand, the institutional setting seems to make fewer demands on legislators and allow as many as 73 per cent to settle for a single orientation. But the differences between Tennessee, Ohio, and California are so small in this respect that any definite conclusion about the relationship between the complexity of the political system and legislative role orientations cannot be drawn.

Secondly, the data suggest that the Ohio political system, at least as it was in 1957 under Republican control, does not require legislators to be especially concerned with innovating policies or responsiveness to popular demands—at least not as much as legislators in the other states. The relatively small number of tribunes and inventors in Ohio suggests that, in the absence of the kinds of commitments engendered by these roles, legislators may be in a more favorable position to perform the balancing-integrating function which is so often considered the main goal of lawmaking activity in the modern legislature.

ROLE TAKERS' SENSE OF LEGISLATIVE EFFICACY

The possibility that historical conceptions of what is appropriate legislative behavior may be at variance with actual requirements of the contemporary position of the legislature in the structure of power would seem to create certain problems for effective role taking. The legislator may see himself as an inventor even though the opportunity for independent policy making has slipped from the legislature's domain. He may see himself as tribune even though, in actuality, he may be subject to strict party discipline which prevents him from behaving in line with his self-image. He may think of himself as broker, balancing conflicting interests, though in reality his job calls only for the performance of the legislative routine.

It is, of course, difficult to determine just what roles or combination of orientations are functional or not. A role functional from the point of view of the legislator's private objectives may be dysfunctional from the point of view of institutional goals. Moreover, each orientation refers to different aspects of the legislative business. In all of these respects, the various roles that can be taken are really non-comparable and their relative effectiveness difficult to judge, for they refer to different functions.

Direct appraisal of the effectiveness of roles would require observations of actual behavior. For instance, one could find out whether the tribune's mail is particularly heavy, as it should be if his role is adequate; one could compare the kinds of bills introduced by the inventor with those of other legislators; or one could determine whether the broker is especially inclined to offer amendments to bills as a means of expediting compromises. Our resources did not allow us to collect these kinds of behavioral data, and it is questionable, indeed, whether the collection of such data is the most economical way to evaluate the appropriateness of legislative roles. But indirect tests and inferential judgments of the functionality of legislative roles can be made by appraising them in terms of the legislator's sense of efficacy, his own feeling of whether or not he is effective in the legislative process.

On the basis of the theoretical and historical elaborations of the different purposive-role orientations presented earlier, we might hypothesize that, under modern conditions, the broker will most likely show a relatively high sense of legislative efficacy compared with other role takers. On the other hand, we could assume that those taking the ritualist role would be least likely to evince a sense of legislative efficacy precisely because the behavior enjoined by this role is probably very unimaginative. We could also expect that the tribunes would feel more efficacious than the inventors, though less so than the brokers. For we could assume that the grass-roots atmosphere of state legislative politics is especially congenial to the tribune, while the inventor would feel frustrated by a political situation in which policy making has, in fact, come to be mainly the concern of the executive.

Table 11.3: Sense of legislative efficacy of singular role takers

Role Types	N.J.	Ohio	Calif.	Tenn.
Broker	+60	+42	+22	+25
Tribune	+47	+25	−10	+ 4
Inventor	0	+21	−26	+ 9
Ritualist	0	−15	0	0

Table 11.3 presents the index scores[14] on the legislative efficacy scale of those legislators who held only one role orientation. In general the data seem to support our hypotheses. Regardless of state, brokers score consistently higher on the efficacy index than the other role takers. The tribunes, except in Tennessee where the difference is very small, score higher than the inventors, but lower than the brokers. And the inventors score higher than the ritualists, but lower than the tribunes. In other words, those roles which, from a theoretical and historical standpoint, were assumed to be more functional to contemporary legislative behavior and the legislative process,

[14] See Appendix 2.2 for an explanation of the construction of this index.

are associated with a higher sense of legislative efficacy than the roles which seem to be less viable under modern conditions.

In the case of the multiple role takers, as Table 11.4 shows, the pattern is less clear, but by no means arbitrary. In the first place,

Table 11.4: Sense of legislative efficacy of multiple role takers

Role Types	N.J.	Ohio	Calif.	Tenn.
Inventor-broker	+40	+26	+60	−20
Tribune-broker	+15	−20	0	+33
Tribune-inventor	+ 7	+13	− 7	−29
Tribune-inventor-broker	+45	0	+34	−33

again with the exception of Tennessee, inventor-brokers score considerably higher on the index of efficacy than do tribune-brokers. This may come as a surprise. For, from the rank order of roles noted in Table 11.3, one might expect that the tribune-broker would score higher on the index than the inventor-broker. How, then, explain the result? It suggests the possibility of conflict between orientations. There is nothing in the broker and inventor roles that would make for conflict when they are combined in a new set. This cannot be said of the tribune-broker combination. By definition, the broker orientation means that the legislator holding it is prepared to make compromises; yet, again by definition, the tribune orientation enjoins him from doing just that: the tribune is expected to take an intransigent stand on behalf of "the people" against the government and the interests. We can assume, therefore, that the tribune-broker experiences conflict resulting from his diverse orientations, and this conflict is likely to affect his feelings of legislative efficacy. In the case of the inventor-broker set, on the other hand, the broker component has ample room to effect a relatively high sense of efficacy, even though it is combined with the low-efficacious inventor role. There is no opportunity for sense of legislative efficacy to be impaired by role-conflict as is the case with the tribune-broker set.

Secondly, it may be noted that in three states—the exception now being Ohio—the tribune-brokers score higher than the tribune-inventors. Assuming that the small differences in these three cases are meaningful, one plausible explanation might be that in the tribune-broker set, even though it involves role conflict, the broker component is more potent in generating a sense of efficacy than is the tribune component in the tribune-inventor set. This interpretation would be in line with the original findings that of all the purposive roles that of broker is by far the most salient under modern conditions and generates the highest sense of legislative efficacy.

CONCLUSION

The roles which the legislator may take as a decision maker—ritualist, tribune, inventor, and broker—both define and refine the purposive role as such. They may be indicators of political conditions in the contemporary structure of power or residues of past power patterns. Some, therefore, may be more functional under modern conditions than others. In all states, regardless of differences in the distributions of these roles, the broker role is accompanied by a higher sense of efficacy on the legislator's part than the others. Not surprisingly, the role of inventor is probably more frustrating than the others in systems where policy initiative has largely passed to the executive. But it is the ritualist role which is least accompanied by a sense of legislative efficacy. If taken alone, its political neutrality seems to prevent the legislator from feeling as effective as the other types in terms of policy, in terms of satisfying what he may conceive to be his mandate, or in terms of balancing conflicting interests. But as the ritualist appears, more often than not, in combination with some other orientation, and the number of "pure" ritualists is relatively small, it does not have seriously dysfunctional consequences for the legislature. Indeed, it is an orientation at the very core of the lawmaking role.

The orientations we have reviewed here are indicative of what the legislator sees as goals of his legislative behavior. They do not necessarily refer to the critical point in the legislative process where the "ayes" and "nays" are counted, nor tell us how he will decide to pursue whatever goals he seeks. Roles appropriate in this respect we shall discuss in the next chapter.

CHAPTER 12

The legislator as representative: representational roles

THE PROBLEM OF REPRESENTATION is central to all discussions of the functions of legislatures or the behavior of legislators. For it is through the process of representation, presumably, that legislatures are empowered to act for the whole body politic and legitimized. And because, by virtue of representation, they participate in legislation, the represented accept legislative decisions as authoritative. It would seem, therefore, that legislation and representation are closely related.[1] And if they are related, the functional relevance of representation to legislative behavior needs to be articulated.

But agreement about the meaning of the term "representation" hardly goes beyond a general consensus regarding the context within which it is appropriately used. The history of political theory is studded with definitions of representation, usually embedded in ideological assumptions and postulates which cannot serve the uses of empirical research without conceptual clarification.[2]

Many familiar formulations treat representation as something valuable in itself, and seek to discover or specify its "nature" or "essence." Functional theory, on the other hand, deals with representation from the point of view of the political system as a whole or its component

This chapter drafted by Eulau.

[1] For an excellent historical analysis of the relationship between legislation and representation, see Benjamin Akzin, "The Concept of Legislation," *Iowa Law Review* 21:713–750 (1936).

[2] For a convenient and comprehensive summary of definitions, see John A. Fairlie, "The Nature of Political Representation," *op. cit.* An effort at conceptual clarification is made by Alfred De Grazia, *op. cit.* See also above, Chapter 1, pp. 24–25.

units. Finer, for instance, has suggested that "responsibility is the chief and wider aim, and representativeness merely a convenient means to attain this. . . . The desire for responsible government is paramount; people not merely wish to represent their views, but actually to make and unmake governments."[3] But failure to test functional propositions by empirical research leaves the problems raised by theory in the realm of conjecture rather than reliable knowledge. Once relevant concepts are clarified, a functional formulation of representation may open up areas of research which, in turn, may contribute to theoretical cumulation.

A FUNCTIONAL VIEW OF REPRESENTATION

The relationship between the representative and the represented is at the core of representational theory. The term "representation" directs attention, first of all, to the attitudes, expectations, and behaviors of the represented—to their acceptance of representatives' decisions as legitimate and authoritative for themselves. More particularly, representation concerns not the mere fact that they do accept such decisions, but rather the reasons they have for doing so, their rationalizations of the legitimacy and authority of the decisions made by their representatives.

Sometimes the adjective "representative" denotes nothing more than the publicly approved process by which representatives are chosen—as when a distinction is made between a "representative body" (meaning a group of men elected by specific modes of popular election) and a "non-representative body" (meaning a group of men selected by royal or executive appointment, entailed inheritance, or some other non-electoral process). Such usage implies that citizen's attitudes and expectations include, and may extend no farther than, the belief that representatives' decisions must be accepted as legitimate and authoritative if the representatives have been selected in the approved manner. In other words, elected officials are called "representatives primarily because of the way they have been chosen. Even in a looser usage an appointed commission may be approvingly called a body of "representative" citizens, or may be attacked as "unrepresentative," depending on whether its members might conceivably have been chosen had they been subject to election rather than appointment; and their views will correspondingly be accorded or denied a measure of authority and legitimacy.

But the appropriate process of selecting public decision makers

[3] Herman Finer, *op. cit.*, p. 219.

has never been the really fundamental question for theories of representation. Behind every proposal for altering the method of selecting officials is some assumption, at least, about the effect of such changes on what decision makers or decision-making institutions do, and how they do it. Proposals for reform must assume or show that the proposed change will bring about that what representatives decide and the way they reach decisions is more nearly in accord with expectations and demands of the represented than has been the case under the system to be reformed. The various defenses of existing systems of selection which postulate "virtual representation" have in common some shading of the belief that the process of selection is not of major significance in determining what representatives do or how they do it, or that decisions made by representatives can be brought in harmony with public expectations, without altering whatever process of selection is being defended by the advocacy of virtual representation.

The relationship between the process of selection of legislators and the modes and consequences of legislative behavior, or the relationship between public expectations and legislative decisions, offer wide and fertile fields for empirical research. Our purpose here, however, is less ambitious than a full-scale investigation of such relationships. It is to eliminate those particular ambiguities in the concept of representation which concern the actions or behavior of representatives, by use of the concept of "role," and to demonstrate the utility of this approach for further research relevant to the theory of representation.

A distinction between focus and style of representation. A convenient and useful starting point in theoretical clarification is Edmund Burke's theory of representation. For, in following his classic argument, later theorists have literally accepted Burke's formulation and ignored its contextual basis and polemical bias. Burke ingeniously combined two notions which, for analytical purposes, should be kept distinct. In effect, he combined a conception of the focus of representation with a conception of the style of representation. "Parliament," Burke said in a famous passage,

. . . is not a congress of ambassadors from different and hostile interests; which interests each must maintain, as an agent and advocate, against other agents and advocates; but Parliament is a deliberative assembly of one nation, with one interest, that of the whole; where, not local purposes, not local prejudices ought to guide but the general good, resulting from the general reason of the whole.[4]

[4] Edmund Burke, "Speech to the Electors of Bristol" (1774), Works, II, 12.

The sentence indicates that Burke postulated two possible foci of representation: local, necessarily hostile interests, on the one hand; and a national interest, on the other hand. He rejected the former as an improper and advocated the latter as the proper focus of the representative's role. But in doing so, he also linked these foci of representation with particular representational styles. If the legislature is concerned with only one interest, that of the whole, and not with compromise among diverse interests, it follows that the representative cannot and must not be bound by instructions, from whatever source, but must be guided by what Burke called "his unbiased opinion, his mature judgment, his enlightened conscience." Moreover, Burke buttressed his argument by emphasizing the deliberative function of the legislature, presumably in contrast to its representational function. Yet if one rejects his notion of the legislature as only a deliberative body whose representational focus is the whole rather than its constituent parts, the logic of Burke's formulation is no longer necessary or relevant.

Today, many "publics" constitute significant foci of orientation for the representative as he approaches his legislative task. Under the conditions of a plural political and social order, these foci of representation may be other than geographical interests, be they electoral districts or the larger commonwealth. The modern representative faces similar choices concerning the style of his representational role not only vis-à-vis his constituency or state and nation, but vis-à-vis other clienteles, notably political parties, pressure groups, and administrative agencies. From an analytical point of view— though not, of course, from an empirical standpoint—the style of the representative's role is neutral as far as these different foci of representation are concerned. Regardless of his focus of representation— a geographical unit, a party, a pressure group, or an administrative organization—he is not committed to take either the role of free agent, following his own convictions, or the role of delegate, bound by instructions. In other words, Burke's linkage of a particular areal focus of representation with a particular representational style constitutes only a special case in a generic series of empirically possible relationships between different foci of representation and appropriate styles of representation.

Of course, different foci of representation need not be mutually exclusive. They may occur simultaneously, and appropriate role orientations may be held simultaneously. For instance, a party may be so strong in a district that, in the representative's mind, the interests of district and party are identical. Or a pressure group may have such pervasive influence (as, for example, the Farm Bureau in a predominantly agricultural constituency, or the AFL–CIO in a predominantly working class district) that, again, the interests of district and pressure group become identified. Moreover, it is possible that different focal role orientations are activated seriatim as circumstances require. In particular, one may assume that on matters of no relevance to the legislator's district, roles oriented towards party or lobby as foci of representation may serve as major premises of choice.

The generic extension of Burke's special case, broken down into analytic components, suggests that the focal and stylistic dimensions of representation must be kept separate in empirical research. Burke combined them for polemical reasons: he was writing in opposition to the idea of mandatory representation which had much popular support in the middle of the eighteenth century.[5] But the fact that a representative sees himself as reaching a decision by following his own convictions or judgment does not mean that the content of his decisions is necessarily oriented towards a general rather than a particular interest, just as his acceptance of instructions from a clientele group does not necessarily mean that he is oriented towards a special rather than the public interest. A representative may base his decisions on his own conscience or judgment, but the cause he promotes may be parochial. Or he may follow instructions, but the mandate may be directed towards the realization of the general welfare.

The distinction between the focal and stylistic dimensions of the representative's role allows us to suggest that representation is not concerned with what decisions should be made, but with how decisions are to be made. Now, it is axiomatic that decisions made in institutional contexts, such as legislatures provide, are made in terms of a set of premises which guide the behavior of decision makers. The notion—explicit in Burke and other traditional formulations— that legislative decisions can be purely rational is not tenable in view of the fact that rationality, while not altogether absent, is invariably bounded by the legislature's institutional environment.[6] One of these boundaries is the representational fabric of the legislature. The

---

[5] See Samuel H. Beer, "The Representation of Interests in British Government," *American Political Science Review*, 51 (Sept., 1957), 613, who points out how little general legislation was proposed or enacted in those days.

[6] For the conception of "bounded rationality" as well as the notion that roles constitute some of the premises of decision-making behavior, we are indebted to Herbert A. Simon's writings, notably *Models of Man, op. cit.*

representative system provides the legislator with some of the assumptions in terms of which he defines his representational role. The roles he takes, in turn, whether in the focal or stylistic dimensions of representation, provide the premises for decision.

Premises underlying decisions made by legislatures, then, may be of two kinds: (1) they may be premises relevant to the focus of representation; and (2) they may be relevant to the style of representation. With regard to the first kind, for instance, a legislator may be guided by premises such as that legislation should benefit either his district or the state, that it should be "liberal" or "conservative," that it should or should not favor special interests, that it should or should not be in performance of his party obligations, and so on.[7] With regard to the second kind of premises, the legislator's choices may be circumscribed by his stylistic orientation as a representative, whether he sees himself following his own conscience or instructions. In this dimension the premises involved in his decisional behavior refer not to the focus but to his representational style.

PERCEPTIONS OF THE REPRESENTATIONAL ROLE

Representational-role orientations were derived from responses to the following two questions:

How would you describe the job of being a legislator—what are the most important things you should do here?

Are there any important differences between what you think this job is and the way your constituents see it?

Responses to these questions yielded three major representational-role orientations: trustee, delegate, and politico.[8] In the following we shall describe these orientational types as they were defined by legislators themselves.

Trustee. The role orientation of trustee finds expression in two major conceptions of how decisions ought to be made. These conceptions may occur severally and jointly. There is, first, a moralistic interpretation. The trustee sees himself as a free agent in that, as a premise of his decision making behavior, he claims to follow what he considers right or just, his convictions and principles, the dictates of his conscience. In proceeding along this path of moral righteousness, trustees may give different "reasons" for their interpretation of

[7] These foci of representation will be treated in Chapters 13–15 below.
[8] For more detailed description of how these role orientations were constructed from interview responses, see below, Appendix 1.2, pp. 467–468.

this role. First, the trustee's ideas, attitudes, or legislative objectives are in harmony with those of the represented. And because they are in harmony, he need not pay attention to instructions—for no instructions are forthcoming, and he can follow the dictates of his conscience:

No, there are no differences between my idea of the job and that of the type of people I represent. They accept my philosophy which I have frequently expressed to them. Once when I was campaigning one of my constituents came up and asked if I had voted so that I would get sent back. I told him no, I voted the way I felt was right.

I have never been under pressure once to go against my convictions. I've always stuck to them and I've won more friends than I've lost. I feel I have the confidence of my constituents so that when a problem comes up, I will make a decision that will be in accordance with their best interests.

Secondly, the trustee claims that he must fall back on his own principles in making decisions because those from whom he might take cues—constituents, lobbyists, leaders, or colleagues—cannot be trusted:

His most important and difficult job is to vote according to his conscience without letting other things interfere—even his own constituents. They are axe-grinding elements.

No, wherever differences do exist, you'll get along if you do what you know is right—they usually go along with it. Sometimes you get complaints, but they're usually just emotional appeals which you should be suspicious of: they should be avoided. You shouldn't waver in your convictions because of them.

Finally, if the representative as a man of principle finds himself in conflict with the represented, he should not submit but try to persuade them to his convictions. The trustee here sees himself as a "mentor." He is not in agreement with his constituents, but he does not turn his back on them. Sticking to his ideas, he tries to bring others around to his point of view:

There are often personal differences. The people in the district often express their views one way. It's best to do what you feel should be done. I usually go by my own convictions and depend on being able to convince them when I get back that I did the right things.

There is also a judgmental conception of the role of trustee. The trustee is not bound by a mandate because his decisions are his own considered judgments based on an assessment of the facts in each decision, his understanding of all the problems and angles involved, his thoughtful appraisal of the sides at issue. He may feel that he must follow his own judgments because the community from which he comes expects him to do so:

There are two theories of representation. The first is the delegate theory. Here you are the voice of the community from which you come. Then there is the representative theory. That is, the man is elected for his own capabilities in the solution of problems. I am inclined to this theory. I would say that my community is also of this mind.

Or, representation may be spontaneous in this conception, a product of agreement between representative and represented without any active communication of opinions or beliefs. The representative shares the outlook of his constituents:

As to what should be accomplished here, I think it should be what I think should be done rather than the people here. I've lived in this town 39 years, and you think like the town does. They might show me that this isn't true, but until I find out I assume that they feel the same way as I do.

Or the trustee may follow his own judgment because he cannot afford to allow himself to be influenced by persons who are committed or ill informed:

The most important job is . . . an ability to reach decisions, to solve problems without being unduly influenced by the feelings of persons who are committed or paid, or who for lack of information or ability are incapable of reaching a decision. I do not consider myself as a delegate. People are not capable to tell me what to do—not because they are stupid, but because they have limited access to the facts. If they had the facts, their decision would be the same.

The crucial point in this response is, of course, that if people had the facts, their judgment would be the same as that of the representative. But the theme that constituents and others are ill informed because they have no access to the facts in terms of which decisions must be made is recurrent:

I spend a lot of time looking at both sides. I have the time to do it. People back home are busy and see only one side. My job is to check all angles of a problem, and they want me to use my best judgment.

I think I'm elected by the people to be their representative, and they must have confidence in my judgment, assuming that I have studied the situation in making my decisions. I can't please everyone all the time, even my best friends. I believe in a republican form of government. You elect people to represent you and then abide by their decisions. If they make too many wrong decisions, you elect others. There is a tendency in some cases by some people to return all decisions to the people. I'm not in agreement with that: it's not that they are incapable, but that they don't take time to inform themselves. It's not true of all, but the majority do this.

A related view sees the trustee role as inevitable not because the represented do not understand the problems which the representative faces, but because the representative cannot find out the preferences of his clientele, even if he tried to do so. He must, therefore, fall back on his own judgment:

Well, of course, I have never subscribed to the theory that I'm here to reflect the views of my constituents. I'm here to vote as I see it. You can't vote by what you think the constituents' thinking is. You don't know what that thinking is. Even if you receive 100 letters on a bill, this is a very small proportion in respect to the size of the district. . . . A bill might be opposed by interests which I represent, but if I personally agree with the bill, then I will follow my principles, even if they don't agree with certain Republican interests which might have contributed to my election.

But his own difficulty in ascertaining constituents' preferences, or the clientele's lack of information, does not mean that the trustee should be oblivious of the ideas or opinions of others. He may listen before arriving at a decision:

He should regard the laws for which there seems a need partly in the light of public opinion, but partly on his own judgment. If he refers only to his constituents, why be here at all? I represent the welfare of my community as I see it. Otherwise they can get another boy. Of course, at times you want advice—if you are not sure what the effect of a proposed law may be. Mostly I prefer to do my own thinking.

I'm open to intelligent ideas from my constituents. I'm not interested in simple notes from them saying "vote yes" or "vote no" on bill X. When I get letters like that I sometimes answer them asking for their reasons so that I may be better able to make my own decisions. They seldom reply.

Finally, it seems to be an important aspect of the trustee's role orientation that he should be willing to accept the political consequences of his refusal to be swayed by public opinion. The trustee may be aware of the implications of his conception of representation for political responsibility:

I found out long ago you can't poll your constituents. You can't supply them either with the information so that they can make intelligent decisions. So I haven't concerned myself with them. I try to inform myself and vote as I please. If they don't like it they have a chance to get me at the next election.

I operate on the principle that I'm here to use my own judgment. A representative is as good as long as his ideas coincide with the constituents' wishes. If they don't, it's up to them to throw me out, not for me to change. Not that I don't think you should listen to them. Still I think a legislator should do what he thinks best regardless of public opinion. I do pretty much what I think is best. . . . You see guys here who follow the whims of the people. What's wrong with that is that they're not smart enough to figure out what the people think.

Vote your convictions rather than voting for what you think someone else thinks or wants. Let them defeat you if they want, and can. My first year here I tried to ask everyone's point of view and find out how I should vote. But that doesn't work; they don't know themselves what they want. They may tell you to vote for bill 121 but after talking to them you find out that what they really want would not be accomplished by the bill. Now I vote for what I think they want. I don't ask them anymore. I do it for them.

Evidently, a great variety of conceptions of representation are involved in the role orientation of the trustee. In particular, it seems that this orientation derives not only from a normative definition of the role of the representative, but that it is also often grounded in interpersonal situations which make it functionally inevitable. The condition that the represented do not have the information necessary to give intelligent instructions, that the representative is unable to discover what his clientele may want, that preferences remain un-expressed, that there is no need for instructions because of an alleged harmony of interests between representative and represented—all of the circumstances may be acknowledged as sources of the role orien-tation of trustee, at times even forced on the representative against his own predilection for a mandate if that were possible.

Delegate. Just as the trustee role orientation involves a variety of conceptions of representation, so does the orientation of delegate. All delegates are agreed, of course, that they should not use their independent judgment or principled convictions as decision-making premises. But this does not mean that they feel equally committed to follow instructions, from whatever clientele. Some merely say that they try to inform themselves before making decisions by consulting their constituents or others; however, they seem to imply that such consultation has a mandatory effect on their behavior: "I do ask them (i.e., constituents) quite often, especially where there's doubt in my mind." Others frankly acknowledge instructions as necessary or desirable premises in decision making: "I do what they want me to do. Being re-elected is the best test"; or, "A majority of the people always gets their way with me." More emphatic is this response:

What the district wants me to do is my most important job. I carry out their decisions. I'll put any bill in the hopper they give me. If they wanted me to move this capitol, I'd break my neck to do it.

Finally, there is the representative in the delegate role who not only feels that he should follow instructions, but who also believes that he should do so even if these instructions are explicitly counter to his own judgment or principles: "Some things I'm not particularly sold on, but if the people want it, they should have it"; or, "Reflect the thinking of my district even if it is not my own private thinking." The following two responses are more explicit than most in this connection:

I want to express their views rather than my own. On a controversial matter I'll vote the way I think the majority want even if I personally disagree.

I voted once against my own will to favor my constituents. I wrote a letter to the papers about whether they wanted a State Board of Education appointed or elected, and asked them what they wanted me to do. I favored an appointed board, but they, a preponderance of them, said an elected board. When it came to the decision, I voted for the elected board. I feel that when a fellow represents a section, he should represent their feelings and try to find out their feelings.

What strikes one in these comments, in contrast to those made by trustees, is the failure to elaborate in greater detail the problem of why the representative should follow instructions in his decision-making behavior. Delegates, it seems, have a simpler, more mechanical conception of the political process and of the function of representation in legislative behavior. Perhaps most noticeable, in contrast to the trustee orientation, is the omission of delegates to raise the question of political responsibility under conditions of strict instructions. Apparently, the problem is ignored by the delegate precisely because he rejects the possibility of discretion in his decision making. It is a matter of speculation whether the role orientation of delegate is based on a conscious majoritarian bias which he could elaborate and defend if necessary, or whether it simply reflects lack of political articulation and sophistication. On the other hand, the fact that the delegate seems to have so little doubt about his role suggests that, whatever his reasons and regardless of whether his decisions are really in accord with the views of different groups among his clientele, he is likely to be characterized by a fairly high sense of personal effectiveness in his approach to lawmaking.

Politico. As suggested earlier, the classical dichotomization of the concept of representation in terms of independent judgment and mandate was unlikely to exhaust the empirical possibilities of representational behavior. In particular, it would seem to be possible for a representative to act in line with both criteria. For roles and role orientations need not be mutually exclusive. Depending on circumstances, a representative may hold the role orientation of trustee at one time, and the role orientation of delegate at another time. Or he might even seek to reconcile both orientations in terms of a third. In other words, the representational-role set comprises the extreme orientations of trustee and delegate and a third orientation, the politico, resulting from overlap of these two. Within the orientational range called politico, the trustee and delegate roles may be taken simultaneously, possibly making for role conflict, or they may be taken seriatim, one after another as legislative situations dictate.

Because our data do not permit us to discriminate too sharply between these two possibilities, we shall speak of legislators who express both orientations, either simultaneously or serially, as politicos.[9] In other words, in contrast to either trustees or delegates as relatively "pure" types, representatives holding the role orientation of politico exhibit a certain amount of flexibility in their representational relationships. A qualitative review of the interview protocols may serve to articulate the two possibilities.

Both role orientations—that of trustee and that of delegate—may be held serially, depending on whether the legislator's focus of attention is centered in one clientele or another. For instance, he may see himself as a delegate in matters of local interest, and as a trustee in all other matters:

As a member there are certain things you should do. First you have a specific responsibility to the people of your own constituency on matters of local interest. Second, you should use your own judgment on all matters pertaining to benefits for the people within the framework of governmental policy and should think of what's best for the state as a whole. It's not necessary to follow the will of the people always as you should decide what most benefits the present and future and hope history proves you right.

Or the legislator may feel that he must follow his party's instructions in political matters, though on others he can be a free agent:

My conception of party responsibility—there's a responsibility to the party to vote with them, with respect to administration bills—there's responsibility to go along with the governor. On matters removed from the political category I would vote my convictions.

These comments suggest that both the trustee and delegate roles may be taken, depending on the character of the issue involved or the legislator's focus of attention. But no attempt is made to reconcile the two orientations. They coexist side by side and may be invoked as political circumstances require. These legislators do not seem to feel that they are facing a situation which makes for conflict

[9] Provision for such discrimination was made in the coding of responses, but differences among the coders seemed to introduce a good deal of bias in this connection. Hence it seemed preferable to combine these responses in a single category—politico. See Appendix 1.2, below, pp. 467–468.

of roles, largely because they succeed in avoiding conflict by not attempting to reconcile the two orientations. As one representative clearly put it:

> Well, that gets you into a major philosophical question. Is it the duty of the representative simply to do what people want, or is it his duty to figure out what's in the best interest of people and state, and persuade them that it is? *Uniformly, I have not taken either one position—sometimes one, sometimes the other.* . . . The evidence of success is that I'm still here.

On the other hand, some legislators may be more sensitive to the potential conflict to which they may be exposed by the ambiguity of the representational relationship and seek to come to grips with it. These representatives are not only aware of the problem, but, instead of solving it by sometimes taking the trustee role, sometimes the delegate role, they seek to balance simultaneously the instructions or preferences of clienteles against their own judgment:

> There is a line of demarcation between what they want at home and what you think is good for them. I haven't been too disturbed by that yet but it could become a major problem. I don't think I could ever settle just where the line is. It is too flexible. Each piece of legislation must be considered individually to determine it.

> My job is to look after their interests (i.e., of constituents) and carry out what they want done. But this is subject to the limitation that they can't possibly know all I do if I'm doing my job. They are very understanding. I haven't been threatened that if I don't do what they want I won't be re-elected.

While these respondents leave the possible resolution of conflict between representational-role orientations open, some politicos tend to resolve it, when the chips are down, in favor of the trustee role:

> There is an age-old question—should I vote according to my convictions, or according to the people back home? I think I should follow my convictions but consider the people back home. However, their views are not necessarily best. They get biased views on issues—all of them are members of some pressure groups. A legislator hears both sides. . . . Public opinion is subject to change; it can't be ignored or you won't come back.

> A good many think that you should do what the majority wants, regardless of your personal feelings, and I think what you do is to consider their desires as *one* of the elements in arriving at a conclusion. But you also have to consider the other elements presented here. In other words, you are in a better position to see the relative merits of the bill here than they are. The basic question is: are you elected to do what the majority wants or what you think is best?

Finally, there may be an explicit defense of independent judgment as the more important criterion in decision making, precisely because instructions from particular groups have to be integrated in the legislative process. Here the representational role of politico blends smoothly into the purposive role of broker:

It's difficult to use the term "constituents" to give a composite picture. . . . Particular groups have particular interests that sometimes interfere with the common good. Most constituents feel I am their representative rather than a common representative, and, as a result, I must weigh the conflicting desires of various groups to determine what will benefit the most people in my district. A legislator should realize that in most cases the sincerity and desires of others are just as genuine as his own. He has to try as far as possible—even by giving in sometimes on his own obstinate opinions—to work out the best solution possible without sacrificing principle.

In general, then, the politico as a representational-role taker differs from both the trustee and the delegate in that he seems to be more sensitive to conflicting alternatives, more flexible in the ways in which he tries to resolve the conflict among alternatives, and less dogmatic in his orientation towards legislative behavior as it is related to his representational role. Whether he is or can be successful in performing the role is a matter to which we shall turn later on.

DISTRIBUTION OF REPRESENTATIONAL-ROLE ORIENTATIONS

The spell of the Burkean formulation on the interpretation of representation tended to create reactions which, it seems, are almost as arbitrary as Burke's formula itself. In particular, the functional notion, itself quite realistic under modern conditions, that the legislature is an agency for the coordination and integration of diverse social, economic, and political interests makes apparent the simple-mindedness of Burke's theory, now as then. Friedrich, for instance, has pointed out that "the pious formula that representatives are not bound by mandate, that they are subject only to their conscience and are supposed to serve the common weal, which is repeated in so many European constitutions, while significant as a norm, may lead to differentiating as well as to integrative results."[10] Yet, once the distinction is made between the style of the representative's role and its focus, Burke's "pious formula" may still be relevant. Both the focus and the style are likely to be influenced by the character of politics at a given time and by the demands of contemporary political circumstances on the representative as a decision maker.

[10] Carl J. Friedrich, *op. cit.*, p. 297.

We may, for instance, assume the following: the exigencies of modern government, even on the relatively low level of state government, are exceedingly complex. Taxation and finance, education and public welfare, legal reform, licensing and regulatory problems, transportation, and so on are topics more often than not beyond the comprehension of the average citizen. Unable to understand their problems and helpless to cope with them, people are likely to entrust the affairs of government to the elected representatives who, presumably, are better informed than their constituents. Many of the comments made by trustees about their constituents articulated this set of reasoning. People themselves may pay lip service to the notion that a representative should not use his independent judgment,[11] but in fact they are unlikely to be able, or may not care, to give him instructions as was possibly the case at an earlier time when the tasks of government were comparatively simple. It is likely, therefore, that the representative has become less and less a delegate and more and more a trustee as the business of government has become more and more intricate and technical as well as less locally centered. Rather than being a "pious formula," the role orientation of trustee may be a functional necessity. We might expect, therefore, that it is held by state legislators more frequently today than the role orientation of delegate, with the politico orientation in a middle position.

Table 12.1: Distribution of representational-role orientations

Role Orientation	Calif. $N = 49$	N.J. $N = 54$	Ohio $N = 114$	Tenn. $N = 78$
Trustee	55%	61%	56%	81%
Politico	25	22	29	13
Delegate	20	17	15	6
Total	100%	100%	100%	100%

Comparative analysis of the distribution of representational-role orientations in the four states seems to support these considerations. As Table 12.1 shows, the role orientation of trustee is held by greater proportions of legislators in all four states than either the politico or delegate orientations. Moreover, the politico appears somewhat more often in all four states than the delegate.

The trustee orientation, Table 12.1 indicates, appears more frequently in Tennessee than in the other three states, a fact that seems

[11] See Hadley Cantril, Ed., *Public Opinion, 1935–1946* (Princeton: Princeton University Press, 1951), p. 133.

to contradict the proposition that the orientation of trustee varies with the complexity of governmental affairs. As Tennessee is less urbanized and industrialized than the other states, one might expect Tennessee legislators to be less often trustees and more often delegates than legislators in California, New Jersey, or Ohio. But it may be that "complexity" is a function of perceptions, regardless of the real situation. If so, then to Tennesseans the relatively less complex character of socio-economic life may appear more complex than it actually is, compared with the other states. The more frequent appearance of the trustee there may only be symptomatic of an even greater feeling of helplessness and inefficacy on the part of people vis-á-vis governmental problems, as it is perceived by their representatives. It may also be a reflection of the lower educational level in Tennessee. In all these cases, the political character of Tennessee constituencies would seem to make it very difficult for a legislator to be a delegate for his constituency, forcing him to act as either a trustee or a politico. But to demonstrate this is beyond the limits of this analysis.[12] But the most surprising feature of Table 12.1 is the very small proportion of legislators in each state subscribing to the role orientation of delegate. If one assumes that the extent to which any role is taken is a function of its difficulty, it would seem that the role orientation of delegate is, indeed, most difficult to hold. We noted in the review of responses regarding different orientations made in the interviews that legislators repeatedly gave as a reason for their taking the role of trustee the fact that it was impossible to find out what people really wanted, and that, therefore, the delegate role was unrealistic. Whether realistic or not, the data reveal that very few legislators took the delegate role. Whether it is the most difficult role to take is a problem to which we shall return shortly.

REPRESENTATIONAL ROLES IN THE LEGISLATIVE PROCESS

An obviously important question for future research concerns the differences in behavior which follow from legislators' taking one or another of the representational roles in different legislative situations.

[12] As the trustee orientation includes responses stressing traditional moral values, it might be assumed that these virtues—such as following one's conscience or what one feels to be "right"—are more valued in rural Tennessee than in the three more urbanized states. But inspection of the frequency with which this attitude appears in Tennessee as against the other states does not reveal significantly different distributions of relevant responses: California—18%; New Jersey—8%; Ohio—28%; and Tennessee—23%.

Again, such a question lies beyond the scope of our research. But some of the results of the various orientations are suggested by the way respondents described the influence of different factors in their thinking about one particular subject-matter area—that of school needs. Table 12.2 presents a rough index of the influence attributed

Table 12.2: Comparative influence of different factors in legislators' thinking about school needs problem for legislators taking different representational roles

Influencing Factor	Ranked*	Trustee N = 161	Delegate N = 38	Politico N = 42
Views of friends in legislature	Highest	27%	16%	26%
	Lowest	32	32	26
		−5	−16	0
Advice of party leaders	Highest	12	8	12
	Lowest	55	55	62
		−43	−47	−50
Word from people in district	Highest	55	74	67
	Lowest	12	3	5
		+43	+71	+62
Legislative Commission, Legislative Council	Highest	38	11	19
	Lowest	16	21	10
		+22	−10	+9
Committee recommendations	Highest	29	16	24
	Lowest	32	42	43
		−3	−26	−19
Views of administrative agencies	Highest	25	26	31
	Lowest	28	18	29
		−3	+8	+2
Views of interest groups	Highest	14	18	19
	Lowest	52	37	29
		−38	−19	−10
Others	Highest	16	8	14

* "Highest" are those rated "very important" or "important"; "lowest" are those rated "not very important" or "not at all important," in response to the question, "Just to get an overall picture, how important would you rate each of these items in leading you to see this *school needs* problem as you do?"

to each factor by legislators of each type—the simple arithmetic difference between the proportion of a group attributing most importance and the proportion attributing least importance to it as a consideration in their own thinking about the problem.

Relatively speaking, as the table shows, trustees stand out in the greater emphasis they give to recommendations of the Legislative Commission, Legislative Council or cognate agency, to committee recommendations, and to a variety of other agencies volunteered by them as important. Delegates are noteworthy in their relatively greater emphasis on word from people in their district and their relatively lesser emphasis on intralegislative sources such as committee recommendations or friends in the legislature. Politicos, as might be expected, give relatively more emphasis to the views of interest groups and lobbies, although the influence given them in absolute terms is still rather slight. In most other respects, politicos rank the influence of any given factor somewhere between the extremes of influence ranking found for trustees and delegates. Even though the character of the data does not justify further inferences about the effects on legislative processes of possible distributions of the various representational-role orientations, the differences are at least suggestive of the kinds of effects which might be found in research more carefully designed to investigate them.

REPRESENTATIVES' SENSE OF LEGISLATIVE EFFICACY

It was suggested earlier that the delegate role is probably more difficult under modern conditions of inaccessibility to the mass electorate than the other two representational roles. It would seem feasible for a legislator to take the delegate role only if he feels that he can be effective in its actual performance. One should expect, then, that delegates as a group in each state would score higher on the index of legislative efficacy than either trustees or politicos.[13] This does not mean that the role of delegate is more functional than the others (it probably is not), or that the delegate is in reality effective in performing the representational function as he sees it. It only means that the delegate must make a special effort if he wants to live up to his orientation as a representative who seeks and follows instructions, an effort not required at all by trustees and only as circumstances demand by politicos. Sense of legislative efficacy may thus be considered as an indication that the effort is felt to be successful.

[13] For a more detailed discussion of the "sense of legislative efficacy," see below, Appendix 2.2, pp. 474–475.

Table 12.3 presents the scores obtained by the different types of representational-role takers in the four states. The results of the test support our speculations only in part. California and New Jersey delegates do, indeed, exhibit a higher sense of legislative efficacy than trustees and politicos, but this is not the case in Ohio and Tennessee. We note, too, that politicos in California and New Jersey score even lower on the efficacy index than trustees. At first sight this would seem to be surprising, for the politico role partakes, as we found, of the delegate orientation, and we might expect this to be reflected in the scores. Moreover, we also suggested that this role might be more flexible than the others. But what the California and

Table 12.3: Sense of legislative efficacy of legislators as representatives

Role Types	Calif.	N.J.	Ohio	Tenn.
Trustee	+19	+34	+28	−10
Politico	0	+16	+25	+10
Delegate	+35	+40	+13	0

New Jersey scores seem to suggest is that this flexibility is won only in the face of considerable uncertainty as to what the role of representative involves. Evidently, politicos feel themselves pulled in opposite orientational directions, subject to cross-pressures which give rise to their relatively low sense of legislative efficacy. But the Ohio and Tennessee data are contrary to this hypothesis. In Ohio, politicos have a score similar to that of trustees, and in Tennessee they have the highest efficacy score.

It may be, of course, that the differences in the scores of representational-role takers are expressions of real differences between the four states with regard to the meanings representational orientations have in the four states. The data, however, are at most suggestive for the purpose of entertaining alternate hypotheses. We can reach no conclusions here about the relationship between efficacy and representational-role orientations.

CONCLUSION

Three major role orientations—trustee, politico, and delegate— seem to be characteristic of the legislator's representational style, i.e., of how he relates himself to his decision-making behavior. The trustee claims to rely on his own conscience, on what he thinks is right, or on his considered judgment of the facts involved in the issue which he has to decide. The delegate claims that he seeks and follows instructions from his constituents or other clienteles. The politico claims that he will adopt one or the other orientation as conditions call for, and that he must balance one against the other.

Under modern conditions, the trustee orientation is probably more realistic. Given the complexity of governmental problems, on the one hand, and the difficulty of finding out what clienteles may want, the delegate orientation is probably least functional from the point of view of effective representation. In the four states, many more legislators take the role of trustee than the roles of politico or delegate. If extent of role taking is an indication of the degree of difficulty involved in a given role, it would seem that the trustee role is the easiest and the delegate role the most difficult to take.

An attempt to appraise the three roles in terms of role takers' sense of legislative efficacy proved inconclusive. In two states, delegates showed the highest sense of efficacy and politicos the lowest. But this was not the case in two other states. How the representational roles are related to those roles which are focused on the legislator's clienteles will be treated in Chapter 16.

CHAPTER 13

The legislator
and his district:
areal roles

Rᴇᴘʀᴇsᴇɴᴛᴀᴛɪᴏɴ ᴏғ ɢᴇᴏɢʀᴀᴘʜɪᴄᴀʟ ᴀʀᴇᴀs introduces a certain amount
of ambiguity into the relationship between representative and represented.[1] Part of this ambiguity involves the widely held expectation, contested by Edmund Burke but shared by many citizens and
politicians alike, that the legislator is a spokesman of the presumed
"interests" of his district. Implicit in this expectation is the assumption that a geographical unit has interests which are distinct and
different from those of other units. This assumption has been
challenged on a variety of grounds: that the geographical area as
such, as an electoral unit, is artificial; that it cannot and does not
generate interests shared by its residents; that it has no unique
interests; and so on. Schemes of proportional or vocational representation have been advanced to make possible the representation
of allegedly more "natural" interest groupings, such as minority, skill,
or economic groups

Yet, the assumption that geographical districts have unique interests
which are, or ought to be, taken into consideration when legislative
decisions are made, continues to be shared not only by voters, politicians, and others involved in policy making, but also by scientific
students of the political process. It underlies many studies which
seek to relate legislative roll-call votes to socio-economic character-

This chapter drafted by Eulau.

[1] For a perspicacious discussion of ambiguities in representation, see Harold
F. Gosnell, *Democracy—The Threshold of Freedom* (New York: The Ronald
Press Company, 1948), pp. 124–142.

istics of electoral districts,[2] as well as those studies which analyze the socio-economic composition of legislatures.[3]

Such an interpretation is most tenuous under modern conditions. Electoral districts tend to be so heterogeneous in population attributes, so pluralistic in the character of their group life, so diverse in the kinds of values and beliefs held, that whatever measures of central tendency are used to classify a district are more likely to conceal than to reveal its real character.   The notion that elections are held as a method to discover persons whose attributes and attitudes will somehow mirror those most widely shared by people in their district appears to be of dubious validity.   The function of representation in modern political systems is not to make the legislature a mathematically exact copy of the electorate.

But the difficulty of finding an identity between representative and represented does not mean that a legislator's point of reference in making decisions cannot be his district.   It may or may not be, and whether it is or not is a matter of empirical determination.   We may doubt that what orients a legislator towards his district rather than some other focus of attention is the similarity between his district's characteristics and his own.   Or we may assume that a legislator incorporates in himself the characteristics of his district—which, for argument's sake, may be admitted when he comes from a relatively homogeneous area.   But it is still an empirical question whether or not the legislator is subjectively concerned with his district and seeks to discover its "interests."

THE AREAL-ROLE SET

In spite of the considerations just mentioned, state legislators perceive representation of the interests of some geographical area as a proper function of their legislative activities. Responding to our questions about what they thought were the most important things they should do in the legislature and how their constituents felt about it, more than two-thirds in the three states of California, New Jersey, and Ohio spontaneously mentioned either district or state, or both,

[2] See, for instance, Julius Turner, *Party and Constituency: Pressures on Congress* (Baltimore: The Johns Hopkins Press, 1951); or Duncan MacRae, Jr., *op. cit.*

[3] See, for instance, Donald R. Matthews, *The Social Background of Political Decision-Makers, op. cit.;* or Charles S. Hyneman, "Who Makes Our Laws?," *op. cit.* See also John C. Wahlke and Heinz Eulau, *Legislative Behavior* (Glencoe: The Free Press, 1959), pp. 239–280.

as clienteles (though in Tennessee almost two-thirds failed to do so). Of those who took cognizance of a geographical unit, some would mention only their district or county, others only the state, and still others would mention district and state as equally important foci of attention. On the basis of their responses, we classified legislators into "district oriented," "state oriented," and "district-state oriented."[4]

District oriented. District-oriented legislators indicated two types of response patterns: some simply mentioned their district or county as an important focus of their areal role orientation; others explicitly placed district above state in defining this orientation. Among the former, the most frequent responses suggested that it is the legislator's job to sponsor and pass legislation which would benefit his district. This type of response might be rationalized to the effect that "what would be of benefit to my county would usually also benefit others," or, "the conditions there (i.e., in the district) are the ones I am most familiar with." Some respondents were inclined to generalize this position: "The average member usually thinks first of his own district, of course."

Others in this group of district-oriented legislators emphasized particular policy problems and the importance of protecting what they considered to be the policy interests of their district:

The job is to represent his constituents in matters that vitally affect his district. This usually involves the urban against rural issue. Matters for metropolitan areas—my county is metropolitan—are difficult because rural Republican counties dominate.

The most important thing is that one is elected by his constituents to give them good government. One should study all the bills that pertain to his county. It is hard to have an understanding of all bills since bills range from schools to mental health to highways.

Or the emphasis might be on the services which district-oriented legislators think they are expected to render for their constituents:

I think he should represent his district and see that the members of his district are properly taken care of. And I think the prime function of a legislator is to provide adequate service to his constituents, such as providing good education and getting aid for the local government.

A second major group of district-oriented legislators specifically pointed to the importance of placing the interests of their district above those of the state. Their concern with the state's interests usually appeared as an afterthought. But, as one respondent put it, "you

[4] For further discussion of how these roles were constructed, see Appendix 1.3 below, pp. 465, 468.

cannot actually disassociate one from the other." The following responses are typical of this group:

Well, first, on the basis of contacts with your constituents, you should see which laws you should change to directly help your county. Find out what they need and then introduce the necessary legislation. Your second duty is the job of considering all of the bills before your committee with a view to how they affect the whole state. This is secondary in your thinking but still important.

You should take care of your own backyard first, but think about the whole state too.

State oriented. State-oriented legislators either mentioned the state alone as the salient focus of their areal orientation, or they also mentioned the district, but clearly tending to place the state above district in importance. Some of them emphasized the need for state policy or state program as an over-riding consideration:

The basic job of the legislature is state policy . . . , to set the over-all state policy, that is, whether you're going to emphasize schools, roads, or both.

The most important thing is to settle and provide for the state budget. Next to that I suppose I would consider legislation in the field of public welfare as rather important. . . . I feel that legislators should consider anything important that has to do with the welfare of the people of the state.

A second group of state-oriented legislators pointed to both the state and the district as relevant foci of their role orientation, but tended to give the benefit of doubt to the state:

Well, I consider the state legislature to be like a board of directors of a great state on the same plane as in a large corporation. I feel the legislator has two basic responsibilities—to represent their own section, but beyond that to exercise judgment in representing all the people of the state. You should look at a problem in terms of what is best for the state today and in the future.

Where the general good would conflict with the county interests, I would go with the general good of the state over the county, I think though, definitely.

He should study carefully every piece of legislation and decide to support or oppose only on the ground of whether it is good or bad for the people of the state—and, of course, of his district. First the state and then the district.

Finally, some of the state-oriented legislators explicitly stressed the desirability of overcoming parochial considerations in favor of the state:

To legislate on the basis that there's a direct relationship and fairness to all parties, segments of the state, groups and the state generally. Get away from purely local legislation at penalty to other sections.

I'm from a rural county and the problems are different from urban counties. . . . I'm willing not to narrow myself to county interests, but to consider and vote on urban and state problems also.

District-state oriented. A third group of legislators who spontaneously concerned themselves with the areal focus of their legislative role mentioned both district and state as equally relevant to their legislative or service activities. Apparently, they did not envisage the possibility of conflict arising out of these orientations and thought that they could attend to the interests of both state and district without undue complications. Most of them, however, expressed themselves in very general terms:

Every legislator is faced with two facts. He should be interested in legislation, primarily as it affects the whole state. And legislation as it affects his own district.

It is my job and duty to introduce laws of interest to my constituents which, of course, are not detrimental to the state. Then I have to make decisions on prospective laws on the basis of how they affect my constituents and the state as well as the nation, though that is more or less taken for granted.

Each man here has a dual obligation. He must keep in mind the needs of his constituents and how every bill would affect them, but he also must look at the state as a whole and try to determine what is beneficial for the whole area.

The generality of these and many similar responses may be deceptive, and treating them as indicative of "district-state orientations" may be somewhat arbitrary in a number of cases. Although the actual language used tends in the direction of the state as the focus of attention, the tone often appears to be more suggestive of a latent district orientation. One should not be surprised to find, therefore, that these hyphenated legislators may more resemble district-oriented then state-oriented respondents in attitudes and behavior.

AREAL-ROLE ORIENTATIONS AND POLITICAL COMPETITION

In so far as the district rather than some other unit, such as the entire state, is at the legislator's focus of attention, it is more likely to be a function of political than of demographic or socio-economic considerations. The problem is one of discovering under what conditions the representative can afford to disregard his district and still hope to maintain the confidence of his constituents. We might speculate, for instance, that in so far as he cherishes the position of power he holds, he is unlikely to ignore his district. We should expect, therefore, that what tends to orient the legislator towards his district is likely to be the mechanism of political responsibility effectuated by political competition.

The hypothesis needs further elaboration. Political responsibility— a set of relationships in which the elected are sensitive to the power of the electors over them, and in which the elected are aware of the sanctions which make responsibility a reality—is predicated on the existence of a competitive political system where the represented have genuine choice, and where legislators are periodically confronted

Table 13.1: **Political character of electoral districts and areal-role orientations in three states**[*]

	Political Character of District		
Areal Role Orientation	Competitive $N = 72$	Semi-competitive $N = 77$	One-party $N = 96$
District	53%	48%	33%
District-state	28	34	33
State	19	18	34
Total	100%	100%	100%

* California, New Jersey, and Ohio. "Not ascertained" respondents are omitted.

with the possibility of removal from office. The sanction of removal inherent in a competitive party system serves to focus legislators' attention on their district rather than the state as the crucial point of reference. Legislators from competitive areas are therefore more likely to be district-oriented than legislators from one-party areas, while the latter are more likely to be state-oriented than the former.[5]

A test of this hypothesis is possible by relating areal role orientations to the degree of party competition in legislators' home districts. Because party competition as an independent variable has no room for operation in predominantly one-party Tennessee,[6] Table 13.1 presents the combined data for California, New Jersey, and Ohio alone. As

[5] For a description of how the districts were classified in terms of party competition on the electoral level, see Appendix 2.1, below, pp. 471–474.

[6] Of the 46 Tennessee respondents who mentioned an areal orientation, only four came from competitive and five from semicompetitive districts. Tennessee seems to be a special case, in that Tennessee legislators tend to be more district oriented than legislators elsewhere, regardless of the political or ecological character of the districts.

the table shows, 53 per cent of the representatives from competitive districts are district oriented, while only 33 per cent of those from one-party districts are so classified. On the other hand, one-party district legislators are more likely to hold a state orientation than those from competitive districts. The data seem to support the hypothesis that areal orientation varies with the political character of the district in which legislators are elected.

However, this finding may be spurious. It may be less a function of the political character of the district than of certain demographic district characteristics. For one thing competitive districts are, more often than not, located in metropolitian or urbanized areas, while one-party districts are more frequent in rural or less urban areas.

Table 13.2: Political character of electoral districts, controlled by ecological character, and areal-role orientations in three states*

Areal Role Orientation	Metropolitan			50% + Urban		
	C. N = 48	S-C. N = 38	O-P. N = 39	C. N = 20	S-C. N = 35	O-P. N = 50
District	52%	47%	31%	60%	46%	30%
District-state	24	32	28	30	40	42
State	24	21	41	10	14	28
Total	100%	100%	100%	100%	100%	100%

* California, New Jersey, and Ohio.
Key: C. = competitive; S-C. = semi-competitive; O-P. = one party.

Therefore, to control the political character of the district by its ecological character, the districts were grouped as follows: (1) districts in metropolitan areas as defined by the 1950 Census; (2) districts with an urban and rural non-farm population of 50 per cent or more; and (3) districts with an urban and rural non-farm population of less than 50 per cent, including those without an urban place of 2,500 population or more. As Table 13.2 indicates, the hypothesis is clearly maintained in the metropolitan and urban districts.[7] Regardless of whether they are located in a metropolitan

[7] Our data are not sufficient to test the hypothesis with regard to the less urbanized or "rural" districts. The actual numbers of legislators involved are so small that any inference from the data is extremely hazardous. Of the two respondents from competitive districts, both indicate a district-state orientation. Of three respondents from semi-competitive districts, two are district oriented and one is district-state oriented. Of six legislators from one-party areas, four are district oriented and two are state oriented.

area or not, the competitive districts are more likely to produce legislators who are district oriented than the one-party districts, while the latter produce more state-oriented legislators than do the competitive districts. The semi-competitive districts fall in the middle. In the 50 per cent and more urbanized areas, we note again that the more competitive the district, the more likely it is that legislators will be district oriented. However, greater proportions of district-state-oriented legislators appear in the 50 per cent or more urban than in the metropolitan areas, suggesting a greater pull towards dichotomization of areal-role orientations in the metropolitan districts. In other words, while the political character of the district seems to be of primary importance in shaping areal-role orientations, ecological characteristics have a secondary effect. Apparently, legislators are forced to look to certain elements in their district to maintain their position as representatives.

THE DISTRICT AS A SOURCE OF POLICY

The geographical electoral district is probably the most practical and, from the point of view of competitive politics, the functionally most viable unit of representation. But can it serve as a significant source of public policy? It is often alleged either that legislators hear nothing from their district on policy matters, or that the district and its presumed interests are the major source of legislators' policy stands. But, an either–or formulation of the problem does not seem empirically tenable. As Dexter has pointed out in a qualitative study of the relationship between the Congressman and his district:[8]

On numerous important policy matters, he hears nothing from his constituency. But whether he hears anything on an issue, what he hears, whom he hears from, or how he interprets what he hears all *vary* depending upon the kind of person he is, the kind of associations he has had and has in the constituency and in Washington, the public image of his interests and concerns, and the background information or misinformation which he possesses.

The Congressman's role is, of course, more professionalized than that of the state legislator whose district contacts are likely to be more intimate, partly because of the comparatively smaller period of time he is away from home, partly because, unlike the Congressman, he rarely moves his residence from his district to the capitol. If people in his district have policy views, therefore, the state legislator should be in a better position than the Congressman to discover and appraise

[8] Lewis A. Dexter, "The Representative and His District," *Human Organization* 16:2–37 (1957), p. 2.

such views. For these reasons, it is not surprising that, in answer to the question whether there are "any important differences between what you think this job is and the way your constituents see it?" both district-oriented and state-oriented legislators discussed the district as a source of policy in almost equal proportions (data not shown).

However, if areal-role orientations have any meaning, we should expect that among those who discussed the district as a policy source,

Table 13.3: Perception of district as a source of policy by legislators in four states

	Areal-Role Orientation		
Perception of District	District $N = 88$	District-State $N = 71$	State $N = 48$
Difficulties perceived	63%	64%	79%
No difficulties perceived	37	36	21
Total	100%	100%	100%

Table 13.4: Reasons for policy difficulties between constituents and legislators in four states*

	Areal-Role Orientation		
Reasons for Difficulties	District $N = 55$	District-State $N = 45$	State $N = 38$
Policy views difficult to ascertain, apathy, etc.	25%	22%	3%
Policy views are selfish	24	42	32
Policy views are provincial, uninformed, narrow	49	53	55
Differences on particular issues and bills	13	7	24

* Percentages total more than 100 since some respondents gave more than one answer.

state-oriented legislators would be more likely to envisage difficulties in ascertaining what that policy is than district-oriented respondents. As Table 13.3 shows, this is the case. It may also be noted that the district-state-oriented respondents appear to be similar to the district oriented, as had been anticipated earlier in the theoretical discussion of this hyphenated type.

Just what difficulties are involved in ascertaining the policy views prevalent in a district? And do district-oriented legislators differ in this regard from state-oriented legislators? Table 13.4 presents the data. The table shows, in the first place, that both district-oriented and district-state-oriented respondents are more likely to complain about the fact that district policy views are difficult to find out, that their constituents are apathetic in regard to policy matters, or so divided on policy issues that the district cannot serve as a policy guide. One may assume that they would like to see this changed, that they would like to be able to get cues from their district with regard to policy issues. Not knowing or not being able to ascertain what the people back home may think on policy matters may be expressed as follows:

I don't know how my constituents see things. I don't have a crystal ball that tells me how my constituents feel. After there are hearings and various reports given on a bill I know more about it than my constituents do.

You can't vote by what you think the constituents' thinking is. You don't know what that thinking is. Even if you receive a hundred letters on a bill, this is a very small proportion in respect to the size of the district.

Part of the difficulty in knowing what constituents think seems to be that they are divided. In other words, there is no such thing as a "district point of view":

There are always some groups who see things differently and don't agree with the way you vote. Union people want us to vote one way and get mad if we don't. The doctors and insurance people act as a group and want you to vote certain ways and they all want favors from you.

You can only represent the majority, you can't represent all of your constituents, they are too divergent. For instance, the very radical labor people, or those who are conservative to the nth degree.

Or the constituents may be seen as apathetic and disinterested, or ignorant. They cannot possibly know what the legislator knows and are, therefore, useless as source of policy suggestions:

There isn't much interest in my county. The local newspaper gives me the only indication as to how my constituents feel.

I think I'd say they were disinterested. If they are not affected by the legislation, they don't care.

Sometimes someone will tell them to come up here and tell me how to vote on a certain bill, but they don't know what the bill is about.

They are pitifully ignorant of how you spend state money. People often fight for legislation, like education, that would hurt the county tax-wise. Thirty PTA women once came to see me about education. I explained to them my position, but they don't know and don't care.

While district-oriented legislators express these complaints more frequently than state-oriented legislators, the latter, as Table 13.4 shows, are somewhat more inclined to see their constituents as being narrow in viewpoint or selfish in objectives. Respondents would hint at this in a rather vague sort of way:

Often individual viewpoints fail to be cognizant of the responsibility of the legislator for the interests of the whole constituency.

Constituents consider you a personal representative of theirs, and you're wrong if you don't vote as they personally wish.

People have a way of attaching great importance to their own personal problems. I find it disappointing to have constituents turn against me because I can't accommodate them in some particular matter.

More specifically, people in the district are seen as becoming active in policy matters only if their pocketbooks are involved, or if they have a particular stake in the legislation:

The majority are uninterested, unless it affects their pocketbooks or jobs.

They are interested in certain bills, not the legislature as a whole. Last Saturday a man in the sawmill business in my county came to see me about this bill on industrial insurance. I argued that he didn't really understand the bill and that as it stood I couldn't see my way clear to vote for it as he wanted.

Finally, there are those constituents who, apparently, believe that there is a "county interest" and who will push it in disregard of the legislator's other obligations:

Selfish individuals want laws to aid them at someone else's expense. Some want the county to benefit at the expense of the rest of the state.

Usually they are more interested in their own local problems rather than state problems.

To them it is the county over everything else.

A general feeling of alienation from their constituents expressed by some legislators is well articulated in the following remark:

It's hard to tell what the constituent wants. I have a pretty dim view of the constituency. They want economy if it doesn't hurt them; they want lower taxes for themselves, but higher for other groups. All your motives and intentions are suspect and your actions misinterpreted; we are also subjected to the irresponsible and crank elements; they pick up your name from somewhere and start writing. Some letters, though, are very thoughtful and considerate, but others are pretty rough.

As Table 13.3 indicated, about one-third of those respondents who perceived their district as a source of policy maintained that they had no policy differences or difficulties with their constituents. What are the reasons given by these legislators for feeling that their own policy views and those of their constituents are essentially in agreement? We might expect that state-oriented legislators (who tend to come from non-competitive districts) are more confident about their relationships with constituents in regard to policy views than district-oriented legislators (who come from competitive areas, or urbanized areas, where policy agreement among constituents is presumably less pronounced and more difficult to ascertain). Though the numbers of respondents are small, Table 13.5 tends to bear

Table 13.5: Reasons for policy agreement between constituents and legislators in four states*

Areal-Role Orientation

Reasons for Policy Agreement	District N = 33	District-State N = 26	State N = 10
Constituents rely on legislator's judgment	12%	27%	40%
Constituents and legislator think alike on policy	15	23	20
Legislator's views are satisfactory, is re-elected	24	31	50
Vague, miscellaneous	70	35	30

* Percentages total more than 100 since some respondents gave more than one answer.

out this expectation. It may be noted, first, that district-oriented legislators are considerably more vague in giving reasons for policy agreement between themselves and their constituents than state-oriented respondents. It will be recalled that more of them also reported that they find it difficult to ascertain policy views in their district (Table 13.4). Secondly, it appears that state-oriented respondents who see themselves in agreement on policy with their constituents are much more definite in the reasons they give. Forty per cent of them as against only 12 per cent of the district oriented claim that their constituents rely on them in policy matters. While the difference is small, state-oriented legislators also tend to emphasize that they and their constituents think alike more than district-oriented respondents. Such agreement may be attributed to shared beliefs and understandings:

In my opinion, the great majority of my constituents feel that I'm their voice and vote in the legislature, and are willing to delegate the responsibility to me that I'm willing to accept. We are all common folks, living in a common habitat, having the same desires and needs.

My constituents think like I do, mainly because they too are small businessmen and farmers.

The agreement may be said to stem from the isolation or remoteness of some districts:

I don't think no man has had as little trouble—as far as demands from the district go—as I had. They left it up to my judgment in major matters. I get letters, of course, but I use my own judgment. You know when you come from a rural district you don't have the party chairman interfere all the time. The boys from the city districts are being dictated to.

My constituents are in accord with my ideas. We are a remote county and have the lowest percentage of college educated. It's shameful.

The legislator may feel that there are policy disagreements but also feel that his constituents will go along with him:

You know, I'm pretty independent. I don't necessarily hold the same ideas as the constituents. I tell 'em that. . . . But they seem to humor me and go along.

If my constituents were fully informed, there would be no discrepancy between their views and mine.

Still others interpret their constituents' failure to write them letters as evidence of policy harmony between themselves and their district:

I probably have the least amount of mail of anybody in the legislature; at least, so they tell me. So apparently there aren't any differences.

I'm in a unique position. Others get a constant flock of mail. But I don't have so much trouble. It's a pat on my back—they elected me and have confidence in my judgment. Some senators get letters and get excited and get bothered. I let the seas roll on.

Table 13.5 also shows that state-oriented legislators seem to be more sensitive to the residue of power that is inherent in their constituents, and they point to the sanctions of the electoral process. Having been elected and re-elected is taken as proof that the legislator's policy views must be satisfactory:

My vote has always been high in my constituency. They must like me. While I don't suit politicians, I sure suit my constituents.

Well now, before you write anything down, there are constituents and constituents. There are all types of constituents and you can't satisfy them all. But the people back home sent me back three times—my sincerity has convinced them I deserve re-election. The majority of my constituents are satisfied.

The impression one gets from these replies about the relevance of the legislator's district and constituents in decision making, regardless of whether difficulties and differences or agreements are perceived, is one of considerable malaise. The electorate is seen as an essentially inactive mass which rather passively goes along, or it is seen as so divided that no policy views can be ascertained. The data explain, in part, why it is that the representational role of trustee, as we saw in Chapter 12, is taken by so many legislators in all four states. They suggest that if the legislator claims to follow his own convictions or judgment rather than a mandate, he does not simply express himself in political stock-in-trade cliches. Rather, it seems that the role of trustee is foisted on the legislator by virtue of the difficulties he has in determining the policy views of his constituents in his district. Moreover, though there are characteristic differences between those who are district oriented and those who are state oriented, the differences are small, and both groups seem to face similar problems vis-à-vis their districts, as does the hyphenated group of district-state-oriented legislators. This makes the areal focus of their role orientations all the more important as they approach the task of lawmaking. The whole tone of a legislature's discussions and deliberations may be influenced by prevailing areal-role orientations.

ROLE CONSENSUS AND DISSENSUS: PERCEPTIONS OF THE DISTRICT'S VIEW

The difficulties which the legislator faces in receiving meaningful policy cues from his district may, in part at least, spring from disagreement between himself and his constituents over his central role as a legislator. Conflict in the role expectations concerning the representational role between legislator and constituents is likely to be dysfunctional for the legislator's effectiveness.

From all we know so far about areal-role orientations, we should expect that district-oriented legislators will generally be more sensitive to differences between themselves and their constituents in regard to a conception of the legislative job than state-oriented legislators. In fact, there is a slight tendency of district-oriented legislators to mention differences of various kinds between themselves and the people in their district in somewhat greater proportion than state-oriented legislators—53 per cent as against 44 per cent. But if we look at the content of the differences as they are seen by legislators who mention them, we not only find no coherent pattern in responses, but we also find no consistent differences in the perceptions of district-oriented and state-oriented legislators. It should be noted that the percentages in Table 13.6 may be deceiving because the actual numbers in most of the categories are very small. The most revealing result is that majorities of all three areal-focus groups are agreed that their constituents are uninformed on government, politics, legislative functions and processes. About one-fifth in each group feel that their constituents underestimate the difficulties of the legislative job and the importance of personal relationships in the legislature. And others complain about their constituents' lack of respect for the legislative job, their making unfair moral judgments, and their not appreciating the importance of the job, and so on. In some categories, state-oriented

Table 13.6: Differences between legislators' and constituents' conceptions of the legislative job in four states*

Perception of Constituents' View of Job	Areal-Role Orientation		
	District $N = 70$	District-State $N = 37$	State $N = 31$
Uninformed on government, politics, legislature	59%	57%	68%
Underestimate difficulty of job, personal aspects	20	19	26
Don't appreciate importance of job	11	5	16
Show no respect, make unfair moral judgments	10	3	6
Make unreasonable demands on legislator as errand-boy	7	5	3
Exhibit occasional differences	13	8	3
Have different views about job among themselves	4	16	3
Underestimate party demands	1	5	3
Other comments	7	5	6

* Percentages total more than 100 since some respondents gave more than one answer.

legislators are more outspoken and severe in their own appraisal of constituents than are the district-oriented respondents, but the differences are small and by no means consistent throughout. Expressions of these grievances in the interview protocols may shed further light on the dynamics of the relationships between legislators and their districts.

There is, of course, an abundance of comment to the effect that constituents are uninformed:

I don't think my constituents have the slightest idea of what the legislature is for. They're very poorly informed, speaking in general terms, of course. There are always the people who are close to you and they come to ask questions, so they know a little more, but there is just too much apathy on the part of the rank and file.

Constituents have the impression that we're in session all the time and are surprised to learn that we have only one session every two years. This is because they see Congress news all year. I am thought of like a representative in Washington. People ask me to support federal bills, and, ten to one, ask me "How are things in Washington?"

I haven't heard anything. I haven't been approached. I call it legislation or government, they call it "politics." Let's not kid ourselves, they don't know about the specifics of it. They think of the office as "being in politics," and I think they don't know what they mean by that.

That constituents underestimate the difficulties involved in the legislative job and the importance of personal relations in the legislature may be expressed as follows:

Some constituents think I should know all about each of the 1,300 bills. The public expects a lot of knowledge from the legislator that he doesn't have. A lot of the constituents are interested in just one thing, but I must have a general picture.

Oh, yes . . . now the rank and file don't know what the job entails. They feel that a Senator can sway the thinking of the body of men at his will. They don't realize that I'm only one out of thirty-four. Also they don't realize the many long hours of hard work the consideration of legislation demands. Also poor publicity will cause them to have a misconception of what legislation means.

Other legislators complain that their constituents do not appreciate the importance of the legislature as an institution:

The average person doesn't realize the importance of the position in any legislative body. And after all the position is important because all legislatures make laws by which people live. We pass laws which reach right into the home of a family. Social, business, labor, farmers, all walks of life are affected by legislation passed or defeated. And by taxation.

The opportunities for service, the demands and qualifications that make for an effective representative far exceed the concept of the man in the street. The man in the street has little appreciation of the duties, obligations, and requirements for a qualified representative.

There is especially much bitterness in the expressions of those who feel that their constituents don't respect the job of the legislator and make unfair moral judgments about it:

The average constituent often feels something sinister and basically tainted about politics—the average person thinks that because you hold a political job you can get away with murder—it's difficult to explain the limitations to them. They think there's an overabundance of money and that the legislator has the key to the U.S. mint.

There are two types of constituents: those who think we are here for our own personal good, not knowing that it costs many of us money to come here. The others are those who think that if they wave a magic wand they'll get what they want. A lot of them feel that we're here in session a couple of hours a day and that we play all night.

Another group of legislators felt that their constituents make unreasonable demands on their time by asking them to be errand boys:

They ask for a great deal and are very reluctant about paying for it. They want everything without paying more taxes. There is one difference. Many want state jobs. It is often impossible for me to get them for them. It is not my job. This is one of my biggest problems down here. Getting jobs ought to be the job of the party chairman.

Some think I should be their advocate or errand boy. I make no calls on state offices to seek favors. If I get a request I send it to the proper office, but I don't go out and plead.

A few respondents mention that constituents do not understand the demands made on legislators by their party. As one of them put it:

They think that a senator or representative can carry legislation through by himself. They don't see the minority-majority set-up, that the majority leaders determine whether or not legislation becomes law particularly with regard to policy matters, and that's most bills. They don't see that the legislature works through mechanics which favor the majority party.

Of course, some legislators are more discriminating and point out that different constituents may have different views of the legislator's job:

The general public is too little informed as a whole on the way the government operates. They know the broad principles, but the general citizenry judges on results. Of course, this doesn't apply to those who are informed and active. Elections, though, are often determined by the pleasant smile—someone in the small counties who "talks" to the people and the cities by a "name." There are two people in this legislature who even changed their names, and they changed them to good political ones too. Still I would be lying to say that my father's and grandfather's names have not helped me.

Some think we are doing a magnificent job, others don't. It's hard to tell. Some don't know the workings of the legislature, think we are doing nothing, and have gripes. Civic leaders in the city report to the people through their organizations—that's more important to us than what a few individuals think.

There is an almost tragic element of self-pity in most of these remarks about constituents. Quite clearly, dissensus rather than consensus is the dominant theme in legislators' perceptions of the constituents' views of the representative role. If constituents are as ill informed, ill judging, confused, and apathetic as legislators say they are, it is indeed difficult for the legislator to "represent" his areal clientele in any mandatory sense of the term. What prevents this dissensus about the representational role from being wholly dysfunctional is, of course, the nature of modern government. Expert judgment of what is necessary rather than public opinion or understanding makes for the effective performance of governmental functions. In this situation it is all the more necessary for elected officials to be trustees.[9]   But one of the main consequences of the continued vitality of district orientation is awareness of the electoral district as the source of political power and of elections as the decisive sanctioning mechanism to enforce political responsibility. The district as such may not serve as a useful focus of policy or even as a source of status and prestige, but it clearly serves as a political subsystem whose chief function is, through creating a competitive politics, to enforce political responsibility.   For it is political competition which, as we have seen, makes for areal roles which are district oriented, and which guarantees that the geographical district continues to be a viable unit of representation.

THE LEGISLATOR AS A SERVANT

The notion that the legislator is not only a lawmaker, but also the people's servant, is widely held, but probably considerably less so by legislators themselves than by their clientele.   Of the 474 legislators interviewed in the four states, only 27 per cent spontaneously mentioned what one may call "service functions" as important aspects of their legislative job, and not all of these functions are in the nature of "service," literally interpreted.   There are those who, indeed, perceive the job of legislator as including the "errand-boy" function.   But there are others who would limit service to communication about what they are doing.   And there are those who, strictly speaking, are not servants at all, but who see it as one of their tasks to persuade, convince, and educate their constituents.   While one could speak, therefore, of errand boys, communicators, and mentors as subtypes of the servant role, the number of respondents who could be so classified is too small for meaningful analysis in role terms.   However, the servants as a group may be inspected in terms of various functions they claim for this general role.

From the varying character of areal roles, one may expect that district-oriented legislators will mention service functions more frequently

[9] See below, Chapter 16, pp. 395–397, concerning the interpenetration of areal and representational roles.

than state-oriented respondents. This is, in fact, the case. The differences are small, but 31 per cent of the district-oriented legislators mention service functions of one kind or another, and only 21 per cent of the state-oriented respondents do likewise. However, district-state-oriented legislators exceed both (36 per cent).

How are the more specific service functions perceived by those areal-role takers who mention them? We should expect that errand-boy and communication work will be more often cited by district-oriented respondents, and the mentor function more by state-oriented legislators. Table 13.7 presents the data. In general, our expecta-

Table 13.7: Different service functions mentioned by areal-role takers in four states*

Areal-Role Orientations

Service Functions	District $N = 41$	District-State $N = 32$	State $N = 15$
Errand-boy functions			
Helping people with problems: general	39%	40%	20%
Contacting state administration	32	22	27
Entertaining, shepherding visitors	2	9	—
Getting jobs for people	12	—	—
Communication functions			
Writing letters, keeping people posted	41	22	27
Making speeches in district, at clubs	17	19	13
Reporting via mass media: columns,			
radio, TV	12	13	—
Mentor functions			
Persuading, educating constituents	15	22	40

* Percentages total more than 100 since some respondents gave more than one answer.

tions are met. Almost twice as many district-oriented as state-oriented respondents mention "helping people" as part of their service role, and generally more of them mention other errand-boy and communication functions. On the other hand, more than twice as many of the state-oriented than of the district-oriented legislators mention mentor functions. But, again, the numbers in each category are small, so the data cannot be treated as anything but suggestive and interesting. But qualitative review of the interview protocols may give more insight into the service aspects of the areal-role orientations of the respondents and the relations between legislators and their district in regard to expectations of service.

Errand-boy functions. General statements about helping their constituents with "problems" were made by all three areal-role groups, but more by district-oriented and district-state-oriented respondents than state-oriented legislators:

> To be of service is definitely the most important thing. He who is the greatest among you, serves the best. You try to help out those at home by answering questions and handling problems for them for whatever difficulties they may be up against.

> Little things you do for small people back home, many have nothing to do with legislation, that's the biggest job and the most time consuming.

> To keep my finger on the pulse of the people, I say I will be available to anyone Friday or Saturday at my place of business. I try to make them feel I can help them. I feel that's part of the job.

The notion that the legislator brings his areal clientele into contact with various agencies of the state government is articulated as follows:

> The legislator can be of help to his people in many ways. He is the go-between for the people and the officeholders. They need things done which the representative can do better for them. I'm able to help them in other ways also. I just came from a committee hearing where they are hearing a bill I'm putting up for the people of my county.

> You're the contact between the people back home and the state government. They wouldn't come up here to speak for themselves, but they will come to you. In a way we're sort of an errand boy for the people.

> A good legislator in my opinion should be willing to serve as a contact man between his constituents and the various departments of state government; in other words, he should be a sort of walking directory so that he can at least refer his citizens to the right person or department when they have a problem at the state level. That I feel is a part of the service he should be willing to render when he takes the oath of office.

Communications functions. Communication between themselves and their district is seen by some legislators as another important service as part of their legislative role. Keeping people informed by punctilious answering of one's mail is considered essential:

> I religiously answer mail. I answer everything. I get postcards such as, "Vote against the dog bill. It is a bad bill." In this case I answer them asking why it is bad, and sometimes they don't even know—they were asked by someone to write the card.

> One of the most important jobs, from the standpoint of public relations, is to take care of your correspondence properly and promptly. They know us and we must answer.

Making speeches at home is another form of communication between the legislator and his district:

Just the other week I was asked to speak before the Daughters of the Grand Union. Well, I had to do some research on their organization and it made me very happy that they were so pleased with what I said, and I learned something besides.

It's always my policy to meet with rural people in my district, with city officials, people of the Chamber of Commerce, and so on. I go to many meetings and banquets to learn what they think. I even go to meetings of colored groups.

Finally, a number of these servants are aware of the use they can make of the mass media in communicating with their constituents:

I have a session at my house every week, where the people can come and talk to me. I also do a broadcast every week, and write a column in the paper back home. You've got to let the people know it's their government.

I made up my mind I'd try and keep the people informed. I feel that I have a personal mission to restore and maintain faith in our government. I prepare a weekly news report and send it to my local paper so that the people can know what's going on up here.

Mentor functions. The mentor function does not, in some respects, involve service at all, though in order to be able to persuade and convince his constituents of the importance of what he is doing and bring them around to his conceptions, the legislator must maintain communication with his district. The following examples illustrate this function (other instances have been cited earlier in connection with other aspects of the areal role):

I always listen to my constituents, anyone who wants to talk to me. I listen to whatever goes on here and then *debate* issues with them. Either of us may be right or wrong.

I usually go by my convictions and depend on being able to *convince* the constituents when I get back that I did the right things.

It's the job of a legislator to *explain* and *educate* his constituents, show them that what's good for the state is also good for them. I try to *convince* them that local interests sometimes have to be sacrificed to the common good.

If it serves a useful purpose, you have the duty to *lead* your constituency as well as to follow it.

The qualitative material concerning "service functions" we have reviewed suggests some of the expectations which might make for a servant role if one were to be constructed. For some legislators, these errand-boy or communication services are essential aspects of the job, partly because the maintenance of democratic government is assumed to be bound up with the performance of services for the electoral clientele. Other legislators may look on the service functions as a chore, foisted on them by their constituents and carried out only unwillingly.[10] Finally, there are those who see political advantages in performing service functions, whose service orientation to their district is opportunistic: it gives them publicity and promises re-election. It is quite likely that this is particularly true of state-oriented legislators, but our data do not permit us to explore this proposition.

However, there is some evidence to the effect that commitment to district and constituents is more genuine on the part of district-oriented than state-oriented legislators. Each legislator was asked whether he agreed with the statement that "the job of a representative is to work for what the constituents want even though his may not always agree with his personal views." The statement is ambiguous because it is not clear whether constituents' "wants" refer to policy demands or services. But, as Table 13.8 shows, district-oriented legis-

Table 13.8: Areal-role orientations and attitude concerning constituents' wants in four states

"The job of a representative is to work for what his constituents want . . . "	Areal-Role Orientations		
	District $N = 127$	District-State $N = 86$	State $N = 70$
Agree	76%	53%	57%
Disagree	24	47	43
Total	100%	100%	100%

lators agree with this attitude item in significantly greater proportions than do state-oriented legislators.

AREAL-ROLE ORIENTATIONS AND SENSE OF LEGISLATIVE EFFICACY

In some respects, of course, all three types of areal-role orientations are vital to the functioning of the legislature as an institution: district orientation because it is a continual guarantee of political responsibility; state orientation because it directs attention to problems which require representation; and district-state orientation because it serves the important function of integrating district and state interests in the legislative process.

[10] For negative evaluation of the "errand boy" role, see above, p. 303.

Yet, it appears as a pervasive theme of this chapter that district-oriented legislators seem to have more troubles with and to be more troubled by their constituency relations than state-oriented legislators. This was most apparent in two connections: first, in regard to the problem of the district as a source of policy; second, in regard to the problem of consensus between legislators and constituents involving their conception of the legislative job. On the one hand, district-oriented legislators were more inclined to point out their difficulties in ascertaining the policy views of their district than were state-oriented legislators. They seemed to feel frustrated by their failure to do so, while state-oriented respondents evidently wrote their district off as inconsequential for legislative policymaking. On the other hand, state-oriented respondents seemed to sense more agreement between themselves and their constituents with regard to the role they should play in the legislature than did district-oriented legislators. They seemed to be more confident and assured of themselves with regard to their proper role in the legislative setting.

On the basis of these observations, we might expect that state-oriented legislators will exhibit a higher sense of legislative efficacy than district-oriented respondents. One would expect them to feel more at home in their jobs, more in control of the legislative situation. And one would expect that district-state-oriented legislators will occupy a middle position on the index of efficacy.[11] As Table 13.9

Table 13.9: Areal-role orientations and sense of legislative efficacy

Index of Sense of Legislative Efficacy

Role Orientation	Calif.	N.J.	Ohio	Tenn.
District	+5	+19	+13	0
District-state	+7	+22	+36	+11
State	+12	+82	+16	+27

indicates, this is in fact the case, with the single exception of Ohio where the district-state-oriented respondents scored higher than the state-oriented legislators. But in all four states, the state-oriented respondents have consistently higher scores on the efficacy index than do the district-oriented legislators, and in all but Ohio the district-state-oriented respondents occupy a middle position.

[11] For fuller discussion of the "sense of legislative efficacy" index, see Appendix 2.2, below, pp. 474–475.

But it may also be noted that, Ohio excepted, the efficacy scores of the district-state-oriented group are closer to those of the district-oriented than those of the state-oriented respondents. We noted earlier that the state component of this orientation may be weaker than its district component. In other words, it would seem that these legislators, their declarations notwithstanding, are more district than state oriented. This may affect the nature of the legislature as a role system and the interpenetration of different role sets—problems with which we shall deal in Chapter 16.

CHAPTER 14

The legislator
and the interests:
pressure-group roles

THE ONCE PREVALENT VIEW that "special interest groups," by their very existence, constitute a threat to the general "public interest" has generally given way to a belief that interest groups collectively constitute a legitimate clientele in the formulation of policy.[1] As V. O. Key says:

> Pressure groups fill a gap in our formal political system by performing a function of representation beyond the capacities of representatives chosen by the voters in geographical districts. If it is the duty of government in a democracy to give regard to the wishes of the people, means have to be found to ascertain those wishes. . . . Special interests came to be recognized so that, in part, the cheese makers, the laborers, the drys, or others of like views and interests might have representatives who could state their attitudes authoritatively before the government and the public.[2]

The central problem in representation posed by pressure groups for the modern legislature, therefore, is the problem of relating to each other, and to a public interest espoused by no organized group, the

---

This chapter drafted by Wahlke.

[1] That organized interest groups and group activity occur in all developed Western systems is now widely accepted. See, for example, the comments of G. Heckscher in Henry W. Ehrmann, Edit., *Interest Groups on Four Continents* (Pittsburgh, Pennsylvania: University of Pittsburgh Press, 1958), p. 170, and Joseph LaPalombara, "The Utility and Limitations of Interest Group Theory in Non-American Field Situations," *Journal of Politics* 22:29–49 (1960), at pp. 29–30. This is *not* to say, however, that the *legitimacy* of pressure-group activity is universally admitted, even in Western systems.

[2] V. O. Key, Jr., *Politics, Parties and Pressure Groups*, p. 152.

multitudinous particular interests voiced by countless organized groups. In the words of Belle Zeller:

Before the legislature, this mighty array of pressure groups clashes; . . . Just what should be the role of the legislature while all this is going on? The legislature should serve as impartial referee in seeing that these opposing groups do not take unfair advantage of one another. But it should do more than that. It should protect the interests of the general public.[3]

Yet there are surprisingly few theoretical explanations or cumulative and comparative empirical data about this phase of the representative process.[4] The notion that legislative decisions are simple mathematical resultants of "pressures" by lobbyists, parties, and constituents, all impinging on passively reacting legislators, has often been criticized.[5] Much research on pressure politics attempts to explain the actions of supposedly "pressured" legislatures and legislators by looking not at them but at the pressuring groups. Little is said about how or why the legislator is influenced by the supposedly critical characteristics of pressure groups—size of membership, geographical distribution, wealth and resources, extent and character of leadership and organization, strategic position in society, and so on.[6]

To do his job the legislator must answer such questions as: How much, and in what way, should one take into account the activities, demands, and attitudes of all these groups and their agents? What behavior is appropriate, on the part of the legislator, in encounters with lobbyists? How does a particular group, a particular part of the public, fit into the whole? How can or should one evaluate

[3] Belle Zeller, *Pressure Politics in New York* (New York: Prentice-Hall, 1937), p. 264.

[4] See Samuel J. Eldersveld, "American Interest Groups: A Survey of Research and Some Implications for Theory and Method," in Henry W. Ehrmann (ed.), *op. cit.*, pp. 173–196; Oliver Garceau, "Interest Group Theory in Political Research," *Annals of the American Academy of Political and Social Science* 319: 104–112 (1958). For discussion of some of the general problems of research, theory, and conception, see also Gabriel A. Almond, "A Comparative Study of Interest Groups and the Political Process," *American Political Science Review* 52: 270–282 (1958); Alfred de Grazia, "The Nature and Prospects of Political Interest Groups," *Annals of the American Academy of Political and Social Science* 319:113–122 (1958); W. J. M. Mackenzie, "Pressure Groups: The 'Conceptual Framework'," *Political Studies* 3:247–257 (1955).

[5] Peter Odegard, "A Group Basis of Politics: A New Name for an Ancient Myth," *Western Political Quarterly* 11:689–702 (1958); Robert M. MacIver, *The Web of Government* (New York: Macmillan and Company, 1947), pp. 220–221; Truman, *The Governmental Process*, pp. 332–333.

[6] See, for example, Bertram M. Gross, *op. cit.*, p. 143; Truman lists these and similar group characteristics, adding to the list "group cohesion," *The Governmental Process*, pp. 159–167.

the comparative merit of diverse and competing demands coming from different groups? How rank these alongside proposals which have no organized spokesmen supporting or opposing them, or which introduce still further contradictions? What characteristics of groups or their demands are relevant to the function of a legislature as a representative and authoritative decision-making body? How can the busy legislator ascertain what they are for any given group? Legislators' answers to such questions and their rules for perceiving the world of pressure groups are reflected in their role concepts respecting representatives of organized groups.

To inquire into these and thereby to explore analytical questions about the function and process of representation, we asked a series of questions (Nos. 20–22, Appendix 6, pp. 498–499 below). At a later point in the interview schedule, respondents were questioned at length concerning their views on one issue, the problem of "school needs." Several questions from this context are also used in the analysis which follows (the principle one being No. 34b, Appendix 6, p. 500, below).

PRESSURE GROUPS IN THE FOUR STATES

Just as the party system varies from one state to another, with corresponding differential effects on the behavior of legislators, so too the world of pressure groups faced by the members of one legislature differs from that of others. It is more difficult to describe that background and to make comparisons among the states than is the case with respect to party systems. But viewed collectively, the replies to the above questions provide one approach to the problem.

In the course of the interviews, California legislators referred to a total of 125 interest groups, including 56 specifically named organizations; New Jersey legislators named 101 groups, of which 38 were specifically named organizations; Ohio legislators mentioned 144 groups, of which 68 were specific organizations; and Tennesseans referred to 102 different groups, including 40 specific organizations.[7] It must be assumed these represent only a fraction of the groups and organizations which at one time or another appear politically important in legislators' eyes.[8] But differences in the relative salience of various interests and groups in the four states can tell us something about the differences of pressure-group systems in them.

[7] References to "groups" include such responses as "farmers," "labor," "cattle interests," etc.

[8] Dayton McKean found 164 groups active in New Jersey in the mid-1930's. *Pressures on the Legislature of New Jersey* (New York: Columbia University Press, 1938), Ch. 3.

Salient interests and organizations. Because we are dealing with legislators' perceptions and not with the perceived objects themselves, we must take into account the circumstances making respondents aware of different groups. Presumably, groups which are quite salient in one situation may be overlooked and forgotten in others.

We therefore constructed indices of group salience for each of the different contexts of questioning about pressure groups—indices of *generalized power* salience (based on the question asking what groups are powerful), of *constituency power* salience (based on the question about groups powerful in the constituency), of *group merit* salience (what groups are worth listening to), and of *school issue* salience (groups named in the school issue responses). A summary index of *general salience* was devised from replies to all questions except those concerning school needs (which came after all the other pressure-group questions in the interview).[9]

In terms of the general salience of broad interest classes, there are relatively small differences among the states. Business interests are the most salient in all four states (from 28 per cent in California to 42 per cent in Ohio). Surprisingly, educational interests rank second in general salience in three states and tied for third in the other (12 per cent in Ohio, exactly matching labor interests' salience there, and 20 per cent in each of the other three states).[10] This suggests that legislators' perceptions of the group world are highly sensitive to the degree of organization and the legislative activity of groups. Labor interests rank third (or tied for it) in all four states (from 12 per cent in Ohio to 16 per cent in New Jersey). That labor interests rank so similarly, in spite of the differences among the states in economic diversity and industrial development, is perhaps less surprising than the relatively low rank in salience of agricultural interests for legislators in most rural Tennessee—only 4 per cent, the

[9] Each index is a simple percentage, based upon the total number of references to each set of groups under consideration at each point in the discussion. The criteria and procedures used for classifying interests and groups were entirely pragmatic, categories being devised to fit the manifest content of responses. But the resulting classification is similar to many used in other studies. See for example, Truman, *The Governmental Process*, pp. 33–43; Gross, *op. cit.*, pp. 21–22; Key, *Politics, Parties and Pressure Groups*, pp. 119 *et seq.* For discussion of some general problems in classification of groups by such criteria and others, see G. DeGre, "Outlines for a Systematic Classification of Social Groups," *American Sociological Review* 24:22–29 (1959); and G. A. Lundberg, "Some Problems of Group Classification and Measurement," *American Sociological Review* 5:351–360 (1940).

[10] Not an artifact of the interview, since the education-issue questions were asked only *after* the questions on which this index is based.

same as professional interests. Governmental interests (city and county governments, governmental or government-employees associations, etc.), ethnic and demographic interests, and religious, charitable, and civic interests make up the rest of the legislators'

Table 14.1: Interstate differences in salience of selected classes of interests when viewed by legislators in four different contexts*

Salience Indices for Four Contexts

Class of Interest	School Issue	Generalized Power	Power in Constituency	Group Merit
Business	Calif. 34%	Ohio 50%	Ohio 29%	
	N.J. 26	Tenn. 48	Tenn. 21	
	Ohio 25	Calif. 35	Calif. 10	
	Tenn. 17	N.J. 35	N.J. 9	
	Range 17%	Range 15%	Range 20%	
Educational	Ohio 50		N.J. 43	
	Calif. 41		Calif. 30	
	N.J. 43		Tenn. 30	
	Tenn. 36		Ohio 12	
	Range 14%		Range 31%	
Governmental	Tenn. 26			Tenn. 22%
	N.J. 9			N.J. 15
	Calif. 4			Ohio 14
	Ohio 5			Calif. 10
	Range 22%			Range 12%
Agricultural	Ohio 11	Ohio 13	Ohio 23	Calif. 12
	Calif. 5	Calif. 6	Calif. 17	Ohio 9
	Tenn. 3	N.J. 4	N.J. 12	Tenn. 5
	N.J. 1	Tenn. 2	Tenn. 7	N.J. 2
	Range 10%	Range 11%	Range 16%	Range 10%

* The numbers on which percentages are based for each state are the total number of references to all groups in the particular context.

worlds in all four states, with little difference among the states in the salience of any of these interest classes.

Differences among the states are better shown, however, by examining the salience of groups in particular contexts. Table 14.1 shows the interstate comparisons for each class of interest and in each context where the range among state indices was 10 per cent or greater. It appears that business and agricultural groups are relatively more salient for Ohio legislators than for those in the other three states, when viewed in the context of group power, either general or in the constituencies. But in both contexts, agricultural interests again rank surprisingly low in Tennessee. It may be that farm groups are not particularly salient there because proportionately many legislators come from wholly agricultural districts, thus providing some measure of "direct" representation of agricultural interests which legislators do not perceive as interest-group based. On the other hand, it is also likely that agriculture in Ohio is a much more diversified enterprise than in Tennessee, and that because business, labor, and other interests are highly organized there, agricultural interests have likewise been impelled to greater organization and activity.

Governmental interest groups are more salient for Tennessee legislators than for those of the other three states both as groups particularly worth listening to and with respect to the school issue. On the other hand, educational interest groups are less salient for Tennessee legislators in the school issue context than for legislators in any other state.

There are fewer differences among the states with respect to groups seen as powerful or as meritorious than there are in the other two contexts. This suggests that legislators in different states see significantly different constellations and combinations of interest when they deal with specific issues. The great range (31 per cent) in the context of groups powerful in the constituencies suggests another important difference in the specific impact of group activities from one state to another.[11]

Much the same conclusions can be drawn from examination of the indices of salience for specific interest-group organizations as for the classes of interest. Because of the large number of organizations involved it is impossible to present such data in full. But a comparison of organizations which ranked among the top five in salience in any context and in any state is presented in Table 14.2. Of particular interest is the very high salience of the principal teachers'

[11] All the salience indices, of course, reflect both fairly permanent gross differences in the group life of the four states and more transient differences in the activity and visibility of different groups and interests according to the issues before each legislature during the time of the study. Questions relevant to the contexts of general power, constituency power, and merit of groups presumably get at characteristics which are relatively more stable over time; those regarding school issues presumably reflect more the particular form and content taken by that issue at the time of interviewing.

association in all four states and in all contexts, indices for the specific organizations being substantially greater than for the more vague class of "educational interests." On the other hand, although "business interests" collectively and generally rank high in all states, specific business organizations are relatively much less salient in all. It appears that organizational monopoly or multiplicity in the various fields of interest is a dimension of considerable importance.

Significance of pressure politics. While the foregoing discussion gives some idea of the qualitative differences in group life among the four states, it would be useful to obtain some more precise measure of the comparative development of pressure politics as such in the four systems. Simplicity or diversity of interests and interest organization is one dimension of this, for which several rough measures are obtainable from our data, as shown in Table 14.3.

Comparison of Columns 2 and 4 of the table suggests that Tennessee's group life appears least diverse and Ohio's somewhat more so, whether we consider specific organizations or vaguer interest aggregations. In terms of vague interest classes, New Jersey appears most diverse of the four states, but in terms of specific organizations, California would appear to be somewhat more diverse than New Jersey. In terms of the degree to which group life appears to be organized (Column 5 of Table 14.3), group life appears to be most complex in New Jersey and least so in Tennessee, with Ohio ranking very close to Tennessee in this respect.

Because all three of the indices just described are constructed in the same way and attempt to index closely related aspects of the same general characteristic, they have been combined into a composite Index of Group Diversity and Complexity, by averaging them, with the results shown in Column 6 of Table 14.3. By this standard, which may be taken as a more reliable measure than any one of them singly, it appears that group life is most diverse and complex (in legislators' eyes) in California and least so in Tennessee.

Another dimension of pressure politics in any system is the degree to which legislators or other actors can discriminate and differentiate among the various interests and groups in their surroundings. In general, we should suppose pressure politics to be most developed where legislators are most sophisticated and discriminating in this respect. The potential of pressure politics is limited, in other words, by the ability of legislators to recognize, identify, and make distinctions among the various contending groups and interests. An index of potential for pressure politics based on such assumptions shows again that Tennessee ranks at one extreme and California at the other,

Table 14.2: Relative salience of selected (most salient) interest-group organizations in various contexts as seen by legislators of four states

Index of Salience in Context of

Organization	General	School Issue	Generalized Power	Const. Power	Group Merit
California (56 organizations named)					
California Teachers Assoc.	35%	47%	42%	34%	5%
AFL–CIO	12	4	16	7	2
California Farm Bureau	11	3	4	25	20
California Medical Assoc.	8	—	8	5	2
League of California Cities	8	1	8	5	12
California Supervisors Assoc.	7	1	9	3	8
Chamber(s) of Commerce	5	17	4	2	12
PTA(s)	5	8	4	10	5
League of Women Voters	3	—	1	2	12
California State Grange	2	1	2	5	2
Friends Legislative Committee	2	—	1	—	12
California Taxpayers Assoc.	2	18	1	2	8
	100%	100%	100%	100%	100%
New Jersey (38 organizations named)					
New Jersey Education Assoc.	28%	35%	30%	47%	11%
Chamber(s) of Commerce	20	11	20	12	25
AFL–CIO	20	14	23	24	10
N.J. Municipal League	9	7	7	—	17
N.J. Taxpayers Assoc.	8	14	5	—	21
N.J. Manufacturers Assoc.	5	4	7	4	2

League of Women Voters	5	4	3	4	12
N.J. Farm Bureau	3	—	4	5	2
PTA(s)	2	11	1	4	—
	100%	100%	100%	100%	100%
Ohio (68 organizations named)					
Ohio Farm Bureau	24%	12%	22%	37%	17%
Ohio Education Association	18	53	24	9	9
Chamber(s) of Commerce	15	17	14	15	21
Ohio State Grange	9	4	7	15	8
AFL–CIO	8	—	9	8	4
Ohio Manufacturers Assoc.	8	6	12	3	2
Ohio Council of Retail Merchants	7	—	6	4	14
Ohio Medical Association	6	1	5	3	11
League of Women Voters	3	2	—	2	11
PTA(s)	2	5	1	4	3
	100%	100%	100%	100%	100%
Tennessee (46 organizations named)					
Tennessee Education Assoc.	37%	46%	37%	53%	25%
Tennessee Municipal League	17	17	16	8	23
Tennessee Manufacturers Assoc.	15	5	18	7	16
Tenn. County Services Assoc.	14	19	14	6	19
Tennessee Farm Bureau	5	3	4	7	6
"Trading Stamps" (ad hoc group)	4	—	6	2	—
AFL–CIO	3	—	2	13	—
Tennessee Taxpayers Assoc.	3	5	1	—	9
PTA(s)	2	5	2	4	2
	100%	100%	100%	100%	100%

319

Table 14.3: Indices of diversity and complexity of group life in four states

State	(1) No. of Interest Categories Named	(2) Index: Diversity of Categories Named*	(3) No. of Specific Organizations Named	(4) Index: Diversity of Organizations Named*	(5) Index: Complexity of Organization†	(6) Combined Index: Mean of Cols. 2, 4, 5
California (N = 109)	125	1.15	56	.57	.53	.92
New Jersey (N = 78)	101	1.28	38	.43	.68	.80
Ohio (N = 160)	144	.90	68	.42	.49	.60
Tennessee (N = 115)	102‡	.89	40‡	.35	.48	.58

* The number in the preceding column divided by the number of respondents.

† Ratio of references to specific organizations to all references to groups, interests, and organizations.

‡ One Tennessee respondent named six closely related labor organizations, which have been counted as only one.

so far as the relative importance of pressure politics is concerned.[12] (See Table 14.4.)

Another dimension of pressure politics might be called its "legitimacy."[13] We have alluded earlier to the once-prevalent view,

Table 14.4: Indices of relative discrimination in legislators' perceptions of pressure politics and of relative potential influence of pressure politics

Coefficients of Correlation between Salience Indices in Paired Contexts for All Interests and Organizations*

State	Gen'l. Power and Const. Power	Gen'l. Power and Merit	Gen'l. Power and School Issue	Const. Power and Merit	Const. Power and School Issue	School Issue and Merit	Index of Potential for Pressure Politics† (Mean of Columns 1-6)
Calif.	+.72	−.32	+.81	+.10	+.68	−.64	+.23
N.J.	+.90	+.48	+.78	+.05	+.93	+.24	+.57
Ohio	−.28	+.68	+.80	+.51	+.20	+.16	+.32
Tenn.	+.82	+.82	+.90	+.56	+.84	+.79	+.79

* For organizations named in Table 14.3.

† *High* value indicates comparatively *less* discrimination. See footnote 12.

classically stated by Rousseau, that expression of conflicting private interests is inimical to the public interest. An opposing view, that of many "pluralist" theorists, holds that "the public interest" is never more than the harmonization of partial interests and that

[12] It is assumed that wide variation in salience of a particular group from one context to another indicates discrimination on the part of legislators naming the groups. High positive correlation would indicate very little discrimination (naming the same groups in the same frequency whatever the context). High negative correlation would indicate alertness to certain characteristics of a particular set of groups, a more discriminating view than that just described. Still more discrimination, however, would be indicated by zero—or very low correlation, either positive or negative. Because zero values represent maximum discrimination and negative values a very specialized, single-aspect sort of discrimination, the arithmetic mean based on the actual rather than on absolute values of the coefficients seems to approximate best the values we are seeking to index.

[13] Since this was written, Angus Campbell and his associates have utilized a strikingly similar concept—legitimacy of interest groups in the eyes of voters. It is interesting to note, too, the use of a concept of *salience* of groups in the same discussion. The theoretical assumptions behind the Survey Research Center group's handling of voter perceptions and pressure politics and our own seem quite parallel. See *The American Voter, op. cit.*, pp. 313 ff.

Index	Least		Significance		Most
Diversity and Complexity	Tenn.	Ohio	N.J.		Calif.
(Table 14.4)	.58	.60	.80		.92
Potential for Pressure	Tenn.	N.J.		Ohio	Calif.
Politics (Table 14.5)	.74	.57		.32	.23
Legitimacy of Pressure	Tenn.	N.J.		Ohio	Calif.
Politics (p. 322)	3.5	3.8		4.1	4.4

Figure 14.1. *Comparative significance of pressure politics in four states.*

organized groups, therefore, play an indispensable part in defining the public interest. Legislators' views on the subject likewise differ widely. Some agree with the member who said, "Hell! we wouldn't have a government if there were no interest groups. It would be a form of anarchy if groups and parties didn't do their job." Or, as another said, when asked about the desirability of having the individual citizen participate in government directly, rather than through interest groups, "How's he going to do it 'directly'? You have to organize or go into an organization to do anything." But others agree with the legislator who said, in response to the same question, "Stop right there (after the word 'directly') and you've got the whole story about our citizens and what they should do." Some share the suspicion of interest groups in general, as expressed by the member who said, "I've heard of them all my life, but I didn't aim to fool with that, and I don't know nothing about it."

The relative legitimacy of pressure politics in the four states can be measured by averaging the scale scores given individual legislators to measure their friendliness to pressure politics in general.[14] On this index of legitimacy the four states rank as follows (a score of 5.0 being the maximum possible and indicating greatest legitimacy, a score of 0 being the minimum, indicating the least): California 4.4, Ohio 4.1, New Jersey 3.8, Tennessee 3.5.

Interstate comparisons for the three dimensions of pressure politics are summarized graphically in Figure 14.1. Pressure politics in all three respects appears to be least developed in Tennessee and most in California, with Ohio and New Jersey ranking in between. An indirect but independent test of the validity of such a ranking is provided in legislators' answers to a question asking them to name

[14] See below, Appendix 1.4, for details concerning construction of the Likert-type scale of friendliness toward pressure politics.

the sources of information or advice they considered most reliable on the issue of school needs—a question asked, it might be repeated, only after completion of all questions dealing directly with pressure groups. Indices of reliance on information from pressure groups[15] show that, at least on this one issue, pressure groups would seem to play the greatest part in California (0.54) and the least in Tennessee (0.35), with New Jersey (0.45) and Ohio (0.41) ranking second and third, respectively. The rank order is quite consistent with our conclusions based on the three dimensions of pressure politics discussed above.

While all the measures used are extremely crude, to say the least, the consistent pattern they yield invites speculation. So far as concerns California, New Jersey, and Ohio, the findings are consistent with the often stated hypothesis that the influence of pressure groups is weakened by the existence of a strong party system, since among these three states the parties are least organized and active in the California legislature but comparatively more active and well organized in the legislatures of New Jersey and Ohio.

The fact that pressure politics seems comparatively least significant in Tennessee, even though the legislative party system there is even weaker than in any of the other states, suggests the extent to which other factors than the party system may be important in determining the relative influence of pressure politics. Here it would seem that both the comparatively less developed character of pluralistic group life and certain negative attitudes toward pluralistic phenomena which are part of legislators' cultural equipment contribute to lessen the significance of pressure politics for the legislators. (These two factors are, of course, no doubt interdependent upon each other to a considerable extent.)

While all such conclusions must be judged highly tentative insofar as they are based on the data of this particular study, they do agree with similar generalizations based frequently on even fewer data and even more speculative reasoning.

LEGISLATORS' ROLE ORIENTATIONS TOWARD PRESSURE GROUPS

Further insight into the character and function of pressure politics requires examination of individual legislators' postures toward pressure

[15] The number of references to interest groups as "most reliable sources" of advice or information on problems of school needs as a percentage of all references to all such sources. (From responses to Question No. 33, Appendix 6. p. 500 below.)

groups and their reasons for them—both "reasons" they adduce and correlations between legislators' postures and analytic variables established by analysts. We are concerned here, it should be emphasized, with the functioning of the legislative *institution* and not with unique historical events or outcomes. Similarly, we are concerned with legislators' orientations toward pressure groups as a *generic* class of "significant others," not with their particular individual group affiliations and identifications.

With respect to the bearing of pressure politics on the function of representation, the basic question is, how, and how much, are demands of interest groups considered by a legislature in the course of its decision making? In general some members will accommodate the demands of organized interest groups in the legislative process.[16] Others will resist consideration or accommodation of these demands. Still others, presumably attuned to other persons or factors, will play a neutral or varying and indeterminate role toward such group demands.

It seems obvious that a legislator's reaction to the activities of pressure groups and lobbyists will depend in part upon his general evaluation of pressure politics as a mode of political activity in the world he lives in. It likewise seems obvious that legislators' reactions to pressure groups or lobbyists will vary with their different degrees of knowledge or awareness of group activities. The legislator who knows what the Municipal League is, what it wants, who speaks for it and when, will react differently to cues from the League than one who never heard of it and doesn't identify anyone as its spokesman.

Assuming, then, that any given legislator's behavior with respect to pressure groups will depend largely upon his general affective orientation toward pressure politics and his awareness of such activity when it occurs around him,[17] one can construct the following very

[16] "Accommodation" does not necessarily mean "accession," although that is, of course, one form accommodation may take. Accommodation here means conscious consideration, of the sort implied in J. D. Stewart's discussion of "consultation" [*British Pressure Groups* (Oxford: Oxford University Press, 1958), pp. 3–27)].

[17] These two dimensions are suggested not only in numerous general social-psychological discussions of role concepts and self concepts, but also by two of the very few empirical and analytical studies of group politics. Garceau and Silverman (*op. cit.*, pp. 685 ff.) suggest that differences in legislative behavior toward groups as well as legislators' ideas about appropriate behavior toward them are associated with different levels of information about groups. Samuel H. Beer, in his analysis of operative theories of interest representation in Britain (*op. cit.*), suggests a number of respects in which legislators' different concep-

simple typology of legislators' role orientations toward pressure groups:

Facilitators: Have a friendly attitude toward group activity *and* relatively much knowledge about it.

Resisters: Have a hostile attitude toward group activity *and* relatively much knowledge about it.

Neutrals: Have no strong attitude of favor or disfavor with respect to group activity (regardless of their knowledge of it), or, have very little knowledge about it (regardless of their friendliness or hostility toward it).

By the measures of friendliness or hostility and awareness described elsewhere each of the legislators interviewed was classified under one of these three headings.[18]

The relevance of this classification to all questions concerning the functioning of the legislature is convincingly shown in Table 14.5. Almost two-thirds of the facilitators think the legislature could not function without pressure groups, whereas a substantial number of resisters (40 per cent) expressed much less favorable opinions about their functional value.   Still, it should not be overlooked that the data also indicate rather widespread acceptance by all legislators of the functionality of pressure politics to their business—even among resisters, some 60 per cent ventured opinions (numbers 1 and 2 in the table) which are quite favorable to such activity.

We have presented elsewhere[19] the data concerning some of the specific kinds of behavior associated with each of the three pressure-group role orientations, but they may be summarized here.   In the first place, facilitators are readier to recognize and seek out from many groups cues which would indicate their desires to legislators. On specific issues, as already mentioned, facilitators consciously attribute more importance to the views of interest groups than do the other two types.   They are also more ready to use, or at least to admit to using, the aid of lobbyists both in drafting bills and in lining up support for their own bills.

---

tions of the appropriate place of interest groups (described as Old Tory, Old Whig, Liberal, Radical, and Collectivist theories) imply different conceptions of how legislators should behave toward such groups or their agents.   Beer singles out for special attention one facet of the legislator-group role relationship—that involving the activity of the legislator as agent of a group (the "interested M.P.").

[18] See Appendix 1.4 for details concerning construction of these role types.

[19] See the authors' "American State Legislators' Role Orientations toward Pressure Groups," *Journal of Politics* 22:213–215 (1960).

The patterns are sharper for the facilitators and resisters, since they are attuned, favorably or unfavorably, to group behavior, and they perceive, understand, and react in characteristic fashion. The neutrals, a category consisting of those who apparently fail to perceive, understand, or formulate a coherent standard for judging groups in general, demonstrate, as one might expect, a more erratic, less distinct

Table 14.5: Judgments of legislators with different role orientations concerning functionality of pressure-group activity in the legislative system

| Most Favorable Opinion Expressed* | Role Orientation† | | |
	Facilitator $N = 124$	Neutral $N = 105$	Resister $N = 76$
1. Groups are indispensable	63%	39%	14%
2. Group activity is in general good, though certain "bad practices" of groups are undesirable.	23	41	46
3. Other less favorable opinions: e.g., group activity may be objectionable but one ought not interfere with the democratic right to be heard; group influence is over-rated, it is not an important factor; group activity is a wholly disruptive force which ought to be eliminated.	14	20	40
	100%	100%	100%

* In response to Question 21b (Appendix 6, p. 498, below).

† Total is only 305 because some legislators failed to give reasons when answering the question and others expressed appraisals not codable in these categories. When respondent made more than one codable comment, only the most favorable (highest in the table) was counted.

and consistent pattern. It is possible that each individual neutral, at his own level of awareness or concern, behaves toward some or all group representatives in a manner that could be characterized as "role behavior," but that these patterns cancel each other out in the statistical treatment of responses. In any case, facilitators are more likely to be aware of the nature of the group demands and respond to them; resisters to be aware of them but deliberately fail to respond; neutrals to respond or resist, but for assorted other reasons, without caring or without knowing that a demand has been made by a group.

Role orientations and pressure politics. The general working hypothesis underlying this entire chapter is that legislators' role conceptions are a crucial factor governing their behavior and thereby affecting the access, influence, or power of all groups.[20]   To show how examination of legislators' role orientations relates and adds insight to the kinds of gross institutional differences discussed earlier in this chapter, the distribution of the various role orientations toward pressure groups in the four states is shown in Table 14.6.   Comparison

Table 14.6: Distribution of role orientations toward pressure groups in four state legislatures

Role Orientation	Calif. $N = 97$	N.J. $N = 78$	Ohio $N = 157$	Tenn. $N = 116$
Facilitators	38%	41%	43%	23%
Neutrals	42	32	35	37
Resisters	20	27	22	40
	100%	100%	100%	100%

of these figures with Figure 14.1 (p. 322 above) reveals that in Tennessee, which ranked lowest in the significance of pressure politics, substantially more legislators are resisters than in any other state. In California, which ranked highest in pressure politics significance, proportionately fewer legislators than in any other state are resisters. Although California has slightly fewer facilitators than either New Jersey or Ohio, it has more neutrals than either, while Tennessee, as might be expected, has considerably fewer facilitators.   In other words, the distribution of legislators' role concepts in each state logically matches the gross differences in pressure politics previously described.

The connection between role concepts and gross system charac-teristics may be further elaborated.   Facilitators, for example, are more attuned than either neutrals or resisters to the diversity and complexity of modern group life.   Thus, even though interviewers

[20] This proposition is intimated in Truman's discussion of the influence of office (*The Governmental Process, op. cit.,* pp. 346–350), and Latham's discussion of officiality (*op. cit.,* pp. 33–40).   It is more directly suggested in Huitt's discussion of the way in which legislators' differing conceptions of their roles *pro* or *con* interest groups lead them to bring "competing versions of the facts" to their dis-cussions of conflicting group demands (*op. cit.,* p. 350).   It is the basis for em-pirical research in one very important instance (Garceau and Silverman, *op. cit.*), which differentiates faction-oriented, policy-oriented, program-oriented, and non-generalizers' conceptions of the appropriate mode of behavior for legislators, although not formally utilizing role theory or role concepts to do so.

sought, by probing, to have all respondents name six groups when asking what groups were generally powerful, facilitators nevertheless named significantly more groups than either neutrals or resisters—62 per cent naming five or more, compared with 57 per cent of the resisters and 45 percent of the neutrals who were able to name that many.[21] Similarly, the facilitators in all four states tend to perceive group activity in specific, associational terms, whereas resisters tend to perceive it stereotypically, in terms of broad interest aggregations.[22]

These findings lead to the hypothesis that it is facilitators who are the principal vehicles for pressure politics in the overall system. Further support for this hypothesis is found in the importance attributed by the different types of legislator to the views of interest groups in shaping their individual opinions on the problem of school needs. Of the facilitators, 70 per cent rated these views "very important" or "important," compared to 57 per cent of the neutrals and only 40 per cent of the resisters making the same rating, the differences being consistently in the same direction in all four states.

Role orientations toward pressure groups and the function of representation. An important problem of interest-group representation is the extent to which individual legislators act expressly as agents ("ball carriers") for groups of which they happen to be members or with which they are otherwise affiliated. It is commonly alleged that this type of "overlapping membership," by providing direct "representation" of the group in the legislative chamber, is an important source of pressure-group influence.[23] If this type of influence is actually prominent in any given legislature, then the process of interest-group representation, involving above all the effort by legislator-group spokesmen to write the demands of their respective groups into law, is a process of outright combat between the hostile groups thus represented.

Some good theoretical reasons for not accepting such an interpretation too hastily, however, have been succinctly stated by Gabriel Almond during a discussion of this very problem:

I wonder to which [sic] extent over-lapping membership in interest-groups, Parliament, and government agencies can truly be defined as "ac-

[21] The differences were consistently in the same direction in all four states.

[22] In response to the question concerning generally powerful groups, 56 per cent of the facilitators, but only 36 per cent of the resisters, referred only or mainly to specific organizations or lobbyists; similarly, only 36 per cent of the facilitators but 58 per cent of the resisters referred only or mainly to broad interest aggregations.

[23] Truman, *The Governmental Process, op. cit.*, pp. 338–339.

cess" to parliament and to these agencies. This raises an important problem for research. In the past, when it has been found that memberships did in fact overlap, this was interpreted as indicating interest group representation in Parliament or in a given agency. I do not believe this can always be so construed. Even a trade union member who is a member of Parliament has to distinguish between his two roles.[24]

While our data permit no direct attack on the problem, they do make possible an inferential judgment on it.

We have suggested that, insofar as the accommodation of group demands is accepted as legitimate, facilitators play a larger role than other legislators in the performance of the representative function. But assuming this to be so, what is the relation between a legislator's role orientation as a facilitator, neutral, or resister, and his affiliation or other form of identification with specific groups making contradictory and conflicting demands?

Facilitators, neutrals, and resisters cannot be thought to "represent" different kinds of people in the general public in the sense of acting in the place of, or as agents of, individuals or groups with whom they share certain characteristics, any more than can legislators as such (see above, Chapter 13). Role orientation of legislators is associated with none of the demographic characteristics for which data about legislators are most often collected and tabulated—not with socioeconomic status (whether indexed by income, occupational type, or occupational status), not with urban-rural status (whether indexed by present residence or place of upbringing), not with legislators' ages, nor with their religion.[25]

There is a relation, however, between legislators' education and their role orientations toward pressure groups, as Table 14.7 shows: better-educated legislators tend more than others to be facilitators.[26]

[24] Ehrmann, op. cit., pp. 273–274. Some empirical evidence to support Almond's view with respect to one legislator is provided in John H. Millett, "The Role of an Interest Group Leader in the House of Commons," Western Political Quarterly 9:915–926 (1956).

[25] It has been suggested that the lawyer may stand out in something closely resembling what has been described as the facilitator's role. See, for example, David R. Derge, "The Lawyer as Decision Maker," Journal of Politics 21:408–433 (1959), at p. 433. But this hypothesis is not supported by the present data, which show lawyers no more likely than members of any other occupation or profession to assume the role-orientation of facilitators.

[26] There are some intrastate departures from the pattern: California non-college-educated legislators are less likely to be resisters than are college-educated and are more likely to be facilitators than to be resisters, and college-educated Tennessee legislators are less likely to be facilitators than to be either neutrals or resisters.

This association appears quite plausible, on the assumption, advanced by many educators, that education liberates the mind, eliminates excessive faith in the dogmatic truth of simple ideas, and provides increasing factual understanding of the social and physical world. On such an assumption, better-educated legislators would possess the greater knowledge and greater acceptance of group diversity necessary to make them facilitators. An important effect of different distributions of the three role orientations, therefore, so far as representation is concerned, would be to make different world views or

Table 14.7: More-educated legislators tend more to be facilitators and less to be either neutrals or resisters than do the less-educated legislators

| | Level of Education | |
Role-Orientation Type	Less than Completed College (N = 201)	At Least Completed College (N = 247)
Facilitators	26%	45%
Neutrals	44	31
Resisters	30	24
	100%	100%

different styles of thinking about the world more or less predominant among the legislators making decisions on various issues, even though such different views were in no way "representative" of the thoughts, views, or "interests" of politically significant groups in the population represented.

That differences in role orientation reflect ("represent") certain fundamental differences in complex styles of thought rather than specific differences in "interest" among identifiable population groups is further suggested by the fact that differences in education by no means totally explain differences in role orientation. Thus interstate differences in the distribution of role-orientation types (see Table 14.6) persist even when groups of comparable educational backgrounds are compared. As Table 14.8 shows, there is, on the whole, at least as much variation from state to state within each educational level as there is between educational levels within any given state.[27]

[27] Interstate differences are greater than intrastate, interlevel differences when California or Tennessee is compared with either New Jersey or Ohio, but interlevel differences are slightly greater than interstate differences when Ohio or New Jersey is compared with either of the other two states. It must be remembered that the knowledge dimension of role orientation was normalized in the four states; for this reason the discussion here is directed toward the affective dimension, degree of friendliness (see Appendix 1.4, below p. 468).

This suggests that "political culture"[28] is a significant variable differentiating the states' modes and styles of pressure politics. Quite possibly norms and expectations peculiar to each state system are transmitted and circulated more or less generally among the population of that system, so that legislators, like citizens or occupants of other roles in the system, have acquired some role orientations and potential responses appropriate to their own specific legislature and state political system before they actually become legislators. If so, then legislators collectively, by the interactional effects of the given

Table 14.8: Interstate differences in friendliness toward pressure politics are as great as differences between legislators of different educational backgrounds

Legislator's Education	Mean Score for Friendliness Toward Pressure Politics*				
	Calif. $N = 106$	N.J. $N = 79$	Ohio $N = 160$	Tenn. $N = 117$	Interstate Range
Less than college	2.65	3.17	3.09	3.76	1.11
At least college	2.51	2.52	2.32	3.24	.92
Intrastate, Interlevel range	.14	.65	.77	.52	

* Scores represent quintile groups, score 1 being the most friendly, score 5 the least, on the scale described in Appendix 1.4.

distribution of role orientations, may be said to be "representative" of certain fundamental and characteristic attitudes of the entire state population. Of course, all such reasoning is highly speculative at this stage.

A similar line of reasoning, however, leads to some closely related conclusions. To inquire into the extent to which and the circumstances under which legislators act as agents for ("represent") groups in the population with whom they identify, legislators were classified as either pro-business, pro-labor, or economic neutrals.[29] One would expect individuals committed to some particular interest group (business, labor, etc.) to be less likely than individuals not so committed to view other groups or interests favorably, especially if these others are in conflict with their own group. On the other hand,

[28] For discussion of the concept of "political culture" see Gabriel A. Almond, "Comparative Political Systems," *Journal of Politics* 18:391–409 (1956).

[29] The process of classification is summarized in the authors' "American State Legislators' Role-Orientations toward Pressure Groups," *op. cit.*, pp. 219–221.

assuming they are aware of the group basis of their own interest, one should not necessarily expect the more committed legislators to be especially resistant to group activity in the abstract. From this it can be inferred that economic neutrals will tend more than either pro-business or pro-labor legislators to be facilitators and will tend less to be resisters. Or, to state the same relationship in corollary fashion, facilitators will appear in proportionately greater numbers among the ranks of uncommitted legislators (economic neutrals) than among the committed legislators (either pro-business or pro-labor). Table 14.9 shows these hypotheses are significantly supported.

Table 14.9: Relationship between role orientation and interest orientation of legislators

Role Orientation	Economic-Interest Orientation		
	Pro-Business $N = 239$	Economic Neutral $N = 130$	Pro-Labor $N = 51$
Facilitator	34%	49%	26%
	(51%)*	(41%)	(8%)
Neutral	36	33	33
	(59%)	(29%)	(12%)
Resister	30	18	41
	(62%)	(20%)	(18%)
	100%	100%	100%
	(57%)	(31%)	(12%)

* Figures in parentheses show percentage of role-orientation type having each economic-interest-orientation; figures not in parentheses show percentage of economic-interest-orientation type having each role orientation. Differences are consistent in all four states.

It seems clear, then, that the representation of interest groups in the legislative process involves more than the mere support of various groups by legislators who are personally identified with and committed to granting their claims. The fact that legislators collectively, through their role orientations, may represent certain cultural beliefs of the entire community with respect to pressure politics suggests one way in which legislators "represent" the public even while a multitude of particular groups press their demands in the legislature. The fact that the legislators most sensitive to and most sympathetic with the particular desires of all groups (the facilitators) are the very ones who are least identified with partisans in the group struggle suggests that the vague and undifferentiated "public" may be "represented" by legislators who can act as arbitrators or umpires because they are not themselves partisans in particular group struggles.

This element of the role of legislator may often conflict with the requirements of other roles a legislator may hold as a member of some interest group pressing its demands upon legislators. Our data provide only inferential evidence that the legislative role tends to take precedence over the interest-group-member role in cases of conflict. But neither empirical evidence nor theory supports, as yet, the contention that it is the legislative role which loses out in those cases.

Legislators' evaluations of groups. Further insight into the place of pressure groups in the representative process can be gained by examining the reasons given by legislators for some of their judgments about specific groups. Tables 14.10 and 14.11 show, respectively, the total number of times various reasons were given for the power of specific groups or for legislators' especially listening to certain groups. The individual items in these tables are based on the manifest content of legislators' replies, but they have been grouped into four general categories for purposes of analysis.

While there are some variations in the distribution of responses[30] from state to state and in their distribution among the different types of role orientations (neither of these sets of data are shown), the differences are not great in either case. The comparative uniformity from state to state in legislators' reasoning about both the relative power and the relative merit of pressure groups reflects certain basic agreements about the character of American politics.

As might be expected, the explanation of a group's power or merit is not the same for any and all groups. Thus, the group's size, geographical distribution, pervasiveness, or potential electoral influence looms large as an explanation of the power of religious (and related) groups, but appears comparatively minor as a source of power for business groups; entertainment of legislators and other forms of outright "lobbying" or pressuring activity appears almost as important as a group's size or related characteristics as a source of power for a miscellaneous variety of groups, but neither their wealth nor activity in the electoral districts are given any credit for whatever power such groups have.

The data permit no conclusions about the process or the criteria by which legislators put together the various possible bases of power

[30] Again, to avoid great mechanical difficulties in the manipulation of the data, the analysis has been based upon the total number of *references* made by all legislators, rather than upon the number of *respondents.*

Table 14.10: Number of references to various reasons for power

A. Classes of Interest

Reasons Given by Legislators	Any group, Groups in general N = 479	Agricultural Groups N = 87	Business Groups N = 464	Labor Groups N = 188	Professional Groups N = 367	Governmental Groups N = 88
Groups Representational Claim	(23%)	(43%)	(19%)	(34%)	(44%)	(39%)
Size, geographical distribution, potential electoral influence	16	27	8	29	26	23
Importance, prestige, public favor	7	16	11	5	18	16
Group's Functional Utility	9%	6%	5%	3%	4%	8%
Provides reliable information, facts, knowledge, research						
Group's Lobbying Activity	(31%)	(9%)	(41%)	(20%)	(7%)	(20%)
Entertainment; personal help and favors to legislators	4	0	9	1	0	8
Lobbyists' skill, tact, character, experience, activity	16	7	13	9	5	10
Money	11	2	19	10	2	2
Group's Extra-Legislative Political Activity or Power	(33%)	(40%)	(30%)	(40%)	(41%)	(30%)
Particular legislators friendly to, identified with group	3	8	5	5	4	10
General "organization," "activity," not otherwise specified	16	18	11	14	16	11
Publicity, opinion-influencing activities	5	8	3	4	7	2
Activity in districts: campaign activity, letter-writing campaigns	9	6	11	17	44	7
Other Reasons	4%	2%	5%	3%	4%	3%
	100%	100%	100%	100%	100%	100%

for each group in arriving at their individual estimates of its rank in influence. But reasons connected with a group's claim to be represented or with its general political power appear, in almost every case, to be more significant than reasons associated with its lobbying activities in the legislative arena itself. The fact that reasons in-of specific groups given by legislators in four states

B. Specific Organizations

Religious, Charitable and Civic Groups N = 22	Miscellaneous Groups N = 19	Total, all groups N = 1714	Education Association N = 280	AFL-CIO N = 70	Manufacturers Assoc.(s) N = 67	Farm Bureaus N = 66	Medical Assoc.(s) N = 54	Chamber(s) of Commerce N = 48	Municipal Leagues N = 47	County Government Associations N = 42
(64%)	(31%)	(31%)	(42%)	(36%)	(25%)	(44%)	(35%)	(25%)	(33%)	(47%)
41	26	19	26	30	7	29	20	8	15	26
23	5	12	16	6	18	15	15	17	18	21
0%	11%	6%	5%	4%	9%	8%	4%	21%	13%	7%
(9%)	(26%)	(25%)	(9%)	(20%)	(28%)	(6%)	(11%)	(25%)	(14%)	(12%)
0	21	4	0	1	5	0	0	4	4	0
9	5	11	6	12	5	6	9	8	8	12
0	0	10	3	7	18	0	2	13	2	0
(27%)	(27%)	(34%)	(40%)	(37%)	(38%)	(39%)	(50%)	(27%)	(38%)	(29%)
4	11	4	4	3	6	6	9	4	15	5
18	11	14	16	16	10	20	13	13	10	14
5	5	5	9	4	3	9	8	2	0	0
0	0	11	11	14	19	4	20	8	13	10
0%	5%	4%	4%	3%	0%	3%	0%	2%	2%	5%
100%	100%	100%	100%	100%	100%	100%	100%	100%	100%	100%

volving the group's usefulness to the legislature rank extremely low here (6 per cent for all groups) suggests that the most powerful groups appear to legislators to be external forces, posing problems for the legislature to deal with, and not agencies intimately associated with the legislature in the business of lawmaking.

Table 14.11: Number of references to various reasons for

A. Classes of Interest

Reasons Given by Legislators	Agricultural Groups $N = 78$	Business Groups $N = 266$	Labor Groups $N = 64$	Professional Groups $N = 142$
Group's Representational Claim	(47%)	(26)%	(36%)	(41%)
Size, importance; representation of public opinion or segment of it	17	6	12	10
Group is widely affected, concerned with important problem	20	10	19	16
Group is unselfish, "public-spirited," appeals on moral grounds	10	10	5	15
Group's Functional Utility	(34%)	(56%)	(46%)	(42%)
Group has "right" views, opposes "wrong" views (by respondent's definition)	1	4	0	2
Consistently gives reliable information (on any or many subjects)	16	29	19	13
Is specially expert, only source of information on particular subjects	17	23	27	27
Group's Lobbying Activity	(7%)	(14%)	(7%)	(9%)
Lobbyists' skill, knowledge, character	6	10	6	7
Personal help to legislators	1	4	1	2
Group's Extra-Legislative Political Activity or Power	6%	1%	3%	2%
Ability to affect respondent (elections, constituency relations)				
Other Reasons	6%	3%	8%	6%
	100%	100%	100%	100%

There is likewise considerable discrimination among different classes of interest with respect to the reasons legislators see justifying their claim to special attention. Reasons associated either with the group's usefulness to the legislature in its lawmaking functions or with the group's claim to be represented as a significant element of the public far outweigh all other types of reasons. Legislators do not think

especially listening to specific groups given by legislators in four states

B. Specific Organizations

Governmental Groups N = 127	Religious, Charitable and Civil Groups N = 75	Miscellaneous Groups N = 19	Total, All Groups N = 771	Municipal Leagues N = 70	Chamber(s) of Commerce N = 58	Education Associations N = 53	Farm Bureaus N = 44	Taxpayers Association(s) N = 40	County-Government Associations N = 39	League of Women Voters N = 33
(37%)	(52%)	(42%)	(36%)	(31%)	(31%)	(36%)	(49%)	(33%)	(41%)	(64%)
11	9	26	10	7	9	15	20	7	13	15
13	11	5	13	8	7	3	20	7	8	3
13	32	11	13	16	15	8	9	19	20	46
(51%)	(34%)	(43%)	(47%)	(58%)	(55%)	(49%)	(28%)	(52%)	(46%)	(36%)
0	8	11	3	0	0	2	3	7	0	6
26	13	11	21	35	40	23	16	40	18	21
25	13	21	23	23	15	24	9	5	28	9
(8%)	(8%)	(10%)	(11%)	(7%)	(9%)	(6%)	(11%)	(5%)	(10%)	(0%)
5	5	5	8	6	9	6	9	5	5	0
3	3	5	3	1	0	0	2	0	5	0
2%	2%	0%	2%	1%	2%	0%	7%	3%	0%	0%
2%	4%	5%	4%	3%	3%	9%	5%	7%	3%	0%
100%	100%	100%	100%	100%	100%	100%	100%	100%	100%	100%

lobbying activities as such entitle groups to any special claim. A group's general political power is even less important in this respect.

The two main classes of reasons given for paying particular heed to various groups correspond very closely to what Truman lists as a major "informal determinant" of a group's access in the legislative process—"the legislator-politician's need of information and the ability of a group to supply it," both in the sense of technical information and in the sense of political information.[31]   The kinds of "political information" sought by legislators are well indicated in some of their own comments:

It's more important to get the views of the group adversely affected than the group sponsoring the bill.   They can show implications that go beyond anything that meets the eye.   Objectors don't draft the bill.   . . .

So many members don't know and couldn't know the *effects* (of a bill) if lobbyists didn't tell them.

When the representative comes to (the capitol) he can't possibly know everybody's needs.   Also, everybody can't come to talk to the legislator. The lobbyist knows these needs and can give the legislator some valuable information to judge the problem of his group.   You take into consideration that a lobbyist for a particular group is prejudiced in their favor and reconcile it with the general good.

Legislators' comments on the usefulness of interest groups show that their own conceptions of groups' functional utility include the provision of "technical information" as described by Truman.   But legislators frequently went beyond this to admit a general readiness to use lobbyists as briefing agents who save legislators time by doing some of their research work for them:

Lobbyists are a vital part of the legislative process.   Without them to explain, you couldn't get a clear picture of the situation.   They can study and present the issues concisely—the average legislator has no time or inclination to do it, and wouldn't understand bills or issues without them. A professional lobbyist in ten minutes can explain what it would take a member two hours to wade through just reading bills.   Both sides come around to you, so you can balance off all one-sided presentations (and they're all one-sided).   A definite function is performed by lobbyists.   . . .

[The legislature] would work slower.   You can't possibly watch 7,000 bills.

[Without lobbyists] we'd be doing the research ourselves and always fighting for more money to do the job.   I'd have to hire professional research people and they cost money.

The general picture which emerges, then, shows legislators preferring pressure groups to serve as indicators of sentiment in significant elements of the population and, perhaps even more preferably, as supplementary staff sources which legislators can call on as needed. Direct representation of powerful and important groups as such does not seem widely accepted as a principal function of the legislators.   Pressure groups are most welcome in the legislative arena when they go beyond a mere assertion of demands and interests and

[31] Truman, *The Governmental Process, op. cit.,* p. 33.

present information and data which help legislators to work out compromises and adjustments among the most insistent demands of groups on the basis of some vague conception of a public interest against which particular claims can be judged.

J. D. Stewart has described a relationship of "consultation" between British pressure groups and the British government, in which government officials seek political and technical information from the groups:

In a society in which the major demands appear to have been satisfied, both the main political parties realize the necessity of securing cooperation from all sections of society.   The government seeks by consultation to build up where possible a responsive attitude to its proposals.   It seeks cooperation and elimination of open discontent.

This then is the philosophy of consultation as a part of the political system.   This philosophy does not imply that the consultation must be with groups, but in fact this was the only way in which it could be kept within reasonable bounds or take place without obvious injustice.[32]

American states do not, any more than the American national government, have the kind of disciplined party systems in which "The Government" can assume the kind of responsibility and take the kind of initiative in policy making which would make such a conception of "consultation" directly applicable to the American state legislative scene.   But the similarity between the functional components of Stewart's concept of "consultation" and the clear functional imperatives of political and technical information desired by American state legislators are unmistakable.   They suggest that American state legislators like to picture themselves operating somehow or other as "the government" (or as a significant part of it), somehow or other "representing" the total body politic, and utilizing pressure groups in the process rather than being used by them.

Such a picture, admittedly, is a picture of what legislators prefer, so far as pressure group activity is concerned.   Our data do not permit any conclusions with respect to the extent to which they are able to achieve such a Utopian state of affairs.   The popular stereotype of legislative politics maintains that, whatever legislators might wish, the application of power and pressure by interest groups prevents legislators' carefully balancing and adjusting group conflicts and forces them, on most occasions, to submit to the demands of pressure groups.   But very few of the legislators interviewed felt such a picture to be accurate.   Most of them would go no farther than the Tennessee Senator who said,

[32] Stewart, *op. cit.*, pp. 6–7.

Lobbyists do affect the vote. Maybe they don't change your vote— lobbyists are only effective with those who are undecided—but they can sure make you bleed.

Even while expressing discomfort at the extent they might be made to "bleed" by pressure groups, most legislators would agree with the judgment expressed in the following remarks:

It all boils down to persons expressing their opinions. It's hard for any- one to be "influenced"—all the members now use their own best knowledge about what is best for the public when voting on anything.

Legislators aren't really influenced much by lobbyists in the way people think. We go to their parties because we like free meals and parties. But no one expects that to affect your vote. I don't know that any lobbyist ever really could buy anything.

Cynics will no doubt write off such comments as platitudinous talk for public consumption, but the impression of interviewers in all four states was that such views represent genuine convictions. Legislators themselves seem to be not only much more sophisticated in their estimates of the relative power and merits of various groups than they are generally given credit for, but also much more adept at parrying the thrusts of those groups and devising their own counterpressures against them.

ROLE ORIENTATIONS TOWARD PRESSURE GROUPS AND THE LEGISLATURE

Political scientists distinguish between the different functions of legislature, executive, administration, and judiciary vis-à-vis pressure groups. As Earl Latham has said:

The legislature referees the group struggle, ratifies the victories of the successful coalitions, and records the terms of the surrenders, compromises, and conquests in the form of statutes. . . . The function of the bureaucrat in the group struggle is somewhat different from that of the legislator. Administrative agencies of the regulatory kind are established to carry out the terms of the treaties that the legislators have negotiated and ratified. . . . The function of the judge is not unlike that of bureaucrat.[33]

The preceding section has suggested that the legislature does indeed "referee" the group struggle, and that, while so doing, legislators may stand much more apart from the parties to the struggle, viewing them with a much more impartial or "public-minded" eye, than is generally recognized. Even those who vehemently deny the adequacy of such

[33] Latham, *op. cit.*, pp. 35, 38, 39.

a view as a complete account of the governmental process generally admit that the function of taking into account the expressed demands of organized interest groups belongs more properly to legislative than to executive, administrative, or judicial agencies. It is therefore appropriate to conclude this exploration of legislators' role orientations toward pressure groups with a glance at their import for the continuing structure and functioning of the legislature.

To begin with, it is reasonable to assume that commitment to legislative purpose increases with increasing service in the legislature. If this is so, and if the legislature is the principal agency deemed responsible for the adjustment of group conflicts, then legislators with most tenure should tend more than those with little tenure to be facilitators. Table 14.12 shows that, except for Tennessee resisters, this is the case.

Table 14.12: Legislators with the most legislative service tend most to be facilitators and least to be neutrals

Role-Orientation Type	Median Number Years' Legislative Service Prior to 1957			
	Calif. $N = 99$	N.J. $N = 79$	Ohio $N = 155$	Tenn. $N = 115$
Facilitators	7.3	5.6	6.2	2.2
Neutrals	4.8	2.5	4.4	2.1
Resisters	5.3	3.8	4.6	2.4

The same problem can be looked at from the viewpoint of the individual legislator's conception of himself as a legislator. It seems reasonable to suppose that the number and pervasiveness of groups in American political life are so great that the individual legislator can work effectively and feel he is working effectively as a legislator only if he makes his peace with the world of pressure groups. In other words, other things being equal, the facilitator will probably be a more effective legislator, and will feel himself to be so, than will the neutral or the resister.

The efficacy index scores of the three groups (see below, Appendix 2.2) bear out the hypothesis with respect to legislators' sense of efficacy. Facilitators score +24 per cent on this index, as compared with +8 per cent for neutrals and —6 per cent for resisters.[34]

[34] Tennessee resisters have a higher efficacy sense than do Tennessee facilitators, but they also outrank the latter in low efficacy sense. Tennessee facilitators, i.e., tend more towards a moderate sense of efficacy.

In other words, evidence from several directions points to the conclusion that a central function of the American state legislature is the accommodation of interest-group demands in the legislative process. Experience in the legislature tends to produce in individual legislators, whatever their previous background and experience, the attitudes most appropriate to this function; individuals who possess those attitudes feel themselves to be more effective as legislators than their colleagues who do not.

That such a tendency is found in American state legislatures should not obscure the fact that role orientations other than that of facilitator do occur in significant numbers, indicating that interest-group accommodation is by no means universally accepted as a legislative function, let alone the only one. Our data permit no conclusions about the kinds of major cultural changes which might enhance or diminish recognition of such a function as legitimate. They can do no more than point to relatively widespread acceptance of that function as an empirical fact, given the cultural milieus of the four legislatures studied, and emphasize the extent to which legislators' role concepts lead them to seek accommodation of group interests not by direct embodiment of group demands in public policy (either as group agents or as unwilling pawns) but by attempts to conciliate and harmonize them into an authoritative decision meeting legislators' criteria of the public interest.

CHAPTER 15

The legislator
and his party:
majority and minority

THERE IS AN ALMOST INEVITABLE PARADOX "built into" the roles which
Americans take in the American party system. Regardless of whether
he is an officeholder, a party functionary, or a voter, what we seem
to know best about an American's political roles is that he is either a
Democrat or a Republican. But party labels, as external symbols of
partisan roles, do not seem to involve corresponding expectations concerning behavior appropriate to the labels. There is little consensus
on what it means to be a Democrat or Republican.[1]

Our research therefore included a series of questions (No. 16,
Appendix 6, pp. 496–497) to elicit legislators' descriptions of the roles
they feel called upon to take by virtue of their membership in one or
the other of the two major parties.[2] The term "party" has so many
different meanings in American politics that it is difficult to guess
exactly how response patterns might vary from state to state. But,
in general, we anticipated that party-role descriptions would be related to certain "objective" institutional or structural characteristics of

This chapter drafted by Eulau.

[1] For evidence concerning the mass electorate, see Angus Campbell, Philip E.
Converse, Warren E. Miller and Donald E. Stokes, *The American Voter, op. cit.*
For evidence concerning behavior, in the Congress and state legislatures, see
Julius Turner, *op. cit.*; Duncan MacRae, Jr., *op. cit.*; and William J. Keefe,
"Comparative Study of the Role of Political Parties in State Legislatures," *Western
Political Quarterly* 9:726–742 (1956).

[2] All respondents in the four states carried the label Republican or Democrat,
though in California a number of legislators had been elected on both party
tickets as a result of that state's cross-filing law, now abolished.

a state's legislature, particularly the degree of party competition on the electoral level and the relative majority-minority status of the parties. Within the limits set by such structural conditions, legislators' own "subjective" definitions of the place of party in the state's legislative system, their responses to their cultural environment, might also be expected to influence their party-role orientations.

THE STRUCTURAL ENVIRONMENT

Party competition as a variable. It is often taken for granted that legislators coming from competitive districts are more dependent on their party's support than legislators coming from one-party areas. Partisanship would seem to be more salient, therefore, in competitive systems. But it is also possible that competitive politics may have the opposite effect: the politician in competitive situations may try to play down his party label in the hope of attracting lukewarm supporters of the other party or independents.

As a first step in analysis of this problem, Table 15.1 summarizes the competitive situations encountered by the sixteen party delegations, using an index which may range from a score of zero to a score of one. A zero score would mean that all of the delegation's members come from one-party districts, and a score of one would indicate that they all come from competitive districts.[3] The range of scores varies considerably within each state, but except for the two Ohio Republican delegations, the New Jersey and Ohio as well as California Democratic party groups were more likely to face competitive situations in their home districts, whereas the California Republican and Tennessee delegations tended to encounter less competitive, more one-partyish politics in their districts. The Ohio House Democrats ranked first among all delegations in confronting competitive conditions, and Tennessee Democrats had almost no competition from the Republicans in their districts.

Majority-minority status as a variable. Analyses of roll-call votes in competitive systems show that the majority party is generally more cohesive than the minority, though there may be exceptions—for instance, when the minority party controls the governorship.[4] The ratio

---

[3] Party competition in district was severally defined in the four states. For full definitions of the standards used see Appendix 2.1.

[4] The consequences of majority or minority status have not been much explored. But see David B. Truman, *The Congressional Party, op. cit.*, especially pp. 280–286; 308–316. See also Malcolm E. Jewell, "Party Voting in American State Legislatures," *op. cit.*

Table 15.1: Competition in legislators' districts, by state,
chamber, party, status, and rank

State	Chamber	Party	Status*	Score†	Rank
N.J.	Senate	Dem.	Min.	0.79	2
	House	Rep.	Maj.	0.70	3
	Senate	Rep.	Maj.	0.54	5
	House	Dem.	Min.	0.48	7
Ohio	House	Dem.	Min.	0.80	1
	Senate	Dem.	Min.	0.67	4
	Senate	Rep.	Maj.	0.34	10
	House	Rep.	Maj.	0.21	14
Calif.	Senate	Dem.	Spl.	0.50	6
	House	Dem.	Min.	0.45	8
	House	Rep.	Maj.	0.31	12
	Senate	Rep.	Spl.	0.28	13
Tenn.	House	Rep.	Min.	0.40	9
	Senate	Rep.	Min.	0.33	11
	House	Dem.	Maj.	0.07	15
	Senate	Dem.	Maj.	0.02	16

* Key: Maj. = majority
Min. = minority
Spl. = evenly split
† The scores were obtained by multiplying the number of delegation members coming from one-party districts by zero, the number of those from semi-competitive districts by 0.5, and of those from competitive districts by 1. The individual scores were summed and averaged for each delegation.

of majority-minority strength may be an additional factor influencing legislators' party orientations. As Table 15.2 indicates, the ratios differed considerably from state to state. In California the parties were evenly split in the Senate, and in the House the ratio was ten to nine in favor of the Republican majority. In both New Jersey and Ohio the majorities outnumbered the minorities by about two to one. In Tennessee, Democratic preponderance over the Republican minority was about four to one.

It appears from many interview protocols that legislators were quite sensitive to the sheer difference in status and its strength. "No bill passes," said a New Jersey respondent, "unless the Republicans are for it." In Ohio, a legislator pointed out, "the Democrats have nothing to say because the Republicans have the majority." It is reasonable to assume that in competitive structures where the majority is strong, as was the case during the 1957 sessions in New Jersey and Ohio, a member's majority status would stimulate his partisanship: by "playing ball" with the members of his own team, the legislator is more likely to achieve whatever personal objectives he may have or whatever constituent stakes he may wish to promote. His own legislative success is more likely to be assured by his taking a partisan role.

That belonging to the majority may strengthen a party member's personal feeling of effectiveness appears from the scores obtained by majority and minority delegations on our "legislative efficacy" scale.

Table 15.2: Ratio of majority-minority strength in four state legislatures

State	Chamber	Minority/Majority Ratio	Organized by
Calif.	Senate	1.00	Democrats*
	House	0.91	Republicans
N.J.	House	0.53	Republicans
	Senate	0.50	Republicans
Ohio	Senate	0.55	Republicans
	House	0.43	Republicans
Tenn.	House	0.27	Democrats
	Senate	0.22	Democrats

* The 1957 California Senate was evenly split between the parties, but two Republicans voted in support of a Democratic President pro Tempore. See above, Chapter 3, for an institutional description of the situation.

This scale, it will be recalled, was designed to test legislators' feelings concerning their ability to meet successfully the many demands made on them by their legislative office. A score of one for any delegation means that all its members have a high sense of efficacy, and a score of zero that all have a low sense of efficacy. It is evident from Table 15.3 that, in general, members of the majority parties seemed to feel more efficacious in their lawmaking activities than the members of the minorities. Even California Senate Republicans, though even in strength with the Democrats, obtained a higher score than did the Senate Democrats—possibly a reflection not only of Republican control of the lower chamber and the governorship, but also of half a century of virtual Republican control of the state. Ohio Senators constitute one exception. But only in one-party Tennessee does the difference in efficacy feelings between majority and minority practically disappear. Indeed, the minority Republicans scored slightly higher than the factionalized Democrats.

The interview protocols suggest some of the effects of majority-minority status on partisanship. Minority members, finding partisanship an obstacle to their legislative success, may be inclined to minimize their party distinctiveness and support majority measures to win majority support for their own legislation. But there seem to be limits to such tactics. Only if the majority needs organized minority support because it cannot muster enough support within its own party for exceptional votes (as the two-thirds required for emergency

Table 15.3: Legislators' sense of efficacy, by state,
chamber, party, status, and rank

State	Chamber	Party	Status	Score	Rank
N.J.	House	Rep.	Maj.	0.74	1.0
	Senate	Rep.	Maj.	0.68	2.0
	Senate	Dem.	Min.	0.50	10.0
	House	Dem.	Min.	0.48	13.5
Ohio	House	Rep.	Maj.	0.64	3.0
	Senate	Rep.	Maj.	0.55	5.5
	House	Dem.	Min.	0.55	5.5
	Senate	Dem.	Min.	0.54	7.0
Calif.	Senate	Rep.	Spl.	0.56	4.0
	House	Rep.	Maj.	0.53	8.0
	House	Dem.	Min.	0.45	15.0
	Senate	Dem.	Spl.	0.41	16.0
Tenn.	House	Rep.	Min.	0.50	10.0
	Senate	Rep.	Min.	0.50	10.0
	House	Dem.	Maj.	0.49	12.0
	Senate	Dem.	Maj.	0.48	13.5

legislation or defeat of the governor's veto), does the minority have an opportunity to bargain to its advantage. As an Ohio Democrat pointed out:

It is strictly one sided. Since the Republicans are in the majority, they take the attitude of take it or leave it. The Republicans present a bill in committee and, if they want the bill to go through, it goes through. The Democrats would do the same if they were in the majority, though.

On the other hand, if the minority party controls the governorship, as it did during the 1957 session in New Jersey, party discipline and partisanship may be more highly valued because, in the competitive system, the minority is more visible. The governor's record becomes the legislative minority's record. The New Jersey Senate minority leader seemed quite aware of his party's relationship to the governor:

The Democrats have to work with the governor who is the leader of the party. As minority leader I push his program in the Senate and participate in the battle over the governor's budget.

Yet, control of the governorship by the minority party may be a frustrating experience. A glance at Table 15.3 will show that the New Jersey Democrats in both chambers scored very much lower on the efficacy scale than did the majority Republicans. In other words, New Jersey's minority Democrats did not seem to derive advantage from their party's control of the executive office, and the majority Republicans did not seem to be too greatly hampered by their lack of controlling it.

The prospect that the majority's control of the executive may increase the minority's helplessness appears in this Ohio Democratic comment: "If the governor is of the same party as the majority, then there is nothing we can do. The majority rules—what can we (i.e., the minority) do?" This remark (as several others) suggests failure to recognize a particular function for the minority in the legislative process. Another Ohioan expressed it this way:

When the governor is of the same political party as the majority in the houses, the opposition (minority) party believes it has its hand "in the lion's mouth" and doesn't expect much.

But a majority's lack of control of the governorship need not mean that its members are less partisan than when the executive office is in its hands. Ohio Republicans frequently recalled the fact that during Democratic Governor Frank Lausche's terms they were not any less party oriented. A Senate Republican explained:

From the time Ray Bliss was state chairman until this year, he used to preside at weekly dinner meetings with the leadership of the Senate and the House, and we would have an exchange of views. We used to hammer out a program. We then proceeded to get it enacted and go home. This year he has not participated; he felt that with a Republican governor this was no longer his job.

In other words, a state chairman may serve as a functional equivalent of the governor if the majority fails to win possession of the executive office. In giving guidance to a non-gubernatorial majority, he may be effective in cementing party discipline. Similar leadership from the state chairman might strengthen minority party ties as well. If it is not forthcoming, the minority seems rudderless. This lament of an Ohio House Democrat is to the point:

This session the Democrats haven't been too much of a party. We're really a small minority this time. At the state level there is very little at this time. There wasn't much last time, either. The reason we're floundering is that the state chairman isn't taking any interest in the legislature.

Finally, where the majority is overwhelming but highly factionalized, as in Tennessee, the concept "majority" has almost no meaning and majority "partisanship" is quite irrelevant. It is in this context of factionalism, then, rather than vis-à-vis a recognizable majority, that minority legislators may find in partisanship a source of political strength. By forming a more united front than the majority is capable of forming, minority legislators may succeed in constituting what they perceive as a "balance of power" between the majority's factions and so secure for themselves a share of the spoils. Two comments from Tennessee House and Senate Republicans illustrate the point:

The only part the Republicans play is that the Republicans are a balance of power between the old Clement and Browning factions at some time.

If the Democrats are split, Republicans have some bargaining power. If they are evenly split, the Republicans are the balance of power.

The slightly higher scores of the two Tennessee Republican minority delegations on the efficacy scale probably reflect this assessment of their situation.

The comments we have cited were made in response to this open-ended question: "How would you describe the part played by political parties in the [state] legislature?" By coding responses in terms of whether the parties were seen to have "impact" or not on the legislative process as a whole (rather than "influence" on individual legislative behavior), we are further able to assess the consequences of majority power. Table 15.4 presents the state-by-state specification of majority and minority impact. In New Jersey somewhat over half of the responses acknowledge the impact of the Republican majority, and in Ohio almost a third of the responses do likewise. But what is particularly interesting in Ohio is that, in contrast to New Jersey, twice as many of the responses emphasize the weakness of the minority or minimize party impact generally. In other words, while in New Jersey the majority is recognized as being strong, but the minority party is not counted out as a legislative force, in Ohio the Republican majority is evidently opposed ineffectively by a weak minority. In California and Tennessee over half of the responses minimize party impact generally, but it is noteworthy that in Tennessee the Republican minority is more often acknowledged to have impact than the majority Democrats.

The two features in legislators' structural-institutional environment which may have major effects on legislative behavior can be summarized briefly: competitiveness in the structure of the party system on the electoral level and majority-minority status and strength. Tables 15.1, 15.2 and 15.4 indicate an interesting pattern. Although within a state structural features may differently affect different party delegations, and although there may be overlappings from one state to the next, the striking aspect of the tabulations is the stability of rankings and results from one state to the next. New Jersey has not only the most competitive electoral structure, but its majority delegations scored

Table 15.4: Specification of majority and minority impact
on legislature, by state

Specification	N.J. $N = 77$	Ohio $N = 158$	Calif.* $N = 111$	Tenn. $N = 117$
Majority has impact	53%	30%	9%	8%
Majority has no/little impact	1	1	2	3
Minority has impact	9	3	4	12
Minority has no/little impact	7	15	4	6
Both parties have impact	26	29	28	8
Both parties have no/little impact	4	22	53	63
	100%	100%	100%	100%

* For the purposes of this tabulation, California Republicans were treated as the majority party, Democrats as the minority party.

high on legislative efficacy feelings and were deemed to have considerable impact on the legislative process. Moreover, its Democratic minority delegations by no means felt themselves faced with a hopeless situation. New Jersey was followed by Ohio with somewhat lower competition scores, more limited feelings of efficacy among its majority delegation, less wholehearted recognition of majority impact, and greater recognition of minority weakness. But both states differed distinctly from California and Tennessee in these respects. In both these states electoral party competition is considerably less widespread; and in both, for different reasons, of course, party impact on the legislative process seems minimal, making majority or minority status a less significant factor, although Tennessee's Republicans, especially in the Senate, represent a special case. But in all four states, excepting the New Jersey House Democrats, the minority delegations faced more competitive electoral situations; and in all states, except Tennessee where there was hardly any difference, the majority delegations recorded a greater sense of legislative efficacy. It is within these institutional parameters, then, that legislators' political-cultural environments give rise to particular party-role descriptions and attitudes.

THE CULTURAL ENVIRONMENT

Cognitive orientation to party. It is reasonable to assume that the political party must be perceived as a differentiating factor in the legislative struggle before partisanship can have much meaning at all. Legislators were therefore asked to rank particular conflicts which, in their opinion, divided the legislature of their state in the voting on crucial issues—Republican versus Democratic conflict, conflicts between the governor's supporters and his opponents, between the cities and the rural areas, between liberals and conservatives, between labor's friends and opponents, and between one part of the state and another. The different rankings given to party conflict by the different delegations may be considered indicators of legislators' cognitive orientations towards party and components of a legislature's political culture.

Table 15.5 presents the results. As can be readily seen, conflict along party lines was ranked uniformly highest in New Jersey and consistently second-highest in Ohio. The pattern is somewhat less clear between California and Tennessee, where some overlap in scores may be noted. In these two states party conflicts were evidently perceived as less critical than other alignments. But the lowest delegation score in California is slightly higher than the lowest score in Tennessee. It is interesting to note that in California both Democratic delegations ranked party conflict somewhat higher than the Republicans, further evidence of greater Democratic sensitivity to the emergence of two-party politics during this transitional phase of state politics. In Tennessee, on the other hand, though the score differences are small and party conflict was generally seen to be of little importance, the vastly outnumbered Republican minority delegations ranked party conflicts somewhat lower than the majority Democrats. On the other hand, in a highly competitive system like New Jersey's, the minority delegation in either chamber seems to be more inclined to recognize party differentiation than does the majority delegation, probably because it can only benefit from sharpening its appeal to the electorate in party-cleavage terms. In summary, party conflicts are perceived as highly relevant in New Jersey, moderately important in Ohio, and of little significance in California and Tennessee. We would expect, therefore, that partisanship would be similarly more salient in New Jersey and Ohio than in the other two states.

Affective orientation to party. For appropriate roles to be taken in the party system, it would seem necessary not only that a party be perceptually salient, but also that it be an object of emotional involvement or attachment, that the legislator prefer the party as a cue giver to other possible sources of reference, and respond to expectations that

Table 15.5: Perception of conflicts between Democrats and Republicans, by state, chamber, party, status, and rank

State	Chamber	Party	Status	Score*	Rank
N.J.	House	Dem.	Min.	5.7	1.0
	House	Rep.	Maj.	5.5	2.5
	Senate	Dem.	Min.	5.5	2.5
	Senate	Rep.	Maj.	5.1	4.0
Ohio	Senate	Rep.	Maj.	4.1	5.0
	House	Dem.	Min.	3.6	6.0
	House	Rep.	Maj.	3.5	7.0
	Senate	Dem.	Min.	3.4	8.0
Calif.	House	Dem.	Min.	2.8	9.0
	Senate	Dem.	Spl.	2.6	10.5
	Senate	Rep.	Spl.	2.5	12.5
	House	Rep.	Maj.	2.3	14.5
Tenn.	House	Dem.	Maj.	2.6	10.5
	Senate	Dem.	Maj.	2.5	12.5
	House	Rep.	Min.	2.3	14.5
	Senate	Rep.	Min.	2.0	16.0

* Scores are averages of the individual conflict-ranking scores, which ranged from 6, for party conflict being ranked first, to one, for its being ranked last. If party conflict was tied in the rankings with one or more other conflicts, intermediate values were assigned.

he behave "like" a partisan Republican or Democrat in situations where the parties are in conflict. To compare the affective orientation toward party of legislators in the various delegations, a summary Likert-type score was constructed, based on three questions (Nos. 39-f, k, w, Appendix 6, pp. 502–503 below) dealing with the most obvious functions parties might be expected to perform in a competitive and disciplined party system—recruiting and electing candidates, defining public-policy positions, and influencing members' legislative votes. The higher a delegation's score (theoretical maximum, 5), the more positive the delegation's affect toward party; the lower the delegation's score (theoretical minimum, 1), the less its affect toward party.[5]

As Table 15.6 shows, the Ohio Senate Republicans outscored all New Jersey delegations, but the scores within the two more competitive states are quite similar and indicate orientations generally more favorable to party than orientations in California and Tennessee. Of particular interest is the fact that the lowest score among the New

Table 15.6: Affective orientations towards party, by state, chamber, party, status, and rank

State	Chamber	Party	Status	Score	Rank
N.J.	Senate	Rep.	Maj.	3.62	2.0
	Senate	Dem.	Min.	3.35	4.0
	House	Rep.	Maj.	3.30	5.5
	House	Dem.	Min.	3.20	8.5
Ohio	Senate	Rep.	Maj.	3.95	1.0
	House	Rep.	Maj.	3.50	3.0
	Senate	Dem.	Min.	3.30	5.5
	House	Dem.	Min.	3.13	10.0
Calif.	House	Dem.	Min.	3.22	7.0
	Senate	Dem.	Spl.	2.84	11.0
	House	Rep.	Maj.	2.36	15.0
	Senate	Rep.	Spl.	2.00	16.0
Tenn.	Senate	Rep.	Min.	3.20	8.5
	House	Dem.	Maj.	2.74	12.0
	House	Rep.	Min.	2.63	13.0
	Senate	Dem.	Maj.	2.46	14.0

Jersey and Ohio delegations is recorded for the Ohio House Democrats who, we noted earlier, were weakly organized and quite demoralized. On the other hand, surprisingly high affect scores are recorded for the California House Democrats and the Tennessee Senate Republicans. Indeed, both California Democratic delegations showed more affect towards party than did the Republicans, further evidence of Democratic preference for stronger two-party politics in traditionally non-partisan California. And the Tennessee Senate Republicans once

[5] A pro-party "agree" response to each question was scored 5, a pro-party "tend to agree" response 4, a neutral "undecided" response 3, an anti-party "tend to disagree" response 2, and an anti-party "disagree" response 1. The average of the respondent's three scores constitute his individual score. The delegation scores are merely the averages of the individual scores for each delegation.

more indicated by their score that they have only to gain and little to lose from a positive affective stance toward party as an instrument of influence in the factional milieu of Democratic politics. Moreover, it is noteworthy that party still seems to mean more as an object of gratification to all Tennessee delegations than to California's two Republican delegations.

Evaluative orientation to party. Just as party must be perceived as a significant factor in legislative combat and invested with emotional meaning for partisan roles to be taken, so party influence on legislative behavior must be positively evaluated. Where legislators evaluate party influence as significant, they are likely to find partisan roles agreeable. Where evaluations of party influence are negative, partisan roles are not likely to be considered assets in legislative performance.

It was possible to construct a measure of "evaluative orientation to party" by classifying responses concerning party influence on behavior of the individual legislators into three categories: first, the parties are judged to have much or considerable influence; second, they are judged as having some or increasing influence; third, they are seen as having little or no influence.[6] Table 15.7 presents the findings for the 16 party delegations. The data differentiate sharply between the two-party states, but also suggest that the difference may be due to the generally more competitive character of New Jersey. For the New Jersey delegations, regardless of chamber or status, revealed a very high degree of consensus in their very positive appraisal of party influence on legislative behavior. In Ohio, on the other hand, the delegations not only scored lower, but indicated much less consensus. Moreover, the House Republican delegation which, we noted earlier, faced the least competition in Ohio, was the most positive in its appraisal of party influence. In California, the scores suggest, party influence is not judged to be important, but at least three delegations, as we shall see, were evidently impressed by increasing party influence on legislative behavior in that state. In Tennessee, finally, the Senate Republicans again exhibit their deviant ways. But it is well to keep in mind that their evaluations refer to their party alone.

If we examine legislators' evaluative orientations by taking account of the specific party as the object of judgment, some interesting findings emerge. Table 15.8 presents, by state, the distribution of re-

---

[6] The data on which this measure is based come from the same questions as those used in assessing "party impact" on the legislative process. The present measure is derived from legislators' evaluations of party "influence on *individual behavior*," while "impact" was interpreted to mean effect on the legislative *process as a whole.*

Table 15.7: Evaluations of party influence on party members' behavior by state, chamber, party, status, and rank

State	Chamber	Party	Status	Score*	Rank
N.J.	Senate	Dem.	Min.	0.95	1.0
	House	Rep.	Maj.	0.93	2.5
	House	Dem.	Min.	0.93	2.5
	Senate	Rep.	Maj.	0.88	4.0
Ohio	House	Rep.	Maj.	0.67	6.0
	House	Dem.	Min.	0.55	7.0
	Senate	Rep.	Maj.	0.54	8.0
	Senate	Dem.	Min.	0.50	9.0
Calif.	House	Rep.	Maj.	0.35	11.5
	House	Dem.	Min.	0.35	11.5
	Senate	Rep.	Spl.	0.31	14.0
	Senate	Dem.	Spl.	0.22	15.5
Tenn.	Senate	Rep.	Min.	0.84	5.0
	Senate	Dem.	Maj.	0.48	10.0
	House	Rep.	Min.	0.38	13.0
	House	Dem.	Maj.	0.22	15.5

* Respondents judging party influence to be much or considerable were given a score of one; those judging it to be moderate or increasing were given a score of 0.5; and those judging it to be little or none were given a score of zero. A delegation's score represents the average and may range, therefore, from one to zero.

Table 15.8: Evaluation of party influence on legislative behavior, by state

Evaluation	N.J. $N = 98$	Ohio $N = 134$	Calif. $N = 111$	Tenn. $N = 118$
Much/considerable influence				
Republicans have	37%	34%	1%	16%
Democrats have	22	1	5	3
Both parties have	33	16	—	1
Some/increasing influence				
Republicans have	—	7	5	16
Democrats have	1	6	15	4
Both parties have	—	5	34	3
Little/no influence				
Republicans have	1	2	8	2
Democrats have	—	17	—	4
Both parties have	6	12	32	51

sponses referring to evaluations of party influence.   In New Jersey, a little more than a third of the responses credit the Republican Party with much or considerable influence on its members; another third appraise both parties as influential; and a fifth attribute to the Democratic Party much or considerable influence on its members.   At the same time, only 6 per cent of the responses deny that the parties have influence.   By way of contrast, responses in Ohio reveal a quite different pattern.   Whereas the majority Republican Party is credited with having much or some influence by 41 per cent of the responses, only seven per cent of the responses judged the minority Democrats as having much or some influence.   But, in stark contrast to New Jersey, 17 per cent of the Ohio responses evaluated the Democratic Party as having no or little influence.

The California evaluations are, of course, quite different from those in the two-party, competitive states.   The most significant aspect of the distribution is that one third of the responses find both parties to have some or increasing influence, and another third judge both parties to have no or little influence.   These results are probably indicative of the ambiguity of the party situation in the California legislature during the 1957 session.   But it is also interesting to note that almost three times as many of the responses refer in positive terms to Democratic as to Republican influence.   And 8 per cent deny any influence or acknowledge little influence to the Republicans, but not to the Democrats.   In Tennessee, finally, half of the responses judge either party to have little or no influence, but, conspicuously, 32 per cent, equally divided, appraise the Republican Party as having much influence or some and increasing influence over its members.

Again, comments made in the interviews will serve us to present a more qualitative description of these evaluative orientations.   In New Jersey, Democratic influence in the 1957 session was explained by the fact that the governor was a Democrat:

Having a Democratic governor we are influenced by his wishes and we try to pick the side that he would like.   Most members try to go along with party policy.

A Republican saw it likewise: "the Democrats try to support the governor, and we support our side."   Republican influence was primarily attributed to the caucus: "In our legislature most bills are supported by both parties, but Republicans seldom go against the caucus."

In a two-party, competitive legislature, party influence on individual members is seen as a function of a party's numerical strength.   The low influence on its members attributed to the Ohio Democratic minority, as the following response suggests, may have been due to the fact that it was so greatly outnumbered, especially in the House:

> No one has told me to vote for or against something because I'm a Democrat. I don't know, though; it may be different with the Republicans. I think that they are closely associated with their party because they are in control. No one bothers us (i.e., the Democrats) because they know that the Democrats can't deliver.

Republicans in Ohio were also inclined to undervalue their party's influence on their behavior. With a strong majority in both houses, deviations were permissible. A Republican leader stated:

> I would say that there are about five out of the ninety-seven members in the House who are not interested in supporting any party position. But, members are rarely called upon or required to support a party position. Some people are not inclined to place any weight on the two-party system; others recognize the responsibility involved.

The fact that the Republicans controlled the governorship was felt to involve an obligation to support the party:

> The difference in Republican and Democratic influence stems from the fact that the party had to reorganize to help the new governor, a Republican, rather than to oppose a Democratic governor. Thus a period of hesitation was caused. Things moved slowly at first. We owe support to him because the people of Ohio had faith in him and elected him. There is a line of demarcation in how far to go in supporting him. I opposed both bills (i.e., bills involving salary measures for top administrative personnel), but I owed him support. The line is difficult to establish.

California, as we noted before, was characterized by a party politics in transition during the 1957 session. The situation was still ambiguous enough for a large proportion of the responses to give party influence a rather low or negative evaluation. An Assemblyman who judged the parties to have little or no influence put it this way:

> Some men come in here with considerable party spirit, but it wears off. They find there isn't time for it—you have to get results right away and the job is too big. The luxury of playing at parties doubles the time you have to spend on a bill.

Another legislator explained: "They wave the flag about party principles, write the platform—but we never see it during the session." Even some who reluctantly evaluated party influence as increasing were cautious:

> To a degree you are a captive of your party because you have to depend on it for help—you go along when you can do it without hypocrisy.

Others might point out that party influence is restricted to certain issues alone:

> The only time we have a partisan fight is on public versus private power. On the rest it's just the "ins" versus the "outs." On an appropriation bill the Democrats will vote against, the Republicans for. If the balance changed it would be the other way.

The interesting aspect of this comment is that party influence coming from one's party's control of the governorship is not admitted as such. "Ins" and "outs" are still considered more appropriate labels than Republican and Democrat. As a California legislator phrased it, "your party designation is strictly a matter of personal pride, like Rotary, Lions or Kiwanis." Another felt that "a lot of them talk party but they're willing to work in the coalition." Phrases like "playing at parties," or "captive of your party" in these responses attest to the persistence of anti-party bias in California.

But quite a few responses appraised party, particularly Democratic, influence as on the rise. The Democrats, reported a legislator, "have a news service for us; they'll send speakers up on some phases of the program." Another reported that "there's a Democratic party manager sitting in the rear of the chamber. That's never happened before in a hundred years." That increasing Democratic influence is due to an increasingly active state organization appears from this comment:

> We maintain liaison between the State Democratic Party and the legislature on the basis of a paid secretary who correlates data and information for Democratic Assemblyman. He studies how our bills relate to or differ from the state platform. We don't have time to check it.

Like California, but for different reasons and under different conditions, Tennessee legislators' negative evaluation of party influence is particularly reflected in lack of articulate responses. A response more explicit than most suggested:

> I don't remember but one instance when the parties had any influence or when a plea was made to the members on the basis of party.

In contrast to California, party label as such is, for well-known historical reasons, more highly valued in Tennessee. Yet, as this response suggests, it may not mean too much in actual behavior:

> The members are proud of their party affiliation. It affects their attitude. They don't always vote together, but sometimes they do.

Tennessee responses acknowledging party influence usually specified that it involved matters which were either considered "national issues," such as segregation, or local concerns, such as redistricting or apportionment. A number of comments indicated that the Democrats might occasionally set factionalism aside because of suspicion of Republican tactics:

You never thought about the Democratic Party unless the Republicans were trying something—for example, reapportionment.

Some few Republicans think they can join up with the niggers to beat us.

The Republican Party was united over bills of interest to their members personally. The Democrats are always leery of long-drawn-out Republican bills, wonder what they are trying to put over.

DESCRIPTIONS OF PARTY ROLES

From this examination of "objective" structural features of the political environment and of legislators' own "subjective" definitions of party orientations, it would seem that the "meaning" of party is most approximate to an ideal-type conception in New Jersey. It is somewhat less close in Ohio, and quite remote in California and Tennessee, though we found California party orientations to be in a state of transition and Tennessee orientations to be vestigial remainders of an earlier, more intense two-party situation.

We should expect legislators' descriptions of party roles to be more or less congruent with these meanings. For instance, "partisan" as a viable political role should be most widely recognized and accepted in New Jersey, somewhat less so in Ohio, and very little in California and Tennessee. But, depending on particular circumstances, there might also be variations from one delegation to the next within a given state. The organizational weakness of the Ohio House Democrats, the emergent vitality of California's Democratic delegations, and the self-conscious morale of the Tennessee Senate Republicans should be reflected in the descriptions of party roles.

We asked our respondents whether the distinction between "party man" and "independent, maverick or nonpartisan" was made in their particular chamber of the legislature, and if it was to "describe the difference between the way a party man acts and the way the others act." We shall, in the following, compare only the profiles drawn in New Jersey and Ohio. In California, where only 12 of the 113 interviewees made the distinction, the few comments are so scattered as not to permit us to present a coherent image of the party man. In Tennessee, it appeared, partisanship actually did not so much mean being a Democrat or Republican as being a supporter or opponent of the Administration.[7]

Table 15.9 presents the profiles of the "party man" as they emerge from the descriptions of his behavior in the competitive two-party states. In both states, it appears, "voting with party" is a minimum criterion for being considered a party man. But this minimal description does not tell us very much.

The decisive difference in the "meaning" of the partisan role between the two states appears to involve notions about the place of the caucus in the party scheme of things. In Ohio, participation in caucus discussion serves apparently as a further criterion, but the party man, in the conception of some, can remain in good party standing without being bound by his party's caucus decisions. In New Jersey, on the other hand, more legislators than in Ohio seemed to feel that being bound by caucus decisions and voting with party on crucial issues is the critical characteristic in the behavior of the party man. However, this criterion seemed to be more relevant in the New Jersey House than in the Senate and is more frequently mentioned by Democrats than Republicans, possibly because, with their control of the governorship, Democrats were more sensitive to party discipline than Republicans. This also appears in the greater proportions of Democrats who saw in support of or in opposition to the governor a further test of partisanship. In Ohio, on the other hand, this criterion is mentioned by only a handful of House Republicans, who have never seen a governor of their party face a hostile legislature.

The profile of the "party man," is that of a legislator who "votes with his party" or "sticks to the party program." For "the purpose of the party is to have people pulling in the same direction. Many times you submerge your personal likes and dislikes." The theme of personal disinterestedness is given a variety of expressions. The party man "goes along even when he's not in favor of a bill." More concretely, this means that "he follows the leadership. He votes with them even though at times he does not feel it the thing to do." He sticks with his party "despite pressures or possible political conse-

---

[7] In Tennessee, 17 per cent of the House Democrats and Republicans described the "party man" in terms of the minimum criterion that seems possible—as a man who "votes with his party" or "sticks to party program." In the Senate, only 8 per cent of the Democrats gave a similar reply, as did two of the five Republicans who, we noted, represent a very special case. On the other hand, 24 per cent of the House Democrats, 17 per cent of the House Republicans, and two Senate Republicans made the distinction between Administration–supporter and Administration–opponent, evidently perceiving partisanship in terms of this distinction.

Table 15.9: Description of the behavior characteristics of the party man in New Jersey and Ohio*

Description of Party Man's Behavior	New Jersey				Ohio			
	House		Senate		House		Senate	
	Rep. $N=28$	Dem. 16	Rep. 11	Dem. 7	Rep. 57	Dem. 25	Rep. 12	Dem. 7
Votes with party, sticks to program	57%	44%	91%	72%	65%	68%	83%	72%
Participates in caucus, but not bound by decision	7	0	0	0	9	12	17	14
Votes with party after caucus decision; on crucial issues	39	63	9	29	25	24	8	29
Supports party principles	0	0	0	0	5	4	0	0
Supports Administration of own party, opposes that of other party	7	19	9	29	9	0	0	0
Other descriptions	7	6	36	14	4	4	0	0

* Percentages total more than 100 because more than one response possible.

361

quences," and he will not "sell or barter his vote" with the opposite party. He may be a reluctant follower, but he is prepared "to subordinate his own belief to that of the party." Yet, this need not mean that he is "a rubber-stamp: he is a fellow who, unless something is violently against his personal convictions and beliefs, comes to the aid of his party."

If the partisan disagrees with his party's leadership and feels that he "has to change the thinking of the party, he does it within the framework of the party." Here the caucus becomes critical. The party man participates in caucus discussions because it is here where he has the proper place "to change the party's plans." In the caucus "he argues for his beliefs, but he goes along." The party man "'Will go along,' quote, unquote, and influence intelligently from within, in the caucus." If he is not successful in the caucus, "he makes his position known in private and explains why he cannot support the party's stand on the issue." Few of those who felt that following caucus decisions was the true test of the party man's role argued that exceptions were not possible. "If the party announces a policy measure he will in most cases, though not always, vote the way it has been decided in party caucus," but a good deal depends on the tactical situation in the chamber. Defection from caucus decision "does not matter too much to the leadership so long as they have a sufficient number of votes for favorable passage or defeat of a bill." Another put it this way:

When the chips are down and the party has caucused, a party man will mostly go along with his party. Many times good party men won't follow and, if they give their sincere views, they are respected. A maverick disregards all the rules and lines of voting.

These comments make it quite clear that being a "good" party man in New Jersey or Ohio does not involve blind party loyalty. This also appears from responses to the question, "Under what circumstances do you think it is *not* necessary for a member to vote with his party?" As Table 15.10 shows, only very few legislators in the two states felt that it is always necessary and very few felt that it is never necessary to vote with the party. Reasons for not voting with the party referred to a variety of circumstances. Evidently, the party man is quite free to abstain or vote against his party if it would violate his personal convictions, morals, or ideals:

Except in matters of principle I think it is necessary, or where the issue isn't very important to the overall legislative program. Last week I voted against the party on a bill for four-year registration. It was passed down the line that the party was against it, and I thought the party was wrong. I will diverge from the party line, but I'm thought a good party man by and large, I think.

First, if you have a strong personal conviction on a matter of consequence. Second, if you are convinced that a policy is detrimental or wrong. Third, and this is of less importance, if your vote is meaningless, that is, if there is a safe majority. You find out from the leaders how many votes can be counted on.

Table 15.10: Reasons given by New Jersey and Ohio legislators for not voting with party*

| Reasons | New Jersey | | Ohio | |
	Rep. $N = 52$	Dem. 27	Rep. 111	Dem. 51
When contrary to personal conviction, morals, or ideals	50%	41%	48%	35%
If it is a constituency problem	40	30	39	20
When it is a "bad" bill, not in the public interest	12	7	15	31
Not necessary except on organization matters	0	7	1	8
Not necessary except on policy bills, or when caucus has taken stand	12	30	25	14
When leadership is wrong	2	4	10	2
Not necessary on certain types of bills	0	4	0	2
Never necessary to vote with party	8	0	4	10
Always necessary to vote with party	0	0	5	4
Other reasons for not voting party	13	19	2	2
No answer	2	0	2	2

* Percentages total more than 100 because more than one response possible.

Party regularity may be broken if a bill touches what the party man may consider a constituency problem. Because of a particular situation in a county, "pressure from constituents is heavy and he can't vote party." Or if the bill involves expenditures "too costly to his county or district, he should not vote with his party." A number of Ohio legislators mentioned the axle-mile tax.

Certain members violently disagreed with the party. Take the Summit delegation, they have a large rubber concern. If your constituents are opposed to a party measure, it's a real hard situation. On the trucking issue, a large per cent of the majority voted against it while there were only two dissenting votes on the Democratic side. There's no set rule, though.

Some respondents suggested that breaking party discipline in favor of one's constituency may actually be helpful to the party. For going against the constituency may mean defeat at the polls and weakening of party strength. Members "must first represent their constituency, or they don't return." Such anti-party voting is understood by the party leadership: "If it involves something that would give me a black eye in my county, then the leadership would like to know it and would excuse you from your obligation."

Only a few legislators in New Jersey and Ohio felt it was never necessary to go along with the party, but somewhat more pointed out that it was not necessary unless the vote involved organizational matters, policy bills, or caucus decisions.[8] "Well, as I said, 90 per cent of the bills are not party measures. On those you can vote as you damn please. On the remaining 10 per cent that are party measures there is almost no exception for not voting with the party." But even in this connection party discipline is not iron-clad:

He (i.e., the partisan) is expected to vote with his party only on party policy matters. Even then, the leadership has not demanded 100 per cent adherence to the decision of the party caucus. We have never been bound on anything. They could have done it on the Pay Rise and Decrease bills, but they didn't. They strongly encouraged us all to vote yes, but we were not bound. The same thing happened on the budget.

Sanctions for party role performance. Effective partisan role performance is, of course, stimulated by the sanctions at the disposal of those whose expectations are to be met—notably the party leaders. In order to discover what these sanctions are, we asked legislators what they thought were "some of the advantages of going along with your party leaders when they seek your support on a bill?" As Table 15.11 shows, there was one rather interesting difference in the response patterns between New Jersey and Ohio. New Jersey legislators of both parties, in greater proportions than Ohio legislators of both parties, saw it to their advantage to support party leaders because it would help their party or be helpful in carrying out the party's program, and because it would insure predictable behavior and maintain the two-party system. By way of contrast, Ohio legislators of both parties tended to see advantages in more personal terms. Getting one's *own* bills passed, getting election support for *oneself*, getting *personal* favors such as committee assignments and patronage are advantages more frequently mentioned in Ohio than in New Jersey. These

[8] Of those Californians (34) who discussed the problem at all, 27 per cent said it is never necessary to vote with the party—an interesting confirmation of the anti-party bias in the California system previously noted.

results once more underline the more individualistic, less party-oriented character of Ohio legislative politics (though we should always keep in mind that we are speaking in relative terms). The party is seen in Ohio much more as an *instrument* of personal politics than as an *object* of politics that should be aided by appropriate role taking in the party system.[9]

Table 15.11: Advantages seen by New Jersey and Ohio legislators in supporting party leaders*

	N.J.		Ohio	
Advantages	Rep. $N = 52$	Dem. 27	Rep. 111	Dem. 51
Get own bills passed (local/others)	20%	11%	32%	26%
Get support in elections	13	22	17	29
Get patronage	0	4	2	8
Get committee assignments	4	0	18	24
Get favors for district	0	0	3	8
Get personal favors (unspecified)	10	7	32	20
Help party, help carry out program	37	55	29	18
Insure predictability, two-party system	12	19	14	16
Party a good guide, safe to follow	6	4	3	2
No advantages in supporting leaders	6	0	2	12
Other advantages	16	15	2	0
No answer	2	0	2	4

* Percentages total more than 100 because more than one response was possible.

Support of the leadership for party and organizational reasons was articulated in a number of ways. Some legislators pointed to the need for party discipline as a way of translating the party's program into policy: "By going along with your party leaders, you may be able to lend your influence or weight to bringing about a good program." Moreover, if one's party is in the majority, support of party leadership means "maintaining an efficient majority which can effectuate their program." Some respondents invoked the classical theory of party responsibility:

[9] That 64 per cent of the twenty-two Tennesseans discussing the subject mentioned "getting support of one's own bills" as a major reason for supporting their party tends to confirm the picture of individualistic, undisciplined legislative operations in Tennessee which we have noted earlier.

If everyone went off on a tangent there would be no responsibility to the people.

I look on this from the point of view of party responsibility. I belong to the old school: if the party does something wrong, throw them all out.

We got to go back to the fundamental concepts of representation. Either you adopt the view that the representative is elected by the people to use his own judgment, with the electorate relying that he'll do it intelligently, which presupposes knowledge. Or people vote for him because of his party affiliation. They don't know enough about the candidate and vote for party principles generally. In the first case, you forget about any party policy; in the second, if people vote because of his party affiliation, they expect you to follow the party.

Others referred to the obligation to work toward future electoral success for the party or to repay the party for its past electoral support through partisan support in the legislature:

You can't forget this is still political. You aren't on the ticket without the support of the party; if you aren't on the ticket you won't get elected. Everyone who is elected owes an obligation to the people and the party.

There has to have been some force to hold the majority together, so that you go home and can say, "This is our program."

Some others who took this kind of organizational view went further and asserted the need for maintaining the two-party system and its consequences for legislative action:

Ours is a two-party system and we need two parties, which you can't have if the members don't stand by their parties.

Well, our country is essentially a two-party system. If the legislature weren't organized on a party basis, it would be in a terrible state, and there would be little legislation. There would be a chaotic condition.

Legislators mentioning personal advantages in going along with the party leaders would give a variety of reasons. Getting one's bills passed was uppermost in the minds of many:

You're a member of the club, which you won't be if you don't go along with the party leaders. The non-conformists are given some consideration, but their bills don't get anywhere. If you're in good standing with the Speaker and others, they can influence the members and put in a good word for you. They can do a lot toward seeing whether your bill will get on the calendar and pushing the hearings along. Since most members are simply followers, it helps a bill along tremendously if the leaders are for it.

Other favors to be gained by supporting the party were frequently mentioned. As one Ohioan said, "if you are in the doghouse with the leaders you can't expect to get good committee assignments and things of that type." What he may have meant by "things of that type" was spelled out in these comments:

You get better committee assignments, and you get appointed to interim committees and all kinds of easy assignments like that. There are lots of things they can appoint you to—special committees to take trips and things like that.

If you stick with the party, they'll take care of you. Get you a job after defeat. If you look for security, better be a good boy and do what [you are] told.

Among the favors available as sanctions for proper partisan behavior are benefits to the legislator's district. An Ohio Republican leader gave a lively illustration:

Of course, being a party man, I think a member can do more for his district over the long haul by going along in any legislative body. A fellow, who's dead now, from Hamilton, was always afraid to vote. We had a little meeting, and somebody said: "B. hasn't gone with us,"—he wanted a $500,000 appropriation for his district. We sent somebody to him and explained we had cut him to $200,000.

A variety of other advantages were mentioned. Among these, endorsement by party leaders, for re-election or another government position, figured prominently:

The chief advantage is when you want something they can recommend you to. You might want something like a judgeship of the Supreme Court and might want their endorsement. They might say, "He didn't go along." And they would pick one who did follow, although the other man might be his equal or better qualified.

Politically, if you fail to line up with the party, in all probability that failure will be brought to the attention of your county chairman. He, in turn, could make it rough on you if you wanted to run again. Your local party wants to know if you can be counted on to support party principles.

Finally, the party is seen as an anchorage point to guide behavior in doubtful situations. As one legislator said, "If one is in doubt or not informed, the party leaders are more likely to be right." Another put it this way: "If you are in doubt, right or wrong, follow the party— and there's always something that's in doubt."

Definitions of the "independent." Our expectation that the terms "independents, mavericks, or nonpartisans" might be given particular definitions in the four states did not quite turn out as we had expected. Ninety-four per cent of the Tennessee, 70 per cent of the New Jersey, 61 per cent of the California and 50 per cent of the Ohio legislators failed to define independents of one sort or another at all. Of those who did, most simply reversed their descriptions of the party man. But a few peculiarities may be noted. California legislators more than those from Ohio and New Jersey stressed that independents were men who follow their own principles:

I'd say I was independent. I don't know, but I don't do what they tell me. A party man finds out what the county and state chairman and party want and then goes along. I guess he hopes that if he goes along he may get an appointment or he may go along just to be a good fellow, or he may think they are right. The others (i.e., independents) determine right and wrong and then follow the right. These men usually last longer, for in the ultimate end they are right. The public eye is always on you, and if you do something wrong and blame it on the party, they, the public, will say you should have known better. They blame you, not the party.

An independent is one who refuses to be dictated to if he feels he has good judgment and is willing to stand on it. The party man allows himself to be cajoled and coerced to support the organization against his own better judgment.

In general, however, the profile of the independent is confused. Some defined him as a man not only uncommitted to vote with his own party, but consistently voting with the other party. This kind is sometimes called "maverick," but the distinction is not clear between him and the principled independent. One legislator attempted to make this distinction: "A party man adheres strictly to party politics, always votes the party line. A maverick jumps party lines. An independent votes the way he feels he should vote." Others put it somewhat differently:

The maverick is usually an individual more concerned about the effect on his own political life than on the party as a whole. The role of the independent sounds good, but they usually think in terms of "I" and not how it affects others.

A maverick is sounding off frequently. A true independent will keep his mouth shut but vote his convictions.

A few Ohio House Republicans, having some of their own party members in mind, occasionally defined the independent as one who consistently votes "no," as an essentially negative person who opposes whatever the majority is for: he "votes no on every god-damn thing, even if you are right. He votes against anybody." "Most of our independents," said another Ohioan, "are fellows who do not believe in any kind of discipline—party, economic, urban-rural. They are not constructive." Another said: "They always differ from others. If they don't know how to decide, they say no." It seems that the maverick rather than the independent is the opposite of the party man. A party man can be an "independent" of sorts, but he cannot be a maverick:

A maverick disregards party politics, he acts as he sees fit. He doesn't consider himself as part of any party—could vote any way on controversial matters.

A maverick is indifferent, by definition. He is neither less nor more sincere. He does not see the relationship of the problem to the party. The maverick speaks more often than the partisan. The reaction to the maverick is that he is taken with a grain of salt. The behavior of the maverick is more unpredictable than the partisan's.

More often than not, the descriptions of independents or mavericks, even in California, involved much negative judgment about the role. He "is out to get newspaper publicity. He talks to the press when he's making a speech, not for the benefit of the members here. When he speaks on the floor, it's to the gallery." The independent, said another, "seeks the popular view. He seeks the headlines rather than anything else. Some people think you will stand out, if you are out of step. It's one way of getting attention." A California respondent summed it up this way: "They simply make a lot of noise, try to make headlines for the personal gratification of being courted by both sides." But a favorable description would say that the maverick "is a free-thinker. He makes his own determination of the issues. He makes his own decisions. Maverick isn't exactly the right word for those who don't conform."

APPRAISAL OF PARTY ROLES AND POLITICAL CULTURE

Among those legislators who described the roles of the "party man" and the "independent," some spontaneously expressed attitudes of approval or disapproval concerning the roles. By assigning values to the entire set of response patterns, it is possible to present an over-all appraisal of the roles made by 14 of the 16 delegations. A score of +1.0 would mean that a delegation was wholly favorable to the role of party man and unfavorable to that of independent; a score of —1.0 that its appraisal wholly favored the independent and disfavored the party man. As Table 15.12 shows, all of the New Jersey and Ohio delegations, except Ohio Senate Democrats, were more or less favorable or at least neutral to the role of party man, while the California and Tennessee delegations, except the California House Democrats, were more or less favorable or at least neutral to the role of independent.

But the most significant aspect of the summary scores is their rather restricted range. In absolute terms, the uppermost score of +0.54, reached by the New Jersey Senate Republicans, means that

Table 15.12: Appraisal of roles of party man and independent, by state, chamber, party, status, and rank

State	Chamber	Party	Status	Score*	Rank
N.J.	Senate	Rep.	Maj.	+0.54	1.0
	House	Rep.	Maj.	+0.50	3.5
	Senate	Dem.	Min.	+0.50	3.5
	House	Dem.	Min.	+0.25	6.0
Ohio	House	Rep.	Maj.	+0.52	2.0
	Senate	Rep.	Maj.	+0.46	5.0
	House	Dem.	Min.	+0.12	7.0
	Senate	Dem.	Min.	−0.03	10.0
Calif.	House	Dem.	Min.	+0.11	8.0
	House	Rep.	Maj.	−0.05	11.0
	Senate	Dem.	Spl.	−0.19	13.0
	Senate	Rep.	Spl.	−0.20	14.0
Tenn.†	House	Dem.	Maj.	−0.02	9.0
	House	Rep.	Min.	−0.13	12.0

* The following values were assigned to possible response patterns:

Attitude towards:

Party Man	Independent	Score value
Favorable	Unfavorable	+1.0
Favorable	Neutral	+.75
Favorable	Favorable	+.50
Neutral	Unfavorable	+.25
Neutral	Neutral	0.0
Neutral	Favorable	−.25
Unfavorable	Unfavorable	−.50
Unfavorable	Neutral	−.75
Unfavorable	Favorable	−1.0

Delegation scores were obtained by multiplying the number of party members in each response-pattern category by the score value and averaging the totals.

† No scores could be computed for Tennessee Senate Democrats and Republicans because insufficient numbers of them expressed clearly defined attitudes.

this delegation, though not enthusiastic about the role of partisan, gave moderate encouragement to those who might choose to play it. And the lowest score of −0.20, by California's Senate Republicans, means that this delegation, though not enthusiastic about the role of independent, was more tolerant of independents than of partisan role-players. In any case, the delegations most favorable to the party man in their appraisal were not overwhelmingly favorable to this role.

It would seem, then, that both roles are of mutually limiting effect, that expectations concerning them are not very rigid. The distinction between the party man and the independent is essentially ambiguous and their appraisal ambivalent. Apparently, the party man may act independently, and the independent may yet be more or less of a party man. In general, the New Jersey and Ohio legislators were more in favor of the party man's role, and the California and Tennessee delegations more in favor of the role of the independent.

The distribution of scores also shows that, with one exception, the majority party delegations were more inclined to favor the role of the party man than were the minority delegations. The only exception, again, is the appraisal of the two roles made by the California House Democrats who, as we have repeatedly seen, were generally more favorable to party phenomena than were their Republican colleagues.

Although majority or minority status seems to be an institutional-structural factor of some significance for the ways in which legislators appraise partisan or independent roles, the degree of competition encountered on the electoral level appears to be of less importance. The coefficient of rank-order correlation between delegations' score on the index of competition and the role-appraisal index is $+0.28$, that is, positive but low. In other words, delegations coming more from one-party than competitive districts, like Ohio's Republicans, may yet place high value on the party man's role in preference to that of the independent's.

On the other hand, rank-order correlations between role appraisal and what we characterized as elements of a legislature's political culture are exceptionally high. For affective orientation the coefficient was $+0.85$; for evaluative orientation it was $+0.82$; and for cognitive orientation $+0.81$. The more a legislature's political culture is party-oriented, the more likely will legislators look on the role of the party man as a positive asset of his total legislative position. In other words, partisan or independent roles will be favored or disfavored in line with those other orientations which constitute a legislature's cultural environment.

PARTY ROLES AND IDEOLOGICAL HOMOGENEITY

We have so far been dealing largely with the form and functions of the roles of partisan and independent in the party scheme of things, but not with their content. Partisanship, we noted, is likely to be activated in only two types of situations: first, when party discipline is absolutely essential for the survival itself of the party as an "organization"; and, second, when members are to be mobilized, for the sake of the party's "record," in support of vaguely felt programmatic objectives. But even then, as many roll-call studies have shown, the crossing of party lines is, more often than not, a widely practiced behavior pattern in American legislatures.

It is, therefore, surprising to find that Democratic and Republican legislators differ quite sharply in ideological terms. A Guttman-type scale designed to differentiate between "liberals" and "conservatives" served the purpose of giving us a measure of the party delegations' ideological commitments.[10] Table 15.13 presents the

Table 15.13: Ideology of legislators, by state, chamber,
party, status, and rank

State	Chamber	Party	Status	Score	Rank
N.J.	Senate	Dem.	Min.	0.79	3.0
	House	Dem.	Min.	0.55	6.0
	Senate	Rep.	Maj.	0.50	8.0
	House	Rep.	Maj.	0.41	10.0
Ohio	House	Dem.	Min.	0.69	4.0
	Senate	Dem.	Min.	0.54	7.0
	House	Rep.	Maj.	0.28	15.0
	Senate	Rep.	Maj.	0.15	16.0
Calif.	House	Dem.	Min.	0.85	1.0
	Senate	Dem.	Spl.	0.82	2.0
	House	Rep.	Maj.	0.42	9.0
	Senate	Rep.	Spl.	0.38	13.0
Tenn.	Senate	Dem.	Maj.	0.56	5.0
	House	Dem.	Maj.	0.39	11.5
	House	Rep.	Min.	0.39	11.5
	Senate	Rep.	Min.	0.30	14.0

scores obtained by the 16 delegations on the index of ideology. A score of 1.0 would mean that a delegation is solidly "liberal," and a score of 0.0 that it is solidly "conservative." As the table shows, the scores ranged from 0.85 for the most liberal delegation, California's House Democrats, to 0.15 for the most conservative delegation,

[10] For a discussion and construction of the "ideology scale," see Appendix 2.3 below, p. 475.

Ohio's Senate Republicans. Two facts stand out: first, that in every state, even in Tennessee, the two Democratic delegations are invariably more liberal than the Republican delegations. And, second, that in terms of over-all rankings, seven of the eight upper "more liberal" delegations are Democratic. Only Tennessee's House Democrats are outranked by three Republican delegations.

How shall we interpret these consistent ideological differences between Republicans and Democrats in view of the general belief that American political parties differ little, if at all, in their positions on political principles? First, it may be true that the average Republican voter is ideologically not very unlike the average Democratic voter, a fact which forces the parties to appeal to the electorate in very similar terms. But it does not follow, as recent research shows, that those who make up the core of party workers are also ideologically more alike than different.[11] Second, statistical differences between Republicans and Democrats in the matter of ideology should not blind us to the fact that both parties are ideologically more heterogeneous than homogeneous, i.e., each contains both liberals and conservatives.

For these and other reasons, ideological beliefs are not necessarily linked to party policy stands. They may exist quite apart from party considerations. What may be true of individuals may not be true of the aggregates of which individual persons are members. Our findings about ideological differences between Republican and Democratic legislators, just as similar findings on other levels of the party hierarchies, need not mean, therefore, that the parties as organizations will behave in ideological terms. Of course, they may. The condition for doing so exists. But whether they actually will do so might depend on whether ideological preferences have been assimilated into party orientations and party roles.

In order to determine whether ideological position is related to party orientations and roles, we transformed the scores on the ideology scale into measures of ideological homogeneity or consensus. A score of one (1.0) or zero (0.0) on the ideology scale would mean that a delegation is completely or 100 per cent agreed; a score of 0.50 on the ideology scale would mean that a delegation is sharply divided, that its consensus is non-existent. In other words, homogeneity scores may range from 100, for full consensus in ideology, to zero, for complete

[11] See, for instance, Herbert McClosky, Paul J. Hoffman and Rosemary O'Hara, "Issue Conflict and Consensus Among Party Leaders and Followers," *American Political Science Review* 54:406–427 (1960.)

dissensus.[12]   Table 15.14 shows that 12 of the delegations have homogeneity scores of less than 50, which means that ideological consensus in these delegations is rather low.

If partisanship were identified with a given ideology—Democratic with liberalism or Republican with conservatism—we should expect fairly high positive correlations between the scores recorded for the

Table 15.14: Legislators' ideological homogeneity, by state, chamber, party, status, and rank

State	Chamber	Party	Status	Score	Rank
N.J.	Senate	Dem.	Min.	58	4.0
	House	Rep.	Maj.	18	11.0
	House	Dem.	Min.	10	14.0
	Senate	Rep.	Maj.	0	16.0
Ohio	Senate	Rep.	Maj.	70	1.5
	House	Rep.	Maj.	44	5.0
	House	Dem.	Min.	38	7.0
	Senate	Dem.	Min.	8	15.0
Calif.	House	Dem.	Min.	70	1.5
	Senate	Dem.	Spl.	64	3.0
	Senate	Rep.	Spl.	24	8.0
	House	Rep.	Maj.	16	12.0
Tenn.	Senate	Rep.	Min.	40	6.0
	House	Dem.	Maj.	22	9.5
	House	Rep.	Min.	22	9.5
	Senate	Dem.	Maj.	12	13.0

party delegations on the ideological homogeneity measure and their scores on the various indices involving party orientations.   This, as the following tabulation shows, is not the case:

Ideological homogeneity with respect to:

		rho
Evaluation of party influence		—.16
Appraisal of party roles		—.06
Cognition of party conflict		—.05
Affect towards party		+.19

[12] This measure is, of course, the same as Rice's famous "index of cohesion." The index measure for any delegation equals the deviation of the ideological score from 0.50 multiplied by two.   See Stuart A. Rice, "The Behavior of Legislative Groups," *Political Science Quarterly* **40**:60–72 (1925).

Except in the case of affective orientation towards party where the co-efficient of correlation is positive but negligible, the coefficients for the three other measures are negative and negligible. The relationships suggest that ideology, insofar as it does differentiate between Republicans and Democrats, does not enter their definition of the legislative situation in which party orientations and party roles are salient considerations.

This, in our view, is a most significant finding. Just as the traditional belief that there is little or no ideological difference between the Democratic and Republican parties may be an overstatement, so the recent discoveries, including our own, that party leaders and functionaries of the two parties differ significantly as individuals in terms of ideology, do not necessarily mean that these differences will be activated in the performance of partisan roles. Depending on the particular legislative issue, there may or may not be an association between ideological and party-line thinking or partisan role taking. Our data suggest that, in general, there is no association. Though Republicans and Democrats differ when confronted with alternatives involving ideological commitment, as in the case of our ideology scale, their party orientations and partisan role expectations seem to constitute a definition of the legislative situation in which ideological considerations are simply not mobilized.

That this is a valid interpretation of the data is substantiated by legislators' comments relating to policy issues. We found none explicitly linking party policy concerns with ideological divisions between the two parties. Either these comments suggest that party differences on issues are, for one reason or another, unimportant:

> We don't follow any party policy to any great extent. We attempt to have a party policy, but for the most part I don't think we have it. We should have more specific policy than we do. That way people would have a better choice between the parties.

> Except for a few party bills, most legislation doesn't follow party lines. Most good bills and some controversial bills usually have Democratic and Republican sponsors. Party lines just don't mean much except for organizational purposes.

Or, even if "party stands" may be considered important, the comments do not specify their ideological content:

> Party considerations are important in the matters of major legislation enacted in any session, that is, party stands on taxation, workman's compensation, highways, conservation and welfare. The two-party system is of great importance in the success or failure of major legislation—their major programs. Any member elected as a party candidate has an obligation to vote along party lines and philosophy.

CONCLUSION

Partisanship enters the legislative process in the various states in different ways and different degrees. The extent of partisanship in a legislature varies with both the structural-institutional context and the political-cultural environment. In particular, it depends upon the competitive situation and the majority-minority status of the legislators and upon their orientations toward party acquired through their cultural background.

Partisanship and the impact of party on the legislative process clearly seem greatest in New Jersey and somewhat less in Ohio. (California and Tennessee were omitted from the analysis except at a few points because of incompleteness in the data.)   But the influence of partisanship differs markedly not only from state to state but from chamber to chamber and even from party delegation to delegation within a chamber.   For example, California Democrats and Tennessee Republicans tend to respond in exceptional ways, but for different reasons, to the demands of partisanship.

Variations in the meaning of partisanship are perhaps of even greater importance to the political analyst than variations in its extent.   The role of "party man" is a highly ambiguous one.   It is not the same from one state or party to another.   The line between a "party man" and an "independent" or a "maverick" is a tenuous one.   On the whole, the role of "party man" tends to be defined in terms of minimal activities—e.g., roll-call voting—in response to party cues.   In spite of the fact that ideological differences among party members appear to be much sharper than are such differences among average citizens, there is little correspondence between ideological attitude and party role.

These findings point to the past neglect and the present need of research into the roles of legislators as party members.   They are at best suggestive of some of the directions such research might take.   At the same time, they undoubtedly report an important characteristic of American state legislative politics: ambivalence and uncertainty about the meaning of "party" is a fact of political life, felt by the legislators themselves; it is not just a reflection of the state of political research.

PART FIVE

The legislative system

In CONTRAST to the burgeoning body of sophisticated theoretical writings about organizational or administrative behavior,[1] the legislative process and legislative behavior, and especially the legislature's environment, have been given little theoretical attention. Most of the writing is descriptive of either formal or informal structural arrangements or of functions; or it is concerned with pathological and therapeutic aspects. There has been little concern with analytic theory of the legislative process.[2]

What theory there is involves a series of inarticulate assumptions centered in the notion, well expressed by Stephen K. Bailey, that "legislative policy-making appears to be the result of a confluence of factors streaming from an almost endless number of tribu-

---

This introduction drafted by Eulau.

[1] See James G. March and Herbert A. Simon's codification in *Organizations* (New York: John Wiley and Sons, 1958), and the works cited there. Also P. Wasserman and F. S. Silander, *Decision-Making: An Annotated Bibliography* (Ithaca, N.Y.: Cayuga Press, 1958).

[2] Jean M. Driscoll, "Some Analytic Concepts for the Comparative Study of State Legislatures," paper presented at the Annual Meeting of the American Political Science Association, Boulder, Colorado, September 7–9, 1955. Indicative of the state of affairs is the fact that organizational theorists have a specialized medium of communication in the *Administrative Science Quarterly*. No equivalent journal is devoted to the study of legislative behavior and processes. The scientific lag is most evident if one compares legislative with electoral research. Concerning the latter, compare Samuel J. Eldersveld's early critique, "Theory and Method in Voting Behavior Research," in Heinz Eulau, Samuel J. Eldersveld and Morris Janowitz, eds., *Political Behavior* (Glencoe: The Free Press, 1956), pp. 267–274, with Peter H. Rossi's recent "Four Landmarks in Voting Research," in Eugene Burdick and Arthur J. Brodbeck, Eds., *American Voting Behavior* (Glencoe: The Free Press, 1959), pp. 5–54.

taries. . . ."   Bailey's "attempt to make a vector analysis of legislative policy-making" is suggestive.[3] The "tributaries" most frequently
recognized, and probably correctly so, are parties, pressure groups,
constituencies, and administrative agencies. But the vector model
implicit in most studies is essentially a one-way street. It assumes
that the actions of "outside" forces are the independent or causal factors having direct effect on legislative decisions as dependent variables.
Studies along this line are not concerned with how the external factors
are themselves related to each other, how these forces are received
by legislators and, in turn, related to by them or transformed into
legislative results.

More specific theoretical formulation conceives of the legislative
process as a struggle among groups in conflict.[4] But most studies
using the "group-influence model" seem to be primarily devoted to
the group character of political conflict in the legislative setting, not
with the place of the legislature in the political system.[5] The same is
largely true of those studies which focus on party and constituency as
influences on the legislature.[6] This does not mean that other assumptions are absent from the many descriptive studies of legislatures. The
legislature is variously conceived as a "decision-making mechanism,"
"a structure of power," or an "equilibrium system," but suggestive as
these notions are, they have only rarely been tested in the crucible of
empirical research.

Perhaps most valuable in understanding the concrete reality of
legislative behavior within the larger political system are the studies
which concentrate on particular decisions.[7] But the notion of the
legislature as a decisional system tends to limit the focus of inquiry
more than seems appropriate for the purpose of specifying just how
legislature and political system are interdependent. In the main
limited to case studies, the decisional approach ignores the fact that a

[3] Stephen Kemp Bailey, *Congress Makes a Law, op. cit.*, pp. x, 236.

[4] The most notable works are: Bertram M. Gross, *op cit.;* Earl Latham, *op. cit.;*
and David B. Truman, *The Governmental Process, op. cit.* It may be noted that
all of these works deal with the Congress of the United States.

[5] Garceau's and Silverman's study of the Vermont legislature, *op. cit.*, represents
a definite shift in conceptualization from the conventional "group-influence
model" to a more complex model of interaction between a legislature and its
clientele.

[6] William J. Keefe, *op. cit.*, summarizes relevant formulations and critically
appraises the deficiencies of this approach.

[7] See, for instance, Bernard C. Cohen, *The Political Process and Foreign Policy
—The Making of the Japanese Peace Settlement* (Princeton, N.J.: Princeton
University Press, 1957).

good deal of legislative behavior does not involve decision making at all. Much of what happens between legislatures and other institutions or organizations in the political system, and between legislators and their clients, is not a matter of decision processes. The legislature may serve as a channel of executive information, as a tool for maintaining community consensus, or as an investigating agency. The many services legislators perform—the errand-boy function—are not covered by the decision-making scheme. As Roy C. Macridis has remarked, "we may discover that the function we took for granted, i.e., legislation, is only incidental to the other functions that it may perform."[8]

Indeed, the decisional model, at least as borrowed from organizational theory, does not really seem applicable to the legislative process, even if the latter calls for decision making. In organizational theory a decision involves a choice of a preferred project from among a number of clearly specified and numerically limited alternative projects. But in the legislative process it is often by no means clear what the alternatives are. In fact, it is one of the objectives of the legislative process to evolve and identify alternatives, and the whole process is much less rational than the organizational decision-making model assumes. The legislative process is political precisely because the choices facing legislators may be ill defined. In contrast to bureaucratic organizations, the legislature is, by its very nature, compelled to be rooted in conflict. For just this reason the criteria used in appraising administrative behavior—efficiency and effectiveness—seem out of place. If the resolution of conflict is the goal of legislative decision making, an "effective" legislature is one in which the lines of cleavage can be expected to be sharply drawn so that issues may be crystallized and clarified. Of course, cleavage is not absent from other types of governmental institutions, such as courts of law or even administrative agencies. But here division is not formally expected and institutionalized. Even in a court a unanimous opinion is preferred to a close decision. Conflict may characterize informal relations in an administrative organization, but it cannot be formally acknowledged: indeed, "unity of command," fictitious though it may be, is the formally recognized mode of interaction. But in a legislature unanimity, though perhaps present more often than expected, is suspect. Only in "emergencies" is consensus the predicate rather than the goal of legislative decision making.[9]

[8] Roy C. Macridis, *The Study of Comparative Government* (Garden City, New York: Doubleday and Company, 1955), p. 66.

[9] It can be argued that the conflict hypothesis does not account for significant

A model linking the legislature's internal structure and functioning to its external environment must make provision for conflict as an immanent feature of legislative behavior. The theoretical difficulty in determining this linkage lies in appropriate conceptualization. For "legislature" is not a particularly serviceable analytic concept.[10] It may define a concrete group of particular political actors, but it does not specify just how the behavior of these actors is a function of the legislature's position in the larger political system. How legislature and other institutions relevant to its functioning are linked remains the critical problem to be explored. Yet, the very notion of linkage may point the way. For it suggests that the legislature may be thought of as a subsystem of the political system coupled to parties, pressure groups, constituencies, or administrative agencies, also now conceived as subsystems. Rather than thinking of the legislature as genetically and organically apart from these other components of the political system, we may treat them all as legislative subsystems and speak of "legislative system." Legislative system, in contrast to legislature, is an analytic concept. It directs attention to a number of properties of the system which are directly relevant to the problem of linkage.[11]

In the first place, the notion of system implies analytical boundaries. It aids in defining what to include and exclude in research. Insofar as legislative behavior is purposeful and goal oriented, the boundaries of the legislative system may be drawn in terms of communications, services, and decisions relevant to the institutionalization, crystalliza-

---

and numerically frequent patterns of behavior in state legislatures. Keefe, for instance, points out that unanimity and consensus in many cases "may not be so much a matter of 'leadership' as simply a case of like-minded legislators moving from bill to bill in the broad fields of state public policy where consensus rather than conflict obtains." (*Op. cit.*) But this interpretation is possibly deceptive. As Truman points out, in *The Governmental Process*, (*op. cit.*, p. 392), "even a temporarily viable legislative decision usually must involve the adjustment and compromise of interests. Even where virtual unanimity prevails in the legislature, the process of reconciling conflicting interests must have taken place—*though perhaps at an earlier stage wholly or partly outside the legislature* and the formal institutions of government. When this happens, the legislature merely registers the decision. . . . " (Italics added.)

[10] See Driscoll, *op. cit.*

[11] For system analysis of politics, see David Easton, "An Approach to the Analysis of Political Systems," *World Politics* 9:383–400 (1957), and Talcott Parsons, "'Voting' and the Equilibrium of the American Political System," in Burdick and Brodbeck, *op. cit.*, pp. 80–120. Also see Morton A. Kaplan, *System and Process in International Politics* (New York: John Wiley and Sons, 1957).

tion, and resolution of social and political conflicts. Only behavior appropriate to the achievement of these goals is included in the system, all other behavior is excluded. For instance, electoral behavior in a legislator's constituency on the Presidential level may be considered irrelevant to the functioning of a state legislative system and may be considered "external," while electoral behavior on the state legislative level is "internal" to the system. This is, of course, a purely arbitrary theoretical matter. In many cases, inclusion or exclusion of variables may be a matter of empirical determination. Constituents' electoral behavior on the Presidential level may be included as a legislative-system variable if it demonstrably affects party control of a legislative seat through the working of the Presidential candidate's "coat tail." Or, whether friendship relations in the legislature are to be considered system variables depends on whether or not such relations are relevant to the goals of the system. In other words, not all behavior occurring within or between concrete structures such as legislatures, parties, pressure groups, or constituencies is necessarily conducive to the functioning of the legislative system.

Second, the concept of system directs attention to the units of analysis. What units are chosen depends on the level of inquiry one wishes to pursue. The unit of inquiry may be a whole system in relation to another system, an institutionalized group, or an individual person. Because the legislative system is a system of human action, we have chosen roles taken by one set of actors—legislators—as our units of analysis. In Part Four we suggested why we think that legislators as role takers are particularly useful units of analysis in a study of legislative behavior. And we shall suggest, in the following two chapters, that it is by virtue of their taking roles in all legislative subsystems that the relationship between these subsystems can be empirically scrutinized. But this leads directly to the next aspect of the concept of system.

Third, a system is a set of variables which are related to each other, in contrast to external variables, in such a way that behavioral regularities can be described. In other words, the notion of system implies that relevant variables are interdependent in a structure which is not arbitrary or random but, again, relevant to the goals of the system. A system has, of course, an identity through time. Ideally it would seem desirable to describe the system at different times in order to show how changes in one variable affect changes in another variable. This only longitudinal analysis can do. But by describing the "state" of the variables at any one time the structure of the system can be identified.

Fourth, the actions of a system have antecedents and consequences. The former can be thought of as "inputs" and the latter as "outputs." Without inputs the system cannot function. In the case of the legislature as a subsystem, typical inputs are, for instance, the votes harnessed by parties in support of candidates, the requests for services from constituents, or the demands made by pressure groups for favorable legislation. Outputs, in turn, are, from the point of view of the legislature as a subsystem, all its actions in response to inputs—bills passed, requests forwarded, letters answered, constituents introduced, and so on. These outputs from the legislature as a subsystem become, of course, inputs into the other subsystems of the legislative system, just as the legislature's inputs are outputs from these subsystems.

Fifth, it is through the input-output transactions that subsystems are coupled to constitute a whole system—in our case the legislative system (as a whole, itself a subsystem of the political system). Outputs from one system are "fed back" as inputs into another system and generate fresh outputs from that system. The process through which inputs are transformed into outputs is, of course, at the core of inquiry into what is usually called "the legislative process." In this process, however, the legislature's own needs for maintenance and survival make for characteristic outputs as well. Legislative behavior, therefore, is not simply a response to "pressures" brought to bear on the legislature from outside (inputs), but involves absorption of these pressures and their integration with the legislature's own needs before they are "processed" into outputs.

Finally, the process of transforming inputs into outputs is facilitated by both differentiation and integration within the system. Differentiation is occasioned by the propensity of actors to take different roles. In the case of the legislature some of these roles, we pointed out in Part Three, such as formal or informal leadership roles, or such roles as "friend" and "expert," are taken in response to the legislature's internal structural and functional requirements. Other roles, like those described in Part Four, are taken in response either to the sources of input or with a view on outputs, depending on the legislator's relationships in other subsystems of the legislative system. But not all available roles are taken simultaneously by all legislators. There is a division of labor, so to speak, in role taking. However, differentiation carried too far would probably have dysfunctional consequences for the system. If the taking of roles were completely random, the resulting chaos would interfere with the production of outputs necessary for the functioning of the system. The division of labor in terms of role differentiation is offset, therefore, by countervailing tendencies for legislators to take roles in such combinations as are conducive to the integration of the legislature as a system. Insofar as analytically differentiated roles are empirically related to each other in a theoretically meaningful manner, we can speak of the legislature as a "role system." This notion underlies the analyses presented in Chapter 16.

This model of the legislative role system is, of course, very difficult to adapt in its full concreteness to the purposes of empirical research. If it were to be attempted, it would be necessary to assemble data concerning the mutual expectations which all the actors in the legislative system—constituents, pressure-group representatives, administrative officials, political-party leaders, as well as legislators—have of each other's behavior. The task, if not insurmountable, would be time consuming and expensive. But by choosing legislators' own role orientations relevant to these expectations, we have appropriate units of analysis. If the notion of a legislative role system is at all empirically viable, concrete reality should be reflected in those perceptions of their roles which legislators must hold as reasonably effective actors in the legislative arena. For self-images and the expectations of others are mutually interdependent by virtue of the fact that any system of action is also a system of interaction.

The underlying design is, of course, essentially identical with the model of the legislative system as we have sketched it, and even though role orientations must not be confused with roles, they can be analyzed in terms of the legislative system. Some roles represent what we have called "sources of input"; others are focussed on the legislative process; and a third group relate to legislative output. If role orientations relevant to legislative input, process, and output hang together in an identifiable structure, there is reason to believe that they reflect the reality of the legislative role system. In this system legislature and other subsystems—notably constituencies, pressure groups, and political parties—are linked or coupled because legislators take appropriate roles in each subsystem.

Finally, each concrete legislative system may be assumed to have its characteristic "political role structure." This structure is expressed in legislators' role orientations, their frequency of occurrence in any particular system, and their more or less typical combinations. In Chapter 17, therefore, we shall compare the political role structures of the four state systems—not all their aspects, of course, but those embedded in legislators' role orientations.

CHAPTER 16

The network of legislative
role orientations

THERE ARE A NUMBER OF WAYS in which a legislator's roles can be combined into a coherent network of role orientations. Roles taken in different systems may be harmonious and complementary. This is largely the case if one system overlaps with or is included in a more embracing system. For instance, in an electoral district dominated by a single industry, role orientations towards areal clientele and group clientele may be identical because there is no conflict among relevant expectations.

But in other cases there may be real conflict between expectations made on the legislator from one type of clientele to another. In part, such conflict is ameliorated by the differential intensity or differential pervasiveness of the various roles. In a competitive party system, for example, the party role is likely to be both pervasive and intense, and it is likely to be more salient in the legislator's orientations than the role he may take in the system of pressure groups. In case of conflict, the legislator will select the more pervasive or more intense over the less pervasive and less intense roles in orienting himself to action.

Role conflict may also be lessened by the degree to which roles in conflict are specified. Some roles are clearly defined, others are blurred. The more blurred a role is, the greater the likelihood of its yielding to a more clearly defined role. Such roles as neutral in the pressure group system, of district-state-oriented in the areal system, or of politico in the representational system are likely to be less clearly related to more precisely defined roles than the latter are among themselves. Predictability of behavior in performance of blurred

This chapter drafted by Eulau.

384

roles is more difficult because the orientations involved are both very flexible and complex.

Finally, role conflict may be adjusted by the genetic origins of different roles. Usually, "ascribed" roles are both more pervasive and clearly defined than "achieved" roles. Of the roles discussed in Part Four, party and areal roles are probably the most ascriptive, and the latter less so than the former. It is rare that a legislator deserts his party, becomes an independent, or even joins the other party, whereas he may well give up a district-oriented role in favor of a state-oriented role.

In general then, role-conflict solution is likely to be in favor of the more ascribed, more pervasive, more intense, and more clearly defined roles. Of course even logically contradictory role orientations may be held without the experience of conflict. The legislator may take roles seriatim, one role in one connection but not in another, without any feeling that a problem of consistency is involved. Indeed, it is this kind of behavior which has probably earned, if unwittingly, the politician's contemptuous reputation as a shifty and deceitful "man with a thousand faces."

INTERPENETRATION OF CLIENTELE-ROLE ORIENTATIONS

Theoretically it is more difficult to anticipate how clientele-role orientations—focussed on parties, areas, and pressure groups—are likely to be related to each other than how these orientations may interpenetrate with representational and purposive legislative orientations. In some respects, the three clientele-oriented components of the legislator's total role are three potentially independent influences on his behavior. Which component of the three is more salient for any given legislator would seem to depend almost as much on typical situations and circumstances (such as degree of party competition in a district or state, size and character of district population, power of pressure groups, party control of a legislative chamber or the governorship, and so on) as upon the logic of role compatibility. Yet, typical patterns, even if different from state to state, may tell us something about generic problems involved in role relations.

Party- and areal-role orientations. Of all his roles, that associated with the legislator's party membership comes closest to being ascriptive. In comparison with other clientele roles, it is also pervasive. But party roles, though ascribed and pervasive, are quite blurred and have quite different meanings in different political systems.

Both party competition and majority status, we have seen, make party-oriented roles more critical as influences on behavior. But there may be exceptions, as is the case with respect to the small Republican minority delegations in Tennessee, the morale-imbued Democratic delegations in California, and the New Jersey minority Democrats whose party controlled the governorship. All of these special circumstances should be expected to affect the relationship between party- and areal-role orientations in particular ways and obviate any general hypothesis about it.

Of all the four states, therefore, Ohio has the most "normal" conditions for party orientations to be effectively and systematically related to areal-role orientations. With Republican control of the state government firmly established and with gubernatorial initiative in legislative policy making accepted as right and proper, one should expect that as members of the majority, Ohio Republicans will be more state oriented than the minority Democrats. On the other hand, the latter may be expected to be more district oriented: to survive in the next election and possibly even be victorious may make minority legislators particularly sensitive to their district constituents.[1]

Table 16.1 presents the data by chamber. In general, the Ohio results are in line with expectations. The minority Democrats are considerably more district-oriented than the majority Republicans. Yet, large proportions of the majority members—44 per cent in the House and 36 per cent in the Senate—are district-state oriented, evidence of a healthy respect for the local constituencies, as one might well expect in a competitive party system like Ohio's. As a result, the majority members are only barely more state oriented than the minority Democrats in the House, if somewhat more so in the Senate.

One might expect similar results in competitive New Jersey, except for the fact that minority control of the governorship may somehow affect the role of the minority. Indeed, the New Jersey data differ from the Ohio results in some interesting respects. In the New Jersey Senate the Ohio pattern is unmistakable, but in the House, the minority Democrats are only barely more district oriented than the majority Republicans, and considerably less so than their Ohio fellow partisans. But New Jersey House minority members are more state-oriented than the majority Republicans, a clear break of the Ohio

[1] Strong Democratic district-orientation in Ohio is, of course, also related to the fact that more of the Democrats than of the Republicans come from metropolitan districts where party competition is keen. The limited number of cases does not allow us to control the party-areal role orientation relationship by "party competition in district." But see Table 15.1, above, p. 345.

pattern. Here the minority's obligation to support their governor would seem to direct their attention to state matters and make for the difference between the New Jersey and Ohio results (though this is not the case in the New Jersey Senate, where the small numbers involved must be reckoned with, however). Finally, like their fellow

Table 16.1: Interpenetration of party- and areal-role orientations, by chamber and state

Areal-Role Orientation	House		Senate	
	Majority	Minority	Majority	Minority
Ohio	$N = 66$	$N = 28$	$N = 11$	$N = 7$
District	33%	58%	36%	57%
District-State	44	21	36	29
State	23	21	28	14
Total	100%	100%	100%	100%
N.J.	$N = 25$	$N = 13$	$N = 10$	$N = 6$
District	32%	38%	40%	67%
District-State	52	31	30	33
State	16	31	30	0
Total	100%	100%	100%	100%
Calif.	$N = 28$	$N = 22$	$N = 14*$	$N = 14†$
District	45%	72%	50%	36%
District-State	14	19	21	36
State	41	9	29	28
Total	100%	100%	100%	100%
Tenn.	$N = 31$	$N = 7$	$N = 6$	$N = 2$
District	52%	58%	67%	50%
District-State	29	14	0	0
State	19	28	33	50
Total	100%	100%	100%	100%

* Democrats.
† Republicans.

partisans in Ohio, New Jersey House Republicans include a sizable proportion of district-state-oriented legislators, again suggesting that a majority party cannot easily ignore its local ties.

In California, traditionally more non-partisan and with the majority-minority roles poorly defined, yet undergoing change towards a more characteristic party pattern, the nature of the relationship between

388   The legislative system

party- and areal-role orientations should be confused. Yet, California follows the Ohio pattern to a surprising extent, especially in the House. In the Senate, where an additional complication is due to the fact that the two parties were evenly split (though the Democrats had organized the chamber with some Republican support, making them formally the controlling party), there is almost no difference between party members in state orientation, but the Democrats (the "majority") are more district oriented than the Republicans (the "minority"). It may be that the Democrats in spite of their formal status perceived themselves as minority members, since their House colleagues were in the minority, the governorship was in Republican hands, and they were long used to minority status. This observation is, of course, purely speculative.

How the relationship between party-status and areal-role orientations may be conditioned by a non-competitive political structure is suggested by the data from Tennessee. As too few Senators could be classified on the areal dimension, only House results will be examined here.[2] It appears that more than half of both majority and minority members are district oriented, and the latter only slightly more so than the former. But the minority members are also somewhat more state oriented. They may see in activity on the state level a more fertile field of operation than do the factionalized

[2] The proportion of respondents who could be used in the different analyses of this chapter fluctuates a good deal from analysis to analysis within a chamber and between chambers as well as between states, as the following table shows. The data for New Jersey and Ohio are proportionately very similar and more complete than the California and Tennessee data:

Size of Samples Used in Analyses of Chapter 16, by Chamber and State

Table Numbers	Houses				Senates			
	Calif.	N.J.	Ohio	Tenn.	Calif.	N.J.	Ohio	Tenn.
16.1	62%	66%	68%	38%	70%	76%	53%	24%
16.2	85	98	90	88	72	100	94	88
16.4	41	67	68	62	30	71	59	52
16.5	29	45	54	31	30	62	38	15
16.6	40	67	66	60	30	71	59	52
16.7	97	100	93	90	88	100	94	94
16.8	61	64	68	37	70	76	50	24
16.9	85	98	90	88	73	100	94	88
16.10	59	95	86	67	43	100	71	55
Total Members:	80	58	139	99	40	21	34	33

members of the majority party in a one-party system. As we noted in Chapter 15, Tennessee Republicans are quite sensitive to their occasional balancing function between warring Democratic factions. Their greater state orientation seems to be congruent with this function.

Party- and areal-role orientations seem to be related to each other in different patterns, depending on the structure of the party system and other special circumstances in a particular system. In general, in a competitive system, minority members seem more likely to adopt a district orientation than majority members. It seems that the responsibility for running the state government which goes with majority control makes for state orientation. However, in a competitive political system majority-party members cannot ignore their districts altogether. They tend to respond to their cross-pressured circumstances by adopting the blurred district-state role. It seems to be a highly functional solution: district-state oriented legislators, we noted in Chapter 13, are more similar in attitudes to district oriented than to state oriented.

Party- and pressure-group-role orientations. Legislators' orientations towards pressure groups are less specific and more diffuse than their areal orientations. They are highly generalized orientations, not directed to special clienteles. Though more diffuse than party and areal orientations, pressure-group roles are probably quite stable. They are geared to long-range developments rather than to immediate contingencies.

The relationship between party and pressure-group roles is likely to vary a good deal from state to state with the relative significance of pressure politics in a state. In a competitive two-party system, therefore, where pressure politics is particularly relevant to the majority's ability in carrying through a successful and acceptable legislative program, it is likely that majority members will be more inclined to facilitate the play of pressure politics, while minority members are more likely to resist the demands of pressure groups.

Table 16.2 presents the cross-tabulations of party- and pressure-group-role orientations in the four states. In both the Ohio House and Senate, the majority Republicans include larger proportions of facilitators and neutrals than the minority Democrats who are more likely to be resisters. The New Jersey data are partly similar to and partly different from the Ohio results. The majority members in both chambers include more facilitators, but the House majority also includes somewhat more resisters than the minority. House minority Democrats include more neutrals, and only in the Senate are minority members more likely to be resisters. Apparently, New Jersey's minority Democrats feel somewhat more restrained in opposition to pressure groups, possibly due to their control of the governorship which may serve as a countervailing influence on the minority's

Table 16.2: Interpenetration of party- and pressure-group-role orientations, by chamber and state

Pressure-Group-Role Orientation	House		Senate	
	Majority	Minority	Majority	Minority
Ohio	N = 87	N = 38	N = 20	N = 12
Facilitator	46%	39%	45%	33%
Neutral	39	24	40	34
Resister	15	37	15	33
Total	100%	100%	100%	100%
N.J.	N = 37	N = 20	N = 14	N = 7
Facilitator	43%	30%	43%	28%
Neutral	30	50	29	29
Resister	27	20	28	43
Total	100%	100%	100%	100%
Calif.	N = 36	N = 32	N = 14*	N = 15†
Facilitator	33%	34%	43%	53%
Neutral	50	38	36	40
Resister	17	28	21	7
Total	100%	100%	100%	100%
Tenn.	N = 69	N = 18	N = 24	N = 5
Facilitator	25%	17%	25%	20%
Neutral	36	55	29	20
Resister	39	28	46	60
Total	100%	100%	100%	100%

* Democrats.
† Republicans.

tendency to include more resisters and fewer facilitators and neutrals in a competitive party system.

Majority and minority party status should be of less relevance in the pressure-group-role orientations of California legislators, and there in no reason to assume that the general pattern observed in Ohio and New Jersey should appear here. Indeed, in the California House, almost equal proportions of majority and minority are facilitators, but more of the minority Democrats are resisters. In the Senate the pattern seems reversed, but it should be recalled that the Democrats here can only very tentatively be considered the "majority." As in the case of areal-role orientations, the Republicans indicate the orientations characteristic of a majority party, and the Democrats of a minority party.

Finally, we find the majority-facilitator relationship present even in one-party Tennessee, though it is very slight. But otherwise Tennessee deviates from the Ohio pattern. Large proportions of the majority Democrats in both chambers are resisters (the minority data, particularly in the Senate, are quite unreliable because of the small numbers involved—a shift of a single case would change the picture). The results for the majority are not surprising: though in the "majority," the Democrats are factionalized, and Tennessee legislators, we noted in Chapter 14, are generally least hospitable to pressure politics. Given the numerical superiority of the Democrats in Tennessee, this can only mean that, though in the majority, they are resistant to pressure groups at least as much or even more so than the minority Republicans.

Though the state-by-state results do not represent a single pattern, the deviations seem to confirm a systematic relationship between party- and pressure-group-role orientations. In competitive systems, majority partisans are more likely to be facilitators and minority partisans to be resisters. Unfortunately, since all of the majority delegations are also Republican, the suspicion remains that, perhaps, facilitation of pressure-group operations is not so much a characteristic of majority status as an attitudinal attribute of Republicans. Only comparative analysis of other states can clarify the problem involved.

Areal- and pressure-group-role orientations. There are at least two ways in which legislators' areal- and pressure-group-role orientations might be systematically related. District-oriented legislators, sensitive to their constituency as the source of power, would want to facilitate the adjustment of pressures that impinge on them from local groups. But state-oriented legislators would also be inclined to be facilitators because the adjustment of conflicting pressures on the state level is predicated on group access to those whose legislative focus is the state. However, analysis along these lines is impossible because our pressure-group-role types were not constructed for the purpose of discriminating between those who see pressure politics as a primarily local matter and those who see it as a primarily state matter. There is no reason to assume, therefore, that our data would reveal any consistent relationship between the legislator's areal- and pressure-group-role orientations. It is more reasonable to assume that these orientations are randomly related from chamber to chamber and state to state (though some combinations may be more typical of a given house or state than another, telling us something about a chamber's or state's "political role structure"—a concern to which we shall turn in the next chapter).

The results of arraying interpenetrations of areal- and pressure-group-role orientations in each of the eight chambers are inconclusive (data not shown). No pattern is evident, either within a state or between the states. Although aggregation of such heterogeneous data cannot be accepted as being indicative of any true correspondence with the universes from which they come, it may be suggestive. Table 16.3 presents, therefore, the aggregated data for the four state

Table 16.3: Aggregate relationships between areal- and pressure-group-role orientations in four states

	Orientation towards		
Pressure-Group-Role Orientation	District $N = 125$	District-State $N = 84$	State $N = 66$
Facilitator	38%	38%	44%
Neutral	34	41	35
Resister	26	21	21
Total	100%	100%	100%

legislatures. The table suggests a tenuous relationship between areal- and pressure-group-role orientations. Although the differences are extremely small, somewhat more of the state oriented than of the other two groups are facilitators (44 per cent); somewhat more of the district oriented than of the other areal types are resisters (26 per cent); and more of the district-state-oriented legislators are neutrals (41 per cent). In some respects, the pattern evident here (rather than the distributions) may be considered theoretically plausible— if one assumes that pressure politics is primarily perceived by legislators as taking place on the state level. But the aggregated data cannot be thought of as more than suggestive, for they disguise a great deal of the actual variations among the eight chambers. The plausibility of the hypothesized relationship between areal- and pressure-group-role orientations may be supported, however, by the whole network of all role orientations. (To this we shall return in the concluding chapter.)

CLIENTELE ORIENTATIONS
AND REPRESENTATIONAL STYLES

Although analytically the foci and the style of the representative's role are distinct,[3] they can be expected to be related empirically in a system of mutually interpenetrating orientations. Just as we need not assume that an orientation toward a given clientele (say his district) invariably involves the representative's following instructions from this clientele (the role orientation of delegate), or that a representative not so oriented is invariably a free agent (the role orientation of trustee), so also we need not assume that the foci of a representative's role are invariably unrelated to his representational style.

Party- and representational-role orientations. In a political system where party discipline is very strict, as in the British House of Commons, the legislator's party orientation is so intense that he is unlikely to have much leeway in assuming a representational role other than that of delegate. The voting instructions received from party leaders and whips are so binding that his own conscience or judgment, even if different from the party's mandate, must be subordinated to his party obligations.[4] Moreover, the party's hold over the legislator is equally strong regardless of whether he belongs to the majority or minority.

In American state legislatures, by way of contrast, party discipline is weak, even in the more competitive systems, like New Jersey's or Ohio's. As we noted in Chapter 15, in spite of the pervasiveness of partisan roles, partisanship as such is not a critical orientation in the role perspectives of state legislators. Under these conditions, party membership as such should not be expected to make for one rather than another representational style. Representational-role orientations should not differentiate between Republicans and Democrats as such.

However, some differences might occur by virtue of the legislator's belonging to the legislative majority or minority. Of the many functions which the party performs in the political system, that of coordinating and integrating the multiplicity of divergent demands made on government by individuals and groups is central. This is more likely to be a function of the majority than of the minority party, particularly if the majority party also controls the executive establishment. We might expect, therefore, that the majority party will include a greater

---

[3] See above, Chapter 12, p. 269.

[4] See Leon D. Epstein, "Cohesion of British Parliamentary Parties," *American Political Science Review* 50:360–377 (1956).

proportion of politicos than the minority.   As a politico the legislator is particularly aware of the fact that he must reconcile instructions he may receive from different clienteles, including his party, with his own conscience or judgment, if he is to carry out successfully the coordinating-integrating function expected of him as a party politician. On the other hand, we have no reason to assume that majority and minority members will differ in their taking the roles of either trustee or delegate.

Table 16.4: Interpenetration of party- and representational-role orientations, by chamber and party

Representational-Role Orientation	House		Senate	
	Majority	Minority	Majority	Minority
Ohio	$N = 66$	$N = 28$	$N = 14$	$N = 6$
Trustee	50%	61%	71%	67%
Politico	33	25	29	0
Delegate	17	14	0	33
Total	100%	100%	100%	100%
N.J.	$N = 26$	$N = 13$	$N = 10$	$N = 5$
Trustee	62%	76%	50%	20%
Politico	23	16	30	20
Delegate	15	8	20	60
Total	100%	100%	100%	100%
Calif.	$N = 20$	$N = 17$	$N = 6*$	$N = 6†$
Trustee	55%	54%	66%	50%
Politico	20	23	17	50
Delegate	25	23	17	0
Total	100%	100%	100%	100%
Tenn.	$N = 48$	$N = 13$	$N = 14$	$N = 3$
Trustee	75%	85%	92%	100%
Politico	17	7	8	0
Delegate	8	8	0	0
Total	100%	100%	100%	100%

* Democrats.
† Republicans.

Table 16.4 shows that, indeed, Ohio's majority Republicans in both houses include larger proportions of politicos than do the minority Democrats.   But no consistent differences exist between the parties in respect to the other representational-role orientations.   The same is true in New Jersey and Tennessee, but the pattern is reversed in California. In some senate parties the number of legislators is very small and the data are not very satisfactory. Yet, in all states other than California the same direction in the distributions of politicos is maintained. Apparently, where party patterns of either the competitive or noncompetitive type are firmly established, an orientation derived from the party's status seems to be related to the politico orientation. In non-partisan California, majority and minority status have less meaning, and we miss the relationship between majority-minority status and the politico role noted elsewhere. But it must again be pointed out that the observed differences are small, and that the number of cases on which proportions are based is in some instances very small indeed.

Areal- and representational-role orientations. Analytically, stylistic role orientations are quite separate from areal-role orientations. But they may well be correlated empirically. With respect to areal clienteles, district-oriented representatives by definition feel ultimately responsible to their constituents, while state-oriented representatives cannot feel similarly—for they cannot point to a state-wide areal clientele from which they could possibly receive a mandate.[5] We should expect, therefore, that state-oriented legislators are more likely to be trustees than district-oriented legislators, whereas the latter are more likely to be delegates than the former.

Table 16.5 presents the interpenetration of areal- and representational-role orientations in the eight chambers. Because of the small numbers involved, the Senate data are less satisfactory than the House data. In all four houses and in the Ohio and New Jersey Senates, greater proportions of the state oriented than of the two other areal types are trustees. Moreover, the proportions of trustees among the areal-role types declines progressively through district-state and district-oriented legislators in the four houses and in the New Jersey Senate. On the other hand, in the four houses and in the New Jersey and California Senates, the district-oriented groups include larger proportions of delegates, and no delegate appears among any of the state-oriented legislators in any one of the eight chambers. The fact that district-oriented legislators at the opposite pole may be trustees means that though they may clearly have their attention focussed on their districts, these legislators see themselves acting on behalf of their districts as free agents. These district-oriented trustees will say, it

[5] They might, of course, receive instructions from a state-wide clientele such as a state-wide pressure group or political party, but these constitute non-areal foci of attention.

will be recalled from Chapter 13, that they know and understand what their districts need and want, and they reject the notion that anybody in their districts can tell them what to do. On the other hand, that state-oriented legislators fail to be delegates probably stems from their inability to recognize an appropriate state-wide clientele from which they could receive instructions.

Table 16.5: Interpenetration of areal- and representational-role orientations, by chamber and state

Representational-Role Orientation	House			Senate		
	District	District-State	State	District	District-State	State
Ohio	$N = 28$	$N = 29$	$N = 18$	$N = 6$	$N = 3$	$N = 4$
Trustee	29%	48%	84%	50%	33%	75%
Politico	32	41	16	33	33	25
Delegate	39	11	0	17	33	0
Total	100%	100%	100%	100%	100%	100%
N.J.	$N = 11$	$N = 8$	$N = 7$	$N = 6$	$N = 4$	$N = 3$
Trustee	36%	75%	86%	17%	50%	100%
Politico	18	25	14	17	50	0
Delegate	46	0	0	66	0	0
Total	100%	100%	100%	100%	100%	100%
Calif.	$N = 14$	$N = 5$	$N = 4$	$N = 4$	$N = 6$	$N = 2$
Trustee	21%	20%	100%	50%	67%	50%
Politico	29	60	0	25	33	50
Delegate	50	20	0	25	0	0
Total	100%	100%	100%	100%	100%	100%
Tenn.	$N = 17$	$N = 9$	$N = 5$	$N = 4$	$N = 0$	$N = 1$
Trustee	53%	78%	80%	100%	0%	100%
Politico	29	22	20	0	0	0
Delegate	18	0	0	0	0	0
Total	100%	100%	100%	100%	100%	100%

Finally, if the legislator's areal focus embraces both his district and the state, one might expect that he will hold the role orientation of politico more frequently than either of the other two "pure" areal types. For, because he stresses both foci, he is likely to feel cross-pressured: as a district-oriented representative he will tend to hold the delegate orientation; as a state-oriented legislator he will subscribe to the trustee orientation. We should expect, therefore, that this hyphenated type will not only hold the politico orientation in greater proportion than do the other two areal orientational groups, but that he will also be a trustee more often than a delegate. Both expectations are at least partially met in Table 16.5. In three of the houses (Ohio, New Jersey, and California), the district-state-oriented legislators include greater proportions of politicos than do either of the other two areal role types. And in the Ohio, New Jersey, and Tennessee Houses they include more trustees than delegates.

The data presented in this section suffer a great deal from their numerical limitations. Moreover, the differences observed between the areal-role types are often small. Nevertheless, the over-all pattern, especially in the Houses where the numbers are more adequate, is surprisingly similar from one state to the other, and it supports the notion that the areal and representational components of the legislator's total role, though analytically distinct, constitute an order, and that this order gives the process of representation both its structure and its function.

Pressure-group- and representational-role orientations. It is important to keep in mind the generalized quality of pressure-group orientations in appraising their interpenetration with the representational-role orientations. For concealed in these relationships are quite probably those particular connections between a legislator and a particular group which the generalized group orientations possibly embrace, but which they are not designed to articulate. For instance, delegates may have a propensity to be at the disposal of a particular pressure group, but delegates who are facilitators are generally favorable to group operations, as neutrals they are more likely to be unconcerned, and as resisters they are generally opposed. It is, therefore, difficult to anticipate just how pressure-group-role orientations, as defined and constructed in this study, are related to the representational-role orientations. But the findings may be suggestive for theoretical development.

Table 16.6 presents the cross-tabulation of the two sets of role orientations for the eight chambers. A first glance at the table suggests that California and Tennessee may have to be treated separately from each other and from Ohio and New Jersey. In Tennessee, the pervasiveness of the trustee orientation (81 per cent are trustees) evidently leaves little room for differentiation between the pressure-group-role types. But the distributions in Ohio and New Jersey indicate some recurring patterns.

In the first place, facilitators in Ohio and New Jersey, but also in the California House, tend to include greater proportions of politicos than do either the neutrals or resisters. This is as one might have expected: recognizing the numerous and divergent, if not conflicting, demands of pressure groups, facilitators are apparently more prepared to weigh instructions from these groups against their own principles

Table 16.6: Interpenetration of pressure-group- and representational-role orientations, by chamber and state

Representa- tional-Role Orientation	House			Senate		
	Facilitator	Neutral	Resister	Facilitator	Neutral	Resister
Ohio	$N = 39$	$N = 33$	$N = 20$	$N = 9$	$N = 7$	$N = 4$
Trustee	56%	55%	50%	56%	86%	75%
Politico	31	30	30	33	14	0
Delegate	13	15	20	11	0	25
Total	100%	100%	100%	100%	100%	100%
N.J.	$N = 17$	$N = 12$	$N = 10$	$N = 8$	$N = 3$	$N = 4$
Trustee	59%	75%	70%	38%	67%	25%
Politico	29	8	20	50	0	0
Delegate	12	17	10	12	33	75
Total	100%	100%	100%	100%	100%	100%
Calif.	$N = 10$	$N = 14$	$N = 8$	$N = 7$	$N = 4$	$N = 1$
Trustee	40%	71%	50%	86%	0%	100%
Politico	30	8	25	14	75	0
Delegate	30	21	25	0	25	0
Total	100%	100%	100%	100%	100%	100%
Tenn.	$N = 10$	$N = 25$	$N = 24$	$N = 4$	$N = 5$	$N = 8$
Trustee	90%	84%	67%	100%	100%	88%
Politico	10	4	25	0	0	12
Delegate	0	12	8	0	0	0
Total	100%	100%	100%	100%	100%	100%

or judgment. And for just this reason few of them take the role of delegate. Some, of course do. In all probability, they are bound to a particular group, yet as facilitators they recognize the activities of other groups as legitimate operations.

Secondly, in spite of its apparently being a theoretical anomaly, resisters in Ohio and the New Jersey Senate include more delegates than do facilitators and neutrals. Speculating on this fact, we might consider the hypothetical case of a legislator who is very close to a labor union and who "represents" (as a delegate) the union in the legislative arena. Yet, he may be opposed to the operations of pressure groups in general, particularly if he feels surrounded and hemmed in by the great variety of business lobbies opposed to his own objectives.

Thirdly, in all chambers (except the New Jersey Senate) the trustee orientation predominates among the three pressure-group-role types, but somewhat more so among the neutrals. Neutrals, being less involved in the politics of interest groups, are apparently more likely to fall back on their own convictions or judgment in groping their way among divergent and conflicting groups.

Although the Ohio and New Jersey patterns are similar, they are erratic enough to suggest that the different emphases placed on pressure politics in different states may mobilize different representational-role emphases as well. The pervasiveness of pressure-group politics in California, for instance, may be reflected in the fact that a greater proportion of California facilitators are also delegates. In Tennessee, where pressure-group politics is less pervasive but more emotionally intense, the relatively large groups of resisters take the politico role more than do facilitators or neutrals. Apparently, while the over-all Tennessee political culture is hostile to pressure-group politics, the inevitability of pressure-group activity and the need to take the groups into account force some of the resisters to adopt the flexible politico representational style (in contrast to the resister-trustees who may be considered anti-group intransigents).

These interpretations may seem to get more theoretical mileage out of numerically limited and distributionally erratic data than might be justified. No claim can be made that the results are in any way "true" beyond the data on which they are based. But they do seem plausible in the light of theoretical assumptions made about both pressure-group- and representational-role orientations as well as in terms of what we know about the nature of pressure politics in the four states.

CLIENTELE ORIENTATIONS AND PURPOSIVE ROLES

Purposive roles, we noted in Chapter 11, are focussed on three major types of legislative substance: first, the creation of public policies necessary to adjust the political system as a whole to the ever-changing needs of the larger social system; second, the coordination and integration of conflicting interests and demands in terms of a minimum conception of the public interest; and, third, the articulation and achievement of popular needs, wants, or preferences.[6] If one were to organize the content of most legislative activity, it could probably be located in one of these categories. Theoretically, as we suggested in Chapter 11, each legislator can take more than one role geared to legislative output. In practice there is a division of labor, with some legislators taking only one role and others taking more than one. But the choice of roles that will be taken depends on the legislator's clientele orientations. We shall be concerned, therefore, with the problem of who, among particular clientele-role types, takes what purposive roles geared to the content and output of legislative action.

Party- and purposive-role orientations. In some respects, parties and legislatures perform very much the same functions for the maintenance of the political system, even though they are legally different structures. Among their shared functions three stand out: first, sensitizing the political system to the needs and requirements for decisions and services; second, adjusting, coordinating, and integrating a multiplicity of divergent demands; third, articulating and projecting issues into the political system, defining the boundaries of political conflict, and seeking to translate issue positions into governmental policies.[7] The purposive-role orientations relevant to these functions are readily apparent: the tribune is particularly sensitive to the demands reaching the legislature from outside. The broker coordinates and integrates these demands in the legislative arena. And the inventor translates demands into public policies from a broader point of view. As each of these roles involves behavior which is directly related to action in the performance of party functions, we should expect that purposive-role orientations and party-role orientations are likely to interpenetrate in characteristic ways.

As simultaneous role takers in the party and legislative systems, majority and minority partisans should be expected to take purposive roles geared not only to the functioning of the legislature in general, but also of their party in particular, depending on whether it is in the majority or in the minority. What particular purposive-role orientation will be held by virtue of his party's majority or minority status is likely to depend on the nature of the party system and those special conditions in a given state party noted in Chapter 15. In general, Ohio and New Jersey might be expected to resemble

---

[6] A fourth category—the ritualistic acceptance and processing of whatever reaches the legislative mill and which produces the widely held role orientation of ritualist—will be omitted from the analysis because it does not yield meaningful differences vis-à-vis the other categories.

[7] See Robert M. MacIver, *The Web of Government, op. cit.*, p. 213.

each other more than either will resemble California or Tennessee. But even an Ohio-New Jersey comparison must keep in mind that New Jersey's minority party controlled the governorship, a factor which may affect the behavior of New Jersey's minority.

Table 16.7 presents the data for the eight chambers in the four states. The table immediately reveals dissimilar patterns from one state to the next. In Ohio, perhaps the outstanding feature is the

Table 16.7: Interpenetration of party- and purposive-role orientations, by chamber and state*

Purposive-Role Orientation	House		Senate	
	Majority	Minority	Majority	Minority
Ohio	$N = 91$	$N = 39$	$N = 20$	$N = 12$
Inventor	29%	33%	35%	58%
Tribune	39	44	30	50
Broker	52	39	45	50
N.J.	$N = 38$	$N = 20$	$N = 14$	$N = 7$
Inventor	47%	50%	57%	43%
Tribune	71	50	50	86
Broker	34	35	36	14
Calif.	$N = 42$	$N = 36$	$N = 18†$	$N = 17‡$
Inventor	45%	31%	44%	18%
Tribune	45	62	67	53
Broker	19	22	33	47
Tenn.	$N = 71$	$N = 18$	$N = 26$	$N = 5$
Inventor	28%	22%	42%	20%
Tribune	61	17	50	40
Broker	14	61	12	40

* Percentages total more than 100 since more than one purposive role orientation could be held.

† Democrats.

‡ Republicans.

relatively great proportion of brokers among the House majority Republicans in contrast to the minority Democrats. In the Senate, the direction is reversed but the difference is small, and proportionately almost as many majority as minority members are brokers. In New Jersey, it is the Senate Republican majority partisans who tend to be brokers more than the minority members, while in the House almost equal proportions of both parties are brokers. The data are inconclusive, therefore, but it is plausible to assume that the broker role in competitive systems is more likely to be taken by the majority members. The legislature's success in bringing about political integration by satisfying diverse interests is more crucial to the majority than to the minority's party record. But, as consideration of the New Jersey House minority suggests, control of the governorship might make coordination and integration also critical in the minority's appraisal of the legislative situation.

This pattern is clearly reversed in California and Tennessee, although just why this should be so in California is difficult to tell. In the California House the difference is very small; in the Senate, the Republicans, by taking the broker role in greater proportion than the Democrats, may yet think of themselves as being in the majority (given the fact that their party was in the majority in the House and controlled the governorship). In Tennessee, on the other hand, the minority Republicans' preference for the broker orientation is in line with what we already know about the minority's role in that state. The Republican minority derived strength from its being a balancing power in the midst of struggling Democratic factions.

The other two purposive-role orientations are even more difficult to interpret in majority-minority terms. In Ohio, minority members tend to be inventors or tribunes in greater proportions than the majority Republicans. That these roles should be taken by minority members in a competitive system is plausible. As inventors, the minority members are more apt to pump fresh ideas about desirable policies into the legislative system. As tribunes, they are inclined to sponsor popular demands or defend what they think are popular causes. Both orientations are particularly conducive to the minority's success at the polls. Just as the majority's record may be judged in terms of success in translating diverse and conflicting interests into public policy, so the minority's record may be judged in terms of its sensitivity to new ideas and popular causes.

But in New Jersey this plausible interpretation does not hold. In the House, almost equal proportions of majority and minority partisans are inventors, and a greater proportion of the majority than of the minority are tribunes. In the Senate, majority Republicans are inventors and minority Democrats are tribunes in greater proportions than their opposites. Whether the confusion of roles is a function of the confusion brought into the legislative system by the divided control of the executive and legislative branches we cannot say. But it may have something to do with it.

The California results are equally puzzling in this respect. In the House, the minority Democrats are more likely to be tribunes, but the Majority Republicans are more likely to be inventors. In the Senate, where the parties were evenly split, the Democrats are both inventors and tribunes in greater proportions than the Republicans. Evidently, their organizational control of the Senate seems to have little effect on their purposive orientations, and they hold orientations more characteristic of a minority as in Ohio. It may be that the introduction of new ideas and the propagation of popular causes in any state by the Democrats is due to their party's generally more liberal point of view, but this interpretation is difficult to maintain in the analytical context we have provided.

The Tennessee data clearly reverse the Ohio pattern. In both chambers, the majority party includes greater proportions of inventors and tribunes than does the Republican minority. Evidently, in a one-party state the minority feels helpless in either promoting policy legislation or in claiming a popular mandate. Its function is predominantly one of brokerage, and the data seem to reflect this situation.

In some respects, the findings about the interpenetration of party- and purposive-role orientations are quite satisfactory, in other respects they are not. Clearly, conditions in the party systems of the four states are so diverse as to obviate the possibility of generalizing about all of them. On the other hand, the clean reversal in patterns between competitive, two-party Ohio and non-competitive, one-party Tennessee is suggestive of just how different conditions may affect the relationship between party and purposive roles. That the California results are not equally plausible may be due to the transitional nature of the state's party system at the time.

Areal- and purposive-role orientations. Insofar as the tribune orientation remains viable under modern conditions, we should expect that district-oriented legislators will hold the tribune orientation in greater proportions than any other, and that they will differ in this respect from the other areal-role types. As Table 16.8 shows, this is indeed the case in all but two of the eight chambers—the exceptions being the New Jersey and California Senates (but the numbers involved are so small as to make the results quite arbitrary in these two cases). Moreover, if we compare the proportions of district-oriented tribunes with the total percentage of tribunes in each of the four states (Table 11.1), it appears that they are generally greater than the proportion of tribunes at large. The results seem to support the theoretical conception of the tribune as a man who looks on the content of the legislative business and output in terms of his preoccupation with his geographical constituency.

Not surprisingly, we find a reversal of the pattern in connection with the role orientation of inventor. As Table 16.8 indicates, the connection between a state-oriented perspective and the inventor orientation is maintained in four of the eight chambers. In three lower Houses and one Senate, greater or at least equal proportions of state-oriented legislators are inventors. And just as the tribunes are distributed among the areal-role types in descending order from

Table 16.8: Interpenetration of areal- and purposive-role orientations, by chamber and state*

Purposive-Role Orientation	House			Senate		
	District	District-State	State	District	District-State	State
Ohio	$N = 38$	$N = 35$	$N = 22$	$N = 8$	$N = 6$	$N = 3$
Tribune	55%	43%	23%	88%	0%	0%
Inventor	16	20	54	50	17	0
Broker	42	74	59	25	100	100
N.J.	$N = 12$	$N = 17$	$N = 8$	$N = 8$	$N = 5$	$N = 3$
Tribune	83%	71%	50%	78%	100%	0%
Invento ·	25	41	63	38	80	67
Broker	17	65	88	0	60	67
Calif.	$N = 27$	$N = 8$	$N = 14$	$N = 12$	$N = 8$	$N = 8$
Tribune	85%	50%	14%	67%	50%	100%
Inventor	26	50	50	25	38	38
Broker	7	50	14	50	63	13
Tenn.	$N = 20$	$N = 9$	$N = 8$	$N = 5$	$N = 0$	$N = 3$
Tribune	90%	89%	88%	100%	—	100%
Inventor	5	11	0	0	—	0
Broker	10	0	0	20	—	67

* Percentages total more than 100 since more than one purposive role orientation could be held.

district- through district-state- to state-oriented groups, so the inventors distribute in the same order but in a reversed direction. The fact that four chambers fail to confirm the pattern is probably due to the small number of state-oriented legislators in these houses.

Finally, Table 16.8 suggests that district-state-oriented legislators have a preference for the broker orientation. If we omit Tennessee where tribunes dominate among areal types, the tendency for the district-state-oriented legislators to be brokers is most evident in the two Ohio houses, but it is also apparent in California. In New Jersey, the district-state oriented are more likely to be brokers than inventors in the House, but they are proportionately least frequent in the Senate. Evidently, the strong attraction of the tribune orientation in the state (New Jersey has 63 per cent tribunes as against only 40 per cent in Ohio), is also characteristic of the district-state-oriented subgroups in the two New Jersey chambers.

That district-state-oriented legislators should be brokers is quite plausible. The broker orientation allows the legislator with a dual focus to reconcile possibly conflicting demands on him from different areal clienteles in terms of legislation or services whose substance is the product of compromise and balance.

The patterns evident in Table 16.8, though not satisfactory in all cases, suggest that the legislator's areal orientation influences the way in which he approaches the content of his legislative activities. The areal- and purposive-role orientations are related because both perform a vital function in linking interests "outside" of the legislature with legislative performance.

Pressure-group- and purposive-role orientations. In terms of role taking, the legislator's connection with pressure groups is probably more tenuous than his connection with political party or geographical area. He is elected by voters in districts under an electoral system traditionally developed as a method of reflecting the political views of residents in specified areas; and he is elected in campaigns waged under party banners and labels. We should expect, therefore, that the linkage between legislators and pressure groups in general is weaker than the linkage between them and areal or party clienteles. Moreover, pressure-group-role orientations are more diffuse and blurred than either areal or party orientations. In other words, the relationships between pressure-group- and purposive-role orientations are likely to be less systematic. Finally, because of the differential significance of pressure politics in the four states, a pattern noticeable in one state need not necessarily occur in another state.

However, at least one hypothesis might be found to hold more universally: facilitators should be more likely than neutrals or resisters to be brokers in their purposive orientations. If facilitators recognize the legitimacy of pressure groups in the legislative arena and are prepared to serve as points of access for pressure groups, they are at least one long step ahead of neutrals and resisters in the effort to coordinate and integrate possibly conflicting interests and demands into substantive legislation. Moreover, if facilitators see these "external" demands as determinants of public policy, they may well find it difficult to think of the policy issues involved in as abstract or intellectual terms as would inventors. And if they perceive the multiplicity of organized groups as vehicles for the articulation of public needs in the legislative process, they are unlikely to subscribe to the tribune's undifferentiated conception of "the people" as the source of public policy.

Table 16.9 presents the data. No easily recognizable pattern similar from state to state is evident. In the two Ohio chambers facilitators

Table 16.9: Interpenetration of pressure-group- and purposive-role orientations, by chamber and state°

Purposive-Role Orientation	House			Senate		
	Facilitator	Neutral	Resister	Facilitator	Neutral	Resister
Ohio	$N = 55$	$N = 43$	$N = 27$	$N = 13$	$N = 12$	$N = 7$
Tribune	42%	47%	33%	46%	33%	29%
Inventor	31	21	41	38	50	43
Broker	55	44	55	54	42	43
N.J.	$N = 23$	$N = 20$	$N = 14$	$N = 9$	$N = 5$	$N = 7$
Tribune	56%	60%	78%	89%	40%	43%
Inventor	48	50	50	67	60	29
Broker	30	25	50	45	20	14
Calif.	$N = 23$	$N = 30$	$N = 15$	$N = 14$	$N = 11$	$N = 4$
Tribune	52%	50%	53%	43%	73%	75%
Inventor	26	40	53	36	27	50
Broker	17	23	20	43	36	50
Tenn.	$N = 20$	$N = 35$	$N = 32$	$N = 7$	$N = 8$	$N = 14$
Tribune	45%	69%	63%	43%	50%	57%
Inventor	30	20	31	29	63	36
Broker	20	11	16	0	25	21

* Percentages total more than 100 since more than one purposive role orientation could be held.

hold the broker orientation in greater proportions than do neutrals and resisters, as is also the case in the New Jersey Senate and the Tennessee House. But the numbers involved and the differences are small. Comparative inspection does not give much ground for support of the hypothesis that facilitators are especially prone to serve as brokers. But this judgment may reflect more on the quality of the data than the validity of the hypothesis.

But Table 16.9 shows some other interesting results. It appears that in five of the chambers resisters tend to be brokers in greater proportions than do neutrals. Indeed, in the Ohio House brokers appear in the same proportion among resisters as among facilitators, and in some other chambers their percentage is surprisingly high. How can this be interpreted? It will be recalled that resisters, though unfavorable to the politics of pressure groups, are highly aware of their activities. It is as if the resisters, when confronting pressure groups, accept the inevitable: precisely because they are hostile to pressure groups in general, they seem to find in the broker orientation a way to make their hostility felt. The broker orientation serves as a means of resistance because it allows legislators to face the situation head on rather than with head in the ground.

It appears that the coupling of pressure groups and legislature in terms of a systematic relationship between the generalized pressure-group- and the purposive-role orientations is rather incomplete. It would seem that insofar as such coupling must take place, it may well occur in terms of concrete contacts between a particular legislator and a particular group rather than in terms of the very general pressure-group-role orientations developed in this study. This does not mean that these orientations are ineffective: they represent generally pre-dispositional rather than immediately behavioral components of the legislator's total role.

INTERPENETRATION OF PURPOSIVE AND REPRESENTATIONAL ROLES

As clientele roles are more or less systematically related to both representational and purposive roles, one should expect that the latter, also are systematically connected. The classification of representatives as trustees, politicos, and delegates—their orientations to the "how" of the legislative process—would make little sense if these representational roles were not meaningfully related to roles relevant to the "what for" of the legislative process. It is only as the tribune, inventor, or broker roles interpenetrate with the trustee, delegate, and politico roles that the concept "legislator" is given its full empirical content.

This does not mean, of course, that any one purposive role cannot effectively influence behavior unless one single appropriate representational style is related to it. It only means that the legislator whose purposive and representational roles "fit" is more likely to be consistent in his legislative behavior and less exposed to role conflict than the legislator whose roles do not "fit." Just what degree of "fit" or lack of it among purposive and representational roles is desirable or tolerable from the point of view of a system's integration and maintenance is, of course, a normative problem difficult to specify. It is probable that the limits are rather flexible and variable from one system to the next. But it is, nevertheless, the "fit" in the relationship between purposive and representational roles which gives the legislature as an institution its characteristic quality.

Inventors, unlike brokers or tribunes, perceive themselves as "movers and shakers," ahead of the multitude and immune to special pressures. It is reasonable to assume, therefore, that, if at all possible, they will eschew instructions from whatever source, and that they will refuse to make easy compromises. They are more likely than either tribunes or brokers to be guided in their legislative behavior by their own convictions or judgment of what public policies and innovations ought to be. They should, therefore, include more trustees and differ in this respect from tribunes and brokers.

The tribune's goals are less high-flown and more limited. He seeks to satisfy immediate popular needs and wishes, either by promoting limited objectives or by opposition to programs he considers detrimental to the people's interests. He is, therefore, more prone than the inventor or broker to look for instructions from his preferred clienteles. We should expect that tribunes are more likely to be delegates than will be the case with inventors or brokers. But he may also feel that he need not explicitly seek instructions and that he can rely on his own convictions or judgment in sensing the popular cause he has built into his role. There is no reason to suppose that he cannot be a trustee, yet he is less likely to be one than the inventor or even the broker. In other words, the tribune has at his disposal more than one major representational style, and the "fit" is likely to be more flexible than in the cases of inventor or broker.

The broker's role is to weigh, balance, and reconcile conflicting interests. In performing this role, the legislator must necessarily pay attention to instructions that may reach him, and he may even allow these instructions to guide his conduct. But precisely because these instructions are probably conflicting, the broker cannot often be a delegate. Rather, he must act as a trustee and use his own judgment in discovering widely acceptable solutions. We should expect, therefore, that brokers will include more politicos proportionately than will either tribunes or inventors. But we should also expect that many brokers will see in the role of trustee an appropriate representational style.

Table 16.10 presents the cross-tabulation of purposive- and representational-role orientations. The results are not equally satisfactory in the houses and the senates. But in all lower chambers and two of the senates the inventors invariably include greater proportions of trustees than do brokers and tribunes. Only in the New Jersey Senate do brokers include proportionately more trustees than the inventors, while in the Tennessee Senate, trustee orientations are distributed in the same proportions among the three purposive-role types. But the number of cases in the four senates is so small that the results

Table 16.10: Interpenetration of purposive- and representational-role orientations, by chamber and state

Representational-Role Orientation	House			Senate		
	Inventor	Broker	Tribune	Inventor	Broker	Tribune
Ohio	$N = 25$	$N = 54$	$N = 41$	$N = 8$	$N = 10$	$N = 6$
Trustee	60%	52%	39%	75%	60%	50%
Politico	32	43	34	0	30	33
Delegate	8	6	27	25	10	17
Total	100%	100%	100%	100%	100%	100%
N.J.	$N = 21$	$N = 12$	$N = 22$	$N = 7$	$N = 5$	$N = 9$
Trustee	81%	67%	59%	43%	60%	22%
Politico	19	25	18	57	40	33
Delegate	0	8	23	0	0	45
Total	100%	100%	100%	100%	100%	100%
Calif.	$N = 14$	$N = 12$	$N = 21$	$N = 3$	$N = 7$	$N = 7$
Trustee	65%	50%	33%	100%	57%	28%
Politico	14	33	29	0	29	57
Delegate	21	17	38	0	14	15
Total	100%	100%	100%	100%	100%	100%
Tenn.	$N = 16$	$N = 11$	$N = 39$	$N = 6$	$N = 3$	$N = 9$
Trustee	94%	90%	69%	100%	100%	100%
Politico	0	10	18	0	0	0
Delegate	6	0	13	0	0	0
Total	100%	100%	100%	100%	100%	100%

there, whether in support or opposition to our expectations, must be treated with much caution.

Secondly, in three of the houses—Ohio, New Jersey, and California —the brokers include proportionately more politicos than do the inventors and tribunes. The differences are small, but the data clearly follow the expected pattern. In the Tennessee House, the tribunes include somewhat more politicos than do the brokers, and in all four senates the results are quite arbitrary, probably due to the small number of cases involved. But we also find that, as expected, in all eight chambers the brokers include proportionately more trustees than the tribunes, and they also include proportionately fewer delegates.

Thirdly, tribunes, as suspected, are more likely to be delegates than the inventors or brokers. This is the case in all four houses and the New Jersey and California Senates. But we also find that tribunes evidently find the trustee orientation congenial in fashioning their representational style. Overall, the tribunes show a more balanced distribution of representational-role orientations than do the inventors and brokers, suggesting that almost any representational style is considered "fit" for performing the role of tribune.

These generally very satisfactory results support the assumption that the legislature as an institutionalized system of behavior gains coherence not only through formal, legal processes, but also through legislators' tendency for consistency in the taking of those roles most immediately relevant to legislative performance—what we have called the purposive and representational roles. It is the tendency for consistency which finds expression in a network of interpenetrating purposive and representational roles. By taking these roles in systematic fashion, legislators come to act in a reasonably predictable manner.

If this is so, legislators cannot be assumed to bend automatically to the force of the strongest pressures which impinge on them from the "outside" as circumstances may occasion. The existence or impact of such pressures may be admitted. But it is imperative to recognize that what pressures are brought to bear are absorbed by legislators in a meaningful manner by their taking those purposive and representational roles which serve them as immediate premises in their behavior. And if these roles are related to each other in a "fit," the influences brought to bear on legislators from the outside can be expected to be reorganized in such a way that the legislature can operate as a system rather than being a neutral battle ground of pressures in conflict.

THE NETWORK OF ROLES: AN IDEAL-TYPE CONSTRUCT

The analytical distinction between clientele, representational, and purposive roles is helpful in dissecting the legislator's total role. Actual behavior, however, is not a function of discrete roles, but of a system of roles. It is the network of interpenetrating roles which gives structure and coherence to the legislative process. To demonstrate the empirical reality of such a network, it would seem necessary to relate clientele, representational, and purposive roles to each other in a single multidimensional matrix. Only then could it be established that the great variety of roles available to legislators do, in fact, constitute an integrated pattern of mutually interpenetrating roles.

A multi-variate analysis of this kind would require many more individual cases than are available in this study. With the limited number of cases at hand, we are able to relate only two sets of role orientations at any one time. Even then, as has been evident, analysis is handicapped by lack of numbers, partly due to the small size of some chambers, partly due to response failures. Nevertheless, although the evidence is not always satisfactory, comparative analysis of the eight chambers of four states included in this study supports the notion that roles are meaningfully related to each other. Moreover, the patterning of observed relations and differences is such that it is possible to develop an ideal-type construct of the total network. Such an ideal-type construct is, of course, an exaggeration of empirical reality, but it can serve two valuable purposes: first, it can demonstrate the logic of the postulated network; and, second, it can serve as an independent criterion for comparing the concrete, empirical role systems.

Figure 16.1 presents a diagram of the ideal-type network of legislators' roles suggested by the clustering of role orientations empirically found in the four states and by the theoretical considerations discussed in this chapter. The diagram reflects the observed tendency of certain orientations in one sector to be associated with particular orientations in others. Thus, the upper half of the diagram idealizes the following pairs of role orientations: majority-state-oriented, majority-facilitator, state-oriented-facilitator, facilitator-politico, majority-politico, majority-broker, state-oriented-trustee, state-oriented-inventor/broker, facilitator-broker, broker-trustee/politico, and inventor-trustee. The lower half idealizes these pairs: minority-district-oriented, minority-resister, district-oriented-resister, resister-delegate, minority-delegate, minority-inventor/tribune, district-oriented-delegate, district-oriented-tribune, resister-tribune, and tribune-delegate. The diagram thus suggests two essentially reciprocal sets of relationships or dimensions, one represented in the upper, the other in the lower half of the diagram. The neutral and district-state orientations do not associate readily in theory (nor, as we have seen, empirically) with either of these, but, as the diagram shows, stand more or less outside and between them.

Any individual legislator is likely to be located more in one than another dimension of this network of available roles. Moreover, it is the network as such, rather than simple adoption of one orientation instead of another, which is crucial to the individual's behavior. That is to say, the difference between one role and another in a given sub-

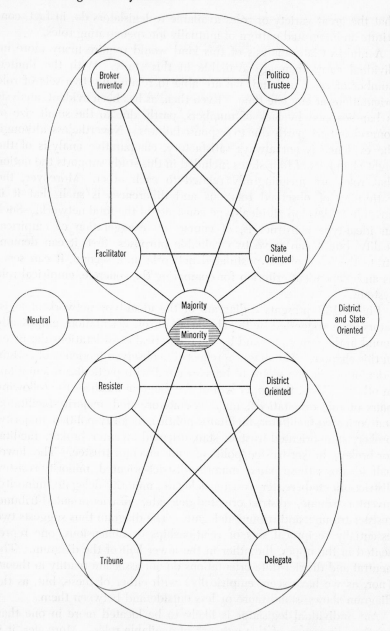

Figure 16.1 *Ideal-type network of roles.*

system—such as, for instance, the difference between facilitator and resister, or between trustee and delegate—is a function of the total network of roles. In such a network, each role is somehow related to every other role, and the character and extent of these relations gives any one empirical legislative role system its peculiar character.

We have not attempted to characterize the different patterns or clusterings of role orientation which might be manifested by the individual legislator, in terms of the ideal-type network illustrated in Figure 16.1. We have, instead, sought to characterize the system differences resulting from the various constellations of role orientation found to prevail in the four legislatures. In other words, although the diagram represents the coincidence of particular role orientations for the individual legislator, we are interested in it as a representation of the aggregates of role orientations and role relationships constituting a system of role relationships among legislators in particular legislatures. We wish to use the ideal-type construct of the network of roles to characterize differences among legislative systems. It is to this that we turn in the next chapter.

CHAPTER 17

Legislative role structure
and political conflict

Among the legislature's purposes and goals the crystallization and resolution of political conflicts is central, for politics is rooted in conflict. Capacity to facilitate the crystallization and resolution of political conflicts is therefore one important criterion of the "functionality" of the legislative structure. Functionality of the formal institutional elements of the modern democratic legislature has not been our research concern. The fact that legislatures continue to exist as vital centers of decision making in democratic political systems may be taken as face-value evidence that, in spite of possible needs for reform, the formal institutional structure remains viable. Our interest here is with the problem of whether the legislative role structure, in so far as we can specify it, is conducive to the task of crystallizing and resolving political conflicts.

Of course, because the legislature is an institutionalized group with varied functional requirements, a "division of labor" in role taking occurs. This division of labor permits individual legislators to choose from among available roles those which are germane to the legislature's functions. Some of these roles, we noted in Part Three, are particularly conducive to the functioning of the "internal" legislative arena. Other roles, reviewed in Part Four, are particularly functional for the maintenance of the legislature in the larger "legislative system" and for the task of solving conflicts among the legislature's different clienteles. They provide the premises in terms of which legislators orient themselves to the "input-output" process at the core of legislative action. This process is "systemic" in that it takes place within and is facilitated by the legislative role structure.

This chapter drafted by Eulau.

414

As we saw in Chapter 16, legislators' self-conceptions of their roles are evidently related in a network of role orientations which, we can assume, mirrors the legislature's role structure. The data suggested the construction of an "ideal-type" network of role orientations which seems to make sense theoretically, and which may be useful heuristically in identifying particular empirical role structures. But whether these structures are functional from the point of view of the legislature's task to crystallize and resolve political conflicts requires independent proof. We shall, therefore, outline in this chapter what we think are the characteristic role structures of the four legislatures or eight chambers, and appraise their functionality in terms of legislators' own specifications of the conflict situation prevailing in their respective houses.

LEGISLATIVE ROLE STRUCTURES

Ideally, it would be desirable to identify and specify the entire matrix of all role combinations in a given legislative system. For instance, just how many members of the majority are also trustees, brokers, facilitators, and state oriented? Does this combination constitute the dominant pattern? What secondary and tertiary patterns exist? Unfortunately, even the largest chamber in this study includes too few cases to isolate empirically the theoretically possible matrix of roles in combination. However, we can construct a partial framework by dealing with the most frequent individual pairs of roles that are taken in a legislative chamber. Each of these "dominant pairs" may or may not be linked because any one role in one pair may also be linked with a third role in another pair.

Table 17.1 presents the dominant (i.e., the most frequent) pairs of roles in the two chambers of each state legislature. The base of the proportions is the total number of legislators whose individual roles appeared in the dominant pairs. For instance, of the California House members for whom data were available, 30 per cent are district-oriented minority members, 26 per cent are majority-neutrals, 27 per cent are district-oriented facilitators, and so on. The tables from which these proportions are derived are those presented in Chapter 16.

House role structures. The distributions in Table 17.1 yield some interesting results, but they are difficult to inspect and appraise. There are two ways in which we can simplify the emerging structures—one numerical, the other graphical. First, we can single out the number of times a given role appears in a dominant pair. Table 17.2 presents this alternative. The patterns for each role set are clear. They sen-

Table 17.1: Proportions of dominant role pairs in the four legislatures

Lower Chambers

Ohio	N =	% =	N.J.	N =	% =	Calif.	N =	% =	Tenn.	N =	% =
Ma/Di-St	94	31	Ma/Di-St	38	34	Mi/Di	50	30	Ma/Di	38	42
Ma/Fa	125	32	Ma/Fa	57	28	Ma/Ne	68	26	Ma/Re	87	31
Di-St/Ne	89	19	Di-St/Fa	37	19	Di/Fa	44	27	Di/Re	38	23
Ma/Tr	94	35	Ma/Tr	39	41	Ma/Tr	37	30	Ma/Tr	61	59
St/Tr	75	20	Di-St/Tr	26	23	Di/De	23	30	Di/Tr	31	29
			St/Tr	26	23						
Fa/Tr	92	24	Fa/Tr	39	26	Ne/Tr	32	31	Ne/Tr	59	36
Ma/Br	130	36	Ma/Tri	58	47	Mi/Tri	78	28	Ma/Tri	89	48
Di-St/Br	95	27	Di-St/Tri	37	32	Di/Tri	49	47	Di/Tri	37	49
Br/Tr	125	24	Fa/Tr	57	23	Ne/Tri	68	22	Ne/Tri	87	28
	120	23	In/Tr	55	31	In/Tr	47	19	Tri/Tr	66	41

Senates

Ohio	N =	% =	N.J.	N =	% =	Calif.	N =	% =	Tenn.	N =	% =
Ma/Di-St	18	22	Ma/Di	16	25	Ma/Di	28	25	Ma/Di	8	50
Ma/Di	18	22	Mi/Di	16	25						
Mi/Di	18	22									
Ma/Fa	32	28	Ma/Fa	21	29	Mi/Fa	29	28	Ma/Re	29	38
Di/Fa	19	27	Di-St/Fa	16	31	Di/Ne	24	21	Di/Re	8	38
Ma/Tr	20	50	Ma/Tr	15	33	Ma/Tr	12	33	Ma/Tr	17	76
Di/Tr	13	23	Di/De	13	31	Di-St/Tr	12	34	Di/Tr	5	80
St/Tr	13	23									
Ne/Tr	20	30	Fa/Po	15	27	Fa/Tri	12	50	Re/Tr	17	41
Ma/Br	32	28	Ma/In	21	38	Ma/Tri	35	34	Ma/Tri	31	42
Di/Tri	17	41	Di/Tri	16	44	Di/Tri	28	29	Di/Tri	8	63
Fa/Br	32	22	Fa/Tri	23	38	St/Tri	28	29	Re/Tr	29	28
In/Tr	24	25	In/Po	21	19	Ne/Tri	29	28	Tri/Tr	18	50
Br/Tr	24	25	Tri/De	21	19	Br/Tri	17	24			
						Tri/Po	17	24			

Key:
Ma = majority
Mi = minority

Br = broker
De = delegate
Di = district
Di-St = district-state

Fa = facilitator
In = inventor
Ne = neutral

Po = politico
Re = resister
Tri = tribune
Tr = trustee

416

sitize us to the significance of particular distributions in the more complex array of Table 17.1. In the first place, in the New Jersey and Ohio Houses, where "party government" has genuine meaning, the role of majority member appears among the dominant pairs, but the role of minority member does not. In California, where "party control" has little meaning, both the roles of majority and minority member are encountered in the dominant pairs. Tennessee represents

Table 17.2: Number of times a role appears in combination with another in a dominant pair, lower chambers

Role	Ohio	N.J.	Calif.	Tenn.
Party				
Majority member	4	4	2	4
Minority member	0	0	2	0
Representational				
Trustee	4	5	3	4
Politico	0	0	0	0
Delegate	0	0	1	0
Purposive				
Inventor	0	1	1	0
Broker	4	0	0	0
Tribune	0	3	3	4
Areal				
State oriented	1	1	0	0
District-State oriented	3	4	0	0
District oriented	0	0	4	4
Pressure group				
Facilitator	3	4	1	0
Neutral	1	0	3	2
Resister	0	0	0	2

a special case: although formally the role of "majority member" alone occurs in the dominant pairs, we know that the "majority" is faction-alized and not a majority in the same sense as in the competitive party states. The Tennessee House is actually composed of competing "minorities," and though the role of majority member seems present in the dominant pairs, it cannot be taken in a literal sense.

Second, in the representational-role set, the role of trustee occurs in the dominant pairs almost exclusively, with the single exception of California, where the delegate role appears in one dominant pair. This role of trustee is, as we noted earlier, so universal that it is neces-sarily linked to any cluster in the total network of dominant pairs. In other words, it does not serve as a discriminating factor in a typology of role structures.

Third, in the purposive-role set, the Ohio House role structure differs from the other three lower chamber structures in the pervasiveness of the broker role in dominant pairs, while elsewhere the tribune role is more prominent, suggesting a more "populist" milieu than prevailed in 1957 in the Republican-dominanted Ohio House.

Fourth, of the areal-role set, the district role is present in dominant pairs in California and Tennessee, but not in Ohio and New Jersey. In the latter two states, the district-state role occurs in the dominant pairs, as does the state role in one pair, but neither of these two roles is present in the dominant California and Tennessee pairs. The pattern suggests that the areal-role orientations held by legislators may serve as critical discriminating devices in the characterization of legislative role structures.

Finally, the pressure-group-role set seems to perform a similar function. The facilitator role is prominent in Ohio's and New Jersey's dominant pairs, and the neutral role in California. Only in Tennessee does the resister role appear in dominant pairs, and it does so twice, while the facilitator role is altogether absent from dominant pairs.

The frequency of a role's appearance in dominant pairs, and the pattern of occurrences from state to state, give a first view of what one might expect when the linkages between those roles which constitute the dominant pairs are constructed graphically. The diagrams of the House structures presented in Figure 17.1 can be readily compared with the ideal-type construct of the role structure developed from the bivariate analyses in Chapter 16 (Figure 16.1, p. 412 above). This comparison makes it possible to develop an empirical typology of legislative role structures.

The Ohio diagram of Figure 17.1 shows a relatively highly integrated role cluster of what we may call the "majoritarian type." Almost all the ideal-type linkages are present, and where they are not they are replaced by "intermediate" roles in the dominant pairs (such as the district-state instead of the "pure" state role, or the neutral role instead of the facilitator role). But the linkages in no way penetrate into the reciprocal "minoritarian" cluster of the ideal-type model. Minority members are totally eclipsed as role takers in the dominant structure, as are such minority-linked roles of the ideal-type model as tribunes, resisters, delegates, and district oriented.

In the New Jersey House structure, also, the role of minority member and its ideally associated roles of delegate, resister, and district oriented are missing from the dominant majority-centered cluster.

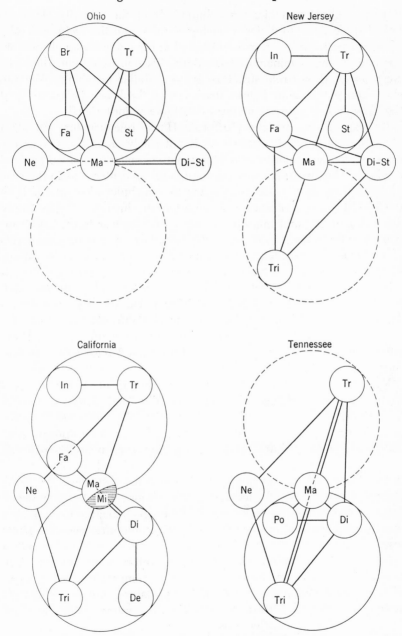

Figure 17.1. *Role structures of four lower houses.*

But, in contrast to Ohio, the tribune role of the minority cluster is linked three times to majority-anchored roles, and the reciprocal roles of the purposive-role set, ideally located in the majoritarian cluster, are not among the dominant pairs. With this one exception, then, the New Jersey House role structure is very similar to Ohio's. We can characterize the Ohio House structure as "broker-majoritarian" and the New Jersey House structure as "tribune-majoritarian."

By way of contrast, the California House role structure reveals a bipartisan pattern. The structure is not solely, as in the Ohio case, centered in the majority role (though the "majority" had organized the lower chamber), nor is it predominantly so centered as in the case of New Jersey. The California structure includes elements of both the ideal-type majoritarian and minoritarian clusters. And not only do both majority and minority member roles appear in the dominant pairs, but the linkages cut across the boundaries of the reciprocal sets of the ideal-type model. The "populist" component is outstanding: the tribune and district-oriented roles are linked across cluster boundaries, but the majority-related roles of inventor and facilitator each appear in dominant pairs. The California House role structure reflects the strongly "atomistic" orientation of California legislators, and it is indicative of the low salience of party roles as premises for legislative behavior. We may term the California House role structure "populist-bipartisan."

Finally, the Tennessee House role structure is altogether different from the previous types. Though formally "majoritarian," it is in fact minority geared: the tribune and district roles are most pervasive, and, alone among the four chambers, the role of resister appears in at least one dominant pair. At the same time, such majority-anchored roles as inventor or broker in the purposive-role set, facilitator, and state oriented are missing altogether in the Tennessee House structure. Only the trustee, ideally located in the majority cluster, is present. Apparently, it is a role which cannot be shed in contemporary empirical reality, even in a system which is so clearly minority geared. These results, we already suggested, are easy to explain, and they confirm that the "majority" in Tennessee is only a pro forma majority. In fact, the "majority" Democrats are divided into competing factions, none of which can permanently control the legislature, and which behave more like minority parties in a multi-party system. We can characterize this structure as "populist-minoritarian."

Senate role structures. Tables 17.1 and Table 17.3 show that in the four Senates more pairs are tied for dominance, making the overall picture somewhat more complex. But a glance at Figure 17.2 will indicate that, in spite of the greater complexity, the general patterns observed in the role structures of the lower houses are maintained from state to state, but a number of differences may be noted.

In the first place, in the Ohio and New Jersey Senate the role of minority member seems to be somewhat more integrated into the dominant majority pattern than is the case in the respective Houses. This is quite plausible. In the smaller chambers, the minority is

Table 17.3: Number of times a role appears in combination with another in a dominant pair, senates

Role	Ohio	N.J.	Calif.	Tenn.
Party				
Majority member	5	4	3	4
Minority member	1	1	1	0
Representational				
Trustee	6	1	4	4
Politico	0	2	1	0
Delegate	0	2	0	0
Purposive				
Inventor	1	2	0	0
Broker	3	0	1	0
Tribune	1	3	5	4
Areal				
State oriented	1	0	1	0
District-State oriented	1	1	1	0
District oriented	5	4	3	4
Pressure group				
Facilitator	3	4	2	0
Neutral	1	0	2	0
Resister	0	0	0	4

more likely to be in closer contact with the majority, it is more likely to be given attention, and it is more likely to play an active role in the legislative process. As a result, ideally minority-centered roles are likely to be more frequently linked to majority-anchored roles. In New Jersey, for instance, we may note the facilitator-tribune combination among the dominant pairs, or in Ohio the facilitator-district pair.

Secondly, we note that in the Ohio and New Jersey Senates the district-oriented role appears in dominant pairs, while this is not the case in the respective Houses. Also, in New Jersey the delegate role and in Ohio the tribune role are paired with some other roles, while this pairing does not occur (with the exception of the tribune in New

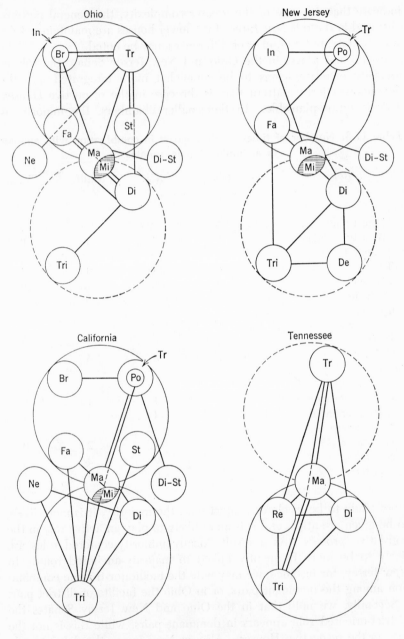

Figure 17.2. *Role structures of four senates.*

Jersey) in the lower chambers. These three roles—tribune, delegate, and district-oriented—seem to loom as latent premises of their behavior in Senators' self-conceptions of their legislative role in general. Senates have been historically looked on as performing more distinctly "ambassadorial functions" in the representative system. And though now popularly elected just as the members of the "popular" lower houses, the notion that Senates are, in part at least, conclaves of ambassadors from geographically-based constituencies may linger on in Senators' self-definitions. This, of course, we cannot prove, but as a hypothesis it is congruent with the fact that in the lower houses these "populist" roles are minority centered. Minority members are likely to perceive themselves as "ambassadors"—spokesmen of the "outs"—vis-à-vis the controlling majority with its predominant state orientation.

The "constructions" of legislative chambers as role structures suggest that through the use of non-conventional analytical categories, in our case derived from a role analysis of legislators, we can describe the structure of a legislative chamber, not as it is embodied in rules and bylaws (which are important parameters for behavior), but as it represents a system of action. Are the structures we delineated "functional," then, in being adapted to and, in turn, facilitative of conflict crystallization and resolution? Before investigating this question, we must describe the patterns of conflict in the four legislatures as they were perceived and rated by the legislators.

PERCEPTIONS OF CONFLICTS

For the purpose of analysis, we can assume that the conflicts of concern to a legislature originate in the other subsystems of the legislative system from where they are transmitted for legislative disposal. A number of major conflict areas—between the parties, urban and rural interests, sectional groupings, or ideologies—have been identified by previous studies as matters of theoretical and empirical inquiry. It is usually assumed in these studies that the analysis of legislators' stands on roll calls is helpful in determining just what influences are most important, in the aggregate, in legislative decisions and in whose favor conflicts are most likely to be resolved.[1] The hypothesis is advanced here that the roles legislators take in the legislative arena are adapted to the conflict situation which prevails in particular state contexts, as this is reflected in legis-

[1] The number of such studies is now legion. For the formulation here given to these studies, see especially Julius Turner, *op. cit.*

lators' definitions of the range and importance of different types of conflict.

At least two aspects of legislators' perceptions of characteristic conflicts are important here: first, what type of conflict they see as more important than others; and, second, the amount of agreement or consensus in their ranking of the importance of various types of conflict. Low consensus is indicative of perceptual confusion, in the sense that legislators either cannot or do not differentiate among the issues at stake. Where this is the case, the legislature will fail as an agency of conflict clarification, and though unanimous votes occur, they cannot be considered indicators of genuine consensus[2] about what is at issue. In other words consensus about what conflicts exist and are important is a rough indicator of the degree of conflict-crystallization in the chamber.

To examine the relationship between role structure and the legislative conflict situation as they defined it, legislators were asked to rank a number of "opinion conflicts":

1. Between Republicans and Democrats;
2. Between the Governor's supporters and opponents;
3. Between the cities and the rural counties;
4. Between liberals and conservatives;
5. Between labor and the opponents of labor; and
6. Between region and region.

Table 17.4 presents the proportions of legislators ranking a given conflict as important and rank orders the various conflicts in each state in terms of these proportions.[3] It also presents a measure of consensus which is used as an index of conflict crystallization. This measure can range from zero for complete dissensus or poor crystallization (i.e., a 50–50 division) to 100 for full consensus or sharp crystallization (i.e., no division).[4] The data reflect rather accurately

[2] See above, Introduction to Part Five, note 13.

[3] For the exact wording of the question asked, and the particular inter-regional conflicts in each state, see below, Question No. 17, Appendix 6, p. 497. For purposes of analysis, an opinion conflict ranked first, second, or third, or tied for these rankings was considered "important."

[4] The measure is essentially the same as Stuart A. Rice's "index of cohesion," *op. cit.* If 50 per cent of the legislators rate an opinion conflict "important" (as defined in the text) and 50 per cent rate it "not important," the amount of consensus is zero; if all legislators rate a conflict either "important" or "not important," the amount of consensus is 100. Any intermediate index number represents the degree to which the proportion of those considering a conflict "important" deviates from 50 per cent in either direction toward 0 or 100.

Table 17.4: Opinion conflicts, by chamber and state

	Houses			Senates	
Conflict	% Important	Crystalli- zation	Conflict	% Important	Crystalli- zation
	N = 76		California	N = 34	
Regional	69	38	Urb-Rural	74	48
Urb-Rural	65	30	Lib-Cons	74	48
Labor	65	30	Labor	62	24
Lib-Cons	58	16	Regional	44	12
Party	26	48	Party	26	48
Governor	18	64	Governor	24	52
	N = 51		New Jersey	N = 20	
Party	96	92	Party	85	70
Governor	76	52	Governor	70	40
Urb-Rural	53	6	Urb-Rural	50	0
Lib-Cons	22	56	Regional	40	20
Regional	18	64	Lib-Cons	25	50
Labor	18	64	Labor	15	70
	N = 121		Ohio	N = 29	
Urb-Rural	79	58	Urb-Rural	65	30
Labor	61	22	Lib-Cons	59	18
Lib-Cons	52	4	Party	59	18
Party	49	2	Labor	55	10
Governor	36	28	Governor	38	24
Regional	17	66	Regional	10	80
	N = 83		Tennessee	N = 30	
Urb-Rural	91	82	Governor	96	92
Governor	89	78	Labor	67	34
Labor	54	8	Urb-Rural	63	26
Lib-Cons	29	42	Lib-Cons	37	26
Party	23	54	Regional	20	60
Regional	13	74	Party	17	66

Houses	M =	Mean Crystallization Evaluation		Senates	M =
California	38	0–19	Little	California	39
New Jersey	56	20–39	Low	New Jersey	42
Ohio	30	40–59	Moderate	Ohio	30
Tennessee	57	60–79	Considerable	Tennessee	51
		80–100	Strong		

what we already know about the "political characteristics" of the four legislatures. But they also reveal a good deal more that may be helpful in appraising the legislative role structure as an adaptive mechanism in the political conflict situation.

First, in regard to conflict between the parties, the legislators in at least three states show a great deal of "reality-consciousness." In California and Tennessee, as we should expect, only small proportions in either chamber consider party conflict important. But there is only moderate consensus in this respect, suggestive of some ambiguity in perceptions. In New Jersey, on the other hand, very large proportions deem party conflict important, and crystallization is sharp but more so in the House than in the Senate. The surprising finding involves Ohio. Though Ohio has a reasonably competitive party system on the state legislative level, and though in fact party divisions are significant in legislative voting, there is a good deal of perceptual confusion in regard to the importance of party conflict. In the House, conflict crystallization is very poor—49 per cent considering party conflict important and, correspondingly, 51 per cent considering it not important. In the Senate, party conflict is deemed important by 59 per cent, indicative of little consensus. Evidently, the majority's grip on the legislative situation was so firm in 1957 that legislators could not see effective minority opposition. In this situation other types of conflict are likely to be perceived as more salient, making for an adaptive role structure somewhat different from New Jersey's, though in general the structures of the two states, as we have seen, are more similar than different.

Secondly, combat between the Governor's supporters and opponents is considered important in both Tennessee and New Jersey by large proportions, with moderate crystallization in the latter but sharp crystallization in the former state. These results reflect, of course, quite different realities. In Tennessee, they confirm the very active role which the Governor as a factional leader usually plays in the legislature. In New Jersey, on the other hand, the results probably mirror a special situation, due to the fact that in 1957 the office of Governor was controlled by the minority party. In this situation, as already noted in Chapter 3, the Governor is more involved in legislative affairs because his legislative record is a most visible element in the struggle between the parties for popular support. In California and Ohio this type of conflict is considered important by only small proportions, but whereas consensus in this regard is moderate in California, it is low in Ohio.

Conflicts stemming from the cleavage between urban and rural areas are rated important by majorities of legislators in all four states. This type of conflict ranks first in the California Senate, the Tennessee House, and both Ohio chambers. It ranks second in the California House, and third in the Tennessee Senate and both New Jersey chambers. But, as the crystallization indices suggest, there is a good deal of difference between chambers in the degree of agreement on the importance of urban-rural cleavage. In New Jersey, Senators are evenly split, indicating no consensus at all, and the House members, too, show almost no agreement. There is slightly more crystallization in the Ohio Senate, the California House and the Tennessee Senate. Consensus concerning the importance of urban-rural cleavage is moderate in the California Senate and Ohio House. Only in the Tennessee House is there pronounced conflict crystallization.

Regional conflicts are considered important by only small proportions in three of the states, although consensus varies somewhat. It ranks first among opinion conflicts only in the California House, but crystallization is only moderate. Here the fact that 31 of the 80 members come from Los Angeles County alone may tend to accentuate regional differentiation. But in the California Senate only a minority consider regional conflict important, and there is little crystallization.

Conflict arising out of labor issues is deemed important by majorities in California, Ohio, and Tennessee, but not in New Jersey. However, consensus in this regard is little or low in the states where these majorities consider it important.

Finally, ideological differences between liberals and conservatives are quite variously assessed in the four states. In California, with its weak party system, ideological conflict is deemed important by more legislators than elsewhere, but in Ohio, too, majorities consider it important, though crystallization there is less than in California. In New Jersey and Tennessee, on the other hand, only small percentages of legislators rate this type of conflict important. Evidently, in the more competitive situations—whether of the party type as in New Jersey or the factional type as in Tennessee—ideology counts for less than in situations where organized competition is less keen.

But the most striking feature of the data is the relative lack of widespread crystallization of the conflict situation in all chambers. This is reflected not only in the relatively low indices for each particular opinion conflict in the various chambers but in the mean crystallization scores for each chamber given at the bottom of Table 17.4. What are the consequences of this for the legislative role structure?

POLITICAL CONFLICT AND LEGISLATIVE
ROLE STRUCTURE

Ohio. The Ohio role structure is centered in a strong, well-organized majority which, in the House, eclipses the minority in giving the legislature its characteristic format, though in the Senate the minority-centered roles of tribune and district-oriented are joined in the dominant pattern. But the outstanding and distinguishing feature in both Ohio chambers is the presence of the broker in the role structure. Legislators' rankings of types of conflict may be relevant to the emergence of the broker as a dominant role. Although Ohio's legislature is organized as an unequivocal two-party system, in the 1957 session, at least, a variety of conflicts, especially those involving urban-rural cleavage, labor problems, and ideological disagreement, were seen as more important than party conflict. Apparently, majority members, feeling free from conflict with a minority, come to function as brokers among interests whose conflicts are deemed more important than party conflicts. Moreover, as we saw, both Ohio chambers have the lowest mean consensus score in regard to the conflicts deemed important. Again, if this is the case, the brokerage function becomes critical, and the role structure tends to be adapted to the situation as it is perceived. The characterization of the Ohio role structure as "broker-majoritarian" is predicated on its functionality in regard to the kinds of conflict deemed important and the low consensual quality of the legislature. In a system in which highly differentiating conflicts, as those between city and country, business and labor, liberals and conservatives, are considered important, but in which legislators are little agreed, the functions associated with the broker role seem to serve the needs of political integration. The prominence of the broker role in the role structure gives the system its characteristic ability to function effectively in a complex conflict situation.

New Jersey. The role structure of this state's legislative system is similar to Ohio's, but, in contrast to Ohio, party conflict is considered as the most important among all others, and there is strong consensus in this respect. The conflict situation mirrored in legislators' perceptions is strongly focussed also on tensions arising out of the minority's control of the governorship. In such direct combat between organized and disciplined sides decisions are less likely to require the taking of the broker role in the dominant structure. Rather, conflict is centered on those popular mandates which the majority receives in its competition with the minority. And if governmental control is divided between the parties—one controlling the legislature, the other the governorship—the functional requirements of the system seem to incline towards a role structure in which the populist orientation finds expression. The appearance of the tribune role in the dominant New Jersey role structure seems to meet these requirements. Just as in Ohio the solution of the perceived conflicts seems to generate the adaptation of the role structure through emphasis on the broker role, so the solution of the centrally perceived New Jersey conflicts—those between the parties and between the minority Governor and the legislative majority—seems to fit into what we have called a role structure of the "tribune-majoritarian" type.

California. The California role structure, we noted earlier, is not singularly anchored in either majority or minority. Majority and minority roles seem to have little meaning, with the result that the role structure partakes of elements found in both major role clusters of the ideal-type model. Party and gubernatorial conflicts ranked lowest in both chambers, and there was a good deal of crystallization in this respect. Instead, other conflicts—involving regional differentiation, urban-rural cleavage, labor, and ideological difficulties—were judged important. Why, then, does the broker role not emerge as a component of the dominant role structure in California, as it does in Ohio?

An answer to this question is difficult. It may be suggested that the broker role is missing in the California structure because it is linked to the role of majority member. But as party roles are essentially meaningless in the California system, the brokerage function fails to be performed. For this function is predicated on the presence of a fairly stable point of reference—the majority's stand on issues in terms of which the brokerage function must be performed. If this stable point of reference is missing, the brokerage function cannot be readily executed, and there is relatively little need for legislators to take the broker role.

Instead, the populist component dominates in the California role structure. The large number of bills introduced and passed in California, in contrast to the other states, seems to confirm our characterization of the California system as "populist-bipartisan." Unable to select and sift among the huge amount of legislation introduced by legislators in behalf of particular interests, the California role structure is adapted to the demands made on the legislature from "outside" by providing a counterbalance to group pressures in the form of a populist component. It is interesting to note that in California the pressure-group role of neutral rather than that of facilitator appears more often in the dominant pairs. California politics of an earlier period than the one studied here had been notorious for its submissiveness to special interests and group pressures. By 1957, evidently, the role structure had developed in a direction which permitted legislators to off-set pressure-group influence by taking roles more responsive to popular demands. Being under cross-pressures from both organized interests and grass-roots influences, California legislators take the role of tribune rather than broker in the purposive-role set and the role of neutral in the pressure-group-role set. Conflicts are resolved by way of negotiation in terms of popular demands rather than by way of brokerage in terms of a majority's stand on issues.

Tennessee. To speak of a "majority" in Tennessee is merely using a figure of speech. In actuality, the effective organized units of the legislature are factions, usually centered in the Governor. If anything, therefore, the Tennessee system is a multi-minority system par excellence. The dominant role pairs which serve to "build" the legislative role structure converge in the minority-anchored cluster of roles. The structure seems reasonably adapted to the prevailing appraisal of the importance of different conflicts by the legislators themselves. Party conflict is considered of little importance, but conflicts involving the Governor are given prominent rank. As a multi-minority system in which the Governor's faction is only a transient clique, the Tennessee system is strongly populist: urban-rural and labor-business conflicts perceived in the legislative arena reflect popular tensions, and legislators take roles as minority proponents of diverse popular interests. The roles of tribune and district-oriented, as well as other minority-centered roles, such as delegate and resister, tend towards what we have termed a "populist-minoritarian" role structure.

CONCLUSION

The legislature is a human group with a determinate role structure which serves two interdependent functions: (a) to link the legislature as a subsystem with other subsystems of the political system, notably electoral constituencies, parties, pressure groups, and administrative agencies; and (b) to institutionalize and resolve the social, economic, and political conflicts generated as legislative inputs in the various subsystems. We find that American state legislatures, so similar in their formal structures and processes, differ significantly in their adaptations to political reality, depending on the types and importance of conflicts encountered in particular contexts within and among the other political subsystems with which the legislature is linked. The roles taken by legislators in different political contexts (such as the degree of competition between parties or factions, or the relative strength of majority and minority) constitute a role structure of consequence for the performance of legislative tasks, especially the resolution of conflicts, and for the achievement of democratic integration.

PART SIX

Legislative research

CHAPTER 18

Strategy and tactics
of legislative research

In CHAPTER 2, and at appropriate points throughout the book, we have
sought to supply enough information about our methods of collecting
and analyzing data to facilitate interpretation of our results. Some
methodological problems, however, deserve more explicit and detailed
consideration because of the distinctive or novel features of the research—design, conduct, and analysis of research by a team of coequal
researchers cooperating without formal organization or direction by a
single responsible research administrator; the effort to relate empirical
data about legislators' behavior to a broad range of theoretical questions posed in essentially institutional and functional terms; the
attempt to collect thoroughly comparable data in four different settings
and apply comparative methods to study of general problems; and
heavy reliance upon direct interviews with the total populations of
complex institutionalized groups.

PROBLEMS OF COLLABORATIVE RESEARCH

We have described elsewhere[1] the development of patterns and
techniques of collaboration among a team of equals, but we may
summarize here our principal conclusions on this point. The methods
of collaboration were, of course, worked out gradually, as the group
took shape, in a series of ad hoc decisions. The experience proves at
least that it is possible to weld together a research team whose in-

This chapter drafted by Eulau and Wahlke.

[1] "The Annals of Research: A Case of Collaboration in Comparative Study of
Legislative Behavior," *The American Behavioral Scientist*, 4, No. 9, (May, 1961),
3–9.

dividual members come to the common task with different theoretical orientations, different substantive concerns, different approaches, and without even mutual acquaintance at the beginning.

The initial plans, calling for the loosest sort of cooperation in only the initial, or design, phases of the research, were continually modified as each successive stage of the work called for closer and closer teamwork. The group was very tentatively formed when the Committee on Political Behavior of the Social Science Research Council encouraged its four members to meet for four days (in September, 1955) to explore the possibilities of bringing their four individual projects, then just begun, into some kind of common framework. The group's original proposal to the Committee, developed at this and a later meeting (three days in October, 1955), envisaged little more than a common research instrument, meeting the separate research needs of the four individuals, to be used by each researcher in a different state. It was thought, at this time, that data would be exchanged and each member, using the data from four states, would proceed to a comparative analysis of the particular problem of primary interest to him.

Development of an interview schedule meeting the needs sketched out in the original proposal early forced the group into much closer collaboration than anticipated. It called for extensive correspondence and elaborate working papers for circulation among the group, in preparation for the task of merging the interests of the four researchers into a single questionnaire. An entire month (August, 1956) was spent in conference to draft the questionnaire. Still further correspondence and another short meeting (in December) were required before the final draft was completed. Discussions at this stage indicated it would be desirable during the field stage of research (January–June, 1957) for the team members to leave their own interviewing briefly and familiarize themselves with the other three states by visiting and interviewing in each of them, if possible.

Closer collaboration than ever was imperative once the data were collected. The group faced the task of coding open-ended questions where each set of legislators had answered with a slightly different terminology and a slightly different set of institutions as referents. The entire summer of 1957 was spent in conference developing the code categories and the common understanding necessary to use them. At this point the group belatedly recognized that a unified analysis of the project was needed, rather than a series of disjointed individual studies. The summer of 1958 was, therefore, devoted to still another conference of the group for purposes of planning such an analysis. From this point on, until its final meeting (a week, in September,

1960), the group worked in closest collaboration, though communicating primarily by mail.

The experience suggests that collaboration, to be successful, must at some point become much more than casual mutual aid, even though it can at least begin with something less than common subservience to a group goal. At each stage of development, it was the need to solve theoretical, rather than practical or technical problems, which impelled the group to ever-closer collaboration. This is reflected in the fact that the field stages of the research, in which the work was least collaborative, required no more than about 25 per cent of the total time and energy of the project. Design (planning, development of instruments) occupied about 15 per cent of it; coding and analysis, about another 20 per cent; and analysis and writing of reports, some 40 per cent.

The most obvious advantage of collaborative operation is undoubtedly efficiency and economy in data collection. No one in the group could have obtained the relatively enormous volume of interview data which the four of them (aided by a few interviewers, mostly students) did in six months. No one of them could have become familiar so quickly with the details of procedure in four so widely scattered legislatures, but four of them could approximate familiarity with such facts by concentrating on one legislature each and pooling their experience in constant correspondence and frequent conferences.

Other advantages, though less obvious, are more far-reaching. The collective product almost inevitably represents more than the mere sum of individual cogitations, thanks to the constant interplay of different perceptions and different interpretations. Moreover, the process of collaboration tends to force attention to hidden or conflicting theoretical premises which might pass unnoticed in either individual or more highly centralized research operations.

We should be less than candid if we did not point out that a certain price must be paid for these and other advantages of collaborative methods. In such an operation the failure of one member can jeopardize the group's work. The inevitable differences of personality among members can occasion lengthy controversy quite irrelevant to the purposes of the research. More meaningful differences of intellectual interest and outlook are bound to appear. One in particular deserves comment. More than once the theoretically oriented members felt that collaboration was forcing them to compromise objectives and substitute a fuzzy eclecticism for clean-cutting analysis. At the same time, the empirically oriented felt that potentially rewarding areas of investigation were being sealed off and that valid and potentially useful observations were being dismissed or cut to fit pre-constructed theoretical pigeonholes.

Nevertheless, on balance, the capabilities of this type of "headless" collaboration are distinctive and potent. Despite its hazards and its hardships, it offers advantages which are not to be obtained by mere centralization or more hierarchic management.

INTERVIEW SCHEDULE: CONSTRUCTION AND PRE-TESTS

Theoretical considerations and the practical requirements of a viable schedule constantly affected each other in the over-all design of the project.[2] The following table, offering a rough comparison of the number and kind of questions included in the three major drafts of the instrument, shows that, in general, a highly structured questionnaire consisting predominantly of a variety of closed questions was transformed into a decidedly open-ended, though focused, interview schedule.[3]

Number and kind of questions in three drafts of the interview schedule

	Open-ended	Multi-ple choice	Scale Items	Yes-No	Name Lists	Per-sonal Data
First (August, 1956)	23	59	35	51	25	22
Third (October, 1956)	29	32	31	41	27	23
Final (December, 1956)	34	27	25	12	10	21

The first draft was by far the longest, most detailed, and most directly theory geared of the various schedules. To insure that appropriate empirical data would be forthcoming for most of the variables which had been of theoretical concern, it included a great number of multiple-choice questions (various rating devices, and simple yes-no questions, etc.). It was hoped that the interviews could be completed in one-and-a-half to two hours. A few pretests,

[2] At the time our project was begun only one interview study formulated in role terms had been published—by Corinne Silverman, "The Legislator's View of the Legislative Process," *Public Opinion Quarterly*, 18:180–190 (1954). Ralph K. Huitt had used documentary data from transcripts to reconstruct the roles taken by Congressional Committee members, (*op. cit.*); and Duncan MacRae had used roll calls in "The Role of the State Legislator in Massachusetts," *American Sociological Review*, 19:185–194 (1954).

[3] The interview schedule and accompanying interview instructions are set forth in Appendix 6.

however, showed that time ran out in each case long before the interview was completed. Furthermore, respondents either reacted unfavorably to forced-choice questions or they could not be contained from freely elaborating on them after having given us the desired closed response. These first few pretests also showed, on the other hand, that, whether they were open or closed, the questions stimulated pretest respondents to articulate whatever they had on their minds that they thought we ought to know, and that respondents of the kind we were dealing with were quite willing to cooperate with the project.

Two successive revisions resulted, by October, 1956, in a third draft, which served as the main pretesting instrument. In the revision process, a great many questions were reworded, rephrased or simplified. The order of the questions was rearranged, since pretesting had shown certain orderly ways in which legislators themselves were thinking and we sought to have our questions follow this order. Finally, the number of closed-type questions was somewhat reduced and the number of open-ended questions increased. But, as the tabulation above shows, the third draft still included a great many closed items. Evidently we were still unwilling to sacrifice data for variables we considered essential.

This third draft was pretested throughout October and November on twenty-eight respondents—some of them incumbent legislators in states not included in the study, some of them former legislators in the states of the study.[4] These pretests confirmed our earlier experience: the open-ended questions proved more useful and insightful and, in the end, more economical than the closed-answer ones. The final draft, therefore, further reduced the number of all types of questions other than the open-ended ones which were increased.

Despite the great care taken in making the interview not longer than an hour and a half, the time problem continued to prove troublesome even after the pretests. Indeed, our experience in this connection well illustrates the need for close cooperation between team members lest misunderstanding jeopardize a project such as this. Inability of one member to participate in the conference where the semi-final draft had been hammered out left him unaware of decisions presumably made somewhat implicitly either then or later. A consensus had been reached by the other three members that one-and-a-half hours was the optimum time. The missing member's protests and his insistence on a shorter version (45 minutes to an hour) had to be

---

[4] Eight each of these pretest interviews were taken in Tennessee and Michigan, six in Indiana, and three each in California and New Jersey.

overruled in correspondence. This difference over strategy led to temporarily unresolved tensions which, judging from other instances, would rapidly and easily have been worked out in a face-to-face situation. There was something less than complete quadrilateral acceptance of responsibility for this decision when interviewing had to be begun in February. Some respondents did refuse to be interviewed but only a few, and these not necessarily because they objected to the time demanded of them; some terminated the interview before it had run its full course; and some gave laconic answers. But these, as shown in Chapter 2, were a very small minority, and the schedule became an important rapport-building device in the field. A shorter schedule would probably not have yielded any better results. But the difficulties which resulted when one member had to miss one conference made painfully clear to all members of the group the crucial necessity of extensive and frequent face-to-face negotiation in a collaborative project such as ours.

In any case, the major time-saving cut was elimination of one "issue series" from the semi-final draft. The original intention was to ask respondents what three issues they thought were the most important facing their own legislature, what "solutions" they favored and what influenced their positions on these issues. The "issue series" responses were to serve as dependent variables in the study, serving as substitutes for actual vote decisions. The pretest phase suggested that three such series were too many, and that the comparative objectives of the project would be better served by one series about the same issue in all four states and another one to be specified by the respondent himself. The fourth draft included questions formed on this basis. But concern over the length of the interview led to elimination of the spontaneous issue series as the easiest way out. Only one series was to be included, and it was to be the same for all four states. The issue finally chosen was education which, we had reason to believe, was the only one likely to come up in all of the states. In many respects, this was an unfortunate choice because in some states the issue generated less conflict than might have been wished for. Moreover, the results obtained in this connection were the least satisfying of the whole interview, and we have not made much use of the data in this book.[5]

Drafting an interview schedule for application to a specialized population like state legislators requires a subtle blending of theoreti-

[5] See, however, the unpublished report to the United States Office of Education, 1960, by LeRoy C. Ferguson: "How State Legislators View the Problem of School Needs."

cal and practical considerations. If cutting was not to be altogether arbitrary—just because a question did not seem to "work"—it required constant reference back to the theoretical variable which would give the data meaning. In some cases, rewording was absolutely essential; in other cases, it was more feasible to develop open-ended questions which would hopefully produce data relevant to a number of theoretical variables. At the same time, the tendency to proceed in a brutish-empirical manner was ever present: "Wouldn't it be nice to know this or that?" It was forever necessary to bring such questions back to the theoretical design of the project.

This interplay of theoretical and practical considerations is best illustrated in the continual "opening up" of questions during the revision process. Although open-ended questions have the advantage of making for spontaneity and a wide range of response, and of allowing the respondent himself to formulate or "structure" the topic under investigation, certain drawbacks limit their usefulness for statistical analysis. Heterogeneous answers make statistical controls difficult and raise problems of inference. Moreover, many respondents gave more than one answer to many questions, thus preventing the possibility of assigning priorities within particular response patterns. (We shall deal with some of the statistical problems in more detail later in this chapter.) Then, too, the respondents differed greatly in a number of personal characteristics which are significant in answering open-ended questions. A few were suspicious of the interview and gave minimum, if not evasive answers. Others, more favorably inclined, were more candid. Some were genuinely pressed for time and failed to elaborate as fully as those who were willing to devote a great deal of time to the interview. Still others—especially those with relatively little education—were unable to articulate answers to open-ended questions about which they had evidently thought little prior to the interview. Fluctuations in mood, in attitude towards the interview, in verbal facility, or in self-consciousness contributed to considerable variability in answer patterns to the open-ended questions. These differences, inherent in the open-ended type of interview question and in the interview situation, are discussed in more detail in the next section of this chapter.

INTERVIEW PROCEDURES AND EXPERIENCES

Previous research has accumulated a certain amount of experience in the use of systematic interviews with politicians, especially legislators. Selected Congressmen and Senators have been interviewed in

connection with various institutional studies of Congress.[6] Samples
of state legislators have been interviewed,[7] and the mailed questionnaire has at times been employed.[8] The noteworthy report on the
experiences of interviewers who collected data for V. O. Key's
Southern Politics in State and Nation broke through the traditional
bias against interviewing politicians to assert "the conviction that
much significant political information could be obtaned only from
politicians themselves or from their close associates."[9] But the attempt
to collect thoroughly comparable data by means of a rigidly uniform
interview schedule involves certain difficulties which stem from the
requirements of comparability more than from the interview process
itself.

During the interviewing, unanticipated practical problems arose in
each state which could be solved only by adjusting ad hoc to local
circumstances. Often the responsible researcher in each state was
uncertain whether he faced a generic problem common to all states
or a problem unique to his own state. Time pressures and distance
forestalled consultation on such problems. Under these circumstances
the uniform interview schedule was a valuable asset. Without it, the
interviews might well have diverged to a point where comparability
was made impossible. Moreover, as was discovered during coding
and analysis, even questions that might have struck both interviewer
and respondent in a particular state as inappropriate or nonsensical
were yet quite useful for comparative purposes. For instance, "no
answer" responses in a state could be more significant from the comparative point of view than positive responses in that state. It was
the difference in the local legislative contexts that made some questions
meaningless, but this would not have been discoverable unless apparently irrelevant questions had been asked and equally irrelevant
responses recorded.

Interview staff. The interviews were conducted by either the four
senior researchers themselves or by graduate and undergraduate
students under close supervision. Staff requirements were largely

[6] But reports of these efforts were not available to us when our project was
planned or executed. See David B. Truman, *The Congressional Party, op. cit.;*
Donald R. Matthews, "The Folkways of the United States Senate: Conformity to
Group Norms and Legislative Effectiveness," *op. cit.*

[7] Most useful to us were Corinne Silverman, *op. cit.,* and Oliver Garceau and
Corinne Silverman, *op. cit.* See also John B. McConaughy, *op. cit.*

[8] See, for instance, Leon Epstein, *Politics in Wisconsin* (Madison: University
of Wisconsin Press, 1958).

[9] Alexander Heard, "Interviewing Southern Politicians," *American Political
Science Review,* 44: 886–896 (1950), p. 886.

dictated by the number of legislators who had to be interviewed in the different states.   In New Jersey, Ferguson interviewed 77 members, Buchanan and Wahlke one each.   In California, 102 of the 113 interviews were made by Buchanan, the others by two paid graduate students at the University of Southern California.   In Ohio, where the task of interviewing a potential 173 legislators could clearly not be completed by a single person, 45 interviews were completed by Eulau, eight by other senior researchers, and 99 by students from Antioch College.   Similarly, in Tennessee, with its 132 legislators and short legislative session, staff assistance was needed.   Fifty-nine interviews were completed by Wahlke, 4 by Ferguson, and 6 by Mrs. JoAnn Bennett.   The remainder were secured by graduate and undergraduate students at Vanderbilt University.   Interviewers in all states were, of course, carefully briefed in the research objectives and trained in interviewing techniques.

Studies of interviewing situations in public opinion research have shown that distortions in interview results may be occasioned by differences, such as of sex and social class, between interviewer and respondent, or by the attitudes of the interviewer.   Questions may be raised, therefore, about the use of students in the conduct of interviews with men and women considerably older, with quite different backgrounds, and occupying positions of some authority in the political system.

In introducing themselves to respondents, junior interviewers stated that they were "on the staff of the State Legislative Research Project" or "on the staff of Professor X who was studying the legislature," and they generally took the role of the professional interviewer. Only in a very few isolated instances did respondents inquire into the professional status of the junior staff.   How this may have affected the interview may be surmised from the following thumbnail sketch:

Respondent was a rather difficult subject.   He seemed extremely bored and disinterested throughout the entire interview, often yawning and looking around the room, and forgetting the questions, forcing the interviewer to repeat.   . . . Once he asked the interviewer if she was going to receive a grade on what he said.   When she gave a negative answer and explained that she was only an assistant, he replied that, in that case, his answer was long enough, and even though there was more he could say, he wouldn't bother to say it since there weren't any grades involved.   At this point the interviewer really started pressing R, assuring him that we were very anxious to receive any information he could give, but R refused to budge. Throughout the interview he would intersperse his answers with questions to the interviewer, asking her where she was from, how old she was, etc. He expressed real puzzlement over the fact that she came all the way from California to attend school in Ohio.

As this sketch suggests, had the interviewer taken the role of student rather than that of professional interviewer she might have secured a fuller interview. In fact, in some cases, legislators were probably more candid in facing a young student than "the professor" for whom, they thought, they would have to have the "right" answers. In general, the differences in interviewers' status did not seem seriously to affect interview results. Both senior and junior staffers faced the same difficulties, and advantages of one over the other were offset by the difficulties.

Access and rapport. The most immediate problem of the field phase was to gain access to the legislators. Several techniques were used in the four states, but it does not appear that differences in procedure to gain access have greatly affected the results.

Appointments with the legislators were sought in a variety of ways. In New Jersey, an effort was made to interview the officers and more influential members early in the interview period, so that their assistance could be harnessed to make other contacts. In Ohio, a letter describing the project and including a postal card for reply was sent to the members who were to be interviewed in a given week. Those who did not respond to this or to follow-up letters were finally contacted through personal introductions solicited from members already interviewed—usually those whose desks were located in the prospective respondent's vicinity. That this generally worked out very satisfactorily suggests that breaking the floor up into "neighborhoods" might be a very efficient strategy in interviewing legislators. Interviews were first sought with members who had five or more terms, then with those who had three or four terms, and so on, for the purpose not only of gaining the support of senior members in approaching others, but also of allowing the freshmen to become familiar with the legislative routine and their legislative roles. This strategy subsequently proved advantageous for still another reason: as the session progressed, the senior members and committee chairmen were even more busy, while freshmen or second termers were relatively less engaged and easier to reach.

In California, members were approached for appointments on a schedule that equalized regions, party, and tenure so far as possible for any given period, while in Tennessee interviews during the session were arranged by catching available respondents on the floor. The different ways in which the legislators in the different states were approached may have affected the interviews, but just how we cannot say.

Although some legislators shied away from the interview altogether, for most the only major problem was finding a mutually agreeable time for the interview. A number of appointments were necessarily broken because of unexpected circumstances. Other interviews were interrupted and had to be completed at a second or third setting. In some cases a great deal of time was spent by interviewers in securing interviews, as shown by this plaintive note from one interviewer's report:

The next four times I went to the capitol my luck changed. I spent as much as 14 hours just waiting around for an interview to start or to contact the representative assigned to me to set up a time. These experiences left me with a discouraged outlook on the job of the professional interviewer. It's not so much the time involved or the waiting around that bothered me. It's rather that after all the waiting, and you don't get an interview, it all seems like such a waste.

After the interview, respondents were rated in terms of the degree of cooperation which, according to the interviewer, they had shown during the interview. As Table 18.1 shows, remarkably few respondents in all four states were judged "not very cooperative" or "very uncooperative." In a number of cases where respondents would agree, somewhat reluctantly or impatiently, to give the interviewer a few minutes of his time, they would become so interested in the process of answering the questions that it was difficult to terminate the interview. Here the interview schedule itself was probably the best rapport-building device that the interviewer had. Dozens of very colorful descriptions of respondents' behavior could be cited here. One each for every rating category must suffice to convey some of the flavor of the appraisals reported in Table 18.1:

Table 18.1: Interviewer ratings of respondents' cooperation

	N.J.	Calif.	Ohio	Tenn.
Very cooperative	17	38	86	70
Cooperative	55	52	61	42
	72	90	147	112
Not very cooperative	6	16	12	7
Very uncooperative	1	3	2	0
	7	19	14	7
Not recorded	0	4	1	1
Total	79	113	162	120

Very cooperative:

He went out of his way to set up the interview time, and was almost overly generous in giving his answers. He seems to be a rather thoughtful, sensitive person who is very serious about assuming his responsibilities. R is almost unnaturally loquacious, occasionally giving the impression of a public speech. His thoughts are well organized and he frequently enumerated his answers. He was, in general, quite relaxed—he smoked and leaned back in his chair and took his time answering.

Cooperative:

R was interviewed without prior letter after interviewer had been introduced to R by Senator Y. Interviewer said it would take an hour or so. R said, "well, maybe we can get started for half an hour." But the interview went on for an hour and a quarter. It was a difficult interview. R had a tendency to wander off. Took things either for granted or was very positive. Translated the questions as to how they pertained to himself. A very pleasant person.

Not very cooperative:

I continually had the feeling the respondent was neither honest nor interested. He opened and read letters during the interview. He seemed interested in answering only in terms of what he thought would make him appear in the best light. According to the pages he is a heavy drinker and not too well liked. His emphasis throughout the interview was on the value of mixing with his fellow legislators. He seems to have moved from the backroom of a pool hall or bar into the legislature without much visible change.

Very uncooperative:

Resentful of his constituents, contemptuous of some of his colleagues. He mentioned an infection, and has been out recently, which could account for his abruptness. Very perceptive and well-formulated answers, but resentful of questions even when he gave the answers. Quite annoyed at any attempts to probe or even clarify answers. I don't really know what's eating at him.

An effort was made in all states to interview all legislators. In fact, 100 per cent of the New Jersey, 94 per cent of the California and Ohio, and 91 per cent of the Tennessee legislators were finally interviewed.[10] Only three legislators in California and Ohio, and two in Tennessee, refused outright to be interviewed. One each of the California, Ohio, and Tennessee refusers variously demonstrated hostility to academic research. They were rather inarticulate men who spoke only very rarely in the legislature. The second Ohioan was quite articulate and spent a good deal of time with the interviewer discussing things political, but steadfastly refused a formal interview. A third Ohioan broke off the interview in progress and asked that the schedule be destroyed after becoming very irritated over a scale

[10] See Table 2.3, p. 36 above, for details.

question. One Californian, a busy and influential member, refused
point blank to take the time. The other, an aged and crochety gentleman, simply stumped down the hall muttering: "God damn!
Interview! God damn!" A number of other legislators not interviewed, in spite of frequent attempts, evaded the interview, usually
by pleading lack of time or by failing to keep appointments. A few
others were not interviewed simply because mutually convenient
arrangements could not be made despite sincere efforts on both sides.
In New Jersey, one legislator refused to arrange for a formal appointment. However, he answered most of the questions in the course
of informal talks with the interviewer at various times. At the end
of the interview period he was mailed the series of scale items and
told that all the other legislators had answered them. He responded
and returned the questionnaire.

Evaluation of the characteristics of the non-respondents indicates
that in California they were fairly evenly distributed with regard to
party and tenure. However, three of the senators not interviewed
were quite powerful senior members, a fact which constitutes a
distinct bias. In Ohio, of the eleven members not interviewed, eight
were Republicans and three were Democrats, two were senators and
nine were representatives. The most serious omission was the Democratic minority floor leader in the House, a man who "successfully"
(and, the interviewer felt, deliberately) evaded the interview for
reasons of his own, in spite of at least a half dozen attempts to
arrange for an appointment, including promises by his secretary. The
twelve members not interviewed in Tennessee comprise eight Democrats and four Republicans, four from East, five from Middle and
three from West Tennessee, a set quite representative in terms of
urban-rural characteristics of their districts; however, these twelve
members also included the House Republican Floor Leader, the
Senate Democratic Co-Leader, and a very senior Republican senator
who is a former Floor Leader. The loss of interviews with officers,
of course, was more serious than the loss of member interviews. The
organizational structure of an institutionalized group cannot be
"sampled," nor "substitutes" or "replacements" found for missing respondents, since each officer, by virtue of his official role, is "unique."

Length of interviews. Especially during the closing days of the
legislative sessions, the problem of completing interviews in the face
of intense pressures on members was a critical one. It was particularly pronounced in California, but it arose also in the other three
states.

As the time schedule of the whole project did not allow postsession interviews in California, there was no really satisfactory means in that state for securing an interview geared for completion, on the average, to an hour and a half. The strategy adopted was to seek an appointment, however brief, with each member, and delete portions of the interview as the particular situation demanded. As a result, interview time in California for the early recess interviews ranged from one and a half to five hours, the average being about two and a half hours. Early in March, it was still possible to secure interviews in members' offices that lasted from an hour and a half to two hours and covered all questions. After April 1, the average length of the California interviews declined to 45 minutes, though only two lasted less than half an hour, and these were with busy members who were brief and to the point in their responses.

The time difficulties encountered in California were largely avoided in Ohio by the fortuitous circumstance that, for other reasons already mentioned, an effort had been made to interview legislative leaders, committee chairmen, and senior members early in the session. But even here time pressure in the last few weeks required, in a number of cases, elimination of the "education issue" series. Interviews ranged from one to five hours, the average being about two hours. In New Jersey the length of interviews varied from one to five hours, with the average being about an hour and a half; in fifteen interviews the "education issue" series was dropped because of pressure of time. In Tennessee, except for six interviews omitting the "education issue" series, and occasional failures to answer one or another question, all interviews were successfully completed. As has already been mentioned in Chapter 2, the shortest interview—surprisingly full despite its brevity, thanks to this respondent's terse and rapid-fire manner— took barely half an hour, the longest somewhat over four hours. Nine interviews were completed in an hour or less, and the average length of the interviews was an hour and a half.

How the length of the interview affected results—and, possibly, the results obtained affected the interview situation—is difficult to say. Undoubtedly, differential probing by interviewers introduces a good deal of variability into data derived from open-ended questions, affecting the quality and length of interviews and creating certain statistical problems with which it is very difficult to deal (see below, p. 459). Our general impression is that length of interview bears less relation to the "quality" of the data for useful analysis, however, than to the personal characteristics of the respondents—

garrulity, timidity, deafness, egoism, senility, or experience, for example.

The various ways in which interviews had sometimes to be abridged have been referred to in Chapter 2 (Table 2.2, p. 35). Of the various abridgement procedures, only elimination of the "education issue" series had been agreed on beforehand as a possible way of shortening the interviews. The problem of cutting the interview was most acute in California where several additional modifications were sometimes made in the order of the interview schedule: (1) the biographical questions were put at the end of the interview, rather than at the beginning, where they tended to divert respondents into reminiscences about their private lives; they could be held a few extra minutes to answer questions about themselves which were easier and required less thought than questions about the legislative process; (2) the scale items were handed to the respondent at the end of the interview with the request that he fill them out at his convenience and give them to his secretary where they could be picked up later (only three respondents out of the 113 failed to do so).[11] With these abridgements and modifications, the interview could be completed in approximately one hour. Where the time available was known in advance to be less than this, other questions were omitted, and sometimes unexpected interruptions terminated the interview before it was completed,

Summary. Our experience suggests that there is little justification for believing that politicians are unapproachable for interview, or that, if they can be approached and subjected to formal interview by a stranger, they will be evasive if not deceitful in responding to questions concerning themselves and their activities.

We have already reported our confidence in the reliability of legislators' answers to our questions, and the interviewers' evaluations of respondents' frankness which provide one important basis for that confidence (see Table 2.4, above, p. 37). A fuller understanding of what interviewers considered frankness or lack of it on respondents' part can be gained from comments from interviewers' thumbnail sketches accompanying the reports giving different ratings to particular legislators:

[11] This raises the question, of course, whether the items were actually completed by the respondent himself. It is known that Congressmen habitually delegate such form-completion chores to their staff assistants, with instructions to "answer as you think (or know) I would answer them." We doubt that state legislators with little or no staff are apt to follow this procedure.

Very frank:

He answered with a minimum of words and never gave two reasons until he was probed. Even then he often said, "Well, I'm pretty sure that's all." On certain questions such as how he became interested in politics, or his criticism of the Speaker of the House, he spoke freely and fluently. He didn't seem to have any really well developed ideas about the legislature, and when he jokingly said he was there for the money I perceived the truth. He was concerned with organizational matters as he often brought up procedural things where they weren't called for. I feel that all the answers he gave were sincere and that he wasn't holding back—he merely didn't have much more to say. Even though he only mentioned three people as his friends, several men came over to him during the interview and spoke to him about meeting at the Athletic Club; so I'm under the impression that he only gave me the names of his friends in long standing even though I had made it clear to him that we wanted the names of those people he was more friendly with than others.

Frank:

R's estrangement from the vital core of legislative activity (meager knowledge of lobbies, inability to see even after constant probing that the House splits along certain divisions) might in part be attributed to his poor sight and hearing at the age of 69. He seemed friendly and willing to give information if he had it. His hesitancy to name those he respected and personal friends was not from fear of any indiscretions on our part, I feel, but because none came to mind as particularly close, and he didn't seem quite sure whom to name among his secondary acquaintances. On questions where there is no answer, or one that is almost irrelevant, the difficulty was usually that, although I repeated the question changing the wording, he had just never thought of these problems and had no reply.

Not very frank:

He is verbal and expresses himself well. His jokes often tend to relax the situation. However, I did not feel that R was at all relaxed. He was very conscious of what he was saying, and what I was writing. He constantly looked at what I wrote and several times asked to see it. At one point he said, "You write down everything, don't you?" He seemed rather worried about what he might say. Several times he said, "I'm not giving you much, am I?", or "I'm probably the worst interview you ever had."

Very evasive:

I find it difficult to give my impression of R, for his answers at times appeared to be very evasive. Our rapport seemed excellent, but I felt he was giving me pat phrases as a means of not answering certain questions. He seemed to be a collector of descriptive phrases and little quotes. He was extremely hesitant to commit himself to any one viewpoint that might in the least be considered controversial. Yet, he appeared to be a very sharp and alert person who is aware of what is going on about him and knows whom to see to get what he wants accomplished.

A major conclusion, then, is that a specialized population like American state legislators will provide reliable data when directly and intensively interviewed. Although both the quality and the frankness of answers may vary from one respondent to another, we believe the aggregate of data obtained is more than adequate for purposes of basic research. All other conclusions, of course, assume such reliability of the interview data. The most important of these conclusions may be summarized as follows:

1. Useful research in political institutional settings may be done by the technique of interviewing finite populations (rather than samples) to gather data for comparative analysis. (The problem of population versus sample interviewing is discussed in more detail in the last section of this chapter.)

2. Particular attention should be paid to the situation in which politicians work, the constant demands made on their time and energies, and the time or place when they are most available for interviewing. Advance efforts to communicate the nature and objectives of the project, receive formal endorsement for conducting the interviews from leaders, build up confidence in the integrity of the project, and convey an understanding of it are well repaid.

3. Individual recalcitrant personalities set an upper limit on attempts to interview an entire population. But initial reluctance to be interviewed does not necessarily mean that a respondent will not give frank and complete (or even enthusiastic) responses. Patience and persistence help to overcome this. On the other hand, there is evidence that the small percentage of persons who make a sustained effort to avoid being interviewed (perhaps from 2 to 5 per cent), include some whose unwillingness to cooperate comes from their inability to communicate and articulate generally. The quality of the results obtained at this extreme is likely to be low, from the standpoint of coherence, frankness, and completeness.

4. The actual interview time is a rather small proportion, perhaps 25 per cent, of the time and expense involved in nearly complete coverage of a universe like a legislature. For an interview of an hour and a half or more, one should be prepared to spend one man-day per respondent of field time to achieve an over-all coverage of 90 per cent or better. The larger part of this "field day" must be spent in laying the groundwork for interviewing, arranging appointments, being "stood up," being interrupted, pursuing respondents down corridors, and cultivating pages or secretaries.

Finally, the systematic interview technique has a very important ancillary advantage. Interviewing numerous politicians in their natural habitat gives the researcher insight into the institution and the dynamic environment in which they work, as well as into their attitudes and perceptions, that is second only to that obtained from holding office. Yet it preserves the detachment and provides the broad view that must be the mark of the observer scholar.

CONSTRUCTION OF THE MASTER CODE AND CODING

A code is a set of roles for "translating" raw data into a "language" understandable to machines. Basically, each category of data must be associated with a unique punch hole or pattern of punched holes in a Hollerith card. The problem of designing a code must not be confused with the prior problem of determining the categories into which the data must be classified for purposes of analysis. But the construction of a code often stimulates the researcher to clarify and define more sharply the analytical categories of his design. In a study which relies heavily on open-ended questions, the construction of the master code and the coding process go far toward determining the quality of the results.

In developing codes for our abundance of data we sought to steer around these traps: (1) providing categories only for what our theoretical framework called for; (2) providing categories for everything in the interview protocols, even if the material was not or did not seem to be directly relevant to our research design; and (3) exhausting the theoretical possibilities by including categories with few or no responses. In general, we leaned over backwards to provide codes for almost all empirical data that might be of some use, on the assumption that it was probably better to know what we had and what could be finally ignored than not to know what we might possibly have missed. In some cases this strategy paid off in valuable data; in other instances, it did not.

The procedure of developing codes directly from interviews—a procedure to which we saw no alternative—may lead to inconsistencies in code construction, such as overlapping codes and bi-dimensionality within a code. In general, the empirical material in a particular open-ended question was continually referred to the theoretical objectives and concepts of the study and to our previous specifications of data requirements. However, systematic ordering of the data along a single dimension is not easy to achieve with responses from persons who are not a random sample of the American people, but who are, on the whole, highly motivated, highly articulate, and at times highly ambiguous respondents—masters in "the fine art of seeming to say something without doing so." For instance, the responses to Question 16—asking respondents to "describe the job of being a legislator: what are the most important things you should do here?"—yielded six different codes as follows:

> Card 3
> Col. 6 Characterization of job
> Col. 7 Objectives of job
> Col. 8 Criteria of decision
> Col. 9 Lawmaking functions
> Col. 10 Non-lawmaking functions
> Col. 11 Service functions

Codes for open-ended questions were developed by going over a number of interviews to find out what kinds of things were said by respondents with sufficient frequency to warrant a code or an item in a code.   In general, proliferation of items or categories to catch minor variations in responses is undesirable because it reduces coding reliability.   On the other hand it is desirable to leave some categories narrow enough to catch some of the linguistic flavor of a particular response pattern. We inclined in the latter direction especially in connection with those data which were to be used primarily as "descriptive variables."   For instance, the data concerning the "rules of the game" (see Chapter 7) produced 42 specific categories distributed in six code classes.

Wherever possible, specific response items were classified into broad code categories whose limits were clearly defined theoretically, although this required care to ensure that separate responses would have easily recognized equivalence.   For this purpose, we sometimes used a column on the IBM-card as a generic category.   In the case of the 42 "rules of the game," for instance, the rules were classified in the following codes:

Card 3
Col. 21 Rules regarding predictability of behavior
Col. 22 Rules regarding restraint and canalization of conflict
Col. 23 Rules which expedite legislative business
Col. 24 Rules which promote group cohesion or solidarity
Col. 25 Tactical rules primarily for benefit of individual member
Col. 26 "Rules" which are primarily desirable personal qualities

This procedure made it possible to use the column as a single analytical category.   In other words, the form and general content of our master code was in accord with the theoretical objectives of the study, while the specific items within each code were more likely to be based on actual responses to the questions themselves.   This allowed us to combine categories in the analysis without running the risk of producing illogical or unnatural combinations.

Code revision and coding process. Since the major part of the coding was to be done by the researchers themselves, code revision could go hand-in-hand with coding. In order to make sure that the researchers understood the definitions of the categories, four interviews were coded collectively but secretly. Agreement was reached on about 90 per cent of the items coded. The researchers then coded about 40 interviews individually. No test of intercoder reliability was made, but disagreements were discussed and the codes continuously revised in the early stage of the coding process. Finally, twelve interviews were coded and check-coded before production coding began.

The master code was given its final form after the bulk of the interviews had been coded throughout the Fall of 1957. During this period of individual coding each researcher recorded responses he was unable to code or about which he felt uncertain. These difficulties were subsequently dealt with one by one in conference and assigned to an appropriate category by joint decision. In a few cases, new codes or categories were added to the master code. In general, the main difficulty was not agreement on definitions of codes or categories, but rather interpretation of ambiguous responses and their assignment.

The California interviews were partly coded by two senior researchers, partly by graduate students. They were rechecked by the California researcher. New Jersey interviews were coded by the senior researcher in that state and check-coded by a research assistant. Ohio interviews were coded by the senior researcher and checked by himself and a research assistant. Tennessee interviews were coded by the principal researcher; two graduate students check-coded 10 per cent, and other interviews were spot-checked for coding errors.

In spite of the many preparations and precautions, it would have been preferable if the coders had been together during the entire coding period. This was impossible. Undoubtedly, the main problem involved was not so much one of the usual coding errors as of classificatory judgments which could have been easily ironed out by immediate consultation. Of course, this might have tended to make for systematic group bias in assigning responses to particular categories rather than systematic individual bias. To what extent systematic coding bias crept into the coding process we do not know. A particular source of such bias may have been the particular analytical interests of a researcher who may have read more into responses falling into a given category than the other researchers. One alternative might have been to distribute the 474 questionnaires among all four coders. But this would have involved a significant cost: some references to procedures, events, and political phenomena would have been unintelligible to or misinterpreted by a coder familiar with only one state. Coding this sort of material is not a mere mechanical process, but requires both political insight and analytical judgment.

There may be some biases due to interviewer and coder being the same person in each state. Any such biases are most likely to appear in gross interstate comparisons, however. Where related differences appear as well between parties, chambers, or other groups within a state, we know they do not result from this kind of bias.

STATISTICAL PROBLEMS

The kind of data used in our analyses, as well as the procedures used in collecting and processing them, create a number of statistical problems, most of them relevant to the question: Why are tests of significance not reported in this volume, as they were in some of the earlier articles using the same data? The answers are not simple or obvious, and the way they were finally reached demonstrates once again that in the present state of political science research one cannot draw a clear line between *what he learns* and *how he learns it*. Our research technique involved a unique combination of three familiar methods: (1) a *comparative* study of *more than two* similar institutions, (2) by *personal interviews* (following a fixed schedule), (3) with nearly the *entire population* (universe) of persons constituting the institution. Not being statiticians, we do not intend to enter the recent and continuing controversy among experts better qualified than are we to decide how statistical tests should be used.[12] But a candid discussion of our statistical problems in dealing with data which does not fit neatly into any of the usual categories of surveys may not only show why we treated our data as we did but also contribute to establishing agreed-upon tests for this sort of research effort.

[12] See, in particular, Hanan C. Selvin, "A Critique of Tests of Significance in Survey Research," *American Sociological Review,* **22**:519–527 (1957); and Leslie Kish, "Some Statistical Problems in Research Design," *ibid.,* **24**:328–338 (1959). See also Seymour H. Lipset, Martin Trow and James Coleman, *Union Democracy* (Glencoe: The Free Press, 1956), pp. 427–32: "Statistical Problems;" and Hanan C. Selvin, "Statistical Significance and Sociological Theory," mimeographed revision of a paper read at the American Sociological Association, Chicago, 1959.

Initially the Chi-square test was used to determine whether differences implied a statistically significant relationship. Frankly, the initial decision to use this and related significance tests was made because it never occurred to anyone that they should not be used in what was then conceived to be a survey research project. But the more the data were analyzed, the more the whole process by which they had been collected and handled was re-examined, the more it became clear that Chi-square and other significance tests might not be properly applicable.

The "sample" and the "universe." Tests of statistical significance are based on the assumption that the data come from a random sample of the population which is analyzed. The initial decision to interview the entire memberships of the four legislatures was taken precisely to avoid the familiar sampling worries of the survey researcher. If all legislators were interviewed, the problem of making statistical inferences from a sample to a population would not arise. There would be no reason, then, to make any statistical tests of significance. Although we did not succeed in interviewing our entire populations, we did come close enough to the 100 per cent mark in order not to worry about a sampling problem on that score.

Let us suppose we calculate Chi-square by the customary method for a difference of 11 per cent between, say 53 per cent giving a certain response in California and 42 per cent giving it in Ohio. Assuming 112 of the 120 members in California and 162 of the 173 members in Ohio were interviewed, the difference would fall short of significance at the usual levels ($X^2 = 2.45$, D.F. $= 1$, $.20 > p > .10$). Yet if all the 8 Californians and 12 Ohioans not interviewed had been interviewed and had given the "wrong" answers (from the standpoint of the hypothesis), this would reduce the California percentage to 49 per cent and increase the Ohio percentage to 46 per cent, still leaving a difference (for the universe!) of 3 per cent. Thus the Chi-square test would, in this hypothetical case, have rejected a "genuine" difference between two groups in the universe. We would have done better to assume that we interviewed the universe and that any difference between the two groups was "genuine." Chi-square and similar tests do not measure the importance of such differences as "genuinely" existing whatever their magnitude may be.

On the other hand, it often became desirable to combine data from all four states in a single set in order to have sufficient cases for studying bivariate or multivariate relationships—e.g., the interpenetration of role orientations. But when this is done the problem of sampling and statistical tests arises all over again, for we are no longer dealing with four particular universes but with 474 interviews as a "sample" of some larger entity. This larger universe might conceivably be defined in various ways. One possibility is that it comprises the 7,000 persons sitting in the 48 American legislatures in 1957. But if this is our universe we have a very bad sample of it. We have a two-stage sampling design, selecting 4 out of 48 clusters and sampling them at the rate of about 90 per cent. No statistician would recommend such a lumpy sample. Furthermore, our four states were not selected at random: three were selected because of accessibility, the fourth to complement these. By combining them without weighting, we give Ohio legislators twice the influence on the total percentage that we give New Jersey legislators, simply because there are twice as many of them. Altogether, without even considering response biases characteristic of our survey along with all others, we must conclude that the assumption of random sampling implicit in the application of significance tests is hardly justified if we are sampling the universe of legislators in the year 1957.

Another possibility is that we were sampling a universe of legislators past and present. The concept of such a "hypothetical" universe makes explicit a point often overlooked by political scientists in the past. Any case study or comparative study is in a sense a sample ($N = 1$) of a universe of political phenomena. The precise limits of this universe are not well-defined, but there is a consensus on their location in rough terms. We say certain studies "pertain to another culture," or they "are out of date" or they deal with "atypical conditions." The interview method forces one to at least consider this problem, of which students of comparative government of the anecdotal school often seem to be unaware. If the writer does not define his universe, the reader must. From our standpoint, since we wish some generality attached to our findings, this "universe" is attractive. We should not like to believe our conclusions are confined to four legislature that adjourned over four years ago, many of whose members have retired from public life by this time. On the other hand, this is not a satisfactory universe to justify mathematical calculations of significance. Chi-square would certainly overestimate the accuracy of our sample of this universe.

In short, whenever we are dealing with some universe other than the particular legislative groups in office in the four states in 1957 we have a sample which is far from random. But random sampling is essential for significance testing precisely because not all factors of possible relevance in an analysis are controlled. This is, of course, an overstatement of the sampling requirement, for *all* factors are never controlled even in carefully designed experiments. But we can certainly assume that in our study not all factors of possible relevance were even considered due to the exploratory character of the project. It deserves emphasis, therefore, that randomization is necessary for valid statistical inference because through random sampling uncontrollable but constant factors will be so distributed that they have an equal chance to influence results. Even if, for certain broad comparative purposes, we may regard the four legislatures as "typical," the conditions of random sampling assumed by tests of significance were not fulfilled.

The statistical quandary for comparative studies such as ours can be expressed oversimply as follows: significance tests underestimate the accuracy of our interviews as they apply specifically to the 1957 sessions of the four legislatures studied, but they overestimate it when generalizations are made to other legislative bodies and other times. We see no easy solution to this problem.

The problem of ex post facto hypotheses. There is a further reason for not employing tests of significance in this study. Although the project was designed with theoretical considerations in mind, and although we had specified a limited number of particular hypotheses prior to the field work, an exploratory investigation of this nature cannot possibly formulate in advance all the hypotheses for which data may be available. In actual fact, even if there are a priori hypotheses, they are likely to be modified once initial tabulations are examined, and further hypotheses are developed on inspection of the data. But if hypotheses are adjusted or newly proposed after the data have been looked at, it is certainly unnecessary to test such ex post facto hypotheses for statistical significance of the differences or relations between variables which have been discovered by inspection. The process is circular: what is to be proven has already been proved. This procedure gives a spurious impression of validity. It in no way tells us anything significant about the real distribution of the differences or relations in the population.

We do not contend that there is anything improper about the construction of such a posteriori hypotheses. On the contrary, it was one of the objectives of our project, as of any exploratory effort. But our data permit us only to formulate hypotheses; new data must be collected to test them.

Even in the specification of hypotheses there is a possible statistical fallacy. The investigator has in his mind a number of alternative hypotheses. He has at his disposal a great many tables, and the possible comparisons run into the hundreds of thousands. Some of these tables support, others reject a hypothesis. Some tables may be discarded because they are unsatisfactory from a measurement point of view; some are based on often vague, sometimes contradictory, and at times altogether foolish ideas. To report only those tables which seem substantial may be quite legitimate, but to subject them to tests of significance is another matter. Mercifully, most reports spare the reader mention of the hypotheses which have been rejected and present him with only the remainder, properly documented with Chi-squares. But, even though Chi-square may document these hypotheses as "not due to chance," it is quite possible that they are due to chance because of the use of probability standards in eliminating all the others.

Non-response bias and related problems. Statistical difficulties arise also in connection with the data derived from open-end questions. Such questions created great heterogenity in answer patterns for a variety of reasons. As a result, many respondents could not be classified in appropriate categories: their failure to give answers coordinate with the bulk of responses from other respondents, even if they had been asked a question and then thoroughly probed, made them "not ascertained" cases—in effect, non-respondents. Because of such non-response, it was often advisable to use as the base for computing percentages only those respondents whose answers could be coded in a particular category. In such instances, it would not be justifiable to assume that these "effective" respondents constitute a random sample of all possible respondents, nor even of all those we interviewed or of all the members of the particular legislature treated. It is impossible to make inferences from those limited data to possible distributions which might have been obtained if we had asked only direct, closed questions and had received a full quota of responses. For this reason, the distributions in many of our tables are, at most, suggestive indicators of the way legislators might respond if all were "forced," by closed questions or otherwise, to do so.

Statistical tests of significance are intended to measure whether differences observed between two or more groups have been produced by random error of sampling, not to appraise the effects of incidental variations in response patterns which are uncontrolled and, by virtue of the open-end interview question, uncontrollable. Some such biases could, of course, be controlled ex post facto, and frequently have been so controlled—as, for instance, the effect of lower education on articulateness. But how can one control for a respondent's hostility to a question, or his general mood? Indeed, this type of bias arising from the "not ascertained" categorization of respondents may influence results more effectively than random errors of sampling. A test designed to measure the latter is in no way relevant to the former.

There are other difficulties stemming from the interview situation which may have affected responses and which may disturb relationships between variables that are analyzed. These are themselves factors difficult to control. For instance, though we believe, as pointed out earlier in this chapter, that the age and status of different interviewers did not significantly disturb the results of an interview, we have no possible way to control for possible bias in this respect. Similarly, the time and place of the interview may introduce a good deal of bias. We cannot measure the effect of place on interview results. We could possibly control ex post facto for the time factor, but, again, the size of our samples makes this quite unfeasible.

Random errors other than sampling errors. The possible interference of extraneous uncontrolled factors—"random variables," i.e., errors assumed to be randomized in survey research—which are confounded with the main analytical variables is not the sole source of disturbance in relationships among the latter. Much attention has been given to random errors of sampling, but not so much to errors of recording, coding, or processing the data. Research seeks to be on guard against such errors, of course, and some studies have been made of the extent of such errors. In our own work, as has been indicated, we took great care in these respects, but the extent to which errors of this sort occurred we really do not know.

The problem of data manipulation, stemming from the researcher's freedom to handle his data in certain ways which may facilitate finding support of a hypothesis, is the most obvious point where such errors might occur. They seem particularly likely in the case of tables based on scales and other continuous variables, where collapsing of categories is often necessitated by the small numbers of cases in particular cells. But when this is resorted to, it should be done independently of the relationship which is investigated. If the cutting points are made where they tend to support a hypothesis, thus increasing the size of a relationship, the subsequent test of statistical significance can only be considered spurious. To the best of our knowledge, we did not set the cutting points of our scales in this fashion, though some columns or rows in tables may have been collapsed on inspection of the data in such a way that they would unintentionally tend to maximize support for some theoretical assumption or inference.

How significance was evaluated. For a variety of reasons, then, we came gradually to the conclusion that the usual tests of statistical significance were of little use in our analysis. In the process, we were sensitized to certain inadequancies and flaws in our data which had to be taken into account whatever statistical use we might make of the data. Absolving ourselves of the necessity to report Chi-square or other significance-measures, however, only made the problem of standards of discrimination more acute. Without some such standards we should have had no basis for deciding what differences to report, what differences to consider interesting or important, or what conclusions to draw from differences discovered. The standards we used, as they emerged from our continual wrestling with the kinds of problem we have been describing, can be summarized briefly:

1. *Consistency of finding with preliminary expectations* (for a priori hypotheses only): Did legislators behave as our preliminary expectations (theory) indicated they would? If they did we felt they had in fact demonstrated a conclusion and significance tests were justified. If they did not, the absence of a difference was a meaningful finding, and we have called attention to it.

2. *Size of difference:* Statistical significance does not necessarily mean substantive importance. A very large sample may generate a high level of significance but the difference between the proportions being compared be very small from a substantive point of view, and of little interest to the political scientist. On the other hand, a large difference in proportions may of necessity be based on small numbers (e.g., if it involves the behavior of a small but critical group, like legislative officers), but the difference, though not statistically significant may be of considerable theoretical interest and suggestive of possible hypotheses to be treated elsewhere.

3. *Size of subsample:* Since all of us had previous experience with survey analysis, we performed a substantial part of our analysis with significance tests in view, and actually calculated hundreds of chi squares and estimated hundreds more from nomographs. Even though we eventually chose not to report these differences, it would be idle to contend we were unaware of them. Moreover, we were chary of reporting even substantial differences if they were based on small N's (normally less than 20) unless they qualified by one of the other criteria used.

4. *Internal replication:* Even a weak tendency, if it had theoretical relevance and if it reoccurred, in the same direction, in all four legislatures, all eight chambers, or all 16 parties-in-chambers (or for that matter in all but one of the chambers or parties) has some validity.

This is in fact a variation of the "sign test" which is another measure of statistical significance. This sort of evaluation is particularly adapted to a series of surveys where independent interviewer and coder bias are possibilities.[13] To the extent that our interviewing and coding errors were personal this served as a check on biases as well as random errors. We feel more confidence in a small difference that is consistent than in a large difference in the aggregate sample that is made up of strong differences in one direction and weak ones in the other.

5. *Consistency of results:* We are interested in functional relationships between variables—causal and others. The existence of such relationships may be increasingly supported by the discovery of other, logically connected relationships. In other words, patterns in the appearance of correlations may support a finding more meaningfully, given the kind of data we have, than some quite independent set of tests applied to discrete but disjointed relationships. Moreover, a single hypothesis is not demonstrated by a single table, but by a network of tables. But such testing is difficult. Though we tried to discover an integrated system of roles, for instance, the particular hypothesized relations among discrete role-orientations are relatively imprecise and loose. The fact that one table does not support the whole hypothesized system does not mean that the whole system collapses. Some relations in different tables may be quite independent. But we cannot determine the degree of such interdependence or independence. Acceptance of the null hypothesis, it must be recalled, does not mean a relationship does not exist, merely that we cannot find support for it.

The criteria that have just been given are admittedly flexible. Two analysts can justifiably disagree (and members of the team did so at several preliminary stages). At the present time we have no answers to this problem; only a hope that the statisticians will eventually provide us with some.

Use of the comparative method. Finally, we must not overlook the fact that this study combined the survey and the comparative method. The latter has a longer and not unillustrious history in the hands of political scientists and anthropologists studying institutions. The recorded interviews deal with verbal statements, perceptions, attitudes, and inter-relations of persons occupying certain statuses at a particular point in time. Another phase of the study, quite inde-

[13] Selvin, "Statistical Significance and Sociological Theory," *op. cit.*, p. 15; William Buchanan and Hadley Cantril, *How Nations See Each Other* (Urbana: University of Illinois Press, 1953) pp. 109–113.

pendent of these particular occupants, deals with descriptions of certain institutions. These descriptions are embodied in law, precedent, observation of the system in action, and printed matter generated by the system. One of our objects was, by bringing to bear new concepts and different techniques, to more adequately describe and analyze the consequences of these legislative parameters.

Had we not interviewed a single member, but merely observed and absorbed (as we had considerable time to do in the periods between interviews), we would have had a certain amount of data to incorporate into our structure. A great deal may be learned from just this sort of data, as any textbook in comparative government will demonstrate. To make a sharp distinction between our use of the literature on legislatures in general and these legislatures in particular, our observation of the system in action, and our tabulations of interviews recorded on punch cards, or to say which body of data generated hypotheses, which tested them, which confirmed the tests, would be to make unrealistic distinctions. Each source of data and hypotheses contributed in its own way to establishing the "significance" of our findings in the larger, non-statistical sense.

APPENDIX 1

Construction of role types

PURPOSIVE, REPRESENTATIONAL, AND AREAL ROLES were derived mainly from responses to Question 10 (see Appendix 6). Each total answer was broken up into individual statements, according to the manifest content of the statements, and the content items coded under one of the five categories:

a. Characterization of job
b. Objectives of job
c. Criteria of decision
d. Lawmaking functions
e. Non-lawmaking functions

In general, purposive roles were derived mainly from data concerning characterization of job, representational roles from data about criteria of decision, and areal roles from data about objectives of the job, although other categories were also used in each case. All 474 legislators were classified into one of the purposive roles but, because of the open-endedness of the question, there were a number of non-classifiable respondents in each of the other two roles distributed as follows: (a) representational roles: California, 56 per cent; New Jersey, 32 per cent; Ohio, 30 per cent; and Tennessee, 35 per cent; (b) areal roles: California, New Jersey, and Ohio, 31 per cent, respectively; Tennessee, 62 per cent. The following is a summary of the codes and categories from which the different role types were derived.

1.1 PURPOSIVE ROLES

Role Type	Code Category	Content Item
Tribune	Characterization of job	a. Find out (know) will of people
		b. Represent concerns (express needs, demands, will) of people: a public trust, benefit people
		c. Protect (defend) interests of people
Inventor	Characterization of job	d. Solving problems
	Objectives of job	a. General welfare
		b. Specific policies
		c. Better government
Broker	Characterization of job	e. Balance conflicting interests (demands), general: all sides, over-all picture
		f. Balance: constituents versus state (general)
		g. Balance: group versus group
		h. Balance: constituents versus group
		i. Balance: state (general) versus group

Role Type	Code Category	Content Item
Ritualist	Lawmaking functions Non-lawmaking functions	All categories a. Investigation b. Appointments and confirmation c. Review and safeguard of the Constitution: prevent abuse of laws
Opportunist	Not ascertained	Not ascertained

1.2 REPRESENTATIONAL ROLES

Trustee	Criteria of decision	a. Make decisions on basis of conscience: principles, justice, right, etc. b. Make decisions on basis of own judgment and understanding: consideration of facts, appraisal of interests, etc.
Delegate	Criteria of decision	c. Make decisions on basis of instructions or orders: by constituents d. Make decisions on basis of instructions or orders: by interest groups e. Make decisions on basis of instructions or orders: by party

Role Type	Code Category	Content Item
Politico[1]	Criteria of Decision	f. Make decisions by weighing own judgment and/ or conscience versus instructions
		g. Combines "a" or "b" with "c", "d," or "e"

1.3 AREAL ROLES

Role Type	Code Category	Content Item
District oriented	Objectives of Job	d. Interests of district
		e. Interests of district *above* state
State oriented	Objectives of Job	f. Interests of state
		g. Interests of state *above* district
District-state oriented	Objectives of Job	h. Interests of district and state *equal*

1.4 PRESSURE-GROUP ROLES

This typology was constructed inferentially by combining a measure of legislators' friendliness or hostility toward pressure-group activity and a measure of their level of knowledge or awareness of pressure-group activity in their own immediate legislative situations. Attitude toward pressure-group activity was measured by a four-item Likert-type scale[2] based on responses to Questions 21-a, 39-j, 39-u, and 39-y (see Appendix 6). After the scale was constructed and tested, twenty-five respondents who answered only three of these questions were classified into one of five scale types (ranging from "most" to "least friendly to pressure-group activity"), on the basis of the three questions they

---

[1] It will be noted that the role of politico combines a "pure" category—"f"—with combinations of "a" or "b," on the one hand and "c," "d," or "e," on the other hand. Differences among the coders with regard to item "f" introduced a good deal of unreliability in this connection. Hence it seemed preferable to combine all possibly relevant responses, making for a rawer but more reliable classification.

[2] See Rensis Likert, "A Technique for the Measurement of Attitudes," *Archives of Psychology*, No. 140 (1932).

did answer. The value of "discriminatory power" of each item (1.3, 1.5, 2.0, and 1.9 respectively) is well above the 1.0 difference usually considered necessary, in view of the fact that it was measured by comparing the high and low *thirds* (actually top 32 per cent and bottom 35 per cent), rather than the more usual comparison of upper and lower quartiles.

To measure awareness of lobbying activity, respondents were asked to identify the names on a list of eleven (in California, ten) lobbyists. A respondent was credited with a "correct" answer to each name if he identified the organizational tie, the general type of interest represented, or some particular legislative measure of concern for each lobbyist listed. Names on the list had been selected to include lobbyists of varying degrees of presumed familiarity.

To obtain a more precise measure, score values for each lobbyist were weighted to give somewhat greater credit for identifying lesser known than for identifying universally known lobbyists. For each respondent, a total score was computed by adding the score values of each lobbyist he correctly identified.

Because the lobbyist-awareness scores thus obtained cannot be compared directly across state lines, since there is no way of comparing the recognition value of lobbyists in different systems, respondents were rank ordered by their total lobbyist-identification scores and the resulting array divided into quintile groups—the highest fifth being most aware of lobbyists, the lowest fifth being least aware, and so on.[3]

Table A-1 shows the distribution of all legislators among the different awareness-score quintiles, the five scale types of friendliness-hostility to pressure politics, and the three role types constructed from combining the two measures. These legislators in the first four rows of columns I and II were classified as facilitators; those in the first four rows of columns IV and V, as resisters: and those in the inverted-T formed by column III and row V, as neutrals.

The reasoning behind the classification can be briefly summarized. Legislators can be expected to facilitate or to resist the accommodation of group demands according to their relative friendliness or hostility to pressure-group activity. But it seems obvious that the effectiveness of their actions in either facilitating or resisting such demands

---

[3] Garceau and Silverman (*op. cit.*) measured several other dimensions of awareness—ability to identify selected pressure groups and ability to recognize more than one issue on which selected groups had been active. Pretests indicated the single measure based on lobbyist recognition produced results very similar to those obtained by more complex measures; the simple unidimensional measure was therefore used here.

Table A-1: Construction of pressure-group roles from scores for awareness of, and attitude toward, pressure groups

Friendliness-Hostility Scale Types

Awareness Score Quintile	I. (Most)	II.	III.	IV.	V. (Least)	No Answer	Total
I. Top 20%	20	22	19	14	16	4	95
II.	17	25	23	9	15	0	89
III.	17	19	25	15	15	3	94
IV.	28	16	13	13	23	1	94
V. Low 20%	17	18	15	18	16	1	85
No answer	1	7	2	1	3	33	47
Total	100	107	97	70	88	42	504

will also depend upon their knowledge of the actual character of groups and their demands. Behavior which consistently either facilitates or resists group influence in legislative policy making requires at least some minimal knowledge about the world of pressure groups. The uninformed legislator's behavior is likely to be erratic and inconsistent in this respect. Similarly, the legislator who is neutral toward pressure group activity and influence in general can not be expected to behave in any very consistent manner either.

Construction of other scales and measures

2.1 MEASURES OF PARTY COMPETITION IN DISTRICTS

Because the four states differed in the manner and frequency with which district boundaries have been changed, length of terms (Senate), and other respects, it was necessary to define competitiveness of districts individually for each state. The measures take into account both the number of elections won and the percentage distribution of the vote in a given election. Because of the extreme movement of population in California, a supplementary measure was constructed based upon party registration.

California. Definitions for Assembly Districts are based on the elections of 1952, 1954, and 1956; for Senate Districts, on the elections of 1950 and 1954 (even-numbered Senate seats) or 1952 and 1956 odd-numbered Senate seats). Averages, computed for the one, two, or three elections contested, were used only to separate one-party from semi-competitive districts. The definitions of the categories, using election statistics as the basis of classification, are:

One-party Democratic:
    (1) Assembly: seats won three times by Democrats
        Senate: seats won twice by Democrats
    (2) Republicans average 40 per cent or less of two-party vote.

Semi-competitive Democratic:
    (1) Assembly: seats won three times by Democrats
        Senate: seats won twice by Democrats
    (2) Republicans average 41–50 per cent of two-party vote.

Competitive:

> Assembly: Seats won twice by one party, once by other.
> Senate: Seats won once by each party.

Semi-competitive Republican:

> (1) Assembly: seats won three times by Republicans
>   Senate: seats won twice by Republicans
> (2) Republicans average 50–59 per cent of two-party vote.

One-party Republican:

> (1) Assembly: seats won three times by Republicans
>   Senate: seats won twice by Republicans
> (2) Republicans average 60 per cent or more of two-party vote.

Because the general redistricting after the 1950 elections and the gradual elimination of cross-filing after 1952 makes it impossible to compare election statistics before 1950 with those after 1950, current party-registration is used as a further measure of party competition in district. Definitions of categories using this criterion are:

One-party Democratic—Registration 68 per cent or more Democratic
Semi-competitive Democratic—Registration 58–67 per cent Democratic
Competitive—Registration 54–57 per cent Democratic
Semi-competitive Republican—Registration 46–53 per cent Democratic
One-party Republican—Registration 45 per cent or less Democratic

New Jersey. The following definitions of categories were used:

One-party:

> The same party received over 60 per cent of the two-party vote in the last three elections (1951, 1953, 1955).

Semi-competitive:

> The same party received over 55 per cent in the last three elections (but not over 60 per cent in all).

Competitive:

> *Either* different parties won in the last three elections,
> *or*, the dominant party won less than 55 per cent of the two-party vote in one or more of the last three elections.

Ohio. Election data from 1946 to 1956 were used as the base. As a number of districts are multimember districts, i.e., more than one contest takes place in any one election, the total number of contests in the six elections since 1946 was used as an initial device to classify the districts in terms of competition between the two major parties.

For this purpose, the vote cast in multi-member districts was averaged and the mean vote cast for all party candidates was used as the percentage index. Definitions of the categories are:

One party:
>The second party has won less than 25 per cent of the contests (or none), *and*
>
>has won over 40 per cent of the two-party vote in less than four of the elections since 1946.

Semi-competitive:
>The second party has won less than 25 per cent of the contests (or none), *but*
>
>has won 40 per cent or more of the two-party vote in at least four of the elections since 1946.

Competitive:
>Each of the two parties has won at least 25 per cent of all the contests in the six elections since 1946.

Tennessee. As in Ohio, the six elections since 1946 were used in the classification, and, in the case of multimember districts, the percentage was based on the mean vote cast for all party candidates. Definitions of the categories are:

One party:
>(1) The second party has won no more than one contest in the six elections, *and*
>
>(2) Has received 40 per cent or less of the two-party vote in at least four elections, *or* 30 per cent or less in at least five elections.

Semi-competitive:
>(1) The second party has won no more than two contests in the six elections, *and*
>
>(2) Has received more than 40 per cent of the two-party vote in at least four elections *or* at least 30 per cent in at least five elections (but less than 40 per cent in at least four of them).

Competitive:
>(1) The second party has won at least two contests in the six elections, *and*
>
>(2) Has received at least 40 per cent of the two-party vote in at least four of the elections.

Table A-2 shows the number of districts of each type in the four states.

Table A-2: Distribution of state legislators by degree of party competition in electoral districts

District	N.J. N = 79	Ohio N = 173	Calif. N = 120	Tenn. N = 132
Competitive	49%	31%	21%	8%
Semi-competitive	25	30	32	10
One party	26	39	47	82
Total	100%	100%	100%	100%
Index of Competition	+23	−8	−26	−74

2.2 LEGISLATIVE EFFICACY SCALE

This scale, explicitly modeled after the "sense of political efficacy" scale first introduced by the Survey Research Center, University of Michigan, in its study of the 1952 presidential election,[4] is a four-item Guttman-type scale constructed by Ford's method using the counter-sorter.[5] Questions 39-n, 39-i, 39-c, and 39-t furnished the items for the scale, which produced a coefficient of reproducibility of 0.893, barely under Guttman's standard, but sufficiently high to be acceptable. Errors of the individual items remained well within the permissible range of 15 per cent (9 per cent, 11 per cent, 10 per cent, and 13 per cent, respectively). Imperfect response patterns were assigned to perfect scale types by the technique of "minimum error assignment."[6] This procedure yields a five-point scale, but, for analytical purposes, legislative efficacy scale types 0 and 1 were combined into a "low" category, scores 2 and 3 into a "medium" category, and type 4 was left alone as the "high" category, in order to avoid cross-tabulation cells with insufficient numbers of cases. On the basis of this procedure, it was possible to calculate a simple "index of legislative efficacy" by subtracting the proportion of "low" respondents in any tabulation from the proportion of "high" respondents. Table A-3 presents the results of the index for the four states. As the table shows, New Jersey legislators, as a group, had a higher feeling of efficacy than Ohio, California, and Tennessee legislators, and in that order.

An alternative method of securing a summary measure of "sense of legislative efficacy" (used in chapter 13, Table 13.2) multiplies

[4] See Angus Campbell, Gerald Gurin, and Warren E. Miller, *op. cit.*, pp. 187–194.

[5] See Robert N. Ford, "A Rapid Scoring Procedure for Scaling Attitude Questions," in M. W. Riley, J. W. Riley, Jr., and J. Toby, *Sociological Studies in Scale Analysis* (New Brunswick: Rutgers University Press, 1954), pp. 273–305.

[6] See Andrew F. Henry, "A Method of Classifying Non-Scale Response Patterns in a Guttman Scale," *Public Opinion Quarterly* 16:94–106 (1952).

high scorers by a weight of 1.0, medium scorers by 0.5, and low scorers by 0.0. The resulting values are added and averaged, yielding index scores ranging from one to zero. In other words, an index score of 1.0 means that all legislators in a given group are highly efficacious, and a score of zero that all are low in efficacy. The efficacy scores for the four states are also shown in Table A-3.

Table A-3: Index of legislative efficacy for four states

Efficacy Category	Calif. $N = 109$	N.J. $N = 79$	Ohio $N = 160$	Tenn. $N = 118$
High	33%	41%	42%	24%
Medium	33	47	35	49
Low	34	12	23	27
Total	100%	100%	100%	100%
Index of Efficacy	−1	+29	+19	−3
Efficacy Score	0.50	0.64	0.60	0.49

2.3 LIBERALISM-CONSERVATISM (IDEOLOGY)

In spite of the danger of terminological confusion, we combined one political question involving a civil liberties issue (Question 39-s) with two economic items (Questions 39-b and 39-h) in developing a Guttman-type ideology scale. The scale yielded a coefficient of reproducibility of 0.924, with errors for the individual items of 11.7 per cent, 13.8 per cent, and 4.7 per cent, respectively. For purposes of analysis the two types at the "low" end of the original four-point scale were combined into a single "conservative" category. Table A-4

Table A-4: Index of ideology, by party and state

	Calif.		N.J.		Ohio		Tenn.	
Ideology Category	Dem. $N = 50$	Rep. $N = 59$	Dem. $N = 27$	Rep. $N = 52$	Dem. $N = 51$	Rep. $N = 110$	Dem. $N = 95$	Rep. $N = 23$
Liberal	74%	22%	45%	29%	47%	17%	27%	17%
Medium	20	37	33	29	37	19	33	39
Conservative	6	41	22	42	16	64	40	44
Total	100%	100%	100%	100%	100%	100%	100%	100%
Index of Ideology	+68	−19	+23	−13	+31	−47	−13	−27

presents the distribution of respondents on the ideology scale, by party and state. Again, by subtracting the proportion of conservative from the proportion of liberal respondents we can construct a simple "index of ideology." As the table shows, Democrats, even in generally conservative Tennessee, scored consistently "higher" ("more liberal") on the ideology index than did Republicans.

APPENDIX 3

Legislative officers—
how they are chosen
and what they do

OFFICE (generic): State; Chamber; Exact title	FORMAL PROCESS OF SE- LECTION	USUAL PRACTICE IN SELECTION	POWERS, DUTIES, AND FUNCTIONS PERFORMED BY OFFICER

PRESIDING OFFICERS

California Assembly			
Speaker	Elected by members.	Chosen in contest between bipartisan factions prior to opening of session.	Presides over chamber. Appoints committees and chairmen. Refers bills to committee.
Speaker pro Tempore	Same.	Member of Speaker's faction.	Presides in Speaker's absence from floor.
California Senate			
Lieutenant Governor	Elected at polls.		Presides over Senate, successor to Governor.
President pro Tempore	Elected by members.	Selection may take place in caucus of whole prior to for- mal unanimous vote.	Chairs Rules Committee and thus exerts major influence over committee appointments, bill ref- erence, housekeeping, etc. Presides or ap- points member to pre- side in Lieutenant Gover- nor's absence from floor.

New Jersey Assembly			
Speaker	Elected by mem- bers (party vote).	Caucus always picks last year's party leader, rotates between large and small counties.	Presides over chamber. Appoints committees and chairmen. Refers bills to committee. Sets agenda. All these func- tions performed in line with caucus decision.
New Jersey Senate			
President	Same.	Same but does not rotate.	Same. Successor to Gov- ernor, since state has no Lieutenant Governor.

OFFICE (generic): State; Chamber; Exact title	FORMAL PROCESS OF SE- LECTION	USUAL PRACTICE IN SELECTION	POWERS, DUTIES, AND FUNCTIONS PERFORMED BY OFFICER

PRESIDING OFFICERS (*Continued*)

Ohio
House of Representatives

| *Speaker* | Elected by members (party vote). | Elected in majority caucus. | Presides over chamber and in caucus. Appoints committees and chairmen. Leader of majority party. Chairs Rules Committee. Housekeeping. |
| *Speaker pro Tempore* | Same. | Same. | Majority floor manager. Presides over chamber in Speaker's absence. |

Ohio
Senate

| *Lieutenant Governor* | Elected at polls. | | Presides over chamber. |
| *President pro Tempore* | Elected by members (party vote). | Elected in majority caucus. | Presides in caucus. Refers bills to committee. Chairs Rules Committee. Leader of majority party. Housekeeping. Appoints committees and chairmen. |

Tennessee
House of Representatives

| *Speaker* | Elected by members (party vote). | Caucus in fact ratifies governor's nominee. | Presides over chamber. Appoints committees and chairmen. Refers bills to committee. |

Tennessee
Senate

| *Lieutenant Governor and Speaker of Senate* | Elected by members (party vote). | Caucus in fact ratifies governor's nominee. | Presides over chamber. Appoints committees and chairmen. Refers bills to committee. |

OFFICE (generic): State; Chamber; Exact title	FORMAL PROCESS OF SE- LECTION	USUAL PRACTICE IN SELECTION	POWERS, DUTIES, AND FUNCTIONS PERFORMED BY OFFICER
PARTY LEADERS			
California Assembly			
Majority (Rep.) *Floor Leader*	Appointed by Speaker.	Represents Speaker's faction, *not* majority party.	Makes procedural mo- tions, keeps track of agenda, acts as Speaker's floor manager.
Minority (Dem.) *Floor Leader*	Elected in caucus.	May be member of Speaker's faction.	Floor manager for minor- ity party. (Duties not clearly structured.)
Caucus chairmen (both parties)	Elected in caucus.	May or may not be floor leader.	Calls and presides over caucus meetings.
California Senate	(There were no recognized party leaders in the Senate.)		
New Jersey Assembly			
Majority (Rep.) *Leader*	Elected in caucus.	Majority caucus al- ways picks last year's Appropriation Committee chairman.	Presides over caucus. Floor manager for majority.
New Jersey Assembly			
Minority (Dem.) *Leader*	Elected in caucus.		Presides over caucus. Floor manager for minor- ity. Liaison (in 1957) with Governor of same party.
Assistant Party Leaders (both parties)	Elected in caucus.		Function as party whips.
New Jersey Senate	(Same as Assembly, but no assistant party leaders.)		
Ohio House of Representatives			
Majority (Rep.) *Leader*	(Functions performed by Speaker and Speaker pro Tempore. See above.)		
Minority (Dem.) *Leader*	Elected in caucus.		Floor manager. Pre- sides over caucus.

OFFICE (generic): State; Chamber; Exact title	FORMAL PROCESS OF SE- LECTION	USUAL PRACTICE IN SE- LECTION	POWERS, DUTIES, AND FUNCTIONS PERFORMED BY OFFICER

PARTY LEADERS (*Continued*)

Ohio
Senate

Majority (Rep.) *Leader*	(Functions performed by President pro Tempore. See above.)		
Minority (Dem.) *Leader*	Elected in caucus.		Floor manager. Presides over caucus.

Tennessee
House of Representatives

Administration (Dem.) *Floor Leader*	Appointed by Governor.	Co-leaders may be designated.	Floor manager for *administration* program.
Minority (Rep.) *Floor Leader*	Elected in caucus.		Floor manager. Presides over caucus.
Tennessee Senate	(Same as House. Two administration Co-leaders were appointed in 1957.)		

STEERING COMMITTEES	MEM- BER- SHIP	COMPOSITION AND METHOD OF SEL- ECTION	POWER, DUTIES, AND FUNCTIONS PERFORMED BY COMMITTEE

California
Assembly

Rules Committee	7	Speaker appoints chairman. Three members nominated by each party ratified by house.	Housekeeping. Serves as standing committee on resolutions. Technically responsible for agenda.

California
Senate

Rules Committee	5	President pro Tempore is chairman. Two members of each party elected by *whole house.*	Appoints committees and chairmen. Refers bills to committee. Housekeeping.

STEERING COMMITTEES	MEM-BER-SHIP	COMPOSITION AND METHOD OF SEL-ECTION	POWERS, DUTIES, AND FUNCTIONS PERFORMED BY COMMITTEE
New Jersey Assembly			
Conference Committee	17	Senior members of majority (Rep.) party, elected by caucus.	Sets agenda for caucus, guides caucus decisions which determine policy of chamber.
New Jersey Senate		(No significant steering committees.)	
Ohio House of Representatives			
Rules Committee	10	Appointed and chaired by Speaker.	Controls calendar.
Reference Committee	7	Appointed by Speaker.	Refers bills to committee; screens bills for form and legal effect.
Ohio Senate			
Rules Committee	7	Appointed and chaired by President pro Tempore. Includes major committee chairmen and *minority* leader.	Controls calendar.
Tennessee House of Representatives			
Calendar Committee		Speaker and committee chairmen. Elects own chairman.	Meets after adjournment, sets next day's calendar.
Steering Committee		Same, plus additional members appointed by speaker.	Late in session replaces Calendar Committee, takes over all bills from standing committees, acts as substantive and steering committee.
Tennessee Senate		(Same committees as House.)	

Behavior expected of formal leaders

EXPECTED BEHAVIORS	Calif. House	Calif. Senate	N.J. House	N.J. Senate	Ohio House	Ohio Senate	Tenn. House	Tenn. Senate	Total
A-1. *Maintain order:* "be firm," be a "stable leader," "be calm." *Expected of:*									
Presiding officer	13%	—	36%	38%	27%	12%	21%	13%	21%
Committee chairmen	31	23	4	—	38	53	10	6	24
Party leaders	—	*	4	—	1	3	—	—	1
A-2. *Know the rules,* procedures, be experienced. *Expected of:*									
Presiding officer	12	21	23	10	18	3	22	35	18
Committee chairmen	11	3	2	—	3	6	7	—	5
Party leaders	7	*	7	5	12	6	2	13	8
A-3. *Follow the rules:* "be fair," preside impartially, be a referee, arbitrator. *Expected of:*									
Presiding officer	56	32	62	57	59	16	81	94	61
Committee chairmen	35	50	7	—	41	35	34	32	32
Party leaders	4	*	5	10	3	—	15	6	6
A. Mentioning one or more of the above behaviors making the system stable and predictable. *Expected of:*									
Presiding officer	60	47	84	71	75	31	89	94	72
Committee chairmen	53	59	12	—	66	75	47	39	49
Party leaders	12	*	18	14	15	10	17	16	15
Number of respondents	(75)	(34)	(56)	(21)	(130)	(32)	(88)	(31)	(467)
B-1. *Give "due regard" for members' rights:* let them bring out the issues, assign bills fairly. *Expected of:*									
Presiding officer	27%	29%	16%	—	23%	9%	32%	26%	23%
Committee chairmen	31	29	25	5	44	41	30	32	33
Party leaders	23	*	16	5	6	3	16	13	12
B-2. *Focus conflict:* narrow the alternatives, "organize" hearings, "present the issues clearly." *Expected of:*									
Presiding officer	4	—	2	—	7	31	1	—	5
Committee chairmen	31	32	11	—	47	59	9	6	28
Party leaders	9	*	—	—	4	12	3	3	6
B-3. *Promote, defend party or factional positions:* "get the program through," bring up party/administration bills. *Expected of:*									
Presiding officer	8	—	12	33	36	50	2	—	18
Committee chairmen	—	—	12	10	11	16	2	—	6
Party leaders	45	*	48	76	39	66	31	23	42
B-4. *Let the majority rule:* "don't push his personal views," "let the committee determine the fate of the bill." *Expected of:*									
Presiding officer	51	26	21	19	8	9	23	23	22
Committee chairmen	29	29	11	—	32	19	19	23	24
Party leaders	12	*	20	14	15	19	10	3	14

B. Mentioning *one or more of the above behaviors focussing* issues and resolving conflict. *Expected of:*

Presiding officer	67	47	41	52	63	75	51	52	57
Committee chairmen	66	70	48	14	79	82	51	55	63
Party leaders	71	*	71	81	56	75	58	45	63
Number of respondents	(75)	(34)	(56)	(21)	(130)	(32)	(88)	(31)	(467)

C-1. *Guide, lead the group:* "coordinate members' ideas," promote teamwork, be diplomatic with members. *Expected of:*

Presiding officer	49%	76%	36%	48%	59%	34%	17%	13%	43%
Committee chairmen	28	15	4	—	15	3	11	10	13
Party leaders	25	*	20	10	14	3	15	16	16

C-2. *Help individuals:* "be accessible," assist them with their personal problems. *Expected of:*

Presiding officer	23	50	16	24	37	22	14	10	25
Committee chairmen	3	—	—	—	1	3	2	—	1
Party leaders	4	*	4	—	10	3	3	—	5

C-3. *Expedite business:* organize, "be concise," "start on time." *Expected of:*

Presiding officer	24	56	21	38	21	16	12	6	22
Committee chairmen	39	50	14	10	31	19	27	26	29
Party leaders	8	*	21	33	8	6	26	23	15

C-4. *Coordinate, communicate:* provide liaison with other officers and political systems. *Expected of:*

Presiding officer	8	18	12	14	27	9	5	—	14
Committee chairmen	12	27	22	14	15	15	3	3	13
Party leaders	24	*	50	24	35	25	6	3	25

C. Mentioning *one or more of the above behaviors leading and administering the legislative system.* *Expected of:*

Presiding officer	52	85	52	67	76	56	31	16	56
Committee chairmen	62	68	36	19	52	34	40	32	47
Party leaders	49	*	75	57	53	31	47	42	52
Number of respondents	(75)	(34)	(56)	(21)	(130)	(32)	(88)	(31)	(467)

D. Knowledge of the content of legislation. *Expected of:*

Presiding officer	3%	—	5%	10%	10%	9%	6%	—	6%
Committee chairmen	37	12	27	43	15	15	19	16	22
Party leaders	7	*	9	5	7	—	18	19	10

No description made of role of:

Presiding officer	4	9	16	—	2	6	1	3	2
Committee chairmen	5	—	2	43	4	3	12	19	10
Party leaders	13	*	2	10	15	16	18	19	14
Number of respondents	(75)	(34)	(56)	(21)	(130)	(32)	(88)	(31)	(467)

* There are no party leaders in the California Senate.

485

The legislators:
their backgrounds
and characteristics

T HE 504 PERSONS who happened to be sitting at the 1957 sessions of
these four legislatures do not, of course, constitute an accurate sample
of the 7,600-odd American state legislators.   They do compose one of
the larger groups to be studied intensively, with interviews supplementing the data in official biographical sources.   We therefore present here a statistical summary which may be compared with similar
information in such sources as the excellent biographical studies by
Hyneman, Matthews, and others.[7]

Every biographical study has shown that parliaments and legislatures are quite atypical of the populations they represent.[8]   These
are no exceptions.   From the female half of the population were
drawn only 18 women (4 per cent), although there were at least
two women in every legislature.   In other respects, the tendency
was to over-represent majority, and under-represent minority groups.

[7] Donald R. Matthews, *U.S. Senators and Their World* (Chapel Hill: The University of North Carolina Press, 1960), Chapter 2; Charles S. Hyneman, "Who
Makes Our Laws?," *Political Science Quarterly* 55:556–581 (1940); Hyneman,
"Tenure and Turnover of Legislative Personnel," *Annals of the American Academy
of Political and Social Science* 195:21–33 (1938).   A score of other studies in this
vein are cited in Norman Meller's bibliographical article, "Legislative Behavior
Research," *Western Political Quarterly* 13:131–153 (1960).

[8] Studies of parliaments supporting this observation include Peter C. Richards,
Honourable Members (New York: Frederick A. Praeger, Inc., 1959), and J. F. S.
Ross, *Parliamentary Representation* (New Haven: Yale University Press, 1944).
A. W. Martin, "The Legislative Assembly of New South Wales," *Australian
Journal of Politics and History* 2:46–67 (1956), cites others.

Table A-5: Religious affiliation

Religious Affiliation	Calif. N = 116		N.J. N = 78		Ohio N = 162		Tenn. N = 132		Total N = 488	
Protestant	83	72%	45	58%	114	70%	125	95%	367	75%
Methodist	(14)		(9)		(40)		(45)		(108)	
Presbyterian	(13)		(18)		(25)		(13)		(69)	
Baptist	(—)		(5)		(2)		(35)		(42)	
Episcopal	(19)		(8)		(7)		(2)		(36)	
Church of Christ	(1)		(—)		(8)		(12)		(21)	
Lutheran	(6)		(2)		(7)		(1)		(16)	
Congregational	(8)		(—)		(6)		(—)		(14)	
Christian	(2)		(—)		(6)		(6)		(14)	
Other denominations	(8)		(3)		(9)		(8)		(28)	
"Protestant"	(12)		(—)		(4)		(3)		(19)	
Catholic	20	17%	28	36%	37	23%	3	2%	88	18%
Jewish	1	1%	5	6%	1	*	2	2%	9	2%
Other, refused to state	2	2%	—	—	1	—	1	1%	4	1%
"No religious affiliation"	10	8%	—	—	9	6%	1	1%	20	4%

* Less than 1%.

487

There were only four Negroes (1 per cent) to represent the 4 to 6 per cent of the population in California, Ohio, and New Jersey, though there was one or more in each legislature. There were no representatives of the 16 per cent Negro population in Tennessee. Tables A-5 through A-13 summarize a number of other characteristics of the experience and background of legislators in the four states.

Table A-6: Place of birth of legislators and state population

Place of Birth	Calif. $N = 120$	N.J. $N = 79$	Ohio $N = 162$	Tenn. $N = 132$	Total $N = 493$
Legislators					
Born in state	44%	71%	88%	86%	74%
In county represented	(22%)	(62%)	(71%)	(66%)	(56%)
Elsewhere in state	(22)	(9)	(17)	(20)	(18)
Born in another state	53	28	10	14	24
Foreign born	3	1	2	—	2
	100%	100%	100%	100%	100%
*Population**					
Born in state	42%	68%	76%	80%	
Foreign born	8	12	7	†	

* Source: *Statistical Abstract of the United States*, 1960, pp. 33–34; 1953, p. 43.

† Less than 1%.

Table A-7: Residence in district

Length of Residence in District	Calif. $N = 118$	N.J. $N = 79$	Ohio $N = 162$	Tenn. $N = 119$	Total $N = 488$
"All my life"	14%	60%	65%	53%	48%
Most (80%) of life, or over 30 years	42	23	23	23	28
20–29 years	15	7	7	11	10
10–19 years	19	10	3	9	10
Less than 10 years	10	—	2	4	4
	100%	100%	100%	100%	100%

Table A-8: Where legislators lived when they were "growing up"

Place where legislators "grew up"	Calif. (N = 110)	N.J. (N = 78)	Ohio (N = 162)	Tenn. (N = 119)	Total (N = 469)
"In a city"	45%	62%	45%	22%	42%
"In a small town"	23	32	28	34	29
"On a farm"	21	5	24	33	22
Combination of the above	11	1	3	11	7
	100%	100%	100%	100%	100%

Table A-9: Education of legislators, compared with population over age 25

Educational Attainment	Calif. Leg. (N=120)	Calif. Pop.	N.J. Leg. (N=79)	N.J. Pop.	Ohio Leg. (N=162)	Ohio Pop.	Tenn. Leg. (N=120)	Tenn. Pop.	Total Leg. (N=481)	U.S. Pop.
Elementary only	—	33%	—	47%	4%	43%	4%	60%	2%	47%
Some high school	15	45	13	38	19	42	22	29	17	37
Some college*	31	11	24	6	19	7	28	6	26	7
College graduate†	54	8	63	7	58	6	46	4	55	6
Totals‡	100%	97%	100%	98%	100%	98%	100%	99%	100%	97%

* Includes business school, night school, music school, and law school if at post-high school level.
† Includes those with graduate, professional, and legal work at the post-college level.
‡ From *Statistical Abstract*, 1957, p. 112. Less than 100% because of non-reporting.

Table A-10: Occupation of legislators' fathers, legislators themselves, U.S. senators, and the U.S. labor force, 1950

Occupation	Legislators' Fathers	Legislators	Senators*	Labor Force, 1950†
Professional, technical	18%	47%	64%	7%
Proprietors, managers, officials	29	35	29	7
Farmers, farm managers	25	10	7	16
Craftsmen, foremen, operatives	16	2	—	31
Clerical, sales	5	5	—	15
Unskilled labor, servants, farm labor	5	—	—	20
Other, not known	2	1	—	4
	100%	100%	100%	100%

* Source: Matthews, *op. cit.*, p. 282.
† Source: *Statistical Abstract*, 1957, pp. 219–220.

Table A-11: Occupation and status level of state legislators, by state

	Calif. (N = 120)	N.J. (N = 79)	Ohio (N = 173)	Tenn. (N = 132)	Total (N = 504)	
Agriculture, agricultural services	16	2	18	16	52	10 %
Forestry, fishing	1	—	—	3	4	1
Mining, oil extraction	2	1	2	1	6	1
Construction, home building	4	—	4	1	9	2
Manufacturing	1	6	6	2	15	3
Transportation (rail, truck, air)	3	—	1	2	6	1
Utilities	1	—	—	—	1	—
Wholesale trade	1	—	5	9	15	3
Retail trade	7	1	11	16	35	7
Banking, brokerage	—	1	2	1	4	1
Insurance	6	2	7	1	16	3
Real estate, real estate *and* insurance	9	1	12	12	34	7
Speculator, investor, etc.	3	1	—	1	5	1
Communication (press, radio, TV)	2	3	9	4	18	4
Business services (advertising, auditing)	3	1	7	1	12	2
Business and repair services (other)	4	1	3	3	11	2
Personal services	1	—	—	3	4	1
Entertainment, recreation	2	—	—	2	4	1
Law	36	41	63	40	180	36
Teaching, education	4	1	6	4	15	3
Medicine, pharmacy	2	—	2	6	10	2
Other professions (engineer, mining)	1	4	5	—	10	2
Labor union official	—	4	—	—	4	1
"Legislator"	8	3	5	—	16	4
"Politician"	—	—	4	1	5	1
Other government, administration	3	2	—	1	6	1
Other (including housewife)	—	4	1	2	7	*
Managers, proprietors, officials	44 %	23 %	31 %	41 %	35 %	
Professional, technical	39	60	52	38	47	
Clerical, sales	3	9	5	5	5	
Craftsmen, foremen, operatives	1	1	2	2	2	
Unskilled labor, farm labor, servant	—	—	—	—	—	
Farmers, farm managers	13	2	10	13	10	
Other, not classificable	—	5	*	1	1	

* Less than 1 %.

Table A-12: Legislators' previous experience (in either or both houses)

Prior Legislative Experience	Calif. House	Calif. Senate	N.J. House	N.J. Senate	Ohio House	Ohio Senate	Tenn. House	Tenn. Senate
0 or 1 year	17	5	15	4	32	3	46	9
2 to 4 years	17	5	19	5	30	3	32	5
4 to 6 years	10	4	9	3	20	4	12	9
6 to 8 years	9	5	7	—	24	7	2	6
8 to 10 years	7	5	4	3	16	3	4	2
10 to 12 years	6	4	2	1	10	2	1	1
12 to 14 years	3	1	1	1	3	6	1	—
14 to 16 years	4	2	—	3	2	2	1	—
16 to 18 years	3	—	1	—	—	—	—	—
18 to 20 years	2	3	—	1	1	3	—	—
Over 20 years	2	6	—	—	1	1	—	1
Median	5.2	8.4	3.5	5.0	4.8	8.0	2.2	4.6

Table A-13: Age of legislators in 1957

Age	Calif. House	Calif. Senate	N. J. House	N. J. Senate	Ohio House	Ohio Senate	Tenn. House	Tenn. Senate
Under 30	—	—	—	—	3	2	11	—
31–40	20	4	15	5	40	4	29	7
41–50	26	12	25	10	35	9	27	13
51–60	21	9	16	6	27	7	17	6
61–75	13	13	2	—	22	9	11	7
76 and over	—	2	—	—	3	1	2	—
	80	40	58	21	130	32	97	33
Median	48.2	53.4	45.9	46.6	46.9	52.5	44.4	47.0

Interview schedule
and instructions
to interviewers

ON THE FACE-SHEET, interviewers recorded the interview number; interviewer's name; number of call-backs made in process of interviewing; date, time, and place of interview; and number of questions completed. The face-sheet also included the following introduction to the interview: "Several of us at different universities around the country are doing a study of the legislatures of four states, to learn what legislators think of their jobs and how they go about their work. The information and opinions you give me will be tabulated along with material from 500 other legislators. No names will be used, and what you say will be off the record."

(*Note:* QUESTIONS *are in large type;* INSTRUCTIONS *given to the interviewer appear in smaller type.*)

1. First, a couple of questions about your background:
   a. Where were you born?   (city, county, state)
   b. And in what year?

(1) Make sure to get city *and* county *and* state.

2. Where were you brought up?   (city, county, state)
3. Did you spend most of the years when you were growing up in a city, a small town, or on a farm?

(2, 3) If R lived in several places during his youth, take his own choice of reference for terms "brought up" and "most of the years when you were growing up." Object of these questions is urban-rural background, similarity of background to district represented.

4. How many years have you been living in the district you represent in the legislature?

5. Now would you tell me a little bit about your education—where you went to school?

(5) Let R first tell you what he wants to tell, then follow up as his answer requires.   Probe for level of school, place, type, and R's educational status.   *Make sure not to embarrass him.*

6. What was your father's job or occupation?

(6) Try to get realistic description adequate for appraising socio-economic status.

7. a. What is your own principal occupation?
   b. And who is your employer?
   c. Has this been your main occupation all your working life?   (If "no"):
   d. What other work have you done, and for how long?

(7) Get beyond "cover" occupations like "businessman," "farmer," "attorney" that are popular in official biographies.   How does R really make his living?   Get enough on 7c to reveal real or imagined areas of *expertise* or associational ties.

8. How did you become interested in politics?   For example:
   a. What is your earliest recollection of being interested in it?
   b. What other members of your family or close relatives held public or political office before you yourself did?
   c. Just what clinched your decision to go into politics yourself?
   d. Just how did it come about that you became a legislator?
   e. Do you expect to continue to run for the legislature?   Why is that?
   f. Are there any other political or government positions—local, state, or federal—which you would like to seek?   (If "yes" or "perhaps"):
   g. What are they?

(8) The whole series of questions under 8 tries in a variety of ways to get at the problem of how the legislator is related to politics.   It seeks to elicit effective attitudinal and perceptual data about the self.   A combination of responses will, hopefully, yield a reasonably complete profile of the legislator's general orientation to politics.
   (a) Emphasis here is on *earliest* and *interested:* "earliest" refers to childhood memories, however vague, and to possible experiences in schooldays.   Depression or war may loom large in memory.   Or there may be recall to *significant others* who impressed R.   "Interested" may refer to generalized events of "interest" to R, or to awareness of political goings-on in the more immediate environment.   It may refer to motivations—the *why* of interest.   Record anecdotes.   Allow R to

talk freely, encourage him through probes of "how?" and "why?"   The
purpose of the question becomes clearer by comparing it with 8c and
8d.

(b) This question may get at persons in the early environment of R
who were influential in setting his political course.   Make sure to note
any comments that may be made concerning influentials.

(c) This question differs from 8a in that it tries to get at the "trau-
matic" event or situation which decided R to go into politics.   We are
not looking here for "interest in general," but for a more specific condition or circumstances.   If R answers this question in terms of either
8a or 8d, record responses and return to 8c with further probes.

(d) In contrast to 8a and 8c, this question tries to get at the circumstances surrounding R's becoming a *legislator*.   Again, anecdotal information should be recorded.

(e) This tries to get at R's continuing commitment to the job.   In
combination with 8f and 8g it should give us a pretty full profile of
"politics as a vocation."

(f) Here we want to get R's aspirations.   Is he committed to the
legislature alone, or to public service more generally?   Is the legislative
job a stepping stone?

(g) Record all comments volunteered by respondent.

9.   a. What governmental or party positions—local, state, or federal—
had you held before going into the legislature?
b. Do you hold any such positions now?
(What are they?)

(9) These questions should tell us whether R is in fact a professional or
amateur.   Make sure all categories—both *governmental* and *party*, and
levels—are exhausted.

10. Now, a couple of questions about the job of being a legislator:
a. First of all, how would you describe the job of being a legislator
—what are the most important things you should do here?
b. Are there any important *differences* between what *you* think
this job is and the way *your constituents* see it?   (What are they?)

(10) Questions 10b, 35 and 36 are the only ones getting directly at perception of and relation to constituency.   Record anything he says
that shows how he appraises or reacts to his constituents, even
though irrelevant to the question, but go back to the question eventually.   Beware of surface replies indicating complete harmony and
identity with constituents.   Pretests show this appears—is he trying
to fool himself or us, or is it real?

(a) This is a central question.   Probe as fully as possible.   If there
is a difference between what he does and what he thinks he should
be doing, explore adequately, and get *both*.   If no indication of
such, probe to be sure ideal and actual roles are in harmony.

(b) Don't accept a quick "no."   Try: "None of them ever want you
to do something you don't think is worth doing?" or something

similar. Get any existing disagreement between own concept of job and that imputed to constituents. Also get any overtones of resentment toward certain or all constituents.

11. We've been told that every legislature has its *unofficial* rules of the game—certain things members must do and things they must not do if they want the respect and cooperation of fellow members.

a. What are some of these things—these "rules of the game"—that a member must observe, to hold the respect and cooperation of his fellow members?

b. Would you name four or five of your fellow members, regardless of party or position, who are most widely respected for following these "rules of the game"—I mean people that a new member should look up to when he's just learning the ropes?

c. Some members don't seem to have the respect and cooperation of their fellow members because they don't follow the "rules of the game." What are some of the things that may cause a member to lose the respect and cooperation of his fellow members?

d. How do the other members make things difficult for these people when they don't follow the "rules of the game"?

(11) (a) Here we are trying to discover some of the *informal* group norms of the legislature. If R says it is just like any other group situation, probe to find out what kind of behavior he has in mind. Also, probe to determine whether there is any special kind of behavior required in the legislative group.

(b) Here we are seeking to identify those regarded as conformers and perpetuators of group norms. Emphasis should be placed on being respected *for* following the rules of the game, rather than just being generally respected.

(c) This is designed to supplement 11a by asking for *proscribed* behavior. Pretesting indicated that R may mention names if probed for examples of "deviant" behavior. Record names if voluntarily given.

(d) Here we want to discover the sanctions used to enforce the group norms of the legislative body. This may be either individual or group action.

12. Now I'd like to ask you a few questions about the various jobs here in the House (Senate):

a. First of all, what role ought the Speaker of the House (President Pro Tem of the Senate) play in order to be most effective in his job?

b. Now, how about the committee chairmen—what role ought a committee chairman play in order to be most effective in his job?

c. And what about the party leaders—what role ought they play in order to be most effective in their jobs?

(12) (a-c) If R doesn't appear to understand the term *role*, ask him what the Speaker, the committee chairmen, or party leaders *should do* and *should not do* in order to be effective.

13. How do the two houses of the legislature work together in (state)? For example,

a. How does a member of *this house* go about getting support for his bills in the *other house?*

b. When a bill has passed *this house,* what kind of things are most likely to determine its fate in the *other house?*

(13) This series of questions is designed to give an overview of the legislative system as a whole, or, at least, how it is seen.

(a) Designed to tell us about the tactics of individual actors in the system, about informal interaction patterns, as well as the norms guiding such interaction.

(b) This may give us some insight into significant decision-making processes of the system: how powerful actors in the system operate.

14. a. Is there any particular subject or field of legislation in which you consider yourself particularly expert—I mean when it comes to dealing with proposed legislation in that field? (What is that?)

b. Why is that?

c. Could you name five or six members of the House (Senate) whom you consider particularly expert in their respective fields? (In what fields are they expert?)

(14) (a) How does R see himself? If he reacts negatively to the term *expert,* this is important and should be recorded. So should qualifications made by R on the term "expert." We want to know whether *expertise* or other parliamentary skills are more highly valued.

(b) This probe should elicit more specific reasons why R considers himself "expert."

(c) This question, among other objectives, serves as a check on 14a. Be sure to exhaust all six lines.

15. Now, who are some of your closest personal friends in the House (Senate)—I mean the members you see most often outside the chamber, at lunch or dinner, or parties or other social gatherings?

(15) *Try to get six.* This question is designed to obtain sociometric data. We want to determine whether there is any relation between patterns of political association and political attitudes or voting records.

16. We're interested in finding out how parties work at the state level.

a. How would you describe the part played by political parties in the (state) legislature?

b. In some legislatures certain men are described as *party* men, and others are described as *independents, mavericks, nonpartisans,* or similar terms. Is this distinction made in the (state) House (Senate)? (If "yes"):

c. How would you describe the differences between the way a party man acts and the way the others act?

d. Under what circumstances do you think it is *not* necessary for a member to vote with his party?

e. What are some of the advantages of going along with your party leaders when they seek your support on a bill? Anything else?

f. How much cooperation is there between the majority and minority leaders here in the House (Senate)? How is that?

(16) (a) Here we are trying to get R's perception of how political parties influence the operation of the legislature.
(b) If answer is "no," skip to 16d. Record terms used by R to describe "party men" and "others."
(c) Emphasis here is on behavior in the legislature.
(d) This may involve either subject matter or a peculiar constituency situation. We are interested in either one, or in other circumstances that R may mention..
(e) Record disadvantages also, if they are given so as to indicate sanctions applied by party leaders.
(f) We are trying to determine how often and to what extent leaders cooperate across party lines to keep the legislative system going.

17. a. There are always conflicting opinions in a legislature. How would you rank these particular conflicts of opinion in the order of their importance here in (state)?
(1) Republicans versus Democrats
(2) The Governor's supporters versus his opponents
(3) The cities versus rural counties
(4) Liberals versus conservatives
(5) Labor's friends versus the opponents of labor
(6) Section versus rest of the State
(7) Other?

b. Are there any other important divisions that are not on this list?

(17) (a) This question gets at division of opinion *before* a vote is taken. The assumption here is that the issue is still relatively uncrystallized, so the *general opinions* (attitudes?) have an opportunity to operate. It may tell us something about initial approaches to legislative issues.
(b) Follow-up if 17a is not exhaustive.

18. Now let's talk a bit about the governor. What would you say are the main reasons for whatever power or influence the governor has over the legislature of (state)? Anything else?

(18) Likelihood is that R will answer this in terms of the incumbent in the Governor's office. Interviewer might stimulate R to compare incumbent with earlier governors to elicit more generic answers. Give R plenty of time to answer this question. There's much room on page for it.

19. You hear a lot these days about the power of interest groups and lobbies in state politics.

    a. What would you say are the most powerful groups of this kind here in (state)? *Probe:* What particular organizations do you have in mind here?

    b. Now, what would you say makes these groups so powerful— what are the main reasons for their influence?

    c. Are there any interest groups or lobbies that are particularly strong *in your own district?* What are they?

20. We've been told that there are always some interest groups or lobbies whose advice *ought* to be considered, whether they happen to be powerful or not.

    a. Would you name some of these groups here in (state)? *Probe:* What *organizations* do you have in mind?

    b. Could you tell me what there is about these groups that makes them particularly worth listening to?

(19, 20) These two questions seek to ascertain R's specific perceptions of the world of groups around him. We want to know, first, what groups he sees readily and which ones he is blind to, and, second, what characteristics he sees when he looks at them—in particular, what degree and form of power he sees. It is important, above all, to record all answers *fully.*

In 19a, 19c and 20a, if R answers in terms of general interest aggregations, ("labor," "farmers," "gamblers," etc.), record that fact, but probe to see if R is thinking of particular organizations; record these also. The record should indicate (by the order of listing) R's ranking of groups according to power he attributes to them, but do not probe too hard to determine such ranking.

In 19b and 20b, record answers carefully, making clear when R is talking about groups in general and when he is assigning reasons to particular organizations or groups.

21. a. Would you say that, on the whole, the legislature would work much better, somewhat better, about the same, somewhat worse, or much worse, if there were no interest groups and lobbies trying to influence legislation?

    b. Just how is that? *Probe:* What particular organizations or lobbyists do you have in mind here?

(21) Here we want R's *feelings* about the world he has partially described for us in questions 19 and 20—in particular whether he feels this world is hostile or friendly toward the functioning of the legislature.

If R thinks the hypothetical situation is too impossible to consider, ask him something like, "Well, how do you feel about these interest groups and what they do? On the whole, do you think they are very helpful to the legislature, . . . or very much a hindrance?" Do not accept a DK/NA unless there is really no answer forthcoming.

It is important to keep R talking in 21b to get a full record of what he feels and why. ("What sort of thing do they do?," "Do all of them act this way?", "Is this sort of thing pretty common?," etc.) Probe to see if R identifies particular groups or organizations in his affective reactions only after exhausting his general feelings, and do not push if R is reluctant to name specific cases and groups.

22. Here are the names of some persons that people have told us are connected with various interest groups and lobbies. Could you tell me who each of them is, or what he does?

(22) Although this question will be used to measure R's familiarity with groups, their agents, and their interests, be sure not to give R the impression he is being tested, or in any way expected to know any of the names listed. If necessary explain that we want to know how much lobbyists get around among legislators. Be sure to record answers as fully as possible. Do not try to give R any clues or help him in any way.

(THERE ARE NO QUESTIONS 23–29)

30. Now I'd like to ask you some questions about the work of this session of the legislature. The issue of school needs is one almost every legislative session faces. Would you say that this particular matter is of great concern to you personally, of some concern, of little concern, or of no concern?

(30) This question is designed to get a raw measure of R's affect, involvement in the issue of school needs. Note down any comments he may make about his concern.

31. Can you tell me what solution you would personally favor for this general problem? (*Or, if matter is settled:* Can you tell me what solutions you would personally have favored for this general problem?)

(31) Give R as much rope as possible. Record his recommended solutions as faithfully as possible. Probe a good deal.

32. a. Just what have you done, or what do you still expect to do, to promote the solution you favor in this *school needs* matter? Did you:
   (0) nothing?
   (1) author or sponsor a particular bill?
   (2) work for your solution in committee
   (3) speak for your solution on floor?
   (4) offer any amendments favoring your solution?
   (5) try to convince other members in private?
   (6) seek support outside the legislature?
   b. *[If "yes" to (6)]* Just what kind of support did you try to get?

(32) (a) Any number of items may be checked.
     (b) Designed to get R's feeling of his effectiveness in the matter.

33. On this particular subject of *school needs*, where would you get your most reliable information—what source of advice and information would you trust the most? (*Probe:* Try to get specific names of persons, agencies, organizations, as well as general classes of information source).

(33) The question is designed to elicit information on the pervasiveness of functional authority. Hence, as indicated on the schedule, it should be exhaustively probed.

34. a. Now, I would like you to help me find out how members of the House (Senate) generally feel about this *school needs* problem.
    (1) Take the Republicans, for instance. How do you think *most* of them feel about it? Do most of them agree with you, or disagree?
    (2) What about the Democrats? Do you think *most* of them agree with you on this, or disagree?
    (3) Have you any idea how most members from the rural districts feel about it. Would you say *most* of them agree with you, or disagree?
    (4) What about members from the city districts? Would you say *most* of them agree with you in this matter, or disagree?
    b. How do the interest groups or lobbies that are affected by this matter of *school needs* line up on it? Which ones would you say feel pretty much as you do about it, and which ones disagree with you on it?

(34) (b) Note here that we want R to assess the position of interest groups in relation to his *own* suggested solution.

35. How would you describe the attitudes of the voters in your district on this matter or school needs? Which ones agree with your position, and which differ?

(35) If he says all agree, try: "You mean not a single voter in your district disagrees with you on this?" Try for specific description of groups or organizations in both categories.

36. a. Have any of your constituents contacted you to express their views on it? (If "yes"):
    b. About how many communications about this matter—letters, telegrams, phone calls, personal visits, etc.—have you received from people in *your district?*
    c. About what percentage of them agreed with your position?
    d. What *kind* of people were those who contacted you? (*Probe:* Any particular groups?)

(36) (a) "Practically none" or "None to speak of," etc. are *yes* answers, and should be so checked. Follow up a hesitant *no* with "None at

all?"—Though not concerned with his efforts to contact *them,* record
if volunteered.
(b) Pretests indicate reluctance to give numbers, so go beyond surface DK. Ask him to guess. If he doesn't know, no one does. If
he gives unreasonably large number, ask if these are individual contacts. Be sure he doesn't accept spokesmen as representing a whole
group (or if he does, that we can evaluate it correctly).
(c) A number or proportion is just as good as a percentage, but get
beyond "most" or "not many" or such.

37. Just to get an over-all picture, how important would you rate each
of these items in leading you to see this *school needs* problem as
you do? Very important, important, not very important, not at all
important?
(1) Views of friends in the legislature
(2) Advice of party leaders
(3) Word from people in your district
(4) Report of Legislative Commission
(5) Committee recommendations
(6) Views of administrative agencies
(7) Views of interest groups or lobbies
(8) Others (specify)

(37) Exhaust all categories.

38. a. Do you think the solution the legislature is likely to reach (has
reached) in this matter will be (is) satisfactory to you personally?
b. This is the list of different conflicts of opinion we mentioned a
while ago. How would you rank these opinion conflicts in order
of their importance *on* this issue of *school needs?*
(1) Republicans versus Democrats
(2) The Governor's supporters versus his opponents
(3) The cities versus rural counties
(4) Liberals versus conservatives
(5) Labor's friends versus the opponents of labor
(6) Section versus rest of the State
(7) Other?
c. Do you think the solution which the legislature will reach (has
reached) in this matter:
(1) Will involve (has involved) compromises and concessions by
all sides, *or*
(2) Will be (was) pretty much a complete victory for one
viewpoint?
(If "2'):
d. Which viewpoint?

(38) (a) The question is to get R's relative feeling of indulgence or deprivation. Answers may help us explain his position on the issue.

(b) Make sure R understands this to refer to *opinion* on *this issue*. Make sure also the ranking is correct.

(c) This, hopefully, will tell us something about how R sees the *quality*, if you wish, of the legislative process. Make sure to follow up with probe: *which viewpoint?*

39. Now, here are some statements that various legislators and other people have made concerning government and politics in general and the work of a legislator. Would you please read each one and then check just how much you agree or disagree with it?

Instructions: Record any comments R makes about specific items. If he questions meaning of an item, do not interpret it for him but give him appropriate neutral, reassuring answers. Try to commit him on items where he is wavering but not plainly undecided. You can reassure R that we are not testing his opinions in any way. If necessary, say that these are statements we've heard mentioned in many places and that we want to see whether there is any difference of opinions about them from one state to another. Note the "UNDECIDED" and "NO ANSWER" responses are to be recorded on *your* interview schedule— R's sheet does not offer him these alternatives. Enter them on his sheet if necessary after the interview.

a. The job of a representative is to work for what his constituents want even though this may not always agree with his personal views.

b. The government has the responsibility to see to it that all people, poor or rich, have adequate housing, education, medical care, and protection against unemployment.

c. There is so little time during a session to study all the bills that sometimes I don't know what I'm voting for or against.

d. Interest groups or their agents give me valuable help in lining up support for my bills.

e. A legislator can decide how to vote on most issues by asking himself if the proposed law is morally right.

f. If a bill is important for his party's record, a member should vote with his party even if it costs him some support in his district.

g. Often legislators get so involved in affairs at the capitol that they lose touch with their constituents.

h. Business enterprise can continue to give us our high standard of living only if it remains free from government regulation.

i. Many of the bills are so detailed and technical that I have trouble understanding them.

j. The job of the legislator is to work out compromises among conflicting interests.

k. The two parties should take clear-cut, opposing stands on more of the important state issues in order to encourage party responsibility.

l. I seldom have to sound out my constituents because I think so much like them that I know how to react to almost any proposal.

m. The most pressing problems which local governments face cannot be solved without new state taxes.

n. So many groups want so many different things that it is often difficult to know what stand to take.

o. I get valuable help in drafting bills or amendments from interest groups or their agents.

p. It's just as important to be on guard against ideas put out by people of one's own party as against ideas put out by people in the opposite party.

q. Under our form of government, every individual should take an interest in government directly, not through a political party.

r. Almost nobody in my district cares about the big policy issues unless a bill happens to touch his personal or business interests.

s. A man whose loyalty has been questioned before a legislative committee, but who swears under oath that he has never been a communist, should be permitted to teach in our public schools.

t. My district includes so many different kinds of people that I often don't know just what the people there want me to do.

u. Lobbyists and special interests have entirely too much influence in American state legislatures.

v. In the long run, the best way to get along in the legislature is to pick friends and associates whose tastes and beliefs are the same as your own.

w. The best interests of the people would be better served if legislators were elected without party labels.

x. Generally speaking, if you want a thing done right, it is best to do it yourself, for many so-called experts don't know their business.

y. Under our form of government, every individual should take an interest in government directly, not through interest-group organizations.

(THERE ARE NO QUESTIONS 40–49)

50. a. Speaking now of government and politics in general, which would you say interests you most?
   (1) International affairs,
   (2) National affairs,
   (3) State affairs, *or*

(4) Local affairs?

b. And which would you say interests you least?

c. Now, as between the remaining two, which interests you most?

(50) This question is to get R's focus of attention. It is related to the earlier question on aspirations. It should give us an indication of his "provincialism." Make sure to exhaust b and c so that each category in a is finally ranked.

51. a. From a purely financial standpoint, do you think the salary and mileage you get from the state is adequate compensation for the time you spend on legislative business?

b. Now, including your legislative salary, into which of these four income groups would you say your total annual income falls? (Less than $5,000; $5,000–10,000; $10,000–20,000; over $20,000.)

(51) Record all comments made in connection with both a and b.

52. What church do you belong to?

53. a. Do you have any children?   How many?

b. (If "yes") About what ages are they?

54. Is there anything else about the legislature and how it works that you think we ought to pay attention to in our study?   (What?)

(54) Purpose of this question is, among other things, to permit R to let off steam.   Record all he says, probe only mildly.

(TO BE COMPLETED BY INTERVIEWER)

55. Were other persons present or within earshot during the interview? (Yes, throughout; Yes, at times; No)

56. Interviewer's estimate of frankness/sincerity of respondent's replies: (Very frank; Frank; Not very frank; Very evasive).

57. Interviewer's estimate of general cooperativeness of respondent throughout interview: (Very cooperative; Cooperative; Not very cooperative; Very uncooperative).

58. Interviewer's general impressions of respondent, especially concerning (1) his personal characteristics, (2) his general political attitudes, orientation to politics, (3) his conceptions of party, pressure groups, constituents, and administration, and (4) his conception of himself as a legislator.

APPENDIX 7

Bibliographical note

Oᴜʀ ꜱᴏᴜʀᴄᴇꜱ ᴏꜰ ɪɴꜰᴏʀᴍᴀᴛɪᴏɴ on particular states and their legislatures may be broken down into several categories:

(a) Compilations of information on the 48 (50) states, of which *American State Legislatures,* edited by Belle Zeller for the American Political Science Association's Committee on State Legislatures (New York: Thomas Y. Crowell and Company, 1954), and the Book of the States were most useful. Data on apportionment in Gordon E. Baker, *Rural versus Urban Political Power* (New York: Doubleday and Company, 1955), has been brought up to date in Margaret Greenfield, et al., *Legislative Reapportionment: California in National Perspective* (Berkeley: University of California Bureau of Public Administration, 1959) which treats both California and the other states, the former in detail.

(b) Studies of the government and/or politics of individual states or regions.

Several texts on California are kept up to date. The editions used here were Joseph P. Harris and Leonard Rowe, *California Politics* (Stanford: Stanford University Press, 1959); Henry A. Turner and John A. Vieg, *The Government and Politics of California* (New York: McGraw Hill Book Company, 1960); Bernard L. Hyink, Seyom Brown and E. W. Thacker, *Politics and Government in California* (New York: Thomas Y. Crowell and Company, 1959); and Winston W. Crouch, Dean E. McHenry, John C. Bollens and Stanley Scott, *California Government and Politics* (Englewood Cliffs, New Jersey: Prentice-Hall, Inc., 1956). Earlier studies which throw some light on one aspect or another of California legislative politics are David Farrelly and Ivan Hinderaker, *The Politics of California* (New York: The Ronald Press, 1951); and Dean R. Cresap, *Party Politics in the Golden State* (Los Angeles: The Haynes Foundation, 1954). Francis Carney, *The Rise of the Democratic Clubs in California* (New York:

505

Henry Holt and Company, 1958) is particularly useful in bringing California's party system up to date. *Streamlining State Legislatures* (Berkeley: University of California Bureau of Public Administration, 1955) and *California State Government: Its Tasks and Organization* (Stanford: The California Assembly, 1956) are two symposia summaries with information on the legislative process. The Mangore Corporation study of legislative compensation, *The California Legislator: A Report Presented to the Citizens Legislative Advisory Commission* (Los Angeles, January, 1958), has been summarized more accessibly in Richard W. Gable and Alexander Cloner, "The California Legislature and the Problem of Compensation," *Western Political Quarterly* 12:712–726 (1959).

Both New Jersey and Ohio are covered by rather recent volumes in the American Commonwealths series: Bennett M. Rich, *The Government and Administration of New Jersey* (New York: Thomas Y. Crowell and Company, 1957), and Francis R. Aumann and Harvey Walker, *The Government and Administration of Ohio* (New York: Thomas Y. Crowell and Company, 1957). There is a *Handbook of New Jersey State Government* prepared in 1952 by the Bureau of Government Research at Rutgers, and an outline entitled *Your Ohio Government* written by William H. Eells (Columbus, Ohio: Midwest Law Printers and Publishers, 1955). *The Ohio State Law Journal*, Vol. 11 (Autumn, 1950) contains several useful articles on the legislature.

There are no such up-to-date general works on Tennessee government other than William H. Combs and William E. Cole, *Tennessee: A Political Study* (Knoxville: University of Tennessee Press, 1940). The chapter on Tennessee in V. O. Key, Jr., *Southern Politics in State and Nation* (New York: Alfred A. Knopf, 1949) and William Goodman, *Inherited Domain: Political Parties in Tennessee* (Knoxville: Bureau of Public Administration, 1954, University of Tennessee Record, Extension Series, Vol. XXX, No. 1) are the best sources. Henry N. Williams, *The Legislative Process in Tennessee, with Special Reference to Gubernatorial Control* (University of Chicago, Ph.D. Dissertation, 1951) is the only work on the legislature.

(c) Official or semi-official publications of the legislatures provide information about particular sessions, and in some instances about the continuing process.

Legislative publications in California include two politico-legal descriptions of the process that are brought up to date from time to time, one authored by the Clerk of the Assembly, the other by the Secretary of the Senate. They are respectively: Arthur A. Ohnimus,

The Legislature of California, and Joseph A. Beek, *The Legislature of California.* Other useful publications of the Assembly are Jay Doubleday: *Standing and Interim Committees of the California Legislature* (1959); and the annual *Legislators' Orientation Conference,* a transcript of remarks before the freshman legislators, published early in the session. Joint publications for each session include a *List of Legislative Advocates and Organizations,* which lists registered lobbyists, the *Handbook of the California Legislature,* which gives the rules of both houses, the roster of members with brief biographical sketches, primary and general election statistics. Day to day publications have been mentioned on page 51. A comprehensive summary score of measures and their distribution appears in the *Final Calendar of Legislative Business.*

The Ohio legislature publishes at each session a joint *Roster of the Members, Officers, Employees and List of Standing Committees,* and each house publishes its *Rules,* (with joint rules appended). A *Bill Drafting Manual* by the Legislative Service Commission sheds some light on the process.

In New Jersey the Assembly publishes a *Handbook for Members* biennially. The annual *Manual of the Legislature of New Jersey* (in 1957 compiled and edited by J. Joseph Gribbins) is published by Dorothy A. Fitzgerald, Trenton. A *Legislative Index* published weekly during the session by The Legislative Index of New Jersey, Inc., Elizabeth, gives biographical information and committee appointments in its early issues, and keeps score on the progress of measures.

The *Tennessee Blue Book* published biennially carries a few pages of legislative rosters, etc., plus election returns. Committee lists and minimum personal information are appended to *Rules of Order* of the Senate (House of Representatives) prepared for each session by the respective Chief Clerks. A *Legislator's Manual* prepared by the Legislative Council Committee gives elementary information for freshman legislators.

Index

Acting Governor, New Jersey, 56
Administration floor leader, see Party-
    leader role
Administration roles, 13, 243
Age of legislators, 491
Akzin, Benjamin, 267n
Almond, Gabriel A., 6n, 312n, 328, 331n
American Political Science Association,
    Committee for Apportionment of
    Congress, 46
Committee on State Legislatures, 42,
    45, 53
Anderson, W. A., 82n
Apportionment, 46–48
Areal-role orientations, 13, 14, 252n,
    287–310, 465, 468
    interpenetration with party-role orien-
        tations, 385–389
    interpenetration with pressure-group-
        role orientations, 391–392
    interpenetration with purposive-role
        orientation, 403–405
    interpenetration with representa-
        tional-role orientations, 395–397
Attitudes, see Efficacy sense of legisla-
    tors; Ideology; Political socializa-
    tion
Attorney-General, Tennessee, 52
Availability, 105–106

Baily, Stephen K., 4n, 193n, 237n, 256n,
    378n
Baker, Gordon E., 46

Baker, Roscoe, 63n
Barton, Allen H., 80n
Bates, Frederick L., 8n
Beer, Samuel H., 271n, 324–325n
Behavioral approach (behavioral study),
    4–7, 10, 31–32, 70, 141, 239–240,
    243–244, 380–381, 435
Belknap, George N., 239n
Bentham, Jeremy, 139
Bentley, Arthur F., 142, 175, 192n
Berelson, Bernard, 82n
Beyle, Herman C., 219n
Binkley, Wilfred E., 247, 248n
Birthplace of legislators, 488
Bone, Hugh A., 73n
Borgatta, Edgar F., 219, 223n
Broker-majoritarian-role structure, 420,
    428
Broker-role orientation, 248, 256–258,
    280, 466
    see also Purposive-role orientations
Bruck, Henry W., 196
Buchanan, William, 34, 212n, 462n
Burdick, Eugene, 377n, 380n
Burke, Edmund, 9–10, 158, 269–271,
    280–281, 287

Campbell, Angus A., 31n, 82n, 93n,
    321n, 343n, 474n
Cantril, Hadley, 281n, 462n
Caplow, Theodore, 166n
Carney, Francis, 97n
Carroll, Holbert N., 25n, 193n, 195

509

Cartwright, Dorwin, 156n
Case study, 237–238
Catlin, George E. G., 5n
Caucus, 55–58, 61–63, 190, 360–362
Chairman, see Committee chairmen
Child, Irvin L., 78n
Circumstantial variables, 20, 21n
Civic education, see Political socialization
Class, see Socio-economic characteristics
Clientele-roles sector, 12–13, 14
  interpenetration of role orientations in, 385–392
  interpenetration with purposive roles, 399–407
  interpenetration with representational roles, 393–399
Coding, 37–38, 452–455
Cohen, Bernard C., 378n
Cohesion, see Party cohesion
Coleman, James S., 6n, 455n
Committee chairmen, behavior expected of, 484–485
  relation to subject-matter experts, 202, 207, 208, 212–213
  role of, 174, 176–182, 184–188
  see also Officers of legislature
Committees, 50, 53, 60–65, 154–155, 194, 199–200, 206, 238–241, 480–481
Communication functions, 24, 185, 186–187, 305, 306–307
Comparative method, 245–246, 462–463
Conflict, legislators' perceptions of, 423–427
  relation to legislature's functions, 162–164, 172, 174–175, 179–185, 241, 246, 379–381, 414–415
  relation to role structure, 423–424, 428–430
Congress, 6, 41, 141–143, 176, 182n, 192, 193–196, 199, 217, 226, 229n, 238, 294
  legislators' aspirations to, 130–132
Consensual role, 11, 14, 19
  see also Norms; Rules of the game
Constituency, see Apportionment; Areal-role orientations; District
Constituents, legislators' views of, 294–300

Converse, Philip E., 93n, 343n
Core-roles sector, 11–12, 14
  see also Consensual role; Purposive-role orientations; Representational-role orientations
Coser, Lewis A., 8n
Counterposition (counter-role), 11, 12, 19
Cross-filing, 43, 343n
Cureton, Edward E., 219n

Dahl, Robert A., 25n, 195–196, 196n
Decision-making model, 196, 378–379
DeGrazia, Alfred, 248, 312n
DeGrazia, Sebastian, 78n
DeGre, G., 314n
Delegate-role orientation, 276–277, 467
  see also Areal-role orientations
Derge, David R., 46n, 329n
Dexter, Lewis A., 294n
District, legislators' residence in, 488
  see also Apportionment; Areal-role orientations; Constituents
District-oriented-role orientation, 289–290, 468
  see also Areal-role orientations
District-state-oriented-role orientation, 291, 468
  see also Areal-role orientations
Driscoll, Jean M., 377n, 380n

Easton, David, 5n, 19n, 77n, 380n
Education issues in the legislature, friendship role in, 216–217
  representational-role orientations in, 283–284
  subject-matter expert role in, 209–212
Education of legislators, 489
  and articulateness in rules of the game, 166
  and legislative behavior, 23, 72
  and pressure-group-role orientations, 329–331
  and representational-role orientations, 282
  and subject-matter expertise, 206–207
Efficacy sense of legislators, 59, 474–475
  and areal-role orientations, 309–310

Efficacy sense of legislators, and articulateness in rules of the game, 167
and party-role orientations, 346–349
and pressure-group-role orientations, 341
and purposive-role orientations, 263–266
and representational-role orientations, 284–285
and subject-matter expertise, 212–214
Ehrman, Henry W., 311n, 312n, 329n
Eldersveld, Samuel J., 312n, 377n
Enacted role requirements, 21, 22, 23, 171
Epstein, Leon, 442n
Errand-boy functions, 304, 306, 379
"Escalator model" of political careers, 73, 96
Eulau, Heinz, 34, 74n, 288n, 377n
Experience of legislators, *see* Political careers of legislators; Political experience of legislators; Tenure

Facilitator-role orientation, 325–326, 469–470
see also Pressure-group-role orientations
Fairlie, John A., 25n, 267n
Family, *see* Primary groups
Farris, Charles D., 239n
Federalist Papers, 248
Ferguson, LeRoy C., 34, 209n, 217n, 440n
Findley, James C., 43n
Finer, Herman, 193, 194n, 217n, 222, 250, 254, 255n, 268
Fitch, David J., 219n
Floor leader, *see* Party-leader role
Floterial districts, Tennessee, 48
Ford, Robert N., 474n
Formal leadership roles, 13, 14
see also Officers of legislature; specific officers' titles
Friedrich, Carl J., 194n, 258, 280n
Friendship role, 14, 140, 216–235
see also Primary groups
Functional approach, to political study, 5–7

Functional approach, to study of officers of legislature, 172–175, 189–192
to study of representation, 267–272
Functions of legislature, 5–6, 11, 24–25, 136, 245–246, 378–380, 400, 414
and officers' roles, 172–178, 189–192
and rules of the game, 155–165

Galloway, George B., 182n, 193n, 194n
Garceau, Oliver, 255n, 312n, 324n, 327n, 378n, 442n, 469n
Gaudet, Hazel, 82n
"Generalized other," 11
Gerth, H. H., 76n, 114n
Goffman, Erving, 11n, 20n, 145n
Gosnell, Harold F., 287n
Governor (Governorship), 41, 58, 59, 186, 346–348, 358, 402, 425, 426
in California, 54, 346
in New Jersey, 41, 44, 347–348, 356, 386, 390, 401, 429
in Ohio, 44–45, 64, 357, 386
in Tennessee, 56, 57, 58, 65, 430
Graicunas, V. A., 222n
Greaves, H. R. G., 139n
Gross, Bertram M., 193n, 256n, 312n, 314n, 378n
Gross, Edward, 167n
Gross, Neal, 8n, 11n, 15n
Group norms, *see* Norms
Gurin, Gerald, 82n, 474n

Harris, Joseph P., 43n
Heard, Alexander, 442n
Henry, Andrew F., 474n
Hess, Robert D., 77n
Hoffman, Paul J., 373n
Homans, George, 31n, 141, 145n
Homophily, 223
Huges, Everett C., 69
Hughes, James W., 8n
Huitt, Ralph K., 238, 438n
Hyman, Herbert, 71n, 78n
Hyneman, Charles S., 121n, 208, 288n, 486n

Ideology, 475
and party-role orientations, 371–375, 475

Ideology, and political socialization, 93–94
as political motivation, 115
conflict of, 425, 427
Incidental-roles sector, 13–14, 19
Independent-role orientation, 367–369
  see also Party-role orientations
Input-output, 18, 19–20, 24–28, 242, 382–383, 414
Institution, see Legislative institution
Institutional approach to political study, 4–7, 141, 245–246
Interest groups, see Pressure groups
Interest orientation of legislators, 331–333
Interposition consensus, see Role conflict and consensus
Inter-role conflict, see Role conflict and consensus
Interview data, 31–33, 70, 449–451
Interview experience, 34–37, 441–452
Interview schedule, 33, 438–441, 492–504
Intraposition consensus, see Role conflict and consensus
Intrarole conflict, see Role conflict and consensus
Inventor-role orientation, 248, 254–256, 466
  see also Purposive-role orientations

Janowitz, Morris, 71n, 377n
Jewell, Malcolm E., 60n, 266n, 344n

Kaplan, Morton A., 380n
Keefe, William J., 343n, 378n, 380n
Kendall, Willmoore, 42n
Key, V. O., 41n, 42, 43n, 44n, 101n, 311, 314n, 442
Kish, Leslie, 455n
Klain, Maurice, 47n
Koslin, Bertram L., 5n, 141n

Lane, Robert E., 71n
LaPalombara, Joseph, 311n
Lasswell, Harold D., 5n, 10n, 69n, 72n, 73–74, 91n
Latham, Earl, 8n, 256, 327n, 340, 378n

Law Revision and Legislative Services Commission, New Jersey, 52
Lawyers as legislators, 102–103, 110, 115, 119, 120, 198, 200–201, 206–208, 329n
Lazarsfeld, Paul F., 80n, 82n
Leadership, see Formal leadership roles; Officers of legislature
Legislation, concept of, 5–6
Legislative Analyst, California, 50
Legislative Bill Room, California, 51
Legislative Commission, see Legislative Council
Legislative Council, 283, 284
Legislative Counsel, California, 50, 59, 201
  New Jersey, 52
Legislative efficacy, see Efficacy sense of legislators
Legislative functions, see Functions of legislature
Legislative input, see Input-output
Legislative institution, concept of, 5, 10–13, 17–19
Legislative officers, see Officers of legislature
Legislative organization, see Officers of legislature; Organization of legislature
Legislative output, see Input-output
Legislative procedure, see Procedure
Legislative Reference Bureau, New Jersey, 52
  Ohio, 52
Legislative Reference Service, Tennessee, 52
"Legislative Service," Tennessee, 52
Legislative Service Commission, Ohio, 52
Legislative system, concept of, 17–20, 380–383
Leiserson, Avery, 73n
Leites, Nathan, 142n
Lerner, Daniel, 72n
Lieutenant Governor, 56, 177–178, 477–478
Likert, Rensis, 352, 468
Lindzey, Gardner, 8n, 78n, 80n, 219n, 223n

Linton, Ralph, 7n, 8n
Linz, Juan, 80n
Lippit, Ronald, 78n
Lippmann, Walter, 20n
Lipset, Seymour M., 77n, 80n, 455n
Local bills, 61, 62, 64, 65
Loomis, C. P., 219n
Lowell, A. Lawrence, 238n
Lowenthal, Leo, 77n
Lundberg, G. A., 314n

McClosky, Herbert, 373n
McConaughy, John B., 10n, 442n
McEachern, Alexander W., 8n, 11n, 15n
MacIver, Robert M., 312n, 400n
McKean, Dayton D., 313n
MacMahon, Arthur W., 74n
McPhee, William N., 82n
MacRae, Duncan, Jr., 219n, 239n,
    288n, 343n, 438n
Maccoby, Eleanor S., 71n
Mackenzie, Kenneth R., 176n
Mackenzie, W. J. M., 312n
Macridis, Roy C., 379
Majoritarian-role structure, 418–420
Majority leader, see Party-leader role
Majority-minority status, see Party
    balance in the legislature; Party-
    role orientations
March, James G., 377n
Martin, A. W., 486n
Marvick, Dwaine, 72n, 73n
Mason, Ward S., 8n, 11n, 15n
Matthews, Donald R., 72n, 143, 193,
    226n, 288n, 442n, 486n
Matthews, Richard E., 71n
Maverick-role orientation, 368–369
    see also Party-role orientations
Mead, George Herbert, 7n, 11n
Meller, Norman, 8n, 238n, 486n
Melnik, Constantin, 142n
Mentor functions, 305, 307
Merriam, Charles E., 70, 77n, 196n
Merriam, Robert E., 196n
Merton, Robert K., 7n, 17n
Miller, Warren E., 82n, 93n, 343n,
    474n
Millett, John D., 74n
Millett, John H., 329n

Mills, C. Wright, 76n, 114n
Minoritarian-role structure, 418–420
Minority leader, see Party-leader role
Money-Kirle, R. E., 78n
Morton, Alton S., 71n
Motivation, 70, 73, 90–93, 104–105,
    113–119

Nadel, S. F., 7n
Namier, Sir Lewis, 74n
Neiman, Lionel J., 8n
Neutral-role orientation, 325–326, 469–
    470
    see also Pressure-group-role orienta-
        tions
Newcomb, Theodore M., 7n
Nicholls, William L., II, 223n
Non-partisanship in California, 43, 180,
    353, 387
Norms, 8–9, 141–143
North, Robert C., 72n

Observation as a research method, 37,
    218, 239–240
Occupations of legislators, 489–490
    and articulateness in rules of the
        game, 166
    and legislative behavior, 23, 72
    and legislators' career aspirations,
        131–132
    and legislators' commitment to legis-
        lature, 118–119, 128
    and legislators' skills, 102–103
    and pressure-group-role orientations,
        329
    and recruitment of legislators, 102–
        103, 118–119
    and subject-matter expertise, 204–
        205, 207
    as a source of political interest, 87
Odegard, Peter M., 312n
Officers of legislature, 52–59, 170–192,
    477–481
    behavior expected of, 484–485
    friendships among, 226–229
    see also Formal leadership roles;
        Organization of legislature; spe-
        cific officers' titles

O'Hara, Rosemary, 373n
Opportunist-role orientation, 249, 467
Organization of legislature, 13, 170–171, 189–192
  and subject-matter expertise, 196, 199–201
Output, *see* Input-output

Parliament, 175, 271, 324n, 328–329, 393
Parsons, Talcott, 7n, 71n, 380n
Participation, *see* Political participation
Parties, as sponsors of legislative careers, 98–100
  impact on legislative process, 54, 55–56, 58, 60–64, 344–351
  influence on legislators' behavior, 354–359
  in legislative organization, 53
  legislators' evaluations of, 351–354
  participation in, as source of political interest, 86–87
Party balance in the legislature, 344–350
  and concepts of party-leader role, 184
  see also Party-role orientations
Party caucus, *see* Caucus
Party cohesion, 42–45, 60n, 98, 230n, 344, 372
Party competition, 41–46, 344–345, 471–474
  and areal-role orientations, 292–294
  and family influence on political socialization, 83
  and interpenetration of areal- and party-role orientations, 385–389
  and interpenetration of party- and pressure-group-role orientations, 389–391
  and party-role orientations, 343–350
  and political careers, 75
  and recruitment of legislators, 96–106, 109–110, 111, 114–118, 120
  and role consensus on presiding officer's role, 183–184
Party conflict in the legislature, 424–426

Party-leader role, 53–58, 61, 65, 477–480, 484–485
  see also Officers of legislature
Party-man-role orientation, 359–367
Party-role orientations, 13, 14, 359–376
  and legislators' career aspirations, 116–117
  and legislators' friendship choices, 224–226
  and nominations for subject-matter expert, 209
  and perceptions of officer roles, 183–184
  and perceptions of rules of the game, 151–152
  interpenetration with areal- , pressure-group- , representational- , and purposive-role orientations, 385–395, 400–403
Party system, 41–46
  and legislators' career expectations, 121–122, 129–130
  and legislators' commitment to legislature, 121–123, 133–134
  and purposive-role orientations, 259–260, 262
  and Speaker's role, 184
  see also Party balance in the legislature; Party competition
Patterson, Samuel C., 218, 220n, 226
Perceptual data, 31–32, 192
"Personality" as a factor in legislative behavior, 23, 69, 75, 93
  see also Motivation
Personal predispositions, *see* Motivation
Political attitudes, *see* Efficacy sense of legislators; Ideology; Political socialization
Political Behavior, Committee on, 29, 436
Political behavior, *see* Behavioral approach
Political careers of legislators, 71–76, 95–98, 121–129
Political culture, 94
  and party-role orientations, 369–371
  and pressure-group-role orientations, 331
Political events as sources of political interest, 79, 80, 88–90

Political experience of legislators, 491
and subject-matter expertise, 204–
206
see also Political careers of legislators; Tenure
Political interest, sources of, 79–94
Political participation, 79, 80, 84–88
Political parties, see Parties; Party . . .
Political skills, see Skills of legislators
Political socialization, 70–71, 77–94
Political structure, and political careers,
72–75
and purposive-role orientations, 246–
249, 262–263
see also Party system
Politico-role orientation, 277–280, 468
see also Representational-role orientations
Populist-bipartisan-role structure, 420,
429–430
Populist-minoritarian-role structure, 420,
430
President, President pro Tempore, see
Presiding officers' roles
Presiding officers' roles, 54–58, 60, 64,
174, 175–188, 477–478, 484–485
Pressure-group-role orientations, 13, 14,
16, 256–257n, 323–342, 468–470
interpenetration with areal-role
orientations, 391–392
interpenetration with party-role
orientations, 389–391
interpenetration with purposive-role
orientations, 405–407
interpenetration with representational-role orientations, 397–399
Pressure groups, 313–323
as sources of political interest, 87
as sponsors of legislative careers,
100–101
Price, Hugh D., 219n
Primary groups, as sources of political
interest, 79–80, 82–84
as sponsors of legislative careers,
100–101
see also Friendship role
Private legislation, see Local bills
Procedure, 59–66, 136–137, 139–140
and ritualist-role orientation, 249–
250

Procedure, and roll-call analysis, 230n
officers' knowledge of, 176–178
Proctor, C. H., 219n
Progressivism, see Non-partisanship in
California
Purposive-role orientations, 12, 14, 16,
243, 245–266, 465–467
interpenetration with areal- , party- ,
pressure-group- , and representational-role orientations, 399–
410
Pye, Lucian W., 73n, 79n

Ranney, Austin, 42n
Recruitment of legislators, 23, 72, 95–
101, 107–120
Reference Bureau, New Jersey, 52
Religious affiliation of legislators, 487
Representation, 11, 25–26, 46–48, 267–
272, 287–288, 311–313, 328–333
Representational-role orientations, 12,
14, 16, 243, 267–287, 465, 467–
468
interpenetration with clientele-role
orientations, 393–399
interpenetration with purposive-role
orientations, 407–410
Residence, legislators' place of, 488–489
Resister-role orientation, 325–326, 469–
470
see also Pressure-group-role orientations
Respect for following rules of the
game, 167–168
Respondents, frankness of, 36–37
number of, 36
see also Interview experience
Rice, Stuart A., 219n, 238n, 374n, 424n
Richards, Peter C., 486n
Ridgeway, Marian E., 25–26n
Riggs, Fred W., 26n
Riker, William H., 231n
Riley, J. W., Jr., 474n
Riley, M. W., 474n
Ritualist-role orientation, 247, 249–
252, 400n, 467
see also Purposive-role orientations
Rohrer, John H., 7n
Role, concept of, 7–11, 239–240

Role behavior, 9, 31–33, 410
Role concept, 9, 31–33
Role conflict and consensus, 14–17, 77, 384–385
concerning areal role, 300–304
concerning legislative officers' roles, 175, 188, 191–192
concerning party role, 354
in presiding officer's role, 182–183, 191–192
see also Working consensus
Role orientation, concept of, 14–17, 382–383
Role potential, 22, 23, 69
Role sector, 11–14
Role segmentalization, 17
Role set, 17
Role structure, 392, 410–413
of eight chambers, 415–423
relation to political conflict, 423–424, 428–430
Roll-call studies, 230n, 238–239, 423
Rosenberg, Bernard, 8n
Rosenberg, Morris, 121n
Rosenzweig, Robert M., 73n
Ross, J. F. S., 486n
Rossi, Peter H., 377n
Rotation of offices, 44, 48, 55, 62
Rothwell, C. Easton, 72n
Rousseau, Jean-Jacques, 321
Routt, Garland C., 217n, 218n, 239n
Rules of the game, 11, 140, 141–169
and officers' roles, 173–175, 186

Sample (sampling), 30–31, 35–36, 447, 456–458
Samuel, Howard D., 193n
Sanctions, for party-role performance, 364–367
for rules of the game, 152–155
Sapin, Burton, 196
Sarbin, Theodore, 8n
Sargent, Stansfeld, 7n
Schlesinger, Joseph A., 75n
School issue, *see* Education issues in the legislature
Seligman, Lester C., 96n
Selvin, Hanan C., 455n, 462n,
Senators, U.S., *see* Congress

Seniority, 48, 125
see also Tenure
Service functions, 24, 304–308
Sherif, Muzafer, 5n, 7n, 141n
Shils, Edward A., 7n
Shuman, Howard E., 140n
Significance, tests of, 455–456, 461–462
Silander, F. S., 377n
Silverman, Corinne, 255n, 324n, 327n, 378n, 438n, 442n, 469n
Simon, Herbert A., 246n, 271n, 377n
Situational landmarks, 21, 22, 40
Size of legislative chambers, and friendship formation, 226
and purposive-role orientations, 262
Skills of legislators, 101–107
and subject-matter expertise, 202–212
Snyder Richard C., 72n, 196
Social class, *see* Socio-economic characteristics
Social Science Research Council, 29, 436
Social structure, *see* Socio-economic characteristics
Socio-economic characteristics (socio-economic status), of electoral districts, 287–288
of legislators, 23, 72, 329
of states, 66–68
and political careers, 71–72
and representational-role orientations, 282
and subject-matter specialization, 199
Speaker, Speaker pro Tempore, *see* Presiding officers' roles
Speaker's Coalition, California, 54, 184, 231–234, 477, 479
Specialized sub-roles sector, 13, 14, 19, 140
see also Formal leadership roles; Officers of legislature; Subject-matter expert; specific officers' titles
State-oriented-role orientation, 290–291, 468
see also Areal-role orientations
Statistical problems, 38–39, 455–462
Stewart, J. D., 324n, 339
Stokes, Donald E., 93n, 343n

Subject-matter expert, 13, 14, 140, 187, 193–215
System, *see* Legislative system

Tenure, 48–49
and articulateness in rules of the game, 167
and friendship choices, 223–224
and pressure-group-role orientations, 341
and subject-matter expertise, 206–207
see also Seniority
Toby, J., 474n
Tribune-majoritarian-role structure, 420–429
Tribune-role orientation, 247–248, 252–254, 466
see also Purposive-role orientations
Trow, Martin, 455n
Truman, David B., 4n, 8n, 142–143, 189, 192n, 193, 217n, 219n, 226n, 229n, 231n, 256n, 312n, 314n, 327n, 328n, 338n, 344n, 378n, 380n, 442n
Trustee-role orientation, 272–276, 300, 304, 467
see also Representational-role orientations
Turner, Julius H., 288n, 343n, 423n
Turner, Ralph H., 8n, 9n

University of California Bureau of Public Administration, 51
Urban-rural balance, in apportionment, 46–47
in state populations, 66
Urban-rural conflict, 425–427
Urban-rural status of legislators, 489
and areal-role orientations, 293–294
and articulateness in rules of the game, 166
and pressure-group-role orientations, 329

Viet, Jean, 7n

Wahlke, John C., 34, 288n
Walker, Harvey A., 255n
Wasserman, P., 377n
Weber, Max, 76n, 114
Westerfield, H. Bradford, 26n
White, William S., 226n
Wilson, Alan B., 219n
Working consensus, 11, 143–152

Young, Roland A., 142, 175n, 176n, 189, 193n, 194

Zeller, Belle, 42n, 53n, 312n